Lecture Notes in Computer Science   **9734**

Commenced Publication in 1973
Founding and Former Series Editors:
Gerhard Goos, Juris Hartmanis, and Jan van Leeuwen

More information about this series at http://www.springer.com/series/7409

Sakae Yamamoto (Ed.)

Human Interface and the Management of Information: Information, Design and Interaction

18th International Conference, HCI International 2016
Toronto, Canada, July 17–22, 2016
Proceedings, Part I

 Springer

Editor
Sakae Yamamoto
Tokyo University of Science
Tokyo
Japan

ISSN 0302-9743   ISSN 1611-3349   (electronic)
Lecture Notes in Computer Science
ISBN 978-3-319-40348-9   ISBN 978-3-319-40349-6   (eBook)
DOI 10.1007/978-3-319-40349-6

Library of Congress Control Number: 2016940822

LNCS Sublibrary: SL3 – Information Systems and Applications, incl. Internet/Web, and HCI

Printed on acid-free paper

This Springer imprint is published by Springer Nature
The registered company is Springer International Publishing AG Switzerland

Foreword

The 18th International Conference on Human-Computer Interaction, HCI International 2016, was held in Toronto, Canada, during July 17–22, 2016. The event incorporated the 15 conferences/thematic areas listed on the following page.

A total of 4,354 individuals from academia, research institutes, industry, and governmental agencies from 74 countries submitted contributions, and 1,287 papers and 186 posters have been included in the proceedings. These papers address the latest research and development efforts and highlight the human aspects of the design and use of computing systems. The papers thoroughly cover the entire field of human-computer interaction, addressing major advances in knowledge and effective use of computers in a variety of application areas. The volumes constituting the full 27-volume set of the conference proceedings are listed on pages IX and X.

I would like to thank the program board chairs and the members of the program boards of all thematic areas and affiliated conferences for their contribution to the highest scientific quality and the overall success of the HCI International 2016 conference.

This conference would not have been possible without the continuous and unwavering support and advice of the founder, Conference General Chair Emeritus and Conference Scientific Advisor Prof. Gavriel Salvendy. For his outstanding efforts, I would like to express my appreciation to the communications chair and editor of *HCI International News*, Dr. Abbas Moallem.

April 2016   Constantine Stephanidis

HCI International 2016 Thematic Areas
and Affiliated Conferences

Thematic areas:

- Human-Computer Interaction (HCI 2016)
- Human Interface and the Management of Information (HIMI 2016)

Affiliated conferences:

- 13th International Conference on Engineering Psychology and Cognitive Ergonomics (EPCE 2016)
- 10th International Conference on Universal Access in Human-Computer Interaction (UAHCI 2016)
- 8th International Conference on Virtual, Augmented and Mixed Reality (VAMR 2016)
- 8th International Conference on Cross-Cultural Design (CCD 2016)
- 8th International Conference on Social Computing and Social Media (SCSM 2016)
- 10th International Conference on Augmented Cognition (AC 2016)
- 7th International Conference on Digital Human Modeling and Applications in Health, Safety, Ergonomics and Risk Management (DHM 2016)
- 5th International Conference on Design, User Experience and Usability (DUXU 2016)
- 4th International Conference on Distributed, Ambient and Pervasive Interactions (DAPI 2016)
- 4th International Conference on Human Aspects of Information Security, Privacy and Trust (HAS 2016)
- Third International Conference on HCI in Business, Government, and Organizations (HCIBGO 2016)
- Third International Conference on Learning and Collaboration Technologies (LCT 2016)
- Second International Conference on Human Aspects of IT for the Aged Population (ITAP 2016)

Conference Proceedings Volumes Full List

1. LNCS 9731, Human-Computer Interaction: Theory, Design, Development and Practice (Part I), edited by Masaaki Kurosu
2. LNCS 9732, Human-Computer Interaction: Interaction Platforms and Techniques (Part II), edited by Masaaki Kurosu
3. LNCS 9733, Human-Computer Interaction: Novel User Experiences (Part III), edited by Masaaki Kurosu
4. LNCS 9734, Human Interface and the Management of Information: Information, Design and Interaction (Part I), edited by Sakae Yamamoto
5. LNCS 9735, Human Interface and the Management of Information: Applications and Services (Part II), edited by Sakae Yamamoto
6. LNAI 9736, Engineering Psychology and Cognitive Ergonomics, edited by Don Harris
7. LNCS 9737, Universal Access in Human-Computer Interaction: Methods, Techniques, and Best Practices (Part I), edited by Margherita Antona and Constantine Stephanidis
8. LNCS 9738, Universal Access in Human-Computer Interaction: Interaction Techniques and Environments (Part II), edited by Margherita Antona and Constantine Stephanidis
9. LNCS 9739, Universal Access in Human-Computer Interaction: Users and Context Diversity (Part III), edited by Margherita Antona and Constantine Stephanidis
10. LNCS 9740, Virtual, Augmented and Mixed Reality, edited by Stephanie Lackey and Randall Shumaker
11. LNCS 9741, Cross-Cultural Design, edited by Pei-Luen Patrick Rau
12. LNCS 9742, Social Computing and Social Media, edited by Gabriele Meiselwitz
13. LNAI 9743, Foundations of Augmented Cognition: Neuroergonomics and Operational Neuroscience (Part I), edited by Dylan D. Schmorrow and Cali M. Fidopiastis
14. LNAI 9744, Foundations of Augmented Cognition: Neuroergonomics and Operational Neuroscience (Part II), edited by Dylan D. Schmorrow and Cali M. Fidopiastis
15. LNCS 9745, Digital Human Modeling and Applications in Health, Safety, Ergonomics and Risk Management, edited by Vincent G. Duffy
16. LNCS 9746, Design, User Experience, and Usability: Design Thinking and Methods (Part I), edited by Aaron Marcus
17. LNCS 9747, Design, User Experience, and Usability: Novel User Experiences (Part II), edited by Aaron Marcus
18. LNCS 9748, Design, User Experience, and Usability: Technological Contexts (Part III), edited by Aaron Marcus
19. LNCS 9749, Distributed, Ambient and Pervasive Interactions, edited by Norbert Streitz and Panos Markopoulos
20. LNCS 9750, Human Aspects of Information Security, Privacy and Trust, edited by Theo Tryfonas

21. LNCS 9751, HCI in Business, Government, and Organizations: eCommerce and Innovation (Part I), edited by Fiona Fui-Hoon Nah and Chuan-Hoo Tan
22. LNCS 9752, HCI in Business, Government, and Organizations: Information Systems (Part II), edited by Fiona Fui-Hoon Nah and Chuan-Hoo Tan
23. LNCS 9753, Learning and Collaboration Technologies, edited by Panayiotis Zaphiris and Andri Ioannou
24. LNCS 9754, Human Aspects of IT for the Aged Population: Design for Aging (Part I), edited by Jia Zhou and Gavriel Salvendy
25. LNCS 9755, Human Aspects of IT for the Aged Population: Healthy and Active Aging (Part II), edited by Jia Zhou and Gavriel Salvendy
26. CCIS 617, HCI International 2016 Posters Proceedings (Part I), edited by Constantine Stephanidis
27. CCIS 618, HCI International 2016 Posters Proceedings (Part II), edited by Constantine Stephanidis

Human Interface and the Management of Information

Program Board Chair: **Sakae Yamamoto, Japan**

- Yumi Asahi, Japan
- Dennis Coelho, Portugal
- Shin'ichi Fukuzumi, Japan
- Michitaka Hirose, Japan
- Daiji Kobayashi, Japan
- Kentaro Kotani, Japan
- Mark Lehto, USA
- Hiroyuki Miki, Japan
- Hirohiko Mori, Japan
- Shogo Nishida, Japan
- Robert Proctor, USA
- Katsunori Shimohara, Japan
- Jiro Tanaka, Japan
- Kim-Phuong Vu, USA
- Tomio Watanabe, Japan

The full list with the program board chairs and the members of the program boards of all thematic areas and affiliated conferences is available online at:

http://www.hci.international/2016/

HCI International 2017

The 19th International Conference on Human-Computer Interaction, HCI International 2017, will be held jointly with the affiliated conferences in Vancouver, Canada, at the Vancouver Convention Centre, July 9–14, 2017. It will cover a broad spectrum of themes related to human-computer interaction, including theoretical issues, methods, tools, processes, and case studies in HCI design, as well as novel interaction techniques, interfaces, and applications. The proceedings will be published by Springer. More information will be available on the conference website: http://2017. hci.international/.

General Chair
Prof. Constantine Stephanidis
University of Crete and ICS-FORTH
Heraklion, Crete, Greece
E-mail: general_chair@hcii2017.org

http://2017.hci.international/

Contents – Part I

Information Presentation

How to Support the Lay Users Evaluations of Medical Information
on the Web?.. 3
   Katarzyna Abramczuk, Michał Kąkol, and Adam Wierzbicki

Living Globe: Tridimensional Interactive Visualization of World
Demographic Data 14
   Eduardo Duarte, Pedro Bordonhos, Paulo Dias,
   and Beatriz Sousa Santos

Effectiveness of Choosing Dissonant Combination of Tones
for Multivariate Data Sonification 25
   Yukio Horiguchi, Moriyu Nakashima, Hiroaki Nakanishi,
   and Tetsuo Sawaragi

A Trial Cartooning to Promote Understanding of a Scenario............ 34
   Shigeyoshi Iizuka

The Influence of Numerical Displays on Human Performance
in the Manual RVD Task.. 40
   Wang Liu, Yu Tian, Chunhui Wang, Weifen Huang, Shanguang Chen,
   and Jun Wang

A System Description Model Without Hierarchical Structure 48
   Tetsuya Maeshiro and Midori Maeshiro

Knowledge Used for Information Search: A Computer Simulation Study 60
   Miki Matsumuro and Kazuhisa Miwa

Study on the Target Frame of HMDs in Different Background Brightness ... 70
   Jiang Shao, Haiyan Wang, Rui Zhao, Jing Zhang, Zhangfan Shen,
   and Hongwei Xi

A Decision Tree Based Image Enhancement Instruction System
for Producing Contemporary Style Images 80
   Meng-Luen Wu and Chin-Shyurng Fahn

Spatial Conformity Research of Temporal Order Information Presentation
in Visualization Design 91
   Xiaozhou Zhou, Chengqi Xue, Lei Zhou, Jiang Shao, and Zhangfan Shen

Big Data Visualization

Externalization of Data Analytics Models: Toward Human-Centered
Visual Analytics   103
  Arman Didandeh and Kamran Sedig

Investigating Cognitive Characteristics of Visualization and Insight
Environments: A Case Study with WISE   115
  Juliana Jansen Ferreira, Vinícius Segura, and Renato Cerqueira

Support Vector Mind Map of Wine Speak   127
  Brendan Flanagan and Sachio Hirokawa

A Visualization Technique Using Loop Animations.   136
  Takao Ito and Kazuo Misue

Subjective Evaluation for 2D Visualization of Data from a 3D Laser Sensor . . .   148
  Patrik Lif, Gustav Tolt, Håkan Larsson, and Alice Lagebrant

Comparison of Two Visualization Tools in Supporting Comprehension
of Data Trends   158
  Chen Ling, Julie S. Bock, Leslie Goodwin, G. Cole Jackson,
  and Molly K. Floyd

A Visual Citation Search Engine.   168
  Tetsuya Nakatoh, Hayato Nakanishi, Toshiro Minami, Kensuke Baba,
  and Sachio Hirokawa

Visualization of Brand Images Extracted from Home-Interior Commercial
Websites Using Color Features   179
  Naoki Takahashi, Takashi Sakamoto, and Toshikazu Kato

Ergonomic Considerations for the Design and the Evaluation of Uncertain
Data Visualizations   191
  Sabine Theis, Christina Bröhl, Matthias Wille, Peter Rasche,
  Alexander Mertens, Emma Beauxis-Aussalet, Lynda Hardman,
  and Christopher M. Schlick

Towards a Visual Data Language to Improve Insights into Complex
Multidimensional Data.   203
  Jan Wojdziak, Bettina Kirchner, Dietrich Kammer, Martin Herrmann,
  and Rainer Groh

A Graphical System for Interactive Creation and Exploration of Dynamic
Information Visualization.   214
  Jaqueline Zaia and João Luiz Bernardes Jr.

Information Analytics, Discovery and Exploration

Interactive Pattern Exploration: Securely Mining Distributed Databases   229
    Priya Chawla, Raj Bhatnagar, and Chia Han

Effect of Heuristics on Serendipity in Path-Based Storytelling
with Linked Data   238
    Laurens De Vocht, Christian Beecks, Ruben Verborgh, Erik Mannens,
    Thomas Seidl, and Rik Van de Walle

Interaction for Information Discovery Empowering Information Consumers . . .   252
    Kurt Englmeier and Fionn Murtagh

Federated Query Evaluation Supported by SPARQL Recommendation   263
    Gergő Gombos and Attila Kiss

Evaluation of a System to Analyze Long-Term Images from
a Stationary Camera   275
    Akira Ishii, Tetsuya Abe, Hiroyuki Hakoda, Buntarou Shizuki,
    and Jiro Tanaka

The Effect of the Arrangement of Fuzzy If-Then Rules on the Performance
of On-Line Fuzzy Classification   287
    Tomoharu Nakashima

An Efficient Scheme for Candidate Solutions of Search-Based
Multi-objective Software Remodularization.   296
    Amarjeet Prajapati and Jitender Kumar Chhabra

Dynamic Sampling for Visual Exploration of Large Dense-Dense Matrices   308
    Philipp Roskosch, James Twellmeyer, and Arjan Kuijper

Interaction Design

Analysis of Hand Raising Actions for Group Interaction Enhancement   321
    Saizo Aoyagi, Michiya Yamamoto, and Satoshi Fukumori

Content Authoring Tool to Assign Signage Items to Regions
on a Paper Poster   329
    Akira Hattori, Hiroshi Suzuki, and Haruo Hayami

Motion Control Algorithm of ARM-COMS for Entrainment Enhancement . . .   339
    Teruaki Ito and Tomio Watanabe

IVOrpheus 2.0 - A Proposal for Interaction by Voice Command-Control
in Three Dimensional Environments of Information Visualization   347
    Lennon Furtado, Anderson Marques, Nelson Neto, Marcelle Mota,
    and Bianchi Meiguins

A Sketch-Based User Interface for Image Search Using Sample Photos   361
Hitoshi Sugimura, Hayato Tsukiji, Mizuki Kumada, Toshiya Iiba,
and Kosuke Takano

Proposal and Evaluation of a Document Reader that Supports Pointing and
Finger Bookmarking   371
Kentaro Takano, Shingo Uchihashi, Hirohito Shibata, Kengo Omura,
Junko Ichino, Tomonori Hashiyama, and Shunichi Tano

An Advanced Web-Based Hindi Language Interface to Database Using
Machine Learning Approach.   381
Zorawar Singh Virk and Mohit Dua

MapCube: A Mobile Focus and Context Information Visualization
Technique for Geographic Maps   391
Björn Werkmann and Matthias Hemmje

Human-Centered Design

Design Education at the Cross-Roads of Change.   405
Denis A. Coelho

Clarification of Customers' "Demand" in Development Process   413
Shin'ichi Fukuzumi and Yukiko Tanikawa

Product Awareness Between Consumers and Designers – A Family Dining
Table Design as Example.   421
Ming-Hsuan Hsieh and Chia-Ling Chang

User Interface Developing Framework for Engineers   433
Hiroyuki Miki, Kunikazu Suzuki, and Tsuyoshi Suzuki

Agile Human-Centred Design: A Conformance Checklist.   442
Karsten Nebe and Snigdha Baloni

Understanding the Dynamics and Temporal Aspects of Work
for Human Centered Design   454
Kate Sellen

User Centered Design Methods and Their Application in Older Adult
Community   462
Joash Sujan Samuel Roy, W. Patrick Neumann, and Deborah I. Fels

Haptic, Tactile and Multimodal interaction

Effect of Physiological and Psychological Conditions by Aroma
and Color on VDT Task 475
  Takeo Ainoya and Keiko Kasamatsu

Topographic Surface Perception Modulated by Pitch Rotation
of Motion Chair 483
  Tomohiro Amemiya, Koichi Hirota, and Yasushi Ikei

Mel Frequency Cepstral Coefficients Based Similar Albanian
Phonemes Recognition...................................... 491
  Bertan Karahoda, Krenare Pireva, and Ali Shariq Imran

Minimal Virtual Reality System for Virtual Walking in a Real Scene 501
  Michiteru Kitazaki, Koichi Hirota, and Yasushi Ikei

Designing Effective Vibration Patterns for Tactile Interfaces............ 511
  Daiji Kobayashi and Ryogo Nakamura

Relationship Between Operability in Touch Actions and Smartphone Size
Based on Muscular Load 523
  *Kentaro Kotani, Ryo Ineyama, Daisuke Hashimoto, Takafumi Asao,
  and Satoshi Suzuki*

Why Is Tactile Information not Accurately Perceived? Accuracy
and Transfer Characteristics of Visualized Schematic Images Induced
by Perceived Tactile Stimuli................................ 531
  *Keisuke Kumagai, Kazuki Sakai, Kentaro Kotani, Satoshi Suzuki,
  and Takafumi Asao*

Multimodal Information Coding System for Wearable Devices of Advanced
Uniform... 539
  *Andrey L. Ronzhin, Oleg O. Basov, Anna I. Motienko, Alexey A. Karpov,
  Yuri V. Mikhailov, and Milos Zelezny*

Increasing User Appreciation of Spherical Videos by Finger Touch
Interaction 546
  *Yuta Sakakibara, Ryohei Tanaka, Takuji Narumi, Tomohiro Tanikawa,
  and Michitaka Hirose*

Production of a VR Horror Movie Using a Head-Mounted Display with a
Head-Tracking System...................................... 556
  Kenichi Sera, Takashi Kitada, and Nahomi Maki

Basic Investigation for Improvement of Sign Language Recognition
Using Classification Scheme................................ 563
  Hirotoshi Shibata, Hiromitsu Nishimura, and Hiroshi Tanaka

Empirical Study of Physiological Characteristics Accompanied by Tactile
Thermal Perception: Relationship Between Changes in Thermal Gradients
and Skin Conductance Responses   575
   Takafumi Shinoda, Kouki Shimomura, Kentaro Kotani, Satoshi Suzuki,
   Takafumi Asao, and Shigeyoshi Iizuka

Using the Office Desk as a Touch Interface   585
   Hirobumi Tomita, Simona Vasilache, and Jiro Tanaka

Author Index   597

Contents – Part II

Communication, Collaboration and Decision-Making Support

Collaborative Modes on Collaborative Problem Solving.   3
    Yu-Hung Chien, Kuen-Yi Lin, Kuang-Chao Yu, Hsien-Sheng Hsiao,
    Yu-Shan Chang, and Yih-Hsien Chu

Modelling Information Flow and Situational Awareness in Wild Fire
Response Operations.   11
    Laila Goubran, Avi Parush, and Anthony Whitehead

Supporting Analytical Reasoning: A Study from the Automotive Industry . . .   20
    Tove Helldin, Maria Riveiro, Sepideh Pashami, Göran Falkman,
    Stefan Byttner, and Slawomir Nowaczyk

Towards More Practical Information Sharing in Disaster Situations   32
    Masayuki Ihara, Shunichi Seko, Akihiro Miyata, Ryosuke Aoki,
    Tatsuro Ishida, Masahiro Watanabe, Ryo Hashimoto,
    and Hiroshi Watanabe

Prototype of Decision Support Based on Estimation of Group Status
Using Conversation Analysis   40
    Susumu Kono and Kenro Aihara

Preventing Incorrect Opinion Sharing with Weighted Relationship
Among Agents.   50
    Rei Saito, Masaya Nakata, Hiroyuki Sato, Tim Kovacs,
    and Keiki Takadama

The Temporal Analysis of Networks for Community Activity.   63
    Yurika Shiozu, Koya Kimura, and Katsunori Shimohara

Method to Evaluate Difficulty of Technical Terms   72
    Yuta Sudo, Toru Nakata, and Toshikazu Kato

Essential Tips for Successful Collaboration – A Case Study of the
"Marshmallow Challenge"   81
    Noriko Suzuki, Haruka Shoda, Mamiko Sakata, and Kaori Inada

A Mechanism to Control Aggressive Comments in Pseudonym Type
Computer Mediated Communications   90
    Hiroki Yamaguchi and Tetsuya Maeshiro

Information in e-Learning and e-Education

One Size Does Not Fit All: Applying the Right Game Concepts for the
Right Persons to Encourage Non-game Activities   103
   Hina Akasaki, Shoko Suzuki, Kanako Nakajima, Koko Yamabe,
   Mizuki Sakamoto, Todorka Alexandrova, and Tatsuo Nakajima

Gaze-Aware Thinking Training Environment to Analyze Internal
Self-conversation Process.   115
   Yuki Hayashi, Kazuhisa Seta, and Mitsuru Ikeda

Educational Externalization of Thinking Task by Kit-Build Method.   126
   Tsukasa Hirashima and Yusuke Hayashi

Student Authentication Method by Sequential Update of Face Information
Registered in e-Learning System.   138
   Taisuke Kawamata, Susumu Fujimori, and Takako Akakura

An Open-Ended and Interactive Learning Using Logic Building System
with Four-Frame Comic Strip.   146
   Kayo Kawamoto, Yusuke Hayashi, and Tsukasa Hirashima

Construction of a Literature Review Support System Using Latent
Dirichlet Allocation.   159
   Yusuke Kometani and Keizo Nagaoka

Design for Adaptive User Interface for Modeling Students' Learning Styles. . . .   168
   Ashery Mbilinyi, Shinobu Hasegawa, and Akihiro Kashihara

An Adaptive Research Support System for Students in Higher Education:
Beyond Logging and Tracking   178
   Harriet Nyanchama Ocharo and Shinobu Hasegawa

Investigation of Learning Process with TUI   187
   Natsumi Sei, Makoto Oka, and Hirohiko Mori

A Method for Consensus Building Between Teachers and Learners in
Higher Education Through Co-design Process.   197
   Ryota Sugino, Satoshi Mizoguchi, Koji Kimita, Keiichi Muramatsu,
   Tatsunori Matsui, and Yoshiki Shimomura

Association Rules on Relationships Between Learner's Physiological
Information and Mental States During Learning Process.   209
   Kazuma Takehana and Tatsunori Matsui

Access to Cultural Heritage, Creativity and Art

Listening to Music and Idea Generation.   223
    Wen-Chih Chang and Chi-Meng Liao

Application of Co-creation Design Experiences to the Development of
Green Furniture   235
    Chia-Ling Chang and Ming-Hsuan Hsieh

Well-Being of Decolonizing Aesthetics: New Environment of Art
with BCI in HCI.   244
    Hyunkyoung Cho and Jin-kyung Paik

Creation of Shadow Media Using Point Cloud and Design of Co-creative
Expression Space   256
    Maho Hayashi, Yoshiyuki Miwa, Shiroh Itai, Hiroko Nishi,
    and Yuto Yamakawa

Image Mnemonics for Cognitive Mapping of the Museum Exhibits.   268
    Yasushi Ikei, Ken Ishigaki, Hirofumi Ota, and Keisuke Yoshida

AR Reference Model for K-Culture Time Machine   278
    Eunseok Kim, Junghoon Jo, Kihong Kim, Sunhyuck Kim, Seungmo
    Hong, Jea-In Kim, Noh-young Park, Hyerim Park, Tamás Matuszka,
    Jungwha Kim, and Woontack Woo

Encouraging People to Interact with Interactive Systems in Public Spaces
by Managing Lines of Participants   290
    Takuji Narumi, Hiroyuki Yabe, Shunsuke Yoshida, Tomohiro Tanikawa,
    and Michitaka Hirose

Visualization of Composer Relationships Using Implicit Data Graphs   300
    Christoph Niese, Tatiana von Landesberger, and Arjan Kuijper

Crowd-Cloud Window to the Past: Constructing a Photo Database
for On-Site AR Exhibitions by Crowdsourcing.   313
    Sohei Osawa, Ryohei Tanaka, Takuji Narumi, Tomohiro Tanikawa,
    and Michitaka Hirose

Backend Infrastructure Supporting Audio Augmented Reality and
Storytelling   325
    Kari Salo, Diana Giova, and Tommi Mikkonen

Creativity Comes from Interaction: Multi-modal Analyses of Three-Creator
Communication in Constructing a Lego Castle   336
    Haruka Shoda, Koshi Nishimoto, Noriko Suzuki, Mamiko Sakata,
    and Noriko Ito

Co-creative Expression Interface: Aiming to Support Embodied
Communication for Developmentally Disabled Children.   346
  Takuto Takahashi, Ryutaro Hayashi, Yoshiyuki Miwa, and Hiroko Nishi

High-Resolution Tactile Display for Lips   357
  Yuhei Tsutsui, Koichi Hirota, Takuya Nojima, and Yasushi Ikei

Fortune Air: Interactive Fortune-Telling for Entertainment Enhancement
in a Praying Experience   367
  Ryoko Ueoka and Naoto Kamiyama

e-Science and e-Research

Prioritizing Tasks Using User-Support-Worker's Activity Model
(USWAM)   379
  Hashim Iqbal Chunpir

Improving User Interfaces for a Request Tracking System:
Best Practical RT   391
  *Hashim Iqbal Chunpir, Endrit Curri, Luciana Zaina,
  and Thomas Ludwig*

Strategic Knowledge Management for Interdisciplinary Teams -
Overcoming Barriers of Interdisciplinary Work Via an Online
Portal Approach   402
  *Tatjana Hamann, Anne Kathrin Schaar, André Calero Valdez,
  and Martina Ziefle*

Data Integration and Knowledge Coordination for Planetary Exploration
Traverses   414
  Jordan R. Hill, Barrett S. Caldwell, Michael J. Miller, and David S. Lees

Gauging the Reliability of Online Health Information
in the Turkish Context.   423
  Edibe Betül Karbay and Hashim Iqbal Chunpir

How to Improve Research Data Management: The Case of Sciebo
(Science Box).   434
  *Konstantin Wilms, Christian Meske, Stefan Stieglitz, Dominik Rudolph,
  and Raimund Vogl*

Information in Health and Well-being

Well-Being and HCI in Later Life - What Matters?.   445
  *Arlene J. Astell, Faustina Hwang, Elizabeth A. Williams, Libby Archer,
  Sarah Harney-Levine, Dave Wright, and Maggie Ellis*

Improving Sense of Well-Being by Managing Memories of Experience   454
Mark Chignell, Chelsea de Guzman, Leon Zucherman, Jie Jiang,
Jonathan Chan, and Nipon Charoenkitkarn

Towards Understanding Senior Citizens' Gateball Participations Behavior
and Well-Being: An Application of the Theory of Planned Behavior   466
Chia-Chien Hsu, Yu-Chin Hsu, and Ching-Torng Lin

Video Recommendation System that Arranges Video Clips Based
on Pre-defined Viewing Times   478
Mitsuhiko Kimoto, Tomoki Nakahata, Takahiro Hirano,
Takuya Nagashio, Masahiro Shiomi, Takamasa Iio, Ivan Tanev,
and Katsunori Shimohara

Diminished Agency: Attenuating a Sense of Agency for Problem Finding
on Personal Physical Performance   487
Sho Sakurai, Yuki Ban, Nami Ogawa, Takuji Narumi,
Tomohiro Tanikawa, and Michitaka Hirose

Evaluating Hedonic and Eudaimonic Motives
in Human-Computer Interaction   494
Katie Seaborn

Personalized Real-Time Sleep Stage from Past Sleep Data to Today's Sleep
Estimation   501
Yusuke Tajima, Tomohiro Harada, Hiroyuki Sato, and Keiki Takadama

Exploring Dance Teaching Anxiety in Japanese Schoolteachers   511
Rina Yamaguchi, Haruka Shoda, Noriko Suzuki, and Mamiko Sakata

Case Studies

Sensory Evaluation Method with Multivariate Analysis
for Pictograms on Smartphone   521
Naotsune Hosono, Hiromitsu Inoue, Miwa Nakanishi,
and Yutaka Tomita

Exploring Information Needs of Using Battery Swapping System for Riders. . .   531
Fei-Hui Huang

Detecting Multitasking Work and Negative Routines from Computer Logs. . .   542
Hirofumi Kaburagi, Simona Vasilache, and Jiro Tanaka

A Leader and Media Spot Estimation Method Using Location Information. . .   550
Koya Kimura, Yurika Shiozu, Ivan Tanev, and Katsunori Shimohara

What Kind of Foreign Baseball Players Want to Get Japanese
Baseball Team?   560
   Hirohito Matsuka and Yumi Asahi

Effect of Changes in Fresh Vegetables Prices Give Consumers   569
   Ryota Morizumi and Yumi Asahi

Tacit Skills Discovery by Data Mining   579
   Makoto Oka and Hirohiko Mori

Basic Observation About the Difficulty of Assembly Wood Puzzle
by Wooden Joint.   589
   *Takamitsu Tanaka, Masao Tachibana, Thongthai Wongwichai,
   and Yen-Yu Kang*

Livelog: Sensing and Inducing Japanese Idol Fan Activities with
Smartphone   599
   *Tomohiro Tanikawa, Rihito Hashido, Takuji Narumi,
   and Michitaka Hirose*

Author Index   607

Information Presentation

How to Support the Lay Users Evaluations of Medical Information on the Web?

Katarzyna Abramczuk[1]([✉]), Michał Kąkol[2], and Adam Wierzbicki[2]

[1] Institute of Sociology, University of Warsaw, Warsaw, Poland
`k.abramczuk@uw.edu.pl`
[2] Polish-Japanese Academy of Information Technology, Warsaw, Poland
`{michal.kakol,adamw}@pjwstk.edu.pl`

Abstract. In this paper we present a study on the credibility of lay users evaluations of health related web content. We investigate the differences between their approach and the approach of medical experts, analyse whether we can increase their accuracy using a simple support system, and explore the effectiveness of the wisdom of crowds approach. We find that a support system based on expert ratings is effective while relying on the wisdom of crowds can be risky. There is a clear positive bias in lay evaluations that is very difficult to correct. Moreover lay users perceive health related web-content differently than medical experts.

Keywords: Web credibility · Wisdom of crowds · World wide web · Information retrieval · Health information

1 Introduction

People often search the Web for medical information. As a matter of fact eight in ten people browse the Internet for health related content, which makes it one of the most common Internet activities. Unfortunately, what the users ultimately find is often misleading, incomplete, and non-credible. The Web is filled with a myriad of humbug therapies, mysterious super-drugs and pseudo doctors. As it can be easily guessed it may, and often does, lead to grave consequences for both private and, as can be seen by the example of the anti-vaccine movement, social matters.

We present a study on the process by which people evaluate the credibility of medical web content and a system supporting lay evaluations. We try to understand what guides peoples decisions, to what extent we can influence them and how a supporting system should be constructed in order to maximise its positive effect.

The paper is structured as follows. Firstly, we introduce the concept of web content credibility and describe the study design. Then we contrast expert and lay evaluations to see how they differ and whether lay users are able to discern credible and non-credible medical content on their own. Finally, we analyse whether and to what extent lay users are prone to following advice provided by

© Springer International Publishing Switzerland 2016
S. Yamamoto (Ed.): HIMI 2016, Part I, LNCS 9734, pp. 3–13, 2016.
DOI: 10.1007/978-3-319-40349-6_1

a supporting system. We do this by comparing how accurate and inaccurate system suggestions affect users, while contrasting this with the power of the wisdom of crowds.

2 Related Work

Credibility is a multifaceted concept. The majority of researchers agree that it is composed of at least two components: expertise and trustworthiness. Both these components are naturally associated with the source of the information being assessed [1]. Expertise is defined in terms of the competency or experience of the author and trustworthiness in terms of the goodwill and agenda of the source [2]. There is also a number of other source characteristics that are related to the concept of credibility such as completeness of information or information accuracy. One of the dimensions which was assessed in our study is controversy of the information on the page. In fact this dimension turns out to be important for explaining the differences between lay and expert evaluations. Jankowski-Lorek et al. in their work make attempts to automatically detect controversy in the content based on crowdsourced ratings distributions [3] or Wikipedia category structure [4].

Apart from the correlates of credibility related to the information piece and its source a number of viewer traits influence the individual process of credibility assessment. For example Rafalak et al. [5,6] investigated how different psychological and demographical traits of Internet users affect the credibility perception. Flanagin and Metzger [7] add the internet/web experience of the viewer as being one of the crucial factors. Similarly in [8] it is pointed out that Internet usage efficacy is an important determinant of the assessment of credibility of web sources. Another obvious viewer related factor is the viewers familiarity with the assessed information [9]. Lucassen et al. [10] also found that various user characteristics such as domain expertise and information search skills affect credibility evaluations. The effect of the viewers traits has also been reported specifically in the health domain e.g. Crawford et al. [11] have explored health information search behaviors in this context.

The usefulness of Google as an indicator of medical Websites credibility has been evaluated by Frick et al. [12] who evaluated the PageRank score as one indicator of quality. Their results show that it is not inherently useful for discrimination or helping users to avoid inaccurate or poor information. Griffiths et al. [13] evaluated PageRank scores with evidence based quality scores for depression websites (expert ratings). Again PageRank scores correlated weakly with the evidence based scores. This shows that, considered alone, PageRank indicator is clearly insufficient to account for the quality of medical Websites.

In this paper we address the problem of increasing the accuracy of lay credibility evaluations. We evaluate the usefulness of a system supporting credibility evaluations and test the reliability of the wisdom of crowds approach. The idea of augmenting web content in order to enhance credibility judgments is not new. For example Schwarz and Morris [14] present visualizations based on expert user

Table 1. The list of medical topics used in the study together with the number of webpages and the number of lay user evaluations.

Category	No. of webpages	No. of evaluations
Celiac disease treatment	23	1112
Depression treatment	17	776
Diabetes treatment	22	1023
Heart disease treatment	19	901
Hormonal contraception	21	979
Norovirus treatment	21	979
Twitch eye treatment	24	1143
West Nile virus	19	913
Whooping cough treatment	24	1152

behavior additionally to search results. Yamamoto and Tanaka [15] also augment web search results with visualizations and re-rank the results according to the users predicted credibility model. A simpler augmentation in a similar setting is also described in an Amin et al. [16] study covering culture related web content.

3   Study Design

The study we present is based on an experiment. A single task in this experiment consisted of evaluations of three websites drawn randomly from a corpus of 190 webpages on 9 health-related topics. We chose websites using most popular, and those increasing the most in popularity, medical searches performed on Google from the US in 12 months preceding the study and chose 9 topics. We constructed corresponding search phrases aimed at finding both credible and not credible information. We selected random websites from those that were shown on the first results pages (as searched for in the US) and filtered out those that did not contain any meaningful content that could be subject to credibility evaluation. The list of medical topics used in the study together with the number of webpages and the number of lay user evaluations used in this paper for each topic is presented below (Table 1):

To run the study we used the Reconcile[1] (Robust Online Credibility Evaluation of Web Content) system which is a product of a joint research project of two universities: Polish PJIIT and Swiss EPFL. The system is a prototype of an online support platform for credibility evaluations.

Two types of users took part in our study: lay users recruited via Amazon Mechanical Turk and medical experts from the Medical University of Warsaw. The medical experts took part in the study during two medical congresses and from their houses. Based on their evaluations each website was assigned one

---
[1] http://www.reconcile.pl.

unique expert rating that was a result of experts consensus. The lay users were MTurk workers from English-speaking countries (mostly US). All users were paid accordingly for their participation in the study.

The lay user data presented in this paper is based on 3 experimental treatments that were part of our study. Participants were assigned to the treatments randomly. In each case they were asked to evaluate three websites with respect to 6 dimensions: credibility, expertise, intentions of the authors, completeness, controversy of the information provided, and appearance of the website. For all the dimensions except for controversy we used a 5-point ordinal scale where choices were labeled (e.g. 1 completely not credible 2 mostly not credible etc.). Controversy was measured using dichotomous choice (controversial vs. not controversial).

The experimental treatments we are reporting here were as follows:

NH (No Hints) Treatment: In this condition we asked participants to evaluate the webpages without any external support.

EH (Expert Hint) Treatment: In this condition we used Reconcile interface to present the suggested evaluations of the webpages. The suggested evaluations were based on previously gathered expert ratings of the given page and were presented in a form of a traffic light (e.g. green corresponded to credible and red to not credible content) next to the field where the user was submitting his own rating. This mimics the workings of most of the existing support systems.

RE (Reversed Expert) Treatment: This condition was identical to the EH condition except for the fact that the suggested ratings were exactly opposite to the ratings provided by the experts. We chose 158 webpages that received expert credibility ratings other than 3 (the middle of the scale) and marked the credible websites as not credible and vice versa.

To avoid learning that the system suggestions are misleading in RE conditions, this condition and the EH condition were joined. The participants were served either three webpages in the EH condition or two pages in the EH condition and one (the last in the package) in the RE condition. In all the conditions we tracked the subjects activity i.e. page clicks, time spent on each task, going back and forth within the quest etc.

4   Lay and Expert Evaluations

The distribution of credibility ratings for the experts and for the lay users in all the experimental conditions is presented in Fig. 1. 45 (24 %) out of the 190 webpages in the corpus were rated by the experts as not credible (evaluations 1 and 2). 113 (60 %) were rated as credible (evaluations 4 and 5). This distribution for the experts shows a familiar skew that is present in most of the online assessment

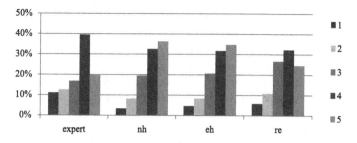

Fig. 1. The distribution of credibility ratings for the experts and for the lay users in all the experimental conditions.

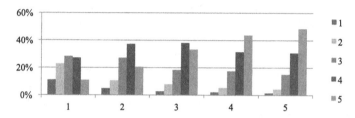

Fig. 2. The distribution of unsupported lay ratings (NH) in the subgroups of web-pages grouped by expert evaluation.

systems. In this case it probably results from the fact that websites were chosen using Google search which successfully filtered out much of the noncredible content.

There is a visible and statistically significant (p = 0,01) difference between expert distribution and lay distributions in any of the conditions presented. In particular the experts are much less prone to using the maximal (5) rating and use the negative (1 and 2) ratings more often. The maximal rating is the most popular choice for the lay users both without any support (NH) and with an expert suggestion (EH). It is slightly different for the RE treatment which will be discussed in the next section. The remaining part of this section is based entirely on the data from the NH treatment.

The lay evaluations and the expert evaluations are correlated. Figure 2 presents the distribution of unsupported lay ratings in the subgroups of webpages grouped by expert evaluation. The share of negative ratings rises systematically with the falling expert rating, starting with 7 % for the most credible and ending with 34 % for the least credible content. Unfortunately, even in the latter case there are more positive (4 and 5) than negative ratings. They amount to 38 % of all the evaluations of the completely noncredible web pages. As a result, the ratings distribution in this case is highly dispersed. The Leik measure [17] of ordinal dispersion equals 0.47 here while in the other cases it oscillates around 0.40.

There are clear limits to the ability of the individual lay users to discern the valuable and trash health information on the web. When no support is provided only 27.72 % of all their evaluations are exactly the same as expert evaluations of the given webpages while 49.72 % are higher. The main problem is therefore a tendency to overestimate the credibility of the medical information encountered on the Internet. If we take into account the fact that both values 4 and 5 indicate credible content while choosing ratings between 1 and 3 indicates various amounts of doubt, the problem becomes much less dramatic. For the following analyses we divided all the ratings into positive (4 or 5) and negative (other values). In this case 62.53 % of the lay evaluations are the same as expert evaluations i.e. both groups think the content as (generally) credible or both group consider it (generally) not credible. The share of overly positive ratings equals 23.43 % and the share of overly negative ratings equals 14.03 %.

The situation improves even further when we rely on the wisdom of crowds. Under this approach individual lay ratings are aggregated to produce a group-based evaluation that in theory should be more accurate as it eliminates the individual biases. As [18] suggests that when imperfect judgments are aggregated in the right way, the collective intelligence is often excellent. To test this supposition we computed median lay ratings for each page. Two facts became clear. First, the share of accurate lay ratings did indeed increase from 62.53 % to 70.52 %. Second, the share of overly optimistic ratings remained practically unchanged and equaled 23.68 %. In other words, while the wisdom of the crowds approach can help to evaluate accurately the websites that the individual users tend to unjustifiably see as not credible, it does little to identify the content that is seen as credible and is in fact treacherous. This is due to a clear positive bias in lay evaluations.

We investigated the possible sources of the differences between expert and lay evaluations. In particular we wanted to know which other characteristics that were rated by the participants of the study are most useful when predicting their credibility evaluations. Towards this purpose we ran logistic regressions with the dichotomised credibility rating as the dependent variable and the dichotomised other ratings provided by the same group as the independent variables. The results are presented in Table 2. In general all the evaluated dimensions are very

Table 2. Logistic regressions results. Dichotomised credibility rating dichotomised other dimensions.

	Lay users				Experts			
	Coef.	Robust std. error	Z	Sig.	Coef.	Std. error	Z	Sig.
Appearance	0.562	0.15	3.80	<0.001	0.973	0.47	2.06	0.04
Completeness	1.101	0.15	7.44	<0.001	1.210	0.58	2.09	0.04
Expertise	2.604	0.15	17.38	<0.001	1.265	0.59	2.14	0.03
Intentions	1.372	0.16	8.38	<0.001	1.657	0.48	3.44	<0.001
Controversy	−1.213	0.15	−8.11	<0.001	−1.696	0.48	−3.57	<0.001
Pseudo R squared	0.5232				0.5060			

strongly correlated in both groups. For the lay users clearly the most important factor is the perceived expertise of the author. The content in which the author is thought of as an expert has 13.5 (OR) times higher chance of being rated as credible than the content written by someone not perceived as an expert. The least important determinant of the perceived credibility for this group is the evaluation of the website appearance. In the case of experts the role of all the other dimensions is weighted in a more balanced way. The most important factor being the perceived intentions of the author. The content in which the author is thought to have good intentions has 5.2 (OR) times higher chance of being rated as credible than the content written by someone whose intentions seem dubious. Once again the websites perceived appearance is of least importance.

The relatively small role of a websites appearance may come as a surprise and, as it shall be shown later, its actual influence is much larger. Please note that appearance is a characteristic that can in principle be evaluated with equal competence by both the medical experts and the lay users. We therefore computed the correlation coefficient between appearance evaluations made by the experts and the lay users. They are significantly (p=0,01) correlated, but the correlation coefficient is only 0,135. It is small in comparison to correlations between different dimensions rated by the same group, virtually all of which exceed 0,3. Moreover the same pattern applies to all other evaluated characteristics i.e. all of them are tightly connected within the group (the experts or the lay users) and loosely related to the same characteristics as seen by the other group. Both the experts and the lay users form very coherent images of the content they evaluate but their images do not correspond with each other. In other words the experts and non-experts almost literally see medical web content differently.

5   To Follow or to Resist

In this section we will investigate whether the lay evaluations can be improved by a support system offering simple suggestions concerning the contents reliability. In general the answer is positive. The share of lay evaluations that are exactly the same as the expert evaluations rises by almost 10 % points (from the previously mentioned 27.72 % to almost 37 %). Unfortunately the share of overly positive ratings falls only slightly (from the 49.72 % to 46.22 %). When concentrating on the dichotomous evaluations (4–5 credible, 1–3 not credible) the share of accurate ratings equals 74.51 % and the overly positive ratings amount to only 17.63 % of all the ratings. When using the wisdom of crowds approach an impressive 87.9 % of the webpages are generally classified adequately. The remaining 12 % is however still overrated.

We compared median evaluations of all the webpages in the NH and the EH treatment. We found that all the webpages that were underrated when no suggestions were made got positive evaluations when the support system was available. However, from the webpages that were spontaneously overrated by the lay participants only 53 % got negative evaluations when the system revealed that they were not trustworthy. Once again it appears that the positive evaluation bias is exceptionally persistent.

Table 3. The average shares of webpages that got positive evaluations on the remaining four dimensions within the webpages with corrected and uncorrected group ratings.

	EH treatment			NH treatment		
	Corrected	Not corrected	Sig.	Corrected	Not corrected	Sig.
Expertise	0.125	0.762	<0.001	0.875	0.952	0.181
Intentions	0.750	0.952	0.031	1.000	1.000	-
Completeness	0.125	0.667	<0.001	0.750	0.905	0.088
Appearance	0.250	0.762	<0.001	0.750	0.952	0.031

Trying to understand which mechanism stands behind this unfortunate case, we inspected the differences between those webpages overrated in the NH treatment where the ratings were and were not corrected when the support system was available. First we note that almost all the webpages that were wrongly thought credible when no suggestions were offered were rated as controversial by the lay people. We therefore computed the average shares of webpages that got positive evaluations on the remaining four dimensions within the webpages with corrected and uncorrected group ratings. The results are presented in Table 3.

Three facts are worth noticing. First, in the EH condition the measured characteristics are once again highly correlated with the credibility rating. In the case of the websites whose ratings were corrected to not-credible, the mean share of positive ratings on all the other dimensions is significantly lower. Second, the general image of the analysed websites in the EH and NH conditions is visibly different. When the support system suggests that the website is a bad one the mean share of positive evaluations becomes much lower. Last but not least, if we were to predict, the image of which overrated websites will be corrected when we put the support system to work, relying solely on the ratings provided without this system, the only useful cue would be the perceived website appearance. Only in this case there is a statistically significant difference between the websites with corrected and uncorrected group ratings. We conclude that the bad webpages that look good are less likely to receive negative evaluation even if a support system reveals their treacherousness. The website appearance is therefore more important than it seems to be.

So far we have been analysing only reliable system feedback. Now we will explore whether the wise crowd can fight off system suggestions that are plainly wrong. Here we must analyse data from the RE condition. The accuracy of the lay evaluations in this case is the lowest. Only 23.4 % of all of them is exactly the same as the corresponding (correct) expert evaluations, After dichotomising the ratings this share reaches 50.88 % and when using the wisdom of the crowd approach it rises by a further 3 % points.

Similarly to the case of completely noncredible content in the NH treatment the best sign of the ongoing fight for correct evaluation is the dispersion of ratings in this condition. The Leik measure of ordinal dispersion in this case, irrespective of the actual website credibility, oscillates around 45 % of the

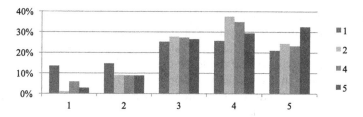

Fig. 3. The distributions of the lay evaluations (horizontal axis) for all the possible values of false suggestions made by the system (colours).

Table 4. The average time in seconds spent on a single evaluation in the RE condition.

	Mean estimation time	Std. Err.	95 % Conf. Interval	
Negative suggestions followed	36.947	2.396	32.215	41.679
Negative suggestion rejected	43.683	1.352	41.012	46.353
Positive suggestion rejected	46.152	3.471	39.296	53.008
Positive suggestion followed	43.341	2.162	39.070	47.612

maximum. Figure 3 depicts the distributions of the lay evaluations for all the possible values of false suggestions made by the system (as explained at the beginning the middle ratings were excluded). It can be seen that not all lay users are keen on following the deceitful advice. However, once again there is a visible asymmetry in how positive and negative information is treated. The probability that deceptive positive advice will be rejected equals 13 % if the rejection is defined as choosing either 1 or 2, and equals 39.8 % if we also include 3 as a negative evaluation. At the same time the probability that deceptive negative advice will be rejected equals over 53.3 %. It looks as though the subjects relied on some decision heuristics that are particularly sensitive to all the positive cues and they disregarded the warning signs.

The disregard for the warning signs, however, is costly as indicated by the time spent on evaluation. Table 4 presents the average time in seconds spent on a single evaluation in the RE condition. The rejection of the system suggestion is always more time consuming than following it. Interestingly this difference is statistically significant only in the case of negative system suggestions. The decision to follow them takes on average about 37 s while when deciding to reject it the subjects need on average about 44 s.

6 Summary

In this paper we presented a study on how the lay users evaluate the credibility of health related content on the web. We investigated the differences between their approach and the approach of medical experts and analysed whether we can increase their accuracy using a simple support system.

The general conclusion is positive. A simple support system based on expert choices does visibly increase the share of accurate evaluations. Even the wisdom of crowds is effective to some extent. Yet in this case it is important to pay attention not only to the central tendency measures for the group but also to the dispersion of ratings that is indicative of an inner struggle for better evaluations in the most problematic cases. These problematic cases can aslo be identified by asking for controversy evaluations.

We learned that lay users exhibit a clear positive evaluation bias that cannot be easily corrected under the wisdom of crowds approach. Moreover, it is fairly resistant to support system suggestions. On one hand, it prevents the lay users from correcting their overly positive evaluations when informed about their inaccuracy. On the other, it leads them to believe the false positive suggestions more keenly than the false negative suggestions.

Furthermore, we saw that lay users and experts both form coherent images of the evaluated web content that have much less in common than expected. It seems that these two groups literally see the evaluated medical websites differently. The lay users seem to perceive their evaluations as based mostly on the expertise of the source. However, when we analysed the predictors for their resilience against (rightfully) negative system suggestions, the perceived appearance of the websites becomes important.

Acknowledgments. This project has received funding from the European Unions Horizon 2020 research and innovation programme under the Marie Skłodowska-Curie grant agreement No. 690962.

References

1. Fogg, B.J., Tseng, H.: The elements of computer credibility. In: Proceedings of the SIGCHI Conference on Human Factors in Computing Systems, pp. 80–87. ACM (1999)
2. Fogg, B.J.: Persuasive technology: using computers to change what we think and do. Morgan Kaufmann Publishers, San Francisco, CA (2003)
3. Jankowski-Lorek, M., Nielek, R., Wierzbicki, A., Zieliński, K.: Predicting controversy of wikipedia articles using the article feedback tool. In: Proceedings of the 2014 International Conference on Social Computing, p. 22. ACM (2014)
4. Jankowski-Lorek, M., Zieliński, K.: Document controversy classification based on the wikipedia category structure. Comput. Sci. **16**(2), 185–198 (2015)
5. Rafalak, M., Abramczuk, K., Wierzbicki, A.: Incredible: is (almost) all web content trustworthy? Analysis of psychological factors related to website credibility evaluation. In: Proceedings of the Companion Publication of the 23rd International Conference on World Wide Web Companion, pp. 1117–1122. International World Wide Web Conferences Steering Committee (2014)
6. Rafalak, M., Bilski, P., Wierzbicki, A.: Analysis of demographical factors' influence on websites' credibility evaluation. In: Kurosu, M. (ed.) HCI 2014, Part III. LNCS, vol. 8512, pp. 57–68. Springer, Heidelberg (2014)
7. Flanagin, A.J., Metzger, M.J.: The role of site features, user attributes, and information verification behaviors on the perceived credibility of web-based information. New Media Soc. **9**(2), 319–342 (2007)

8. Kakol, M., Jankowski-Lorek, M., Abramczuk, K., Wierzbicki, A., Catasta, M.: On the subjectivity and bias of web content credibility evaluations. In: Proceedings of the 22nd International Conference on World Wide Web Companion, pp. 1131–1136. International World Wide Web Conferences Steering Committee (2013)

9. Kakol, M., Nielek, R.: What affects web credibility perception? An analysis of textual justifications. Comput. Sci. **16**(3), 295–310 (2015)

10. Lucassen, T., Muilwijk, R., Noordzij, M.L., Schraagen, J.M.: Topic familiarity and information skills in online credibility evaluation. J. Am. Soc. Inform. Sci. Technol. **64**(2), 254–264 (2013)

11. Crawford, J.L., Guo, C., Schroeder, J., Arriaga, R.I., Mankoff, J.: Is it a question of trust? How search preferences influence forum use. In: Proceedings of the 8th International Conference on Pervasive Computing Technologies for Healthcare, pp. 118–125. ICST (Institute for Computer Sciences, Social-Informatics and Telecommunications Engineering) (2014)

12. Frické, M., Fallis, D., Jones, M., Luszko, G.M.: Consumer health information on the internet about carpal tunnel syndrome: indicators of accuracy. Am. J. Med. **118**(2), 168–174 (2005)

13. Griffiths, K.M., Tang, T.T., Hawking, D., Christensen, H.: Automated assessment of the quality of depression websites. J. Med. Internet Res. **7**(5), e59 (2005)

14. Schwarz, J., Morris, M.: Augmenting web pages and search results to support credibility assessment. In: Proceedings of the SIGCHI Conference on Human Factors in Computing Systems, pp. 1245–1254. ACM (2011)

15. Yamamoto, Y., Tanaka, K.: Enhancing credibility judgment of web search results. In: Proceedings of the SIGCHI Conference on Human Factors in Computing Systems, pp. 1235–1244. ACM (2011)

16. Amin, A., Zhang, J., Cramer, H., Hardman, L., Evers, V.: The effects of source credibility ratings in a cultural heritage information aggregator. In: Proceedings of the 3rd Workshop on Information Credibility on the Web, pp. 35–42. ACM (2009)

17. Leik, R.K.: A measure of ordinal consensus. Pac. Sociol. Rev. **9**(2), 85–90 (1966)

18. Surowiecki, J.: The Wisdom of Crowds. Anchor, Garden City (2005)

Living Globe: Tridimensional Interactive Visualization of World Demographic Data

Eduardo Duarte[1(✉)], Pedro Bordonhos[1], Paulo Dias[1,2],
and Beatriz Sousa Santos[1,2]

[1] Department of Electronics Telecommunications and Informatics,
University of Aveiro, Aveiro, Portugal
{emod, bordonhos, paulo.dias, bss}@ua.pt
[2] Institute of Electronics and Informatics Engineering of Aveiro/IEETA,
Aveiro, Portugal

Abstract. This paper presents Living Globe, an application for visualization of demographic data supporting the temporal comparison of data from several countries represented on a 3D globe. Living Globe allows the visual exploration of the following demographic data: total population, population density and growth, crude birth and death rates, life expectancy, net migration and population percentage of different age groups. While offering unexperienced users a default mapping of these data variables into visual variables, Living Globe allows more advanced users to select the mapping, increasing its flexibility.

The main aspects of the Living Globe model and prototype are described as well as the evaluation results obtained using heuristic evaluation and usability testing. Some conclusions and ideas for future work are also presented.

Keywords: Information visualization · Demographic data · 3D globe · WebGL Globe · Usability evaluation · Heuristic evaluation

1 Introduction

This paper presents Living Globe, a 3D web visualization application meant to support the study of demographic data allowing users to compare data corresponding to several countries along the years. Living Globe allows the visual exploration of demographic data represented on a 3D globe and offers functionality not available in other demographic data visualization applications.

While 3D data visualization may have advantages and disadvantages regarding 2D solutions [1], and may be more appropriate in specific contexts, we consider the visualization of demographic data on a 3D globe to potentially be a more intuitive and useful approach. There are already other applications allowing the 3D visualization of demographic data on a globe mapping total population or population density (for example) into the height of bars positioned on the globe at the corresponding location. "World Population" [2] and "China and US Population" [3] are two such applications, both based on WebGL Globe [4]; however, the applications we have found and analyzed are very limited regarding the represented demographic data, its interactivity and its usability. Throughout this paper we describe the main aspects of our proposal in

© Springer International Publishing Switzerland 2016
S. Yamamoto (Ed.): HIMI 2016, Part I, LNCS 9734, pp. 14–24, 2016.
DOI: 10.1007/978-3-319-40349-6_2

Sect. 2, the prototype built to test it in Sect. 3, and the results obtained with heuristic evaluation and tests involving users performed to test usability in Sect. 4. Finally, conclusions and ideas for future work are presented in Sect. 5.

2 Related Work

In the following section we present 3D data web applications that allow data visualization on a globe and provide interaction to some extent which have inspired our proposal (Fig. 1). All except one allow visualizing total population or population density mapped as vertical bars with variable height on a globe.

Fig. 1. Related Visualizations (from left to right): 'WebGL Globe - World Population', 'WebGL Globe - China and US Population', 'World Population Density - 2010' and 'Small Arms and Ammunition'.

These applications were implemented using the WebGL technology or other APIs allowing 3D representations in Javascript, like three.js [5]. These technologies allow the creation of interactive 3D visual objects with textures and shaders in a canvas, and make the solution compatible with various types of devices, requiring only internet access and a browser supporting these technologies (such as the most currently used browsers). One such platform is the WebGL Globe developed in the scope of the "Chrome Experiments" project based on the native API of WebGL, which is an open platform that allows the visualization of any set of spatial data in a tridimensional globe. Using this API, a user can easily map any data to available graphical elements (a bar by default) and positioned in an interactive 3D globe.

As mentioned, two projects featured at the WebGL Globe site allow visualizing demographic data: "World Population" [2] and "China and US Population"[3]. While both represent data provided by the Socioeconomic Data and Application Center (SEDAC), "China and US Population" represents a more limited data set; "World Population Density" [6] is another example that presents SEDAC demographic data on a globe, implemented in three.js. In these three examples the population of all countries is represented by the height of vertical bars. While the first two offer as single functionality, the possibility of rotating the globe, the latter is not interactive, since the globe rotates continuously which implies that the user has to wait until the globe assumes an adequate position to visualize the population of a specific country.

Another example that has inspired us in spite of visualizing non-demographic data is "Small Arms and Ammunition - Imports & Exports" [7]. It is an interactive visualization of government-authorized small arms and ammunition trades from 1992 to 2000. The year is selected through a slider and, unlike the previous examples, this visualization supports selection and search with automatic completion of countries. The traffic between any two countries is represented by curved lines connecting the two, taking advantage of the third dimension to prevent it from occulting countries and the selection feedback.

The analyzed demographic data visualization applications have limitations regarding interaction when compared to "Small Arms and Ammunition", which features searching and selection functionality that might be easily integrated in a demographic data application resulting in a higher usability. Moreover, the tri-dimensionality of the user interface might be further explored. These ideas were incorporated in our proposal, the Living Globe, described in the next section.

3 Living Globe: The Proposal

Living Globe allows the visual exploration of the following demographic data along a set period of time: total population, population density and growth, crude birth and death rates, life expectancy, net migration and population percentage of different age groups. It is targeted to users that have some computer and statistics literacy. While offering unexperienced users a default mapping of these data variables into visual variables, Living Globe allows more advanced users to select the mapping they intent to use. This means that these users have the possibility of acting upon an earlier stage of the visualization reference model [8] making Living Globe a more flexible tool. In order to support this feature, three visual variables may be selected to map a data variable: (i) height of vertical bars (directly proportional to the data value) (ii) color of vertical bars (in a color scale ranging from blue to yellow) and (iii) color of the countries on the globe (in a scale ranging from red to green). An adequate selection of the data variables and their mapping to the visual variables may help the identification and study of potential relations among data variables.

According to Robertson et al. [9], it is likely that using 3D visualization can "maximize effective use of screen space", as it enables the simultaneous representation (in a single view) of a larger part of the data (even if it implies distortion). These authors also deem that interactive animation supports object constancy; for instance, when the user rotates a representation of complex data, it will be easier to remember the relationships of what is visualized. Cognitive load is shifted to the perceptual system, which frees users' cognitive capacity to perform tasks with the application.

After the user customizes the mapping of the variables to analyse (or simply uses the default mapping), Living Globe allows the visualization of the selected demographic data on an interactive 3D globe (users can freely rotate the globe) while offering the following filtering functionality: (i) selection of the country to analyze; (ii) selection of the year to analyze; (iii) definition of minimum and maximum data values that should be visualized; (iv) search with dynamic suggestion of the country names. The time selection provides support for analysis of temporal evolution of data; the value interval selection is important, for instance, when visualizing the population of small countries (e.g. Portugal) leaving out countries with large population (e.g. China). The dynamic search allows users to look more efficiently for countries when they do not know their location. Moreover, to ease the analysis of temporal evolution of data variables mapped to the three visual variables, it is possible to maintain configured limits to filter each variable when the selected year changes. Also, some variables can be displayed numerically on the user interface using country selection, supporting a more accurate analysis of the data. All of this functionality may be picked by the user according to the task at hand and instantiate to some extent Shneiderman's "Visualization seeking mantra" [10], namely, overview first, filter and details on demand.

Figure 2 shows the main aspects of the Living Globe user interface (UI), featuring the 3D interactive globe at the center, and various widgets allowing the selection of the above mentioned functionality: a search box for countries (upper left), sliders to set the filtering limits of the three variables mapped to the visual variables on the globe (middle left), numerical data corresponding to the selected country (top right), and a slider to select the year (beneath the globe).

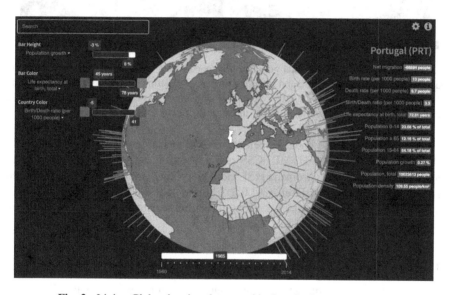

Fig. 2. Living Globe showing demographic data for Portugal in 1985

Figure 3 illustrates the filtering functionality regarding the data value interval to visualize as the countries color. On the left all the countries are visualized and most countries are represented with similar colors; on the right countries with large population (as China and India) are filtered out resulting in a visualization of the remaining countries with much more diverse and distinguishable colors.

4   Implementing the Prototype

To test the Living Globe proposal a prototype was developed allowing the visualization of data corresponding to the period between 1980 and 2014, obtained from the World Bank [11] with an open license for non-commercial usage.

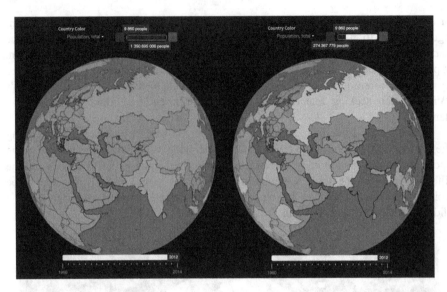

Fig. 3. Living Globe showing total population mapped to the country color: the data from all countries is displayed on the left, and filtering out large population countries (such as China and India) on the right (resulting in a representation with much more diverse and distinguishing colors for the remaining countries). (Color figure online)

The prototype (whose code is open-source and available at [12]), was built using web technologies such as HTML, CSS and Javascript, as well as some Javascript libraries such as three.js, chroma.js [13] and jQuery [14], and was successfully tested for the following browsers: Firefox 44.0.2, Chrome 48.0.2564.109 (64-bit) and Safari 9.0.3. In this section some details concerning the implementation of the prototype are described.

4.1   Data

Data is structured in a table where each country-indicator corresponds to a line and a column corresponds to a year. The net migration indicator is registered only every five years. Countries are identified by their official name as well as by their ISO 3166 alpha-3 code, a three letter code identifying univocally each country [15]. The geographic location of the countries used to create the vertical bar representations are characterized by latitude-longitude pairs obtained from the Sokrata Open Data Portal [16] a portal providing data for non-commercial purposes also in tabular format. All data is collected asynchronously using Ajax technology and analyzed to obtain the data variables minimum and maximum values, which are used for data normalization.

4.2   Globe and Countries

The country selection and their coloring according to a variable implies the identification of and drawing over country areas on a tridimensional object. As a first solution for this challenge, a CSV (Comma Separated Values) file containing a set of latitude-longitude pairs defining the polygonal border of each country was used [17]. To identify a selected country the cursor location was converted to latitude-longitude and compared with the country borders; however, this implementation was not efficient as drawing multiple polygons (whose properties change whenever the year or the filtering settings change) was resource-heavy and negatively affected the user experience.

A second solution, which is less computationally expensive, yielding a better user experience, uses textures and a raycaster, and was inspired by the "Small Arms and Ammunition" example mentioned in Sect. 2. Five different textures are superimposed on the globe (Fig. 4): (a) blend, using an image (Fig. 4A) with a gradient effect over the sea area for aesthetical purposes; (b) outline, using an image (Fig. 4B) with lines over the countries frontiers, allowing a better differentiation of different countries when these are displaying the same color; (c) lookup, using an image (Fig. 4C) that colors country territories with a unique luminosity level of grey; (d) ratio, initially transparent and where country territories are colored with the color corresponding to the value of the mapped data variable; and (e) select, initially transparent and where country territories are colored in white to provide feedback corresponding to the selected country.

A manually generated JSON file mapping grey levels to ISO 3166-1 alpha-3 codes was used. Since the demographic data used the same code per country, it was easy to associate them to each grey color.

A color scale obtained from a gradient between red and green (representing the minimum and the maximum values respectively) was created using the chroma.js library to represent the normalized value (V_{norm}) of the data variable mapped to the country color, according to the mathematical expression 1, where dv is the data variable to represent, c is the country and y is the selected year.

$$V_{norm}(dv, \ c, \ y) = (V \ (dv, \ c, \ y) \ - \ Min(dv, \ y)) \ / \ (Max(dv, \ y) \ - \ Min(dv, \ y) \tag{1}$$

4.3   Vertical Bars

A similar procedure was used to map another variable to the color of the vertical bars. A gradient between blue and yellow (representing the minimum and the maximum values respectively) was used for this mapping.

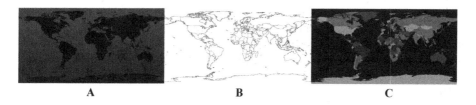

A   B   C

Fig. 4. Images used as textures in Living Globe: blend, outline and lookup (from left to right)

Finally, the height of the bars (mapping a third data variable) is also obtained using expression 1 and representing the maximum data value with a height of 100 pixels, which was found adequate taking into consideration the initial camera position and the globe scale.

5 Usability Evaluation

This section presents the main results obtained using an evaluation approach that we have been employing in our previous work [18] using two widely known and applied usability evaluation methods: heuristic evaluation [19], and usability testing used in order to improve the prototype (i.e. as a formative evaluation) [20]. The heuristic evaluation was performed using the Nielsen's usability heuristics by two evaluators, and three different sets of heuristics by one evaluator, all having some experience in using the method to analyze Information Visualization applications. During the usability test four users were observed while performing five tasks with different degrees of complexity, answered a post-task questionnaire, and gave some feedback concerning possible improvements. The most relevant findings are discussed in the following sections.

5.1 Heuristic Evaluation

Heuristic evaluation is a usability evaluation method extensively used to find potential usability problems proposed by Nielsen [19, 21]. It is performed by examining a user interface taking into consideration a set of heuristics that should be complied with. A list of problems corresponding to noncompliant aspects, categorized according to their estimated impact on user performance or acceptance and rated according to their severity is produced. This list is supposed to be used by the development team to prioritize the fixes to improve the user interface.

According to Tory and Möller [22, 23] heuristic evaluation is a useful expert review method to evaluate visualization applications and they recommended the use of visualization-specific heuristics. Several visualization-oriented heuristic sets have been proposed and used to evaluate visualization applications [24]. We have used the Nielsen's heuristics, a general heuristics set and two visualization-specific sets of heuristics [25, 26]. Several positive aspects were found as well as several minor potential usability problems and four issues with a severity equal or higher than 3 (in a scale of 1–5, where 5 is a catastrophic usability problem). Figure 5 illustrates one such problem related with the perception of the color used to represent visually a variable as the color of the country on the globe: the different colors of the scale used may be difficult to discriminate by color blind people. This can be alleviated by offering alternative color scales that the user can pick for both the bar colors and the country colors.

The ·remaining potential usability problems found having a higher severity grade were related to a deficient spatial organization that may occur when the browser window does not have enough size to accommodate all the visual elements of Living

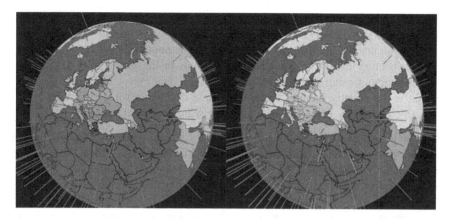

Fig. 5. Living Globe as seen by normal observers on the left, and color-blind observers (with Green-Blind/Deuteranopia) one the right, simulated by the Coblis simulator [27].

Globe and several elements are superimposed, and when the filter sliders are so close to each other that the numerical value on the right starts to occlude the values on the left (Fig. 6A). To lessen the first issue, the widgets layout was slightly changed, and to solve the latter issue, the numerical values were displayed on different sides of the sliders, one over and one under (Fig. 6B).

Most of the potential usability problems detected by the evaluators have been corrected or alleviated in the subsequent versions of Living Globe.

A   B

Fig. 6. Usability issue: version A has a slider whose numerical value on the right partially occludes the value on the left. Version B is the solution found for the latest version of Living Globe.

5.2 Usability Test

A simple usability test was achieved with a small set of tasks to be performed by participants while observed by the experimenter, a questionnaire, and a short interview to obtain participants' feedback concerning the application. Before executing these tasks, the participants where allowed to test the visualization at will and without any time limit in order to experiment with all of its features.

The questionnaire included questions regarding the difficulty and confidence in performing each task, and the overall satisfaction with the application.

The tasks corresponded to answering the following five questions:

1. What is the total population of Portugal?
2. What is the population growth of Benin?
3. Which country has the highest crude birth rate (without using search or selection)?
4. Which country has the highest birth/death ratio in the year 1990: Argentina or Brazil (without using search or selection)?
5. What is the country having the highest crude death rate value (representing this variable as country color and without using search or selection)?

The first three tasks are relatively easy and their main goal was to let the participants become more familiar with the application while encouraging them to explore the available functionalities (such as search). The last two tasks are more complex and were included in the test to find if they are understandable by the users and usable enough.

The usability test was performed with the collaboration of four participants, two having low computer literacy and no experience with information visualization applications, aged 23 and 59, and two being students at the Masters level in the Computing field, with high computer literacy but no experience with information visualization evaluation procedures, both aged 23.

In general, all tests lasted approximately 7 min and all participants completed all tasks without requiring assistance. The fourth and fifth tasks were answered with less confidence, and two of the participants completed task number five incorrectly.

Additionally, all users preferred to observe the data variables using country colors and text over bar colors and bar heights, which leads us to believe that vertical bars are not an appropriate visual variable to represent spatial data when compared to area coloring and text.

Along with the tasks, users also tested and provided feedback on a few variants of the visualization with additional widgets, like the inclusion of box-plots that represent the minimum, maximum and median values of the data variables before and after filtering, and the possibility of showing the numerical data in a tooltip that follows the mouse cursor instead of being placed statically in the top right corner. For the first variant, none of the users found the box-plots particularly useful. For the second variant, user preferences were split between static and tooltip.

Observation and participants' feedback suggest that the application was easy to learn and use, the filtering functionality was very useful, but the color scale used to colorize the countries might be misinterpreted (as green and red may have different cultural meanings). Once again, the addition of alternative color scales could mitigate this problem since the users could pick a more appropriate color scheme to represent the displayed data variables.

6 Conclusions and Future Work

This paper describes a 3D interactive visualization tool that allows users to visually explore demographic data represented on a globe. The general outcome of the evaluation is that Living Globe is an interesting tool to visualize demographic data and has potential to become more useful. The evaluation pointed out some negative points that were corrected in future versions, such as allowing the user selection of custom color scales, and provided some ideas for future work, such as the automatic adjustment of the widgets to the data characteristics (e.g. if the data does not allow the selection of a time period, the corresponding slider should not be present in the interface). Moreover, the conceptual model of Living Globe may be used beyond demographic data visualization and we consider it as a step to a more general API, allowing interactive representation of any kind of spatial data on a globe.

Acknowledgments. The authors are grateful to Beatriz Quintino Ferreira, Bruno Andrade, Bruno Garcia, Isabel Nascimento, Luís Afonso, Luís Silva, Pedro Miguel, Rui Simões e João Pedrosa for their valuable contribution to the usability evaluation of the prototype. This work was partially funded by National Funds through FCT - Foundation for Science and Technology, in the context of the projects UID/CEC/00127/2013 and Incentivo/EEI/UI0127/2014.

References

1. Dubel, S., Rohlig, M., Schumann, H., Trapp, M.: 2D and 3D presentation of spatial data: a systematic review. In: Proceedings of 3DVis@IEEEVIS2014: Does 3D really make sense for Data Visualization? pp. 11–18 (2014)
2. World Population. http://data-arts.appspot.com/globe/
3. China and US Population. http://newnaw.com/pub/js/webglglobe/chinaanduspop/
4. WebGL Globe. http://globe.chromeexperiments.com/
5. Three.js. http://threejs.org/
6. World Population Density. http://www.smartjava.org/examples/population/
7. Small Arms and Ammunition - Imports & Exports. http://armsglobe.chromeexper-iments. com/
8. Mazza, R.: Introduction to Information Visualization. Springer, London (2009)
9. Robertson, G., Card, S., Mackinlay, J.: Information visualization using 3D interactive animation. Commun. ACM **36**(4), 57–71 (1994)
10. Shneiderman, B.: The eyes have it: a task by data type taxonomy for information visualizations. In: Proceedings of the IEEE Symposium on Visual Languages, pp.336–343 (1996)
11. World Bank. http://data.worldbank.org/
12. Living Globe. https://github.com/edduarte/living-globe/
13. chroma.js. http://old.driven-by-data.net/about/chromajs/
14. jQuery. https://jquery.com/
15. ISO 3166 alpha-3. http://www.iso.org/iso/country_codes/
16. Sokrata Open Data Portal. https://opendata.socrata.com/dataset/Country-List-ISO-3166-Codes-Latitude-Longitude/mnkm-8ram/
17. World countries in JSON, CSV and XML and Yaml. https://mledoze.github.io/countries/
18. Santos, B.S., Dias, P.: Evaluation in visualization: some issues and best practices. In: SPIE Conference on Electronic Imaging, Visualization and Data Analysis 2014, vol. 9017, pp. 90170O-1–8. SPIE, San Francisco (2014)
19. Nielsen, J.: Heuristic evaluation of user interfaces. In: Proceedings of the ACM CHI 2090 Conference, pp. 249–256 (1990)
20. Dix, A., Finlay, J., Abowd, G., Beale, R.: Human-Computer Interaction, 3rd edn. Prentice Hall, Upper Saddle River (2004)

21. Nielsen, J.: Finding usability problems through heuristic evaluation. In: Proceedings of the SIGCHI Conference on Human Factors in Computing Systems, pp. 373–380 (1992)
22. Tory, M., Möller, T.: Human factors in visualization research. IEEE Trans. Vis. Comput. Graph. **10**(1), 72–84 (2004). IEEE
23. Tory, M., Möller, T.: Evaluating visualizations: do expert reviews work? IEEE Comput. Graph. Appl. **25**(5), 8–11 (2005). IEEE
24. Carpendale, S.: Evaluating information visualizations. In: Kerren, A., Stasko, J.T., Fekete, J.-D., North, C. (eds.) Information Visualization. LNCS, vol. 4950, pp. 19–45. Springer, Heidelberg (2008)
25. Zuk, T., Schlesier, L., Neumann, P., Hancock, M. S., Carpendale, S.: Heuristics for Information Visualization Evaluation. In BELIV 2006, pp. 1–6. ACM, New York (2006)
26. Forsell, C., Johanson, J.: An heuristic set for evaluation in information visualization. In: Proceedings of AVI 2010, pp. 199–206. ACM, New York (2010)
27. Coblis simulator. http://www.color-blindness.com/coblis-color-blindness-simulator/

Effectiveness of Choosing Dissonant Combination of Tones for Multivariate Data Sonification

Yukio Horiguchi$^{(\boxtimes)}$, Moriyu Nakashima, Hiroaki Nakanishi, and Tetsuo Sawaragi

Department of Mechanical Engineering and Science, Kyoto University, Kyoto, Japan
{horiguchi,nakanishi,sawaragi}@me.kyoto-u.ac.jp,
nakashima.moriyu.23z@st.kyoto-u.ac.jp

Abstract. In the present paper, additive syntheses of two tones are examined in order to look into what data-to-sound mapping design is better to acoustically communicate varying quantities of a multivariate system. The research focus is placed on the effectiveness of mappings for listeners to discriminate one variable component of sonified data from another. Dyads of pitches are tested through a couple of experiments where a special attention is paid to the "dissonance" of two tones. The first experiment investigates its effects on the perception of two static tones presented simultaneously. The second experiment investigates the effectiveness of choosing dissonant pitch combinations to sonify two quantities of a system being controlled manually. Experimental results demonstrate that the dissonance of tones can improve the perception of changes in individual variates out of a synthesized sound but that the frequency interval between two tones has stronger effects in dynamic situations.

Keywords: Tonal dissonance · Sonification · Parameter mapping · Auditory display

1 Introduction

Sonification is a subset of auditory display to convey information using non-speech audio [1–3]. By means of sonification, data relations are transformed into perceived relations in acoustic signals. While it has been successfully deployed in a wide range of application domains, general guidelines for sonification design are yet to be developed [2–4].

Parameter mapping is one of the most commonly used techniques to produce a sonification, which defines a set of mappings between data dimensions and acoustic dimensions (e.g., loudness, pitch, tempo, etc.) [1–4]. The authors have been doing empirical studies to examine parameter mappings to make audible the gap between desired and current state of dynamic systems being controlled. Various data-to-sound mappings were tested using a one-dimensional, invisible target tracking task [5, 6]. The experimental results clarified preferable polarity and scaling function of the mapping for a type of sonification that has a target to pursue. Reducing the sound intensity as the

© Springer International Publishing Switzerland 2016
S. Yamamoto (Ed.): HIMI 2016, Part I, LNCS 9734, pp. 25–33, 2016.
DOI: 10.1007/978-3-319-40349-6_3

gap decreases and making no sound at the goal state are found to be the most effective mapping among those that have intensity and pitch as acoustic parameters to use. These results are, however, limited to univariate systems. In order to extend the application domain, knowledge of designing sonification for multivariate systems needs to be explored.

In the present paper, additive syntheses of two tones are examined in order to look into what mapping design is better to communicate quantities of a multivariate system that changes dynamically. The research focus is placed on the effectiveness of data-to-sound mappings for listeners to discriminate one variate of sonified data from another. On the basis of empirical findings mentioned above, quantitative variables are mapped onto the amplitude of different tones so that the intensity of each tone represents the difference of the corresponding variable value from its reference. The pitch of tones is therefore the acoustic parameter to examine. Parameter mappings independent of the physical configuration of the task space are explored in this study.

Dyads of pitches are tested through a couple of experiments where a special attention is paid to consonance and dissonance of two tones. Consonance had been studied in the field of musical aesthetics and is a matter of tone quality playing an important role in determining a level of pleasantness/unpleasantness of sounds [7]. The tonal consonance is defined as the sensation of "clearness" while the dissonance is "turbidity". The consonance of a chord changes according to the frequency ratio of its components. Two tones sound consonant only if their frequency ratio is integer; otherwise they are dissonant. According to Stumpf's tonal fusion theory of consonance [8], two consonant tones may be perceptually fused into a single harmonic series. The research question here is whether or not dissonant combinations of tones can improve the listener's perception of changes in individual auditory components out of a synthesized sound.

2 Experiment 1: Discrimination of Static Tones

2.1 Experimental Setup and Procedure

The first experiment was carried out to examine the loudness perception of two *static* pure tones with different pitch levels. Participants were requested to judge the loudness of individual tones that were simultaneously presented to them.

The frequencies of the tones are defined as shown in Table 1. Frequency difference (3 levels) and consonance vs. dissonance (2 levels) are factors of the experiment. Combinations #1 through #3 consist of consonant tones with the 250, 500, and 750 Hz frequency difference, respectively. Combinations #4 through #6 consist of dissonant tones that have the same variations of the frequency difference.

The experiment employed a within-subject design. It consists of six sections that correspond to different tone combinations and each section is divided further into two blocks. In the first block, participants were exposed to individual tones of the combination separately to learn the reference sound level and the sound intensity variation range. The amplitude of each tone was set to 0.5, 0, and 1 by turns to illustrate to participants the intermediate, minimum (i.e., silent), and maximum sound levels of the tone, respectively.

Table 1. Combination of frequencies in Experiment 1

Combination #	Frequency of Tone 1 (Hz)	Frequency of Tone 2 (Hz)
1	750	500
2	1000	500
3	1500	500
4	763	513
5	1013	513
6	1513	513

In the second block, four static tones were presented in sequence that were composites of two pure tones of the same frequency combination but they were different combinations of amplitudes. Each time they heard a static tone, the participants were requested to tell their judgment of each constituent tone's loudness by placing a check mark on the scale shown in Fig. 1. Errors between presented and perceived sound level were evaluated for comparison. Twenty-four samples in total (6 frequency combinations × 4 amplitude combinations) were collected and the order of the test combinations was randomized across participants to balance the order effect.

Silent ├─────────────────┼─────────────────┤ Loud

Fig. 1. Linear scale to answer the loudness of each tone

For this experiment, Max/MSP 5 was used for sound synthesis and auditory stimuli were presented though a BOSE Quiet Comfort 15 active noise canceling headphone.

2.2 Results

Ten undergraduate and graduate students (aged from 22 to 24 years) participated in the experiment from the department of mechanical engineering and science in Kyoto University. They are normal in hearing ability. The experimenter told them sufficient instructions about the purpose and procedure of the experiment as well as the designs of the auditory displays. All of them gave informed consent to the experiment.

Figure 2 presents a summary of the experimental results. A two-way ANOVA found no effect of the frequency difference but a significant effect of the consonance/dissonance factor ($p < 0.001$) onto the perception error. A post-hoc Tukey's test shows that, compared to the consonant combination, the perception error decreases by the dissonant combination of tones significantly when the frequency interval is 1,000 Hz ($p < 0.01$) and marginally significantly when the frequency difference is 500 Hz ($p = 0.070$). The perception error also decreases significantly with dissonant combinations as the frequency difference increases from 250 Hz to 1,000 Hz ($p < 0.05$).

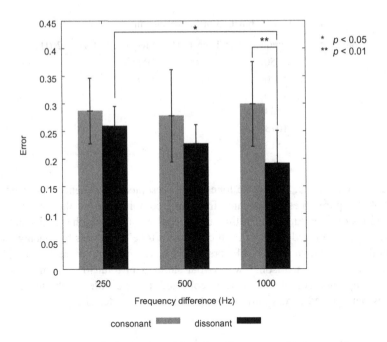

Fig. 2. Loudness perception error (mean + SD)

The above result indicates that the participants can achieve more accurate loudness perception when the two tones are given in a dissonant combination than in a consonant one. This effect becomes stronger when the tones have a larger difference in the frequency. On the other hand, some of the participants made comments that they could hardly measure how much amount of intensity difference the stimulus tones had relative to the reference sound level. They could only hear whether they sounded larger or smaller.

3   Experiment 2: Discrimination of Dynamic Tones for Control

3.1   Experimental Setup

In the second experiment, the same pitch combinations were tested using a kind of tracking task where the system being controlled had two dimensions of the state, one of which was controlled manually and the other was defined automatically. Both dimensions were sonified by different pure tones so that their intensity changed dynamically with the corresponding state variable. Human operators needed to specify the status of each variable from auditory signals for successful control of the system.

Figure 3 shows a visual representation of the experimental task. The two bars represent non-negative quantities to be displayed acoustically by the intensity of two tones. The operator's task is to make both values zero at the same instant. On the one

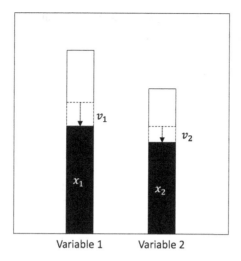

Fig. 3. Visual representation of the auditory tracking task

hand, Variable 1 corresponds to the system dimension the operator tries to control and its behavior is defined as a second order system. The input device is a joystick whose displacement is mapped onto the acceleration of the system being controlled. Variable 2, on the other hand, gives a reference signal to the operator. Its value automatically decreases at a constant rate that varies randomly from trail to trail. Participants were requested to control the position of the Variable 1 bar so that it reached zero exactly when the Variable 2 bar got vanished. The difference in the timing of reaching zero between the two variables is the main evaluation metric in this experiment.

On the basis of findings in our previous studies [5, 6], the data-to-sound mapping for each dimension was designed so that the loudness of a generated sound represents a quantity to be diminished. The amplitude of the tone is given by

$$A(d) = C \ d^{\frac{1}{2\log_{10}2}} \tag{1}$$

where d represents the quantity of interest and C is a constant coefficient. Through this mapping, the sound intensity decreases as the quantity decreases and the "loudness" [9] of the sound changes proportional to the quantity.

The tested tones are defined in Table 2, which consist of the same pitch combinations as the first experiment. Frequency difference (3 levels), consonance vs. dissonance (2 levels), and higher vs. lower pitch for the control dimension (2 levels) were factors of this experiment. Combinations #1 through #6 consist of consonant tones while combinations #7 through #12 consist of dissonant tones. Within combinations #1 through #3 and #7 through #9, lower frequencies are assigned to the control dimension, i.e., Variable 1; otherwise, higher frequencies are assigned. The frequency difference of the two tones is chosen from 250, 500, and 750 Hz.

Same as Experiment 1, Max/MSP 5 was used for sound synthesis and auditory signals were presented though a BOSE Quiet Comfort 15 headphone. The sound

Table 2. Combination of frequencies in Experiment 2

Combination #	Frequency of Tone 1 (Hz)	Frequency of Tone 2 (Hz)
1	500	750
2	500	1000
3	500	1500
4	500	500
5	750	500
6	1000	500
7	513	763
8	513	1013
9	513	1513
10	763	513
11	1013	513
12	1513	513

pressure level of the generated sound ranged from 55 dB (no audio output) to 86 dB (the maximum output).

3.2   Procedure

The experiment employed a within-subject design and consisted of two sections. The first section is the practice session for participants to get familiar with the tracking task itself. In this section, the participants practiced the auditory tracking task with a visual aid for 3 min and then 15 trials with no aid. The visual representation of the tracking task, which was shown in Fig. 3, was provided as the visual aid.

The second section is divided into three blocks. The first block is the rehearsal session, in which the participants performed the auditory tracking task using a particular combination of tones. They rehearsed 6 trials without the visual aid to learn the tones to be tested in this section. At the beginning of this block, the experimenter told the participants which pitch in the combination was assigned to the control dimension. The second block is the recording session. The participants did 10 trials for the same configuration of the auditory display. The last block was prepared for collecting participants' evaluation of the mappings. The participants were requested to fill in a NASA-TLX subjective workload questionnaire sheet. The second section lasted until all of the tone combinations listed in Table 2 were tested.

One hundred and twenty trials per participant were recorded for performance evaluation. The order of the test combinations was randomized across participants to balance the order effect. Tracking error and workload measure are evaluation functions to compare different parameter mappings. The former aspect is evaluated by the amount of the time difference of reaching zero (time difference) and the remaining quantity when the other quantity has reached zero (position error). The NASA-TLX Weighted Work Load (WWL) score is used for the latter evaluation aspect.

3.3   Results

Twelve undergraduate and graduate students (aged from 22 to 31 years) participated in the experiment from the department of mechanical engineering and science in Kyoto University. All of them are normal in hearing ability and gave informed consent to the experiment.

Figures 4, 5 and 6 show experimental results described with respect to the time difference, position error, and WWL score, respectively. Both of the performance measures (Figs. 4 and 5) indicate that the listener can achieve more accurate control when the component tones are given with a larger difference in the pitch level. The more similar frequencies two tones have, the more difficult for listeners to discriminate them. This phenomenon, known as "auditory masking" (in the frequency domain) [10], obviously provides a solid rationale for the observed performance degradation with a smaller frequency difference. The WWL score (Fig. 6) shows the same trend, demonstrating that the participants' subjective evaluation of the task difficulty is congruent with their task performance.

Three-way ANOVAs with repeated measures found significant effects of the frequency difference ($p < 0.05$) onto all of three dependent measures. Post-hoc Tukey's tests show that there are significant mean differences in these measures between the frequency difference of 250 Hz and 1,000 Hz ($p < 0.05$). No effect was found with respect to the consonance/dissonance of the tone combination or the higher/lower pitch assignment to the control dimension. The mean difference in the time difference, however, approached significance between the consonant and the dissonant tone combination at the frequency difference of 500 Hz ($p = 0.088$). Although its effect is limited, there was a trend for performance improvement by choosing dissonant pitch combinations to sonify two quantities.

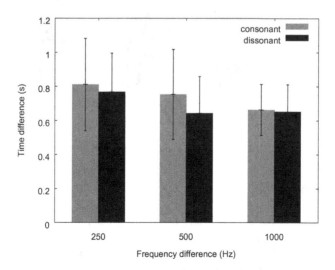

Fig. 4. Time difference (mean + SD)

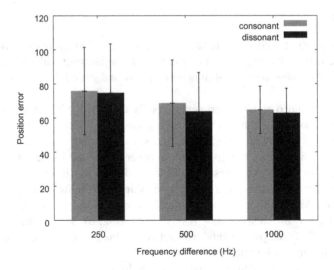

Fig. 5. Position error (mean + SD)

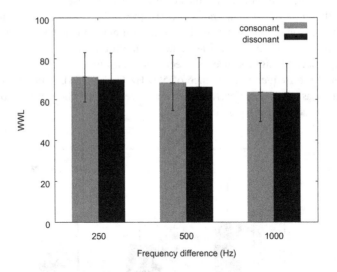

Fig. 6. WWL score (mean + SD)

4 Conclusions

The overall results of the present study demonstrated that choosing dissonant pitch
combinations can make a difference in sonification of multivariate data. The tonal
dissonance is beneficial for listeners to differentiate one variate from another although
the findings are limited to two variate systems.

The first experiment revealed that two tones in a dissonant combination are easier to
recognize the intensity of each tone from their additive synthesis than those in a

consonant combination. On the other hand, the second experiment showed that this effect is limited to cases where the tones have no temporal variation in their intensity. Increasing the pitch interval of the tones has much stronger effects for dynamic situations than their tonal dissonance. The result implies that intensity variations of partials may cause substantial changes in tone quality. The second experiment, however, confirmed a trend for performance improvement by the tonal dissonance. The dissonance does not deteriorate the perception of varying quantities in a synthesized tone.

Because the experiments were designed to use equal frequency intervals, the most dissonant point [7] was not chosen to determine pitch combinations. The effectiveness therefore could be increased if the most dissonant combinations are employed for pitches to map. The more variates to sonify, the more difficult to determine pitch levels of individual quantities. Considering not only the frequency interval but the frequency ratio may help design decision making for such cases.

Acknowledgements. This work was supported in part by JSPS KAKENHI Grant Number 15K00269. The authors are grateful for their supports.

References

1. Kramer, G.: An introduction to auditory display. In: Kramer, G. (ed.) Auditory Display, Sonification, Audition, and Auditory Interfaces, pp. 1–7. Addison-Wesely, Boston (1994)
2. Eldridge, A.: Issues in auditory display. Artif. Life **12**(2), 259–274 (2006)
3. Peres, S.C., Best, V., Brock, D., Frauenberger, C., Hermann, T., Neuhoff, J.G., Nickerson, L.V., Shinn-Cunningham, B., Stockman, T.: Auditory interfaces. In: Kortum, P. (ed.) HCI Beyond the GUI: Design for Haptic, Speech, Olfactory, and Other Nontraditional Interfaces, pp. 147–195. Morgan Kaufmann, Burlington (2008)
4. Dubus, G., Bresin, R.: A systematic review of mapping strategies for the sonification of physical quantities. PLoS ONE **8**(12), e82491 (2013)
5. Horiguchi, Y., Yasuda, K., Nakanishi, H., Sawaragi, T.: Data-to-sound mapping to sonify ongoing system status in continuous manual control task. In: Proceedings of Human Factors and Ergonomics Society Annual Meeting, vol. 55, pp. 1235–1239 (2011)
6. Horiguchi, Y., Miyajima, K., Nakanishi, H., Sawaragi, T.: Parameter-mapping sonification for manual control task: timbre and intensity manipulation to sonify dynamic system state. In: Proceedings of the SICE Annual Conference 2013, pp. 2341–2346 (2013)
7. Kameoka, A., Kuriyagawa, M.: Consonance theory part I: consonance of dyads. J. Acoust. Soc. Am. **45**, 1451–1459 (1969)
8. DeWitt, L.A., Crowder, R.G.: Tonal fusion of consonant musical intervals: the oomph in Stumpf. Atten. Percep. Psychophy. **41**(1), 73–84 (1987)
9. Stevens, S.S.: The measurement of loudness. J. Acoust. Soc. Am. **27**(5), 815–829 (1955)
10. Moore, B.C.J.: An Introduction to the Psychology of Hearing, 3rd edn. Academic Press, Cambridge (1997)

A Trial Cartooning to Promote Understanding of a Scenario

Shigeyoshi Iizuka[✉]

Faculty of Business Administration, Kanagawa University,
Hiratuska, Kanagawa, Japan
iizuka@kanagawa-u.ac.jp

Abstract. A cartoon is a mode of expression already accepted by all age groups, from children to adults. It is generally believed that expressing by a cartoon makes it possible to convey something that is easy to understand or interesting to readers, or both. This paper describes a trial cartooning of a scenario that reveals how to improve a scenario through cartoons. In this trial, four scenarios were chosen; they were cartooned using a digital cartooning, instead of being hand-drawn. This paper describes the details and results of the cartooning trials, as well as the implications of the results. Further research may estimate the validity of the produced cartoon and develop an approach for cartooning of a scenario in the future.

Keywords: Persona-based scenario methodology · Cartoon expression · User experience · Digital cartooning tool

1 Introduction

The persona-based scenario methodology is followed in the analysis of user requirement in an upstream process of design; this methodology is followed to develop a product that a user would like to use. The advantage of using a person to draw upon users' behavior is that all the members of the design and development team can together determine the target users, setting, timing; and purpose of their product as well the method to use it. The persona-based scenario methodology helps a design team to focus on users' needs. Further, it helps to change the concept of the designer's work from a mere product or website to a thoughtfully designed users' experience of using the product or the website. The scenario-based method need not involve text written in sentences. When applying the method that can help to visualize a user's behavior more intuitively, something like a storyboard with pictures or illustration will be more effective.

Hence, for the designers to share the contents of a scenario more effectively and gain a better understanding of it, a trial in which a scenario was depicted in a cartoon was conducted. The trial is described in this paper.

© Springer International Publishing Switzerland 2016
S. Yamamoto (Ed.): HIMI 2016, Part I, LNCS 9734, pp. 34–39, 2016.
DOI: 10.1007/978-3-319-40349-6_4

2 Trial Cartooning

The tool used for cartooning in this trial is introduced. Additionally, the application of cartooning is described.

It is thought that "expressing by a cartoon" affects the sensitivity of a person more than "expressing by sentences" does. Hence, I thought that the trial of "cartooning a scenario" was suitable to express the value the user appreciates by using the target design equipment or system, that is, the contents equivalent to "value scenario" in the framework of the structured scenario method [1]. Indeed, I made "value scenario" the subject of cartooning. Thus, "scenario" means "value scenario" in this paper (Table 1).

Table 1. Three types of scenarios in the structured scenarios method

Classification of scenario	Content
Value scenario	The value and essential request for the user: the offer policy for business provider
Activity scenario	The user's activity: one scene of a value scenario
Interactive scenario	Operation in detail to the target: one scene of an activity scenario

2.1 Cartooning Tool

The one who is not good at drawing a cartoon is not inadequate. Therefore, it is necessary to reduce the psychological burden at least a little bit.

In recent years, cartoons have been often drawn digitally; general users have been offered certain digital cartooning tools. This trial involves a digital cartooning tool "ComiPO!" [2]. ComiPO! is a cartoon design tool involving 3-D characters. It has various presetting systems. We can illustrate various expressions and poses through transformation with the shape of the hand and slight adjustment of the inclination of the head simply by choosing the characters and basic parts from the presetting feature. The balloon, MANPU, and the effect line peculiar to a cartoon expression are also developed (Fig. 1).

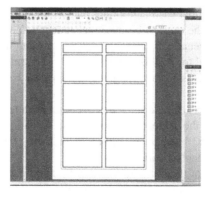

Fig. 1. Authoring Screen of ComiPO!

2.2   Implementation 1

In this trial, the following four patterns were created.

Only one college student applies the cartooning technique. The scenario indicated in Table 2 is used as the material, and the cartooning technique is applied by using ComiPO!

Table 2. Implementation targets

Scenario and persona	Volume of the scenario (Number of characters in Japanese)	Maker (*)
Pattern A	3,020	Same
Pattern A'	2,287	Same
Pattern B	895	Different
Pattern C	710	Different

*It denotes whether "persona and scenario creator" and "the person who applies the cartooning technique" are identical personalities.

First, regarding Pattern A, the student created the scenario and persona that were cartooned. Therefore, one individual created the scenario and persona as well as cartooned it; this pattern demonstrated the cartooning of a design-related aspect of the scenario and persona without misunderstanding. The scenario and persona of Pattern A' are created by a different student. Regarding Pattern B and Pattern C, the scenario and persona were created by different individuals. In other words, in this trial, one individual cartooned for all the patterns, but different individuals made each set of scenario and persona.

In fact, a storyboard was once created using a scenario according to a student's judgment of cartooning, and the scenario was cartooned based on that (Fig. 2). A storyboard contains panel layout, composition of each panels, serif, arrangement of characters, and so on.

2.3   Results

Figure 3 shows the hours that each cartooning pattern took. As expected, the working hours for Pattern A were the shortest because the student who was assigned cartooning created the persona and scenario as well as understood its aim well. Moreover, she was cartooning using ComiPO! for the first time, when she performed the task of Pattern A. The fact that the process was so fast implies that there was less time than that for the other patterns.

On the other hand, considerable time was needed for Pattern B and Pattern C, but less time was needed for the sentence volume of the scenario than that for Pattern A and Pattern A'. Therefore, the relative volume of scenario-related sentences may not always affect the hours spent in cartooning.

Conversely, in terms of the hours spent in cartooning, Pattern C took longer than the other patterns took, although Pattern C was performed at the end and its volume of

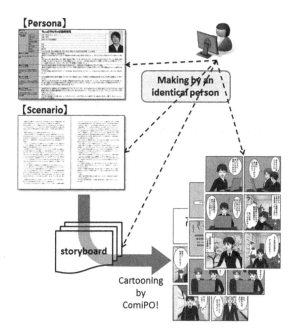

Fig. 2. Work flow of cartooning

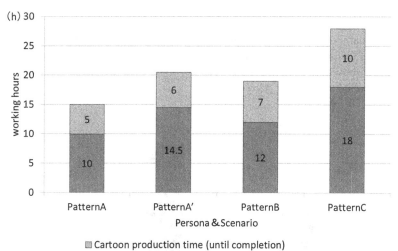

Fig. 3. Working hours for each pattern of cartooning

scenario was less. The interview of the student in charge revealed that she needed time because she was fussy about detailed visualization and repeated her trial-and-error attempts. However, the result that is evident in such a detailed expression for readers is noteworthy. Therefore, this extra time cannot be deemed unnecessary.

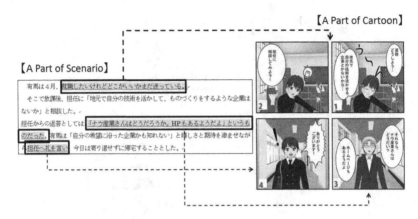

Fig. 4. Interaction of scenario and produced cartoon (excerpt)

In this trial, the judgment of how to visualize specific parts was entrusted to the student in charge. Figure 4 shows how the interaction in specific parts of the scenario was expressed in the cartoon.

2.4   Implementation 2

In addition, to reveal the difference among the cartoon creators, another student performed the cartooning. In this case, the targets of cartooning were Pattern B and Pattern C. That is, scenario was not created; it was only cartooned. Until that stage, she had not used ComiPO! She used it in this trial for the first time.

Figure 5 shows the comparison between the hours spent by these two students who were assigned cartooning.

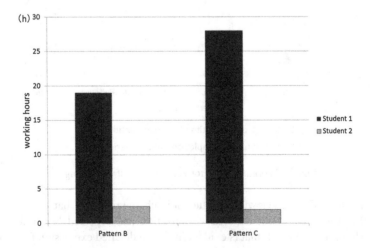

Fig. 5. Comparison between hours spent by the two students who were assigned cartooning

Figure 5 shows that even when cartooning was conducted for the same scenario, there was a difference in the working hours spent by a person.

Furthermore, there was also a difference in terms of the quality of the completed cartoon.

3 Discussion

Regarding the visualization of a scenario, how to visualize each part can be considered a crucial element. This element is evident in the working hours and cartoon. As indicated in the previous chapter, the hours spent in cartooning can differ substantially among individuals. Furthermore, there is also a difference in the quality of the completed cartoon. As stated above, the difference in the quality of the completed cartoon or the considerable time needed in cartooning can hinder the cartooning of a scenario. Therefore, a technique that considerably varies among individuals is needed. Such a technique will be a one-solution method to enable the cartooning of a scenario.

4 Conclusion

It is generally believed that expressing through a cartoon influences the process of conveying something that is easy-to-understand or interesting to people. Further, cartoons appeal more to the sensitivity of people than sentences do.

This paper describes a trial cartooning of a scenario. In this trial, a digital cartooning tool "ComiPO!" was used instead of the hand-drawing technique. "Value scenario," which expresses the value appreciated by a user, was the target for cartooning. Four kinds of scenario were created. A student cartooned all of those and checked the difference between the working hours. Furthermore, another student cartooned the two kinds of scenario, and the difference between the working hours was seen. The results showed that

- The relative volume of the scenario sentence may not always influence the hours spent in cartooning
- Even when a scenario was cartooned, there was a difference between the working hours spent by a person.

I aim to develop a method involving cartooning of a scenario in the future.

References

1. Yanagida, K., Ueda, Y., Go, K., Takahashi, K., Hayakawa, S., Yamazaki, K.: Structured scenario-based design method. In: Kurosu, M. (ed.) HCD 2009. LNCS, vol. 5619, pp. 374–380. Springer, Heidelberg (2009). Special issue of Japanese society for the science of design, vol. 18-2, no. 70 (2011) (in Japanese)
2. http://www.comipo.com/en/index.html

The Influence of Numerical Displays on Human Performance in the Manual RVD Task

Wang Liu[1,2], Yu Tian[1(✉)], Chunhui Wang[1], Weifen Huang[1],
Shanguang Chen[1], and Jun Wang[2]

[1] National Key Laboratory of Human Factors Engineering, China Astronaut
Research and Training Center, Beijing 100094, China
{acc_liuwang, hwf_2006}@sina.com,
{cctian, shanguang_chen}@126.com, chunhui_89@163.com
[2] School of Aviation Science and Engineering, Beijing University
of Aeronautics and Astronautics, Beijing 100191, China
wangjun@buaa.edu.cn

Abstract. The present study aims to identify the influence of the display of numerical data on human performance in the manually controlled rendezvous and docking (manual RVD) task. Two display schemes were designed and developed in a RVD simulator, one display scheme with numerical data (Display A) and the other without numerical data (Display B). Twelve male subjects completed four trials of RVD simulations on the RVD simulator each, two trials observing Display A, and two trials observing Display B. Deviation data, such as the horizontal deviation (Y), the vertical deviation (Z), the roll deviation (∅), the pitch deviation (θ), the yaw deviation (φ), are automatically recorded. Results show that the display of the numerical data are helpful for the diminishing of the pitch deviation (θ) and the yaw deviation (φ), while the roll deviation (∅) does not change significantly in the two conditions, the horizontal deviation (Y) and the vertical deviation (Z) indices seem to be affected negatively by the numerical display. Based on analysis of the results, we suggest that numerical data of the pitch deviation (θ) and the yaw deviation (φ) should be highlighted on the interface, meanwhile operators should pay more attention to the control of horizontal deviation (Y) and the vertical deviation (Z) when there are numerical displays.

Keywords: Manually controlled rendezvous and docking (manual RVD) · Numerical display · Human performance

1 Background

Manually controlled rendezvous and docking (manual RVD) of space vehicles is a complex human computer interaction (HCI) task for astronauts. Manual RVD task generally involves two spacecrafts, namely, a chaser spacecraft and a target spacecraft. In the manual RVD task, the operator, displays, and controllers form a closed loop [1], as shown in Fig. 1. Video image of the target spacecraft obtained from the cameras is

© Springer International Publishing Switzerland 2016
S. Yamamoto (Ed.): HIMI 2016, Part I, LNCS 9734, pp. 40–47, 2016.
DOI: 10.1007/978-3-319-40349-6_5

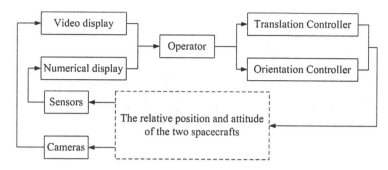

Fig. 1. The display-human-controller loop in the manual RVD task

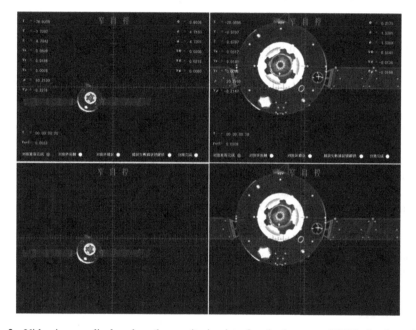

Fig. 2. Video images displayed on the monitoring interface in the manual RVD simulator. Left column: When the distance between the two spacecrafts is around 80 m, the whole profile of the target spacecraft can be seen; Right column: When the distance between the two spacecrafts is around 20 m, the cross drone on the target spacecraft can be viewed clearly, meanwhile only part of the target spacecraft profile can be seen. First row: Interface with numerical displays; Second row: Interface without numerical displays.

displayed on the monitoring interface, numerical data obtained from the sensors which indicate the relative position and attitude of the two spacecrafts can be overlaid on the edge of the interface (displaying the numerical data is optional in the manual RVD system) [2], as shown in Fig. 2. The operator observes the information displayed on the monitoring interface and manipulates the controllers to complete the manual RVD task. The system includes two controllers in the chaser spacecraft: one translation controller,

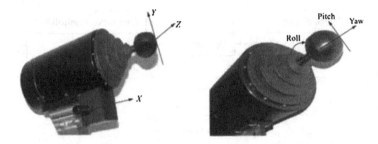

Fig. 3. The two controllers of the manual RVD system. (a) Left: the translation controller which controls the X, Y, and Z axes of the chaser's position. (b) Right: the orientation controller which controls the yaw, pitch, and roll of the chaser's attitude.

shown in Fig. 3a, which controls the X, Y, and Z axes of the chaser's position, and one orientation controller, shown in Fig. 3b, which controls the yaw, pitch, and roll of the chaser's attitude [3].

Researches have shown that human performance in the manual RVD tasks are influenced by many factors, such as the ergonomic design of the manual RVD system [4], the cognitive abilities of the operator [2, 5], and the complexity of the RVD tasks [3].

Researches concerning the influence of ergonomic design on human performance in manual RVD task have investigated several key factors in the display and control loop, such as the polarity of the controllers, the gain of the controller, the delay time for the system to respond, the size, shape, and color of the target cross-drone on the object space vehicle [6]. However, the influence of the display of numerical data on human performance in the manual RVD task has not been clearly indentified in previous studies, while displaying the numerical data on the interface is optional in the manual RVD system in China. So the present study aims to indentify the influence by empirical data, and to provide helpful guidance for the design of the monitoring interface of the RVD task.

2 Methods

2.1 Experiment Design

The current empirical research was conducted on a RVD simulation system. The manual RVD simulation system was designed and developed by technicians at the China Astronaut Research and Training Center [7]. The simulation system was established by modeling and simulating the Guidance, Navigation, and Controls Systems (GNC), the docking mechanisms, the instrumentation, the TV video system, and the cabin environment. The experimental schemes and initial parameters of the simulated RVD tasks can be configured.

Two display schemes were designed and developed in a RVD simulator, namely display scheme with numerical data (Display A) and display scheme without numerical data (Display B), as demonstrated in Fig. 2.

Each subject had to complete four trials of RVD simulations, two trials observing Display A, two trials observing Display B. The sequences of the trials were balanced among the subjects. The initial deviations of the two space vehicles in the four trials were set as Table 1. The four trials are at the same difficulty level. Deviation data, such as the horizontal deviation (Y), the vertical deviation (Z), the roll deviation (∅), the pitch deviation (θ), the yaw deviation (φ), are automatically recorded every 40 ms by the simulation system. Deviations of the Y, Z, ∅, θ, φ at the distance of 80 m, 50 m, 30 m, 20 m, 10 m, 5 m, 2 m were selected to indicate the dynamic control performance of the operators. The performance outcome of Display A and Display B were compared to analyze the influence of numerical display on human performance in RVD tasks.

Table 1. The initial deviations of the two space vehicles in the four trials of manual RVD simulations.

Task ID	Numerical display	X (m)	Y (m)	Z (m)	∅ (°)	θ(°)	φ(°)
T1	With	100	−10	10	−5	−6	−6
T2	With	100	−10	−10	5	6	−6
T3	Without	100	10	10	−5	−6	6
T4	Without	100	10	−10	5	6	6

2.2 Subjects

Twelve male subjects, technicians from the China Astronaut Research and Training Center, participated in the experiment. The subjects' ages range from 27 to 38 years. The subjects are all right-handed, have normal sight and hearing, and hold at least a bachelor's degree. The subjects had at least 6 h of training and practice before the current experiment, and had adequate knowledge and skills for completing the manual RVD simulations.

3 Results

3.1 The Orientation Deviations

The roll deviation (∅), the pitch deviation (θ) and the yaw deviation (φ) are three orientation parameters and are manipulated by the orientation controller. If any of the three orientation deviation at the docking moment exceeds 4°, the RVD task will fail. The orientation deviation data were shown in Figs. 4, 5 and 6. From the figures, we can see that:

(1) The orientation deviations of the subjects observing displays with numerical data are generally smaller than that without numerical data. However, there is an exceptional case, the roll deviations (∅) of the subjects observing displays with numerical data at the distance of 80 m is significantly larger than that without numerical data.

(2) Averagely, the pitch deviation (θ) and the yaw deviation (φ) are reduced to be less than one degree when the distance (X) between the two space vehicles is around

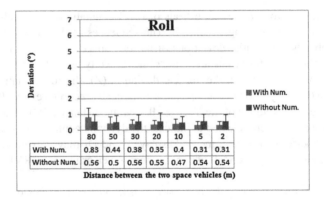

Fig. 4. Roll deviations at the distance of 80 m, 50 m, 30 m, 20 m, 10 m, 5 m, 2 m (Mean and STD of the twelve subjects). (Color figure online)

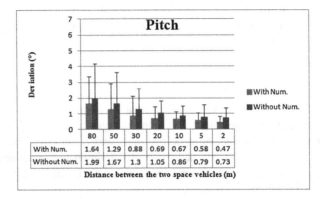

Fig. 5. Pitch deviations at the distance of 80 m, 50 m, 30 m, 20 m, 10 m, 5 m, 2 m (Mean and STD of the twelve subjects). (Color figure online)

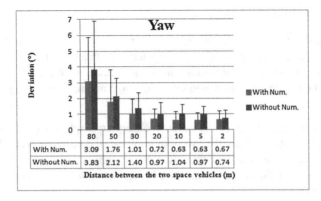

Fig. 6. Yaw deviations at the distance of 80 m, 50 m, 30 m, 20 m, 10 m, 5 m, 2 m (Mean and STD of the twelve subjects). (Color figure online)

30 m, while the roll deviations (Ø) is reduced to be less than one degree when the distance (X) between the two space vehicles is as far as 80 m.

(3) The roll deviations (Ø) are significantly smaller than the pitch deviations (θ) and the yaw deviations (φ) in the whole task process, especially when the distance (X) between the two space vehicles is over 30 m.

(4) The orientation deviations (Ø, θ, φ) are mainly diminished before the distance reaches 30 m, there is no significant decrease of orientation deviations when the distance is closer than 30 m.

3.2   The Translation Deviations

The horizontal deviation (Y) and the vertical deviation (Z) are two main translation indices indicating human performance, and are manipulated by the translation controller. The distance (X) between the two space vehicles is always diminished to approximately zero at the moment of docking, so it is not listed as a performance index in the current paper. If the translation deviation (calculated by $\sqrt{Y^2 + Z^2}$) at the docking moment exceeds 0.15 m, the RVD task will fail. The translation deviation data were shown in Figs. 7 and 8. From the figures, we can see that:

(1) The translation deviations of the subjects observing displays with numerical data are bigger than that without numerical data in the early stage, when the distance (X) between the two space vehicles is over 30 m. When the distance (X) between the two space vehicles is less than 20 m, there is no significant difference between the translation deviations of the subjects observing displays with numerical data are bigger and that without numerical data.

(2) At the very early stage of the task, that is when the distance is over 80 m, the horizontal deviation (Y) have been reduced more than the vertical deviation (Z). When the distance (X) between the two space vehicles is less than 50 m, there is no significant difference between the horizontal deviation (Y) and the vertical deviation (Z).

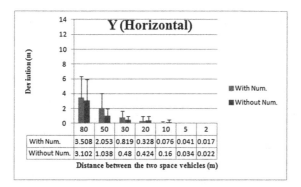

Fig. 7. Horizontal deviations at the distance of 80 m, 50 m, 30 m, 20 m, 10 m, 5 m, 2 m (Mean and STD of the twelve subjects). (Color figure online)

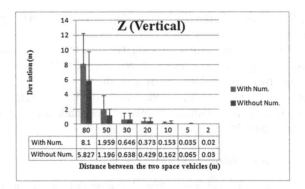

The table within the figure:

	80	50	30	20	10	5	2
With Num.	8.1	1.959	0.646	0.373	0.153	0.035	0.02
Without Num.	5.827	1.196	0.638	0.429	0.162	0.065	0.03

Distance between the two space vehicles (m)

Fig. 8. Vertical deviations at the distance of 80 m, 50 m, 30 m, 20 m, 10 m, 5 m, 2 m (Mean and STD of the twelve subjects). (Color figure online)

(3) Averagely, the translation deviations have been decreased in the whole task process, and meet the success criteria when the distance (X) between the two space vehicles is closer than 10 m.

4 Discussions

From the empirical data we can deduce that the display of the numerical data are helpful for the diminishing of the pitch deviation (θ) and the yaw deviation (φ), while the roll deviation ($\varnothing$) does not change significantly in the two conditions, the horizontal deviation (Y) and the vertical deviation (Z) indices seem to be affected negatively by the numerical display.

By interviewing with several manual RVD experts, the results were interpreted. The pitch deviation (θ) and the yaw deviation (φ) are difficult to perceive and judge from the video images of the target space vehicle, especially at a far distance, so numerical data of the pitch deviation (θ) and the yaw deviation (φ) reduce the perceiving workload and improve the judge accuracy, thus the pitch deviation (θ) and the yaw deviation (φ) are consistently lower in Display A than Display B. The roll deviation ($\varnothing$) can be judged from the angle of the solar panels, which is relatively easy to judge even at a far distance, and the roll deviation is regulated to a quite small scale (less than $1°$ on average) in the first 20 m, so the numerical display does not influence control accuracy of the roll deviation ($\varnothing$) significantly. The situation is quite similar for the horizontal deviation (Y) and the vertical deviation (Z), human operators generally obtain the translation deviation information from the video images and do not rely on numerical displays. Meanwhile, numerical display seems to change the priority of the control dimensions: while the roll deviation ($\varnothing$) is always the first dimension to be controlled, the pitch deviation (θ) and the yaw deviation (φ) are more likely to be controlled more frequently in the early stages of the task when there are numerical displays. As a result the horizontal deviation (Y) and the vertical deviation (Z) receive less attention and the indices are worse in the early stages when there are numerical display.

The empirical data also show although the deviation data of the subjects observing Display A than Display B have significant differences in the early stages of the RVD task (when the distance is over 30 m in the current study), there is no significant difference in the final stages (especially when the distance is less than 10 m). Indicating that the designs of the video image display for the RVD task support effective perception and judgment.

Based on the results of the present study, we suggest that numerical data of the pitch deviation (θ) and the yaw deviation (φ) should be highlighted on the interface, and the operators should pay more attention to the control of horizontal deviation (Y) and the vertical deviation (Z) when there are numerical displays. The present study suggests that the overlying of numerical data on the HCI interfaces may cause complex effects for dynamic control tasks, and when we design interfaces with image displays and numerical displays, the information displayed and the layout of the numerical displays should be considered carefully.

Acknowledgements. This work was supported by the Feitian Foundation of China Astronaut Research and Training Center (No. FTKY201505) and the funding of Key Laboratory of Science and Technology for National Defense (No. 9140C770102140C77313). The authors would like to thank Dongxu Han for the collection of the experimental data.

References

1. Jiang, T., Wang, C., Tian, Z., Xu, Y., Wang, Z.: Study on synthetic evaluation of human performance in manually controlled spacecraft rendezvous and docking tasks. In: Duffy, V.G. (ed.) ICDHM 2011. LNCS, vol. 6777, pp. 387–393. Springer, Heidelberg (2011)
2. Wang, C., Tian, Y., Chen, S., Tian, Z., Jiang, T., Du, F.: Predicting performance in manually controlled rendezvous and docking through spatial abilities. Adv. Space Res. **53**(2), 362–369 (2014)
3. Zhang, Y., Xu, Y., Li, Z., Li, J., Wu, S.: Influence of monitoring method and control complexity on operator performance in manually controlled spacecraft rendezvous and docking. Tsinghua Sci. Technol. **13**(5), 619–624 (2011)
4. Wang, C., Jiang, T.: Study on ergonomic design of display-control system in manual-control rendezvous and docking. Manned Spaceflight **17**, 50–53, 64 (2011). (in Chinese)
5. Du, X., Zhang, Y., Tian, Y., Huang, W., Wu, B., Zhang, J.: The influence of spatial ability and experience on performance during spaceship rendezvous and docking. Front. Psychol. **6**, 955 (2015)
6. Wang, C., Jiang, T. Tian, Y., Chen, S.: Human factors in manually controlled rendezvous and docking: implications for engineering better designs. In: Human Performance in Space: Advancing Astronautics Research in China, Science/AAAS, Washington, DC, pp. 26–27 (2014)
7. Wang, B., Jiang, G., Chao, J., Wang, X., Wang, Y., Wang, C., Lian, S.: Design and implement of manned rendezvous and docking ergonomics experimental system. Space Med. Med. Eng. **24**, 30–35 (2011). (in Chinese)

A System Description Model Without Hierarchical Structure

Tetsuya Maeshiro[1,2(✉)] and Midori Maeshiro[3]

[1] Faculty of Library, Information and Media Studies,
University of Tsukuba, Tsukuba 305-8550, Japan
maeshiro@slis.tsukuba.ac.jp
[2] Research Center for Knowledge Communities,
University of Tsukuba, Tsukuba 305-8550, Japan
[3] School of Music, Federal University of Rio de Janeiro, Rio de Janeiro, Brazil

Abstract. In order to simulate and analyze the properties of a phenomena from systems point of view, a proper description is necessary, otherwise these objectives cannot be accomplished. We are currently describing two superficially distinctive phenomena, the feeding process of living organisms and music composition process by composers, but they share some fundamental properties from the system description point of view. Here we discuss these common characteristics and the requirements for the system description model.

1 Introduction

This paper focuses on the description of two different phenomena to elucidate properties that system description model should possess. Descriptions of two phenomena serve to analyze their properties and elucidate the functional relationships among elements. The basic assumption, fundamentally different from conventional system description and theories related to emergence, is the absence of hierarchical relationships among phenomena resulting from elements of different hierarchical levels.

For instance, a bee colony is as set of many bees with diverse roles inside the colony, such as queen and workers. The bee colony as a whole can be treated as a single honey collecting machine, where the number of outgoing worker bees that collect honey and of internal worker bees that receive collected honey are under decentralized control [1]. Bees are elements constituting the bee colony, and the bee colony and bees are in hierarchical relationships (Fig. 1(A)). Conventional studies assume that the phenomena of an entity and its elements also consitute the hierarchical relationship, which corresponds to the mechanism to control the number of collecting and receiving bees, and the behavior of individual bees (Fig. 1(B-1) and (B-2)).

We agree on the existence of hierarchical relationship among structural elements, such as individual bees and the bee colony. However, no hierarchical relationship exists among phenomena (Fig. 1(B-1) and (B-2)), differing from

© Springer International Publishing Switzerland 2016
S. Yamamoto (Ed.): HIMI 2016, Part I, LNCS 9734, pp. 48–59, 2016.
DOI: 10.1007/978-3-319-40349-6_6

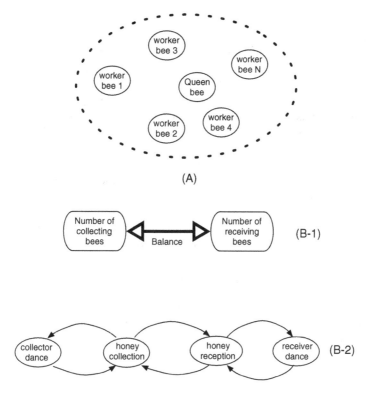

Fig. 1. (A) Bee colony and individual bees. (B-1) Balancing the number of honey collecting bees and honey receiving bees. (B-2) Honey collection and reception.

conventional studies. We assume that the phenomena (B-1) and (B-2) are two different viewpoints to describe the bee colony. The mechanism to control the number of collecting and receiving bees is generated by the interactions among bees and their behaviors, but the number controlling phenomena is independent from the description of individual bees' behaviors.

2 Music Composition Process

We are analysing the music composition process of professional composers, treating the composition process as a sequence of decision makings. We focus on the creation process or composition process, from a blank music sheet to the final work. This is a "creation history" of musical piece. Human being is skillful at creating new concepts and ideas, and imagining non-existing conditions. These abilities are mainly related with sensitivity and emotion. On the other hand, reasoning based on explicit knowledge is also necessary. It is the author's assumption that during the thinking process by human beings, 40 to 50 % is related to sensitivity, treating nonverbal information and imagination, and the rest, 50 to 60 %, treats verbal concepts and explicit knowledge. Our studies suggest that the sole use of either sensitivity or explicit knowledge does not enable the generation of new ideas, but simultaneous employment of both abilities are essential [2]. Conventional research on knowledge representation focused on the explicit knowledge. Our attempt is to unify the two kinds of thinking process.

Musical score is the de facto representation of musical pieces. Musical score encompasses every aspect of the musical piece, and it describes what to be performed, how to be performed, and composer's intentions. Everything is in the score, as some say. John Cage once said that by looking at the music sheet, one can judge the composer's talent, but not by listening to the performance of a musical piece. Music composition process involves a wide range of fields, and the list of fields depends on the music style. Even limiting to fields directly related to music, a composer should be familiar with many disciplines of musical theory including Harmony, acoustics of musical instruments, and genre-dependent articulations of each musical instrument. Many works on music analysis have been published, including the description model of music structure. For instance, Generative Theory of Tonal Music (GTTM) [3] is a model to describe the structure of musical pieces based on linguistic theory. Conventional works try to represent this type of knowledge as the static entity, usually treating as a structure of notes, chords and groups of these elements [3]. Typical structure is hierarchical, where the whole musical piece is positioned at the top of the hierarchy.

Music composition process presents following properties: (i) it is a creative process, and because of its artistic nature, sensitivity and emotion is strongly involved; (ii) there is a solid foundation of music theory, differing from other Arts fields such as paintings, sculptures and dances. Harmony of tonal music, for instance, involves mathematics of sound frequencies. The liberty and amount of sensitivity that is involved in music composition is higher than engineering process, industrial design and product design, for example, whith have strong theoretical bases. These are the reason to treat music composition.

In the present work, a musical piece is represented by relationships among decisions. Such a creation history is more valuable than static structures generated by conventional methods. The disclosure of description of intermediate composition process is useful for both composers and players. For composers, it is valuable to overview and clarify his own composition process to improve the composed opus, besides the benefit to reorganize his ideas. For musical instrument players, the acquisition of background and underlying phylosophy is invaluable, because deeper understanding of musical piece is fundamental and crucial for good execution. This kind of information is missing in all available music sheets, but is of fundamental importance for instrument players.

We classify each decision element to the following five facets.

1. Decision type. Related to the process of decision making, and further classified to theoretical, selective and intuitive.
2. Concept. Composer's background idea, related to emotional aspect of decisions.

3. Structure. Related to music theory, which is explicit knowledge thinking.
4. Aesthetic. Mainly involving listeners, related to listening impression of executed music.
5. Playing technique. Mainly related to instrument players.

Each decision is classified into one of five facets, besides the classification into theoretical and intuitive. Theoretical decisions use explicit knowledge, and intuitive decisions belong to sensitivity and emotional thinking process. Then the integration of all decisions offers a global view of a creation process that is a combination of emotional and explicit knowledge thinking processes. After the analysis of description of composition process by the composer, a main decision is subdivided into smaller decisions. Typically a main decision consists of 2 to 5 decisions. The five facets proposed in this paper are representations of a single set of facts and concepts. These facets are dependent to each other, and some elements of a facet are shared by other facet(s). No facet is in hierarchical relationship with other facets, and no facet is totally independent from other facets.

Our analysis indicate that the number of decisions belonging to each facet is approximately similar. No decisions belonging to playing technique were detected, as contents related to techniques were not directly mentioned. However, playing techniques are indicated in musical score using conventional notations. It is interesting that playing technique is not involved in decisions to create musical piece, although this might be a particular case of analyzed musical pieces. Since playing technique is annotated by the composer in music score, playing technique is important element in composed musical piece. However, it is not a factor to consider during the music creation process.

The frequency distribution of decision types indicates that all five facets are necessary to describe a musical piece. It also indicates that the composer devotes his attention to basic concept and musical structure with similar importance, i.e., emotional and explicit knowledge (verbal) thinking has approximately equal ratio. Specifically, the average value of emotional thinking is 40 %, and verbal thinking is 60 %. Therefore, two types of decision making exist in music composition processes, and the representation of both types of thinking process is necessary. The existence of a sequence of multiple decisions applied to the same passage is partially due to the lack of emergency in music composition task, which is fundamentally different from conditions encountered by firefighters, medical doctors and military commands. Such relaxation of constraints results in diversity of decision making process, and consequently of different creative process styles. Some composers do not postedit, while others executes a certain number of revisions.

It would be useful if the detection of similar passages, that is unable to be detected by other representation models, is possible. Conventional description models allow detection of only one type of similarity, which is insufficient for actual use, because they capture just a fraction of existing types. The connection of elements based on similarity among decisions elucidates implicit relationships among musical elements, difficult and time consuming to be clarified by

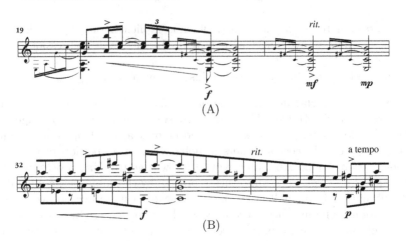

Fig. 2. Two passages created from same decision, although their musical aspects are dissimilar.

conventional music analysis methods. Figure 2 shows two passages from the same musical piece that were generated by identical decision. The decision making by the composer was to introduce release of tension to the movement that the target passage connects, which are measures until 19 and measures after 21 in Fig. 2-(A), and measures until 32 and after 34 in Fig. 2-(B).

Once the generated micro-decisions are connected by various relationships, a connected network of decisions of a musical piece is obtained. The plain network containing all extracted relationships is not primarily used to visualize and understand the structure of the described musical piece. Instead, the user chooses a viewpoint to filter unwanted relationships. The hierarchical structure is treated as one viewpoint. An important relationship in decision representation network is the causal relationship among micro-decisions, because causal relationships elucidate the sequence of decisions enables the analysis of indirect causes and results. By detecting indirect causes, which are obtained by following the decision sequence paths for more than one step, it is possible to clarify common ancestor decisions of diverse level of commoness. Identical operation applies to the detection of indirect results. Since the causal relationships among micro-decisions are independent of temporal sequence of decisions, which is linear, the structure is not a tree, and present ramifications and convergences. There are convergences in decisions, meaning that a decision has multiple decisions as causes. This structure can only be detected using the proposed method.

3   Feeding Process

Similar to the description of music composition described in previous section, we are currently describing the feeding process of human beings. The feeding process refers to all functions, processes and control mechanisms regarding intake

Fig. 3. The network with blue nodes (lower network) represents the genomics layer, and the network with red nodes (upper network) represents metabolomics layer. (Color figure online)

of food, energy absorption and feeding behavior [9–15]. The feeding process influences a wide range of other phenomena, mainly those related with energy. One of most important may be lifestyle diseases represented by diabetes meritus, in a sense that a huge number of people is affected. Other diseases are also related, for instance hyperorexia and anorexia, which are directly related with the control mechanism of feeding. Energy consumption is a fundamental function of organism behavior, thus the fact description of feeding behavior treats one of fundamental aspects of life.

We are compiling data from available papers and open databases, and generated integrated description of genes, RNA, proteins and metabolites. Genes, RNA and proteins were connected using primarily the central dogma. On the other hand, metabolites were integrated primarily to enzymes based on metabolic reactions. Since enzymes are proteins, metabolites are also integrated into the represented model. Figure 3 is a part of the generated network, visualizing the gene and metabolite networks. Figure 3 is the visualization example based on experiment, because genomics data and metabolomics data are the result of independent experiments. These networks can also be visualized as a single network.

Humans possess feeding mechanism partially similar to mouse and monkeys, whose mechanism is closely related to the instinct, so it is an automatic system. Figure 4 is the mechanism to generate appetite, involving three brain regions, which are hypothalamus, ventral tegmental area and nucleus

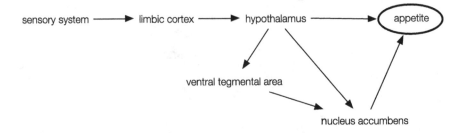

Fig. 4. General mechanism involving brain function area that generate appetite

accumbens. It seems that hypothalamus and nucleus accumbens directly generate the sense of appetite. The control flow to generate appetite by these mechanisms are straightforward because no considerable conflict exists. Humans, however, present a more complex mechanism, but details is still unknown. Anorexia nervosa, bulimia nervosa and the propagation of obesity [4] are three examples of complexity, which are phenomena unique to Humans. The first two are diseases, and the last one is an observed fact. But all three deregulate the basic feeding mechanism (Fig. 4) that is incorporated to the organism, the molecular mechanism that is shared with other mammals.

Transomics has objective similar to our research. There is, however, a fundamental difference, which is the data integration standpoint and basic concepts of the representation model. Transomics is biological experimental data driven. Currently, any high throughput data can measure only one kind of substance class, such as genes, RNA sequence, proteins and metabolites. Data generated from each substance class are treated as a single layer in the integrated representation. Then relationships among same substance class are inferred using some kind of algorithm, and a network of a given substance class is generated, which results in a network representation of one layer. The layer is sometimes referred as a hierarchical level. The use of the term "hierarchy" is misleading because there is no hierarchical relationship among substance classes in strict sense, neither structural nor functional. A layer in Transomics corresponds to a viewpoint in the proposed model. The problem of conventionally used methods in Transomics is that the concept of a layer is directly related to the kind of data that each high throughput experiment can generate, and not to the adequacy to describe biological phenomena. For instance, the description of a very simple gene regulation involves the gene encoding the transcription factor, mRNA transcripted from the gene, the protein synthesezed based on the mRNA sequence, the docking region in the granscription target gene, mRNA transcripted from the target gene, and the target protein. Ribosome and other substances involved in transcription and translation might be also included, but they are omitted for simplicity of explanation.

The feeding process at the molecular level can be viewed as a collection of reactions that correspond to causal relationships. Then feeding process can be described using description model analogous to that used to describe music composition process, described in previous section. Although the same should apply to the mechanism involving the brain, much more experimental data are still necessary. Although the mechanism is still unknown, it seems that brain functions of higher order than those functions directly involved in feeding mechanism of molecular level, mainly activated in hypothalamus. Therefore, it is possible that higher order brain function, present only in Human and denoted here as the "new" brain, overrides and modifies the control signals from hypothalamus and nucleus accumbens, present in other animals and denoted here as the "old" brain, to change the feeding behavior.

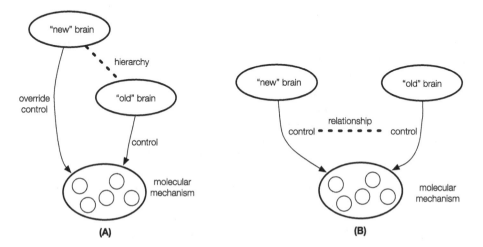

Fig. 5. (A) Conventional (hierarchical) viewpoint and (B) the viewpoint based on the proposed model

Figure 5 illustrates the difference of the viewpoint and representation of the control of feeding mechanism involving control by the two brains, the "new" and the "old" brains. The hierarchical relationship is absent among phenomena. Conventionally, the "new" brain is positioned in the higher level of the "old" brain (Fig. 5(A)), because the model supposes that the basic molecular level control is overridden by the "new" brain. Then the "new" brain is considered to be on the higher hierarchical level than the "old" brain. More precisely, not the two brains, but the involved control mechanism that are in hierarchical relationship, since the "new" brain's control overrides the "old" brain's control mechanism. In the proposed model, both "new" and "old" brains belong to the same level, the level of organs. The relationship between these two brains are basically of functional difference.

4   Common Properties of Analyzed Phenomena

An important aspect of both phenomena treated in this paper is the multi-viewpointness. No single viewpoint of description is sufficient to describe the phenomena, and in extreme cases, one viewpoint is required for each purpose, such as analysis and simulation, including different parameter settings. At least in the two phenomena treated in this paper, multiple hierarchical structures exist and should be described to understand these phenomena.

The hierarchy in system is a remarkable relationship among available viewpoints, and because the concept of hierarchy is natural and obvious, the hierarchy is often not considered as viewpoint, but is treated as an inherent property of system. However, in raw state of description using the proposed model, no hierarchy is present in the system. Because fundamental concepts of system such as emergence assume the existence of the hierarchical structure, where a set of interacting elements generates a phenomenon in higher hierarchical level, the hierarchy seems to be the necessity to a system. However, we treat the hierarchy as one of available viewpoints. Furthermore, multiple hierarchies can be defined, and the elements belonging to the same hierarchical level in a given viewpoint of hierarchy may belong to different hierarchical levels in another viewpoint of hierarchy. Conventional system theory allows only one definition of hierarchy, which strongly limits the phenomena that can be represented.

Another aspect of these phenomena are the dynamism of viewpoints. The most straightforward kind of dynamism is temporal. The dynamism of the system behavior is treated in conventional system theory, but not the dynamism of the viewpoint. As the relationships and interactions among elements constituting a system change, appropriate viewpoint to understand and analyze the target phenomena changes accordingly. Even if the hierarchical structure is maintained, the details of the hierarchical relationships change, including additions and deletions of a hierarchical level and move of elements to a different hierarchical level. Furthermore, emergences and disappearances of interactions among elements of a system change the hierarchical structure.

In the descriptions of both the music composition process and feeding process, causal relationship is the intuitive relationship that is useful in these representations. Each causal relationship description has multiple pre-status or precondition or facts and multiple post-status or postcondition are connected by a relationship that specifies the process, which corresponds to a causal relationship. Thus a process is an N-ary relationship, impossible to be accurately represented by conventional representation models. A process modifies the pre-status to generate the post-status. Generally, the pre-status is varied because it depends on the type of relationship. External facts may also compose the pre-status set. Detecting similar causal relationships is useful to analyze the mechanisms of the feeding process and music composition process, and valuable information is obtained for the understanding and further research of the process. Furthermore, similarity among causal relationship sequences is more important than comparison of single causal relationship.

Currently, the proposed model uses known concepts and semantic relationships among concepts to describe the target phenomena [16,17]. Semantic relationships are specified using other concepts. The describability and understanding of the target phenomena are unrelated. Even if mathematical formula and computer program are able to reconstruct the target phenomena, it does not imply the target phenomena is understood, particularly when so called emergence is involved, where phenomena of different hierarchical levels are involved. This is because no description is provided for phenomena of the emerged hierarchical level, which is usually of upper hierarchical level than the level of described elements.

The proposed model provides direct description of each hierarchical level, treating each level as an independent viewpoint that represents a phenomenon or a process. Therefore, a description is also provided for the "emerged" phenomena, and concepts belonging to the lower hierarchical level may or may not be used in the description. Consequently, only a vague explanation is provided if the phenomena is poorly understood. However, there is a concrete link between the emerged phenomena and the elements that generate the phenomena by interactions. These properties of the proposed model results in the absence of hierarchy in the description. No phenomena belongs to the lower or higher hierarchical level, and descriptions of each phenomenon are interrelated based on the intersections of concepts used in each representation.

Conventional representations provide only the hierarchical relationship among phenomena. In the context of the proposed model, hierarchy is only one facet of the relationship among phenomena. On the other hand, our model enables the definition of varied types of relationships among phenomena, including the hierarchical relationship, which is a clear but simple type of relationship. The hierarchical viewpoint is not emphasized as in conventional models, enabling employment of diverse viewpoints that enables elucidation of new viewpoints to treat the phenomena. Therefore, the proposed model allows description of multiple relationships among different processes. Moreover, the details of a relationship can be further described, because the proposed model allows specification of the relationship entity.

The advantage of the proposed model is the ability to create any viewpoint for representation, analysis and visualization, due to the use of model extended from hypergraph, which presents more representation capability than the conventionally used models that are based on graph model. The hypernetwork model allows creation of links among multiple links, which is impossible with conventional models. Furthermore, the hypernetwork model allows addition of further links from the newly generated link, enabling more freedom in representation than conventional models.

With the representation based on the proposed model, the hypernetwork model, detection of similar subnetworks (cluster of nodes) with varied degree of granularity of description levels is possible. In the case of the music composition process, detection of similar subnetworks (node groups) corresponds to the detection of similar decisions. Granularity of represented decision corresponds to the granularity of concepts and connected concepts to the subnetwork. Similarly, in the case of feeding process, detection of similar subnetworks corresponds to the extraction of similar biochemical processes.

Furthermore, a causal relationship may consist of multiple causal relationships, functioning as elements of a larger causal relationship. Then it is possible to extract similar sequence of causal relationships. The sequence is particularly important in both music composition and feeding processes, because it represents the development of creative process in music composition and sequence of biochemical reactions in feeding process. The similarity among sequences of causal relationships is more valuable than the comparison of single causal relationships. Moreover, the sequences are nonlinear, with ramifications and convergences, and parallel sequences also exist.

The description of the feeding process provides an even more valuable functionality, which is the elucidation of missing relationships, such as biochemical reactions and interactions among elements that constitute the entire feeding process. Prediction of missing links in currently available facts is important to support the design of new biological experiments to fill the unknown facts. This approach is contrary to the traditional approach that is hypotheses-driven. We aim to realize the data-driven research, enabling the detection of missing part in gathered and integrated data. We are currently developing an algorithm to detect the "missing links" in the integrated data representation.

Acknowledgments. This research was supported by the JSPS Grants-in-Aid for Scientific Research 24500307 (T.M.) and 15K00458 (T.M.).

References

1. Jacobsen, R.: "Fruitless Fall : The Collapse of the Honey Bee and the Coming Agricultural Crisis". Bloomsbury, New York (1996)
2. Polanyi, M.: The creative imagination. Chem. Eng. News **44**, 85–93 (1966)
3. Lerdahl, F., Jackendoff, R.S.: A Generative Theory of Tonal Music. MIT Press, Cambridge (1996)
4. Christakis, N.A., Fowler, J.H.: The spread of obesity in a large social network over 32 years. N. Engl. J. Med. **357**, 370–379 (2007)
5. Forte, A.: The Structure of Atonal Music. Yale University Press, New Haven (1977)
6. Klein, G.: Sources of Power: How People Make Decisions. MIT Press, Cambridge (1999)
7. Berge, C.: The Theory of Graphs. Dover, New York (2001)
8. Berge, C.: Hypergraphs: Combinatorics of Finite Sets. North-Holland, Amsterdam (1989)
9. Cone, R.D.: Anatomy and regulation of the central melanocortin system. Nat. Neurosci. **8**, 571–578 (2005)
10. Jordan, S.D., Konner, A.C., Bruning, J.C.: Sensing the fuels: glucose and lipid signaling in the CNS controlling energy homeostasis. Cell. Mol. Life Sci. **67**, 3255–3273 (2010)
11. Porte Jr., D., Baskin, D.G., Schwartz, M.W.: Insulin signaling in the central nervous system: a critical role in metabolic homeostasis and disease from C. elegans to humans. Diabetes **54**, 1264–1276 (2005)
12. Sainsbury, A., Cooney, G.J., Herzog, H.: Hypothalamic regulation of energy homeostasis. Best Pract. Res. Clin. Endocrinol. Metab. **16**, 623–637 (2002)

13. Badmin, M.K., Flier, J.S.: The gut and energy balance: visceral allies in the obesity wars. Science **307**, 1909–1914 (2005)
14. Demuro, G., Obici, S.: Central nervous system and control of endogenous glucose production. Curr. Diab. Rep. **6**, 188–193 (2006)
15. Lam, T.K., Schwartz, G.J., Rossetti, L.: Hypothalamic sensing of fatty acids. Nat. Neurosci. **8**, 579–584 (2005)
16. Karr, J.R., et al.: A whole-cell computational model predicts phenotype from genotype. Cell **150**, 389–401 (2012)
17. Schierenberg, E.: Embryological Variation During Nematode Development. The C. elegans Research Community. WormBook, Placerville (2006). doi:10.1895/wormbook.1.7.1. http://www.wormbook.org

Knowledge Used for Information Search: A Computer Simulation Study

Miki Matsumuro[✉] and Kazuhisa Miwa

Graduate School of Information Science, Nagoya University,
Fro-cho, Chikusa-ku, Nagoya, Japan
muro@cog.human.nagoya-u.ac.jp, miwa@is.nagoya-u.ac.jp

Abstract. In this study, we investigated the types of knowledge utilized by users to search for information. Previous studies have emphasized the importance of acquiring the understanding of a hierarchical information structure. We defined the knowledge about such an information structure as "structural knowledge." Recently, user interfaces (UIs) have provided information in a more graphical manner. Stimuli on the UIs' displays have various properties (e.g., format, color, and size). We predicted that these perceptual features of the stimuli on the display, which we defined as "perceptual knowledge," would be important for information searching. Three computer models were created for simulation: The Structural Knowledge model, which included only structural knowledge; the Perceptual Knowledge model, which included only perceptual knowledge; and the Mixed Knowledge model, which included both perceptual and partial structural knowledge. The simulation results showed that the Mixed Knowledge model could predict how human participants would search for information. We concluded that users utilize both perceptual and structural knowledge to search for information.

Keywords: Information search · Cognitive model · Computer simulation · User interface

1 Introduction

Everyday, we interact with software through various user interfaces (UIs). How the UI design provides users with information is an extremely important topic. To improve UI design, we focused on how users find needed information using a device (i.e., information searching).

1.1 Information Device and Human Cognition

In this study, we define the term "information" as facts that a device stores and provides for users. Information is provided for users through a stimulus or a combination of stimuli on the device display. These stimuli have properties, such as format, color, size, and location.

© Springer International Publishing Switzerland 2016
S. Yamamoto (Ed.): HIMI 2016, Part I, LNCS 9734, pp. 60–69, 2016.
DOI: 10.1007/978-3-319-40349-6_7

The users' process to read information is as follows. The users have to operate the device so that the needed information appears on the device display. They can perceive all stimuli in their visual field (i.e., iconic memory). From these stimuli, they find the location of a stimulus they need, based on the property settings of the stimulus, focus their attention on it, and then recognize its meaning (Anderson and Matessa 2007). From the meaning(s) of the stimulus or stimuli, they obtain their needed information.

We focused on how the users bring up their needed information on the device's display during the first step of the process. In this step, they must utilize some declarative knowledge, that is, facts that a person knows (e.g., "Tokyo is the capital city of Japan"). Declarative knowledge about the device is acquired by the users through their experiences of information searching. In this study, we investigated the types of declarative knowledge acquired and utilized to search for information.

1.2   Two Types of Declarative Knowledge

Two types of declarative knowledge were important to our research efforts: structural knowledge and perceptual knowledge.

Structural Knowledge Previous studies have emphasized the importance for users to acquire an understanding of the hierarchical structure of information or the menu categories (Amant et al. 2007; Jacko and Salvendy 1996; Ziefle and Bay 2004, 2006). For example, Jacko and Salvendy (1996) investigated the influence of the depth of a menu structure on perceived complexity. Ziefle and Bay (2004, 2006) concluded that knowledge of the menu structure is important for the accuracy of the operations.

We defined knowledge about the structure of information as "structural knowledge." To acquire structural knowledge means to construct a mental map of the information, which shows where each piece of information is allocated in the hierarchical information structure of the device. The users can mentally find a path from a current position to a target position in the map.

Perceptual Knowledge. Recently, UIs have provided information in a more graphical manner. The properties of a stimulus have various settings. In older UIs, stimuli are presented in the identical property settings (e.g., the format is textual, the colors are black and white, and the stimuli are sized identically). We defined the property settings of a stimulus used as a cue to finding the target information as "perceptual knowledge."

Previous studies show that the difference in property settings of stimuli affected how users learned and operated a device (Benbasat and Todd 1993; Gittins 1986; Parush et al. 2005). Simon (1975) showed that participants determined which actions to take based on the problem state acquired perceptually. Similarly, users would utilize the perceptual knowledge while searching for information. We investigated the role of perceptual knowledge by simulating users' cognitive processes.

2   Multi-information Display

We used a multi-information display (MID) installed in certain hybrid cars to
provide drivers with driving information. The driving information was presented
graphically, such as the examples shown in Fig. 1. For example, the average speed
of a vehicle was presented by four stimuli: one was an icon (drive meter) format
and the other three were text (AVG, 56, km/h) format, and both in white color,
as shown in Fig. 1(a), and how much money was being saved each month was
shown in a yellow graph with white text, as shown in Fig. 1(b). These property
settings were acquired as perceptual knowledge if needed (e.g., the amount of
money saved in July is presented with a yellow graph).

(a) Screenshot of "Drive Info"   (b) Screenshot of "Saving Money Record"

Fig. 1. Example screenshots of MID. Figure 1(a) shows the "Drive Info" in DI.
Figure 1(b) shows the "Saving Money Record" in Eco (refer to Fig. 2).

The MID information was structured as a hierarchy, as shown in Fig. 2. The
information was categorized into one or both of the higher categories: "Drive
Information (DI)" and "Eco." Furthermore, they were categorized into some
lower categories. The information in an identical lower category was presented
together on the display. The structural knowledge in the MID referred to the
information categorizations and their relationships (Fig. 2).

The drivers could select categories using arrow buttons on a steering wheel.
They selected the higher category using the right and left buttons and the lower
category using the up and down buttons. The lower category was selected in the
order shown in Fig. 2 (i.e., if the driver pressed the down button when DI1 was
selected, DI2 would be selected). Additionally, both higher and lower categories
were selected cyclically. For example, DI1 would be selected after DI4 if the down
button was pressed, and vice versa. In this study, the MID was presented on a
PC monitor and operated using arrow keys on the keyboard.

During the information search task, one of the names of the target information (Table 1) was presented at first. Participants or computer models had to
find the value of the target information from the MID and enter it. If the entered
value was correct, the name of the next target information was presented. We
prepared four sets of the target information (Table 1).

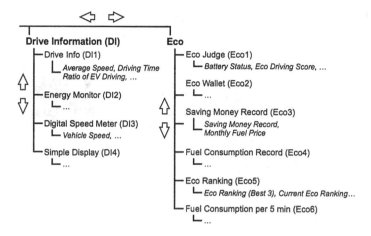

Fig. 2. Hierarchical information structure of MID. Information is shown in italic fonts, the lower categories in normal fonts, and the higher categories in bold fonts. The figure does not describe all information in MID. "EV" in figure means an electric vehicle.

Table 1. Target information

	Target information	Category	
		Higher	Lower
T1	Vehicle Speed	DI	Digital Speed Meter
T2	Driving time	DI	Drive Info
T3	Current Eco Ranking	Eco	Eco Ranking
T4	Saving money in July	Eco	Saving Money Record

3   Human Data

Thirty-eight undergraduates ranging in age from 19 to 23 years ($M = 20.579$ years, $SD = 1.780$ years) participated, and their behavioral data were collected after training (performing eight searches for each set of target information). During training, an initial category for each search was randomly determined. The participants sufficiently, quickly, and accurately searched for the information by the fourth search.

4   Computer Simulation

4.1   Adaptive Control of Thought-Rational

Adaptive Control of Thought-Rational (ACT-R) is a cognitive architecture that consists of modules (Anderson, 2007). Figure 3 shows the structure of ACT-R. The ACT-R model receives the perceptual stimuli from the environment through perceptual modules and changes the environment using motor modules. ACT-R

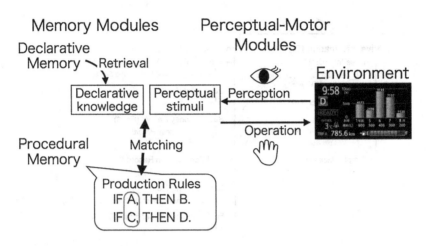

Fig. 3. Structure of ACT-R

has two memory modules: declarative and procedural memory modules. Procedural memory includes the production rule (i.e., "IF ..., THEN ..."). Declarative memory includes declarative knowledge. The structural and/or perceptual knowledge is part of this memory. The production rule whose conditions match the current model's state is executed.

4.2   Three Models

We created three models implementing different types of knowledge in declarative memory, namely the Structural Knowledge model (SK model), the Perceptual Knowledge model (PK model), and the Mixed Knowledge model (MK model). In the following section, we discuss the types of knowledge in declarative memory, as summarized in Table 2, and the search heuristics for each model.

SK Model. The SK model included perfect structural knowledge, which constructed the information structure in Fig. 2. Its structural knowledge consisted

Table 2. Declarative knowledge of each model

Model	Structural knowledge	Perceptual knowledge
SK model	Link knowledge Order knowledge	None
PK model	None	Target-display knowledge DI/Eco-identification knowledge
MK model	Higher-category knowledge	Target-display knowledge DI/Eco-identification knowledge

of link and order knowledge. Link knowledge was the parent-child relationships between the information and the categories, such as "Vehicle Speed is categorized as Digital Speed Meter" and "Simple Display is categorized as DI" (refer to Fig. 2). The order knowledge was the order of the lower categories, such as "Digital Speed Meter is the third lower category" and "Simple Display is the fourth."

For the SK model, we used a means-ends analysis as a heuristic. In this heuristic, the model applied an operation that would reduce the difference between the goal and the current state. The SK model calculated the shortest path from the currently presented category (i.e., current state) to the category including the target information (i.e., goal state), based on the information structure constructed from the link and order knowledge.

For this heuristic, the SK model had to identify the currently presented category based on the presented stimuli. The SK model had no perceptual knowledge. So it recognized the meaning of the stimuli and identified to which information the meaning corresponded. Therefore, we gave the SK model the knowledge to associate stimulus meanings with the information names.

PK Model. The PK model included only perceptual knowledge, which included the property settings of the stimulus important for information searching. Its perceptual knowledge consisted of the target-display and DI/Eco-identification knowledge. The target-display knowledge consisted of the property settings of the stimulus used to identify the lower category that included the target information, such as "Vehicle Speed is presented with a big text stimulus," and "Saving Money in July is presented with a graph stimulus." Note that the knowledge included the property settings of a significant stimulus in the display, not the stimulus representing the target information. The DI/Eco-identification knowledge was the property settings of the stimulus used to identify the currently presented higher category, such as "Graph is the property setting used in Eco" and "big meter is the property setting used in Eco."

The PK model used a heuristic in which it compared the property settings in the target-display knowledge with the property settings of the stimuli currently presented. If the model was not able to find the stimulus that had the searching property settings, it switched to the next lower category. The model repeated this comparison until it found the stimulus that had the property settings in the target-display knowledge (i.e., the model found the lower category that included the target information). We defined this heuristic as a perceptual comparison. Additionally, the PK model switched to the other higher category when the presented category returned to the initial one.

MK Model. The MK model included both perceptual and partial structural knowledge. The perceptual knowledge was identical to that of the PK model. The structural knowledge of the MK model was the higher-category knowledge that showed to which higher category the target information belonged, such as "Vehicle Speed belongs to DI" and "Current Eco Ranking belongs to Eco."

The MK model used a means-ends analysis and a perceptual comparison. First, the model used a means-ends analysis. It detected whether the currently presented higher category, identified using the DI/Eco-identification knowledge, was the higher category that included the target information, shown by the higher-category knowledge. If it was not, the model changed to the other higher category. Then, it used a perceptual comparison until the lower category including the target information was presented.

4.3   Simulation Results

We ran each model 450 times for each set of the target information.

Search Sequence. Using the Levenshtein distance, we compared the search sequence of the categories of each model and those of the human participants. The distance was obtained using the minimal number of operations (insertions and deletions) needed to transfer from one sequence to another. The smaller distance meant that the sequences used by the model and human participants were more similar. Figure 4 shows the mean distance between each model and the human participants. A significant difference between the models was observed ($F(2, 111) = 40.073, p < .001$). The distance of the MK model was smaller than those of other models ($ps \leq .001$). The distance of the SK model was smaller than that of the PK model ($p < .001$). These results indicate that the MK model's sequence was the nearest to the human data, and the PK model was the farthest.

Additionally, no human participant achieved a sequence that was identical to that of the PK model. Considering the farthest distance, the PK model could not explain the process of the users' information search. After that, we compared the SK and MK models.

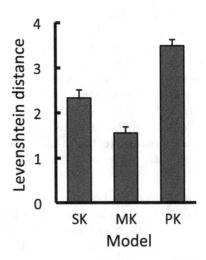

Fig. 4. Mean Levenshtein distance between each model and the human data

Observation Time. Because of the limitation of the analysis method, we used the data from the human participants whose search sequences were identical to those of any model for the target information 1 and 3 (T1 and T3 in Table 1). The details are summarized in Table 3. We calculated the observation time per lower category for the human participants and for each model. We conducted a linear regression analysis. The MK model predicted the observation time in the human data ($r^2 = .951$) to be more than that done by the SK model ($r^2 = .330$).

Table 3. Details of the analyzed data

Model	Target information	Search sequence	The number of participants
SK model	T1	Eco3 → DI4 → DI3	11
	T3	DI1 → Eco1 → Eco6 → Eco5	3
MK model	T1	Eco3 → DI4 → DI1 → DI2 → DI3	19
	T3	DI1 → Eco1 → Eco2 → Eco3 → Eco4→ Eco5	17

5 Discussion

We compared the behavior of the three computer models to investigate the types of declarative knowledge utilized for information search. The MK model could explain the behavior of the human participants, which means that the users utilized both perceptual and partial structural knowledge for information searching.

The PK model, which included only perceptual knowledge, failed to predict the search sequence of the human participants. The PK model observed all lower categories in the higher category selected initially, even when the higher category did not include the target information; the human participants avoided such unnecessary searching. This result implies that the users utilize the structural knowledge to judge whether the current higher category included the target information.

The SK model, which implemented only structural knowledge, could not explain the human participants' time spent observing each lower category. The model took more time to identify the currently presented category when the search started and when the higher category was changed. Because of the lack of perceptual knowledge, the model had to recognize the meaning of the stimuli for the identification. More time was needed to move attention and to understand the meaning of the stimulus. The human participants did not need such a long time. Therefore, they must have utilized perceptual knowledge to judge whether the currently presented category included the target information.

5.1 Cognitive and Physical Load

The results of our simulation show the following user information search strategy. The users narrowed the search area using structural knowledge, and then used perceptual knowledge to judge whether the currently presented category included the target information. Based on the results of several previous studies, it seems the rational strategy.

The means-ends analysis imposes a heavy cognitive load (Sweller 1988). To calculate the shortest path mentally, the users have to keep in mind the goal and current states, and the intermediate states if needed. However, the calculated path is the shortest and most accurate if the structural knowledge is perfect. The users can reach the target information without extraneous key presses, which reduces their physical load.

In contrast, the perceptual comparison reduces the cognitive load (Kirsh and Maglio 1994; Simon 1975). The problem state kept in the users' mind is minimized because the stimuli in the environment are used for perceptual comparison. However, the physical load is increased. The users have to continue to press keys until they find the stimulus that matches with the perceptual knowledge without knowing which category includes the target information and how far category includes the target information.

Our study suggests that users balanced cognitive and physical loads.

5.2 Implications

We should consider both structural and perceptual aspects when designing a UI. The structure of the information is particularly important for classifying information into higher categories. Users utilized structural knowledge when they decide whether they had to switch the higher category or not. Users can easily acquire structural knowledge when an information classification in a device is similar to users' classification.

Users utilized perceptual knowledge to judge whether the currently presented category included the target information. Therefore, a highly similar arrangement of stimuli confuses users. Thus, we should provide significant features that identify each category.

In addition, a computer simulation approach can act as a low-cost usability evaluation. We can calculate the cognitive and physical load of users without recruiting many participants.

References

Amant, T.E., Horton, F.E., Ritter, F.E.: Model-based evaluation of expert cell phone menu interaction. Trans. Comput.-Hum. Interact. (TOCHI) **14**, 1 (2007)

Anderson, J.R., Matessa, M., Lebiere, C.: ACT-R: a theory of higher level cognition and its relation to visual attention. Hum.-Comput. Interact. **12**, 439–462 (1997)

Anderson, J.R.: How Can the Human Mind Occur in the Physical Universe?. Oxford University Press, New York (2007)

Benbasat, I., Todd, P.: An experimental investigation of interface design alternatives: icon vs. text and direct manipulation vs. menus. Int. J. Man Mach. Stud. **38**, 369–402 (1993)

Gittins, D.: Icon-based human-computer interaction. Int. J. Man Mach. Stud. **24**, 519–543 (1986)

Jacko, J.A., Salvendy, G.: Hierarchical menu design: breadth, depth, and task complexity. Percept. Mot. Skills **82**, 1187–1201 (1996)

Jiang, Y., Olson, I.R., Chun, M.M.: Organization of visual short-term memory. J. Exp. Psychol.: Learn. Mem. Cogn. **26**, 683–702 (2000)

Kirsh, D., Maglio, P.: On distinguishing epistemic from pragmatic action. Cogn. Sci. **18**, 513–549 (1994)

Parush, A., Shwarts, Y., Shtub, A., Chandra, M.J.: The impact of visual layout factors on performance in web pages: a cross-language study. Hum. Factors: J. Hum. Factors Ergon. Soc. **47**, 141–157 (2005)

Simon, H.A.: The functional equivalence of problem solving skills. Cogn. Psychol. **7**, 268–288 (1975)

Sweller, J.: Cognitive load during problem solving: effects on learning. Cogn. Sci. **12**, 257–285 (1988)

Ziefle, M., Bay, S.: Mental models of a cellular phone menu. Comparing older and younger novice users. In: Brewster, S., Dunlop, M.D. (eds.) Mobile HCI 2004. LNCS, vol. 3160, pp. 25–37. Springer, Heidelberg (2004)

Ziefle, M., Bay, S.: How to overcome disorientation in mobile phone menus: a comparison of two different types of navigation aids. Hum.-Comput. Interact. **21**, 393–433 (2006)

Study on the Target Frame of HMDs in Different Background Brightness

Jiang Shao[1,3(✉)], Haiyan Wang[2,3], Rui Zhao[2], Jing Zhang[2],
Zhangfan Shen[2], and Hongwei Xi[2]

[1] School of Arts & Design,
China University of Mining and Technology, Xuzhou 221116, China
shaojiangseu@qq.com
[2] School of Mechanical Engineering,
Southeast University, Nanjing 211189, China
[3] Science and Technology on Electro-Optic Control Laboratory,
Luoyang 471000, China

Abstract. Interface of Helmet Mounted Display System (HMDs) will be the major human-computer interaction interface of fighters in the future. Its icons and color design are important for the efficiency of the entire system in operations. This paper focuses on the problem about target frame of HMDs and design of background brightness to research. According to the data of the behavior experiment based on E-prime, impacts of solid and dotted lines upon users' visual cognition are compared under backgrounds of different brightness to analyze key elements of such differences, in order to lay a foundation for improving and optimizing interface design of HMDs. Experimental data have effectively indicated the changes based on background brightness and demonstrated that the design scheme of brightness for optimizing target frame is feasible. On the whole, cognitive effects are better for the target frame with changeable brightness as compared with existing target frame no matter how many disturbances there are. The reaction time is about 12 % shorter on average for the former target frame. Experimental data analysis and conclusions may provide references for future design of HMDS, to effectively avoid misjudgments and omissions of interface information for the final purpose of increasing utilization efficiency of the system.

Keywords: HMDs · Human computer interaction · Background brightness · Interface design

1 Introduction

In the wake of the rapid development of photoelectric technology and human-computer interaction interface, Helmet Mounted Display System (HMDs) has become the key link in information transfer and interaction control of modern fighters, and the research on the system interface is of great importance. HMDs interface, as the sub-interface in the complicated system of fighters, is characterized by large amounts of information, intricate information structure and information continuity, due to that various dynamic changes and targeting system of fighters are centralized in HMDs. In actual combats,

S. Yamamoto (Ed.): HIMI 2016, Part I, LNCS 9734, pp. 70–79, 2016.
DOI: 10.1007/978-3-319-40349-6_8

human-computer system matching shall be more restrict, with more scientific information coding and structure. An irrational and unscientific design of HDMs interface will lead to the wrong decisions of pilots with serious results.

With the transparent HMDs interface, pilots shall not only observe the dynamic change information in it, but also the external targets through it. Thus, the background brightness of the interfaces will impact pilots' observation on destination icons. A long-term literature investigation on existing HMDs has shown that the great majority of HMDs have focused on interface design, including icon shape, size and color and the change of brightness of the entire interface, with little on the brightness changes. In particular, little China's research on HMDs, on the early stage, has focused on the brightness of HMDs interface. This paper proceeds from this aspect aiming at optimizing the brightness of existing icons.

Color is one of the essential elements in traditional interface design of avionics systems. Color coding acts two roles. On the one hand, it can highlight important information in the complicated avionics systems, to guide pilots for quick target lock and upgrade the system efficiency. On the other hand, users have different psychological experience and feelings for different colors and there are related standard requirements in the avionics subsystem interface for the use of different colors, including red, yellow and green. In design of avionics subsystem interface, besides simple use, color coding can also express the logical structure and subsystem of information [1]. The use of color can integrate and classify the functions and levels of interface information, to effectively express the heterogeneousness and similarity among information cells, for the convenience of pilots to get interface information, understand and study the avionics system interface. Icon characters displayed in HMDs interface include flight parameters, tracking and aiming information. Icon characters of flight parameters include: flight path and direction icons, attitude information (pitching and rolling), speed, height, heading and vertical velocity (climbing and diving); tracking and aiming characters include: target line of sight, aiming characters, target guide, velocity of approach and slant-range of target, etc., as shown in Fig. 1.

The development avionics system interface will follow the systematic, complicated and integrated trend. HMDs will be the representative interface of human-computer interaction of fighters in the future. Along with the transformation of war modes and the revolutionary advance of weapon performance, battlefield situation information under the background of bid data will also feature multiple dimensions, dynamics and complication. Hue, brightness, purity and contrast ratio can be used as the features of color coding to express the prosperities of information in different dimensions and upgrade pilots' information understanding and identification efficiency. As Fig. 2 shows, the node design of next generation monitoring interface information network applies the scientific color coding to enhance the use efficiency of monitoring interface substantially.

HMDs interface design enhances the brightness of information color to attract the attention of pilots, in order to highlight and feature the important information. Users will experience the strength of simulation to search and orient the information zone quickly. Similarly, the coordination utilization of color coding, size, shape and layout of icons and characters can function to significantly enhance pilots' performance of information searching and cognition degree of interface information. A scientific and

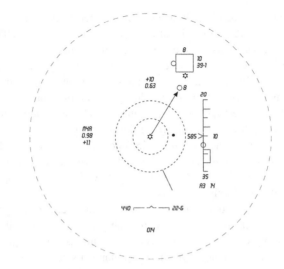

Fig. 1. HMDs interface icons

Fig. 2. The node design of next generation monitoring interface

rational color coding is of great importance for visual guidance of pilots. Many of experts and scholars have conducted researches in this aspect. Laar (2001) suggested that color difference can enhance the visual display and help users search visual clues [2]. Jen-Her Wu et al. (2003) conducted experimental analysis on the cognitive performance of hue, brightness and saturability in foreground and background assortment [3]. Peter (2003) conducted the significance level experiment on the differentiation degree and detectability of colored text [4]. Ahlstrom et al. (2005) adopted hierarchical brightness coding to optimize the design of avionics system interface [5]. Dennis (2008) proposed to structure the visual advantage via color perception; the hierarchical color combination could promote the importance ranking of interface information [6] (Fig. 3).

In terms of complicated system interfaces such s HMDs interface, Wu and Sun [7] proposed to test the azimuth angle and pitch angle of HMD relative to fighters, based on video picture processing methods, in order to optimize the existing angle of HMD for head tracking. Niklas [8] applied multi-sensor information combination to enhance the visual display effect of HMD. Xiaoli et al. [9] conducted experimental research on the visual limitation of target searching in radar situation interface, based on information erroneous judgment and careless omission of pilots. Jing et al. [10] launched the research on information coding of balancing time pressure in complicated system

Fig. 3. Mapping of color anti-interference performance to visual perceptive layer

interface. Zhang and Zhuang [11] analyzed the influence of text and location coding on information cognition based on eye movement data, through measurement of accuracy and respond time of testees to complete operation tasks. Knalb and Többen [12] developed icon system covering barriers and route information and threatening the regional conformal presentation. Wilson et al. [13] measured the prospective memory and attention diversion of pilots based on eye movement tracking technology to confirm the complicated factors influencing cognition. Cheng and Sun [14] proposed the methods for tracking human-computer eye movement oriented to mobile devices. Xiaoping et al. [15] proposed the methods to optimize the layout of human-computer interface layout of vehicles. Haiyan et al. [16] proposed the methods to assess the interface of driving display and control system of fighters, based on eye movement tracking technology. Weinreich et al. [17] conducted the eye movement research on enterprise website and SE interface. The literatures have shown that the research on HMDs interface mainly focuses on helmet mounted display technology and physiological assessment method of eye movement in complicated system interface, with little research on HMDs interface from the perspective of color brightness.

2 Methodology

2.1 Participants

17 subjects (9 males and 8 females) were present undergraduates (n = 5), postgraduate (n = 6) and doctoral candidates (n = 6) from Southeast University. They ranged in age from 20 to 35 years, with a mean age of 24 years. They had no color blindness or hypochromatopsia, with the corrected visual acuity over 1.0. They were required to practice and train to know the experimental procedure and operation requirements. Each participant sat in a comfortable chair in a soft light and soundproofed room, and eyes gazed at the center of the screen. A 17-in. CRT monitor with a 1024 × 768 pixel resolution was used in the experiment. The distance between participant eyes and the screen was approximately 60 cm, while the horizontal and vertical picture viewing angle was within 2.3°.

2.2 Experimental Equipment and Experimental Procedures

Five values of brightness, including 10 %, 30 %, 50 %, 70 % and 90 %, are used in the experiment. There is a horizon in the center of the display, while sky and ground are simulated in upper and lower parts. Five values of brightness of sky are compared with those of ground. The interface is shown in Fig. 4. Through random combination, 25 pictures are obtained for simulating background brightness.

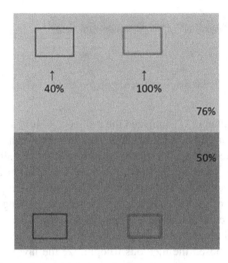

Fig. 4. Simulated picture for comparing brightness between sky and ground

There are two experiments, including Experiment 1 and 2. Experiment 1 focuses on exploring whether pilots' reaction time will be shortened when the target frame is regulated based on background brightness. The target frame used is rectangular. In this experiment, it is designated to be 50*50 large, 0.7 mm wide and green (wavelength: 500–560 mm). In the control group of Experiment 1, brightness is a constant and equals to 100 %, just as shown in Fig. 5. Aforementioned 25 pictures are separately taken for 3 times to simulate brightness. Each time, 3, 5 and 7 disturbances appear in different positions at random. Subjects need to make responses by clicking the button as soon as possible. In experimental group, when background brightness isn't above 50 %, brightness of the target frame will keep 100 %. As background brightness is higher than 50 %, the brightness will be automatically declined to 40 %, just as shown in Fig. 6. Other experimental requirements are completely the same as those of the control group.

Experiment 2 intends to examine if it is more effective to use dotted target frame than the solid one under backgrounds of different brightness. The experimental methods won't be illustrated here in detail because they are completely the same as those mentioned above. In this experiment, dotted target frame is used in the experimental group and solid target frame is utilized in the control group for comparisons.

3 Analysis and Results

The experiment selects 17 testees; removes 10 % of testees with high error rate; and selects 14 groups of available data. Then, the experiment selects the reaction time and accuracy data of each testee for each picture; finally, the experiment summarizes the mean value of reaction time and accuracy of 14 testees in different disturbances to get Tables 1, 2 and 3.

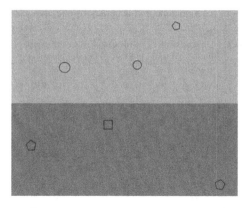

Fig. 5. Simulated picture of control group in experiment

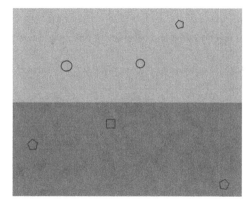

Fig. 6. Simulated picture of experimental group in experiment

3.1 Line Chart Analysis

Summarize the mean values of testees' reaction time in the experiment to get this line chart as in Fig. 7.

The line chart above has visually shown that the existing target frame, target frame with changeable brightness and dotted target frame are increased, along with the increase of disturbance number. The dynamic change of line chart has suggested that the fold lines of design plans of three target frames are roughly paralleled without cross. However, in the wake of the increase of disturbances, the increase trend of reaction time has been slightly reduced. And the dotted target frame features the most significant decreasing trend, compared by target frame with changeable brightness with the most unapparent decreasing trend. In addition, it is visual that the reaction time of dotted target frame is the longest, followed by that of existing target frame, and the reaction time of target frame with changeable brightness is the shortest, among the design of three target frames.

Table 1. Mean values of reaction time and accuracy of effective testees in control group

3 Disturbances RT (ms)	3 Disturbances ACC (%)	5 Disturbances RT (ms)	5 Disturbances ACC (%)	7 Disturbances RT (ms)	7 Disturbances ACC (%)
998.67	0.94	1019.81	1.00	1230.25	1.00
857.56	1.00	927.44	1.00	879.07	1.00
542.50	1.00	587.63	1.00	622.81	1.00
775.89	1.00	838.31	0.94	933.43	1.00
887.44	1.00	1063.81	1.00	1217.93	0.93
696.69	1.00	891.75	1.00	830.44	1.00
693.13	1.00	829.00	0.94	1003.57	1.00
939.44	1.00	1046.81	1.00	767.50	1.00
826.50	1.00	1051.19	1.00	1115.14	1.00
955.83	1.00	978.81	1.00	1081.79	1.00
977.00	1.00	1095.00	1.00	797.00	0.94
860.56	1.00	936.13	1.00	1150.21	1.00
770.78	0.78	1230.25	1.00	870.31	1.00
1220.33	1.00	824.69	0.81	1157.07	1.00

Table 2. Mean values of reaction time and accuracy of effective testees in experiment group 1

3 Disturbances RT (ms)	3 Disturbances ACC (%)	5 Disturbances RT (ms)	5 Disturbances ACC (%)	7 Disturbances RT (ms)	7 Disturbances ACC (%)
929.25	1.00	1169.75	1.00	1323.75	1.00
733.44	1.00	896.13	1.00	806.44	1.00
542.50	1.00	587.63	1.00	622.81	1.00
634.38	1.00	629.19	1.00	688.06	1.00
887.44	1.00	989.00	1.00	1172.31	1.00
696.69	1.00	891.75	1.00	797.00	0.94
693.13	1.00	829.00	0.94	830.44	1.00
1063.50	1.00	790.63	1.00	1147.69	1.00
626.94	0.94	855.94	1.00	683.25	1.00
777.50	0.94	918.13	0.88	819.44	1.00
786.19	0.94	808.94	1.00	881.13	1.00
860.56	1.00	851.25	1.00	870.25	1.00
625.19	0.94	733.31	1.00	677.44	0.94
872.69	1.00	845.25	1.00	895.38	1.00

3.2 Anova

ANOVA on reaction time shows that the between-group main effect shall be significant as (F = 15.772, P = 0.001, P < 0.05), the main effect of disturbances shall be significant as (F = 3.262, P = 0.042, P < 0.05), showing the significant influence of experiment groups and disturbance number on reaction time.

The multi-comparison test results on reaction time based on LSD are shown as Tables 4 and 5. The table has shown that there are significant differences in reaction time of experiment group 1 and 2, compared by reaction time of disturbances only

Table 3. Mean values of reaction time and accuracy of effective testees in experiment group 2

3 Disturbances RT (ms)	3 Disturbances ACC (%)	5 Disturbances RT (ms)	5 Disturbances ACC (%)	7 Disturbances RT (ms)	7 Disturbances ACC (%)
929.25	1.00	1169.75	1.00	1323.75	1.00
733.44	1.00	896.13	1.00	806.44	1.00
542.50	1.00	587.63	1.00	622.81	1.00
634.38	1.00	629.19	1.00	688.06	1.00
887.44	1.00	989.00	1.00	1172.31	1.00
696.69	1.00	891.75	1.00	797.00	0.94
693.13	1.00	829.00	0.94	830.44	1.00
1063.50	1.00	790.63	1.00	1147.69	1.00
626.94	0.94	855.94	1.00	683.25	1.00
777.50	0.94	918.13	0.88	819.44	1.00
786.19	0.94	808.94	1.00	881.13	1.00
860.56	1.00	851.25	1.00	870.25	1.00
625.19	0.94	733.31	1.00	677.44	0.94
872.69	1.00	845.25	1.00	895.38	1.00

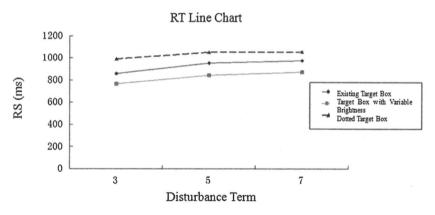

Fig. 7. RT line chart (Color figure online)

when there are 3 and 7 disturbances, showing that the slight change of disturbance number will not bring about significant difference of reaction time.

Conclusions have been made based on the data of 14 effective testes: (1) In case of three disturbances, respondents' reaction time is the shortest regardless of dotted or solid lines. With the increase in disturbances, respondents' reaction time gets longer. (2) In the same background brightness, respondents' reaction time may be effectively shortened when the brightness is 40 %. (3) Under the same experimental conditions, it takes a longer reaction time for respondents to observe the dotted target frame than the solid one.

Table 4. LSD multi-comparison test of experiment groups

(I) Experiment group	(J) Experiment group	Main difference (I–J)	SE	Significance	95 % Confidence interval	
1	2	100.92463*	36.73408	.007	28.2118	173.6375
	3	−105.37201*	36.73408	.005	−178.0849	−32.6592
2	1	−100.92463*	36.73408	.007	−173.6375	−28.2118
	3	−206.29665*	36.73408	.000	−279.0095	−133.5838
3	1	105.37201*	36.73408	.005	32.6592	178.0849
	2	206.29665*	36.73408	.000	133.5838	279.0095

Table 5. LSD multi-comparison test of disturbance number

(I) Experiment group	(J) Experiment group	Main difference (I–J)	SE	Significance	95 % Confidence interval	
3	5	−77.73245	40.12541	.055	−157.1582	1.6933
	7	−96.71428*	40.12541	.017	−176.1401	−17.2885
5	3	77.73245	40.12541	.055	−1.6933	157.1582
	7	−18.98183	40.12541	.637	−98.4076	60.4440
7	3	96.71428*	40.12541	.017	17.2885	176.1401
	5	18.98183	40.12541	.637	−60.4440	98.4076

4   Conclusions

1. Significant differences exist in reaction time among existing target frame, target frame with changeable brightness and dotted target frame. The reaction time also significantly differs for 3, 5 and 7 different disturbances. Experimental data have effectively indicated the changes based on background brightness and demonstrated that the design scheme of brightness for optimizing target frame is feasible. On the whole, cognitive effects are better for the target frame with changeable brightness as compared with existing target frame no matter how many disturbances there are. The reaction time is about 12 % shorter on average for the former target frame.
2. Respondents' reaction time is longer in observing dotted target frame, which reflects that it is more reasonable to design solid target frame.
3. From the increase in reaction time, it may be observed that the longer the reaction time, the smaller the increase, which may be reflected most evidently when the number of disturbances increases from 5 to 7 for the dotted target frame. In addition, it may be discovered from the experimental data that the target frame with changeable brightness narrows by 100 ms on average compared with existing target frame.

Acknowledgement. This paper is supported by National Natural Science Foundation of China (Nos. 71271053, 71471037), Aeronautical Science Foundation of China (No. 20135169016) and Scientific Innovation Research of College Graduates in Jiangsu Province (No. CXLX13_082).

References

1. Laar, D.L.V.: Psychological and cartographic principles for the production of visual layering effects in computer displays. Displays **22**(4), 125–135 (2001)
2. Laar, D.L.V.: Color coding with visual layers can provide performance enhancements in control room displays. In: Proceedings of People in Control. International Conference on Human Interfaces in Control Rooms, Cockpits and Command Centres, Manchester, UK, p. 481 (2001)
3. Jen-Her, W., Yuan, Y.: Improving searching and reading performance: the effect of highlighting and text color coding. Inf. Manag. **40**(7), 617–637 (2003)
4. Peter, B.: Chromaticity contrast in visual search on the multi-colour user interface. Displays **24**(1), 39–48 (2003)
5. Ahlstrom, U.L.F., Arend, L.: Color usability on air traffic control displays. In: Proceedings of the Human Factors and Ergonomics Society 49th Annual Meeting, Oriando, FL, United states, pp. 93–97 (2005)
6. Dennis, M.P.: Perceiving hierarchy through intrinsic color structure. Vis. Commun. **7**(2), 199–228 (2008)
7. Wu, W., Sun, J.: Research on the orientation method of HMD based on image processing. In: 2012 10th World Congress on Intelligent Control and Automation (WCICA), pp. 4160–4162. IEEE (2012)
8. Peinecke, N., Knabl, P.M., Schmerwitz, S, et al.: An evaluation environment for a helmet-mounted synthetic degraded visual environment display. In: 2014 IEEE/AIAA 33rd Digital Avionics Systems Conference (DASC), pp. 2C2-1–2C2-7. IEEE (2014)
9. Xiaoli, W., Chengqi, X., Wencheng, T., Jiang, S., Jing, L.: Experimental study on visual limitation experiment of goal – seeking in radar situation – interface. J. Southeast Univ. Nat. Sci. Ed. **06**, 1166–1170 (2014)
10. Jing, L., Chengqi, X., Haiyan, W., Lei, Z., Yafeng, N.: Encoding information of human – computer interface for equilibrium of time pressure. J. Comput. Aided Des. Comput. Graph. **25**(7), 1022–1028 (2013)
11. Zhang, L., Zhuang, D.: Text and position coding of human – machine display interface. J. Beijing Univ. Aeronaut. Astronaut. **37**(2), 185–188 (2011)
12. Knabl, P., Többen, H.: Symbology development for a 3D conformal synthetic vision helmet-mounted display for helicopter operations in degraded visual environment. In: Harris, D. (ed.) EPCE 2013, Part I. LNCS, vol. 8019, pp. 232–241. Springer, Heidelberg (2013)
13. Wilson, J.R., Hooey, B.L., Foyle, D.C.: Head-up display symbology for surface operations: eye tracking analysis of command-guidance vs. situation-guidance formats. In: Proceedings of the 13th International Symposium on Aviation Psychology, Oklahoma City, pp. 13–18 (2005)
14. Cheng S., Sun Z.: An approach to eye tracking for mobile device based interaction. J. Comput. Aided Des. Comput. Graph. (8), 1354–1361 (2014)
15. Xiaoping, J., Ying, Q., Rongen, M., et al.: Human – research on driving computer interface layout design reasoning system. Trans. Chin. Soc. Agric. Mach. **39**(4), 183–186 (2008)
16. Haiyan, W., Ting, B., Chengqi, X.: Layout design of display interface for a new generation fighter. Electro – Mech. Eng. **27**(4), 57–61 (2011)
17. Weinreich, H., Obendorf, H., Herder, E., et al.: Not quite the average: an empirical study of web use. ACM Trans. Web (TWEB) **2**(1), 5 (2008)

A Decision Tree Based Image Enhancement Instruction System for Producing Contemporary Style Images

Meng-Luen Wu[✉] and Chin-Shyurng Fahn

Department of Computer Science and Information Engineering,
National Taiwan University of Science and Technology,
Taipei 10607, Taiwan, ROC
{d10015015, csfahn}@mail.ntust.edu.tw

Abstract. In this paper, we have proposed an image enhancement method by contemporary aesthetics criteria, which enables computers to produce visually favorable images automatically. The contemporary aesthetics criteria is obtained through data mining algorithms such as decision tree, support vector machine, and neural networks. In order to make computers adjust the images automatically to make them match the contemporary aesthetics criteria, the tree-based classification method is proposed for enhancement instructions. Our proposed system finds the reasons in the tree why an input image is not perceptually favorable and give improvement instructions accordingly. The training features are based on enhancement instructions, such as color component, saturation, sharpness, and so on. Preprocessing methods are also proposed for a more efficient labeling and better accuracy for image classification. The training samples are from both contemporary style high aesthetics quality images and those are not, which more than 15,000 training samples are used. The accuracy of our proposed method is above 95 %. The experimental result shows our system can give users or computers appropriate enhancement instruction efficiently.

Keywords: Professional photographing · Computational aesthetics · Autonomous photographing · Data mining · Image retouching · Image enhancement

1 Introduction

Users who upgrade their camera to high-end ones because they want more appealing pictures. Although high-end cameras provide more functionalities than low-end ones, they are not guaranteed to take better photos. A good image depends on user's handling, and the environmental light sources, as well as the content in the field of view. Automatic image enhancement in real-time can help user take better pictures without any manual operations. In existing camera products, the automatic adjustments focus on image quality enhancement, such as brightness, sharpness, and so on. The existing adjustments help producing clear pictures but will not necessarily produce appealing ones.

Figure 1 shows three images of the same scene. The three images are original raw image from image sensor, image enhanced by camera, and image enhanced by a

© Springer International Publishing Switzerland 2016
S. Yamamoto (Ed.): HIMI 2016, Part I, LNCS 9734, pp. 80–90, 2016.
DOI: 10.1007/978-3-319-40349-6_9

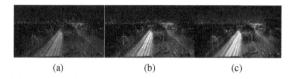

(a)   (b)   (c)

Fig. 1. Three images of the same scene: (a) original raw image from image sensor; (b) image enhanced by camera; (c) image enhanced by software darkroom.

software darkroom, and the difference among them is noticeable. The software darkroom is a key for popular and perceptually favorable images, which the software darkroom enables user to modify the contrast, sharpness, color component, brightness, and so on. The digital darkroom is usually operated manually. The digital darkroom is used for post-enhancement so it has limitations. For example, when an image is underexposure that some pixel values are zero, increasing the brightness of the image is useless for restoring the contents of these pixels. In this case, we know that to produce better images instructing the camera users to handle the cameras well is better than using the software darkroom, and the instructions must run in real-time.

If we deem the software darkroom as a post-enhancement for a popular image, the good handling of professional cameras is a pre-enhancement. Compared to post-enhancement, the pre-enhancement has more possibilities because the environmental conditions are still adjustable. Therefore, our proposed methods focus on autonomous handling instructions, which is the pre-enhancement method. In this paper, we proposed a real-time instruction system for users to adjust their camera parameters appropriately to get better and more appealing pictures. The adjustments can also be performed by machines automatically. The main challenge for this topic is that the concept of a good images differs from time to time, so we have to find out the criterions for popular contemporary style images, which is performed by data mining algorithms.

2 Feature Extraction

Choosing the right image aesthetics features is essential for both clustering and classification of professional and non-professional images, which is used to predict whether an image is possibly favorable [1].

In this paper, we focus on efficient image enhancement instructions that helps an amateur picture become professional. The features include color, brightness, contrast, sharpness, and so on, which are proposed as follows:

The color component is extracted by the following equation:

$$f_{colorcomponent} = \sum_{x=1}^{width} \sum_{y=1}^{height} \frac{D(c_l, c(x,y))}{width \times height} \tag{1}$$

where the width and height in the equation are for the image, and D is the Euclidean distance between two colors in CIELab color space, c_l is the color component to be

82   M.-L. Wu and C.-S. Fahn

extracted in the CIELab color space. c(x, y) is the color value of coordinate (x, y) in the same color space.

The achromatic degree can be obtained by:

$$f_{achromatic} = \sum_{x=1}^{width} \sum_{y=1}^{height} \frac{|\{(x,y)|Ch_R(x,y) = Ch_G(x,y) = Ch_B(x,y)\}|}{width \times height} \tag{2}$$

where Ch_R, Ch_G, Ch_B are for the intensity of red, green, and blue channel of a pixel respectively.

Six features according to this formula, which are red, green, blue, magenta, cyan, and yellow components.

Professional images are usually higher in contrast, which is defined as:

$$f_{contrast} = \sum_{i=1}^{n-1} \sum_{j=i+1}^{n} (1 - d(i,j)) \frac{D(i,j)}{A_i A_j} \tag{3}$$

where $d(i,j)$ is the spatial distance between the centroids of two segmentations i and j; $D(i,j)$ is the color distance between the two segmentations in the CIELab color space.

The color saturation feature is defined as:

$$f_{saturation} = \sum_{x=1}^{width} \sum_{y=1}^{height} \frac{s(x,y)}{width \times height} \tag{4}$$

where s is for the saturation of a pixel in HSV color space.

The degree of sharpness and blur of an image is stated as follows:

$$f_{sharpness} = \frac{|\{(u,v)||F(u,v)| > \xi\}|}{width \times height} \propto \frac{1}{\sigma} \tag{5-1}$$

$$f_{blur} \propto \frac{1}{f_{sharpness}} \tag{5-2}$$

where $I_{blur} = G_\sigma * I$ is the blurred image derived through convolving the original image I with a Gaussian filter G_σ, and $F(u,v) = FFT(I_{blur}(x,y))$ is the blurred image transformed into the frequency domain via the fast Fourier transform. Here, ξ is set to 5.

In [2], the formula of the simplicity feature yields:

$$f_{simplicity} = \left(\frac{|\{l|k(c_l) \geq \gamma k_{max}\}|}{4096} \right) \times 10 \tag{6}$$

where $k(c_l)$ is the color count for color c_l, k_{max} is the maximum color count, and γ is set to 0.001. In this formula, the number of colors in the image is reduced to 4096; that is, the color counts of R, G, and B are all reduced to 16.

For an input image, the global brightness can be obtained by the following equation:

$$f_{brightness} = \frac{\sum_{x=1}^{width} \sum_{y=1}^{height} I(x, y)}{width \times height} \tag{7}$$

where $I(x, y)$ is the intensity of a pixel at (x, y).

The chosen image features are as follows, f1 ∼ f6 are color components, which are red, green, blue, cyan, magenta, and yellow. f7 is the degree of achromatic. f8 is the color contrast. f9 is color saturation. f10 is sharpness. f11 is simplicity. f12 is the brightness.

3 Data Preprocessing

In this paper, the criterions of popular contemporary images are found via data mining. For better data mining results, the training data should be preprocessed properly. In this section, the feature selection and data clustering methods used in our system and are described as follows:

3.1 Feature Selection

The feature selection chooses a useful subset of features from the full subset of the training data. The benefit of feature selection is that less features need to be extracted. In addition, not every features are useful for analysis, which some of them would even influence the accuracy. This is because some feature values are redundant which are useless for analysis according to the information theory. What's worse, data belong to some features can be noisy and not correct. Therefore, feature selection is necessary for better analysis results.

The preliminary goal for feature selection is to find decisive features for data classification. The correlation feature selection (CFS) [3] selects the best feature subsets that have the best contribution to the training set. The CFS assumes that good feature subsets contain features that are highly correlated with the classification, and uncorrelated to others.

3.2 Data Clustering

In our proposed method, data clustering before classification is the major key for the success of training. The training samples are clustered into many groups for labeling. The images in the same group share similar features values, while images belong to different groups are perceptually different. Label the groups which are preferred by professional photographers as "favorable," and the other are labeled as "not favorable." Two preferred images may not be in the same group and they may perceptually different. For example, images under day light and in night scenes are visually different and they will be clustered into different groups, but some groups of both of them are preferred by professionals as they have other subset features in common. To be brief, the purpose of data clustering is to group images with similar features together, and each groups can be labeled as "favorable" or "not favorable."

We choose K-means algorithm for clustering. K-means algorithm is simple yet the number of clusters is controllable. When there are too much groups, the labeling is too detailed and does not give good classification result. On the other hand, when clustered into few groups, the labeling is too rough and still the classifier does not give good accuracy. Empirically, 20 groups is appropriate for labeling.

When the clusters are appropriately labelled, data belong to all labeled groups are set as inputs for the classifier, and the classifier will build separation boundaries for all clusters, which is a means of hybrid learning. The concept is shown in Fig. 2. In next section, the decision tree algorithm is used as one of the classifiers which generates readable rules for classification with the labeling.

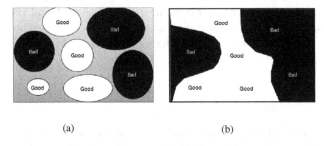

(a)   (b)

Fig. 2. Hybrid learning: (a) clustered data, which two clusters are distributed in the feature space; (b) a possible separation for two classes of data in the feature space with their respective labels. (Good = favorable by experts; Bad = not favorable by experts)

4   Decision Tree Based Instruction System

In this section, the method for autonomous photographing instruction is proposed. The tree based classification method is the core algorithm. In addition to our proposed methods, the limitations are also explained in this section.

4.1   Decision Tree

Decision tree [4] is a popular supervised learning approach because the decision process walks through the path of the tree, and each path can be written as a rule. In a decision tree, the nodes except the leaves represent a feature, and its child edges are predicates for the feature, such as "value larger than," or "value less than." A node without any children is a leaf node. The class labels are put in the leaf nodes of the decision tree.

Decision tree algorithms are based on information theory [5], which the main idea is to calculate the entropy of the classes of data when data are separated using specified feature and branching value.

A major problem for decision tree is over-fitting, [6] which can be solved by pruning. If the degree of the tree is too high, some unnecessary nodes are produced near the leaf, and lowers the accuracy of the decision tree. Therefore, pruning is needed for the tree. When a node is pruned by replacing it with a class leaf, and the accuracy of the tree is better after the replacement, the pruning is accepted, otherwise keep the original sub-tree.

4.2 Instruction Algorithm

When the decision tree is a binary tree, if the value of a node's feature is greater than a specific value, it will be branched to a child, otherwise it will be branched to the other.

The features are abbreviated as f1, f2, f3, ..., fn respectively. For example, in Fig. 3, The red edges is decision path in the tree.

Given a path shown in red in Fig. 3(a), when the value of f4 is less than or equal to 57.46, the image is classified as "bad." (not favorable) If all features are conditionally independent in this decision tree, and f4 has exactly two children, the image can be classified to "good" (favorable) simply by making the value of f4 greater than 57.46, as shown in Fig. 3(b).

Through the decision process, the conditions that cause an photo not favorable can be known by user, and is improved by increasing or decreasing a feature in the image.

The decision path's leaf node should have one leaf node sibling. For example, in Fig. 4(a), an image is classified as "bad." (not favorable) if we adjust the value of f2 to be greater than 41.91, the path will lead to another child of the f2, which is a sub-tree shown as orange in Fig. 4(b). The sub-tree does not guarantee that the adjusted image will be classified as "good," (favorable). Therefore the instruction does not necessarily give expected result in this situation.

A feature in the decision path cannot have multiple occurrences, otherwise the adjustments may lead the path to another sub-tree. For example, in Fig. 5(a), an image is

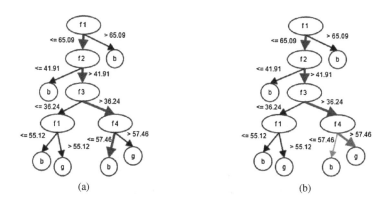

(a)   (b)

Fig. 3. The decision process of a decision tree and the instruction given method: (a) an image is classified as bad (not favored by expert) with the red path; (b) an instruction is given that user changes the environmental condition which makes the last edge in the decision process go to the green edge, and finally the image can be classified as good (favored by experts) 4.3 Limitations. (Color figure online)

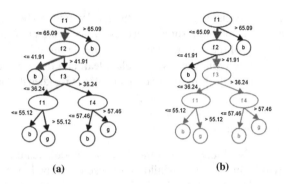

Fig. 4. Limitations for the instruction system: (a) an image is classified as bad (not favored by experts) with the red decision path; (b) alerting the value of f2 is not effective because the decision path will lead to a subtree with two classes at leaves. (Color figure online)

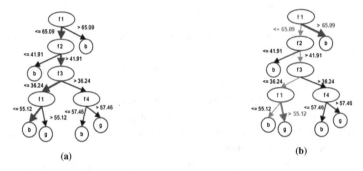

Fig. 5. A limitation that the suggestion cannot be given: (a) an image is classified as bad (not favored by experts) with the red decision path; (b) altering the value of f1 near the leaf node will also change the path of the root node in the tree, which is also branched by f1. (Color figure online)

classified as "bad," (not favorable) and the decision path have two "f1"s in it. If the value of f1 is adjusted to 60, fortunately, it will be classified as "good" (favorable) with the green edge in Fig. 5(b). However, if the value of f1 is adjusted to be greater than 65.09, it will be classified as "bad" (not favorable) with the red edge shown in Fig. 5(b).

Finally, it is recommended that two features in the decision tree must be conditionally independent, which means an adjustment of one feature must not influence another. For example, if "f1" is the feature of "red component" and "f2" is the feature of "green," the enhancement of "red component" also improves "green" at times. Therefore, when training the decision tree, all selected features for training must be conditionally independent. For example, the feature of sharpness does not always influence those of colors.

5   Experimental Result

In this section, the experimental results performed on our proposed system is shown. First, we will introduce the experimental system setup. Second, the accuracy of image classifiers is described.

5.1   Experimental Setup

The experimental setup is as follows: The image sensor is 1/2.3", 20.7 MP image sensor with 27 mm lens and the aperture value is f/2.0. The resolution of the image in the software is 1920 × 1080 when capture and is downscaled to 320 × 240 for processing.

In the experiment, we choose 12 prominent features for training the decision tree, which are red, blue, green, cyan, yellow, magenta, achromatic, contrast, saturation, sharpness, simplicity, brightness. We choose 10,000 images for training, which is first clustered into 20 groups, and only 6 of them are labeled as positive (favored by experts) samples, while the other groups are labeled as bad (not favored by experts).

5.2   Aesthetics Value Prediction

In order to examine the feasibility of out proposed methods, we have verified the accuracy using different classification algorithms other than decision tree, including Naïve Bayesian, Support Vector Machine, Multi-layered Perceptron, Radial Basis Network, Adaptive Boosting, and Random Forest.

The parameters for the classifiers are as follows: For the support vector machine, the RBF function is chosen as the kernel function, the cost is set to 1. For the multi-layered perceptron, the number of hidden layers is set to half the sum of feature numbers and number of classes, which is 7 here. The learning rate is 0.3, and the training iteration is 500. For the Radial basis network, the minimum standard deviation is set to 0.1, clustering seed is 1, number of clusters is 2, and the ridge is 10^{-8}. For the Adaptive Boosting, the weak classifiers are decision stump, the number of iterations is 10, the seed is set to 1, and the weight of threshold is set to 100. For the J48 decision tree, the confidence factor is set to 0.25. For the Random forest, the number of trees is set to 100. Each of the algorithms are verified using 10-fold verification.

5.3   Evaluation of the Instruction System

In this section, the result for the instruction system is shown. Both the input image, the predicted result, and the decision process for the instructions are shown.

The following are good aesthetics value prediction results for the natural images. The images are predicted as accepted. The prediction process is also shown beside the images to be predicted. For cleaner explanation, the "g" in the leaf node means favorable, and "b" represents "not favorable."

(a)   (b)

Fig. 6. A flower image which is classified as "favorable": (a) input image; (b) the decision path of the decision tree.

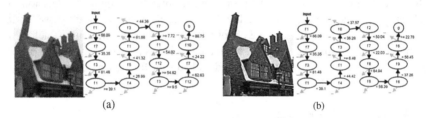

(a)   (b)

Fig. 7. The improvement of an image after applying the instruction from our proposed system: (a) the original image; (b) the improved image after applying the instruction.

In the Fig. 6, the image is classified as "favorable." The decision process are also shown in the figures.

In the figures of the decision path, the black path is the actual path traversed by the decision process, and the gray path in the tree are not traversed. The "…" represents a sub-tree.

The Fig. 7 shows an improvement case after applying the instruction from our system. The instruction asks to improve sharpness, and we use an image editor to enhance the sharpness of the image. In this case, the sharpness is adjusted violently, and the increase of the sharpness also influences other features in the image. The image is classified as "favorable" after applying the instruction. However, the result in this case can be a coincidence because the decision path is not the same as the one before improvement. Fortunately, nodes in four degrees near the root are the same in two paths of the decision tree, which means pruning may be a solution to prevent this kind of problem.

The Figs. 8, 9 and 10 are successful examples that the images are improved by using the instructions from our system. In the three images, the features from the instructions are adjusted carefully that they would not change the decision path of the tree.

In Fig. 23, the feature f4 (cyan degree) is not enough in the image. The image is adjusted to the one which meets the conditions of a contemporary image after increasing the cyan degree of the image. Although the change in the image is subtle, the result is noticeable.

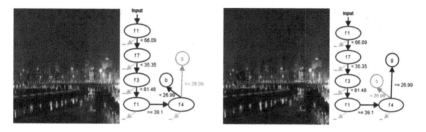

Fig. 8. The improvement of an image after applying the instruction from our proposed system: (a) the original image; (b) the improved image after applying the instruction.

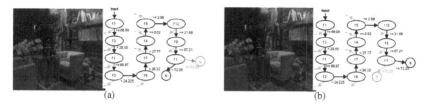

(a)   (b)

Fig. 9. The improvement of an image after applying the instruction from our proposed system: (a) the original image; (b) the improved image after applying the instruction.

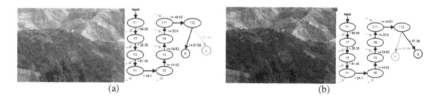

(a)   (b)

Fig. 10. The improvement of an image after applying the instruction from our proposed system: (a) the original image; (b) the improved image after applying the instruction.

In Fig. 9, the feature f1 (red degree) is not enough in the image. The image is adjusted to the one which meets the conditions of a contemporary image after increasing the red degree of the image.

In Fig. 10, the feature f12 (brightness degree) is too high in the image. The image is adjusted to the one which meets the conditions of a contemporary image after decreasing the brightness degree of the image.

6   Conclusion and Future Works

Image enhancement by expert retouching is an effective technique for making contemporary style images which is preferred by professional photographers. Traditionally, the enhancement is performed manually by experience or "trial and error." A good handling of camera can reduce the time of image enhancement. Our proposed methods can effectively tell users directly which features should be enhanced to make a favorable image with single instruction.

There are two issues to be solved for the system. First, when the sibling's leaf node is a sub-tree, the instruction cannot be given in the current method. Second, when changing a feature of the image violently, other features are possibly altered, which also changes the decision path. The solution of these issues would help improve the application and eliminate limitations of the proposed system.

Acknowledgement. The authors thank the National Science Council of Taiwan (R.O.C.) for supporting this work in part under Grant MOST 104-2221-E-011-032-MY3.

References

1. Fahn, C.-S., Wu, M.-L.: An autonomous aesthetics-driven photographing instructor system with personality prediction. In: Proceedings of International Conference on Computer Graphics, Visualization, Computer Vision, and Game Technology, Jakarta, Indonesia, pp. 13–19 (2013)
2. Yeh, C.-H., Ho, Y.-C., Barsky, B.A., Ouhyoung, M.: Personalized photograph ranking and selection system. In: Proceedings of International Conference on Multimedia, Firenze, Italy, pp. 211–220 (2010)
3. Christopher, J.C.: A tutorial on support vector machines for pattern recognition. Data Min. Knowl. Discov. **2**(2), 121–167 (1998)
4. Apté, C.V., Weiss, S.: Data mining with decision trees and decision rules. Future Gener. Comput. Syst. **13**(2), 197–210 (1997)
5. Apté, C.V., Hong, S.J., Natarajan, R., Pednault, E.P., Tipu, F.A., Weiss, S.M.: Data-intensive analytics for predictive modeling. IBM J. Res. Dev. **4**(1), 17–23 (2003)
6. Quinlan, J.R.: C4.5: Programs for Machine Learning. Elsevier, Amsterdam (2014)

Spatial Conformity Research of Temporal Order Information Presentation in Visualization Design

Xiaozhou Zhou, Chengqi Xue[✉], Lei Zhou, Jiang Shao, and Zhangfan Shen

School of Mechanical Engineering, Southeast University,
Nanjing 211189, China
ipd_xcq@seu.edu.cn

Abstract. The topic of dynamic presentation of temporal order information relates to both the node information flowing with time and the location changing in 2D space. In this paper, psychological research methods were applied to research the feasible representation method of temporal order information on the base of human cognitive characteristics. That was the research on relevance of temporal order presentation and space order presentation. We tried to study on the dynamic information presentation processes of the nodes arranged regular in horizontal linear trace. The eye-tracker recorded the performance of 30 valid subjects in different nodes skip way, horizontal moving direction and moving time. Through the analysis of accuracy and reaction time, the conclusion has been drawn that the possible presentation methods with optimal performance.

Keywords: Visualization design · Temporal order · Space coherence · Data type compatibility

1 Information Visualization

In the complex environment of big data, the information interface with visualization is the only effective way for the user to perceive data regardless of any method to deal with the dataset. The target of information visualization is human—the user; therefore, we should discuss the problem of information visualization representation on the point of visual cognition peculiarity of human beings.

The information needs of human are flexible. That means what they want to know is not only the global understanding of the information system but also the detailed characterization of some specific key points. In visualization design, the information we need to representation is not unusual the homogeneous information on different temporal. Thus, it is essential for the user that perceived the situation of information flowing over time to grasp the characteristics of information overall. So, how to define the rule of change to make the user perceive the flow of information of the visualization interface accurately and quickly?

A grounded model of information Visualization sense making should consist of the five major cognitive activities: encountering visualization, constructing a frame,

© Springer International Publishing Switzerland 2016
S. Yamamoto (Ed.): HIMI 2016, Part I, LNCS 9734, pp. 91–99, 2016.
DOI: 10.1007/978-3-319-40349-6_10

exploring visualization, questioning the frame and floundering on visualization, proposed by Lee et al. (2016). Koerner et al. (2014) tried to make the eye trace regular clearly via observing the eye movement under the transformation of hierarchical graphs. Jigsaw provides automatic extraction of entities and a time line to organize them (Gorg et al. 2014). Timeline (temporal order) visualization is an important tool for sense making. And Nguyen's research (2014, 2016) focus on the dynamic interactive time line visualization for sensemaking.

2 Dynamic Display of Temporal Order Information

The perception of spatio-temporal pattern is a fundamental part of visual cognition (Gibson 1966; Schill et al. 2001; Crowder 2014). The topic of consistency of temporal order and spatial coding has been controversy in the field of psychology. The focal point is whether the adding spatial cue could improve the memory performance of temporal order (De Lillo 2004; Parmentier 2006; Körner 2014). And this issue has a strong practical significance in information visualization design.

As far as designers are concerned, data type compatibility (DTC) should be taken into account. That is to build the consistency over the mental models, visual presentation and information characterization (Garnham 1997). With the generation of stream processing technology dataset and the growth of computer performance, we can present the temporal order information in a dynamic way. The so-called dynamic presentation can be regarded as image sets constantly changing on every unit of time (1 frame). While the retinal variables (location, shape, color, size, proportion, etc.) of design element changing at every frame, we can perceive the dynamic change of the design element. And the dynamic variables attracted users' attention most (Tam and Ho 2006; Opach et al. 2014). Differences in the direction and speed of changes of design elements in spatial position have the different influence on the consequent of building the mental model of temporal order. This is the theoretical basis of this paper.

3 Research Methods

3.1 Purpose

In order to find out the most reasonable dynamic skip way of linear nodes, we designed three experiments to compare different nodes skip way, horizontal moving direction and different nodes skip time respectively. The dependent variable was the subjects' cognitive performance, which evaluated by the recall accuracy, reaction time and the skip magnitude of gaze points. Based on this comparison to discriminant the merits of the materials.

3.2 Equipment and Subjects

The Tobii X2-300 compact non-contact eye tracker has been taken to collect eye-tracking data of subjects. The instrument sampling frequency is 30 Hz, the staring accuracy is 0.4°–0.5° and the head movement range is 50 × 36 cm. The resolution ratio of experimental animation material is 1280 × 960 px. The materials were presented by a HP 21 inch screen with the brightness of 92 cd/m². The laboratory was in the normal lighting conditions (40 W fluorescent). The distance between the subjects and the screen was about 550–600 mm.

The valid subjects were 30 graduate students (13 women), aged ranged from 22 to 28. All had normal or corrected- to- normal vision and no color blindness or color weakness. Before the formal experiments, the subjects participated in a practice test to become familiar with the rules of the experiments.

3.3 Materials

At first, we deleted the specific contents of the information nodes for removing the affecting factor of the contents to the subjects. We extracted the most simplified primitive structure of the temporal order information and present it as solid dots. All the nodes were in accordance with the horizontal linear arrangement. The middle node represented the information of the current time at that moment, and the nodes in both ends were arranged with the distance in descending order, to characterized the span of time, as shown in Fig. 1.

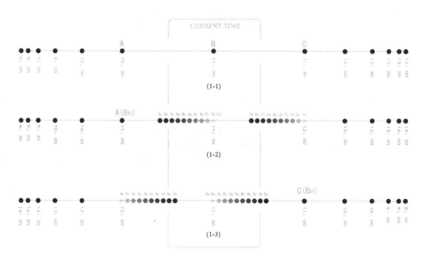

Fig. 1. The dynamic moving skip ways

(1–1) The basic temporal order information presentation structure. (1–2) Dynamic moving skips direction 1: from right to left. (1–3) Dynamic moving skip direction 2: from left to right.

In the experiment, the time information was replaced by the senseless uppercase and lowercase monogrammed (see Fig. 2). A pretest has been done to keep the difficulty of experiment in a reasonable range, in order to avoid the occurrence of "celling phenomenon" and "floor phenomenon".

Fig. 2. The meaningless representation method used in this experiment

The animations and images involving in this experiment were generated by Adobe Flash and the export format was gif with a sequence to ensure the images within the finite size and clarity. In addition to the portion needed to be compared, others were in the same design, including: (1) all the elements were in the linear arranged way; (2) all the elements were moving along the horizontal linear direction; (3) all in the same primitive presentation method, using the solid dots to represent the information nodes; (4) all the images were in the same figure-ground relationship, with the white color (CMYK = 0, 0, 0, 0) was taken as the background and the blue color (CMYK = 90, 60, 0, 0) as the figure one; (5) the uniform application of meaningless upper-case + lowercase letter pairs as the node information elements, such as Gf and the meaningful letter pairs was excluding as If, Or and AB because these letter pairs prone to associative memory.

The experiment designed in the subjects of 3 × 4. The independent variable I was the moving skip way while the independent II was moving skip direction and the variable III was moving skip time, respectively 500 ms, 1000 ms, 1500 ms and 2000 ms. The dependent variable was the cognitive performance of the user. It was synthesized evaluated on the measure index of correct rate of recall questions, the reactive time and the coincidence rate between the eye movement track and the setting track.

3.4   Processes

During the formal experiment, subjects read the guidance language first and pressed any key on the keyboard to start the experiment. At first, the center of the screen presented fixations "+" for 500 ms, then the animation of characterizing linear nodes flowing pattern began to paly. There was a certain space distance between the "+" and the animation information in order to keep the initial viewpoint away from the area of temporal order information. It was benefit for our extracting the eye trace. As shown in Fig. 3, the animation was composed by a sequence of n images in gif format. The first

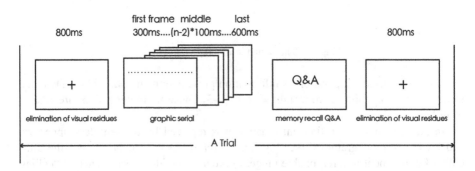

Fig. 3. The experiment process

image presented for 300 ms, the n-2 middle images presented for 100 ms/per page and the last one presented for 600 ms. When the animation finished, the question emerged with 5 options. The subjects could make a judgment by clicking the left mouse button. By this, we could measure the subjects' memories performance of nodes information recall.

In each animation, the nodes were represented by blue dots. The middle node represented the information of current time at that moment, and nodes in both ends were getting close gradually to represent the information with farther distance of time (in the past or in the future), seen in Figs. 1 and 2.

4 Results

4.1 Moving Skip Way

The first section of the experiment was to compare the subjects' behavior in different moving skip way of the nodes. The control group was in the instant moving skip way, that means after displaying a certain period the node information directly changed to the new one. And the experimental group was in the gradually moving skip way, as shown in Fig. 1 (1–2). Both the groups had the same moving skip time of 1000 ms, and the same moving skip direction from right to left (the left node representatives the passing moment). In the instant moving skip condition, we observed an average rate of 43.3 % correct recall responses. In contrast, the average rate of correct node information recall response in the gradually skip condition was 56.7 %. The result shows that both the main effect of accuracy ($t = -1.025$, $df = 58$, $P = 0.310 > 0.05$) and reaction time ($t = -0.9605$, $df = 58$, $P = 0.341 > 0.05$) were not significant.

Subsequently, we improved the experiment by done some adjustments of the moving skip way. The total moving skip time was 1000 ms with 10 frames composing it. In the improved condition, the nodes gradually moved during the first 500 ms(as same as the gradual moving skip way) and then shielded the nodes' information for 500 ms. At last, the last frame presented for 300 ms(as same as the instant and gradual moving skip way). We compared the data of the improved group with the instant group and the gradual group and found that both the main effect of accuracy ($F = 4.602$, $df = 87$ $P = 0.013 < 0.05$) and reaction time ($F = 3.330$, $df = 87$ $P = 0.040 < 0.05$) were significant, seen in Fig. 4. The only different between the gradual moving group and the improved group was the short shield of the old information of the nodes but the data result varied widely. The result can be interpreted as a short blanking allowing the participants to take the initiative to adjust their mental model for preparing a new working memory.

4.2 Moving Skip Direction

The second section of the experiment was to compare the subjects' behavior in different horizontal moving skip direction of the nodes. The control group was in the moving direction from right to left (the left nodes representative the passing moments), while the experimental group was from left to right (the right nodes representative the

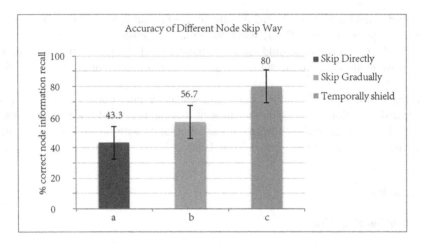

Fig. 4. The accuracy of different nodes moving skip way (The left bar is the condition of instant moving skip way, the middle bar is the condition of gradual moving skip way, the right is the condition of improved moving skip way. In all the conditions, the moving skip is in 1000 ms and the last frame presents for 300 ms)

passing). Both in the two conditions, the total moving skips were in 1000 ms and in the gradual moving skip way.

The result showed that in the same moving skip way and skip time, the different horizontal moving direction influence the subjects' performance very little with the main effect of accuracy ($t = 0.766$, $df = 58$, $P = 0.447 > 0.05$) and of the reaction time ($t = 0.432$, $df = 58$, $P = 0.667 > 0.05$), respectively. That was, the people did not have a clear definition of the positive direction of the horizontal linear direction. And we tend to define the psychological positive direction according to the animation moving direction.

4.3 Moving Skip Time

The third section of the experiment was to compare the subjects' behavior in different moving skip time of the nodes. The subjects observed four kinds of animations with the skip time of 500 ms, 1000 ms, 1500 ms and 2000 ms. Of each group of materials were based on the gradual moving skip way and the horizontal moving direction rom right to left (the left nodes representative the passing moments). The results of this experiment showed that the main effect of accuracy as ($F = 2.818$, $df = 116$ $P = 0.042 < 0.05$), and the main effect of reaction time was ($F = 6.981$, $df = 116$ $P = 0.000 < 0.05$). Both of them were reflected as a significant difference.

This showed that the moving time is one of the key factors for participants' working memory on nodes information. As shown in Figs. 5 and 6, we could get a comprehensive insight of the 30 valid participants' data: the accuracy reached a peak around the moving skip time of 1500 ms between two nodes while the reaction time reached a trough. We could also draw a conclusion that the optimal recall performance is taken place on the moving skip time of 1500 ms.

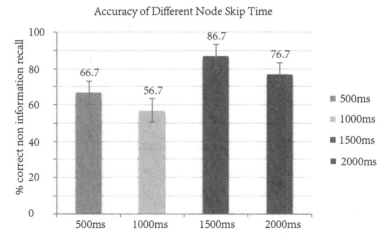

Fig. 5. The reaction time of different node moving skip time between adjacent nodes (from left to right are 500 ms, 1000 ms, 1500 ms, 2000 ms respectively).

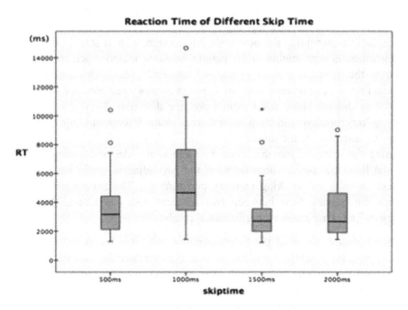

Fig. 6. The accuracy of different node moving skip time between adjacent nodes (from left to right are 500 ms, 1000 ms, 1500 ms, 2000 ms respectively).

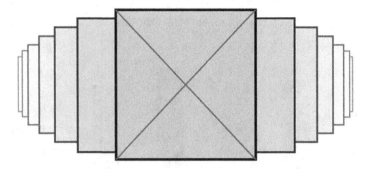

Fig. 7. One of the generalization representation style of the temporal order visualization

5   Conclusions and Generalization

(1) During the dynamic moving process of temporal order nodes arranged in horizontal line, different moving skips way influence significantly on subjects' working memory performance. In the case of controlling other factors and the moving skip time between two nodes equivalently, the performance in the condition of nodes gradually moving in space with the flow of time is better than the condition of nodes instant moving to the next location after presenting a certain time. Before presenting the new node information, a short shield of the old node information is contribution to the people' working memory performance.

(2) During the dynamic moving process of temporal order nodes arranged in horizontal line, we can deduce from the working memory performance of the subjects that they did not show fixed mental positive direction. They always define the psychology positive direction of temporal order information by observing the moving direction of the nodes.

(3) During the dynamic moving process of temporal order nodes arranged in horizontal line, the moving time between the two adjacent nodes has a significant effect on subjects' working memory performance. The experiment proved that when the moving time between two adjacent nodes at around 1500 ms, the subjects' working memory performance reaches the peak.

With the data analysis of the experimental results, we found the relative better performances of the combination of the moving skip way and the moving skip time. As we abandoned the specific content and time information of the temporal order information and used the most simplified coding of meaningless (the solid dots and the meaningless letter pairs), the experience results can be generalized. And it can provide the effective guidance for realization the DTC of the temporal order information visualization design. As shown in Fig. 7, this temporal order information in the form of general representation can be generalized to many visualization cases. So we can directly apply the conclusions to guide the visualization design of the temporal order information.

References

Lee, S., Kim, S.-H., Hung, Y.-H.: How do people make sense of unfamiliar visualizations?: A grounded model of novice's information visualization sensemaking. IEEE Trans. Vis. Comput. Graph. **22**(1), 499–508 (2016)

Koerner, C., Hofler, M., Trobinger, B., Gilchrist, I.D.: Eye movements indicate the temporal organization of information processing in graph comprehension. Appl. Cogn. Psychol. **28**(3), 360–373 (2014)

Gorg, C., Liu, Z., Stasko, J.: Reflections on the evolution of the Jigsaw visual analytics system. Inf. Vis. **13**(4), 336–345 (2014)

Nguyen, P.H., Xu, K., Walker, R.: SchemaLine: timeline visualization for sensemaking. In: IEEE 18th International Conference on Information Visualisation, Paris, pp. 225–233 (2014)

Nguyen, P.H., Xu, K., Wheat, A., et al.: SensePath: understanding the sensemaking process through analytic provenance. IEEE Trans. Vis. Comput. Graph. **22**(1), 41–50 (2016)

Crowder, R.G.: Principles of Learning and Memory, Classic edn. Psychology Press, Hove (2014)

Gibson, J.J.: The problem of temporal order in stimulation and perception. J. Psychol. **62**(2), 141–149 (1966)

Schill, K., Baier, V., Rohrbein, F.: A hierarchical network model for the analysis of human spatio-temporal information processing. In: Conference on Human Vision and Electronic Imaging VI, San Jose, CA: Proceedings of the Society of Photo-Optical Instrumentation Engineers, vol. 4299, pp. 615–621 (2001)

De Lillo, C.: Imposing structure on a Corsi-type task: Evidence for hierarchical organisation based on spatial proximity in serial-spatial memory. Brain Cogn. **55**, 415–426 (2004)

Parmentier, F.B.R., Andres, P., Elford, G.: Organization of visuo-spatial serial memory: Interaction of temporal order with spatial and temporal grouping. Psychol. Res. (Psychologische Forschung) **70**(3), 200–217 (2006)

Körner, C., Höfler, M., Tröbinger, B., et al.: Eye movements indicate the temporal organisation of information processing in graph comprehension. Appl. Cogn. Psychol. **28**(3), 360–373 (2014)

Garnham, A.: Representing information in mental models. In: Cognitive Models of Memory, pp. 149–172 (1997)

Tam, K.Y., Ho, S.Y.: Understanding the impact of web personalization on user information processing and decision outcomes. J. MIS Q. **30**(4), 865–890 (2006)

Opach, T., Golebiowska, L., Fabrikant, S.I.: How do people view multi-component animated maps? Cartographic J. **51**(4), 330–342 (2014)

Big Data Visualization

Externalization of Data Analytics Models:

Toward Human-Centered Visual Analytics

Arman Didandeh[1(✉)] and Kamran Sedig[1,2]

[1] Department of Computer Science, Western University, London, ON, Canada
{adidande,kamrans}@uwo.ca
[2] Faculty of Information and Media Studies, Western University,
London, ON, Canada

Abstract. Visual analytics tools (VATs) can support the execution of complex cognitive activities. Most VATs make use of analytics models in the execution of data-intensive activities. However, due to their non-transparent and black box nature, analytics models are hard to use. This leads to a lower degree of understandability of the models, which then results in a lack of trust and applicability. To overcome this problem and to help bring VATs closer in line with users' mental models, we introduce a framework for the externalization of analytics models in VATs. In doing so, we propose the use of scaffolding to provide the users with visual support in the execution of their cognitive activities. The aim is to make VATs more human-centered. To demonstrate the application of the externalization framework, we present two components of a visual analytics tool named VARSITY.

Keywords: Visual analytics · Cognitive activity · Scaffolding · Externalization · Human-centered computing

1 Introduction

Human-centered computing focuses on research, design, implementation, and evaluation of tools that best suit the perceptual and cognitive needs and abilities of humans to support the tasks and activities that they perform (Huang 2014; Kerren et al. 2006). This paper is concerned with human-centered visual analytics tools (VATs) that support the execution of data-intensive complex cognitive activities (Knauf and Wolf 2010; Sedig and Parsons 2013), such as analyzing financial markets. As the volume, velocity, types, and forms of data multiply, the complexity of data spaces with which users work grows exponentially, making the execution of the complex activities even harder. To overcome these issues, VATs combine automated data analytics and interactive visualization techniques to leverage both the reasoning abilities of humans and the powerful data discovery and modeling strengths of computers (Keim et al. 2008). Accordingly, VATs support distributed cognition (Pohl et al. 2012) by creating a joint cognitive system (Parsons et al. 2015), which reduces the cognitive load of users (Keim et al. 2008). VATs make use of analytics models (e.g., regression analysis, association rule analysis, dimensionality reduction) to enable users to reify the data through engaging with visualizations, making them the epistemic loci of VATs

© Springer International Publishing Switzerland 2016
S. Yamamoto (Ed.): HIMI 2016, Part I, LNCS 9734, pp. 103–114, 2016.
DOI: 10.1007/978-3-319-40349-6_11

(Sedig et al. 2012). In doing so, VATs should provide affordances so that the user can engage with the analytics models through the visualizations (Endert et al. 2012; Sacha et al. 2014).

Interactive steering of analytics models through the given visualizations is not trivial, as the users often view these models as non-transparent black boxes whose behaviors are not easy to understand (Cortez and Embrechts 2013; Keim et al. 2015). If a model is already built without the users being engaged in the process, then interpreting *"what the model is doing"* or understanding the model's application is not easy, resulting in a lack of trust in how the model's outcomes are obtained, in addition to its credibility and applicability. This lack of understandability has a huge impact on final results and the users' hypotheses and conclusions, affecting overall activity performance negatively—e.g., a bioinformatician, using the default parameters of an SVM model to classify clinical outcomes based on their gene signatures, experiences over-fitting in the form of too many false negatives, and thus decides to move on to another less effective classification model. Hence, to make analytics models human-centered, they must be brought closer in line with users' mental models (Endert et al. 2012). Two broad strategies have been suggested in literature: (i) visualizing analytics models to make them more transparent (Bradel et al. 2014; Holzinger and Pasi 2013); and (ii) making analytics models semi-automatic by allowing users to interactively select and adjust their data processing parameters, steer them, and construct their functionality (Keim et al. 2015; Ltifi et al. 2013). However, designing these such that they fit the perceptual and cognitive tasks of the users and create a coupling between analytics models and visualizations is challenging (Sacha et al. 2014) because the design must consider the visual perception and analytical abilities of the users (Kohlhammer et al. 2011). As well, to prevent an increase in the users' mental load when interacting with VATs (Keim et al. 2008), the design must aim to facilitate the cognitive and perceptual processes of the users (Knauff and Wolf 2010; Sedig and Parsons 2013). Making analytics models transparent and conceptually accessible to users requires research and the development of new visualization and interaction techniques that couple them to users' cognitive needs and tasks.

In this paper, to overcome the aforementioned impediments in complex cognitive activities, we briefly introduce the notion of externalizing analytics models through visualization techniques. This approach leads to a more human-centered analytics process, and hence a more human-centered design. To do so, there is a need for collaboration with researchers of disciplines other than visual analytics (Keim et al. 2012, 2015). As a result, users can explicitly engage with the analytics models—not solely with the visualizations of the raw data. To provide a framework for how to externalize analytics models, we briefly introduce an abstract formalization of the models. We also focus on the importance of a human-centered design. In doing so, we employ *scaffolding*, i.e., a human-centered design approach in visualization that provides the users with explicit access to both the data and the analytics spaces, allowing them to construct and evaluate data-based hypotheses. We recommend the proper use of interactive visualizations to gain insight into the analytics model, along with interaction as a means for communicating outputs of the models, for the purposes of education, explanation, and evaluation. Through a scaffolding process, the burdens of engaging with the analytics models, both in the form of model comprehension and model construction can be minimized.

As a testbed for showcasing the externalization framework, we present a brief description of a VAT named VARSITY (*Visual Analytics of university Research networkS and IndusTrY collaborations*). We provide two examples of VARSITY's analytics components which are operationalized according to the externalization framework. These components are: (1) a frequent itemset mining model, and (2) a correlation investigation model (which partially incorporates a textual topic extraction model). These two components are examples of our users' manifold interests in performing data-intensive activities using VARSITY.

The remainder of this paper is structured as follows. The next section provides some terminological and conceptual background to the reader. Then in Sect. 3, we focus on the idea of externalizing analytics models. Next, we briefly introduce the two components of VARSITY to showcase the externalization framework. Finally, Sect. 5 includes a summary and some future ideas.

2 Background and Terminology

2.1 Analytics and Analytics Models

The use of analytics has become popular in different areas, such as business (Chen et al. 2012) and security (Mahmood and Afzal 2013). However, there is a lack of a generally agreed-upon definition for the term. From an etymological standpoint, the suffix *-ics* denotes "the science and/or art of studying something[1]". Therefore, broadly, analytics can be defined as the science and/or art of studying the principles of analysis—and particularly that of the various forms of data within an ecosystem—to be used as an asset in activities such as investigation of underlying patterns and discovery of anomalous behavior. With this definition, an *analytics model* is a computational data model that is built upon a subset of the data space known as a dataset. Techniques and concepts that are incorporated to build such models, specifically in visual analytics, are usually imported from areas such as machine learning, data mining, knowledge translation, and statistics. Since analytics models reduce users' cognitive load and save them time and effort, their use in VATs is strongly advocated. Analytics models are often constructed and utilized in an iterative and multi-step process of the progression of a data-intensive cognitive activity. This might lead to a discourse—i.e., a back and forth communication process between the user and the tool (Keim et al. 2008). This process needs to be transparent (Kohlhammer et al. 2011) to be understandable. On this note, analytics discourse is a process involving the user, the user's tasks, the tool, and the data (in both the raw and intermediary forms and as output). The cognitive activity emerges from the whole process (Sedig and Parsons 2013).

As analytics models support different tasks, they vary in their functionality—e.g., prediction models vs. statistical analysis models. Some models may require intermediary steps in which the initial state of the raw data—either slightly or considerably—changes,

---

[1] http://www.etymonline.com.

resulting in *intermediary data*. Models also vary in complexity—e.g. from a simple model of a sorting algorithm to a fairly complex Bayesian dimensionality reduction model. As their complexity increases, and due to their high dependence on complicated mathematical concepts, they have been dealt with using black box representations (Cortez and Embrechts 2013; Keim et al. 2015). The tools that feature these models usually ask the user for the data upon which the model is to be built, along with some initial setup. Instead of a stepwise construction process, these tools then jump to the fully constructed model. Thus, it is only after the model is built that the user can engage with it—a highly non-optimal and non-trivial action (Keim et al. 2008) with negative effect on the overall execution of the cognitive activity (Wong et al. 2012). Furthermore, many of the state-of-the-art visual analytic techniques and algorithms create results that are unclear to the users, or do not incorporate their preferences, making these techniques less adaptable (Wong et al. 2012). In addition, for models that deal with huge amounts of data, the construction time of the models is a cost to the system. Thus, the understandability of the models might become a huge burden to their users[2]. In particular, this can happen when analytics models are being applied in domains different from mathematics and computer science, such as healthcare, insurance, and security (Meyfroidt et al. 2009). As a result, as the engagement of the users with the models diminish, the level of trust that they have in the outcome of those models dwindles.

Having analytics models paired with visualization techniques to support activities such as learning or decision-making is not a novel idea (Kerren et al. 2006). However, researchers have recently suggested that the design of analytics models be reconsidered (Keim et al. 2012, 2015). As an instance, algorithms must be re-designed, so that they can learn from their users (Endert et al. 2014). Moreover, since the details of analytics models are not well-known among professionals of other communities, there needs to be a way of communicating them (not only their output) without too much complexity (Meyfroidt et al. 2009). We propose that as part of this re-design process, analytics models and interactive visualizations can be paired, which in turn can reduce the disconnectivity between them. In order to do so, we propose the use of *scaffolded design* in externalizing the analytics models within a VAT.

2.2 Scaffolding and Scaffolded Design

Scaffolding is a process that supports the communication of knowledge through guiding, configuring, and/or disciplining a human activity (Alexander et al. 2013). In learning, it is described as "the support given during a learning process" so that learners engage in deeper aspects of information (Marai 2015). In visualization tools, scaffolding is a process in which visual support for a concept gradually transitions "from an intuitive stage of understanding to a reflective one", promoting a higher degree of thought (Sedig et al. 2001). By providing deeper accessibility to embedded concepts and information, scaffolding affects attentive processes, mental load, learning, and decision-making activities of users positively (Alexander et al. 2013). Scaffolded

---

[2] There is an exception for the non-expert users who simply want to use the output of a model. These users are not the focus of this paper.

design is a highly human-centered approach (Quintana et al. 2004), as it minimizes the efforts of the users in interpreting the concepts, and enables users to act independently after mastering the tasks (Jin and Kim 2015).

While scaffolds are visual constructs that provide support and facilitate a user's tasks, scaffolding is the process of providing this support. During the scaffolding process, scaffolds might change, either slightly or drastically, gradually or abruptly, or even remain the same, depending on the user and the activity. Scaffolding is concerned with the design and operationalization of such scaffolds. For instance in analytics models, the characteristics, permanency, and existence of scaffolds that support them might: (1) remain at almost the same level, but change in time—e.g., clusters get updated during a clustering process, but the number of cluster scaffolds might stay the same; (2) increase in quantity—e.g., the cardinality of the set of all frequent itemsets increases throughout the mining process; (3) increase in quality—e.g., association rules are refined throughout their construction process; or (4) decrease in quantity and/or quality—e.g., reduction of visualization structures in progressive elaboration of concepts (Sedig et al. 2001).

Proper design of VATs can result in *human-centered fusion*, human cognition can be engaged, as it both provides support to and receives support from computational processing units (Hall and Jordan 2014). Therefore, it is very important which scaffolding processes are selected for the analytics models. Proper scaffolding can incorporate visual thinking, improve the quality of communication, understandability, and trust. Conjointly, scaffolds may be used as a means of providing feedback. This feedback can be from the tool towards the user through visual perception, or from the user towards the tool, through interaction with visualizations. Hence, scaffolds are good candidates when it comes to externalizing analytics models. In the next section, we focus on incorporating scaffolding in externalization of analytics models.

3   Externalization of Analytics Models

Apart from their outcome, not enough attention is paid to the details of analytics models. This is because many visual analytics experts have mainly focused on the presentation of visual results (Kohlhammer et al. 2011; Marai 2015). As the field advances, end-users are to have a higher degree of engagement with VATs. Thus, designers and researchers have advocated for data-related frameworks, tools, and techniques to adjust and be more human-centered (Endert et al. 2012). In the case of analytics processes, three levels for the involvement of users with the model have been proposed: *automatic* (no control), *user-driven* (partial control), and *user-steered* (full control) analytics (Von Landesberger et al. 2011).

The full control in user-steered analytics is non-trivial and often requires a great deal of effort from the user. Therefore, there is a need for the visual explication of analytics models—i.e., bringing them to the foreground of the analytics process and making them more usable Zhou and Chen (2015). However, when it comes to the construction and improvement of these models, users need to have a certain level of knowledge about their structure and functionality. Since a majority of the users of these models lack such expertise, they might find it hard to engage with the models using current interfaces. This still leaves the users mostly as consumers of the models, resulting in a harder interpretation of the models' application. This results in a lack of understandability of, and consequently a lack of trust, in the results of the analytics models, particularly in the case of complicated models.

We propose the externalization of the analytics models using visual scaffolding. The goal is to help users overcome the aforementioned problems with the understanding of and trust in analytics models and hence support them in the execution of complex cognitive activities. Scaffolding is intended to result in a more balanced information processing load between a VAT and its users as well as smoother flow of interdependent cognitive tasks. Additionally, users with different levels of expertise are meant to have better engagement with the tool, resulting in a more transparent analytics process (Kohlhammer et al. 2011).

In order to externalize analytics models, models of different functionalities and complexity levels need to be described. We propose a simple framework for describing and representing analytics models. The framework conceptualizes models in terms of 5 generic and abstract features: (1) *input*—they receive data; (2) *behavior*—they manifest behavior according to their underlying algorithms; (3) *parameters*—their behavior can be manipulated by adjusting certain internal parameters; (4) *steps*—they generate intermediary data; and (5) *output*—they produce output data. To increase the degree of engagement of users with analytics models, we can use these features and map them onto visual scaffolds. For this mapping, we use two scaffolding techniques: *interpretive* and *constructional*. Interpretive scaffolding mostly uses the externalization of an analytics model to support users with comprehension and understanding. This type of scaffolding helps users engage with scaffolds that represent a model's behavior. Constructional scaffolding requires a higher degree of user engagement. It needs participation in model construction. Both techniques are intended to enable users to engage with externalized representations of the 5 features of analytics models. Each of these features needs to be properly scaffolded according to interactivity considerations (Sedig et al. 2012). To demonstrate an application of our feature-based framework, we briefly present two components of a tool, VARSITY, in the following section.

4   VARSITY

VARSITY is a VAT designed for university administrators (e.g., deans, department chairs, and other stakeholders) to help them analyze research networks and industry collaboration data. Among the many tasks and activities it supports, VARSITY is aimed at helping with decision-making activities involving awards and research directions. Specifically, it helps with gaining insight into the existing large body of data, learning about hidden patterns in data, and, ultimately, making strategic administrative decisions.

Due to space constraints, we do not provide a detailed description of VARSITY's design and implementation. Here, we only provide a brief overview of the technical issues for interested readers. VARSITY runs on a Node.js web server and the implementation follows an AngularJS model-view-controller (MVC) framework. The data space includes publication, awards (i.e., grants), and faculty members' data.

Publications data are retrieved from the Elsevier Scopus API, and the latter two are provided by the university. The data are processed using scripts and are subsequently stored in a MySQL database. The client modules ask for data through secure requests and receive them in JSON format. Our client side is implemented using HTML5, CSS3, and jQuery. We use D3.js to encode data to SVG elements.

Although the interests of the users of VARSITY are manifold, in this paper we focus on two specific activities: (1) detection and investigation of the co-occurring topics among faculty members' publications, and (2) exploration of correlations between publications and awards, and examination of the potential causal relationships among them. These activities and their corresponding implementations are described below.

4.1 Frequent Topic-Sets

The publications data enables administrators to investigate the university's overall research agenda as well as detect the emerging research directions. Publications can be classified in a multi-class setting[3] using 334 distinct topics and 27 topic groups, which are standardized by Elsevier. The topic groups can resemble research disciplines to an accurate degree—e.g. Arts, Business, Computer Science, and Immunology. To detect co-occurring topics, we modified the *frequent itemset mining* model, mainly used for market-basket analysis (Moens et al. 2013). Each publication can be represented as a container (AKA: basket) that includes a number of topics (AKA: items). A topic-set is a group of topics that a number of publications share. Thus, each topic-set corresponds to a numeric value known as the support. Frequent topic-sets are those with a support higher than a threshold. To find the frequent topic-sets, we mine the space of publications with at least one author being a university affiliate.

The input data space can be filtered according to publication attributes such as publication date and the home faculty/department of the authors. Three different behaviors are supported in the current version of VARSITY; the user can choose to see: (1) the overall frequent topic-sets, (2) a specific topic group (i.e., discipline) and mine for frequent topic-sets within, or (3) a number of topic groups to have a directed, yet integrated cross-discipline investigation. In terms of the intermediary data, each topic-set corresponds to a subset of the publication space. These publications can be further investigated as a unit, or individually. As for the parameters (e.g., choice of noise removal method or data structures being used), this analytics model uses a threshold to filter the topic-sets to return the frequent ones.[4] Due to the modified behavior of our model, we no longer incorporate an explicit threshold value. This is as a consequence of the tasks of the user, as in certain scenarios even non-frequent topic-sets also contain valuable information. For example, one might be interested in the fact that recently *Computer Science* and *Immunology* have not co-occurred frequently, and *Infectious Diseases* has replaced *Immunology* in the last five years. Last,

---

[3] In a multi-class setting, each item can be classified as more than one class, as classes are parallel rather than complementary.

[4] Here, we are concerned with internal implementation-level parameters.

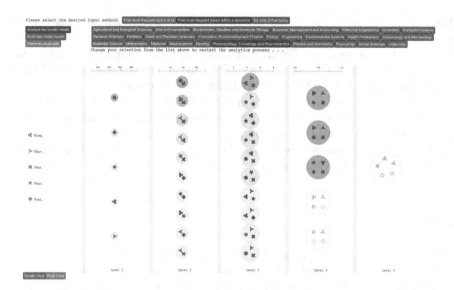

Fig. 1. Frequent topic-sets for *Pharmacology, Toxicology, and Pharmaceutics* under interpretive scaffolding mode: some topics do not co-occur in groups of 4.

but not least, is the output of the model. For the sake of demonstration in this paper, and as a proof of concept, we have limited the maximum number of topics within a topic-set to five. This is because empty topic-sets are also of interest to users, and the total number of possible topic-sets grows factorially.

For this component of VARSITY, we have considered both the interpretive as well as the constructional scaffolding techniques. In the former case, users are provided with support in terms of understanding and—a certain degree of—engagement with the frequent topic-set model. In the case of the latter, users have access to visual affordances that enable them to manually construct different topic-sets according to their needs, hypotheses, and thought processes. These affordances are in the form of empty placeholders for topics and topic-sets and create a dynamic and back-and-forth dialogue between the user and the analytics model. Figure 1 demonstrates the functionality of the component in the interpretive scaffolding mode. The opacity of the topic-set circles encodes their support within their level, while the presence or absence of topics (encoded in different shapes) is demonstrated using color-coding.

4.2 Correlation-to-Causality

Finding correlations is a popular task in visual analytics (Pfaffelmoser and Westermann 2013; Kay and Heer 2016). It usually includes analyzing data items of the same nature—i.e., different instances of the same entity within a dataset. However, when it comes to finding correlations between instances of different entities, and to the best of our knowledge, there has not been a great deal of research in the visual analytics community. For this component of VARSITY, our users are interested in finding potential correlations between publications and awards. This enables them to hypothesize and investigate potential cause-and-effect between the two—i.e., whether awards have led to publications or vice versa. To do so, we have implemented an analytics model that mines the joint space of publications and awards. The model links publications and awards based on attributes such as shared authors/award investigators, their temporal attributes, topics, keywords, and so on.

Our analytics model provides users with three levels of relaxation in the correlation mining process. This is intended to help the model support different degrees of generalization. In the first mode (very relaxed), publications with authors who are also award investigators (whether primary or co-investigators) are detected (the author correlation phase). This is non-trivial due to different formats and language settings of names for the different sources from which the initial data comes. Thus, we have used computational linguistics algorithms, which due to space constraints are not described here. Next, a keyword correlation investigation takes place, using a keyword matching algorithm. A confidence level and a choice of correlation score calculation (either uniform or weighted) are set. The very relaxed mode of the analytics model returns all the possible publications that have correlations with a selected award, regardless of a lack of keyword correlation. The second level of relaxation, however, only returns the publications that have keyword correlations. Therefore, the analysis is less relaxed and focuses on relationships with more possibility of causal detection. To add a new layer of correlation between the awards and the publications, the third level of relaxation (specific mode) incorporates a topic extraction algorithm based on the LDA technique. Topics are represented as a cluster of co-occurring terms, which demonstrate the underlying themes of the documents (Chuang et al. 2012).

In terms of visual support, VARSITY provides users with a treemap of awards (encoded with size according to their amounts) within various departments (encoded with colors). The ability to filter the awards based on different attributes helps users choose the award to be investigated. Upon selection of an award, the user is provided with visual controls to steer the analytics model and analyze both the intermediary data and the output in a back-and-forth manner throughout the analytics discourse. Clues to possible next steps in the analytics discourse are initially visually scaffolded and then disappear gradually; however, they remain available to the user on demand. The correlated publications are grouped based on their years, and a correlation score is provided for each, using a normalized bar. Moreover, the presence or absence of specific keywords/topic terms is scaffolded as well. Furthermore, one can investigate publications in terms of their standard topic groups and topics, as well as their authors. University authors are distinctly visualized to suggest further investigation. For publications with too many authors, further investigation is separated and scaffolded onto a new layer on top of the main canvas. Figure 2 shows the results for the relaxed level of this analytics model. Correlated publications are represented as circles and their correlation score as a bar to their left. Award keywords are color-coded and their existence within a publication is represented as a pie inside the publication circle. Authors of the publications are also shown on demand, along with the topics of the selectd publications. The user can steer the model and analyze both the intermediary and output data throughout the analytics discourse.

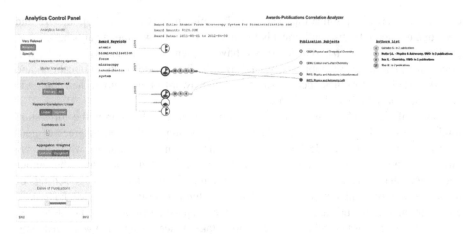

Fig. 2. The output and partial intermediary data of the relaxed mode of the Correlation-to-Causality model for a selected award. Some affordances are activated on demand.

5 Summary and Future Work

The use of analytics models is strongly advocated within the visual analytics community. Yet, due to their complicated nature and standard non-transparent behavior, their understandability, adaptability, applicability, and trust in their outcome have been fairly restricted, specifically when given to non-expert users with little knowledge of the underlying structures and behaviors of these models. In addition, there has been a number of concerns about the lack of a human-centered approach in the design of these tools when it comes to their analytics components. In this paper we introduced a framework for the externalization of analytics models through visualizations. Using human-centered design principles, and in particular, visual scaffolding, designers can externalize different analytics models within VATs. This enables the users of the tools to have a higher degree of engagement with the models through interactive externalized analytics models. Hence, users will be more involved with the analytics discourse, and thus the level of cognitive load in the execution of complex cognitive activities will decrease. Our proposed framework is comprised of 5 general features of the analytics models. These features can be externalized using scaffolding techniques to provide visual support to the users. We provided two examples to demonstrate the feasibility of this framework and the techniques. In future work, we plan to add more elaborate analytics models to VARSITY and solicit feedback from end-users to improve the framework. We also plan on investigating interactivity concerns of the externalization framework.

References

Alexander, E., Eppler, M.J., Bresciani, S.: Knowledge scaffolding: a classification of visual structures for knowledge communication in teams. In: Proceedings of the 13th International Conference on Knowledge Management and Knowledge Technologies, p. 8. ACM, September 2013

Bradel, L, North, C, House, L., Leman, S: Multi-model semantic interaction for text analytics. In: Proceedings of IEEE Conference on Visual Analytics Science and Technology (VAST), pp. 163–172 (2014)

Cortez, P., Embrechts, M.J.: Using sensitivity analysis and visualization techniques to open black box data mining models. Inf. Sci. **225**, 1–17 (2013)

Chen, H., Chiang, R.H., Storey, V.C.: Business intelligence and analytics: from big data to big impact. MIS Q. **36**(4), 1165–1188 (2012)

Chuang, J., Manning, C.D., Heer, J.: Termite: visualization techniques for assessing textual topic models. In: Proceedings of the International Working Conference on Advanced Visual Interfaces, pp. 74–77. ACM, May 2012

Endert, A., Fiaux, P., North, C.: Semantic interaction for sensemaking: inferring analytical reasoning for model steering. IEEE Trans. Vis. Comp. Graph. **18**(12), 2879–2888 (2012)

Endert, A., Hossain, M.S., Ramakrishnan, N., North, C., Fiaux, P., Andrews, C.: The human is the loop: new directions for visual analytics. J. Intell. Inf. Syst. **43**(3), 411–435 (2014)

Hall, D.L., Jordan, J.M.: Human-Centered Information Fusion. Artech House, Norwood (2014)

Holzinger, A.: Human-computer interaction and knowledge discovery (HCI-KDD): what is the benefit of bringing those two fields to work together? In: Cuzzocrea, A., Kittl, C., Simos, D. E., Weippl, E., Xu L. (eds.) CD-ARES 2013.LNCS, vol. 8127, pp. 319-328. Springer, Heidelberg (2013)

Huang, T.W. (ed.): Handbook of Human Centric Visualization: Theories, Methodologies, and Case Studies. Springer, Heidelberg (2014)

Jin, S.H., Kim, T.H.: Visual scaffolding for encouraging online participation. In: 2015 International Conference on Interactive Collaborative Learning (ICL), pp. 685–688. IEEE, September 2015

Kay, M., Heer, J.: Beyond Weber's law: a second look at ranking visualizations of correlation. IEEE Trans. Vis. Comput. Graph. **22**(1), 469–478 (2016)

Keim, D., Andrienko, G., Fekete, J.D., Görg, C., Kohlhammer, J., Melançon, G.: Visual analytics: definition, process, and challenges. In: Kerren, A., Stasko, J.T., Fekete, J.-D., North, C. (eds.) Human-Centered Issues and Perspectives. Lecture Notes in Computer Science, vol. 4950, pp. 154–175. Springer, Heidelberg (2008)

Keim, D.A., Munzner, T., Rossi, F., Verleysen, M.: Bridging information visualization with machine learning (Dagstuhl Seminar 15101). Dagstuhl Reports, vol. 5, no. 3 (2015)

Keim, D.A., Rossi, F., Seidl, T., Verleysen, M., Wrobel, S.: Dagstuhl manifesto: information visualization, visual data mining and machine learning. Informatik-Spektrum **35**(4), 311–317 (2012)

Kerren, A., Ebert, A., Meyer, J.: Human-Centered Visualization Environments. Springer, Heidelberg (2006)

Knauff, M., Wolf, A.G.: Complex cognition: the science of human reasoning, problem-solving, and decision-making. Cogn. Process. **11**(2), 99–102 (2010)

Kohlhammer, J., Keim, D., Pohl, M., Santucci, G., Andrienko, G.: Solving problems with visual analytics. Proc. Comput. Sci. **7**, 117–120 (2011)

Ltifi, H., Kolski, C., Ayed, M.B., Alimi, A.M.: A human-centred design approach for developing dynamic decision support systems. J. Decis. Syst. **22**(2), 69–96 (2013)

Mahmood, T., Afzal, U.: Security analytics: big data analytics for cybersecurity: a review of trends, techniques and tools. In: 2013 2nd National Conference on Information Assurance (Ncia), pp. 129–134. IEEE, December 2013

Marai, G.E.: Visual scaffolding in integrated spatial and nonspatial analysis. In: EuroVis Workshop on Visual Analytics (EuroVA). The Eurographics Association (2015)

Meyfroidt, G., Güiza, F., Ramon, J., Bruynooghe, M.: Machine learning techniques to examine large patient databases. Best Pract. Res. Clin. Anaesthesiol. **23**(1), 127–143 (2009)

Moens, S., Aksehirli, E., Goethals, B.: Frequent itemset mining for big data. In: 2013 IEEE International Conference on Big Data, pp. 111–118. IEEE, October 2013

Pfaffelmoser, T., Westermann, R.: Correlation visualization for structural uncertainty analysis. Int. J. Uncertain. Quantif. **3**(2), 171–186 (2013)

Parsons, P., Sedig, K., Didandeh, A., Khosravi, A.: Interactivity in visual analytics: use of conceptual frameworks to support human-centered design of a decision-support tool. In: 2015 48th Hawaii International Conference on System Sciences (HICSS), pp. 1138–1147. IEEE, January 2015

Pohl, M., Smuc, M., Mayr, E.: The user puzzle—explaining the interaction with visual analytics systems. IEEE Trans. Vis. Comput. Graph. **18**(12), 2908–2916 (2012)

Quintana, C., Reiser, B.J., Davis, E.A., Krajcik, J., Fretz, E., Duncan, R.G., Kyza, E., Edelson, D., Soloway, E.: A scaffolding design framework for software to support science inquiry. J. Learn. Sci. **13**(3), 337–386 (2004)

Sacha, D., Stoffel, A., Stoffel, F., Kwon, B.C., Ellis, G., Keim, D.A.: Knowledge generation model for visual analytics. IEEE Trans. Vis. Comp. Graph. **20**(12), 1604–1613 (2014)

Sedig, K., Klawe, M., Westrom, M.: Role of interface manipulation style and scaffolding on cognition and concept learning in learnware. ACM Trans. Comput.-Hum. Interact. (TOCHI) **8**(1), 34–59 (2001)

Sedig, K., Parsons, P.: Interaction design for complex cognitive activities with visual representations: a pattern-based approach. AIS Trans. Hum.-Comput. Interact. **5**(2), 84–133 (2013)

Sedig, K., Parsons, P., Dittmer, M., Ola, O.: Beyond information access: support for complex cognitive activities in public health informatics tools. Online J. Public Health Inform. **4**(3) (2012)

Von Landesberger, T., Kuijper, A., Schreck, T., Kohlhammer, J., van Wijk, J.J., Fekete, J.D., Fellner, D.W.: Visual analysis of large graphs: state-of-the-art and future research challenges. Comput. Graph. Forum **30**(6), 1719–1749 (2011). Blackwell Publishing Ltd.

Wong, P.C., Shen, H.W., Johnson, C.R., Chen, C., Ross, R.B.: The top 10 challenges in extreme-scale visual analytics. IEEE Comput. Graph. Appl. **32**(4), 63 (2012)

Zhou, J., Chen, F.: Making machine learning useable. Int. J. Intell. Syst. Technol. Appl. **14**(2), 91–109 (2015)

Investigating Cognitive Characteristics of Visualization and Insight Environments: A Case Study with WISE

Juliana Jansen Ferreira[(⊠)], Vinícius Segura, and Renato Cerqueira

IBM Research, Rio de Janeiro, Brazil
{jjansen,vboas,rcerq}@br.ibm.com

Abstract. Data interpretation and insights resources are central for real-time decision-making processes. The combination of different representations and visualizations can help users orchestrate their understanding about data and, therefore, provide the conditions and opportunities for insights. Visualization and insights environments provide conditions for users to make real-time decisions by allowing users to "play with data" – interact with different visualizations, perspectives, and level of details. The human-computer interaction (HCI) design strategy for such environments must consider this data "playfulness" necessity, and also other cognitive characteristics related to that kind of environment. HCI inspection methods generate enriched evidences to designers about cognitive characteristics of interaction that are related to usability features and they can also identify usability issues. We selected two well-known usability inspection methods – Cognitive Walkthrough (CW) and Nielsen's Heuristics (NH) – to perform an evaluation of WISE (Weather InSights Environment). WISE was proposed to improve insightful analysis over weather information, taking full advantage of data. In this work, we discuss the data and knowledge gathered with the comparison of results from CW and NH, and we considered the results from our previous work, which was another HCI evaluation using Cognitive Dimensions of Notations framework (CDNf). Using WISE as a use case, we show and discuss evidences of how a set of specific cognitive characteristics can support HCI evaluation and discussions about the (re)design of visualization and insight environments.

Keywords: Human-computer interaction · Data visualization · Visualization and insight · Cognitive characteristics · Usability evaluation · Usability

1 Introduction

Data visualization and information presentation are key features of systems that support real-time decision-making processes, facilitated by data interpretation and insights resources [1]. The combination of different representations and visualizations can help users orchestrate their understanding about data and therefore provide the conditions and opportunities for insights [2].

Visualization and insights environments provide conditions for users to make real-time decisions by allowing users to "play with data" – interact with different

© Springer International Publishing Switzerland 2016
S. Yamamoto (Ed.): HIMI 2016, Part I, LNCS 9734, pp. 115–126, 2016.
DOI: 10.1007/978-3-319-40349-6_12

visualizations, perspectives, and level of details. The human-computer interaction (HCI) design strategy for such environments must consider this data "playfulness" necessity, and other cognitive characteristics related to that kind of environment. Usability is an important feature for those environments and it needs to be carefully defined and adapted to users' needs regarding data visualization, manipulation, and understanding [3, 4].

The environment evaluated in this work is WISE (Weather InSights Environment), which is a system that gathers and presents weather related information for decision makers. It is a visualization platform that combines data from a weather prediction system with data from a sensor network, presenting them in a web interactive interface. It was proposed to improve insightful analysis over weather information, taking full advantage of data [6]. We selected two well-known usability inspection methods – Cognitive Walkthrough (CW) and Nielsen's Heuristics (NH) [5] – to perform an evaluation of a visualization and insights environment.

WISE was object of a previous HCI evaluation with the Cognitive Dimensions of Notations framework (CDNf) [7]. With the previous evaluation, we started to identify some cognitive characteristics for WISE in particular. We believe, however, that this might be an interesting path to investigate – and possibly define – usability and cognitive characteristics for visualization and insight environments at large: a set of specific usability and cognitive characteristics for a specific nature of environment or system. In this work, we collected more evidences and insights, regarding usability characteristics and issues for that kind of environment by performing two additional HCI evaluations.

The next sections present and discuss our research in more details. First, we begin by introducing WISE, the visualization and insight environment that we evaluated (Sect. 2). Then, we present a summary of NH and CW (Sect. 3). Next, in Sect. 4, we present the results from both usability evaluations and some discussion about them. Finally, we present some remarks and future work in Sect. 5.

2 Weather InSights Environment (WISE)

Data analysis for sense-making, data analysis, and communication are some of the purposes for data visualization, which is the graphical display of abstract information. It has been focus of previous researches in HCI area, considering not only the organization and presentation of information [1, 3], but also the interactive possibilities that systems interfaces can offer to users in order to analyze and manipulate data [4]. Different disciplines in Computer Science investigate visual perception and cognition, such as information visualization, human-computer interaction, as well as disciplines in Cognitive Sciences, especially cognitive psychology [2]. The investigation of usability related to people dealing with data - interpreting, analyzing, and getting insights - is a timely and promising perspective to explore.

In this paper, we present an evaluation of WISE, which is a visualization platform that combines the numerical data generated by a numerical weather prediction with the one generated by a sensor network, and presents the data in a web interactive interface [6]. Its interface was developed keeping in mind the visual information-seeking mantra

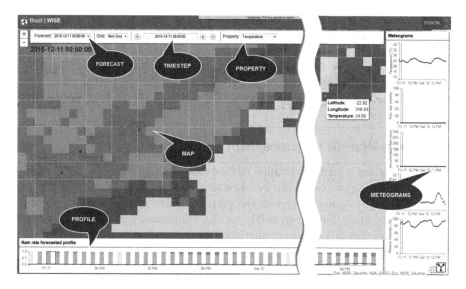

Fig. 1. WISE interface

"overview first, zoom and filter, then details-on-demand" [1]. Its designers provided a valuable interaction environment for the weather experts professionals, specially designed for the daily operations and emergencies as well. For that purpose, WISE presents different visualizations and interaction resources. We highlighted the main concepts related to this paper in Fig. 1.

The first use for WISE was to support analysis over weather information to help mitigate emergencies, but the idea of providing a visual and insightful environment to other kind of data and scenarios (other than weather data) motivated the discussion about the re-design of WISE. To provide inputs for discussions and ideas to improve its interface and interaction, we performed usability evaluations of WISE.

3   Usability Evaluation Through Inspection

We selected two inspection methods to perform our evaluations. Inspection methods are analytical methods, which do not involve users, performed by expert analysts in HCI evaluations. They can be executed as a formative method (during system development) or as a summative method (after the system is delivered to users). This kind of method has been acknowledged as one of the most used in usability evaluations. The common preference for inspection methods is due to their cost-effective ways of evaluating user interfaces to find usability problems. In addition, they are fairly informal methods and easy to use [5].

We selected two inspection methods to guide the evaluations performed in this work: Nielsen's Heuristic evaluation (NH) and Cognitive Walkthrough (CW). Both methods are indicated for the evaluation of visualization environments [3]. We have decided to combine the results from those methods due to their different perspectives and abstraction levels considered for the evaluation. While CW is task-specific, NH takes a holistic view to catch problems not caught by other usability inspection methods. CW takes a more focused approach whereas NH takes a broader one [8]. We believe that those two distinct perspectives provide the analyst with more evidences and knowledge in order to indicate usability issues related to diverse cognitive characteristics of the evaluated system. We present a summary of NH and CW below.

3.1   Nielsen's Heuristic Evaluation (NH)

Heuristic evaluation is a HCI evaluation method created to find usability issues during the interactive design process. It involves having a small set of evaluators examine the interface and judge its compliance with recognized usability principles (i.e. heuristics). These principles guide those responsible for the evaluations (i.e. analysts) during a systematic inspection of the system interface looking to identify problems that may harm the system's usability. During the heuristic evaluation session, the analyst go over the interface several times, interacting with different elements, inspecting various dialogs elements and compares them with a list of usability principles.

It is a holistic method because it goes over the system as a whole looking for usability problems, not focusing on a specific task or part of the system. Since analysts are not using the system as such (to perform a real task), it is possible to perform heuristic evaluation of user interfaces that exist on paper only and have not yet been implemented. This makes heuristic evaluation suited for use early in the usability engineering lifecycle [9]. We selected Nielsen's heuristics (NH) as the set of usability principles for interaction design for our evaluation. The set is composed by ten principles compiled during many years by experienced HCI analysts [10]. The Nielsen's heuristics are presented below:

Aesthetic and minimalist design. Dialogues should not contain information, which is irrelevant or rarely needed. Every extra unit of information in a dialogue competes with the relevant units of information and diminishes their relative visibility.

Consistency and standards. Users should not have to wonder whether different words, situations, or actions mean the same thing. Follow platform conventions.

Error prevention. Even better than good error messages is a careful design, which prevents a problem from occurring in the first place. Either eliminate error-prone conditions or check for them and present users with a confirmation option before they commit to the action.

Flexibility and efficiency of use. Accelerators – unseen by the novice user – may often speed up the interaction for the expert user such that the system can cater to both inexperienced and experienced users. Allow users to tailor frequent actions.

Help and documentation. Even though it is better if the system can be used without documentation, it may be necessary to provide help and documentation. Any such information should be easy to search, focused on the user's task, list concrete steps to be carried out, and not be too large.

Help users recognize, diagnose, and recover from errors. Error messages should be expressed in plain language (no codes), precisely indicate the problem, and constructively suggest a solution.

Match between system and the real world. The system should speak the users' language, with words, phrases, and concepts familiar to the user, rather than system-oriented terms. Follow real-world conventions, making information appear in a natural and logical order.

Recognition rather than recall. Minimize the user's memory load by making objects, actions, and options visible. The user should not have to remember information from one part of the dialogue to another. Instructions for use of the system should be visible or easily retrievable whenever appropriate.

User control and freedom. Users often choose system functions by mistake and will need a clearly marked "emergency exit" to leave the unwanted state without having to go through an extended dialogue. Support undo and redo.

Visibility of system status. The system should always keep users informed about what is going on, through appropriate feedback within reasonable time.

The heuristic evaluation typically has more than one analyst performing the evaluation to have a results' comparison [9]. We only have one analyst performing the evaluation, which could be considered a limitation of our work. However, since our goal was not to perform an exhaustive usability evaluation of WISE, this limitation does not harm our results. We wanted to start by investigating how NH and CW could complement each other in a visualization and insight environment. If the results from that investigation are interesting, we could consider performing further evaluation with more analysts to enrich the usability evaluation.

3.2   Cognitive Walkthrough (CW)

Cognitive Walkthrough (CW) is a HCI inspection method that focus on evaluating a design for easy of learning, particularly by exploration [8, 11]. This task-oriented method mainly considers the relations between the users' conceptual model and the system image, regarding task conceptualization, used vocabulary, and system response to each performed action. CW guides the analyst inspection by users' tasks. The analyst goes over the interface inspecting the projected actions for a user to complete each task using the system. For each action, the analyst tries do put himself in the place of the user and details how his interaction with the system should be. A good interface design should guide the user through the sequence of expected actions to perform his tasks, according to the system designer's intent. If it does not happen, the method raises hypothesis about possible causes and provide suggestion for redesign.

As the method's name indicates, one or more usability experts "walkthrough" a set of the defined user tasks supported by the system, one step at a time to determine the level of usability for that system. At each action or step in a task, the analyst asks himself the following four questions about her expectations of users' behaviors:

- Will the user try to achieve the right effect?
- Will the user notice that the correct action is available?
- Will the user associate the correct action with the effect to be achieved?
- If the correct action is performed, will the user see that progress is being made toward solution of the task?

The analyst attempts to come up with a "success story" for each step in the process. If he cannot come up with one, he instead creates a "failure story" and assesses why the user might not accomplish the task based on the interface design. These insights are then used to improve the usability of the system.

4 WISE Usability Evaluations Results

We executed a preparation phase, as necessary for any inspection method, defining a user profile and evaluation scenario, and describing the actions necessary to perform a selected task. NH does not focus on tasks, but it also needs to define a scope or a portion of the system for the inspection. Our intended user is a meteorologist with previous experience with WISE. We defined the evaluation scenario as follows: a WISE user wants to compare data presented in the meteograms from two different forecasts for the same timestep and same location. Every 24 h a new forecast is generated, covering an interval of 48 h ahead of its generation time. Therefore, consecutive forecasts have data for the same timesteps, but not necessarily the same data. For the comparison, the user first loads WISE with the forecast from 2015-12-11 00:00:00 and selects the timestep 2015-12-11 00:00:00. Then, he loads WISE on another window with the forecast from 2015-12-10 00:00:00 and also selects the timestep 2015-12-11 00:00:00. Then he chooses the same cell (latitude: -22.92 and longitude: 316.83) on both maps to see the meteograms.

The same analyst performed both evaluations, starting from the evaluation with NH and then with the CW. We also considered important to inform that the same analyst performed a previous evaluation of WISE using the CDNf [7]. It might influence the present evaluations or indicate some bias from the analyst. Therefore, we decided to provide this information to readers so they can take it under consideration while analyzing the data from the evaluations presented in this work.

4.1 NH Collected Data

We performed the heuristic evaluation going over WISE's interface, first performing a broader exploration and then a more focused inspection in a portion of the system, considering the proposed scenario. If we identified a usability problem, we went over to the Nielsen's list to check if a heuristic was violated and, if so, we defined the problem as a cosmetic, minor, major, or catastrophic. We organized the identified problems by heuristic as follows:

Consistency and standards. The meteograms show different properties like temperature, rain rate, etc. In Fig. 2, we can see the meteogram for rain rate with a red axis, but the meaning of this "red alert" is not informed to users. The user can see that one meteogram is different from the other and wonder what the difference is, but there is no more information. If the user changes the property to "Rain rate", there is no red zone for that location. The user notices the different color, but does not know what it means, breaking the visual consistency of meteograms, without further explanation. This is a major problem, because the user does not have a clue about the red axis and it can

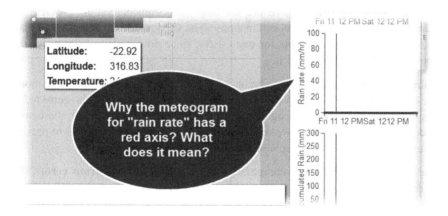

Fig. 2. Meteogram with a red axis

affect his work. A possible solution could be a "see more" option in the meteogram once a red axis appears. The user could check why a red axis was presented and if the red could be signaling a situation of an alert,

Visibility of system status. The timestep details in the profile for the last ones presented are not completely visible to user. The data is hidden behind the meteograms (Fig. 3) breaking the user's interaction. He needs to go to the next timestep to see the complete information. This is a major problem, since it prevents the user to have access to information that could be fundamental to his work.

User control and freedom. The central navigation component for WISE is the map (Fig. 1). The user clicks on a cell and then the meteograms shows the data for that cell. While navigating, user can accidentally click on a cell. If so, there is no "back" or "undo" option to go to the last step of interaction. If the user has an interesting data present on the map and he accidently clicks on another cell, he needs to know that previous cell to go back to it. This is a catastrophic problem because the user might have an interesting insight about the data visualized in the map and he might lose it by a mistaken click. The same analysis may be applied to the profile.

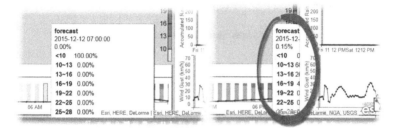

Fig. 3. Timestep details hidden behind meteograms

Help and documentation. There are no help or documentation for WISE. This probably is because the system is still in a pre-alpha version. This is potentially a major problem, once WISE is available for more users, since novice users could need some support to start interacting with it.

Flexibility and efficiency of use. The only mean of interaction is through the mouse. There are no accelerators or ways for user to tailor frequent actions. This seems to be a minor problem. The designer could offer, for example, some keyboard shortcuts to timestep control (*e.g.:* right arrow key to move to the next timestep and left to previous timestep and space key to play/pause the map animation).

Error prevention/Help users recognize, diagnose, and recover from errors. The only error message in WISE is regarding problems to load forecast data (Fig. 4). We can call this an operational error, not related to the user's task with WISE. We need further investigation to determine if this is a heuristic violation or a particular characteristic of a visualization and insight environment, where the user can explore the data from different perspectives to get insights about it. Considering the results from this evaluation, there is no "wrong" action/path for interacting with WISE.

There were no violations for the heuristics **"Match between system and the real world"**, **"Aesthetic and minimalist design."** and **"Recognition rather than recall."** in this evaluation, considering the user profile and scenario.

4.2   CW Collected Data

For the Cognitive Walkthrough execution, we went over the scenario presented in the beginning of this section, listing the action needed to complete the proposed task (compare meteograms of the same timestep from different forecasts):

1. Open WISE on a browser window (w1)
2. Load forecast from *2015-12-11 00:00:00*
3. Select the timestep *2015-12-11 00:00:00*
4. Open WISE on another browser window (w2)
5. Load forecast from *2015-12-10 00:00:00*
6. Select the timestep *2015-12-11 00:00:00*
7. Choose the same cell (*latitude: -22.92 and longitude: 316.83*) on both maps of w1 and w2
8. Compare meteograms on w1 and w2

Error getting Forecast list

OK

Fig. 4. The only one error message from WISE

For each step, the analyst asked himself the set of questions indicated in the CW method (*see* Sect. *3.2*). According to the responses for those questions, the analyst formulates hypothesis for success or failure stories during system interaction, describing usability problems as presented below:

1. **Open WISE on a browser window (w1).** No problems for that step. The user opens WISE in a browser and the latest forecast is loaded in the map and profile.
2. **Load forecast from 2015-12-11 00:00:00.** No problems for that step. The forecast list is presented in a combo box on the left upper side of the screen, which can be easily identified by the user.
3. **Select the timestep 2015-12-11 00:00:00.** The user has two ways to select a specific timestep: by a navigation component (Fig. 5) or by the forecast profile (Fig. 6). In the navigation component, there is no indication (e.g. a label or tips) that indicates to users that those are the available timesteps for that forecast.

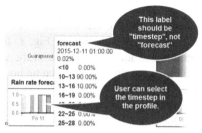

Fig. 5. Navigate to a timestep   **Fig. 6.** Timestep in the forecast profile

In the forecast profile (Fig. 6), we have what it seems to be a design error: where the label or header should be "timestep", it is "forecast". It harms the user interaction, since he can get confused. He might know that the profile presents timesteps, since he had previous experiences with WISE, but the word "forecast" where he would expect "timestep" could get him doubting the data.

4. **Open WISE on another browser window (w2).** The necessity of two browser's windows, as the scenario describes, is already an indication of problem for the proposed task. If the comparison is such an important task to be considered in a usability evaluation, WISE designers should think how the system could support the task in just on instance of WISE. The user resorts to a second browser window to compare different forecasts as a workaround since WISE does not provide the possibility to open two forecast at the same time. This characteristic could have been a conscious design decision, but if the user needs to find a way outside the system to perform the task, it could be an opportunity for reviewing the system design.
5. **Load forecast from *2015-12-10 00:00:00*.** No problem for that step, the same as in step 2.
6. **Select the timestep *2015-12-11 00:00:00*.** This step present the same problems as described in step 3.

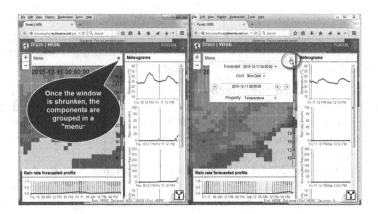

Fig. 7. Meteograms' comparison

7. **Choose the same cell (*latitude: -22.92 and longitude: 316.83*) on both maps of w1 and w2.** As showed in Fig. 1, there are no axis or any indication regarding latitude and longitude values in the map. The user needs to go over the map and look in every tip showed once he hovers the mouse through map's cells. He might need to resort to the zoom-in option to select a specific cell more easily.

8. **Compare meteograms on w1 and w2.** We discussed the need of two browser windows in step 4, but this workaround also presents problems in the comparison step. The analyst opens two browser windows to compare the data in the meteograms, so he places the windows side by side on the screen. Once the windows are resized to fit on half screen, WISE adapts its interface and its interaction components, like forecast combo box, timestep navigator and property combo box. A new "menu" appears (Fig. 7). Originally, there were no menu grouping the interaction options. It might cause the user to get lost, even for a moment. This feature indicates that the WISE designers probably idealized that it could be used in different sizes of windows, like in our evaluation. Here we compared two forecasts, but the comparison could consider more forecasts, which would present more visualization problems.

4.3 Results Discussion

NH allowed the analyst to identify more general problems (lack of help documentation and error messages, interaction totally concentrate on mouse device), and also problems only identified once he took some time to explore and interact with the system (the user cannot go back to a previous state after accidentally clicking on the map, some profile data cannot be visualized properly). Considering the proposed scenario and user profile, to a certain extent, the analyst could also identify more focused problems like the red axis in the meteogram, which the analyst identified using the data of the proposed scenario. A different data could not show the red axis, letting it pass undiscovered by the analyst.

In CW, as a task-oriented evaluation, the analyst could focus on each step asking himself the proposed questions. The analyst could consider each interaction component related to each action or step. This "step-by-step" perspective allow him to take the user's place and observe how the system behaved towards his interactions. The problems were much focused, but with potential of impact to the interaction as a whole (lack of label and incorrect label for timestep, the difficulty to locate a coordinate in the map). The scenario description already indicated a possible problem, since it indicated the necessity of two browser windows with WISE. The analyst identified the same action in two different steps, which allowed him to hypothesize about a potential problem regarding the necessity of two windows to compare data with WISE. The analyst, acting as user, decided how to perform the comparison step by organizing w1 and w2 side by side. This strategy presented other problems during interaction.

The systematic perspective of CW allowed the analyst to observe situations not even presented in the heuristic evaluation with its broader approach. In the NH, the analyst looked at each window in the last step separately, not considering what the user would have done in that situation. For the CW, the analyst arrange both windows side by side to see the meteograms from different forecasts at the same screen and performs the comparison. We highlighted the same problem about the forecast comparison task in our previous evaluation with CDNf [7].

The previous HCI evaluation with CDNf [7] focused on cognitive characteristics of notations used by the interface's designers. CDNf works as a vocabulary that can be used by people to discuss the design of a new system or the redesign of a system already in use. While NH and CW focus on problems (heuristic violations and design error that could harm the learning by exploration process), CDNf offers a more flexible approach where designers can contextualize and discuss cognitive characteristics to explore in a particular environment, for example WISE as a visualization and insights environment. The combination of results from CDNf, NH, and CW provided WISE's designers with a rich source of interaction problems that can be fixed, but also with other problems that might raise questions about some design decisions or trade-offs that might be harming the users' interaction.

5   Final Remarks and Future Work

The results from NH and CW complemented each other as a broader approach and a task-oriented one. The analyst identified different problems for user interaction. Those problems are rich inputs for WISE's redesign, looking to solve some of them. Other results might open some discussions with WISE's designers about design decisions related to what the analyst called "problems". Some of those could be related to a conscious decision from designers, considering some limitation or trade-offs during development. With an evidence of interaction problems related to those decisions, WISE's designers might rethink some points of the current design.

We identified two opportunities for future work. The first one, related to evaluation methods, the analyst was able to map, almost directly, the definition of heuristics to cognitive dimensions during NH evaluation (e.g. NH's "Match between system and the real world" and CDN's "Closeness of mapping"). This relation between NH and CDN needs further investigation. The second one, related to visualization and insights environment's types of errors. WISE does not handle errors *per se* (only handles one operational error), but pointed us to a discussion about the type of errors a visualization and insights environment should handle. Operational and interaction errors need to be handled due to usability issues, but there are the matter of tacit errors, related to the specific tasks of visualization and insights environments that support the decision-making process.

References

1. Shneiderman, B.: The eyes have it: a task by data type taxonomy for information visualizations. In: Proceedings of IEEE Symposium on Visual Languages, September 1996, pp. 336–343 (1996)
2. Few, S.: Data visualization for human perception. In: Soegaard, M., Dam, R.F. (eds.) The Encyclopedia of Human-Computer Interaction, 2nd edn. The Interaction Design Foundation, Aarhus, Denmark (2014)
3. Kulyk, O.A., Kosara, R., Urquiza, J., Wassink, I.: Human-centered aspects. In: Kerren, A., Ebert, A., Meyer, J. (eds.) GI-Dagstuhl Research Seminar 2007. LNCS, vol. 4417, pp. 13–75. Springer, Heidelberg (2007)
4. Fikkert, W., D'Ambros, M., Bierz, T., Jankun-Kelly, T.J.: Interacting with visualizations. In: Kerren, A., Ebert, A., Meyer, J. (eds.) GI-Dagstuhl Research Seminar 2007. LNCS, vol. 4417, pp. 77–162. Springer, Heidelberg (2007)
5. Mack, R.L., Nielsen, J. (eds.): Usability Inspection Methods. Wiley, New York (1994)
6. Oliveira, I., Segura, V., Dos Santos, M.N., Mantripragada, K., Ramirez, J.P., Cerqueira, R.: WISE: a web environment for visualization and insights on weather data. In: WVIS - 5th Workshop on Visual Analytics, Information Visualization and Scientific Visualization – SIBGRAPI (2014)
7. Ferreira, J.J., Segura, V., Cerqueira, R.: Investigating cognitive characteristics of visualization and insight environments: a case study with WISE. In Proceedings of the 14th Brazilian Symposium on Human Factors in Computing Systems (IHC 2015), Brazilian Computer Society, Porto Alegre, Brazil (2015, to be published)
8. Lewis, C., Wharton, C.: Cognitive Walkthroughs. Handb. Hum.-Comput. Interact. **2**, 717–732 (1997)
9. Nielsen, J.: Heuristic evaluation. In: Nielsen, J., Mack, R.L. (eds.) Usability Inspection Methods. Wiley, New York (1994)
10. Nielsen Norman Group: https://www.nngroup.com/articles/ten-usability-heuristics/
11. Wharton, C., Rieman, J., Lewis, C., Polson, P.: The cognitive walkthrough method: a practitioner's guide. In: Usability inspection methods, pp. 105–140. Wiley (1994)

Support Vector Mind Map of Wine Speak

Brendan Flanagan[1](✉) and Sachio Hirokawa[2]

[1] Graduate School of Information Science and Electrical Engineering,
Kyushu University, Fukuoka, Japan
b.flanagan.885@s.kyushu-u.ac.jp
[2] Research Institute for Information Technology, Kyushu University,
Fukuoka, Japan

Abstract. Models created by blackbox machine learning techniques such as SVM can be difficult to interpret. It is because these methods do not offer a clear explanation of how classifications are derived that is easy for humans to understand. Other machine learning techniques, such as: decision trees, produce models that are intuitive for humans to interpret. However, there are often cases where an SVM model will out preform a more intuitive model, making interpretation of SVM trained models an important problem. In this paper, we propose a method of visualizing linear SVM models for text classification by analyzing the relation of features in the support vectors. An example of this method is shown in a case study into the interpretation of a model trained on wine tasting notes.

Keywords: Model visualization · SVM · Support vector weight

1 Introduction

SVM models have often been described as black box models because there is no comprehendible explanation or justification of the trained model and the classifications derived from it [1]. This stems from a lack of evidence as to how the model was derived from the analysis of the input data. Other machine learning methods, such as: decision trees, are easy for humans to interpret classification explanations and justifications by simply observing a visualization of the model. However, there are cases where an SVM trained model is a better fit for a classification problem, and will outperform other methods that generate models that are simple to interpret. A method often used in the interpretation of Linear SVM models for text classification is the extraction of feature weight [2]. However this method does not explain how different features in the model are related. In Sect. 2, we propose that the relation structure of features can be extracted from support vectors to help interpret the characteristics of an SVM model for text classification. Then in Sect. 3, the extracted relation characteristics are analyzed to generate visualizations of the model in the form of positive and negative feature trees. These two trees can be thought of as representing the

© Springer International Publishing Switzerland 2016
S. Yamamoto (Ed.): HIMI 2016, Part I, LNCS 9734, pp. 127–135, 2016.
DOI: 10.1007/978-3-319-40349-6_13

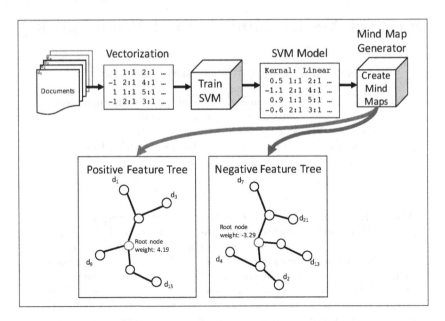

Fig. 1. Overview of the the visualization of SVM models as a Mind Map

support vectors that are placed on the positive and negative sides of the decision hyperplane, and will be referred to as the positive feature tree and negative feature tree respectively. The root node of the trees are the features that have the greatest positive and negative weight across all support vectors respectively. A case study of the proposed method is provided to demonstrate its application on real world data in Sect. 4, and how the generated visualizations can be interpreted. An overview of the proposed method is shown in Fig. 1.

2   Feature Scores and Relations

2.1   Extraction from Support Vectors

The output of linear kernel model trained in SVM^{light} [3] contains the support vectors V that describe the decision hyperplane, in which each support vector $v_j \in V$ is made up of a vector weight $\alpha_j y_j$ and the original feature vector $\{w_1, \ldots, w_n\}$ from the data analyzed in the training process. Equation 1 determines the weight of a feature word w_i.

$$weight(w_i) = \sum_{v_j \in V} \alpha_j y_j TF(w_i, v_j) \tag{1}$$

Where $TF(w_i, v_j)$ is the term frequency of the word w_i in the support vector v_j. To classify a document $d_l \in D$, the $score(d_l)$ in Eq. 2 is evaluated with respect to the model bias b.

$$score(d_l) = \sum_{w_i \in d_l} weight(w_i) \qquad (2)$$

A linear SVM model can be interpreted by analysis and visualization of the feature vectors and $\alpha_j y_j$ weight of support vectors. In the present paper, we propose that visualization by automatically generating trees for the positive and negative features contained in the support vectors of the model. To generate the visualizations, first we analyzed the relation of the feature vectors and apply the vector weight and other characteristics of the features to create a ranking of the features and their relations.

2.2 Feature Scoring and Relation Representation

As described in the previous section, the score of an individual feature word can be calculated from the support vectors contained in the model as seen in Eq. 1. In addition to this method, attributes of features can be used in calculating a word score for ranking. In Eq. 3 the document frequency of a word $DF(w_i)$ is used to give more importance to words that occur in many documents.

$$WS(w_i) = \sum_{v_j \in V} \alpha_j y_j TF(w_i, v_j) DF(w_i) \qquad (3)$$

A word co-occurrence matrix that describes the relations of features can be generated by analyzing the features that occur within the same support vector. A naïve co-occurrence frequency could simply be the number of support vectors in which two feature words have occurred. However this does not take into account the weights of the support vectors in the model. We calculate the values describing co-occurring feature word as seen in Eq. 4.

$$CS(w_u, w_v) = \sum_{v_j \in V} \alpha_j y_j \frac{1}{2} \sum_{w_t \in \{w_u, w_v\}} TF(w_t, v_j) DF(w_t) \qquad (4)$$

3   Visualization Method

By analyzing the relations of features in the support vectors of Linear SVM models, we propose that the visualization of two trees representing the positive and negative features can be useful in model interpretation. A complete graph of the relation of features in the support vectors of the Linear SVM model can be generated by analyzing the Jaccard distance of pairs of features. The similarity of two feature word nodes u and v is calculated using the formula in Eq. 5.

$$Similarity(w_u, w_v) = \frac{CS(w_u, w_v)}{WS(w_u) + WS(w_v) - CS(w_u, w_v)} \qquad (5)$$

Where $CS(w_u, w_v)$ represents the score of support vectors that the two features co-occur in, and $WS(w_u)$ and $WS(w_v)$ represent the score of the support vectors that the features w_u and w_v. Visualization of the relations of the features as a complete graph would be difficult to interpret as there is a large number of edges connecting all the nodes of the graph [4]. To help overcome this problem, we search for a minimum spanning tree of the complete graph that is made up of the strongest relations between the feature nodes. The pseudocode in Algorithm 1 searches for the minimum spanning tree by first creating a matrix of edges that are selected by finding the maximum similarity for nodes of decreasing importance.

Data: w
Result: nodes, edges
sort w in decending order by $WS(w_i)$;
dim relmatrix$[|w|][|w|]$;
for $u = 1; u < |w|; u++$ **do**
  maxsim = 0;
  from = 0;
  for $v = 0; v < u; v++$ **do**
    if $CS(w_u, w_v) > maxsim$ **then**
      maxsim = $CS(w_u, w_v)$;
      from = v;
    end
  end
  relmatrix[u][from] = maxsim;
end
for $u = 1; u < |w|; u++$ **do**
  nodes.addnode(u) unless nodes.u exists;
  for $v = 0; v < u; v++$ **do**
    nodes.addnode(v) unless nodes.u exists;
    edges.addedge(u,v);
  end
end

Algorithm 1. Tree generation algorithm

After the maximum similarity edge matrix is determined the graph is constructed by creating all the nodes and joining the edges found by the search. When generating tree for positive or negative features, the set of features w is limited to only positive or negative features respectively. This ensures that the trees do not contain overlapping features.

4   Case Study: Interpreting SVM Models of Wine Sensory Viewpoints

In previous work, we have analyzed wine tasting notes using SVM [5]. The data analyzed is a corpus that consists of 91,010 wine tasting notes, or 255,966 sentences, that were collected from the Wine Enthusiast website[1]. A subset of the

---

[1] http://buyingguide.winemag.com/.

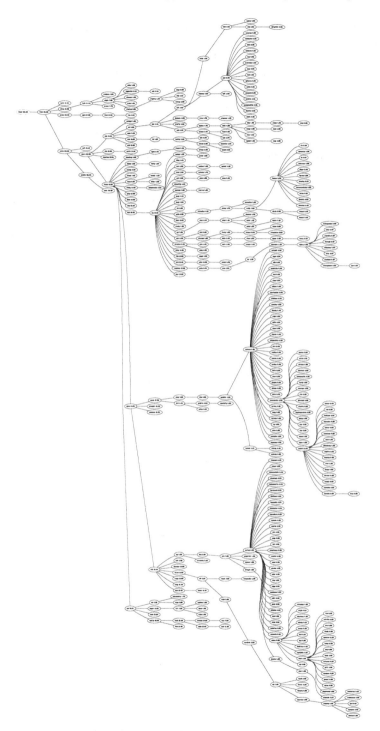

Fig. 2. Positive feature tree of the taste sensory model.

data consisting of 992 sentences from wine tasting notes was randomly selected for use in the training, testing and evaluation of sensory sentiment models. This data subset was manually classified by hand into four different sensory category viewpoints, as defined by Paradis and Eeg-Olofsson [6]. Optimal feature selection was achieved by a subset of 600 top positive and negative features.

In the present paper, we visualize the taste sensory viewpoint SVM model as a case study of interpreting linear models using our system to automatically generate positive and negative feature trees as seen in Figs. 2 and 3. Overall the two trees have quite different structures. The positive tree has groupings of words around hub words, whereas the negative tree has less groupings of features.

A possible explanation for this is that the positive tree only contains features from one class, the taste class, and the negative tree contains features from at least three different classes: smell, touch, and vision. As these trees have

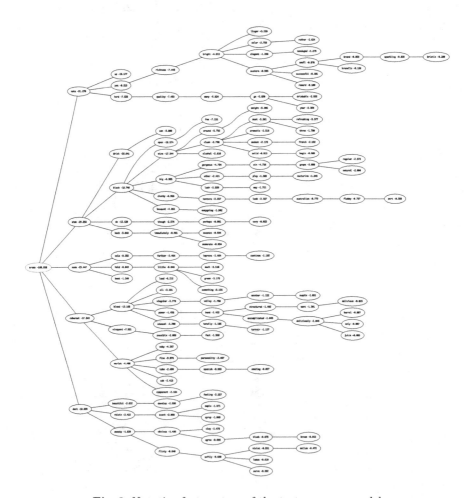

Fig. 3. Negative feature tree of the taste sensory model.

numerous nodes, we will focus our interpretation on a small section of the positive tree. We decided to target the *finish* feature node as it has many first generation child nodes. Table 1 contains a sample of the child nodes and an example wine tasting note that is representative of the support vectors in which the features co-occurred.

The child node word and all the parent node words have been hi-lighted, showing that some of the support vectors extend from the root node, while others are only locally represented by *finish* and a child node. This hierarchal structure represents the *finish* characteristic of a wines taste. This structure would not be apparent just by examining a simple ranking of feature words by WS, as seen in Table 2, as other features in separate surrounding branches share similar scores, but belong to a different taste sub-characteristic. The proposed method enables the interpretation of the structure of related features and their relevance to the SVM model.

Table 1. Child nodes of *finish* feature node from the positive tree and example wine tasting notes they represent.

Child node	Representative wine tasting note
Hint	Its full-bodied, with **hints** of smoke, vanilla and herbs that add complexity to the **cherry fruit**, while on the **finish**, the **tannins** are soft and the **flavors** linger elegantly. (Tapestry 2004 Cabernet Sauvignon)
Spice	The palate is huge and tannic but luxurious, and the **flavors** of tobacco, cedar, lemon peel, **spice** and black **fruit** set up a **finish** with espresso, black **cherry** and a wall of **tannins**. (Numanthia-Termes, S.L. 2009 Termanthia Tinta de Toro)
Sharp	Acidic, with a **sharp finish**, but ultimately it's clean. (Casa Julia 2003 Sauvignon Blanc)
Fruity	It could use more **fruity** concentration, though, as its thin and watery in the **finish**. (Easton 2004 Sauvignon Blanc)
Touch	Snappy on the **finish**, with a **touch** of caramel sweetness. (Llai Llai 2009 Pinot Noir)
Almond	It's a very well-executed wine with softer shades of vanilla and **almond** paste and a smooth, long-lasting **finish**. (Guicciardini Strozzi 2005 Vignarè Red)
Velvety	Thick and smooth, it has a **velvety, fruit**-driven **finish**. (Massolino 2007 Nebbiolo)
Tomato	The **finish** is quite herbal, and there's more than an accent of **tomato**. (Terrapura 2008 Merlot)
Chocolaty	The **finish** is warm and **chocolaty**, and as a whole it's delivering a lot more depth and quality than most $14 wines. (Vinã Santacruz 2006 Chama'n Gran Reserva Syrah)

Table 2. Rank of features by $WS(w_i)$ from *finish* to *hint*.

Rank	Feature	$WS(w_i)$
8	Finish	94.0618744453973
9	Oak	79.9109859470339
10	Vanilla	46.9400117871891
11	Citrus	46.4532939237085
12	Spice	44.0763867784245
13	Tannic	42.5907366996148
14	Taste	39.853999024464
15	Soft	38.1486820604408
16	Chocolate	33.5414635606771
17	Hint	30.7294073932907

5   Related Work

Previous work into the extraction of features for interpretation of SVM models has focused on creating rules that describe the classifications made by the model. Barakat et al. [1], argued that the interpretation of a model is an important step to gaining acceptance when applying black box machine learning techniques in medical settings. They proposed the extraction of rules from models to aid medical understanding into the classifications made for the diagnoses of type 2 diabetes. Few features were used in the study, which would make interpretation by rules applicable. In the present paper, we focus on methods for interpreting text classification models, which have numerous features, making rule based interpretation an unfeasible option.

In other previous work, the authors have visualized the contents of wine tasting notes from the perspective of words describing sensory modalities by a system that automatically generates radar charts of the predicted value by SVM model [5]. This method only analyzes the predicted document $score(d_l)$, and does not provide insight into the interpretation of the model. We previously examined the visualization of a corpus of documents by analyzing the SMART weight of single words and pairs of words selected by AND boolean search [4]. However, it was not possible to use a search engine for the visualization of Linear SVM models as the system needs to take into account both positive and negative scored words. To overcome this problem, we propose analyzing the ranking of features by $WS(w_i)$ and the relation of features by co-occurrence matrix.

6   Conclusion

Blackbox machine learning techniques are difficult for humans to interpret due to the lack of explanation on how classifications are derived. Other machine learning techniques, such as: decision trees offer a model that is easy for human's to interpret. However, a short coming of these techniques is that they are often out preformed by blackbox trained models, such as: SVM. In this paper, we proposed a method for extracting the relations from support vectors contained within a trained SVM model. These relations were then analyzed to automatically generate two trees that represent the positive and negative features of the SVM model. In a case study on the interpretation of an SVM model that classifies the taste sensory viewpoint of wine tasting notes, we found that the proposed method can reveal structures in the model that can be interpreted as sub-characteristics.

In future work, the propose method should be compared to other machine learning methods to evaluate the effectiveness of the visualization for model interpretation.

Acknowledgment. This work was supported by JSPS KAKENHI Grant Number 15J04830.

References

1. Barakat, M.N.H., Bradley, A.P.: Intelligible support vector machines for diagnosis of diabetes mellitus. IEEE Trans. Inf. Technol. Biomed. **14**(4), 1114–1120 (2010)
2. Sakai, T., Hirokawa, S.: Feature words that classify problem sentence in scientific article. In: Proceedings of the 14th International Conference on Information Integration and Web-Based Applications and Services, pp. 360–367 (2012)
3. Joachims, T.: Learning to Classify Text Using Support Vector Machines: Methods, Theory and Algorithms. Kluwer Academic Publishers, Berlin (2002)
4. Hirokawa, S., Flanagan, B., Suzuki, T., Yin, C.: Learning winespeak from mind map of wine blogs. In: Yamamoto, S. (ed.) HCI 2014, Part II. LNCS, vol. 8522, pp. 383–393. Springer, Heidelberg (2014)
5. Flanagan, B., Wariishi, N., Suzuki, T., Hirokawa, S.: Predicting and visualizing wine characteristics through analysis of tasting notes from viewpoints. In: Stephanidis, C., Tino, A. (eds.) HCII 2015 Posters. CCIS, vol. 528, pp. 613–619. Springer, Heidelberg (2015). doi:10.1007/978-3-319-21380-4_104
6. Paradis, C., Eeg-Olofsson, M.: Describing sensory experience: the genre of wine reviews. Metaphor Symb. **28**(1), 22–40 (2013)

A Visualization Technique Using Loop Animations

Takao Ito[1](✉) and Kazuo Misue[2]

[1] Department of Computer Science, University of Tsukuba,
Tennodai, Tsukuba 305-8573, Ibaraki, Japan
ito@vislab.cs.tsukuba.ac.jp
[2] Faculty of Engineering, Information and Systems, University of Tsukuba,
Tennodai, Tsukuba 305-8573, Ibaraki, Japan
misue@cs.tsukuba.ac.jp

Abstract. Animation extends the dimensions of spaces for visual representations by adding a temporal dimension. Although various techniques using animation have been proposed, most of them use a temporal dimension in the representation space only for representing temporal data. To represent quantitative data, an animation technique is proposed. A short animation played repeatedly is called a "loop animation." The frequency of loop animations can represent quantitative data. Four variations of loop animations were designed and an experiment was conducted to evaluate their accuracy in representing quantitative data. In the experiment, loop animations were compared with static visual representations. The results showed that animations, in which either marks were spun or sizes were vibrated, were more accurate than visual representations using brightness and area.

Keywords: Visualization · Loop animation

1 Introduction

Visualization is often used for analyzing and presenting data. It helps in understanding complex data in analyzing tools. By using this in websites, viewers can understand the given data in an easier manner.

It is evident that a large number of various visual representations are required. Many techniques to analyze large-scale and complex data are also required. Attractive representations are required to present data to viewers. In order to meet the increasing demand, extending spaces for visual representations is necessary.

Animation is one of the most effective methods to extend design spaces for visual representations. It extends the dimensions of spaces for visual representations by adding a temporal dimension that can attract viewers. Although various techniques using animation have been proposed, animations are used in most techniques to represent motions or changes [1,10]. In other words, the techniques use a temporal dimension in the representation space only for representing temporal data.

© Springer International Publishing Switzerland 2016
S. Yamamoto (Ed.): HIMI 2016, Part I, LNCS 9734, pp. 136–147, 2016.
DOI: 10.1007/978-3-319-40349-6_14

In this research, a technique to represent quantitative data by using short repeating animations is proposed. We call this technique "Loop Animation." It is proposed that the frequency of cycles or changes in the sizes in loop animations can represent quantitative data. If animations can represent quantity, the dimensions of spaces for visual representations are extended.

Frequency is used to represent quantitative data in the real world, but usage and accuracy of such representations have not been studied enough. For example, a certain battery charger represents state-of-charge by the frequency of the blinking of a lamp. Access lamps of HDD or LAN flash when devices are working. Users of such devices interpret the degree of working from the frequency of blinking. However, it is not understood what kind of representations can show quantitative data more accurately.

The goal is to establish methods to represent quantitative data using animations. First, variations of loop animations based on traditional static visual variables were designed. Then, an experiment to investigate the accuracy of their representations for quantitative data was conducted. In the experiment, loop animations were compared with static visual representations.

2 Related Work

In the present study, we investigated the techniques for representing quantitative data to extend the dimensions of spaces for visual representations. First, we investigated the accuracy of representing quantitative data with traditional visual representations, and then, we study animations in visualization.

2.1 Static Visual Representations and Their Accuracy

Some studies have examined the accuracy of static visual representations for representing quantitative data. Bertin [2] showed that the position, size, and color of a mark are able to represent the quantity. Cleveland and McGill [3] showed that the position is more accurate for representing quantitative data than the length. Mackinlay [8] described that the length and orientation of a mark are also able to represent quantity relatively precisely.

There are some static visual representations that can represent quantity. However, accuracy of animations for representing quantitative data has not been investigated so far.

2.2 Usage of Animations in Visualization

Animations are often used in information visualization. In particular, animated transitions are used in several visualization systems such as ScatterDice [4] and DiffAni et al. [10]. It is known that animation is an efficient method to represent category data. Munzner [9] described that the direction and frequency of spin can represent categorical data.

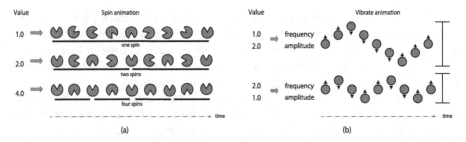

Fig. 1. Examples of loop animations. (a) Values are encoded to the frequency of spins. (b) Values are encoded to the amplitude and frequency of vibrations.

Several researchers have studied various features of animations. Archambault et al. [1] compared the effects of animation and small multiples. Heer and Robertson [5] studied the effects of animated transitions in statistical data graphics. Huber and Healey [6] showed that humans are able to distinguish the presence or absence of a small group of target elements that flicker at a rate different from background elements.

Although some investigations have been carried out on animation techniques for visualization, animation techniques to represent quantitative data have not been researched.

3   Representing Quantitative Data with Loop Animations

Herein, we introduce some examples to represent quantitative data with loop animations. Figure 1(a) illustrates examples of representation methods with loop animations where the marks spin. These loop animations represent quantitative data based on the frequency of the spin according to the quantitative value. Figure 1(b) illustrates some examples where the marks vibrate. These loop animations represent two quantitative values based on the amplitude and frequency of vibration. We believe that the frequency and amplitude of loop animations can represent quantitative data.

It was assumed that loop animations are used together with existing visualization techniques. Visualization designers often consider the use of Bertin's static visual variables for designing visual representations. Therefore, using Bertin's static visual variables as the basis, we designed four variations of loop animations that can represent quantitative data (Table 1).

In Table 1, each row shows a variation of loop animations, and Bertin's static visual variables used for loop animations are written in the column named "Visual Variable." Examples of each variation are drawn in the column named "Example." A Spin animation changes the orientation of a mark according to time. A Blink animation changes the color of a mark according to time. A Vibrate animation changes the position or size of a mark according to time. A Morph animation changes the level of morphing of the shape or texture of a mark according to time.

Table 1. Variations of loop animations

Variation	Visual Variable	Example
Spin	Orientation	spin of a cut circle
Blink	Value, Color	blink of value blink of color(hue)
Vibrate	Position, Size	virtical vibrate horizontal vibrate size vibrate
Morph	Shape, Texture	shape morph texture morph

4 Experiment to Evaluate Accuracy

Accuracy, i.e., how correctly the values can be interpreted from representations, is one of the important aspects of visual representations of quantitative data. Therefore, an experiment was conducted to compare traditional static visual representations with loop animation in terms of accuracy of representing quantitative data.

4.1 Tasks

If the variance of values read from a certain visual representation is low, it can be said that the visual representation has high accuracy. Based on such an idea, a task was designed in which participants read values from visual representations.

In the tasks, five marks were shown on the screen (Fig. 2). The physical parameter of each mark, like the size and brightness of the mark, and the frequency of loop animations, was controlled by a value. This value is called "given value." The physical parameters were proportional to the given values. The given value of the first mark from the left was 0, and the given value of the second mark was 1. Given the values of the third to fifth marks were random values between 0 and 3, a circle was drawn below the fourth mark. It was assumed that loop animations are used in the environment where many marks are drawn, like in Figs. 5 and 6. Therefore, five marks were shown.

The participants were told that the first mark represented 0 and the second mark represented 1. They answered a value represented by the fourth mark by referring he first and second marks. Values read from representations are called "judged values." The participants used the slider bar under the marks to answer.

The range of the slider bar varied from 0 to 3 with 0.1 steps. The participants finished the task by clicking the "OK" button after controlling the slider bar.

There was no time limit set for answers. The participants were told to answer as soon as and as correctly as possible.

4.2   Visual Representations Used in the Experiment

Length, Slope (Tilt), Area, and Density (Brightness) were used as static visual representations (Table 2). Table 3 shows the ranking of the static visual representations for quantitative data provided by Cleveland et al. and Mackinlay. Although this ranking was made by considering various psychological aspects, it is useful as an index of accuracy. Comparison targets were narrowed down to reduce the load of participants. Length was chosen as the delegate of representations, which have high accuracy. The accuracy of Angle and Slope was almost the same [8]. Therefore, Angle was removed from the comparison targets. Volume was excluded from the comparison targets because it is hardly used. Brightness was chosen because it is the most accurate parameter among the color-related representations: Hue, Saturation, and Brightness.

Spin, Blink of Brightness (Value), Vertical Vibrate, Horizontal Vibrate, Size Vibrate, and Shape morph were used as loop animations. The simplest possible variation among the various alternatives was chosen in each type of loop animations. Finally, the variations enclosed with red rectangles shown in Table 1 were used in the experiment. Cut circles were used for Spin. The brightness of gray scale was used for Blink. Circles were used for Vertical Vibrate and Horizontal Vibrate, and squares were used for Size Vibrate. The morph of between a circle and a square was used for Morph. For any animation, "stop" was assigned to 0, and the given values controlled the frequency of animations. For Spin, the frequency was double the given value; for other animations, the frequency was a given value.

Table 2. The list of static visual represents used in the experiment. In figures of Example column, given values fo marks were 0, 0.5, 1, 1.5, 2, and 2.5 sequentially from the left.

Represent	Example	Encode
Length	ı ▪ ▬ ▬ ▬ ▬	The length of a bar is proportional to the given value.
Slope(Tilt)	ı / ╱ — ╲ \	The tilt of a bar is proportional to the given value. A bar is vertical when the value is 0, and the angle of tilt is 30° when the value is 1.
Area	▪ ▪ ■ ■ ■	The area of a rectangle is proportional to the given value.
Density(Brightness)	● ● ● ● ● ●	The brightness of a circle is proportional to the given value. The color is black when the value is 0, and the color is white when the value is 3.

Table 3. Ranking of static visual variables to represent quantitative values. Underlined variables were used in the experiment.

Rank	Visual variable
1	Position
2	Length
3	Angle
4	Slope(Tilt)
5	Area
6	Volume
7	Density(Brightness)
8	Color saturation
9	Color hue

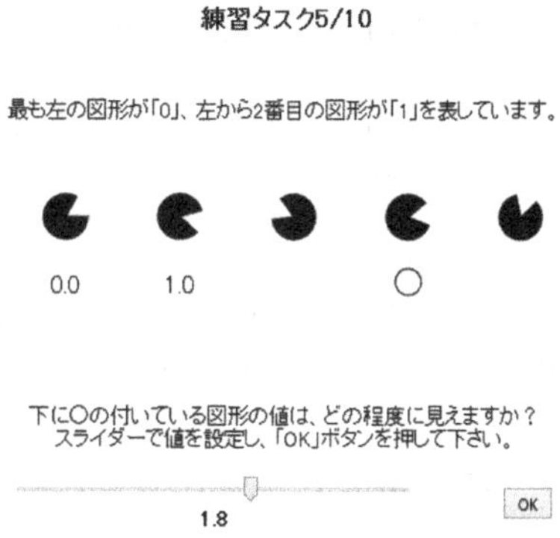

練習タスク5/10

最も左の図形が「0」、左から2番目の図形が「1」を表しています。

0.0   1.0   ○

下に○の付いている図形の値は、どの程度に見えますか？
スライダーで値を設定し、「OK」ボタンを押して下さい。

1.8   OK

Fig. 2. An example of a task screen. The participants selected the value by the slider bar and clicked "OK" button to finish the answer.

For loop animations, there are many variations in marks used in animations, color, and the speed of animation. Such slight differences affect accuracy. To extensively investigate the effects by experiments, the participant were forced with a heavy load. Therefore, experiment conductors selected comparison targets through preliminary surveys of variations of loop animations. Various visual representations were surveyed by using Iv Studio [7], which is a development environment for visualization methods. Iv Studio has a dataflow visual language for designing visual representations, and it supports the implementation and tuning of visual representations interactively. For example, 12 marks were tried for Spin, and animations of hue, saturation, and brightness were tried for Blink. The speed of animations was tuned so that the animations could be read easily and participants do not get tired.

4.3   Procedure

Fourteen students from the Department of Computer Science, University of Tsukuba, participated in the present experiment. Out of these, 8 participants were members of a laboratory whose research field was Information Visualization.

A set consists of 10 tasks for 10 visual representations. The order of visual representations in a set was decided at random to remove the order effect. The given values of the third, fourth, and fifth marks varied from 0.2 to 2.8, and these values were decided at random.

The operations of tasks were explained to the participants; then, one set was given to them for practice. During practice, they were explained how to read each visual representation. For example, they were told that for Density (Brightness), the brighter color represented higher values and in Area, values were represented by the area. After the practice, the participants performed three sets of tasks, rested for 3 min, and then again performed three sets of tasks. In other words, six sets (60 tasks) were carried out. Finally, the participants were told to answer a questionnaire about the free description. It was assumed that the experiment would take about 30 min.

In the experiment, the visual representations implemented by Iv Studio as Lua's scripts[1] were exported, and the scripts were run on web pages with lua.vm.js[2]. The Web browser was Mozilla Firefox 42.0.The monitor used in the experiment was Eizo ColorEdge CG277.

4.4   Result

The result of the experiment is shown as scatter plots (Fig. 3). In these charts, the given values of the fourth marks are represented by the x-axis, and the judged values by the y-axis. Answers were considered "wrong" when the participants answered with a value bigger than 1.0 when the given value was smaller than 1.0, or when they answered with a value smaller than 1.0 when the given value was bigger than 1.0. Twenty five answers were considered wrong, and were excluded from the result.

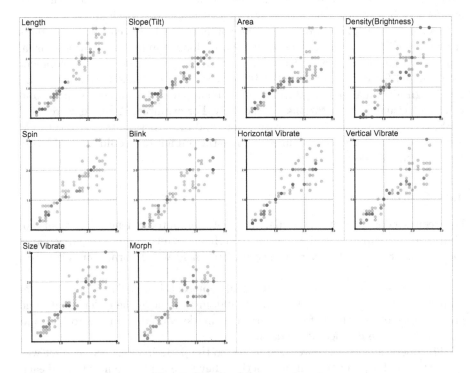

Fig. 3. Result of the experiment

---

[1] http://www.lua.org/.

[2] https://kripken.github.io/lua.vm.js/lua.vm.js.html.

Two indexes were used for computing the variance of answers. The smaller the values of indexes are, the more accurate the visual representation is.

Error of mean square obtained from the given values was used as the first index. Computation was done for the first index $e1$ with Eq. 1, where n is the number of answers for a visual representation; $v = (v_1, v_2, ..., v_n)$ is a sequence of the given values, and $j = (j_1, j_2, ..., j_n)$ is a sequence of the judged values.

$$e1 = \frac{\sum_{k=1}^{n}(v_k - j_k)^2}{n} \qquad (1)$$

Next, the distortion of the sense that humans receive was considered. It is known that the relationship between the magnitude of a physical stimulus and its perceived intensity or strength is based on the power laws (Stevens' power law; Eq. 2).

$$E(I) = kI^a \qquad (2)$$

Using this law, we computed the second index $e2$ (Eq. 3).

$$e2 = \frac{\sum_{k=1}^{n}(E(v_k) - j_k)^2}{n} \qquad (3)$$

Coefficients of the power trendline were taken as k and a in Eq. 2. In Table 4, k, a, $e1$, and $e2$ are shown.

The outcome of static visual representations was analyzed to validate the experimental results. It was found that Length and Slope (Tilt) were more accurate than Area and Density (Brightness). This result matched that of a previous work [3,8]. In particular, the order of $e1$ was almost the same as that of the previous work (Table 3). Therefore, it can be concluded that the present experiment is valid.

Loop animations were compared with static visual representations. The results showed that Spin and Size Vibrate were more accurate than Area and Density (Brightness) in both $e1$ and $e2$. Other loop animations were as accurate as Area and Density (Brightness).

In loop animations, Spin was the most accurate representation, followed by Size Vibrate. The accuracy of Blink, Position Vibrate (Vertical Vibrate and Horizontal Vibrate), and Morph was low.

With regard to k and a, loop animations were closer to 1 than Area and Density (Brightness). The results showed that the distortion of representations by the frequency of loop animations was low.

From the above results, it can be concluded that loop animations can be used to represent quantitative data instead of Area or Density (Brightness). Furthermore, it was found that Spin and Size Vibrate can represent quantitative data more accurately than Area and Density (Brightness). Accuracy ranking of visual representations obtained by considering loop animations and static visual representations is shown in Fig. 4.

Table 4. Result of the experiment

Represent	k	a	$e1$	$e2$
Length	0.950	1.112	0.057	0.048
Slope(Tilt)	1.010	0.739	0.088	0.038
Area	0.906	0.811	0.189	0.104
Density(Brightness)	0.816	1.285	0.116	0.114
Spin	0.967	0.947	0.092	0.081
Blink	0.903	1.005	0.130	0.117
Horizontal vibrate	0.973	0.947	0.114	0.104
Vertical vibrate	0.923	0.923	0.121	0.095
Size vibrate	0.958	0.960	0.097	0.086
Morph	0.938	1.029	0.119	0.114

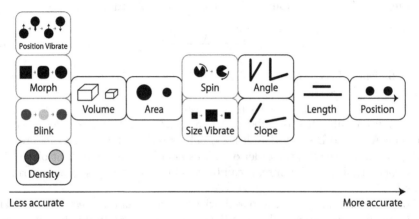

Fig. 4. Accuracy ranking of visual representations for quantitative data. Red visual representations are loop animations. (Color figure online)

4.5 Discussion

Spin was more accurate than other loop animations because it was easy to compare the speed of spin. In order to read quantitative values from the frequency or speed of loop animation, length of the cycles of animations has to be read. Because it was easy to decide the start point of one cycle, it was thought that among our tasks, Spin was the easiest to perform. In Blink and Position Vibrate, the start point of one cycle was not clear; hence, their accuracy was low. It was evident that more accurate representations can be designed by improving the wave to afford clarity to the standard of one cycle.

Many participants commented that it looked like that marks were working together in Blink and Position Vibrate. We believe that it is one of the reasons for the low accuracy of Blink and Position Vibrate. In future, more research should be carried out on the influence of neighboring marks.

Two reasons for low accuracy have been given; however, the reason for low accuracy of Morph has not been determined yet. Representations of Morph used in the experiment were similar to those of Size Vibrate, and a participant commented that Morph's start point of one cycle was clearer than that of Size Vibrate, and therefore, Morph was easy to read. However, the accuracy of Morph was low. More investigation needs to be conducted to determine the reason for the low accuracy of Morph.

The variation of Blink also needs to be investigated more. In order to simplify, only brightness was used for Blink. However, it was evident that hue and saturation affect the readability of Blink. Therefore, it is possible to design more accurate representations by considering hue and saturation.

5   Use Cases

In this section, two examples of visualization using loop animations are shown. Sample videos of these examples are available from the first author's web site[3].

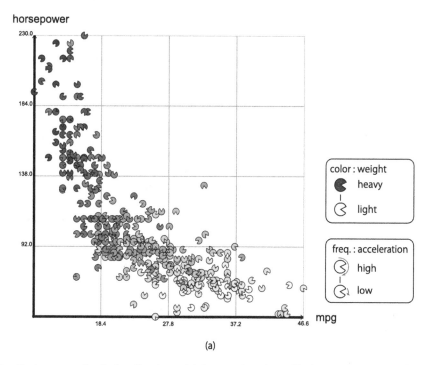

(a)

Fig. 5. An example of visualization with loop animations. Each cut circle spins. (Color figure online)

---

[3] http://www.vislab.cs.tsukuba.ac.jp/members/ito/loopanim/.

Figure 5(a) illustrates the data of cars[4] that contain 406 speculations about these cars. In this figure, X positions represent fuel economy, Y positions represent horsepower, and colors of the cut circles represent weight. In addition, each cut circle spins. The frequency of the spins represents acceleration. This chart was shown to six viewers, and they were asked about the kind of information they could read. The viewers found a trend that cars with higher horsepower had higher acceleration. They also found a trend that horsepower affected acceleration more than the weight. In this way, it was found that the viewers could read trends of data from loop animations.

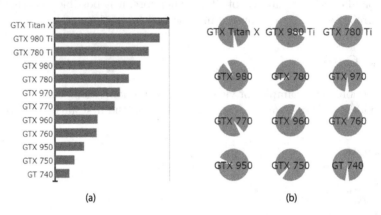

(a)   (b)

Fig. 6. Processing power of GPUs. (a) The processing power is illustrated by a bar chart. (b) The processing power is represented by the speeds of spins.

Figure 6 illustrates processing power of 12 GPUs (graphics processing unit)[5]. Figure 6(a) is a bar chart where x-axis represents processing power (GFLOPS). Such bar charts are often seen on web articles; the charts in Fig. 6 show that displays of GPUs' names are small and white space in the right-bottom is large. In Fig. 6(b), processing powers are represented by spin animations. Spin animations allow visualization designers to use space freely, and hence, designers can display GPUs' name in large fonts. Representation by Area also allows the same layout; spin animations can represent data more accurately. Additionally, spin animations can convey the mean of processing power to the viewer intuitively. It was evident that Fig. 6(b) is suitable for web advertisements where designers want to attract viewers. In this way, loop animations could be used to increase the flexibility of the design and extend the possibility of designing new visual representations.

6   Conclusion

Usage of loop animations was proposed as a method to represent quantitative data. First, four variations of loop animations were obtained. These were

---

[4] http://stat-computing.org/dataexpo/1983.html.
[5] https://en.wikipedia.org/wiki/List_of_Nvidia_graphics_processing_units.

designed based on traditional static visual variables so that loop animations could be used along with other visual variables. Then, an experiment was conducted wherein the accuracy of representations for quantitative data was evaluated. As a result, it was found that Spin and Size Vibrate loop animations were more accurate than Area and Brightness. With the help of use cases, it was found that loop animations could be used to represent the trends of data and increase the flexibility of the design.

References

1. Archambault, D., Purchase, H.C., Pinaud, B.: Animation, small multiples, and the effect of mental map preservation in dynamic graphs. IEEE Trans. Vis. Comput. Graph. **17**(4), 539–552 (2011)
2. Bertin, J.: Semiology of Graphics: Diagrams, Networks Maps. University of Wisconsin Press, Madison (1984)
3. Cleveland, W.S., McGill, R.: Graphical perception: theory, experimentation, and application to the development of graphical methods. J. Am. Stat. Assoc. **79**(387), 531–554 (1984)
4. Elmqvist, N., Dragicevic, P., Fekete, J.D.: Rolling the dice: Multidimensional visual exploration using scatterplot matrix navigation. IEEE Trans. Vis. Comput. Graph. **14**(6), 1141–1148 (2008)
5. Hccr, J., Robertson, G.: Animated transitions in statistical data graphics. IEEE Trans. Vis. Comput. Graph. **13**(6), 1240–1247 (2007)
6. Huber, D.E., Healey, G.C.: Visualizing data with motion. In: Visualization, 2005 VIS 2005, pp. 527–534. IEEE (2005)
7. Ito, T., Misue, K., Tanaka, J.: A development environment for InfoVis system using dataflow visual language. In: IPSJ SIG Technical report, HCI, 2015-HCI, vol. 162(22), pp. 1–8 (2015). (in Japanese)
8. Mackinlay, J.: Automating the design of graphical presentations of relational information. ACM Trans. Graph. **5**(2), 110–141 (1986)
9. Munzner, T.: Visualization Analysis and Design. AK Peters/CRC Press, Boca Raton (2014)
10. Rufiange, S., McGuffin, J., DiffAni, M.: Visualizing dynamic graphs with a hybrid of difference maps and animation. IEEE Trans. Vis. Comput. Graph. **19**(12), 2556–2565 (2013)

Subjective Evaluation for 2D Visualization of Data from a 3D Laser Sensor

Patrik Lif$^{(\boxtimes)}$, Gustav Tolt, Håkan Larsson, and Alice Lagebrant

Swedish Defence Research Agency, Linkoping, Sweden
{patrik.lif,gustav.tolt,hakan.larsson}@foi.se,
alice.lagebrant@live.se

Abstract. The purpose of this study was to increase understanding of how information from a 3D sensor should be presented in two dimensions for users. Stimuli consisted of video footage where people moved in different patterns and carried out various activities. Seven visualizations were used in a simple- and a complex scene respectively. The subjective ratings and interviews shows that various visualizations highlight different parts of the scene and allow the user to prioritize different information. This means that the choice of display must be connected to the application. In future research these results will be supplemented with objective performance metrics, e.g. response time to detect targets and eye movements. Also, to understand end-users and increase their performance in real settings further task analysis will be conducted.

Keywords: 3D laser sensor · Subjective ratings · Human factors

1 Introduction

To build an effective system in a military setting a number of factors must be taken into account. From an ecological approach [1] and representation design [2] there is a cognitive triad between *domain/environment*, *interface* and *humans/users* that must be considered. From a technical perspective the focus is often on technical solutions, such as sensors and their technical performance. From a military perspective the focus is often on the environment where the system should be used. To develop an effective and user friendly system all these three parts must be taken into account, but considerations regarding sensor type are also important. Human factors put the user with abilities and limitations in focus. In our research we aim for an understanding of the whole picture, but here the focus is on how information from sensors shall be presented to make sure that the user gets good situation awareness [3, 4].

In both civilian and military contexts there is a considerable value to depict the environment from sensor information and in many situations it is important to detect and identify people. In this experiment we focus on data from an advanced 3D camera equipped with a pulsed laser so that each pixel acts as a range finder. Range information has proven to be very useful, e.g. for automatic target recognition at long distances and in difficult lighting conditions. The purpose of this study was to increase the knowledge and understanding of how information from a 3D sensor should be presented in two dimensions (2D) for users. The focus was on subjects' ability to

© Springer International Publishing Switzerland 2016
S. Yamamoto (Ed.): HIMI 2016, Part I, LNCS 9734, pp. 148–157, 2016.
DOI: 10.1007/978-3-319-40349-6_15

understand information on the display presentation, not on the sensors *per se* or other technical performance.

2 Method

A within-group design with *three display modes* (distance, intensity, and gated viewing) × *two pseudo-coloring presentation schemes* (jet and gray) × *two scenes* (simple and complex) was used. Moreover, an extra visualization of intensity with red marking was added to highlight items moving towards the observer. Participants watched the video sequences and gave their subjective opinions by answering a questionnaire and attending an interview.

2.1 Subjects

The participants in the experiment consisted of twelve subjects (seven women and five men) with average age 21.58 years and range from 19 to 27 years. The requirement to participate was minimum 18 years of age and adequate vision with or without correction, such as glasses or contacts.

2.2 Apparatus

The data used in this experiment came from the 3D imaging laser sensor ASC 3D-FLASH [5]. This sensor is an advanced camera with its own lighting source in form of a pulsed laser. The detector in the camera consists of 128 × 128 pixels each that acts as a distance meter that gives distance images with an image rate of up to 30 Hz (here: 10 Hz). The number of pixels and the frame rate is much lower than in a normal SLR camera because of the sophisticated electronics in the detector. Apart from a distance assigned to each pixel, there is also an intensity value that corresponds to how much of the emitted laser light is reflected back to the detector.

2.3 Stimuli

Stimuli in the experiment consisted of video footage from a dataset collected during a field trial. Data were collected in a number of scenarios where people moved in different patterns and carried out various activities. From the collected data, movies for one simple and one complex scene were created in MATLAB. In the simple scene, two people walked towards each other, shook hands, passed around each other and went back in the direction they came from. In the complex scene, five people walked irregularly within a limited area, passing a bag between them.

The movies were based on the same data but the visualization varied regarding pseudo-coloration as a function of either *intensity* (the amount of received laser light), *distance* or so-called *gated viewing* (GV). Gated viewing means that the camera shutter opens for a very short period of time, so that only laser light corresponding to a

Fig. 1. The colormaps Gray (above) and Jet (below) (Color figure online)

particular range interval is detected. This technique allows for suppression of disturbing elements such as vegetation, rain, snow and fog. By adjusting the range interval so that it does not include the background, objects can also be made to stand out clearly from the background. Strictly speaking, the 3D-FLASH is not a GV system, but since the collected data contain range values typical GV videos could be simulated.

Seven display configurations for each scene were used. The colormaps "Gray" and "Jet" were adopted from MATLAB colormaps [6] (Fig. 1).

Both scenes were visualized regarding distance (Gray and Jet), gated imaging (Gray and Jet) and intensity (Gray, Gray with red marking for objects moving towards the sensor/viewer, and Jet). The seven conditions are hereafter referred to "distance-gray", "distance-jet", "GV-gray" and "GV-jet", "intensity-gray", "intensity-jet", and "intensity-red". Still images from the simple and complex scene are presented in Figs. 2 and 3. The presentation order between simple and complex scene was balanced between the participants and the order of movies within each scene was randomized.

2.4 Procedure

After welcoming the participants individually and briefing them about the experiment (purpose and procedure), they received some written information and had the opportunity to ask questions to the experiment leader.

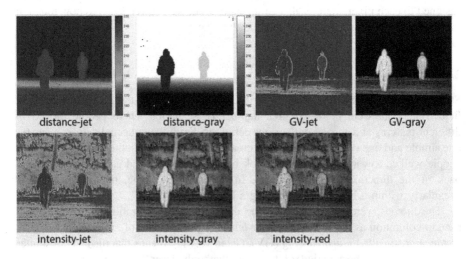

Fig. 2. "Simple scene" conditions (Color figure online)

Fig. 3. "Complex scene" conditions (Color figure online)

Then an introduction was given to make the participants familiar with the situation and the test material. They were introduced to the different types of visualization and then received about ten minutes training, where all types of visualizations to be used in the trial and the survey questions were explained. The participants were informed to focus on the visualizations with different display modes, type of scene, and colormap.

After each scene, subjective information were collected from the participants in the form of a questionnaire. Each question was answered using a seven-point scale, seven being equivalent to the best possible results and one representing the worst case. When the participant had seen all scenes and responded to the related questionnaire, a semi-structured interview was conducted to evaluate participants understanding of the display configurations, e.g. perception of color, distance and direction.

3   Results

The results include statistical analysis of data from the surveys and summarized information from interviews. The data from surveys were analyzed first with a two-way ANOVA [7] with type of visualization (7 types as described in Figs. 2 and 3) and type of scene (2 types as in Figs. 2 and 3) as factors. This was followed by a three-way analysis of variance to analyze the main and interaction effects of type of visualization (distance, intensity, and GV), colormap (gray and jet), and type of scene (simple and complex). In the later analysis the visualization intensity-red were excluded. A Post Hoc test was conducted with Tukey's Honest Significance Test [8]. Only the most important results are presented here. Information from the interview are here presented summarized, highlighting only the most important and frequent answers.

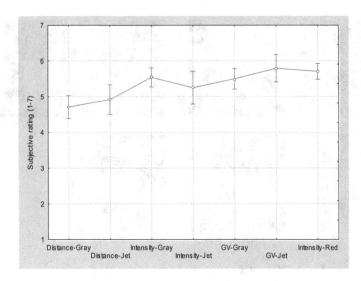

Fig. 4. Mean and standard error of mean for the seven display configurations

3.1 Survey

Here we present data from seven questions (translated from Swedish), five (question 1–5) about the visualization and two about the image quality (question 6–7).

Question 1: How easy/difficult was it to understand what happened in the scene?
A two-way analysis of variance showed that a there were a significant main effect for type of scene, $F(1,11) = 5.22$, $p < .05$. The participants perceived it harder to see which person moved against the observer in the complex scene than in the simple one. There were also significant main effect for type of display, $F(6,66) = 4.63$, $p < .001$ (Fig. 4). Tuckey Post Hoc test shows that display distance-gray were rated lower than intensity-gray, GV-jet, and intensity-red ($p < .05$). Also, distance-jet were rated lower than GV-jet ($p < .05$).

The three-way analysis of variance showed a significant main effect of type of display $F(2,22) = 9.2202$, $p < .005$. Tukey's Post Hoc test showed that display distance were rated lower than displays for intensity and GV ($p < .05$). Also, there was a tendency to significant interaction effect $F(2,22) = 3.3971$, $p = .052$. The post hoc test showed that display distance were rated lower than display intensity and GV in the complex scene ($p < .05$), while all display configuration in the simple scene were rated equal ($p > .05$).

Question 2: How easy/difficult was it to see the different directions that people were moving in?
A two-way analysis of variance showed that there was a significant main effect for type display, $F(6,66) = 4.97$, $p < .001$ (Fig. 5). According to Tukey's post-hoc analysis, participants rated the display intensity-red display higher than intensity-gray, intensity-jet and GV-gray ($p < .05$).

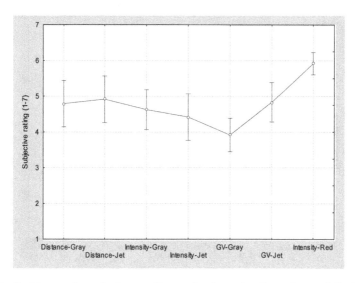

Fig. 5. Mean and standard error of mean for the main effect of type of display

The three-way analysis of variance showed that there was a significant interaction effect between type display and colormap, $F(2,22) = 4.27$, $p < .005$. According to Tukey's post-hoc analysis, participants rated the display GV-jet higher than GV-gray ($p < .05$), and no significant differences due to colormap for distance- and intensity displays.

Question 3: How easy/difficult was it to see which person walked against you?

A two-way analysis of variance showed that there was a significant main effect for type display, $F(6,66) = 9.77$, $p < .001$. According to Tukey's post-hoc analysis, participants rated the display intensity-red higher than all other displays ($p < .05$). The three-way analysis of variance showed that a there was a significant main effect of display type, $F(2,22) = 3.81$, $p < .05$, where display GV was rated lower than display distance. There was also a significant main effect of colormap, $F(1,11) = 9.61$, $p < .05$, and Tukey Post Hoc test showed that colormap gray were rated lower than jet ($p < .05$).

Question 4: How good/bad was your experience of the visualization concerning estimation of distance?

A two-way analysis of variance showed that there was a significant main effect for type display, $F(6,66) = 9.13$, $p < .001$, see Fig. 6. According to Tukey's post-hoc analysis, participants rated the display distance gray and distance jet higher than all other displays ($p < .05$).

The three-way analysis of variance showed that there was a significant main effect of display type, $F(2,22) = 16.51$, $p < .001$, where display distance was rated higher than display intensity and GV ($p < .05$).

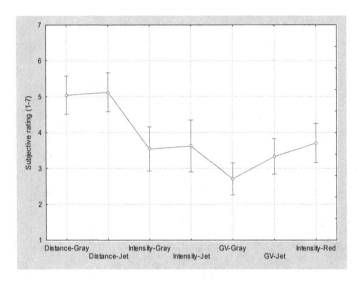

Fig. 6. Mean and standard error of mean for main effect of type of display

Question 5: How did you perceive the risk of confusing different people in the scene?

A two-way analysis of variance showed that there was a significant main effect for type of scene, $F(1,11) = 8.29$, $p < .05$. According to Tukey's post-hoc analysis, participants rated the complex scene lower than the simple scene ($p < .05$). There was also a significant interaction effect between type of scene and type of display $F(6,66) = 3,1943$, $p < .01$, see Fig. 7. Tukey Post Hoc test showed rated display distance-jet and intensity-jet lower in complex- than in simple scene ($p < .001$). Also in complex scene distance-jet were rated lower than display GV-jet and intensity-red ($p < .05$).

The three-way analysis of variance showed that there was a significant main effect for type of scene, $F(1,11) = 8.44$, $p < .05$, the risk to confuse subject between each other was higher in the complex- than in the simple scene ($p < .05$). There was also a significant interaction effect between type of scene and type of colormap, $F(1,11) = 6.91$, $p < .05$ and a three-way interaction effect between type of scene, display and colormap, $F(2,22) = 3.20$, $p < .05$. Tukey Post Hoc test show that display distance-jet and intensity-jet in the complex scene was rated lower than the other displays ($p < .05$). There was no differences between displays coded in gray ($p < .05$), and no differences between displays coded in jet for simple scene ($p < .05$).

Question 6: How good/bad was your experience of the contrast between different persons?

There was no significant differences in the analysis of variance ($p > .05$).

Question 7: How did you experience the image noise?

The three-way analysis of variance showed a significant main effect for type of display, $F(2,22) = 4.27$, $p < .05$, noise was perceived as more annoying with display

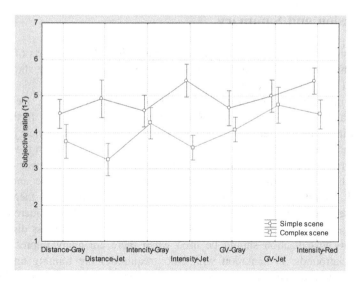

Fig. 7. Mean and standard error of mean for the interaction effect of type of display and type of scene.

intensity compared to GV (p < .05). A tendency to main effect was also found for colormap, F(1,11) = 4.84, p = .050, where Jet was perceived as more disturbing than Gray.

3.2   Interviews

During the semi-structured interview all the visualizations were presented and the participants was instructed to discuss from a number of selected focus areas: scene understanding, the color scale impact, distance and 3D perspective as well as noise and overall quality. In display mode distance-gray the low image detail level made it hard to understand how people moved and interacted with each other. There was an obvious risk to confuse individuals in certain situations (when they were at the same distance), but they stood out clearly from the background. In display mode distance-jet the color scale provided more accurate and precise distance and direction of the assessment than the gray scale which affects the understanding positively. Display mode intensity-gray gives good details and sharp contours and makes objects, people and the background clearly different from each other. Display mode intensity-jet was visually demanding and affected the reference system, mental workload and overall understanding very negatively. The colors, details and noise make the picture chaotic and the interpretation problematic. In display mode intensity-red the understanding of the scene was very high because of detail richness, and this improvement is without noise or workload is affected negatively. The visualization thus becomes very sophisticated and easy to use.

4   Discussion and Summary

This study shows that the various visualizations highlight different parts of the scene and allow the user to prioritize different information. This means that the choice of display must be connected to the application.

Display intensity were considered to be better for tracking people, seeing details and understanding the overall scene. Red marked direction provides further understanding of movement patterns and make the users more confident in their judgments. GV was considered useful mainly when focus was on the individuals in the scene and not on understanding the environment. Coding displays with distance was difficult to use in real-time as it requires a divided attention between the scale and the film sequence. It would therefore be better to use a pause function and then do more qualified assessments from a distance view. Grayscale is generally considered easier to use and perceived as easier to the eyes. Since the noise tends to be less disturbing in grayscale this visualization should be used when there are many impressions, e.g. detailed backgrounds. Presentation with color required more training and initially perceived as more demanding. However, color demonstrated strengths in being more accurate and sensitive. Generally speaking, direction and distance were perceived as easier to determine, but noise became more disturbing. The environment is used as reference to get an understanding of the scene and movement of people. The perception of people's direction and estimation of distances are negatively affected when the environment is absent in the visualization. On the other hand, the absence of disturbing background makes it easier to focus on people.

In this experiment we focused on what users thought of the different visualizations. In the future this will be supplemented with objective performance metrics. Examples of such measures are response time to detect targets, time to solve a task and measurement of eye movements. The basis for our research is to understand the end-users and increase their performance in real settings. With task analysis we can get even better understanding of user needs, and thereby tailor visualizations for specific users and tasks. These results are important to better understand how information from 3D sensors shall be presented for users, e.g. military personal on the ground and unmanned aerial operators.

References

1. Flach, J., Hancock, P.: An ecological approach to human-machine systems. In: Proceedings of the Human Factors and Ergonomics 36th Annual Meeting, pp. 1056–1058, Santa Monica, CA, USA (1992)
2. Woods, D.D.: Towards a theoretical base for representation design in the computer medium: ecological perception and aiding human cognition. In: Flach, J., Hancock, P., Caird, K., Vicente, K. (eds.) An Ecological Approach to Human Machine Systems I: A Global Perspective, pp. 157–188. Erlbaum, Hillsdale (1995)
3. Endsley, M.: Measurement of situation awareness in dynamic systems. Hum. Factors **37**(1), 65–84 (1995)

4. Endsley, M.: Toward a theory of situational awareness in dynamic systems. Hum. Factors **37** (1), 32–64 (1995)
5. ASC. Portable 3D Flash Lidar Camera Kit. http://www.advancedscientificconcepts.com/products/older-products/portable.html (2016). Accessed 11 Feb 2016
6. MATLAB. Colormap (2015). http://se.mathworks.com/help/matlab/ref/colormap.html
7. Hays, W.L.: Statistics. Harcourt Brace College Publishers, Fort Worth (1994)
8. Greene, J., D'Oliveira, M.: Learning to Use Statistical Tests in Psychology. Open University Press, Milton Keynes, Philadelphia (1982)

Comparison of Two Visualization Tools in Supporting Comprehension of Data Trends

Chen Ling[1]([✉]), Julie S. Bock[2], Leslie Goodwin[2], G. Cole Jackson[2],
and Molly K. Floyd[2]

[1] University of Akron, Akron, OH, USA
`cling@uakron.edu`
[2] University of Oklahoma, Norman, OK, USA
`juliesbock@gmail.com`, `gcjackson02@gmail.com`,
`mollykfloyd@gmail.com`, `lesliemgoodwin@yahoo.com`

Abstract. This study compares two commonly used visualization tools, Gapminder and Tableau Public at simple and integrated level, to assess which tool better support user comprehension of data trends in a large dataset. Forty-seven participants were presented with a data set through Gapminder or Tableau Public at either a simple or integrated level. Then each participant was asked to answer questions about what they observed, showing their understanding of the information as well as rate ease-of-use of the tool. The results show that use of animation in Gapminder helped users comprehend data trends, whereas designs that assume prior geographical knowledge of users hampered their performance. Participants achieved higher accuracy with the graphs rated as easier to use. The results suggest that design of visualization tools should use familiar visual features and consider ease-of-use factor to assist user's comprehension of data trend.

Keywords: Data visualization · Display complexity · Data trend comprehension · Ease of use

1 Introduction

With the developments in technological innovation, vast amounts of data are being collected, which creates a need for an effective method of data presentation. In order to meet this need and present data in an effective way, companies around the world have turned to new data visualization tools. Unfortunately, many of these new data visualization software packages are not effective at communicating trends to people without advanced training in their use. There are often multiple views of a dataset or too many variables to show that users cannot distinguish the trends in data easily.

In an effort to simplify these complex datasets, many visualization tools are now using visualization or interactive charts in their presentations. The technique is to engage the viewer and provide statistical analysis using animation to unveil important statistical trends in large datasets over a period of time (Rosling 2007). For example, a tool called Gapminder animates trends that present information throughout time. The graph moves as time is played. This study investigates the effectiveness of two specific,

© Springer International Publishing Switzerland 2016
S. Yamamoto (Ed.): HIMI 2016, Part I, LNCS 9734, pp. 158–167, 2016.
DOI: 10.1007/978-3-319-40349-6_16

commonly used data visualization software packages, Gapminder and Tableau Public. By understanding what techniques work better, software developers can focus on the aspects of the tool that need to be simplified or made more interactive for the user to most effectively interpret the data.

Good visualization tools allow users to filter, sort, and visualize large datasets and then derive new data from the input data (Heer and Shneiderman 2012). Both Gapminder and Tableau Public allow users to interpret and draw conclusions to see trends forming just by looking at the graphs. These systems not only present a picture of the information, but also animate the information to add another dimension of information to be observed and understood by the viewer. Many tools limit the number of items in a display but allow users to select different filters while on the screen to analyze differences between variables (Heer and Shneiderman 2012). Kienle and Muller (2007) found that there should be multiple views present of the data in order to satisfy different stakeholders. It is worthwhile to compare effectiveness of finding data trend by viewing multiple graphs each of which only present trend on a single variable, or viewing a single graph presenting trends from multiple variables.

The goal of this study is to compare the effectiveness of two popular visualization tools-Tableau Public and Gapminder in terms assisting users in understanding data trends. In particular, we are interested in learning how the design of these two tools affect user's comprehension of data trend using multiple simple graph and one integrated graph. Ease of use of the visualization tool is also studied.

2 Literature Review

The goal of data visualization is to present users with data where trends can be detected and relationships can be established. Good visualization tools allow individuals to understand data in order to make hypotheses, look for patterns, and notice exceptions (Rosling 2007). Therefore, each visualization tool has unique design aspects to relay critical information to users.

Each visualization tool takes a distinct approach to aid the understanding of the data to the user. These tools focus on making the important information noticeable (O'Hare and Stenhouse 2008), while allowing users to more easily see the important trends and relationships within the data. While most experts agree that these tools do not intend to bombard the user with repetitive information and visuals, Heer and Shneiderman (2012) believe it can be useful to coordinate multiple or moving views to show different correlations of variables. Combining a clean layout with multiple views, the user can grasp bits of information at a time in order to understand the overall trends in the data. This experiment takes these varying opinions into account by showing the same information using visualization software on an animated display, on multiple simple displays, or all integrated on one display.

In an educational attainment case study, Heer and Shneiderman (2012) combined a bar chart, map, list, and scatter plot to display the ages, locations, education history, and income to help facilitate comparison, which could ultimately lead to a government decision (Heer and Shneiderman 2012). By compiling this information in a visual manner, the user can fully understand the scope of the data and piece together separate information to see the bigger picture. This is just one example of how integrating data with an effective design can minimize distortion, ensure correspondence, and create consistency (O'Hare and Stenhouse 2008).

In order for data trends in the moving display, multiple simple displays, and integrated display to be consistent and represent the global picture, the display could not skew the user's view toward a specific relationship, which would misrepresent the data. For example, if in one view the movement from left to right represents increasing movement and correlates positively, then left to right should represent increasing movement and correlate positively in all views. Inconsistency can cause the user to misinterpret the data and have poor recall and interpretation of the information (O'Hare and Stenhouse 2008). One view may display the data differently from another. It is important to display the data so that users can make correct and unbiased inferences.

In order to visualize useful information, the design of the presented data is vital. Good visualization tools portray the data to aid user comprehension of data trends. For example, the visualization software tool Tableau Public allows users to drop data variables onto "shelve" categories, such as size, spatial position, etc. This particular software then determines a visualization design based on these three categories (Heer and Shneiderman 2012). Another important function of these tools is to allow users to filter through data dimensions. It allows users to look at subsets of data to find trends and correlations without having such broad overviews. In fact, many tools limit the number of items in a display but allow users to select different filters while on the screen to analyze differences between variables (Heer and Shneiderman 2012). By filtering, sorting, selecting, and highlighting different data, the user is able to produce various views with the ultimate goal of finding trends and new conclusions from the dataset. These types of dynamic and moving software tools can be represented in Gapminder software, one of the newest visualization tools.

Gapminder aims to engage the viewer and provide statistical analysis using animation to unveil statistical importance in large datasets over a time period (Rosling 2007). Often these trends and details are hidden under the excess information in traditional data visualization tools, but interactive, moving, or dynamic visualization software has made it possible to present this data in a way that is easier to understand (Battista and Cheng 2011).

3 Methodology

3.1 Participants

A total of 47 participants were recruited from the university. There were about twelve participants for each factor-level combination. Randomness was implemented by randomly assigning a visualization tool and complexity combination to each participant until each group had at least ten different participants. The age range of the participants was between 18 and 22 years old. Overall, 68 % of the participants were in STEM (science, technology, engineering, and math) majors, while the remaining 32 % were non-STEM majors.

3.2   Experimental Design

This study examined the effectiveness of data visualization tools, specifically Gapminder and Tableau Public. Participant's comprehension of trends in data presented by visualization software at different levels of complexity was compared. The independent variables were the visualization tool and the level of complexity. The simple level for a visualization tool presented two dimensions of data on one graph and had a total of three graphs. One graph would have life expectancy across time, another had average income across time, and the last one displayed population across time. All three graph conveyed data for four countries, Brazil, India, China, and Russia. The integrated level for a visualization tool conveyed the same four dimensions, but only on one graph. Information on life expectancy, income, population and time for the different countries are all presented on one graph for the integrated level and relied on more advanced visualization techniques. Tableau Public shows integrated graph in an interactive way, whereas Gapminder shows an animated graph.

The dependent variables were the accuracy of a basic comprehension test, and ease-of-use rating of the tools. The accuracy was a tally of correctly answered questions in a 15-question comprehension questionnaire to evaluate the effectiveness of the tool in assisting participants comprehend trends of data, and the ease-of-use ratings were given by participants at the end of each session.

The experiment used a between-subject design. No participant experienced more than one experimental condition to avoid any learning effect.

3.3   Equipment and Software

Two visualization software- Tableau Public and Gapminder software were used as well as a relevant dataset. An existing dataset already on Gapminder was used; this dataset displayed the average life expectancy, average income, and population size of a particular country per year all across time (year). Data from Brazil, Russia, India, and China was displayed because there was a noticeable trend in the data for each country.

3.4   Hypothesis

The Gapminder/integrated level was expected to yield the highest score due to the use of animation as a visual technique as well as the intuitive nature of the software. The animation utilized the flow of time to show trends. The animation visualization technique effectively sort, filter, and organize multiple dimensions of data onto one cohesive graph (Heer and Shneiderman 2012). Therefore, better performances were anticipated for participants experiencing animation technique. Furthermore, there was expected to be no significant difference between the two tools at the simple level because each used familiar techniques that did not differ greatly.

3.5   Procedure

The participants sat in front of the computer screen and observed the data displayed. The experimenter read instruction to the participant from a script and verbally explained the procedures for the experiment. The participants were not given a tutorial on the software to ensure that the results were reflective of the intuitive nature of the visual display and the tool presented. No one has prior experience with either tool. The proctor experimenter then passed out the paper comprehension test. Then the visualization software was run on a MacBook Pro, and the participants completed the test. The participants were allowed to interact with the software to answer the questions, but a time limit of ten minutes was set as a control. No incentives were used to motivate the participants.

4   Results

4.1   Scores of Comprehension Questionnaire

Based on the ANOVA results of the overall scores of the comprehension test, there was not a significant difference between the two visualization tools ($p = 0.33$) nor the levels of complexity ($p = 0.31$). However, a significant interaction effect was found between the complexity level and the visualization tool ($p = 0.013$; see Fig. 7).

The comprehension scores were affected by the combination of level and visualization tool. The average score for participants using the Tableau Public/Simple was higher than those using the Gapminder/Simple condition, but the Gapminder/integrated average scores were higher than those using Tableau Public/Integrated condition (see Table 1). Note that the Tableau Public/Simple participants answered the questions most accurately overall. Tableau Public/Simple condition had the highest average score along with the lowest standard deviation, meaning that the scores were consistently higher with less variance.

The interaction effect showed that participants scored less accurately with the Gapminder/simple combination, but scored higher using Tableau Public/Simple display. The main difference between the visualization tools at the simple level was the representation of the line that depicts the points between the presented variables (one of life expectancy, income, population) and time. In Tableau Public, the line is continuous, and the colors representing the countries are labeled along the right hand side of the line. In Gapminder, the numerical values of variable versus time were plotted with individual dots and users can click "turning on the trails" to produce a continuous lines. In Gapminder/Simple, the countries were labeled at the beginning of that country's color-coded line on the graph. But because the lines were so close together, it was hard to associate the label with the correct line (see Fig. 2). A map of the countries is located at right of the graph with the appropriate colors, but the software made the assumptions that participants were able to locate the country on the map without labels. This was not as effective and can be confirmed by the number of participants who correctly answered the question related to the identifying countries.

One question in the comprehension test asked what color is correlated to each country. The Tableau Public/Simple had the highest number of participants who

Table 1. Comprehension score for experimental conditions

Tools	Levels	Mean score	SD
Gapminder	Integrated	11.500	3.920
	Simple	10.250	2.491
Tableau Public	Integrated	10.091	2.663
	Simple	13.167	1.992

answered the question correctly, with 12, 10, 11, and 9 participants correctly identifying the colors for countries Brazil, China, India, and Russia, respectively. In comparison, Gapminder/Simple participants answered correctly questions 9, 4, 8, and 3 for the questions correlating to the colors for Brazil, China, India, and Russia. This indicated that participants had a difficult time identifying China and Russia, which could have been due to the close proximity of the countries on the map or the overlapping labels of the countries on the graph. Because of this, answering the questions related to Russia and/or China could also have been compromised if the participant could not correctly identify which trend line represented which country.

4.2 Ratings of Ease of Use

Participants gave ratings of ease-of-use at the end of each session where 1 corresponds to "cannot use", 3 corresponds to "neutral" and 5 corresponds to "very easy". ANOVA analysis on the ratings showed that there was no significant difference between the two visualization tools. But the simple level (M = 3.13, SD = 0.99) was easier to use (p = 0.03) than integrated level (M = 2.55, SD = 1.10). There was also significant interaction (p = 0.0001) between the visualization tools and the complexity level.

Figure 6 shows the interaction plot. It has similar trends as Fig. 5, where Tableau Public/simple had the highest rating of ease-of-use, and Tableau Public/integrated had the lowest rating. Gapminder/integrated condition had slightly higher rating than Gapminder/simple.

4.3 Overall Discussion

The results of this study demonstrate the importance of design features used in visualization tools. At the simple level where users only viewed data for one variable of four countries against time, users comprehended data trends better with Tableau Public. This may be due to the use of simple design features that is familiar to most users (see Fig. 1). In contrast, some users struggled with Gapminder, because it was difficult to tell the color-coded lines for four countries apart. The color coded map at the upper right corner did not have countries name marked, and the tool assume users know where each country is located (see Fig. 2).

At the integrated level, where users view all variables of four countries at the same time, users comprehended data trends better with Gapminder tool. This is mostly due to the use of animation in the tool. The animation utilized the flow of time to show trends.

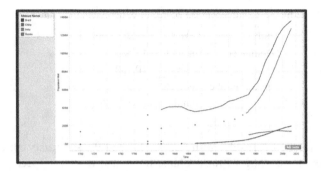

Fig. 1. Tableau Public/simple showing population of countries in a single graph

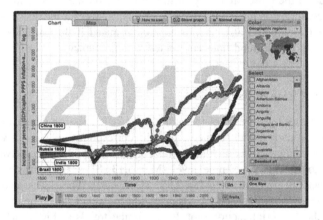

Fig. 2. Gapminder/simple showing income per person of countries in a single graph

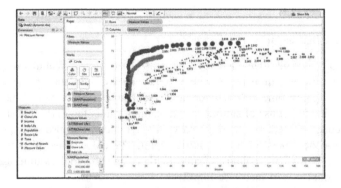

Fig. 3. Tableau Public/integrated showing four variables in an interactive way

Fig. 4. Gapminder/integrated showing all four variables in an animated format

In Gapminder, the year is shown as a light background on each of the graph (see Fig. 4). Users can play animation or slide across time to view changes in other variables across time. The animation utilized the flow of time to show trends. Essentially, this reduced the complexity and clutter of the display by separate out the "year" variable to be handled by animation. For both tools, the x axis was used to show income, y axis was used to show life expectancy, and the size of the data bubble denotes the population. In Gapminder, data of a single year is shown on each graph, but in Tableau Republic, data across all years are shown on one graph with labeling of the year beside the data point. This caused the display to be visually cluttered, and difficult to tell trends across year (see Fig. 3).

It is interesting to see the correspondence between the participant's comprehension questionnaire scores and their ease-of-use ratings (see Figs. 5 and 6). It shows that participant tends to have higher level of comprehend when the visualization tool is easier to use. In particular, it seems that the simple individual graphs clearly labeled

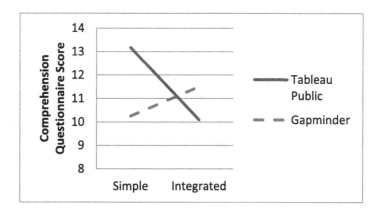

Fig. 5. Observed interaction effect for comprehension questionnaire scores

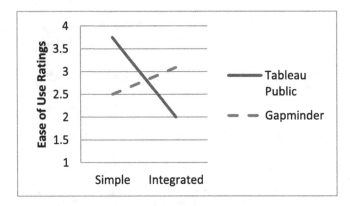

Fig. 6. Observed interaction effect for ease of use ratings

with country names in Tableau/Simple displays helped users to comprehend the data trend. On the contrary, when information about all three variables was shown simultaneously on the same graph with different coding as used in Tableau/Integrated display, it caused difficulty in user's comprehension. The use of animation in the Gapminder/Integrated was helpful for demonstrating data trend, resulting in higher comprehension score and ease-of-use rating than Gapminder/Simple display. Although Gapminder/Simple also displayed each variable with single graphs, the way for displaying country information was not as straightforward, and required prior geographical knowledge of the user. This may explain the worse user performance with the Gapminder/Simple displays.

5 Conclusion

This study demonstrates the importance of design of visualization tools in user's comprehension of data trends. Tableau/Simple display led to the higher level of comprehension and ease-of-use rating because of its use of familiar graphical features to most users-the simplicity of the continuous line to represent trends and the direct labeling of the countries. On the other hand, Gapminder/Simple caused difficulties for some users to correctly associate data line with corresponding countries because the program assumed geographic knowledge of the users. This conclusion contradicts our original hypothesis, but it does make sense that use of familiar visual features has a positive effect on comprehension. Also, the visualization tool should not assume prior knowledge of user and always provide redundant ways to assist users.

Another interesting finding was the correspondence between the comprehension performance and the ease-of-use ratings of users. Users are able to better comprehend data trends when the visualization tool is easier to use. Our results highlight importance of ease-of-use for visualization tool design. When designing visualization tools, we need to consider the ease-of-use factor for the tool to assist user's understandings of data trends.

This experiment collected data from college students with minimum training in data visualization tools. Further study could explore how training in use of visualization tool may change the comprehension scores. Further investigation can also be performed on other visualization techniques used in several different programs to determine the design effectiveness.

References

Battista, V., Cheng, E.: Motion charts: telling stories with statistics. In: Joint Statistical Meetings, Miami Beach, Florida (2011)

Heer, J., Mackinlay, J., Stolte, C., Agrawala, M.: Graphical histories for visualization: supporting analysis, communication, and evaluation. IEEE Trans. Visual. Comput. Graph. **14**(6), 1189–1196 (2008)

Heer, J., Shneiderman, B.: Interactive dynamics for visual analysis. Commun. ACM **55**(4), 45–54 (2012)

Kienle, H.M.; Muller, H.A.: Requirements of software visualization tools: a literature survey. In: 4th IEEE International Workshop on Visualizing Software for Understanding and Analysis, 2007, VISSOFT 2007 (2007)

O'Hare, D.D., Stenhouse, N.N.: Redesigning a graphic weather display for pilots. Ergon. Des. **16**(4), 11–15 (2008)

Rosling, H.: Visual technology unveils the beauty of statistics and swaps policy from dissemination to access. Stat. J. IAOS **24**(1/2), 103–104 (2007)

A Visual Citation Search Engine

Tetsuya Nakatoh[1]([✉]), Hayato Nakanishi[2], Toshiro Minami[3,4], Kensuke Baba[3], and Sachio Hirokawa[1]

[1] Research Institute for Information Technology, Kyushu University, 6-10-1 Hakozaki, Higashi-ku, Fukuoka 812-8581, Japan
nakatoh@kyudai.jp
[2] Graduate School of Integrated Frontier Sciences, Kyushu University, 6-10-1 Hakozaki, Higashi-ku, Fukuoka 812-8581, Japan
[3] Kyushu University Library, 6-10-1 Hakozaki, Higashi-ku, Fukuoka 812-8581, Japan
[4] Kyushu Institute of Information Sciences, 6-3-1 Saifu, Dazaifu, Fukuoka 818-0117, Japan

Abstract. Carrying out the survey of the related researches is an essential part in research activities, the aim of which is to have an overall view of the target field. Generally, we take two approaches toward this aim. One approach is paying attention to selected articles and deeply investigate them. The selection is performed according to some indicators for measuring importance. The other approach is considering the citation relations between articles. One problem is that these approaches cannot be combined straightforwardly. Another problem in carrying out the survey is that there are a huge amount of articles exist already. The aim of this paper is to propose a framework of a visualization system that assists us in surveying related researches. The system displays the important articles together with their key citation relations by displaying not only direct citations between important articles but also the indirect, or weak-tie, citation relations that connect them.

Keywords: Bibliometrics · Research investigation · Citation count · Visualization · Thread-Tree · Weak-tie

1 Introduction

Surveying the related researches is one of the indispensable activities in carrying out academic researches. For new research areas which have no standard textbooks nor survey articles, we have to search a massive amount of scholarly information for related researches. The simplest way to find related researches is searching research articles by some keywords. However, the result of a search often contains too many articles for humans to deal with due to the existence of a large number of articles have been published already, and the number is increasing very rapidly. Thus, novel technologies are needed in order to survey research articles from among the vast amount of scholarly information.

© Springer International Publishing Switzerland 2016
S. Yamamoto (Ed.): HIMI 2016, Part I, LNCS 9734, pp. 168–178, 2016.
DOI: 10.1007/978-3-319-40349-6_17

We generally take two approaches as we survey a research field and grasp their overall view. One of them is selecting articles by considering their *importance* and investigate deeply how they deal with the research topics. A specific feature of research articles is that they are related each other by citations (or references). The number of the citations from other articles, i.e., the number of the articles that cite the target article, is a simple but useful measure for evaluating the importance of the target article; which is called its *citation count*. Actually, the conventional databases, such as Scopus[1], use the citation count of articles in the function of sorting the result of a search. Impact factor [1,3], a popular measure for evaluating academic journals, is calculated using the citation count of the articles published in the target journal. The h-index [4] measure for evaluating researchers is calculated on the basis of the number of the articles written by the target researcher and the citation counts to the articles.

The other approach to get useful information for surveying a research field is investigating the structural features of citations between research articles. In this paper, we call the graph that represents the citation relations between the articles the *citation graph*.

We take the research of Garfield et al. [2] as an example for structural analysis of citation graph. They conducted an analysis on the history of a research area by using a figure of the citation relations between the concerned articles.

Structural analysis can be used as a complement to the approach using the citation count. Suppose there are two articles having the same citation count. It may happen that their citation graphs are contrastingly different; e.g., one may have a long chain of citations in a specific research topic, whereas the other may be cited by the papers relating to a wide variety of research topics. Thus, it is preferable to evaluate the papers on the basis of these two approaches as we perform a survey of a research field.

As we have pointed out, it is an important task to find out important articles and to capture the relations between them for surveying a research field. As a part of "research automation," a search engine system will play a very important role in pursuing our research activities more effectively and more efficiently. Also, since such activities are basically carried out in trial-and-error, such system should be designed as an interactive system, and thus HCI is a crucial part in designing such a system.

In this paper, we propose a system which visualizes the citation relations of important articles in terms of citation count and how they are connected, so that the user can interactively specify which graph to display. In this visualization, the user of the system chooses the nodes and edges of the displayed citation graph by considering the paths from particular nodes. We can interactively choose an article by clicking the node to see detailed information of the article. The graph can be changed by restricting the length of the path or the number of the edges of each node.

The ultimate goal of our study is to develop a search engine with a good HCI interface. As a very beginning toward this goal, we start with proposing a basic

---

[1] http://www.scopus.com/.

mechanism for visualization of articles in this paper. The main contribution of this paper is the proposal of the visualization method which shows the important articles together with the key relations between them. We call this visualization by "Thread-Tree."

The rest of this paper is organized as follows. In Sect. 2, we describe the construction method of Thread-Tree of the citation. In Sect. 3, we show how a search engine can be designed by using the algorithm described in Sect. 2. We also show an example of application to real data. In Sect. 4, we discuss the differences of the features of our system from other related researches. In Sect. 5, we summarize the study in this paper and show some of the research topics for the future.

2   Construction of Thread-Tree

The system proposed in this paper starts with receiving an article as input and displays its Thread-Tree as output. The root of the Thread-Tree represents the article given as input and the other nodes represent the selected articles among the articles citing the root article either directly or indirectly by using the concept of weak-tie.

The whole process of the system consists of the following three small steps:

(1) Construct Thread-Tree from citation graph
(2) Filter important articles
(3) Recover Weak-Tie nodes and edges

In Step 1, the system starts with collecting the articles that cite the article which is given as input. Then the system constructs the citation graph of the articles. The "Thread-Tree" having the given article as the root is generated from the citation graph. In this process, the most important citation link is chosen for each article except the root, and other links are eliminated. Here, the importance is measured by the number of the citing articles, or the citation count, of the article under consideration. In this way, the tree structure (Thread-Tree) is constructed.

In Step 2, the system eliminates the nodes (or articles) which are judged as unimportant on the basis of the citation count; i.e., the citation count is less than the given threshold value. The edges relating to the eliminated nodes are also eliminated. After this process, the obtained Thread-Tree may not be connected even if the original citation graph is connected.

In Step 3, the system recovers some of the articles and their links that were once eliminated in Step 2. The recovered nodes are chosen if they are eliminated in Step 2 as unimportant but still they appear on the paths that connect some of the important nodes and the root node. The edges of them are also recovered accordingly.

2.1   Step 1: Citation Graph to Thread-Tree

Let $\mathcal{A}$ be the set of articles and let $\mathcal{C}$ be the citation relation between the articles in $\mathcal{A}$; i.e., $\mathcal{C} \subseteq \mathcal{A} \times \mathcal{A}$. We will use the notation $b \leftarrow a$ in two senses; as an alternative representation of the binary relation $(b, a) \in \mathcal{C}$ between b and a, and as the element (b, a) of $\mathcal{C}$. The citation graph G is the graph structure consisting of $\mathcal{A}$ and $\mathcal{C}$; i.e., $G = (\mathcal{A}, \mathcal{C})$. We denote $\mathcal{N}(G)$ for $\mathcal{A}$ and $\mathcal{E}(G)$ for $\mathcal{C}$. We assume there are no loops in the citation graph G, because, basically, an article a cites b only after b is published and thus the publication time of a becomes later than that of b. Further, self citation, $a \leftarrow a$, will not happen as well.

We denote the transitive closure of $\leftarrow$ by $\Leftarrow$; i.e., $b \Leftarrow a$ iff there exists a sequence of nodes $a_0, a_1, \ldots, a_{n+1}$ for some $n \geq 0$, and $a_0 = b, a_{n+1} = a$ and $a_i \leftarrow a_{i+1}$ for $i = 0, 1, \ldots, n$. In other words $b \Leftarrow a$ means that the article b is either directly or indirectly cited by the article a. The citation count of an article $a \in \mathcal{A}$ is defined as the number of the articles b that cite a; i.e., $cc(a) = \#\{b \in \mathcal{A} \mid a \leftarrow b\}$, where $\#S$ indicates the number of the elements of the set S.

We define the Thread Graph $TG(a)$ of the specified article a $(\in \mathcal{A})$ as a subgraph of G as follows:

$\mathcal{N}(TG(a)) = \{b \in \mathcal{A} \mid a \Leftarrow b \text{ or } b = a\}$; i.e., the nodes of $TG(a)$ consist of a and the node of $\mathcal{A}$ which directly or indirectly cites a.

$\mathcal{E}(TG(a)) = \{b \leftarrow c \in \mathcal{C} \mid b, c \in \mathcal{N}(TG(a))\}$ $(\subseteq \mathcal{C})$; i.e., the edges which connect the two nodes of $TG(a)$.

The Thread-Tree $TT(a)$ of a is defined as a subgraph of $TG(a)$, which has a as its root node and the edges are chosen so that each node except a has only one edge to another node. We define $TT(a)$ as follows:

$\mathcal{N}(TT(a)) = \mathcal{N}(TG(a))$; i.e., the nodes are the same as of $TG(a)$.

For each node b $(\neq a)$ in $TT(a)$, most important node $\iota(b)$ is chosen so that it satisfies the following conditions: $\iota(b) \leftarrow b$ and $cc(\iota(b)) \geq cc(c)$ for any c such that $c \leftarrow b$. As we take the citation count as the measure for importance of an article, $\iota(b)$ is the, or one of the, most important article(s) among the articles cited by b.

The edges of $TT(a)$ is defined formally as: $\mathcal{E}(TT(a)) = \{b \leftarrow c \in \mathcal{E}(TG(a)) \mid b = \iota(c)\}$.

2.2   Step 2: Elimination of Non-important Articles

As we have already mentioned, we use the citation count as the measure for importance of articles. Thus we set up a threshold value m for judging an article if it is important or not. Now we define the subgraph of $TT(a)$ in which only the important nodes (articles) of $TT(a)$ are left and other nodes together with their edges are eliminated. The resulting graph structure is not necessarily a tree anymore in general, so we call it a "graph."

Let m (≥ 0) be a number. We define the Thread Graph $TG_m(a)$ of the article a with the threshold value m as follows:

$\mathcal{N}(TG_m(a)) = \{b \in \mathcal{N}(TT(a)) \mid cc(b) \geq m \text{ or } b = a\}$; i.e., the nodes consist of the article a and the important articles of $\mathcal{N}(TT(a))$. Where "important article" means its citation count is greater or equals to the threshold value m.

$\mathcal{E}(TG_m(a)) = \{b \leftarrow c \in \mathcal{E}(TT(a)) \mid b,c \in \mathcal{N}(TG_m(a))\}$. The edges of $\mathcal{E}(TG_m(a))$ consist of those in $\mathcal{E}(TT(a))$ so far as their both end nodes are important (i.e., belong to $\mathcal{N}(TG_m(a))$). From the definition, $TG_0(a) = TT(a)$.

Figure 1 shows an example of the Thread-Tree of the article by Newman [10] with the threshold value 10. Unfortunately, the graph is very complicated and it is difficult for us to understand and extract some kind of valuable findings from this graph.

Thus we need to find more sophisticated criteria for restricting the number of nodes so that we are able to have an image for surveying the research field. So, not only the Citation Count, but also a lot of other evaluation criteria have been investigated, so far; e.g., Focused Citation Count, Accumulated Citation Count, Journal Impact Factor, Focused Journal Impact Score, h-index, etc. The combined use of them and evaluation using the length of thread might be useful as well. In this paper, we use Citation Count only for measuring importance and the left possibilities are remained as one of our future work.

2.3   Step 3: Thread-Tree by Recovering the Weak-Ties

As the result of Step 2, the resulting graph $TG_m(a)$ becomes a subgraph of the Thread-Tree $TT(a)$ of a, thus it is a collection of subtrees of $TT(a)$ in general. A problem here is that even though there exist the connections, or indirect citation links between the existing articles, they may not be displayed in the Thread Graph $TG_m(a)$. In order to solve this problem, we rescue the once-eliminated nodes and edges to $TG_m(a)$ so that the resulting graph becomes a subtree of $TT(a)$ and only the important nodes as well as the necessary nodes together with their connecting edges appear in the graph.

The final Thread-Tree $TT_m(a)$ of the article a with the threshold value m is defined as follows:

$\mathcal{N}(TT_m(a)) = \{b \in \mathcal{N}(TT(a)) \mid$ there exists a sequence $a_0, a_1, \ldots, a_{n+1}$ for some $n \geq 0$ such that $a_0 = a, a_{n+1} \in \mathcal{N}(TG_m(a)), a_i = b$ for some $i = 0, 1, \ldots, n+1$, and $a_i \leftarrow a_{i+1} \in \mathcal{E}(TT(a))$ for all $i = 0, 1, \ldots, n\} \cup \mathcal{N}(TG_m(a))$; i.e., the nodes which are either contained in the Thread Graph $TG_m(a)$ or those that appear in the paths from a node in $TT(a)$ on the way to the root node a.

$\mathcal{E}(TT_m(a)) = \{b \leftarrow c \in \mathcal{E}(TT(a)) \mid b,c \in \mathcal{N}(TT_m(a))\}$; i.e., the paths that appear in the Thread-Tree $TT(a)$ and need to be used in the paths to connect an important node to the root a.

We call an edge (link) as a Weak-Tie if it appears in $TT_m(a)$ and does not appear in $TG_m(a)$. As has been pointed out of the importance of Weak-Ties between human beings in social relations, our concept of Weak-Ties for the articles are also important in capturing the overall citation relations among important articles.

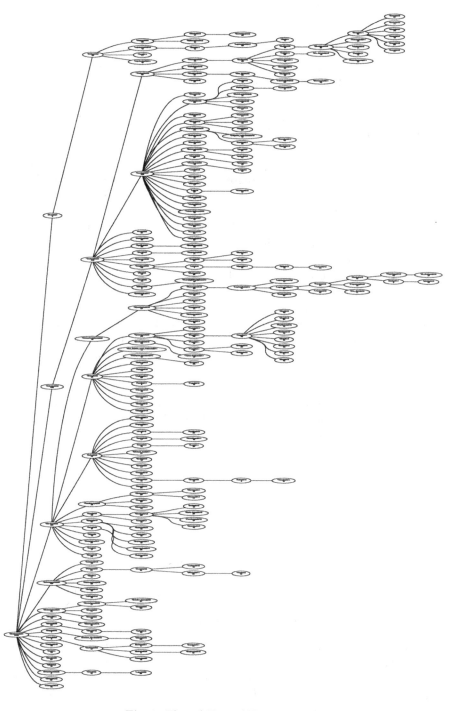

Fig. 1. Thread-Tree of Newman 2001

3   Experiment with Real Data

3.1   Gathering Article Data and Basic Analysis

In this section, we explain the collection method of articles for analysis, and conduct a basic analysis of the data.

The article data were gathered from Scopus. In this experiment, we chose the term "bibliometrics" as the query keyword to specify the research field. We got 10,186 articles with the publishing years range from 1976 to 2015 through the Scopus's search API.

These data are written in JSON format, where the items consist of: "Content Type," "Search identifier," "Complete author list," "Resource identifiers," "Abstract Text," "First author," "Page range," "SCOPUS Cited-by URI," "Result URL," "Document identifier," "Publication date," "Source title," "Article title," "Cited by count," "ISSN," "Issue number," and "Volume."

While some articles have no citation at all, an article has 2,977 citations. The total number of citations becomes 116,743.

Then we gathered the articles which cite other articles. The citation information of an article appears at the "link" item of JSON format in the form of URL. Since the Scopus API does not provide with the sufficient information of the articles at the URLs, we obtained the HTML files using the "wget" command. The number of citation articles obtained by the wget command is limited to 20 at maximum in one HTML file, we called the wget command repeatedly until we got all articles we needed.

Since 3,024 articles have no citations from other articles, we obtained the remaining 7,162 articles as those which have at least one citation counts. The wget command was called 10,719 times for these 7,162 articles and 116,743 citation data were obtained as the result. After eliminating the duplications, 62,265 articles were left.

3.2   Visualized Citation Search Engine

Figure 2 shows a screenshot of the visual citation search engine we are developing. The system displays a citation graph which is explained in Sect. 2. It is built by using the data explained in Sect. 3.1.

The top window of the search system consists of three panes. Articles are obtained according to the given search keyword. Top 20 lists of articles with citation information are displayed on the left pane. Each line looks like as follows:

```
2 Newman2001 1630 png 10 20 30 40 50 60 70 80 90 100
```

The first numerical value shows the ranking in terms of the citation counts. The 2nd item shows the article name in an abbreviated format, which consists of the name of the first author and the publication year of the article. In this case, "Newman2001" represents the article [10] "The structure of scientific collaboration networks" written by Newman and published in 2001. The 3rd item 1630 shows the citation count of the article.

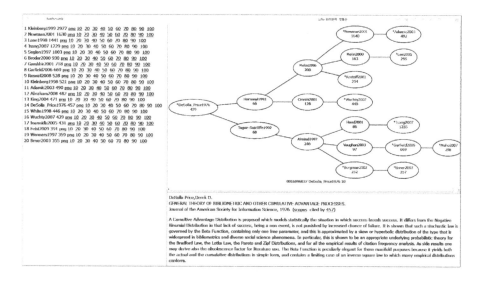

Fig. 2. A screenshot of the visualized citation search engine

The 4th and the remaining items are clickable. The corresponding graph is displayed on the right pane as the user clicks one of them. The 4th item "png" is for displaying the Thread-Tree of the designated article. By default, top 50 articles in terms of the citation count will be displayed. In this case, the whole Thread-Tree is displayed using the whole area of the right-hand pane. It is useful for having the overall view of Thread-Tree.

The 5th and the following items are for specifying the number of articles which appear in the Thread-Tree. As the user clicks the numerical value N, the system will displays the Thread-Tree in the upper part of the right pane, which shows top N articles in terms of the citation count. The displayed image is generated as a Scalable Vector Graphics (svg). At the same time, the bibliographic information of the article, including the author, the title, the journal name, the publication year, the abstract, etc., will be displayed in the lower part of the right pane.

It becomes possible to understand both the global image of research, and the contents of each article because this system visualizes the transition of the articles that cites the specified article displayed as the root.

3.3 Drawing Thread-Tree

In this section, we introduce an example of search by the system, and the effect of Weak-Ties.

Figure 3 is the Thread Graph of the article "The increasing dominance of teams in production of knowledge" written by Wuchty et al. [11] in 2007 (`Wuchty2007` in the graph). The top 10 important articles according to the citation count measure appear in the graph. Although this graph is a subgraph of the Thread-Tree of the article and thus all the articles appearing in the graph cite `Wuchty2007` either directly or indirectly, we cannot see such relations in Fig. 3.

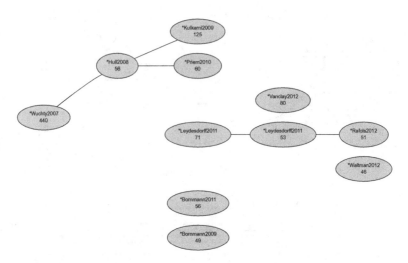

Fig. 3. Thread graph of Wuchty2007 without Weak-Tie

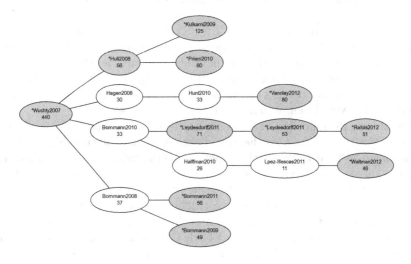

Fig. 4. Thread-Tree of Wuchty2007 with Weak-Tie

Figure 4 shows the graph (tree) obtained by adding the Weak-Tie connections to the graph shown in Fig. 3. See Sect. 2.3 for the definition of Weak-Tie. In this example, 6 articles and 11 citations hidden in the Thread Graph appear and it becomes much easier to capture how the important articles' mutual relations. As we compare these two figures, we easily understand the usefulness of the concept of Weak-Ties.

4   Related Work

There are many work aiming at research investigation. The citation count is useful evaluation for scientific research. Martin [7] has reported that the citation count gained many supports as criteria. Kostoff [5] showed that the citation count as a measure of evaluation has some problems.

It is more appropriate to find out the related articles if we restrict the articles in a specific research area. Nakatoh et al. [9] proposed FCC (Focused Citation Count) which restricts the research area of the cited articles by keywords, and showed that more appropriate articles could be extracted.

Even with such examples of good use of the citation count as a measure for the article's importance, it is not almighty. For example, it is not appropriate to use as a measure to evaluate a new article. Therefore it is common to use the following attribute instead; the evaluation of the scientific journal in which the journal was published or the researcher who wrote the article.

Journal Impact Factor [1,3,6] is one of the most popular evaluation measures of scientific journals. Thomson Reuters updates and provides the score of journals in Journal Citation Reports every year. Hirsch [4] defined the h-index of a researcher as the largest number h such that the researcher wrote h articles and each of the articles is cited from h articles or more. Scopus provides the h-index score of researchers.

For detection of appropriate journals, there are also researches that conduct an analysis focused on a research area. Nakatoh et al. [8] proposed the method of selecting appropriate journals by using the citation which focus on the specific field as evaluation of a journal.

It is one of the further work to combine these evaluation measures with this research.

Garfield et al. [2] visualized the transition of research. They built the network diagram of the articles of DNA research area with the citation index, and showed an analysis. Such research is called "Domain Visualization," "Domain analysis," etc. From the viewpoint of visualization, these researches seem to be close to our research. However, the purpose of these researches is the analysis of research itself, and is not related with the analytic methods. We show the general visualization method for research analysis.

5   Conclusion

It is essential for researchers to survey the related researches as a part of their research activities. They investigate important, or key, articles which have big influence to other articles, and how these articles are related each other. However, a huge amount of scholarly articles exist nowadays and it is practically impossible to find such important articles all by themselves.

Information visualization is used in the system which effectively relieves such time-consuming activity. In this paper, we proposed a new algorithm for displaying important articles and their relations based on the citation information between articles. An advantage of our method is that it solves a dilemma, which is as follows: If you display all the articles and their citation relations as a graph, it becomes too complicated and thus it is impossible to see where the important articles locate and how they are related. On the other hand, if you display important articles and their citation links only, it is hard to recognize how they are related. In our proposed methods, you can get the important articles only and how they are related in terms of their in-direct citation relationships; which we call "Weak-Tie."

We also demonstrated the usefulness of our visualization algorithm by applying it to the articles collected with the term "bibliometrics."

Our future topics include:

– Use and evaluation of other evaluation methods,
– Cooperative use with more complicated search systems,
– Quantitative evaluation and qualitative evaluation of the proposed visualization method,
– Integration to a research assistant system.

References

1. Garfield, E.: Citation indexes for science. Science **122**(3159), 108–111 (1955)
2. Garfield, E., Sher, I.H., Torpie, R.J.: The use of citation data in writing the history of science. Institute for Scientific Information, Institute for Scientific Information, Philadelphia, p. 71 (1964)
3. Garfield, E.: The history and meaning of the journal impact factor. J. Am. Med. Assoc. **295**(1), 90–93 (2006)
4. Hirsch, J.E.: An index to quantify an individual's scientific research output. Nat. Acad. Sci. U.S.A. **102**(46), 16569–16572 (2005)
5. Kostoff, R.N.: Performance measures for government-sponsored research: overview and background. Scientometrics **36**(3), 281–292 (1996)
6. Marshakova-Shaikevich, I.: The standard impact factor as an evaluation tool of science fields and scientific journals. Scientometrics **35**(2), 283–290 (1996)
7. Martin, B.R.: The use of multiple indicators in the assessment of basic research. Scientometrics **36**(3), 343–362 (1996)
8. Nakatoh, T., Nakanishi, H., Hirokawa, S.: Journal impact factor revised with focused view. In: Neves-Silva, R., Jain, L.C., Howlett, R.J. (eds.) (KES-IDT 2015). SIST, vol. 39, pp. 471–481. Springer International Publishing, Switzerland (2015)
9. Nakatoh, T., Nakanishi, H., Baba, K., Hirokawa, S.: Focused citation count: a combined measure of relevancy and quality. In: IIAI 4th International Congress on Advanced Applied Informatics (IIAI AAI 2015), pp. 166–170 (2015)
10. Newman, M.E.J.: The structure of scientific collaboration networks. Nat. Acad. Sci. U.S.A. **98**(2), 404–409 (2001)
11. Wuchty, S., Jones, B.F., Uzzi, B.: The increasing dominance of teams in production of knowledge. Science **316**(5827), 1036–1039 (2007)

Visualization of Brand Images Extracted from Home-Interior Commercial Websites Using Color Features

Naoki Takahashi[1(✉)], Takashi Sakamoto[2], and Toshikazu Kato[3]

[1] Graduate School of Chuo University, Hachioji, Japan
a12.bbt@g.chuo.ac.jp
[2] National Institute of Advance Industrial Science
and Technology, Tokyo, Japan
takashi-sakamoto@aist.go.jp
[3] Chuo University, Hachioji, Japan
t-kato@kc.chuo-u.ac.jp

Abstract. Websites of home-interior brands display many photographs of products that include walls, floors, and furniture. Such photographs, known as image photographs, contain a lot of information about the brand image because the colors of walls, floors, and furniture in a photograph influence the brand image. This paper proposes a method of extracting representative colors of interior photographs by using a hierarchical clustering algorithm and analyzes the characteristics and differences of interior brands with color features. Our proposed method can be used to describe the common characteristics of interior image photographs and differences between eight interior brands (*Ralph Lauren Home, Herman Miller, arflex, Cassina, Carl Hansen and Son, IKEA, Karimoku* and *Nitori*). We measure the similarity or difference between brand images by constructing a brand image space with clusters of representative colors and obtain the relationship between six brand images.

Keywords: Color-analysis · Interior-brand · Visualization

1 Introduction

Data visualization is becoming increasingly important to understand information extracted from the web using data mining technology. The visualized data are considered objective in many research areas [1–3]; however, subjective data can be used to investigate consumers' evaluations of products or companies and understand brand images that they hope to demonstrate to people. In this study, we extracted quantitative features of brand images from specific home interior company web sites and visualized their features. We extracted color features from the images and used them to compare the brands.

1.1 Background

Brand image is a factor of brand value, which is one of the important assets for companies and contributes to driving sales, growing market share, and building

© Springer International Publishing Switzerland 2016
S. Yamamoto (Ed.): HIMI 2016, Part I, LNCS 9734, pp. 179–190, 2016.
DOI: 10.1007/978-3-319-40349-6_18

shareholder value [4]. In this study, we define brand image as affecting the value and impression communicated between the company and customers. The communication is performed in shopping, advertising, and any other scenes of market in real world and on the Internet. Therefore, we regard brand images communicated via the Internet as subjective information of the web, and tried to extract it by web image analysis. However, various images may be formed from a single brand because the brand image is subjective. In such a case, the company would not communicate with customers effectively, because the image the company is expecting to create and the images actually impressed upon the people are different. This paper considers brand images expected by companies, because our final goal is to clarify the brand image desired by the company and evaluate the communication of the company with its customers.

1.2   Related Works

In terms of data mining, there are two types of data, structured and unstructured data. Text and images are mostly unstructured data. Extraction of knowledge from a web image is classified as web content mining or web image mining.

The main focus of knowledge mining from images on the web is the acquisition and application of visual concepts that correspond to the text. The mining of visual concepts generally requires large numbers of tagged images. In this regard, image databases such as ImageNet [5], Google Image Search [6, 7], and photo-sharing services [6, 8] are exploited.

To date, researchers who have studied the extraction of a feature of color automatically from the image data, have proposed the use of techniques such as color histograms and higher order local autocorrelation coefficients. In these studies, because the meaning of each of the variables is unclear, it is difficult to apply to design and marketing. Therefore, we propose methods that use a small number of representative colors in the image as feature followed by their application for estimating the impression.

Wang et al. [9] extracted one color to be perceptually central in the image as the dominant color. Their approach was to remove all colors except the dominant color, which is a good idea in terms of perceptual weight. Nevertheless, for use in the estimation of impression when viewed as a whole photo, it is insufficient. The impression created by products was also evaluated by Niwa and Kato [10], who extracted features from only the product area of the product photo. However, it is considered that the effective analysis of a brand image would necessarily have to include the background area of the image photograph.

We consider color features to sufficiently represent the brand image without the need for information about the composition, object, and shapes. In this study, we describe the analysis of the brand image as conveyed by a photo with color features.

2   Extraction of Color Feature from Image Photograph

We analyzed web images by using representative colors that are used as the main colors in a photograph. In this section, we describe images that are useful to understand the brand image and the method we used to extract the representative colors.

2.1 Image Photographs

Our approach focused on the brand image conveyed by images on the web sites of home interior businesses. We collected the images from their respective websites to analyze the features for comparison purposes. There are mainly three types of images: image photographs, product photographs, and parts of the web page layout. Image photographs do not only show products but also the floor, the wall or other furniture in the background. Product images show only products in contrast. The background of a product photograph is usually a single color such as white. Parts of the page layout also contain images; e.g., small pictures of buttons to click. A product photograph is useful to analyze the features of the products because it is easy to remove the background from the image. However, our focus is on image photographs rather than on product photographs, because image photographs are used to show examples of a combination of items and to express the concept of a product and brand image, whereas product photographs are used explanatorily on catalog pages (Fig. 1).

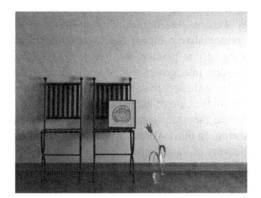 

Fig. 1. Examples of an image photograph (left) and product photograph (right)

2.2 Extraction of Representative Colors

Representative color is one of the ways to express an image feature, and its combination is the color theme. The number of representative colors depends on each individual image photograph. However, the number was assumed to be constant by many researchers, conducting research on color themes, for the purpose of comparing color themes and calculating the dissimilarity between images. The visualization of affective data requires the expression of color features to match human perception. Therefore, we employed hierarchical clustering to extract representative colors without specifying a number of colors.

Extraction of the representative colors from image photographs requires us to determine the amount of space covered by each color. This was calculated for each color cluster, which is created by aggregate hierarchical clustering of a single link method. The aggregate hierarchical clustering algorithm combines a pair of two similar

Fig. 2. Examples of representative colors extracted (Color figure online)

clusters iteratively. This algorithm needs a stop criterion as parameter and the threshold corresponds to perceptual distinction. We used 3.0 as the height of pruning that is obtained as perceptual value in the pre-experiment.

Clusters that covered only one pixel were excluded from this study, and the remaining clusters were extracted as the representative colors of the image photograph. The reason for excluding clusters consisting of one pixel is the following: Clusters obtained by hierarchical clustering are divided into groups of large clusters, small clusters, and very small clusters. In general, large clusters have low saturation, whereas high saturation color is seen in small clusters. In the case of home interiors, vivid colors are not used on the walls and floor, because they are added in the form of small furniture items and accessories for accentuation. In other words, large clusters covering many pixels (e.g., in Fig. 2 the lower left corner of the images in white or gray or the black floor in the bottom right-hand corner) correspond to a wall or the floor, whereas small clusters (the blue green color in the lower left corner, or the yellow in the bottom right) correspond to other furniture. Therefore, a combination of large and small clusters is considered to contain the necessary information for image analysis of the interior images. On the other hand, very small clusters covering only 1 pixel occur in the lower right-hand side of Fig. 2. These pixels are considered to originate from a small amount of visual noise caused by lighting. Although there is a large number of these colors, we do not consider them to be important.

2.3 Materials

The target brands are the typical interior brands of eight companies that are based locally and abroad: arflex (608), Cassina (471), Carl Hansen and Son (360), IKEA (2247), Herman Miller (154), Ralph Lauren Home (615), Karimoku (3985), and Nitori (188). The number in parentheses is the number of images downloaded from their respective websites. However, the variation in these numbers is such that a meaningful comparison of image photographs would not be possible. Thus, we randomly sampled 150 images per brand for analysis purposes.

2.4   Result of Extraction

Firstly, we described the method to analyze. Since the number of representative colors extracted from the image photograph is unspecified, it is difficult to compare the representative colors for each picture. Therefore we analyzed all the representative colors extracted in Fig. 3.

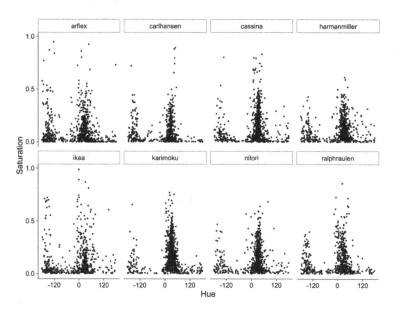

Fig. 3.   Scatter plot of hue and saturation extracted from image photograph of each brand

Figure 3 is the plane of hue and saturation. This distribution has a spread in the direction of orange and the blue at the center of the achromatic color. Such data structure is suitably expressed using hues. Hue is a angular value, and it is difficult to quantitative treatment. However hue is one of scale forming psychological color space, and it is characterized in that intuitively easy to understand the color from the value. For this reason hue is effective as a representation of the features of the color-coordination and design. As seen from the figure, there are two major peaks and spreads around them on orange (hue = 30°) and blue (hue = −150°). These hues are typically used in the pictures of the interior, which is useful in modeling and design the color features.

Also distribution of each brand also had different characteristics. For example, IKEA is widely distributed in some directions. Karimoku was not distributed CB direction when compared to R or O direction. Also Herman Miller and Nitori are distributed in low saturation.

3 Clustering and Scaling Color Feature

3.1 Characteristic of Each Brand (Qualitative Analysis)

The results of analysis of images using hue of Sect. 2, use trend of the representative color of the image photograph in the interior is characterized by the distribution of hue, and two directions are found: orange and blue. Thus parameters need to represent color distribution on the directions as a characteristic of the brand image, and we thought that these parameters, representing the characteristics of each brand and can be used to model the brand image.

It should be noted that, color distribution and interior photos of the color features of the chromaticity diagram, roughly put together it is considered that there is a following of such relevance:

- There are large protrusion in the orange and blue direction of all brands. Specifically. Orange is used in large pieces of furniture or wallpaper, such as a table or sofa. Blue is used in small articles and cushions as accent color.
- Brand distributed in the orange direction in the brand that mainly use the wood, are used warm colors and natural materials. As a background color the color of the wallpaper, as the commodity is considered, such as wooden material corresponds to this.
- If it is widely distributed in each direction using a colorful color scheme.
- Green vivid colors are not used much. Thus, bright purple and green is the color that is not used in most pictures of the interior, it is considered that there is no need to adopt as a parameter.

3.2 Quantitative Scale of Hue Parameters

To evaluate the characteristics as described in the previous section in a quantitative indication, we describe a method for statistically classification of hue and determining the attribution degree of a representative color against a cluster.

Distribution of the hue shown in Fig. 3 represents two peaks, but two colors are too small to express the characteristics of the image photograph. Therefore, in order to further subdivide these colors, using a dendrogram (Fig. 4) of the Word clustering. Because the hue value is represented by the angle, it is difficult such as the average of the calculations, the distance between the hue is determined as the smaller of the two angular difference. Aggregate hierarchical clustering was employed since it is sufficient definitions distance between data. It should be noted that we did not use the colors whose saturation is less than 5 % as data for clustering because a hue of the achromatic color is undefined and a hue of low saturation colors is tend to increase error of hue. In the dendrogram, it can be seen that are created large two clusters. In this study, however, it was divided into four clusters. Table 1 shows sizes and centers of each cluster. The color of low saturation, which did not apply to the hierarchical clustering, were grouped as cluster zero.

It should be noted that the center $\bar{H}_i$ of hue was determined by following equation.

$$\bar{H}_i = atan2\left(\frac{1}{\|c_i\|}\sum_{r \in C_i} cos(H_r), \frac{1}{\|c_i\|}\sum_{r \in C_i} sin(H_r)\right) \qquad (1)$$

Where H_r is the hue of the color r belonging to the cluster C_i, and $atan2(x, y)$ is function for determining the angle against the x-axis from the x and y on the unit circle. What this function does is, after obtaining the average by orthogonal coordinate, transforming it in polar coordinate again. Because hue values inside a cluster are distributed in a limited period, the error does not occur by this calculation method.

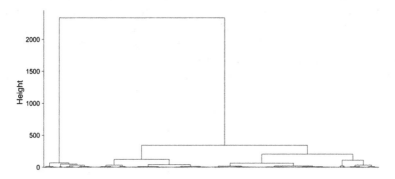

Fig. 4. Dendrogram of word clustering

Table 1. Number of colors and center hue of word clustering

Hue [degree]	Number of colors
Undefined	1985
14.88	1278
34.23	1421
212.6	582
65.65	445

Next, we describe a method to express the color features of the interior pictures of using the result of clustering. As an overview, since one of the representative color extracted from the image belongs to one of the five clusters of Table 1, it calculates the attribution degree of the representative color and the cluster to determine how much used each colors.

Explaining how to determine the attribution degree $A_i(r)$ of the representative color r and cluster C_i. First of all, when $i = 0$ i.e. attributable to the degree of achromatic color cluster is determined as follows.

$$A_0(r) = \begin{cases} 1 - S_r & S_r < 0.05 \\ 0 & otherwise \end{cases} \qquad (2)$$

Where S_r is the saturation of color r. Color with low saturation is about attribution degree is higher close to the achromatic color, color saturation of more than 5 % is attributable degree to zero. Then, the degree of attribution to $i \neq 0$ i.e. colorful cluster is determined as follows.

$$A_i(r) = \begin{cases} b_i(r) \cdot S_r \cdot cosH_r - \bar{H}_i & S_r \geq 0.05 \\ 0 & otherwise \end{cases} \tag{3}$$

H_r is hue of representative color r and $b_i(r)$ is binary function that indices whether r is belong to the cluster C_i. As shown in Eq. (3), the hue of the color r is more close to the center of the cluster, attribution degree higher saturation increases. However, the degree of attribution is exclusive, and all attribution degree of clusters except the nearest to r is zero. Similarly, Attribution degree of low saturation representative colors against non-achromatic clusters is also zero.

Then color feature vector of each image can be formed using the feature quantity. Image features $f = (f_0, f_1, f_2, f_3, f_4)$ is defined as follows.

$$f_i = \frac{1}{\|\{r\}\|} \sum_r A_i(r) \tag{4}$$

$\{r\}$ is the set of representative colors extracted from the image photograph. f_i represents the percentage of clusters which the representative colors in the image belong to, and $\sum_i f_i$ does not exceed 1.

4   Classification of Brand Images Using Color Features

f_i proposed in above is the image feature which has 5 parameters, and can be used to compare or image search among brands. In the study, we show result of visualization of brand images as an application. In particular, the variables from the feature vectors of two selected, mapped on the plane.

In Fig. 6, pictures of each brand mapped on f_1 ($\bar{H}_i = 14.88$, i.e. red) and f_2 ($\bar{H}_i = 34.23$, i.e. orange) plane are shown. As seen in the figure, pictures containing vivid red objects are mapped on lower right, and similarly orange and yellow's ones are on upper left, and proposed f_i is efficient to represent the corresponding color features. Also photos at the bottom left that are not neither orange nor red are mapped. Since the majority of the photos do not have bright colors, the distribution is concentrated in the vicinity of the origin. Regarding difference of each brand, this is able to reflect the analysis discussed in Sect. 3. For example, IKEA is not so much to use the orange, it uses vivid red. Karimoku and Nitori contrary to use well the orange. Further, by using other color variables, it is possible to visualize the relationship between the brand image and color feature.

5   Discussion

5.1   Trend of the Representative Colors in Image Photographs of Home Interior Brands

In Sect. 2, we described the method for extraction of colors and an overview of the distribution of the extracted color features. As a result, achromatic concentration and the distribution of hue of orange and the middle of cyan and blue was observed. In this section, we discuss the relationship with the pictures of each of the color and interior.

Orange or yellow corresponds to the color of the wooden floors and walls. Cyan and blue is opportunity color, thus these colors seem to be used for harmonic. Because in many cases the color of the walls that can not be easily changed in the interior, white or low saturation that is easy to match any other colors is preferred to use in many cases. Further the wall takes a large area in the picture, then the representative color likely to be extracted. Hence the color of low saturation in many image photo believed to have been extracted as a representative color.

And since the middle of the color of red, cyan and blue, both the middle of the achromatic color and is considered to have been used as a harmony color with respect to orange. Cyan and blue that are in a relationship of orange and contrast, many of the images is a color that can be used in photography.

Red is there is a different trend in the use by the brand. In arflex and Cassina, in accordance with the low saturation background, it has been used as a bright red sofa and chairs. On the other hand the color of the massive tree in Ralph Lauren and Karimoku has occurred redness.

In addition, the color of the wood in the pictures of the interior is often seen due to the characteristics of the buildings and furniture. Other furniture in order to further harmonize with the colors were also seen cases be the same color or similar color. Wood has various types and colors, they are the low saturation color to vivid red or orange. Thus, such orange has a rather wide distribution than the particular, and it is considered to be spreading in orange direction in Fig. 3.

And since the red and the middle of cyan and blue, both is considered to have been used as a harmony color with achromatic color and orange. Cyan and blue that are in a opposed relationship of orange, can be used in photography. Red is there is a different usage by the brand. In arflex and Cassina, it has been used as a bright red sofa and chairs with the low saturation background. On the other hand the color of the massive wood in Ralph Lauren and Karimoku has occurred redness.

5.2   Application of Classification of Brand Image

In Sect. 4, we classifies the representative colors into four clusters to construct feature space, and then commonality and difference between brands were observed. These commonality and difference are discussed as qualitative analysis, and in order to carry out the automatic classification of brand image, it is required to have a method of learning the relationship of the feature and the brand, as feature tasks. As remarked in previous discussion, the representative color is used for the particular materials and

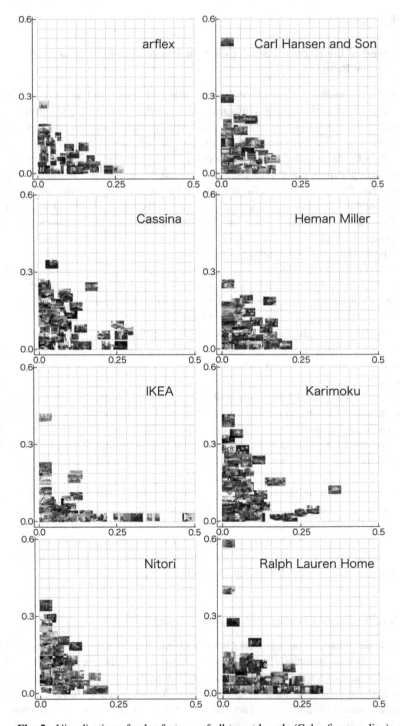

Fig. 5. Visualization of color features of all target brands (Color figure online)

elements as there are things that have been or used to support the harmony of color in a whole image. in this section, color features of each brand of the type is in the image photograph with differences will be discussed based on Fig. 5.

As the common element between the brand, there is a concentration of the distribution of the over the original point and the low-saturation orange. It is considered to be a basic color in pictures of the interior no matter the brand. From the viewpoint of classification and differences of brand, it may be noted the difference in the shape of a distribution as seen in Fig. 5. But it is very difficult to classify the individual image photograph for each brand. The reason is that the majority of pictures of low saturation, and likeness of brand of these pictures is not easy to understand. The purpose of this study is to understand the characteristics of the brand image, not classification and search system of brand image of the picture. However in considering such a service, it would have to be designed in a different concept from the present study.

6 Conclusion

In this study, we have been proposed for the method to design features for visualization of brand images using color features. While traditional approach has been to extract a generic image features, the proposed method by clustering the representative colors is intended to reflect the characteristics of the color scheme of the target contents. In this study, we analyzed eight of the interior brand, constitute a feature vector by four hue clusters and the achromatic color cluster, and use them to visualize the color feature. Proposed method is expected to be constructed by the same procedure for the other brands and content.

In this study, we have been proposed for the method to design features for visualization of brand images using color features. While traditional approach has been to extract a generic image features, the proposed method by clustering the representative colors is intended to reflect the characteristics of the color scheme of the target contents. In this study, we analyzed eight of the interior brand, constitute a feature vector by four hue clusters and the achromatic color cluster, and use them to visualize the color feature. Proposed method is expected to be constructed by the same procedure for the other brands and content.

To analyze the extracted color is from what object quantitatively, object recognition technology is required. Since we used the characteristics of only the color, it was only qualitative analysis mechanisms of the data generation. But for the estimation and image search of the brand image mentioned above, such a detailed analysis is considered to be essential. The proposal of designing the feature is future work such as to achieve this.

In addition, since the representative color to be employed to image photo vary depending on the season and events, the trend of the analysis data is considered to be significantly different depending on the time and the season to collect image data. In this study, we adapted home interior that is not so much affected by seasonal interior. However, When target is other contents, this method was applied to the image data of the same brand for each period of the season and various types of events. And analysis of the change in the brand image of each season analysis and, also, universal brand image not depending on a specific season and various events is considered to be very interesting research theme, which is a topic for future research.

Acknowledgement. This work was partially supported by JSPS KAKENHI grants (No. 25240043), and TISE Research Grant of Chuo University. We would like to thank Hideo Kikuchi from amana Inc. for advice about image photographs and brand images.

References

1. Bollen, J., Mao, H., Zeng, X.J.: Twitter mood predicts the stock market. J. Comput. Sci. **2** (1), 1–8 (2011)
2. Jagan, S., Rajagopalan, S.P.: A survey on web personalization of web usage mining. Int. Res. J. Eng. Technol. **2**(1), 6–12 (2015)
3. Yanai, K.: A review of web image mining. ITE Trans. Media Technol. Appl. **3**(3), 156–169 (2015)
4. Wang, D.: Brand Value. http://www.millwardbrown.com/mb-global/brand-strategy/brand-equity/brandz/top-global-brands/2015/thought-leadership/brand-value
5. Sermanet, P., Eigen, D., Zhang, X., Mathieu, M., Fergus, R., LeCun, Y.: OverFeat: integrated recognition, localization and detection using convolutional networks. In: International Conference on Learning Representations (2014)
6. Ni, B., Song, Z., Yan, S.: Web image mining towards universal age estimator. In: MM 2009, Proceedings of the ACM International Conference on Multimedia, pp. 85–94 (2009)
7. Wang, D., Hoi, S.C.H., He, Y., Zhu, J.: Mining weakly labeled web facial images for search-based face annotation. Knowl. Data Eng. **26**(1), 166–179 (2012)
8. Ginsca, A.L., Popescu, A., Le Borgne, H., Ballas, N., Vo, P., Kanellos, I.: Large-scale image mining with Flickr groups. In: He, X., Luo, S., Tao, D., Xu, C., Yang, J., Hasan, M.A. (eds.) MMM 2015, Part I. LNCS, vol. 8935, pp. 318–334. Springer, Heidelberg (2015)
9. Wang, P., Zhang, D., Zeng, G., Wang, J.: Contextual dominant color name extraction for web image search. In: 2012 IEEE International Conference on Multimedia and Expo Workshops (IC-MEW), pp. 319–324 (2012)
10. Niwa, S., Kato, T.: Modeling relationship between visual impression of products and their graphical features. In: Stephanidis, C. (ed.) HCII 2013, Part I. CCIS, vol. 373, pp. 705–708. Springer, Heidelberg (2013)

Ergonomic Considerations for the Design and the Evaluation of Uncertain Data Visualizations

Sabine Theis[1](✉), Christina Bröhl[1], Matthias Wille[1], Peter Rasche[1],
Alexander Mertens[1], Emma Beauxis-Aussalet[2], Lynda Hardman[2],
and Christopher M. Schlick[1]

[1] Institute of Industrial Engineering and Ergonomics,
RWTH Aachen University, Aachen, Germany
{s.theis,c.broehl,m.wille,p.rasche,a.mertens,
c.schlick}@iaw.rwth-aachen.de
[2] Centrum voor Wiskunde en Informatica (CWI), Amsterdam, The Netherlands
{Emmanuelle.Beauxis-Aussalet,Lynda.Hardman}@cwi.nl

Abstract. Uncertainty impacts many crucial issues the world is facing today – from climate change prediction, to scientific modelling, to the interpretation of medical data. Decisions typically rely on data which can be aggregated from different sources and further transformed using a variety of algorithms and models. Such data processing pipelines involve different types of uncertainty. As visual data representations are able to mediate between human cognition and computational models, a trustworthy conveyance of data characteristics requires effective representations of uncertainty which take productivity and cognitive abilities, as important human factors, into account. We summarize findings resulting from prior work on interactive uncertainty visualizations. Subsequently, an evaluation study is presented which investigates the effect of different visualizations of uncertain data on users' efficiency (time, error rate) and subjectively perceived cognitive load. A table, a static graphic, and an interactive graphic containing uncertain data were compared. The results of an online study (N = 146) showed a significant difference in the task completion time between the visualization type, while there are no significant differences in error rate. A non-parametric K-W test found a significant difference in subjective cognitive load [H (2) = 7.39, p < 0.05]. Subjectively perceived cognitive load was lower for static and interactive graphs than for the numerical table. Given that the shortest task completion time was produced by a static graphic representation, we recommend this for use cases in which uncertain data are to be used time-efficiently.

Keywords: Visualization · Uncertainty · Ergonomics · Efficiency · Cognitive load

1 Introduction

Exploring and analyzing data is often realized with the help of algorithms. Information visualization and data visualization can also help users to interpret the results produced by these algorithms e.g. by reducing information overload and aiding people

© Springer International Publishing Switzerland 2016
S. Yamamoto (Ed.): HIMI 2016, Part I, LNCS 9734, pp. 191–202, 2016.
DOI: 10.1007/978-3-319-40349-6_19

understand (their) data. While many types of data are visualized in order to make them more understandable, uncertainty measures are often excluded from these visualizations to limit visual complexity and clutter, which may lead to misunderstanding or false interpretations or further information overload. However, uncertainty is an essential component of the data, and a trustworthy representation requires it as an integral part of data visualization. Visualizing uncertain data requires us to look initially at different kinds of visual representation and different types of uncertainty. While the graphical attributes are assigned by the visualization developer, the type of uncertainty is often inherent in the data as a predefined feature. In general, uncertainty types are: errors within data, accuracy level, credibility of information source, subjectivity, non-specificity or noise [1]. Pang et al. use a threefold distinction, including *statistical uncertainty*, *error* and *range* caused by data acquisition, measurements, numerical models and data entry [2] while Skeels et al.'s domain-independent classification of uncertainties includes (1) inference uncertainty resulting from imprecision of modelling methods such as probabilistic modelling, hypothesis-testing or diagnosis, (2) completeness uncertainty due to missing values, sampling or aggregation errors and (3) measurement uncertainty caused by imprecise measurement [3].

Like all data, uncertain data can be represented by mapping numerical values to graphical attributes. As a result, an abstract concept can be expressed in a visualization. Uncertainty values can, for example, be represented as tables, glyphs, by geometrical attributes or in terms of colour [2] (Fig. 1).

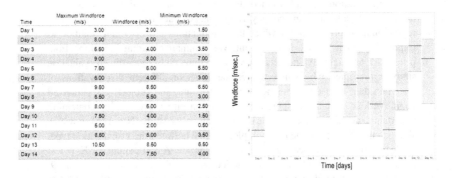

Fig. 1. A table was the baseline in our experiment (left). It was compared to the static visualization condition (right) and the interactive visualization condition (Fig. 2).

In addition, uncertainty measures can, for example, be represented by error bars, boxplots or Tufte Quartile Plots. In principle it is possible to select any graphical attribute as a representation of an uncertain value. This so-called graphical mapping is often brought about by the personal preferences and data experience of the developer or designer [4], by looking for an innovative solution [5], or by user requirements. While the latter studies lead to domain-specific and task dependent visualization, domain-independent studies about the influence of distinct visualizations on human aspects could enable visualization developers and researchers to make their design decisions based on empirical evidence. The need of a design decision is characterized by questions such as for example "Should I use a static or an interactive visualization?" or "Should I use a table instead of a graphic?", "Is cognitive effort lower if I use a bar chart or a line graph?". We believe that design decisions can be supported by general recommendations, resulting from visualization evaluation studies. Unlike domain-specific, user-centered design studies, evaluation studies aim at results domain spanning, thus permitting conclusions about the fundamental character of distinct visualization characteristics. This paper illustrates the characteristics of both approaches. First we derive human aspects relevant to domain-specific visualizations of a marine ecology video retrieval system. Subsequently, we present an example for a more general visualization evaluation aiming at giving general recommendations supporting design decisions in different application fields.

This paper is structured as follows: Sect. 2 summarizes human aspects relevant during the domain-specific development of uncertainty visualizations (marine ecology), Sect. 3 outlines the problem and research questions, followed by a method description in Sect. 4 and experimental results in Sect. 5. We end with a discussion and a conclusion in Sect. 6.

2   Related Work

A user study on trust and data provenance revealed that to be accepted in scientific use, the video analysis tool must provide data provenance information that describes the data collection methods (e.g., sampling methods), as well as the data processing methods and their potential errors (e.g., computer vision software and their confusion matrices). This would allow results to be compared with traditional statistical methods and increase the trust in results [6]. A related study revealed that a high level of user confidence can, however, be subjectively influenced by the visualization. Over-simplifying the visualization had potentially lead to the possibility of negative adverse effects, such as attention tunneling, memory loss, induced misinterpretations and unawareness of crucial information, which can be similar to the effects of uncertainty [7]. In another study [8] it was argue that simplifying expert-oriented visualization of uncertainty, misinterpretations of computer vision errors are less likely to occur. It remains unclear if findings are applicable to other scenarios and how visualization characteristics influence user confidence. But it can be stated that usability evaluation criteria such as efficiency, effectiveness, intuitiveness, intelligibility and trust – which are regularly considered in domain-specific research – are pivotal as a basis for evaluations supporting design decisions. Designing visualization characteristics according to cognitive characteristics are supposed to positively influence the usability [9]. As it is complex to analyze and measure cognitive processes, a more feasible approach is to measure subjectively perceived cognitive load. Cognitive load is strongly related to effectiveness, error rates and learning times [10]. Measured either by EEG or subjective evaluation, it appeared to differ depending on different visualization techniques. It remains unclear if different visualizations of uncertain data also lead to differences in cognitive load [11, 12].

The difference between user-centered design and an ergonomic evaluation is that the former aims at interface development, while the latter produces general recommendations supporting design decisions. Results of evaluation studies are able to shorten the effort for user-centered development activities without completely replacing them. General recommendations for the selection of visualization types require ergonomic evaluations of common visualization types, which usually apply different measures in order to obtain a true understanding of the strengths and weaknesses for all visualizations in the context of a specific task. Performance data provides evidence for the user's ability to use the visualization. Subjective data reflects the opinion of the user, which complements the performance data as often a higher subjective correlates with better performance. Data visualization research focusses on the development of specific tools, tasks or for specific user types. Research on domain independent recommendations for representations of uncertain data is rare. Ergonomics have mainly been involved at an a posteriori stage [13–15] while large part of the work focusses on creating new visual representations and interaction techniques [16], data representations [17, 18] or mathematical foundations [19, 20].

3   Research Question and Hypotheses

The following study therefore aims to generate recommendations for selecting the distinct uncertainty visualization types in terms of task completion time, error rate and cognitive effort by testing the following hypotheses: (1) H_1: There is a significant difference in task execution time per visualization type. (2) H_2: There is a significant difference in error rate per visualization type. (3) H_3: There is a significant difference in cognitive load per visualization type.

4   Method

In order to test our hypotheses we chose a between-group design, testing visualization type as the independent variable and task completion time, error rate and cognitive effort as the dependent variables. Participants were exposed to an experiment website which provided a task description and a task page where participants had to make a decision with the help of visualizations. Afterwards they had to fill in a survey documenting their subjective perceived cognitive load and demographic parameters.

Procedure. During the first phase of the experiment, participants had to accomplish a task using a visualization of uncertain data within the interface of a website. After reading an introduction, the visualization was shown. Participants had to look at the visualization and make a decision based on the information they could derive from it. The time it took each user to come to a decision, as well as the decision value, were recorded. During the second part, conducted to examine the cognitive effort, participants had to fill in a questionnaire.

Task. Weather prediction was chosen as the task topic because it provides uncertain data that is most likely to be easily understood by all participants. We suspected it would deliver the most domain-independent results, because it concerns a major part of the population to which we want to generalize our results. In this case, inference uncertainty [3] was the studied type of uncertainty. In the given case, a task

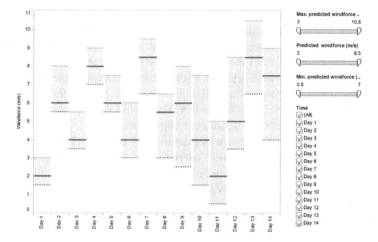

Fig. 2. The interactive visualization was composed of the same visualization as in the static visualization (SG) condition; each measure (max./min./pred. wind force and time) was equipped with control elements (checkbox/slider).

using weather predictions was determined and participants had to make a decision. The task required participants to choose one out of fourteen days to go sailing. They were asked to select the day with the highest estimated wind force and the lowest uncertainty, given one of three visualizations. Daily wind force and uncertainty values, and one radio button for each day as selection options, were provided (see Fig. 2).

Data Set. Weather is usually predicted for the next five to seven days and rarely contains explicit uncertainty values or intervals and if so, only the likelihood of a weather phenomenon (e.g. 60 % chance of wind) is reported. Hence the 10-day ensemble weather predictions published by the KNMI [21] were more suitable for our purpose. The original ensemble predictions show one expected wind value per day and changing minimum and maximum values within the time span of one day. The higher the interval of minimum and maximum estimated wind force, the more uncertain is the estimated wind value. We created an artificial data set, to prevent making any uncertainty related decision too easy, because the more a predicted value is located in the future, the more uncertain it is. Data was shaped, based on the structure (minimum, maximum and estimated wind value) of the ensemble data, according to different possible solution scenarios. In order to design a more difficult task, the original data was extended to fourteen days. 10 days got a lower (2–4 m/s) to medium (4–6 m/s) wind force, serving as distractive noise. Wind forces in the upper third (6–8.5 m/s, days 4, 7, 13 and 14) were designed in order to increase the required attention the participant had to invest for solving the task. These scenarios built a basis for the error rate computation.

Visualizations. On the basis of our artificially created data set, three visualizations were designed. By defining a visualization as visually structured, serving a better perception of its content, we see a table as the simplest form of visualization. The table itself was designed without any colour and graphics in order to distinguish it as much as possible from the graphics. In the graphic visualization the estimated wind value was represented by a horizontal line. The dotted horizontal line represents minimum and maximum estimated wind value and creates a contrast between both lines. The interactive visualization differs from the static one only by the interface control elements, while all graphic attributes were retained. Each of the dimensions time, estimated wind force, maximum and minimum estimated wind force were given a control component, even if this does not contribute to the answer. Each wind value could be restricted by sliders and particular days could be selected with a checkbox.

Questionnaire. Cognitive effort was examined by the SWAT (Subjective Workload Assessment Technique) definition of cognitive effort. This questionnaire tool considers cognitive effort as the amount of concentration (Q8) and automatism (Q13) required by a certain task [4]. The SWAT "cognitive load" subscale with its following items was included: Q7: "The visualization caused low cognitive effort." Q8: "Very little concentration was required to come to a decision." Q13: "Coming to a decision was quite automatic". Answers could be given on a 5-Point Likert scale (1 = "totally agree"). Additionally, demographic and usability questions had to be answered.

Participants. Participants (N = 146) were acquired in two different ways. One part was randomly selected from a research and non-research environment on 5 different locations on 5 different days. The arbitrariness with which participants walked into the experiment situation randomly assigned them to it. The other part was found by distributing the link of the experiment website on research and non-research platforms on the internet (Facebook, Twitter, Researchgate, LinkedIn, Xing) and sent to 4 mailing lists of the University of Amsterdam and at the national research institute for mathematics and computer science in the Netherlands (CWI). 107 participants (Interactive: n = 40, static: n = 33, table: n = 34) also filled in the questionnaire. 68 % of participants who filled in the questionnaire were male, 32 % were female, and they were highly educated (77 % University degree or PhD). 56 data experts and 45 data novices could be identified by participants self-reporting. The mean age was 29.3 years (SD = 4.3 years). Excluding defective entries and incomplete answers lead to a reduction of the sample size for some of the dependent variables.

5   Results

We define an effective and efficient visualization of uncertain data as a visualization leading to a correct decision in the shortest amount of time with least cognitive effort. We analyzed the task completion time, task error rate and cognitive effort for the table (TAB), static graphic (SG) and interactive graphic (IG).

Task Time. The average task time differs per visualization: It took participants with IG 2:19 min on average to come to a decision, while this was only 1:18 min with SG and 1:19 min with TAB. Overall, experts, including students working in research institutions and familiar with visualizations, completed the task faster with a time of 1:28 min than novices with 1:59 min.

A Kolmogorov-Smirnov (K-S) test after log transformation showed that the completion times of the interactive visualization [D(48) = 0.08, p > 0.05] the completion times of the static visualization [D(50) = 0.12, p > 0.05] and the table [D(47) = 0.07,

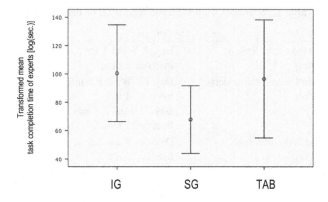

Fig. 3. Mean task completion time (in [log(sec.)]) of **experts** (n = 56) using an interactive visualization (IG, n = 21), a static visualization (SG, n = 21) and a table (TAB, n = 14).

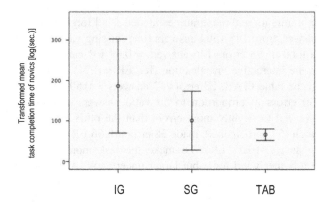

Fig. 4. Transformed mean task completion time [log(sec.)] of **novices** (n = 45) using an interactive visualization (IG, n = 17), a static visualization (SG, n = 9) and a table (TAB, n = 19).

$p > 0.05$] did not significantly deviate from normality. A one-way ANOVA was conducted to compare the effect of visualization types on task completion time. There was a significant effect of task completion time on visualization type for the three conditions [$F(2, 142) = 5.15$, $p < 0.05$]. This confirms our first hypothesis that there is significant difference in task completion time among the different uncertainty visualization types.

A K-S-test after log transformation showed that the task completion time of the experts [$D(56) = 0.08$, $p > 0.05$] and non-experts groups [$D(45) = 0.12$, $p > 0.05$] did not significantly deviate from normality. A one-way between subjects ANOVA was conducted to compare the effect of the group (expert/non-expert) on task completion time (Figs. 3 and 4). There was no significant effect of group on task completion time for the two conditions [$F(1, 99) = 0,85$, $p > 0.05$]. Due to the small group sizes formed by expert group per visualization type we did not test interaction effects.

Table 1. Scenarios used for the computation of the error rate

No	Decision	Options	Rating
1	Highest wind force, lowest uncertainty	Day 4: Wind 8 m/s, Interval: 2 m/s	Right
2	Higher wind force and moderate uncertainty	Day 13: Wind 8,5 m/s, Interval: 4 m/s Day 7: Wind 8,5 m/s, Interval: 3 m/s	Right
3	High wind force und low uncertainty.	Day 14: Wind 7,5 m/s, Interval: 5 m/s	Wrong
4	Low/moderate wind force and/or high uncertainty	Day 1, 2, 3, 5, 6, 8, 9, 10, 11, 12, different intervals	Wrong

Error Rate (ER). Error rates were computed for a strict definition of a right answer (only day 4) as well as for adding day 13 and 7 as the satisfactory right answers (see Table 1). Day 4 was defined as the day with the highest wind force and the lowest interval between minimum and maximum estimated wind force. If day 4 is considered the only right answer, from 145 valid answers (one missing value), 93 gave the wrong answer. Thus, a total of 93 errors/146 answers = 0.64 ER can be stated. Most errors were made with the interactive visualization (IG, ER = 0.74), while the fewest errors were made with the table (TAB, 28 errors/47 answers = 0.59 ER). The static visualization led to 30 errors in proportion to 50 valid answers and an ER of 0.6. The interactive graphic led to slightly more errors than the other two. Experts, including students in research (57 participants), made 38 errors (0.66 ER) while 23 of 45 novices gave the wrong answer (0.51 ER). To make the task more difficult, day 13 was introduced with a higher wind force but larger uncertainty. According to the original task definition it would be a wrong answer but when we consider it as an acceptable second solution we get a much lower error rate for all visualizations. Experts make fewer errors (0.14 ER) than novices (0.22 ER). Then, the interactive visualization would cause a 0.14 ER, the static graphic would have the highest score of 0.22 ER and the table would lead to a 0.19 ER. In order to test the differences error rate if day 4 is right/wrong, a Chi-square test was conducted. There was no significant difference between the type of visualization and whether or not the right answer was given $[X^2 (2) = 2.19, p > 0.5]$. Likewise, there was no significant difference between the different groups (expert/novice) and whether or not the right answer was given $[X^2 (1) = 2.93, p > 0.05]$. Even if day 13 and 7 were considered as right answers, no significant difference was found. *Therefore hypothesis 2 stating that there is a significant difference in errors between different uncertainty visualizations was rejected.*

Cognitive Load. Even if we selected a 3-item subscale of the SWAT questionnaire, these items (see Table 2) had a high reliability, with Cronbach's $\alpha = 0.691$. A K-S showed that all three items did significantly deviate from normality [Q7: $D(97) = 0.19$, $p < 0.001$, Q8: $D(97) = 0.18$, $p < 0.001$ and Q13: $D(97) = 0.21$, $p < 0.001$]. A non-parametric Kruskal-Wallis test found a significant difference in subjective cognitive load between visualization types [Q7: $H(2) = 7.39$, $p < 0.05$]. The effect of visualization type on subjectively perceived concentration was non-significant

Table 2. Mean values of cognitive load items (SWAT) depending on visualization type

	IG	SG	TAB
Q7: the visualization caused low cognitive effort	**2,55**	**2,48**	**3,62**
	n = 38	n = 29	n = 31
Q8: very little concentration was required to come to a decision	**3,00**	**2,55**	**3,18**
	n = 40	n = 29	n = 33
Q13: coming to a decision was quite automatic	**2,79**	**2,95**	**3,06**
	n = 38	n = 29	n = 32

[H (2) = 4.81, p > 0.05] as well as the item automation [Q 13: H (2) = 2.04, p > 0.05]. All three SWAT items together measure cognitive load. Two of them do not show significant difference. *We reject hypothesis 3, which assumes a significant difference regarding cognitive effort between the different types of visualizations.*

Qualitative Feedback. With the interactive visualization most participants used the average wind force slider to find the highest and then select the day with the lowest uncertainty interval without using other control elements (see Fig. 2). The following quote describes the most common procedure: "I sub-selected the three highest wind forces to see them more detailed, compared them and finally choose the one with the highest amount and possible highest prediction."Participants stated that not all controls are really useful for the decision but the one they used made the decision easier. Some would have preferred more explanation and feedback, especially when making unusual selections. The only feedback received given an unusual selection was an empty screen without values. Some participants also grounded their decision on the highest possible maximum value, which showed that they did not take uncertainty into account or did not understand the meaning of the different values. This was more often the case for novice users. Unfortunately the questionnaire only examined the thoughts not the interactions. In some cases it was not clear which, or whether, control elements were used. Colour, interactivity and filtering functions were perceived as the positive attributes of the visualization, while the amount of data was a negative aspect. Few people indicated that they found it difficult to perform the task without having sailing experience. A common thinking process reported by users of the static visualization is similar to the one of the interactive one: in the beginning participants try to understand the meaning of graphical elements by reading the legend. Then they seek out the highest mean values and examine the interval sizes. This process leads in most cases to the right answer. Most of the participants grounded their decision on comparing mean and maximum value of different days. This usually led to the answer of day 13. Most errors occurred as a result of comparing mean, minimum and maximum values independently from each other. While increasing the uncertainty of predictions located further into the future, experts often included this existing knowledge into their process of decision making. Especially when using the table visualization, participants tended to ignore the relationship between minimum and maximum values as an uncertainty interval. Often they started by selecting the highest minimum values and then proceeded by searching for not too high maximum values or just based their decision on the maximum value. For the table visualization, notably fewer participants describe the interval as influencing their decision. The typical cognitive process caused by the

Table 3. Summary table defining which visualization is best (+), worst (−) or in between (o) in terms of error, cognitive load and efficiency for all, experts (ex) and novices (nov).

	IG			SG			TAB		
	all	ex	nov	all	ex	nov	all	ex	nov
Error rate	o	+	o	+	−	o	+	o	o
Cognitive load	o	o	o	+	o	o	−	o	o
Time	−	o	o	+	o	−	+	o	+

interactive and static visualization (searching for the highest means and then deciding on interval size) was rarely documented in the table group. Apparently the table emphasizes independence of values and hides their relation to each other. Overall, it became clear that a majority of participants, especially from the non-researcher group, had problems understanding the concept of uncertainty even though it was briefly described in the introduction.

6 Summary and Future Work

We investigated the influence of three uncertainty visualizations on performance measures and cognitive load. The findings show that task completion time significantly differs per visualization. We found no significant differences in error rates depending on visualization type. Significant differences in explicitly mentioned cognitive load require further investigation. Considering Q7 as single indicator of cognitive load – which would not be in line with our initial hypothesis – would show that data visualizations produce lower subjectively perceived cognitive load than a numerical table representation. We then would recommend data visualizations instead of numeric tables for all cases where data comprehension should result in low cognitive effort. Using the interactive visualization was most time consuming and also leads to a slightly higher error rate than the static visualization and the table. Participants perceived the cognitive effort induced by the interactive visualization as slightly higher than for the SG, but still lower compared to the table. Users stated that the required concentration and automatism during decision making was neutral for IG. Perceiving these attributes is assumed to be difficult. Participants could complete the task most rapidly with the SG, while also making the fewest errors with the lowest cognitive effort. The amount of concentration needed with SG is the lowest. Slightly more time than with the static visualization had to be spent with the table (Table 3).

While the error rate was equal, the table leads to the highest cognitive effort, concentration and the lowest automatism. We found differences between experts and novices. Surprisingly, novices can complete a task much faster with a numerical table than with a SG, whereas experts are faster with a graphical visualization and much slower with a numeric table. Experts make the least mistakes with the interactive and the most with the static graphic visualizations. Novices make the least mistakes in the day 4 scenario with the static visualization. In the day 4 and 13 scenario, this surprisingly alters to the table visualization, while they are again better with the static one when also considering day 7 as a right answer. The number of participants per condition has to be considered in the context of these results. This also applies to the cognitive effort numbers between subjects. According to experts, a table requires both the most cognitive effort and concentration, and could be used with the lowest amount of automation. The static visualization scored best in all three categories. Similar, but less distinctive, results were achieved by novices. **On the basis of our results, we can state the best visualization in terms of task completion time, error rate and cognitive effort for data experts would be a static graphical visualization**. Even if experts complete tasks faster with a table this leads to higher error rates and cognitive effort (assuming that it is more worthwhile to make the right decisions than making them in the shortest period of time possible).

Given results affect visualization of uncertainty as those can be represented as table, interactive or static visualization, but as these characteristics are more a general visualization feature and not only related to the uncertainty, given findings might also apply for data visualizations without uncertainty. Future studies are required to find out whether our findings are also true for data visualization without uncertainty orwhether the results change with an interactive visualization with improved usability, which is more decision related. Moreover, since we found that a static visualization of uncertainty can be recommended to experts, it would be interesting to investigate the detailed attributes. It would be interesting to see if our findings also apply to other types of uncertainties or to analyze cognitive load measurements with objective measures like eye-tracking or pupil dilation or EEG.

Generalizing the findings to the point where designers can confidently rely on them during design decisions would require much more experiments with several datasets, user profiles, and visualization designs including different designs variants like colors, sizes, bar charts or line charts, interactive features, tables with/without heat maps or other graphical features etc.). And further work has to be done to investigate how those features need to be designed for different user types like e.g. elderly whose perception and cognitive functions change during life span. Present work is thus just one of the first struggles within ergonomic evaluations generating general recommendations to support design decisions in data and information visualization.

Acknowledgements.   This publication is part of the research project "TECH4AGE", funded by the German Federal Ministry of Education and Research (BMBF, Grant No. 16SV7111) supervised by the VDI/VDE Innovation + Technik GmbH.

References

1. Griethe, H., Schumann, H.: The visualization of uncertain data: methods and problems. In: Proceedings of Simulation and Visualization, Magdeburg (2006)
2. Pang, A.T., Wittenbrink, C.M., Lodha, S.K.: Approaches to uncertainty visualization. Vis. Comput. **13**, 370–390 (1997)
3. Skeels, M., Lee, B., Smith, G., Robertson, G.G.: Revealing uncertainty for information visualization. Inf. Vis. **9**(1), 70–81 (2010)

4. Bigelow, A., Drucker, S., Fisher, D., Meyer, M.: Reflections on how designers design with data. In: Proceedings of the 2014 International Working Conference on Advanced Visual Interfaces, pp. 17–24. ACM, May 2014
5. Chen, C.: Top 10 unsolved information visualization problems. IEEE Comput. Graph. Appl. **25**(4), 12–16 (2005)
6. Beauxis-Aussalet, E., Arslanova, E., Hardman, L., van Ossenbruggen, J.: A case study of trust issues in scientific video collections. In: Proceedings of the 2nd ACM International Workshop on Multimedia Analysis for Ecological Data (2013)
7. Beauxis-Aussalet, E., Arslanova, E., Hardman, L.: Supporting non-experts' awareness of uncertainty: negative effects of simple visualizations in multiple views. In: Proceedings of the European Conference on Cognitive Ergonomics 2015, p. 20. ACM, Warsaw (2015)
8. Beauxis-Aussalet, E., Hardman, L.: Simplifying the visualization of confusion matrix. In: BNAIC, November 2014
9. Ware, C.: Information Visualization: Perception for Design. Elsevier, Amsterdam (2012)
10. Sweller, J.: Cognitive load theory, learning difficulty, and instructional design. Learn. Instr. **4**(4), 295–312 (1994)
11. Anderson, E.W., Potter, K.C., Matzen, L.E., Shepherd, J.F., Preston, G.A., Silva, C.T.: A User study of visualization effectiveness using EEG and cognitive load. Comput. Graph. Forum **30**, 791–800 (2011). Blackwell Publishing Ltd.
12. Huang, W., Eades, P., Hong, S.-H.: Measuring effectiveness of graph visualizations: a cognitive load perspective. doi:10.1057/ivs.2009.10
13. Rogers, Y., Sharp, J., Preece, J.: Interaction Design: Beyond Human-Computer Interaction. Wiley, Hoboken (2011)
14. Nielsen, J.: The usability engineering life cycle. Computer **25**(3), 12–22 (1992)
15. Tory, M., Möller, T.: Human factors in visualization research. IEEE Trans. Vis. Comput. Graph. **10**, 72–84 (2004)
16. Badam, S.K., Fisher, E., Elmqvist, N.: Munin: a peer-to-peer middleware for ubiquitous analytics and visualization spaces. IEEE Trans. Vis. Comput. Graphi. **XX**(c), 1 (2014)
17. Kang, H., Shneiderman, B.: Visualization methods for personal photo collections: browsing and searching in the PhotoFinder. In: ICME 2000, 2000 IEEE International Conference on Multimedia and Expo, vol. 3, pp. 3:1539–3:1542 (2000)
18. Mullër, W., Schumann, H.: Visualization methods for time-dependent data-an overview. In: Proceedings of the 2003 Winter Simulation Conference, pp. 1:737–1:745. IEEE (2003)
19. Purchase, H.C., Andrienko, N., Jankun-Kelly, T.J., Ward, M.: Theoretical foundations of information visualization. In: Kerren, A., Stasko, J.T., Fekete, J.-D., North, C. (eds.) Information Visualization. LNCS, vol. 4950, pp. 46–64. Springer, Heidelberg (2008)
20. Wilkinson, L.: The Grammar of Graphics. Springer Science & Business Media, Berlin (2006)
21. KNMI, KNMI Verwachtingen, cited 13 July 2011. http://www.knmi.nl/waarschuwingen_en_verwachtingen/

Towards a Visual Data Language to Improve Insights into Complex Multidimensional Data

Jan Wojdziak[1(✉)], Bettina Kirchner[1], Dietrich Kammer[1],
Martin Herrmann[1], and Rainer Groh[2]

[1] Gesellschaft für Technische Visualistik, Dresden, Germany
Jan.wojdziak@visualistik.de
[2] Technische Universität Dresden, Dresden, Germany

Abstract. Data volume is increasing steadily. Visualization helps to handle not only the volume, but the ever increasing diversity of data. Visualization gives answers faster and reveals information that would go unnoticed and therefore unused in decision making. The challenge we address in this contribution is how visualizations can be created semi-automatic without taking the individual human-centered view of the designer on an interface out of the loop. In this paper, we present a tool-supported design process to develop aesthetic and interactive data visualizations in a conceptual, guided, effective way.

Keywords: Information design · Process model · Information visualization · Aesthetics · Tool-support design

1 Introduction

Every information visualization has a very basic need – the narration of a story. Over time, new ways to visualize information were developed. Today, almost everyone is familiar with basic chart types such as line chart or pie chart. Charts are applied to present large amounts of data more understandable than spreadsheets or textual reports. Current visual interfaces that deal with big data only show different charts and graph visualizations arranged in dashboards. Hence, the user has an increased cognitive challenge to merge the visualized datasets in order to get insights into complex information. Visualizations that combine multidimensional data can emphasize answers faster than dashboards and reveal information that would go unnoticed and therefore unused in common chart visualizations. Yet, the design of suitable visual representations of complex and multidimensional datasets requires expert knowledge. The information designer has to employ the right design principles to compose a meaningful story to clarify the complexity of datasets, explaining a process, highlighting a trend, or supporting a specific argument. In consequence, a complex interactive visualization requires months of work by highly skilled professionals. On the other hand, data visualization should be a quick and easy way to convey information. But, it should be remembered that poorly designed data representations can distort the intended message, lose the user's attention, or fail to guide them toward meaningful conclusions.

In this paper, we present a novel tool-supported approach for dealing with complex datasets apart from the well-established charting perspective. The addressed challenge

© Springer International Publishing Switzerland 2016
S. Yamamoto (Ed.): HIMI 2016, Part I, LNCS 9734, pp. 203–213, 2016.
DOI: 10.1007/978-3-319-40349-6_20

is to reduce development time for information visualization by providing tools of the trade to realize information design in a conceptual, guided, and effective way. Common libraries, framework and tools used to create visual interfaces currently lack an overall information design process that addresses a human-centered access to multidimensional data sets. Hence, designers and developers are constrained to a manual design process.

The aim is to enhance the design process by a guided process based on visualization tools. To this end, we present the ViDaLa approach, which is able to create beautifully looking information visualizations without the expert knowledge of software engineers and information designers.

2   Related Work

Information visualization is the representation of data in a graphical form. The concept of using images to understand data has been around for centuries, from maps and graphs in the 17th century to the invention of the pie chart in the early 1800s. Today, information visualization has become a rapidly evolving blend of business, science, and art that is defined as a "visual representations of the semantics, or meaning, of information.[…] information visualization typically deals with nonnumeric, nonspatial, and high-dimensional data." [1]. Designing information visualization can be described as the practice of presenting information in a way that fosters efficient and effective understanding of the fundamental dataset.

There is a vast variety of methods and approaches in information design such as visualization patterns [2], interaction pattern [3], design guidelines in visualization [4] and in interaction design [5]. In [6] Lau and van de Moere present a model that focus on aesthetics as a conceptual influence on the technical implementation of visualizations. It reveals information aesthetics as the conceptual link between information visualization and visualization art. Lang discusses in [7] the importance of aesthetic in visualizations related to its efficiency, whereas Kosara in [8] proposes a classification of several types of information visualization based on aesthetic criteria. Based on aesthetic criteria as well as patterns and guidelines, Fry describes in [9] the process of creating a data visualization in a very accessible way and introduces a tool that simplifies the computational process for beginners. Munzner defined in [10] a layer-based workflow for the design process of visualization and validation.

Among conceptual and theoretical approaches, there are different kinds of tools and visualization libraries available today. Visualization grammars as a declarative format for creating and saving interactive visualizations like Vega [11]. Graph libraries as a set of tools to display and layout interactive graphs, for instance chartist-js or chart.js as well as business intelligence software to create interactive analysis dashboards from any data source and publish them to analyze data, high performance for large data sources, wide device support, multiple sources, and easy publishing of functions e.g. [12].

In conclusion, there are many expert tools and libraries as well as specific methods available that are used to train professionals in the field of information design. Without such training and tool knowledge, it is almost impossible to design and create sophisticated information visualizations of multidimensional data.

3   Approach

This section outlines the concepts of our Visual Data Language (ViDaLa). ViDaLa is the process model to consolidate data into one collective, illustrative, and interactive visualization. Our conceptual model consists of six parts that are built on one another. The ViDaLa design process that is shown in Fig. 1 is based on the steps found in visualization design processes (cp. [9, 10, 13]).

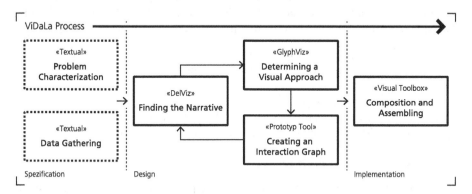

Fig. 1. ViDaLa design process starts with a specification stage, continues with an iterative design procedure and finishes with an implementation of an interactive information visualization.

3.1   Preliminary Considerations

As shown in the related work section, several models of the visualization process have outlined that there is no one way to create visualizations. There are many different paths through the process and most of them can produce useful results. The most remarkable characteristic of the process is that it is always explorative and iterative. The ViDaLa Process Model is intended to serve as a process template based on the conceptual layers of Munzners workflow for creating visualizations. The concept consists of four nested layers: characterize the task and data in the vocabulary of the problem domain, abstract into operations and data types, design visual encoding and interaction techniques, and create algorithms to execute techniques efficiently [10]. Our Process Model enriches the model, excepting the fourth layer by concrete methods and tools to help users to select appropriate design steps based on the intended usage. The following subsection describe these steps of the ViDaLa approach in detail.

3.2   Problem Characterization and Data Gathering

The first step of the ViDaLa process starts with a period of discovery. Preliminary questions should be asked to adequately develop a strategy for the information visualization in order to create a successful design that suits the needs. Only when domain challenges, user needs, and stakeholder requirements are analyzed during the early stage of the information design process, the whole development can be completed successfully and therefore create information designs that fulfil complex interweaved requirements.

In some situations, the story is well-established, but the required data are raw or messy. Similarly, the gathering of information requires additional research of randomly distributed data sources. User-centered methods for getting data and information can take different forms: surveying of users, obtaining data from existing APIs, conducting in-person interviews, or digging on network drives. This can easily be the most time-consuming part of the process. Yet, the full picture of the story is almost always assembled by multiple sources, not isolated in one dataset alone. The objective in this context is to retrieve data and information that answers the following aspects:

- Identify the quantity of data and datasets
- Find out the existing file formats and data sources and whether data need to be scraped
- Discover the complexity of the dataset
- Analyze the data set regarding to numerical range and dimensionality
- Find out if the structure of the dataset is directly usable or if it needs some restructuring
- Identify the quality of the data

In other cases, a visualization projects starts just with a dataset and the initial question is: "What is the best strategy to create a visual representation of the given dataset?" In that case, it is necessary to analyze the data in search of interesting stories and insights. Analyzing data may also require some data mining or statistics in order to come up with interesting insights. Developing a visualization strategy starts with a unique intent and an essential purpose. It might be clarifying a complex set of data, explaining a process, highlighting a trend, or supporting some kind of argument. Finding the narrative of the information visualization results from this challenge. With an existing and familiar dataset, the following basic conditions should be identified to develop a strategy:

- Identify the target audience
- Find out the type of content
- Discover time and place for the information visualization
- Analyze reasons for information need
- Identify the manner of use of the information

To discover necessary requirements and answering initial questions, different kinds of mind mapping tools as well as text editor tools can be used to quickly add records and notes to any part of the problem characterization as well as data gathering step and to reorganize aspects on the fly.

3.3 Finding the Narrative

After describing domain problems and data characteristics, additional design strategies will be applied in the process model to solve the identified problem. In almost any information design approach, there is a central aspect or fact that leads the story.

This piece of data or information will be the key element. If the element is identified, the objective is to organize data structure and story line as well as solidify the hierarchical structure of the information design. Storyboards focus on organizing, structuring, and identifying content in an effective and viable way. The determination of the story can be supported by creating personas and examining scenarios. The goal is to find user journeys to develop an information architecture. The user journey can be developed by merging the captured story pieces to create the larger picture, of how items relate to each other within the given context. The following questions will help to find the narrative:

- How does the designer categorize and structure information?
- How does the designer represent information?
- How does the user interact with information?
- How does the user search information and on which level of detail?

In order to create the story of the visualization, it is necessary to understand the correlations between users, content, and context. To address this problem, an exploration tool for existing information design was developed that illustrates characteristics of visualizations as well as the usage context. The software tool DelViz (Deep Exploration and Lookup of Visualizations) [14] supports searching for information visualizations from various points of view The application allows search and analysis in a collection of information visualizations. The data set used by DelViz currently contains 700 visualization projects which are characterized and stored with title, description, preview picture, and link to a demo of the information visualization or to a related website. DelViz is intended to support different search tasks: finding suitable information visualizations for a given context, and analysis of the underlying structured data set to discover relationships between the visualizations. Due to different search strategies, suitable visualizations and forms of depiction for the story can explored (Fig. 2).

At the end of this step, supporting elements, the level of visual detail to determine degree of interaction, the number of views, and type of views are identified and characterized to tell the story. This becomes a kind of mood board of story points and the picture of the final information design will begin to appear.

3.4   Determining a Visual Approach

After creating the storyboard with the aid of DelViz, the concrete data has to be turned into visuals. Creating a complex information design means evolving a visualization. For this purpose, visual representations for the dataset have to be discovered and determined to tell the given story. In this step of the ViDaLa process, it is an almost 1-to-1 relationship between data and visual representation.

Ware terms the basic building blocks of the visualization as "Preattentive Attributes" [15]. These attributes come into play when we determine the visual representation of data. For instance, position, and length can used to perceive quantitative data with precision. Other attributes are useful for perceiving other types of data such as categorical, or relational data. The choice of representation should address the simplest possible form that conveys the most relevant aspects of the data set. Whatever the case,

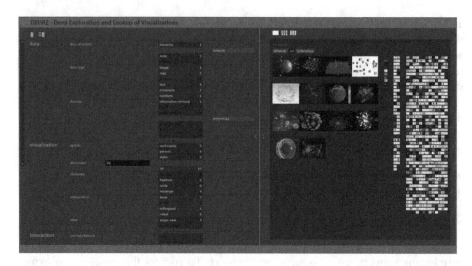

Fig. 2. DelViz interface for exploratory search. On the left-hand side the selected characteristics of information design are displayed, the right-hand side shows the resulting subset of visualizations.

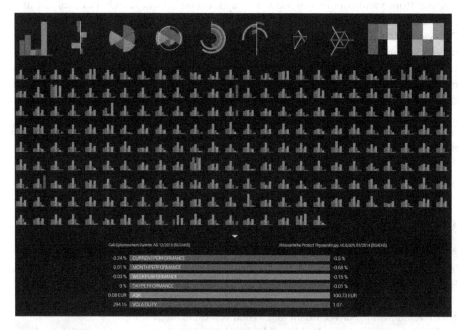

Fig. 3. Different variants of simple glyphs visualized with GlyphViz based on a finance dataset

this decision is guided by the data, which will lend itself to one visual form or a combination of several visual forms. In this design step, many intermediate visualizations have to be designed to end up with the final result. In every iteration, it has to be evaluated, whether the selected basic building blocks of the visualization works for the information design. It is hard to sketch out shape or forms without using real data. Hence, it is very important to walk through this ViDaLa step with real data. To address this problem, a software tool is used that is based on the concept of glyphs, a common form where a data set is depicted by a collection of visual representations [16]. Different properties of the data are depicted as different visual variables of a glyph. To address this challenge of determine the suitability of various visualization dependent on the dataset the GlyphViz was developed.

With GlyphViz different forms can be examined by a fast and flexible creation as well as adaption of glyphs (Fig. 3). Additionally, the tool provides sort functions according to similarity at a pre-selected data. This interactive tool supports decision making by depicting different representations of the data. These decisions should be well-founded due to design and aesthetics, but also based on the dataset and the story of the visualization.

3.5   Creating an Interaction Graph

Interactive data visualizations enable users to focus on interesting parts and details, to customize the content and even the graphical form, and to explore large amounts of data. Therefore, the change in the presentation of a data set fundamentally extends visualization capabilities. Interaction methods involve either how the data interacts with itself or how users can interact and control the data representation. In software, it is easy to provide many options to the user. Yet, it is more difficult, and more important to figure out an efficient and effective interaction in information visualization that is most relevant to the majority of the tasks executed by the majority of users. For instance, highlighting elements and showing details on demand are interactions that are useful for almost all data visualizations. Furthermore, assembling multiple representations in multiple views [17] and coordinating them clarifies different aspects of the data set at the same time. These are only some tangible quality standards for interactions in visualization as described in [4, 18, 19]. The benefit of such a configurable visualization is to display different structurally similar data sets that the user can interactively change. Additionally, when interactions are used in such a manner, an interactive visualization can make a much larger data set accessible than a comparable static graphic.

A software tool to support this ViDaLa step is still under development, yet focused on user-centered interaction within views, linking views as well as easily implement essential transitions and animations. Intended interactions will follow the guidelines of Shneiderman [4], the taxonomy of tools that support visualizations [20] and the seven general categories of interaction techniques described by Yi et al. [3]. Commercial tools such as Spotfire [21] and Tableau [22] provide examples of such interactions in visualization specification by drag-and-drop operations.

3.6   Composition and Assembling

The final stage of an interactive visualization is developed throughout this stage, but it is not only about the design. During this stage, the determined visual representations and the defined interactions are interweaved. During this implementation step, the designer builds with the assistance of the developer an understandable visual representation of the information and its hierarchy. It is an iterative process to realize the narrative of the visualization. In its first iteration it is not the final result, but a design to prove against the storyboard as well as visual elements and interactions. In the following iterations, improvements on the structure as well as refinements of the implemented strategy will take place. The ability for a designer to iterate based on the existing tools is the key to the semi-automatic information design. This might include the addition or removal of features, modification of the visual design, or the improvement of interactions.

The iteration-based implementation of the visualization is supported by our Visual Toolbox. The focus of this tool is to exploit the power and flexibility of the JavaScript visualization library D3 [23] in the user-centered information design of complex and multidimensional datasets. The information design technology is used to provide powerful information visualizations based on the process model of ViDaLa. The Visual Toolbox is an attempt to build re-usable visualization and interaction components for D3 without taking away the power of the library itself based on building blocks of interactive visualizations. The toolbox is a very recent collection of components, with the goal of keeping these components very customizable, staying away from standard chart solutions. It provides an editor based on graphical elements to fulfil the realization step and is currently maintained by a team of frontend software engineers at

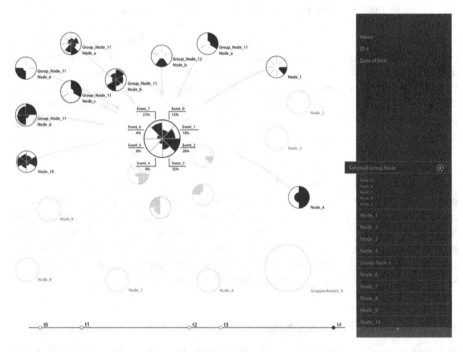

Fig. 4. Information design of the graph-based visualization of a patient model that depicts a detailed node (descriptions and probability of events) in the center of the graph and its relations to other nodes and group nodes as well as a menu on the right side to navigate within the network.

Gesellschaft für Technische Visualistik. The Visual Toolbox harnesses the power of visual intelligence to handle complex and multidimensional data and enables the user to shape them into an interactive visualization.

4 Case Study

To evaluate the ViDaLa design process, digital medical records of patients in a hospital setting were identified as a complex and multidimensional dataset (Fig. 4). The digital patient record consists of a large number of isolated data entries that are provided by various health information systems and medical devices. In order to transfer the digital patient and decision process model into real clinical applications, the ViDaLa process was applied and the digital medical records of patients were visualized in a graph based-visualization. In the context of interactive representations of clinical processes and information management, a user-intended categorization of information architecture was developed. It was decided to visualize digital patient records as a network visualization. A circle glyph combined with a pie chart is used to visualize data of the patient in a network graph to present dependencies, connections and hierarchies.

5 Conclusion

With this paper, we illustrated the importance of visualizing information in business units as well as in research and development. The presented ViDaLa approach constitutes a design process for interactive visualizations using a process model that is based on the analysis of given datasets and analysis of a given problem domain.

The presented tool chain is a consistent set of individual tools that are used to perform information design tasks to create an interactive visualization. In general, all of the ViDaLa tools are executed, however, not necessarily executed consecutively. Moreover, the Visual Toolbox contains a visualization library that consists of graphical elements that can be composed and arranged according to the goals of the visualization. The approach presented in this paper allows developers that are not specifically trained in design and information visualization to create visualizations, which assist users in exploring data in order to gain insights and information. Applying the ViDaLa process model, the development time due to a model-based approach can be reduced, while retaining customization of complex visualizations.

ViDaLa aims to make complex and multidimensional data more focused and more understandable for users via visualizations tools and visual analytics methods. The overall goal is to place a strong emphasis on quality over quantity, especially in the big data world. Visualizing data in an effective, creative way will provide more relevant, understandable information. ViDaLa will help to simplify the design process necessary to create visualizations that focus on the value for the end user.

6 Future Work

With the ViDaLa model as a tool-supported information design process, open research questions about the effective and efficient perception of information can be pursued with great ease. This semi-automatic design process offers possibilities to broaden the range of information design in the context of analytics and business intelligence. With the foundation of the current process model, the aim is to identify more criteria, methods, and techniques that can be integrated into the ViDaLa tools of the trade. Therefore, design and development of a concrete interface can be enhanced and the number of design iterations can be reduced. In addition, the software tools supporting the ViDaLa process model are subject to constant further development and maintenance. Ideally, the tools from specification to implementation form a toolchain that can be executed consecutively, by making the output of each tool or design step the input or starting environment for the next one.

References

1. Chen, C.: Top 10 unsolved information visualization problems. IEEE Comput. Graph. Appl. **25**, 12–16 (2005)
2. Heer, J., Agrawala, M.: Software design patterns for information visualization. IEEE Trans. Vis. Comput. Graph. 12(5), 853–860 (2006) doi:http://doi.ieeecomputersociety.org/10. 1109/TVCG.2006.178
3. Yi, J.S., Youn, K., Stasko, J.T., Jacko, J.A.: Toward a deeper understanding of the role of interaction in information visualization. IEEE Trans. Vis. Comput. Graph., 13, pp. 1224–1231 (2007) doi:10.1109/TVCG.2007.70515
4. Shneiderman, B.: The eyes have it: a task by data type taxonomy for information visualizations. In: Proceedings of IEEE Symposium on Visual Language, pp. 336–343. IEEE Computer Society Press (1996)
5. Borchers, J.O.: Interaction design patterns: twelve theses, pp. 1–6. Workshop Pattern Lang. Interact. Des. ACM Press, Hague, Netherlands (2000)
6. Lau, A., Vande Moere, A.: Towards a model of information aesthetics in information visualization. In: 11th International Conference on Information Visualization 2007 IV07, pp. 87–92. IEEE (2007)
7. Lang, A.: Aesthetics in information visualization. Trends Information Visualization, 8 (2009)
8. Kosara, R.: Visualization criticism-the missing link between information visualization and art. In: 11th International Conference on Information Visualization 2007 IV07, pp. 631–636. IEEE (2007)
9. Fry, B.J.: Computational information design. Massachusetts Institute of Technology (2004)
10. Munzner, T.: A nested model for visualization design and validation. IEEE Trans. Vis. Comput. Graph. **15**, 921–928 (2009)
11. Satyanarayan, A., Wongsuphasawat, K., Heer, J.: Declarative interaction design for data visualization. In: Proceedings of 27th Annual ACM Symposium User Interface Software Technology, pp. 669–678. ACM (2014)
12. García, M., Harmsen, B.: Qlikview 11 for Developers. Packt Publishing Ltd, Birmingham (2012)

13. Fry, B.: Visualizing Data, 1st edn. O'Reilly Media, Sebastopol (2008)
14. Keck, M., Kammer, D., Iwan, R., et al.: DelViz: exploration of tagged information visualizations. In: Interaktion und Visualisierung im Daten-Web (2011)
15. Ware, C.: Information Visualization. Perception for Design, 2. Auflage. Elsevier Ltd, Amsterdam (2004)
16. de Almeida Madeira Clemente, M., Keck, M., Groh, R.: TagStar: a glyph-based interface for indexing and visual analysis. In: Proceedings of 2014 International Working Conference on Advanced Visual Interfaces, pp. 357–358. ACM (2014)
17. North, C.L., Shneiderman, B.: A Taxonomy of Multiple Window Coordinations. Department of Computer Science, University of Maryland, USA (1997)
18. Shneiderman, B.: Designing the User Interface. Strategies for Effective Human-Computer Interaction, 4th edn. Addison-Wesley, Boston (2004)
19. Tidwell, J.: Interaction design patterns. In: Conference on Pattern Language Programming (1998)
20. Heer, J., Shneiderman, B.: Interactive dynamics for visual analysis. Queue **10**, 30 (2012)
21. Spotfire. http://spotfire.tibco.com/de/. Accessed 12 Feb 2016
22. Tableau. http://www.tableau.com
23. Bostock, M., Ogievetsky, V., Heer, J.: D3: Data-Driven Documents. IEEE Trans. Vis. Comp. Graph. Proc. InfoVis **17**, 2301–2309 (2011)

A Graphical System for Interactive Creation and Exploration of Dynamic Information Visualization

Jaqueline Zaia and João Luiz Bernardes Jr.[(⊠)]

Escola de Artes, Ciências e Humanidades, São Paulo, Brazil
{jaqueline.sousa, jbernardes}@usp.br

Abstract. Because of the growing amount of data available for analysis today, it is common to deal with large data sets, often too complex to be interpreted in their brute form. That is why Information Visualization techniques exist, to facilitate the analysis and interaction with data by humans through graphical abstractions. Motivated by the need to allow end users the autonomy to generate and edit visualizations according to their need, this work aims to underscore the importance of end user participation in the creation and support of these graphical abstractions of data. For this purpose, it is developed InterVis – a system for interactive creation of Information Visualizations based on dynamic data. The system is tested to verify whether this interactive creation of Information Visualizations, without programming, allied to the user knowledge of each application's domain, will be more efficient from the perspective of usability without significant loss of flexibility, as expected.

Keywords: Information visualization · Graphical User Interface (GUI) · Data abstraction

1 Introduction

In the last years, it is possible to notice a rapidly growing amount of data available for analysis, resulting not only from process automation but also from the increase in the data storage capacity [1]. Therefore, there is frequent need to deal with large, multidimensional datasets containing large volumes of data, often too complex to be interpreted in their brute form, and execute analytical and exploratory tasks to extract interesting patterns from them. Some of that information is easily understandable by humans when the right presentation is used. That is why plenty of Information Visualization (IV) techniques were developed, in order to provide tools to facilitate the analysis and interaction with data by humans through graphical abstractions and interaction metaphors [2]. Given the need to allow end users autonomy to generate and edit visualizations according to their need and independently of the nature of the information; this work aims to underscore the importance of end user participation in the creation and support of these graphical abstractions of data by providing a tool that supports the interactive creation of visualizations.

© Springer International Publishing Switzerland 2016
S. Yamamoto (Ed.): HIMI 2016, Part I, LNCS 9734, pp. 214–225, 2016.
DOI: 10.1007/978-3-319-40349-6_21

Despite information visualization tools often being indispensable to support data interpretation, there are still deterrents to their use. One of these is the difficulty of visualization development, which often requires advanced knowledge in both programming and math to construct the dynamic visualizations and, ideally, knowledge of the data's domain [3]. Other frequent problem is to find a reusable model in different application domains, since each particular subject demands different presentation layouts and interaction techniques to create successful visualizations [4]. Furthermore, in many cases it is important to preserve the privacy of part of the data, which may include sensitive information in the application's domain, such as personal or financial information [5].

As a solution for this problem, we have specified the graphical interactive system – InterVis – for the creation of interactive Information Visualizations based on dynamic data. Ideally, it does not require technical user knowledge either in information visualization techniques or in code production, being therefore well suited for use by domain experts. The system is tested to verify whether this interactive creation of Visualizations without programming, allied to user knowledge of application domain, is more efficient from the perspective of usability without significant loss of flexibility. To perform the usability test of InterVis, we use a public collection of data about population statistics from Geography and Statistic Brazilian Institute (IBGE) [6]. The volunteers are invited to execute tasks of visualization construction and a qualitative evaluation is made based on their experiences by the application of USE Questionnaire [7].

This paper is organized into sections on Fundamentals of IV and Related Work, followed by the description of InterVis and its Experimental Tests and Results.

2   Fundamentals of Information Visualization

The amount of data that can be shown textually for an average human to interpret is only about one hundred items, which is impracticable when dealing with data collections with millions of items [8]. The field of Information Visualization aims to facilitate the exploration of natural human visual perception and pattern recognition abilities to find and interpret information [9] by providing the communication of abstract data using visual interactive interfaces [10].

The way data is represented depends directly on which problems users are trying to solve, so the visualization can vary according to data types and their relationships [11]. As an example, time line visualizations [12] are ideal to describe personal history while graphs can be very effective in representing relationships [13].

Based on that, Shneiderman [11] proposes one of the most important concepts in Information Visualization, the mantra "Overview first, zoom and filter, then details-on-demand". Thus, in visualization, it is important not only to present information well at first but also to let users interact with it in effective ways to find what is necessary for them to execute a given task.

Another concept is the principle of transparency, which affirms that when the user focuses their energy in the task being executed, the tool seems to disappear [14]. In this context, we can say that the visualization should be noted as a data abstraction rather than a tool, which is the focus of user's attention and helps them to execute tasks and make decisions based on data.

2.1   Components of a Visualization

During the process of creating a visualization, the user has to decide between the diverse visual items and characteristics the visualization may be composed of to represent the data. For instance, each tuple is represented by a visual item in which its variables correspond to the visual item's appearance, such as shape, color, size and interaction function. In addition, we have a visualization, which is the space where related visual items are positioned according to a layout that abstracts their relationship. Lastly, there is the display, which combines one or more visualizations and other visual components; and enables the user to create interaction functions between them.

Keim [15] also classifies visualizations according to three criteria: data to be shown, the way information is laid out and the way users can interact with it.

Data Type. According to Shneiderman [11], data can be organized according to problems the user wants to solve. Therefore, he proposes a taxonomy of tasks by data type, where groups of data can be divided in categories that infer their dimension and relationships; they are uni-, bi- tri- and multi-dimensional data, temporal data, hierarchical data (trees) and relationships (graphs). Besides, data is made up of a number of items, with each one corresponding to an observation that can be represented for diverse dimensions [8]. If we analyze them individually, these variables can be classified as nominal, ordinal, quantitative and intervals [16], or simply as ordinal and quantitative, being at some level considered names and intervals if necessary [17].

Layout. Beyond the data dimension and format, another concept considered in the creation of a visualization is its visual dimension, limited by physical dimensions plus the dimension of time. For this reason, one of the challenges in Information Visualization is to use then the best way possible to represent abstract data. The result generally is bi- or tri-dimensional according to the resulting image; may be animated and allow interaction; and may contain other visual components such as legends, icons, menus and selection boxes [18] that give significance to characteristics of abstraction, such as colors and forms. Harger and Crossno [19] classify the visualizations' layout, similarly to the data classification given by Shneiderman [11], dividing the item's positions in Graph Layouts, Tree Layouts, Tabular Layouts and Georeferenced Layouts.

Interaction. In the context of HCI, interaction can be described as the communication between user and system [20]. Thus, in IV context we consider any way that enables the user to interact with visualization and manipulate data by means of a graphical interface with visual components as icons and figures, and textual components as search boxes, labels and filters [18]. Shneiderman also proposes the essential interaction ways in any IV tool based in seven tasks: overview, zoom, filter, details-on-demand, relate, history and extract [11], and describes models of combining interaction functions, such as zoom and pan, with display space, later evolved to focus

+context and overview+detail [21]. Those models aim to classify the visualization techniques based on the way the granularity levels of information are shown at the same time, providing a system that can answer user questions and allow the progressive refinement of data, known as hierarchical decision-making [11, 18, 22–24].

2.2   Architecture of Graphical User Interfaces

Because of the growth of application development demand, the number of different high-level GUI toolkits has also been increasing, which raises the discussion about how to use them more effectively in order to avoid code replication and provide more integrative systems. When we are dealing with toolkits to help with GUI generation, it is possible to note that, despite their effectiveness in the creation of traditional interfaces, they are insufficient when it is necessary to create interfaces with novel components. This creates the need to write plenty of code to personalize the solution, depending on the toolkit limitations, as is the case with Java Swing [25] and AWT [26], that support the creation of simple components, but is not helpful when a new component solution is necessary. Adobe Flash Builder [27] is a popular example that does not even support different external integrations [28].

For this purpose, Bederson et al. [28] presented the trend in which bi-dimensional toolkits are usually implemented in a more concrete structure and the objects tend to look more like real life. Still, tri-dimensional toolkits have their architectures generally based on specification trees to generate scene graphs. Thus, they exemplified those two architectures with the toolkits Jazz and Picollo. The architectures were called respectively Monolithic, defined as the ones that use primary inheritance in compilation time to extend a functionality, such as in Pad++ [29], Jazz [30, 31] and Swing [25]; and Polilithic, defined as the ones that use primary composition in execution time to extend a functionality, such as in VTK [32], Java 3D [33] and Open Inventor [34]. In Fig. 1 it is possible to observe an example of a fade rectangle, where (a) shows the class hierarchy in compilation time and (b) the runtime scene graph [28].

2.3   Usability

Another important question in IV that frequently does not receive enough attention is the usability of the tool to create the visualizations or of the visualizations themselves and the ways to interact with them. ISO defines this characteristic as the extent to which a product can be used by specified users to achieve specified goals with effectiveness, efficiency and satisfaction in a specified context of use [35]. One of the possible reasons is the particularity of each visualization which, to be properly assessed, may require specific knowledge and tests based on task type to be executed and data to be explored [36].

Information Visualization aims to explore the cognitive capability of human beings and give support to decision making by means of interactive visual interfaces [10]. Consequently, the usability, not only in interactive creation of IVs but also in visualization's exploration, is indispensable to develop the proposed solution.

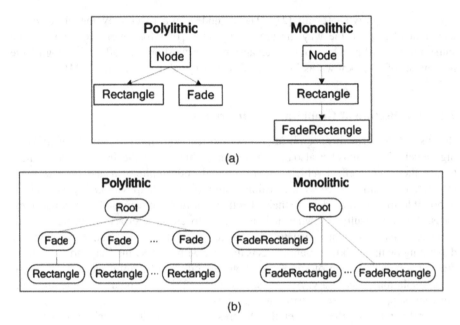

Fig. 1. Class and runtime hierarchies in polylithic and monolithic architectures proposed by Bederson et al. [28].

3   Related Work

Diverse IV techniques have been created to solve the problem of high dimensional massive data analysis. However, in general, those who create the visualization are not those who use it. While those who create the visualization should know how to abstract the data and to implement it, they often lack knowledge of the data or application domain. This makes the process of data abstraction and finding its best representation a more complex problem where the creator of the visualization not necessarily knows the problem nor the data.

In addition, it is possible to find two kinds of tools and libraries to create visualizations: the tools that demand technical knowledge implementing visualizations; and the tools that may have a visual and easy-to-use interface and only require application domain knowledge. The first kind generally provides several reusable components and predefined visualizations and forms of interaction, but requires considerable code production and customization to fulfill IV requirements for a single application. Examples of that are the toolkits VTK [32], InfoVis [37] and prefuse [3], which are fully rich with 2D and 3D visual resources such as different layouts and interactions, but cannot be used to explore data without before being customized.

On the other hand, tools such as TABLEAU [38] and its predecessor Polaris [17], ASK-GraphView [39] and OpenedEyes [40] offer an interactive interface that does not demand code creation or customization, but restrict the visualization by the application's resources and data types. It usually limits users to use the same static graphs or charts instead of allowing creation of dynamic Information Visualizations; and provides solutions only for a predetermined application's domain. In both cases, user autonomy to manipulate data is limited by the tool or application used and their knowledge about them.

In addition, with the increase of new IV techniques, there are a plenty of patterns, guidelines and criteria formulated especially to evaluate information visualization tools [41–44]. In general, these techniques are part of a user interface and include interaction patterns. However, since information visualization's role is to serve as a tool for data exploration, there are bigger issues involved in its evaluation, as the tasks to be accomplished, the users and the data context.

Besides that, since IV aims to support the exploration by users, the usability of the IV tool is one of the major points that requires evaluation in order to guarantee that it not only provides an effective exploration technique, but also a satisfying and easy-to-use interface in each task's context [43]. Following these lines, some works such as [45–49] include usability questionnaires, personal user's feedbacks, logs and observation of tasks.

4 InterVis

The purpose of the InterVis is to be a facilitator tool in the process of creation of Interactive Information Visualizations by users that do not necessarily have experience in programming or technical knowledge of Information Visualization but instead have good domain knowledge. It also aims to guarantee the privacy of raw data by providing a textual abstraction of data, as well as to explore user application domain knowledge during the creation of visualizations.

InterVis is based on a monolithic architecture, which relies on compilation time inheritance, in order to facilitate future extension of techniques, and allows the user to use static or dynamic data. Furthermore, the system's visualization and interaction techniques are mainly supported by prefuse [3].

4.1 Interface

The interface of InterVis works primarily in one of two modes: edition and visualization. Besides these two models, it is possible to configure dynamically the data sources and handle the created reports.

Edition Mode. The edition mode displays graphical tools to select data and associate it with aspects of the visualization (such as type, style, additional components like search boxes and legends) and interaction techniques (such as filters, zoom and pan, connection between two charts etc.). In Fig. 2, it is possible to observe the edition mode of a report. It is composed of a dataset panel, which shows datasets from available data sources to create the report and allows the user to drag and drop information in the visualizations; a preview panel, that generates a preview of how the report should look like; and a tools panel, where the report and their visualizations and interactions can be designed and configured.

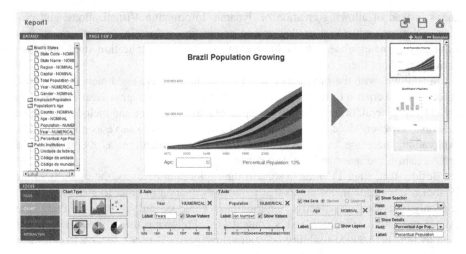

Fig. 2. Edition perspective of InterVis

Fig. 3. Exhibition perspective of InterVis

Exhibition Mode. On the other hand, the visualization mode simply allows interaction with the generated visualization, where the data and interaction tools are predetermined on the edition mode in the form of a slide presentation report, as shown in Fig. 3.

4.2 Data Sources

Users can load their own data in the tool or configure a source to import data from, so it can be dynamically explored according to their metadata. In addition, it is possible to use static data, which is saved with the reports, or dynamic data that reload according to data source updates. The source of data can be a tabular local file, a database configuration or a web service, according to user choice during report creation or edition.

5 Experimental Methodology

Usability is an important factor in software quality. For this reason, different patterns, guidelines and criteria have been created over the years due to the need for more usable interfaces [50]. However, IV tools face some problems when validating their interaction. One of the reasons is that visualizations depends directly on the context, the task to be executed and who is executing it [41], so traditional User Interface evaluation techniques may not be enough in the process of evaluation. Users need to look at data from different perspectives, which may require a long time. Besides, it is common that, during the exploration of visualizations, new questions are formulated and answered dynamically in a collaborative way, making it difficult to observe and measure this process of discovery [44].

Therefore, to validate InterVis, we describe a test in which the process of visualization creation is validated as a task instead of testing only data exploration and interface components per se. The principle is to validate not only the visualization generated, but also the system's tools to create it dynamically from scratch. That way, participants have a compound task, to validate the usability of the creation interface and of the visualization that results from it.

To validate the system's usability we apply the Questionnaire of Usefulness, Satisfaction and Ease of Use (USE) [7] in the end of the test, and collect the user's commentaries during the test, in order to map details of interaction and tasks in the user's viewpoint. The results are evaluated along with their previous comments and task completion, and intends to measure user experience in creating visualizations and not only exploring them.

6 Tests and Results

In order to validate the InfoVis, five participants were selected to represent the target population of likely users. The volunteer group includes system analysts that deal with diverse data contexts and have no specific knowledge in visualization development. The evaluation consists of a short test description followed by some adaptation time when the participants can freely explore the system and make questions. The participants are then encouraged to interact with the system interface and complete a number of compound tasks while describing their preferences and opinions about the experience. Each task takes approximately 15 min and is described as the creation of a new visualization from scratch based on a given dataset (public domain statistical information about Brazilian population provided by IBGE [6]). At the end of the tasks, participants answered the USE questionnaire [7] in order to record the experience from a usability point of view.

Users were asked to explore InterVis tools and use their intuition in choosing which resource would function better to complete each task. The reports resulting from tasks had different presentation according to each user, and it was observed that once a resource was used by some user at one task, the same resource tended to be used again in the following tasks. Despite that, all the users accomplished the task objective in the expected time.

Regarding our experiments, we noticed that despite the initial difficulties of users on the first tasks, their ability was progressive and growing even in just the short time allotted to the experiment, suggesting the system has good learnability. For instance, during the exploration phase users showed some doubts on where to start the visualization and drop the data dragged as well as in the buttons to edit a report and go to the initial page. In the case of the buttons, the default behavior of users was to look for them at the top of the window. However it does not usually take long time or repeats through the tasks.

Another characteristic mentioned is the visualization update when some configuration is changed. According to user reports, depending on what property is changed, it is not obvious what was updated in the visualization, or sometimes this update was not automatic and required saving the report to be applied.

Furthermore, we could observe some user difficulty in finding the data series and adding it to the visualization. There were frequent questions during the tasks about how to classify the data and create a legend. In addition, the section responsible for those resources was frequently the last area in the tools panel to be explored.

Based on the questionnaire results, we may conclude that despite InfoVis ease of use and satisfaction not having the most favorable evaluation, they were still above the expected. Usefulness and learnability were evaluated as pretty close to the ideal by users. We also received some interesting suggestions to implement, such as a filter based on intervals and a horizontal scroll on timelines to facilitate the zoom, resources that could make the visualization richer and more useful.

7   Conclusion

In this work, we describe a GUI for interactive creation of Information Visualizations from scratch and their dynamic exploration. The purpose is to provide a tool that allows the user to create dynamic report presentations without technical knowledge in neither programming nor direct contact with the raw data. In addition, the system's architecture is designed to support easy extension of functionalities and connection to new data sources.

A usability study was conduced using the USE Questionnaire [7] and user's descriptions. The results show that the system was considered above average in providing satisfaction and ease of user but that there is certainly room for further improvement in our tool, particularly regarding highlighting automatic updates, finding data series and creating legends. InfVis was evaluated as highly usable and easy to learn.

As next step, a deeper analysis could also show more gaps that were not explicit in this usability evaluation, such as performance and technical issues. In addition, a richer set of techniques and resources may improve the capacity of InterVis to attend different contexts, such as geographic and graph layouts, as well as different interaction and animation techniques. In spite of those improvements, InfoVis has succeeded in accomplishing the proposed objectives and give support to the easy manipulation of information visualization as expected.

References

1. Alencar, A.B.: Mineração e visualização de coleções de séries temporais. In: Tese de Doutorado. Instituto de Ciências Matemáticas e de Computação (2007)
2. Oliveira, M.C.F., Levkowitz, H.: From visual data exploration to visual data mining: a survey. IEEE Trans. Vis. Comput. Graph. **9**(3), 378–394 (2003)
3. Heer, J., Card, S.K., Landay, J.A.: Prefuse: a toolkit for interactive information visualization. In: Proceedings of the SIGCHI Conference on Human Factors in Computing Systems, pp. 421–430. ACM (2005)
4. Lee, B., et al.: How users interact with biodiversity information using TaxonTree. In: Proceedings of the Working Conference on Advanced Visual Interfaces, pp. 320–327. ACM (2004)
5. Dasgupta, A., Kosara, R.: Adaptive privacy-preserving visualization using parallel coordinates. IEEE Trans. Vis. Comput. Graph. **17**(12), 2241–2248 (2011)
6. Brazilian Institute of Geography and Statistic. http://www.ibge.gov.br/home/
7. Lund, A.M.: Measuring usability with the USE questionnaire. In: Usability Interface 8.2 (2001)
8. Keim, D., et al.: Information visualization and visual data mining. IEEE Trans. Vis. Comput. Graph. **8**(1), 1–8 (2002)
9. Kennedy, J., Mitchell, K., Barclay, P.J.: A framework for information visualisation. ACM SIGMOD Rec. **25**(4), 30–34 (1996)
10. Keim, D.A., Mansmann, F., Schneidewind, J., Ziegler, H.: Challenges in visual data analysis. In: Tenth International Conference on Information Visualization, IV 2006, pp. 9–16 (2006)
11. Shneiderman, B.: The eyes have it: a task by data type taxonomy for information visualizations. In: Proceedings of IEEE Symposium on Visual Languages. IEEE (1996)
12. Plaisant, C., Milash, B., Rose, A., Widoff, S., Shneiderman, B.: LifeLines: visualizing personal histories. In: Proceedings of the SIGCHI Conference on Human Factors in Computing Systems, pp. 221–227 (1996)
13. Gansner, E.R., Hu, Y., Kobourov, S.: GMap: visualizing graphs and clusters as maps. In: 2010 IEEE Pacific Visualization Symposium (PacificVis), pp. 201–208 (2010)
14. Rutkowski, C.: An introduction to the human applications standard computer interface. Byte **7**(10), 291–310 (1982)
15. Keim, D.A.: Visual exploration of large data sets. Commun. ACM **44**(8), 38–44 (2001)
16. Bertin, J.: Semiology of graphics: diagrams, networks, maps (1983)
17. Stolte, C., Tang, D., Hanrahan, P.: Polaris: a system for query, analysis, and visualization of multidimensional relational databases. IEEE Trans. Vis. Comput. Graph. **8**(1), 52–65 (2002)
18. Catarci, T., Costabile, M.F., Levialdi, S., Batini, C.: Visual query systems for databases: a survey. J. Vis. Lang. Comput. **8**(2), 215–260 (1997)
19. Harger, John R., Crossno, Patricia J.: Comparison of open-source visual analytics toolkits. In: IS&T/SPIE Electronic Imaging. International Society for Optics and Photonics (2012)
20. Yi, J.S., Ah Kang, Y., Stasko, J.T., Jacko, J.A.: Toward a deeper understanding of the role of interaction in information visualization. IEEE Trans. Vis. Comput. Graph. **13**(6), 1224–1231 (2007)

21. Plaisant, C., Carr, D., Shneiderman, B.: Image-browser taxonomy and guidelines for designers. IEEE Softw. **12**(2), 21–32 (1994)
22. Card, S.K., Mackinlay, J.D., Shneiderman, B.: Readings in Information Visualization: Using Vision to Think. Morgan Kaufmann, Burlington (1999)
23. Speier, C.: The influence of information presentation formats on complex task decision-making performance. Int. J. Hum Comput Stud. **64**(11), 1115–1131 (2006)
24. Few, S.: Information Dashboard Design, pp. 120–206. O'Reilly, Sebastopol (2006)
25. Eckstein, R., Loy, M., Wood, D.: Java Swing. O'Reilly & Associates Inc., Sebastopol (1998)
26. Zukowski, J.: Java AWT Reference, vol. 3. O'Reilly, Sebastopol (1997)
27. Gassner, D.: Flash Builder 4 and Flex 4 Bible, vol. 683. Wiley, Hoboken (2010)
28. Bederson, B.B., Grosjean, J., Meyer, J.: Toolkit design for interactive structured graphics. IEEE Trans. Softw. Eng. **30**(8), 535–546 (2004)
29. Bederson, B.B., Hollan, J.D.: Pad++: a zooming graphical interface for exploring alternate interface physics. In: Proceedings of the 7th Annual ACM Symposium on User Interface Software and Technology, pp. 17–26 (1994)
30. Bederson, B.B., McAlister, B.: Jazz: an extensible 2D+ zooming graphics toolkit in Java (1999)
31. Bederson, B.B., Meyer, J., Good, L.: Jazz: an extensible zoomable user interface graphics toolkit in Java. In: Proceedings of the 13th Annual ACM Symposium on User Interface Software and Technology, pp. 171–180 (2000)
32. Schroeder, W., Martin, K., Lorensen, B.: An Object-Oriented Approach To 3D Graphics, vol. 429. Prentice hall, Upper Saddle River (1997)
33. JAVA3D, Java 3D API, Java SE Desktop Technologies. http://www.oracle.com/technetwork/articles/javase/index-jsp-138252.html
34. Open Inventor, Silicon Graphics International Corp. http://www.sgi.com/software/inventor/
35. ISO/EIC (1998)
36. Freitas, C.M.D.S., Chubachi, O.M., Luzzardi, P.R.G., Cava, R.A.: Introdução à visualização de informações. Revista de informática teórica e aplicada. **8**(2), 143–158 (2001)
37. Fekete, J.: The infovis toolkit. In: IEEE Symposium on Information Visualization, INFOVIS 2004. IEEE (2004)
38. Tableau System. http://www.tableau.com/
39. Abello, J., Van Ham, F., Krishnan, N.: Ask-graphview: a large scale graph visualization system. IEEE Trans. Vis. Comput. Graph. **12**(5), 669–676 (2006)
40. Almeida, C., Apolinário, A.: OpenedEyes: developing an information visualization framework using web standards and open web technologies. In: Proceedings of the 18th Brazilian Symposium on Multimedia and the Web, pp. 59–66 (2012)
41. Granlund, A., Lafrenière, D., Carr, D.A.: A pattern-supported approach to the user interface design process. In: Proceedings of HCI International, vol. 1 (2001)
42. Plaisant, C.: The challenge of information visualization evaluation. In: Proceedings of the Working Conference on Advanced Visual Interfaces, pp. 109–116 (2004)
43. Luzzardi, P., Freitas, C.M.D.S., Cava, R., Duarte, G., Vasconcelos, M.: An extended set of ergonomic criteria for information visualization techniques. In: Proceedings of the 7th IASTED International Conference on Computer Graphics and Imaging, pp. 236–241 (2004)
44. Shneiderman, B., Plaisant, C.: Strategies for evaluating information visualization tools: multi-dimensional in-depth long-term case studies. In: Proceedings of the 2006 AVI Workshop on Beyond Time and Errors: Novel Evaluation Methods for Information Visualization, pp. 1–7 (2006)

45. Krishnamoorthy, S. North, C.: Learnability of interactive coordinated-view visualizations. In: Proceedings of Ninth International Conference on Information Visualisation, 2005, pp. 306–311. IEEE (2005)
46. Granitzer, M., Kienreich, W., Sabol, V., Andrews, K., Klieber, W.: Evaluating a system for interactive exploration of large, hierarchically structured document repositories. In: IEEE Symposium on Information Visualization, INFOVIS 2004, pp. 127–134. IEEE (2004)
47. North, C., Shneiderman, B.: Snap-together visualization: a user interface for coordinating visualizations via relational schemata. In: Proceedings of the Working Conference on Advanced Visual Interfaces, pp. 128–135 (2000)
48. Perez, C., De Antonio, A.: 3D visualization of text collections: an experimental study to assess the usefulness of 3D. In: Proceedings of the Eighth International Conference on Information Visualisation, 2004, IV 2004, pp. 317–323. IEEE (2004)
49. Vogel, B., Kurti, A., Milrad, M., Kerren, A.: An interactive web-based visualization tool in action: user testing and usability aspects. In: 2011 IEEE 11th International Conference on Computer and Information Technology (CIT), pp. 403–408. IEEE (2011)
50. Mariage, C., Vanderdonckt, J., Pribeanu, C.: State of the art of web usability guidelines. In: The handbook of Human Factors in Web Design, pp. 688–700 (2005)

Information Analytics, Discovery
and Exploration

Interactive Pattern Exploration: Securely Mining Distributed Databases

Priya Chawla$^{(\boxtimes)}$, Raj Bhatnagar, and Chia Han

EECS Department, University of Cincinnati, Cincinnati, USA
chawlapa@mail.uc.edu, {bhatnark,han}@ucmail.uc.edu

Abstract. Interactive patterns embedded and stored in multiple related databases can provide valuable insights into the domain of data exploration. Yet, the owners of individual databases may want to protect the privacy of their data while still allowing enough collaboration for the patterns to be discovered. In this paper, we show how data can be accessed securely through the use of data mining algorithms. We also investigate some methods that discover unique data patterns interactively, while still preserving data and user privacy, as much as possible.

Keywords: Privacy · Interaction · Security · Data · ID3 · Distributed

1 Introduction

Data mining algorithms can be designed to allow us to explore information within multiple independent databases in a secure and proper manner. In the emerging situations of multiple interrelated datasets, many data analysis problems require that these multiple databases be analyzed simultaneously but without any loss of data privacy. There are some algorithms that work with distributed databases to mine patterns embedded in their collective data sets. However, there is a need for algorithms that while mining also preserve data privacy and security. Thus, it is important to devise algorithms for distributed data mining and to create algorithms for mining single databases, while preserving privacy in an interactive manner.

Due to security and privacy concerns, owners of the data impose restrictions on their access; this added layer of protection hinders the collective exploration of datasets because sharing of data becomes limited. Thus, it becomes difficult to discover the valuable patterns of interest in the collective data. The solution to this resides in the design of smart, security-conscious and interactive data mining algorithms. This paper describes intuitive visualization capabilities and interactive strategies to create algorithms to connect patterns across different databases and find out the associations among various types of events and attributes, and utilizing intelligent agents to display the results of mining.

2 Summary of Relevant Research

Through understanding the existing work on the topic of data mining and visualization, we were able to design an efficient and secure algorithm.

© Springer International Publishing Switzerland 2016
S. Yamamoto (Ed.): HIMI 2016, Part I, LNCS 9734, pp. 229–237, 2016.
DOI: 10.1007/978-3-319-40349-6_22

In the paper on "Pattern Discovery in Distributed Databases" [1] we gain a better understanding of learning and pattern discovery algorithms that have been designed for environments in which all relevant data is not available at one network site. The paper goes into detail on this problem of distributed data mining and shows how to develop a decision tree to find meaningful patterns. Our approach takes this idea a step further by introducing the aspects of security and visualization in the decision tree induction process.

Another paper that examines the nature of privacy, the nature of data distribution, and the constraints of collaboration and cooperative computing presents some of the possible mechanisms for collaboration among data sets that we have adapted for our work [3]. This paper introduces tools to preserve privacy while dealing with distributed databases through using secure sum and secure set union techniques. In our research, we use these methods for the larger task of decision tree induction via interactive learning to ensure security and privacy for our datasets [3].

Another topic discussed in the literature is of using data perturbation for privacy preserving data mining. In this approach, permutations of data values are used to secure components of data. The researchers of this type of techniques use random data generation to encrypt and secure their data [9]. We do not adopt this perturbation technique because we want to retain the original data values in datasets, so that shared attribute tests for the decision trees can be discovered.

3   Example Scenarios

According to the National Institute of Health, 60 % of those patients who are seen by multiple physicians are more likely to have chronic visitations to hospitals, compared to those patients who consistently see the same physician [6]. Such associations are embedded in normally collected databases, but for their discovery they need collaboration among the data owned by hospitals, insurance companies, and physician's offices. Each of these data owners is bound by law to non-disclosure agreements, to keep their information about their patients private. Yet, since the patterns are defined over the populations without identifying individual patients, it is possible to develop data mining algorithms, in which we can have these databases exchange higher level summaries of patients and discover the population level patterns. Knowledge of such patterns in medical care datasets can significantly improve care mechanisms and also, reduce overall patient costs in the healthcare system [6].

In the context of healthcare domain, visualization of such patterns using graphically interactive platforms is very helpful. Using GUI frameworks to develop deeper analytical meanings of the medical care datasets can significantly improve care mechanisms and also, reduce overall patient costs in the healthcare system. Other real-world examples where this approach is valuable include, collections of sensor camera datasets for traffic assessment, collections of crime related datasets for improved policing and crime prevention and collections of banking and finance datasets for discovery of money laundering.

4   The Algorithm

In order to create a way to use secure communication with data summaries to perform an analysis of distributed data, we leveraged the original Iterative Dichotomiser 3 (ID3) algorithm [10] to develop our distributed ID3 algorithm, used for distributed datasets in multiple locations. Figure 1 compares the original ID3 algorithm, versus our developed "Distributed ID3" algorithm.

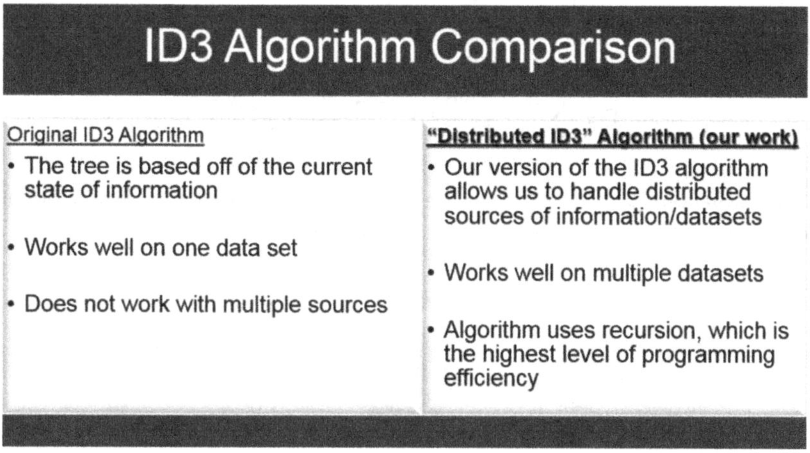

Fig. 1. Chart illustrates key differences between original and cited ID3 algorithm versus the developed ID3 algorithm for distributed data sets and spaces (Source: Monson Paper [10] – for original ID3 algorithm).

The distributed ID3 algorithm, developed by us, is a recursive algorithm that constructs a decision tree from multiple sources of information. The algorithm ensures that the information is encrypted through randomly generated numbers.

Distributed ID3 follows a series of steps, in order to compute the reduction in entropy for each candidate attribute:

1. The algorithm collects the frequency of each class at each component database and uses simple algebraic computations to determine the global frequency for the implicit join formed by the component databases.
2. We initiate from one of the databases all possible combinations of attribute values and class label combinations and send queries to the next database in a round-robin fashion to seek the local frequencies for the combinations. Each combination of attribute-value pairs and class labels sent to local databases is also referred to as a "search criterion" received by a database component.
3. These frequencies can be accumulated as the messages containing frequencies travel from one database to the other.

4. At the end of the cycle the computation can compute all frequencies, and the entropies, and thus the information gain of all the attributes. A choice for the best attribute for the decision tree can thus be made.
5. The process repeats until the decision tree construction needs to be continued.

Figure 2 demonstrates this flow of decisions made using the Distributed ID3 Algorithm.

The main computation that needs to be performed for each node of the decision trees is of the computation of the average entropy for each attribute in case it is to be used as the decision variable in the decision tree. The value of this average entropy is computed by Eq. 1:

$$E = \sum_{b=1}^{m} \left(\frac{Nb}{Nt}\right) \times \left(\sum_{c} \frac{Nbc}{Nb} log2 \frac{Nbc}{Nb}\right) \tag{1}$$

Thus, decisions are made based on the attribute with the highest amount of loss-of-entropy, that is, the most amount of information gain [5].

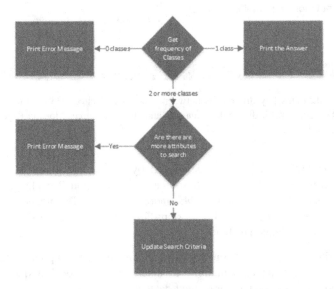

Fig. 2. Diagram explains decision making scheme for Distributed ID3 Algorithm (Source: developed using "Microsoft Publisher" toolkit [7]).

5   Data Compression

Traditionally, decision tree algorithms need all of the information present to construct a decision tree. However, in a distributed problem, this is not possible because of the large amounts of data present at various sites. To overcome this issue, the developed Distributed ID3 algorithm uses search criteria for collecting local frequencies as described above. The search criteria are received by each dataset to determine how many records match the search criteria. The search criteria are a list of values. To utilize real numbers, we split the decision on the average of the attribute from the parent result. An example search criterion would be "[['<', 15.20], [−1, None], ['>', 13.00], [−1, None]]". A dataset would receive this search criterion and check for all records where "column A" is less than 15.20 and where column greater than or equal to 13.00. The dataset would count the number of decisions that meet the search criteria and pass it to the next search query.

The size of the search criteria is computed through Eq. 2:

$$n\,(4\,bytes + 8\,bytes) \tag{2}$$

In Eq. 2, n represents the number of attributes in the dataset. The search criteria consist of either a char or int which is 4 bytes. The value is at most 8 bytes. This is scaled to the number of attributes.

The number of communication is described as m + 1. Where m is the number of devices in the infrastructure, the amount of time we query each database is at most 2^n, where n is the number of attributes in the dataset. This combines to a maximum of amount of data needed to construct a decision tree using Eq. 3, as shown below:

$$2 * (m + 1) * n(12\,bytes) \tag{3}$$

Thus, we can record the number of records that matched against the data with 8 bytes of information. The maximum number an 8-byte double is 1.7 * 10308. We will not exceed this number because 1 yottabyte is equivalent to 1 * 1024 bytes. It can be inferred that since, computers do not need to store data on the order of yottabytes, we can use 8 byte doubles to record the value needed to compress the data.

6 Security Implementation

The premise of the project is to ensure that the datasets are securely mined. In order to ensure this, we have developed the following security measure for our algorithm:

1. We cycle the search criteria for summaries among data sets in a round robin fashion. When the results leave the first database node, a random set of values is added to it. So, the real frequencies of attribute-value pairs in a dataset cannot be inferred by someone even if they capture the message.
2. Every database node in the round robin path adds its frequencies for the search criteria to the frequencies received from the previous node.
3. When the frequencies from all the nodes reach the original node, the random vector of values is subtracted to obtain the actual sums of frequencies.

Figure 3 describes the security aspect of the ID3 Distributed Algorithm in a real world application.

For instance, if we utilize the example of a medical researcher investigating how many patients have a certain symptom for a particular disease from different hospitals,

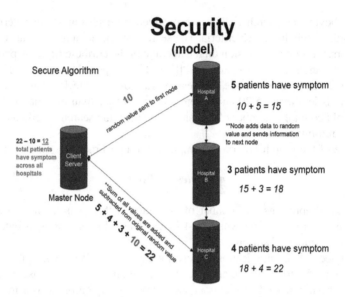

Fig. 3. Visually depicts securely mining information using a healthcare example (Source: example sketch developed for proof-of-concept scenario using "Microsoft Publisher" toolkit [7]).

we would need to ensure that the data is mined securely and does not violate any patient privacy laws. Thus, the researcher (client server) would send a random value to the first hospital's database. The first hospital would then add the number of patients with a certain symptom to the original random value. It would then send its number to the next hospital and so on, until all the values of each hospital dataset has been added to the original random value. The total number of patients with that disease would then be subtracted from the original random value. This will give the researcher the total number of patients with a particular symptom for the disease across all hospitals. Therefore, we have protected patient privacy in this situation, yet, also collected the information needed to relate to interesting demographic patterns.

7 Visualization and Pattern Interaction

To visualize the results of the project, decision trees were created and analyzed to match the projected results. Decision trees allow the users to interactively visualize results of a given pattern [12]. A decision tree consists of a root node, with n number of child nodes and m depth that results in a decision [8]. Our approach was to create decision tree at every step of the process allowing the user to better visualize the pattern interaction at every iterative step of the process. This allows for each decision to be clearly visualized in the decision tree model.

When using a relatively small dataset that consists of about 20 records and three different attributes, it was possible to check the information gain and loss of an expected result (Fig. 4).

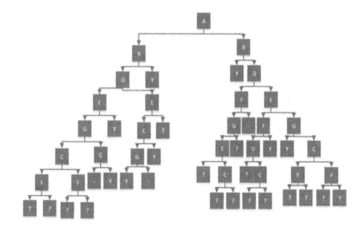

Fig. 4. Decision trees serve as visualization objects for validation of decision making patterns (Source: created using "Orange Data Mining Software Toolkit" [4]).

The notion of decision tree modeling has allowed us to expand the modeling of decision tree learning using heterogeneous datasets that are not stored in the same location [11]. This has allowed us to develop interactive models that allow the user to understand decisions being made in scenarios, in a visual manner.

An example of this type of interaction is the use of demographical case studies. In Fig. 3, we use a healthcare application for explaining the security interaction between datasets. Similarly, we can scale the results of the security model to a develop a decision tree diagram to find out which attributes are the most effective in any given real-life situation for a hospital dataset.

Additionally, the use of graphical user interfaces (GUI) help us to create visual platforms explaining the results of the decision tree models. Thus, allowing researchers to develop interactions and determine patterns in any given case study.

8   Results and Future Work

Essentially, we aimed to design an approach that mined patterns from distributed databases in a secure and privacy preserving manner. This resulted in an ability to connect patterns across different databases and find out the associations among various types of agents or databases.

As discussed in Sect. 4, the idea of visualizing decisions through information gain of an attribute is a critical to users because it gives us a more accurate approach to understanding which decisions and patterns are more meaningful. Through using Orange data mining toolkit, we found that visualizing each decision at each intermediate step is very beneficial to users because it allows us to clearly visualize how much information is being gained with each decision (as shown in Fig. 5).

The results of this research not only helped us to identify and visualize demographic patterns in multiple types of data, but it also allowed us to reduce the incidence of some undesirable events by recognizing their implications based on their associated events.

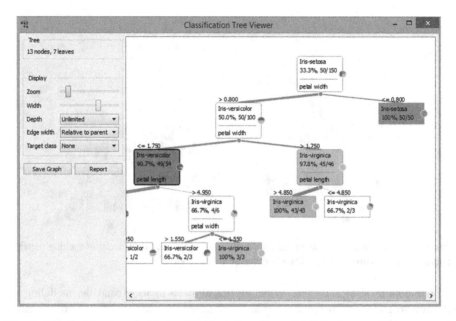

Fig. 5. This decision tree model visualizes the information gain of the plant-petal dataset at each intermediate step. The results of this decision tree model can be applied to research in the area of genetic plant mutations. (Source: screenshots section of "Orange Data Mining Software Toolkit" [4]) (Color figure online).

Further research in the realm of distributed data mining to find interactive patterns can be done using multi-agent bidding approaches [2], while, incorporating additional GUI features to enhance pattern recognition.

9   Conclusion

The broader aim of this research was to find patterns in distributed databases, such that the privacy and security of the participating data is preserved and clearly visualized. The future goals of this type of research are to continue testing the application of the data mining algorithms discovered on real-world datasets to gain collective knowledge and discover patterns in a variety of domains. Ultimately, this research allows us to securely mine datasets in fields such as, medicine, genetics, finance and law while, also maintaining ethical and social concerns of sharing data across multiple owners in an interactive and security-conscious manner.

Acknowledgements. The research was supported in part by the National Science Foundation through the REU program (2013–2014) at the University of Cincinnati. We are also thankful to the reviewers for providing useful comments.

References

1. Bhatnagar, R., Srinivasan, S.: Pattern discovery in distributed databases. In: American Association for Artificial Intelligence (1997)
2. Chattopadhyay, D.: Distributed decision tree induction using multi-agent based negotiation protocol. Electronic thesis or dissertation. University of Cincinnati, OhioLINK Electronic Theses and Dissertations Center (2014)
3. Clifton, C., et al.: Tools for privacy preserving distributed data mining. ACM Sigkdd Explor. Newsl. **4**(2), 28–34 (2002)
4. Demsar, J., Curk, T., Erjavec, A., Gorup, C., Hocevar, T., Milutinovic, M., Mozina, M., Polajnar, M., Toplak, M., Staric, A., Stajdohar, M., Umek, L., Zagar, L., Zbontar, J., Zitnik, M., Zupan, B.: Orange: data mining toolbox in python. J. Mach. Learn. Res. **14**, 2349–2353 (2013)
5. Follmer, H.: On entropy and information gain in random fields. Probab. Theor. Relat. Fields **26**(3), 207–217 (1973). Springer-Verlag
6. Hsiao, C.J., Cherry, D.K., Rechtsteiner, E.A.: Medical care survey. Centers for Disease Control and Prevention. Centers for Disease Control and Prevention (2013)
7. Glinert-Stevens, S.: Microsoft publisher: desktop wizardry. Pc Sources **3**(2), 357 (1992)
8. Kim, H., Koehler, G.J.: Theory and practice of decision tree induction. Omega **23**(6), 637–652 (1995)
9. Liu, K., Kargupta, H., Ryan, J.: Random projection-based multiplicative data perturbation for privacy preserving distributed data mining. IEEE Trans. Knowl. Data Eng. **18**(1), 92–106 (2006)
10. Monson, L.: Dr Dobb's Journal-Software Tools for the Professional Programmer 22(10), pp. 117–120 (1997)
11. Olsen, T.C.: Distributed Decision Tree Learning from Multiple Heterogeneous Data Sources (2006)
12. Quinlan, J.R.: Induction of decision trees. Mach. Learn. **1**(1), 81–106 (1986)

Effect of Heuristics on Serendipity in Path-Based Storytelling with Linked Data

Laurens De Vocht[1(✉)], Christian Beecks[2], Ruben Verborgh[1], Erik Mannens[1], Thomas Seidl[2], and Rik Van de Walle[1]

[1] Department of Electronics and Information Systems, Ghent University - iMinds,
Sint-Pietersnieuwstraat 41 B1,
9050 Ghent, Belgium
{laurens.devocht,ruben.verborgh,erik.mannens,rik.vandewalle}@ugent.be
[2] Data Management and Data Exploration Group, RWTH Aachen University,
Department of Computer Science 9, 52056 Aachen, Germany
{beecks,seidl}@cs.rwth-aachen.de

Abstract. Path-based storytelling with Linked Data on the Web provides users the ability to discover concepts in an entertaining and educational way. Given a query context, many state-of-the-art pathfinding approaches aim at telling a story that coincides with the user's expectations by investigating paths over Linked Data on the Web. By taking into account serendipity in storytelling, we aim at improving and tailoring existing approaches towards better fitting user expectations so that users are able to discover interesting knowledge without feeling unsure or even lost in the story facts. To this end, we propose to optimize the link estimation between - and the selection of facts in a story by increasing the consistency and relevancy of links between facts through additional domain delineation and refinement steps. In order to address multiple aspects of serendipity, we propose and investigate combinations of weights and heuristics in paths forming the essential building blocks for each story. Our experimental findings with stories based on DBpedia indicate the improvements when applying the optimized algorithm.

Keywords: Storytelling · Serendipity · Pathfinding · A* · Linked data · Heuristics

1 Introduction

Algorithmic storytelling can be seen as a particular kind of querying data. Given a set of keywords or entities, which are typically, but not necessarily dissimilar, it aims at generating a story by explicitly relating the query context with a path that includes semantically related resources. Storytelling is utilized for example in entertaining applications and visualizations [21] in order to enrich related Linked Data resources with data from multimedia archives and social media [9] as well as in scientific research fields such as bio-informatics where biologists try

© Springer International Publishing Switzerland 2016
S. Yamamoto (Ed.): HIMI 2016, Part I, LNCS 9734, pp. 238–251, 2016.
DOI: 10.1007/978-3-319-40349-6_23

to relate sets of genes arising from different experiments by investigating the implicated pathways [16] or discovering stories through linked books [7].

The aspects that make a story a good story are captured in the term *serendipity*. The term depicts a mixture between casual, lucky, helpful and unforeseen facts, also in an information context [11]. In fact, users want to be surprised and they want to discover, confirm, and extend knowledge - but not feel unsure while doing so. This means that users can always relate presented story facts to their background knowledge.

In order to generate a story, graph-based pathfinding approaches are typically utilized. The most frequently encountered algorithm to determine a path between multiple resources is the A* algorithm [14]. This algorithm, which is based on a graph representation of the underlying data (i.e., resources and links between them define nodes and edges, respectively) determines an optimal solution in form of a lowest-cost traversable path between two resources. The optimality of a path, which is guaranteed by the A* algorithm, does not necessarily comply with the users' expectations.

By considering for instance large real-world semantic graphs, such as Linked Data graphs, where links between nodes are semantically annotated, users are able to directly interpret the transitions between nodes and thus the meaning of a path. Caused by the inevitable increasing number of nodes and sometimes loosely related links among them, optimal paths frequently show a high extent of *arbitrariness*: paths appear to be determined by chance and not by reason or principle and are often affected by resources that share many links. In addition, large real-world semantic graphs typically exhibit small-world properties. Applying pathfinding approaches increases arbitrariness due to the large number of possible relations that connect two entities in a query context.

In order optimize the serendipity level of the storytelling and to mitigate arbitrariness of a story, we propose an in-depth extension of our algorithm [8], embedded in the Everything is Connected Engine (EiCE) [9]. In fact, our contribution is twofold: (i) We outline the extended algorithm which reduces arbitrariness by increasing the relevance of links between nodes through additional pre-selection and refinement steps; and (ii) we discuss the reorganization of code execution between client and server utilizing Linked Data Fragments. We conclude our paper with preliminary results and an outlook on future work.

2   Related Work

We divide related work into two categories: (i) retrieving associations, and (ii) ranking associations. The former category considers approaches for retrieving semantic associations, with a particular focus on paths, while the latter category considers methods to rank semantic associations.

Retrieving Associations. The original implementation[1] of the "Everything is Connected Engine" (EiCE) [9] uses a distance metric based on the Jaccard for

---

[1] http://demo.everythingisconnected.be/.

pathfinding. It applies the measure to estimate the similarity between two nodes and to assign a random-walk based weight, which ranks more rare resources higher, thereby guaranteeing that paths between resources prefer specific relations over general ones [18]. The A* algorithm is applied for revealing relations between Linked Data resources to recombine data from multimedia archives and social media for storytelling. In contrast to the EiCE system, which heuristically optimizes the choice of relationship explanations, the REX system [10] identifies a ranked list of relationship explanations. A slightly different approach with the same goal of exploratory association search is Explass [5]. It provides a flat list (top-K) clusters and facet values for refocusing and refining a search. The approach detects clusters by running pattern matches on the datasets to compute frequent, informative and small overlapping patterns [5]. All of these approaches where investigated on DBpedia.

Ranking Associations. The number of possible combinations to fill in the bridging resources between entities in the a knowledge base such as DBpedia is much larger than the number of entities themselves. Thus, the likelihood that this type of queries would result in an overwhelming number of possible results for users is increased. Furthermore, it is unlikely that traditional ranking schemes for ranking results may be applied to a graph representation [4]. Ranking semantic associations is different from ranking documents. In general, document ranking according to relevance focuses on the match degree of search keywords (without formal semantics). When ranking semantic associations, approaches semantically reinterpret query results in relation to the query context by using semantic distance (or similarity) to the datasets or search graph. Alternatively, a ranking can vary from rare relationships discovery mode to common relationships in conventional mode [3]. Techniques that support context driven ranking take into account ontological relations of the result instances in respect to the query context [2].

3   Pathfinding for Storytelling

Each path that contributes to a story is determined within a query context comprising both start and destination resources. Our algorithm reduces the arbitrariness of a path between these resources by increasing the *relevance* of the links between the nodes using a domain-delineation step. The path is refined by iteratively applying the A* algorithm and with each iteration attempting to improve the overall semantic relatedness between the resources until a fixed number of iterations or a certain similarity threshold is reached.

3.1   Domain Delineation

Instead of directly initializing the graph as-is by including all links between the resources, we identify the relevance of predicates with respect to the query context. This is done by extracting and giving higher preference to the type of relations (predicates) that occur frequently in the query context. In this way, we make sure that the links included in the story matter because each predicate

Data: start, destination, graph, k
Result: list of important predicates given the context
initialize pf_irf_p_list;
predicates_start = unique predicates start;
predicates_dest = unique predicates destination;
predicates_considered = intersection predicates_start predicates_dest;
foreach *predicates_considered as p* **do**
  | pf_irf_p = compute pf_irf p;
  | add pf_irf_p to list
end
reverse sort pf_irf_p_list;
take the first k elements of the list as important predicated;

Algorithm 1. Important predicate selection

that describes the semantics of a link also occurs in the direct neighborhood of the query context. The selection of the most important predicates for domain delineation is shown in Algorithm 1.

In order to select the links in a graph that are most relevant based on the given start and destination nodes, we utilize an adapted variant of the TF/IDF [1] measure: PF/IRF. The PF/IRF measure reflects the importance of a predicate with respect to a resource in a dataset and is defined as follows:

$$PF(p) = \frac{\text{Number of times predicate } \mathbf{p} \text{ appears in a resource}}{\text{Total number of predicates linked to the resource}} \quad (1)$$

$$IRF(p) = \ln \frac{\text{Total number of resources}}{\text{Number of resources with predicate } \mathbf{p} \text{ in it}} \quad (2)$$

For example, the PF/IRF computation for predicates linked to *Carl Linnaeus* is explained below for the case when PF/IRF is determined in the context of start *Carl Linnaeus* and destination *Charles Darwin* based on DBpedia.

1. We determine predicates that are important in the context. This is done by retrieving the distinct predicates that are linked to the context nodes.
2. For each predicate, we compute its occurrence based on linked nodes. In addition, the total number of predicates linked to the resource *Carl Linnaeus* is determined.
3. As a result, the total number of predicates linked to the resource *Carl Linnaeus* is 9890. For the predicates *binomialAuthority* and *label* we obtain the values 2297 and 12, respectively. The total number of resources (including objects) in the DBpedia is $M = 27,318,782$.
4. We compute the number of resources which are linked using each predicate by counting the distinct number of resources through the predicate *binomialAuthority* and *label* in both directions. This results in $155,207$ and $10,471,330$ respectively.
5. By using the PF/IRF formula above we finally get the following values: PF/IRF(*binomialAuthority*) = $2297/9890 * \ln(27,318,782/155,207) = \mathbf{1.20}$ and PF/IRF(*label*) = $12/9890 * \ln(27,318,782/10,471,330) = \mathbf{0.0011}$

Since the PF/IRF value of *binomialAuthority* is much higher than that of *label*, the predicate *binomialAuthority* is more likely to be included.

3.2   Algorithm

The output of the aforementioned domain delineation step can be thought of a Linked Data graph comprising nodes and predicates which are semantically related to the user's query context. In order to provide a serendipitous story based on this Linked Data graph, the graph has to be traversed via a meaningful path including the start and end destination of the query context. A single or multiple paths are then used as essential building blocks for generating a story.

In order to find a path in a Linked Data graph, we utilize the A* algorithm due to its ability of computing an optimal solution, i.e., a (shortest) cost-minimal path between two nodes with respect to the weights of the linking predicates contained in the path. In order to reduce the number of predicates to be examined when computing the lowest-cost path between two nodes and, thus, to achieve an improvement in the computation time of the A* algorithm, heuristics are frequently used to determine the order of expansion of the nodes according to the start and end node provided within the query context. In addition to a heuristic, the A* algorithm utilizes a weighting function in order to determine paths which are semantically related to source and destination nodes as specified within the query context. Thus, the serendipity of a story generated based on a single or multiple paths is strongly connected to the underlying weighting scheme and heuristic. In the following section, we propose and investigate various heuristics before we will introduce different weighting schemes.

3.3   Heuristics

The objective of a heuristic is to determine whether a node in a Linked Data graph is semantically related to the query context, i.e. source and destination nodes, and thus a good choice for expansion within the A* algorithm. For this purpose, we formally define a heuristic as a function $heuristic : G \times G \to \mathbb{R}$ that assigns all pairs of nodes $n_a, n_b \in G$ from a Linked Data graph G a real-valued number indicating their semantic relation.

Jaccard Distance. The first heuristic we consider is the **Jaccard distance** which is a simple statistical approach taking into account the relative number of common predicates of two nodes. The higher the number of common predicates, the more likely similar properties of the nodes and thus the semantically closer in terms of distance the corresponding nodes. The Jaccard distance $jaccard : G \times G \to \mathbb{R}$ is defined for all nodes $n_a, n_b \in G$ as follows:

$$jaccard(n_a, n_b) = 1 - \frac{\|n_a \cap n_b\|}{\|n_a \cup n_b\|} \tag{3}$$

Normalized DBpedia Distance. Another approach that can be utilized as a heuristic is the **Normalized DBpedia Distance** [13,19]. This approach adapts the idea of the Normalized Web Distance to DBpedia and considers two nodes n_a and n_b to be semantically similar if they share a high number of common neighboring nodes linking to both n_a and n_b. The Normalized DBpedia Distance $NDD : G \times G \rightarrow \mathbb{R}$ is defined for all nodes $n_a, n_b \in G$ as

$$NDD(n_a, n_b) = \frac{\max(\log f(n_a), \log f(n_b)) - \log f(n_a, n_b)}{\log N - \min(\log f(n_a), f(n_b))}, \qquad (4)$$

where $f(n) \in \mathbb{N}$ denotes the number of DBpedia nodes linking to node $n \in G$, $f(n, m) \in \mathbb{N}$ denotes the number of DBpedia nodes linking to both nodes n and $m \in G$, and where the constant N is defined as the total number of nodes in DBpedia, which is about $2.5M$.

Confidence. Another heuristic that has been proposed for semantic path search in Wikipedia is the **Confidence measure** [12]. The Confidence measure is an asymmetrical statistical measure that can be thought of as the probability that node n_a occurs provided that node n_b has already occurred. The Confidence measure $P : G \times G \rightarrow \mathbb{R}$ is defined for all nodes $n_a, n_b \in G$ as:

$$P(n_a|n_b) = \frac{f(n_a, n_b)}{f(n_b)} \qquad (5)$$

As opposed to the heuristics, which affect the expansion order within the A* algorithm by estimating the potential semantic relatedness of a node, weighting schemes are finally utilized in order to asses the quality of a path. We propose different weighting schemes in the following section.

3.4   Weights

The objective of a weighting function is to determine the exact cost of a path, which is the sum of weights of linking nodes. A weighting is formalized as a function $weight : G \times G \rightarrow \mathbb{R}$ between the corresponding nodes from the Linked Data graph.

Jaccard Distance. We apply the **Jaccard distance** in exactly the same way to determine the weights so that the core algorithm prefers similarity in adjacent nodes in each path. We use this distance between two directly adjacent nodes rather than unconnected nodes in the graph.

Combined Node Degree. Moore et al. [18] proposed the **combined node degree** which can be used to compute a weight that encourages rarity of items in a path. It ranks more rare resources higher, thereby guaranteeing that paths between resources prefer specific relations. The main idea is to avoid that paths go via generic nodes. It makes use of the node degree, the number of in and outgoing links. The combined node degree $w : G \times G \rightarrow \mathbb{R}$ is defined for all nodes $n_a, n_b \in G$ as:

$$w(n_a, n_b) = \log(\deg(n_a)) + \log(\deg(n_b)) \qquad (6)$$

Jiang and Conrath Distance. Mazuel and Sabouret [17] suggest to take into account the object property ontology relation between two adjacent items in a path. The base distance measure there is the **Jiang and Conrath distance** [15], which we can interpret in terms of RDF by looking at the classes of each of the nodes and determining the most common denominator of those classes in the ontology. Once this type is determined, the number of subjects that exist with this type is divided by the total number of subjects. The higher this number, the more generic the class, thus the more different two nodes.

3.5 Refinement

After a path is determined by the A* algorithm, we measure the semantic related-ness, corresponding to the lowest semantic distance between all resources occur-ring in the path with respect to the query context. This done for example by counting the number of overlapping predicates (i) among each other combined with those in the start and destination resources; and then (ii) averaging and normalizing this count over all resources. Depending on the threshold and the maximum number of iterations configured, this process is repeated, typically between 3 and 10 times. Finally, the path with the shortest total *distance* (or cost) is selected for the story. The *distance* for a *path* $= (s_1, s_2, ..., s_n)$ is computed based on a weight function w as distance$(path) = \frac{\sum_1^{n-1} w(s_i, s_{i+1})}{n}$.

4 Implementation and Presentation of Stories

The complexity of this approach is enforced by is the centrality of underly-ing graph-indexing and data-processing algorithms. It turns out that server-side query processing degrades the performance of a server and therefore limits its *scalability*. While many approaches are suitable for a small-to-moderate number of clients, they reveal to be a performance bottleneck when the number of clients is increased.

Instead of running the algorithm entirely on the server, we moved CPU and memory intensive tasks to the client. The server translates user queries into smaller, digestible fragments for the data endpoint. All optimizations and the execution of the algorithm are moved to the client. This has two benefits: (i) the CPU and memory bottleneck at server side is reduced; and (ii) the more complex data fragments to be translated stay on the server even though they do not require much CPU and memory resources, but they would introduce to many client-side requests.

A separate index with linked data documents to store the fragments for fast navigating graphs served a first iteration but turned out to be only lim-ited scalable. It required each time a pre-selection of datasets that would need to be manually or semi automatically scheduled to be ingested or updated. The improved algorithm[2] runs using Triple Pattern Fragments (TPFs)[22]. TPF pro-

---

[2] The original algorithm can be found at https://github.com/mmlab/eice and the improved algorithm at https://www.npmjs.com/package/everything_is_connected_engine.

vides a computationally inexpensive server-side interface that does not overload the server and guarantees high availability and instant responses. Basic triple patterns (i.e. *?s ?p ?o*) suffice to navigate across linked data graphs (no complex queries needed).

Obviously a set of paths is not a presentable story yet. We note that even if a path comprise just the start and destination (indicating they are linked via common hops or directly to each other), the story will contain interesting facts. This is because each step in the path is separated with at least one hop from the next node. For example, to present a story about *Carl Linnaeus* and *Charles Darwin*, the story could start from a path that goes via *J.W. von Goethe*. The resulting statements serve as basic facts, which are relation-object statements, that make up the story. It is up to the application or visualization engine to present it to end-users and enrich it with descriptions, media or further facts. Table 1 exemplary explicates the idea of statements as story facts.

Table 1. The statements as story facts

About	Relation	Object
Carl Linnaeus and Charles Darwin	are	scientists
J.W. von Goethe	influenced	Carl Linnaeus and Charles Darwin
J.W. von Goethe and Charles Darwin	influenced	Karl Marx and Sigmund Freud

5   Evaluation

To determine whether the arbitrariness of a story is reduced, we validated that our optimization improved the link estimation between concepts mentioned in a story. To this end, we computed stories about the four highest ranked DBpedia scientists, according to their PageRank score[3]. Resources with a high PageRank are typically very well connected and have a high probability to lead to many arbitrary paths.

5.1   Initial Sample

We have determined the pairwise semantic relatedness of the story about them by applying the Normalized Google Distance (NGD). The results are shown in Table 2.

Table 2 shows that the entities *Aristotle* and *Physics* are included in the story when applying the original algorithm. These entities are perfect examples of *arbitrary* resources in a story which decreases the consistency. Except that they are related to science, it is unclear to the user why the algorithm 'reasoned' them to be in the story. When utilizing the optimized algorithm these entities are replaced by *J._W._Von_Goethe* and *D._Hume*.

---

[3] http://people.aifb.kit.edu/ath#DBpedia_PageRank.

Table 2. The comparison between the original and optimized algorithm shows that the semantic relatedness can be improved in all cases except for the last two when the entities were already closely related, their NGD in the original algorithm was already relatively low.

No.	Query Context	Original Algorithm	NGD	Optimized Algorithm	NGD
S1	C._Linnaeus - C._Darwin	C._H._Merriam	0.50	J._W._Von_Goethe	**0.43**
S2	C._Linnaeus - A._Einstein	Aristotle	0.70	J._W._Von_Goethe	**0.45**
S3	C._Linnaeus - I._Newton	P._L._Maupertuis	0.48	D._Diderot	**0.40**
S4	A._Einstein - I._Newton	Physics	0.62	D._Hume	**0.45**
S5	C._Darwin - I._Newton	D._Hume	**0.38**	Royal_Liberty_School	0.40
S6	C._Darwin - A._Einstein	D._Hume	**0.43**	B._Spinoza	0.44

5.2 Detailed Sample

In order to verify our results, we also include the total semantic similarity of a path by computing the semantic relatedness between all neighboring node pairs in that path. As can be seen in Table 2, the optimized algorithm seemed to be able to improve the link estimation of the resulting paths. To evaluate the results we used three different similarity measures: W2V[4], NGD [6], and SemRank [3,4].

We used an online available Wiki2VecCorpus using vectors with dimension 1000, no stemming and 10skipgrams[5]. We computed the similarities based on that model by using *gensim*[6]. We implemented the NGD - generalized as the normalized web search distance, on top of the Bing Search API, using the same formula as depicted in the heuristic for the algorithm.

We applied SemRank to evaluate the paths, in particular to capture the serendipity of each path. The serendipity is measured by using a factor μ to indicate the so called 'refraction' how different each new step in a path is compared to the previous averaged over the entire path. Furthermore the information gain is modulated using the same factor μ. The information gain is computed from the weakest point along the path and an average of the rest. So that we get as formula for SemRank and a path p:

$$\text{SemRank}(\mu, p) = [\frac{1 - \mu}{I(p)} + \mu I(p)] \times [1 + \mu R(p)], \tag{7}$$

where $I(p)$ is the overall information gain in the path and $R(p)$ is the average refraction. There are three special cases [4]: (i) **conventional** with $\mu = 0$ leading to $\text{SemRank}(0, p) = \frac{1}{I(p)}$, serendipity plays no role and so no emphasis is put one newly gained or unexpected information; (ii) **mixed** with $\mu = 0.5$ leading to $\text{SemRank}(0.5, p) = [\frac{1}{2I(p)} + \frac{I(p)}{2}] \times [1 + \frac{R(p)}{2}]$, a balance between unexpected and newly gained information; and (iii) **discovery** with $\mu = 1$ leading to

---

[4] https://code.google.com/p/word2vec/.
[5] https://github.com/idio/wiki2vec.
[6] https://radimrehurek.com/gensim/.

Table 3. Abbreviations explained and short interpretation of the measures used.

Abbreviation	Description
W2Vs	Word2Vector similarity using Wikipedia English Corpus
NGD	Normalized Web Search Distance using Bing API
SR-C	SemRank - Conventional - No particular role for serendipity
SR-M	SemRank - Mixed - Serendipity plays partly a role
SR-D	SemRank - Discovery - Serendipity has a major role
PR	PageRank - Centrality Degree of a Node

Table 4. Detailed comparison between the original and optimized algorithm.

	Measure	Higher Better?	S1	S2	S3	S4	S5	S6	AVG	STDEV
Original	SR-C	+	6.46	6.70	5.48	9.47	6.50	9.00	7.17	1.59
	SR-M	+	4.04	4.05	3.34	5.25	4.11	5.21	4.35	0.75
	SR-D	+	0.22	0.20	0.25	0.13	0.23	0.14	0.20	0.05
	NGD	−	0.64	0.69	0.48	0.31	0.48	0.29	0.48	0.16
	W2Vs	+	?	?	0.18	0.32	0.21	0.39	0.20	0.02
	PR	−	2631.89	66.27	179.50	62.39	357.36	62.39	166.38	128.58
Improved	SR-C	+	9.19	8.00	7.17	6.74	9.47	6.50	7.78	1.15
	SR-M	+	5.39	4.70	4.00	3.98	5.44	3.95	4.52	0.65
	SR-D	+	0.14	0.16	0.17	0.19	0.13	0.21	0.17	0.03
	NGD	−	0.53	0.22	0.60	0.38	0.32	0.55	0.45	0.14
	W2Vs	+	0.21	0.19	0.20	?	0.34	?	0.27	0.10
	PR	−	40.42	97.11	29.29	0.59	62.39	0.89	33.25	34.08

$SemRank(1, p) = I(p) \times [1 + R(p)]$, emphasizing unexpected and newly gained information.

The DBPedia PageRank[7] (PR) is an indicator for average 'hub' factor of resources and their neighbourhood based links, how 'common' they are [20].

Table 3 summarizes and explains each of the used measures. Table 4 shows the various improvements of the control algorithm using different measures: both the original and optimized algorithms were configured with the same, the Jaccard distance, weight and heuristic.

5.3 Effect of Weights and Heuristics

The results, shown in Fig. 1, confirm the findings in the detailed sample, but this time the original algorithm uses a combination of the Combined Node Degree (CND) and the Jaccard distance, while the optimized algorithm was configured using a variety of heuristics and weights. To be able to compare the results with each other each of the SR measures are normalized as follows: $SRn = \frac{SR}{max(SR)}$.

---

[7] http://people.aifb.kit.edu/ath#DBpedia_PageRank.

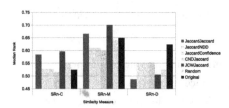 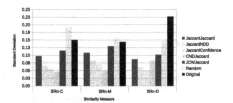

Fig. 1. Effects of the different combinations of weights and heuristics on the measured SemRank. (Color figure online)

Fig. 2. Standard deviation of the measured SemRank when using different heuristics. (Color figure online)

The standard deviation of the results, shown in Fig. 2, highly differs for each case. In particular when using a random number instead of a weighting function and a heuristic leads to a high standard deviation, which is expected - given the randomness. The deviation is also relatively high when using the Jiang-Conrath distance as weight (JCW) and when using the original algorithm.

On the one hand the conventional and mixed mode for SemRank put less emphasis on novelty and focuses mainly on semantic association and information content. The jaccard distance combination used as weight and heuristic is not entirely surprisingly the best choice for this scenario. On the other hand the results of the original algorithm making use of the common node degree as weight together with the jaccard distance is confirmed by the results of the improved algorithm with the common node degree however with a slightly lower rank in the new algorithm. Using the JCW however leads to even higher ranks. In terms of discovery, the original algorithm outperforms the JaccardJaccard combination. The CNDJaccard improved algorithm is able to slightly outperform all the other combinations.

5.4 User Judgments

We presented the output of each of the algorithms as a list of story facts using the scientists example cases S1–S6 as shown in Table 4, typically 1 up to 20 facts depending on the heuristic that was used. As with SemRank, we are interested in the serendipity as a balance between unexpected facts and relevant facts. We asked the users to rate the list of facts in terms of: (i) relevance; (ii) consistency; and (iii) discovery. The users had to indicate how well the list of facts scored according to them on a Likert scale from −2 (None, Not, Very Poor) to +2 (Most, Very, Very Good). A score of 0 (neutral) was only possible in the case of relevance. In total we collected 840 judgments, 20 judgments for each combination of scenario and heuristic. The overall results of the user judgments, rescaled to a score between 0 and 1 are: **relevancy** 0.45; **consistency** 0.45; and **discovery** 0.33. The standard deviations are 0.34; 0.39 and 0.35 respectively. The scores around 0.5 can be interpreted as a disagreement between the users.

The overall score is below 0.5, this indicates that the majority of users judges most of the presented list of story facts below normal or expected relevancy, consistency and with little unexpected new facts. The standard deviation of the user judgments is relatively high, which means that they cover a broad range of judgments some users are very positive while other users are very negative. The mixed results are likely due to varying expectations: some might expected more in-depth results while others appreciated the basic facts about the scientists. The suggested stories that center around a certain via-fact are not always considered relevant by some users even though the algorithms might consider them so. Some examples:

- The users least agreed on the following facts about Carl Linnaeus and Albert Einstein, a score of **0.48** (very little effect) and standard devation of **0.39** when using the JCWJaccard :

      Carl Linnaeus and Baruch Spinoza are Expert, Intellectual and Scholar
      Baruch Spinoza's and Albert Einstein's are both Pantheists Intellectuals and
      Jewish Philosophers

- The most relevant *and* consistent facts were found between Charles Darwin and Carl Linnaeus: a score of **0.65** and **0.6** respectively with CNDJaccard.

      Copley Medal's the award of Alfred Russel Wallace and Charles Darwin
      Alfred Russel Wallace's and Charles Darwin's awards are Royal Medal and Copley Medal
      Alfred Russel Wallace and Charles Darwin are known for their Natural
      selection
      Carl Linnaeus and Alfred Russel Wallace have as subject 'Fellows of the
      Royal Society'
      Carl Linnaeus and Alfred Russel Wallace are Biologists and Colleagues

- In terms of discovery the highest score has relatively little agreement among users: **0.48** and standard deviation **0.42** with JCWJaccard:

      Albert Einstein's and Charles Darwin's reward is Copley Medal.

The scores for relevancy, consistency and discovery as unexpected - but relevant - facts are highly dependent on the user who judges. Some users might be interested in the more trivial path as well in some cases. Nevertheless, we used the overall judgment as a baseline to compare the judgments with the same combinations of heuristics and weights as before.

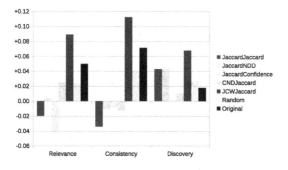

Fig. 3. The effect of the heuristics according to user judgments compared to the overall median. The JCWJaccard confirms already good results with SemRank. The CNDJaccard scores relatively well. (Color figure online)

6 Conclusions and Future Work

We proposed an optimized pathfinding algorithm for storytelling that reduces the number of arbitrary resources revealed in paths contained in the story. Preliminary evaluation results using the DBpedia dataset indicate that our proposal succeeds in telling a story featuring better link estimation, especially in cases where the previous algorithm did not make seemingly optimal choices of links. By defining stories as chains of links in Linked Data, we optimized the storytelling algorithm and tested with several heuristics and weights. The most consistent output was generated with the Jaccard distance used both as weight and heuristic; or as heuristic in combination with the Jiang-Conrath distance as weight. The most arbitrary facts occur in a story when using the combined node degree as weight with the Jaccard distance as heuristic, both in the optimized and the original algorithm. User judgments confirm the findings for the Jiang-Conrath weight and the original algorithm and for the Jaccard distance used as weight and heuristic in terms of discovery. There is no clear positive effect however according the users in terms of consistency and relevancy there.

Future work will focus on validating the correlation between the effect of the link estimation on the arbitrariness as perceived by users and computational semantic relatedness measures such as SemRank. Additionally, we will measure the scalability of our approach by implementing the algorithms (i) solely on the client, (ii) completely on the sever, and (iii) in a distributed client/server architecture.

References

1. Aizawa, A.: An information-theoretic perspective of Tf-idf measures. Inf. Process. Manag. **39**(1), 45–65 (2003)
2. Aleman-Meza, B., Halaschek, C., Arpinar, I.B., Sheth, A.P.: Context-aware semantic association ranking (2003)
3. Aleman-Meza, B., Halaschek-Weiner, C., Arpinar, I.B., Ramakrishnan, C., Sheth, A.P.: Ranking complex relationships on the semantic web. IEEE Internet Comput. **9**(3), 37–44 (2005)
4. Anyanwu, K., Maduko, A., Sheth, A.: Semrank: ranking complex relationship search results on the semantic web. In: Proceedings of the 14th International Conference on World Wide Web, pp. 117–127. ACM (2005)
5. Cheng, G., Zhang, Y., Qu, Y.: Explass: exploring associations between entities via top-k ontological patterns and facets. In: Mika, P., et al. (eds.) ISWC 2014, Part II. LNCS, vol. 8797, pp. 422–437. Springer, Heidelberg (2014)
6. Cilibrasi, R.L., Vitanyi, P.M.: The google similarity distance. IEEE Trans. Knowl. Data Eng. **19**(3), 370–383 (2007)
7. De Meester, B., De Nies, T., De Vocht, L., Verborgh, R., Mannens, E., Van de Walle, R.: StoryBlink: a semantic web approach for linking stories. In: Proceedings of the 14th International Semantic Web Conference (ISWC) Posters and Demonstrations Track (2015)
8. De Vocht, L., Beecks, C., Verborgh, R., Seidl, T., Mannens, E., Van de Walle, R.: Improving semantic relatedness in paths for storytelling with linked data on

the web. In: Gandon, F., Guéret, C., Villata, S., Breslin, J., Faron-Zucker, C., Zimmermann, A. (eds.) The Semantic Web: ESWC 2015 Satellite Events. LNCS, vol. 9341, pp. 31–35. Springer, Heidelberg (2015)

9. De Vocht, L., Coppens, S., Verborgh, R., Vander Sande, M., Mannens, E., Van de Walle, R.: Discovering meaningful connections between resources in the web of data. In: Proceedings of the 6th Workshop on Linked Data on the Web (LDOW2013) (2013)

10. Fang, L., Sarma, A.D., Yu, C., Bohannon, P.: Rex: explaining relationships between entity pairs. Proc. VLDB Endow. **5**(3), 241–252 (2011)

11. Foster, A., Ford, N.: Serendipity and information seeking: an empirical study. J. Doc. **59**(3), 321–340 (2003)

12. Franzoni, V., Mencacci, M., Mengoni, P., Milani, A.: Heuristics for semantic path search in Wikipedia. In: Murgante, B., et al. (eds.) ICCSA 2014, Part VI. LNCS, vol. 8584, pp. 327–340. Springer, Heidelberg (2014)

13. Godin, F., De Nies, T., Beecks, C., De Vocht, L., De Neve, W., Mannens, E., Seidl, T., de Walle, R.V.: The normalized freebase distance. In: Presutti, V., Blomqvist, E., Troncy, R., Sack, H., Papadakis, I., Tordai, A. (eds.) ESWC Satellite Events 2014. LNCS, vol. 8798, pp. 218–221. Springer, Heidelberg (2014)

14. Hart, P., Nilsson, N., Raphael, B.: A formal basis for the heuristic determination of minimum cost paths. IEEE Trans. Syst. Sci. Cybern. **4**, 100–107 (1968)

15. Jiang, J.J., Conrath, D.W.: Semantic similarity based on corpus statistics and lexical taxonomy (1997). arXiv preprint arXiv:cmp-lg/9709008

16. Kumar, D., Ramakrishnan, N., Helm, R.F., Potts, M.: Algorithms for storytelling. IEEE Trans. Knowl. Data Eng. **20**(6), 736–751 (2008)

17. Mazuel, L., Sabouret, N.: Semantic relatedness measure using object properties in an ontology. In: Sheth, A.P., Staab, S., Dean, M., Paolucci, M., Maynard, D., Finin, T., Thirunarayan, K. (eds.) ISWC 2008. LNCS, vol. 5318, pp. 681–694. Springer, Heidelberg (2008)

18. Moore, J.L., Steinke, F., Tresp, V.: A novel metric for information retrieval in semantic networks. In: Proceedings of 3rd International Workshop on Inductive Reasoning and Machine Learning for the Semantic Web (IRMLeS 2011), Heraklion, Greece, May 2011

19. Nies, T.D., Beecks, C., Godin, F., Neve, W.D., Stepien, G., Arndt, D., Vocht, L.D., Verborgh, R., Seidl, T., Mannens, E., de Walle, R.V.: A distance-based approach for semantic dissimilarity in knowledge graphs. In: Proceedings of the 10th International Conference on Semantic Computing (2016, accepted)

20. Page, L., Brin, S., Motwani, R., Winograd, T.: The pagerank citation ranking: bringing order to the web (1999)

21. Vander Sande, M., Verborgh, R., Coppens, S., De Nies, T., Debevere, P., De Vocht, L., De Potter, P., Van Deursen, D., Mannens, E., Van de Walle, R.: Everything is connected: using linked data for multimedia narration of connections between concepts. In: Proceedings of the 11th International Semantic Web Conference Posters and Demo Track, November 2012

22. Verborgh, R., et al.: Querying datasets on the web with high availability. In: Mika, P., et al. (eds.) ISWC 2014, Part I. LNCS, vol. 8796, pp. 180–196. Springer, Heidelberg (2014)

Interaction for Information Discovery Empowering Information Consumers

Kurt Englmeier[1(✉)] and Fionn Murtagh[2]

[1] Schmalkalden University of Applied Science, Schmalkalden, Germany
kurtenglmeier@acm.org
[2] University of Derby, Derby, UK
fmurtagh@acm.org

Abstract. Information Discovery (ID) is predominantly addressed by approaches from Artificial Intelligence (AI). Automatic ID scans large amounts of data and identifies as many potential candidates for discovery as possible. Mass discovery may in fact serve the needs of many information consumers. However, that does not mean that it addresses a broad range of user interests, too. Economies of scale urge the development of automatic tools to address user needs only from a certain critical mass. Hence, many user needs remain unaddressed. This is where HCI comes into play and provides fundamentals for pattern languages that empower information consumers to stage their own information discovery. With this paper we want to draw attention to an approach that is developed around the paradigm of human-centered interaction design. We present an Open Discovery Language that can completely be controlled by information consumers.

Keywords: Information Discovery · Information extraction · Data science · Collaborative work · Interaction design · Participatory design · Pattern languages · Human-centred information management

1 Introduction

A more active role of the information consumers can be enabled by self-service features. This kind of self-service IT may point to user-friendly versions of analytic tools, enabling information consumers to conduct their own analytics. The smooth integration of domain and tool knowledge completes the picture of self-service discovery. The user experience is an important design paradigm, for search engines too. If the users have more impact on the retrieval behaviour of their search engines that leads to an appealing user experience, they are more willing to engage themselves in developing suitable scenarios for their search strategies [1]. When their needs drive design, information discovery engines will provide the insights they require. It is too often the case, that technology as required and described by the users is not quite well understood by designers. There are several ways of human-centred design to overcome this lack of mutual understanding. There is user-centred design where users are employed to test and verify the usability of the system. Participatory design [2] outreaches this form of user engagement, it understands users as part of the design team.

© Springer International Publishing Switzerland 2016
S. Yamamoto (Ed.): HIMI 2016, Part I, LNCS 9734, pp. 252–262, 2016.
DOI: 10.1007/978-3-319-40349-6_24

There are many retrieval methods and technologies that help us to discover the information we need. In general, they serve to detect prominent data in streams of structured or unstructured data. These data are prominent because they are meaningful to us, that is, they reflect information that satisfies our information need. They are also prominent because they follow certain patterns. Data patterns can be quite different, a particular sequence of characters in a string sent by a weather station indicates its location, temperature, and humidity, among others. In texts, an asterisk followed by a date usually indicates a birthdate. Data mining, much like information retrieval, identifies such patterns in structured or unstructured data. With Big Data the focus shifted towards mining of unstructured data. In particular sensors provide their data in unstructured form. The phenomenon, however, to mine unstructured data is not new. Big Data just adds volume, velocity, and variety to it. It addresses the necessity to handle high volumes of data covering a broader spectrum of information and continuously produced by all kind of devices. The Internet-of-things supports the ubiquitous connectivity of these devices and the exchange of data between them.

What qualifies for a prominent or meaningful pattern depends on the logic of the data mining or retrieval algorithms capturing and analyzing the data. The designers of mining features exclusively define this logic and thus the semantics that turn data into information. They determine which data can be meaningful to us. It is the designer, data scientist, or programmer that brings meaning into data, not we. Everything beyond their designs is out of reach for our information needs. What these specialists do not consider in their designs is simply not searchable. That holds for Web search engines in general, but also for individual data collections on the corporate level. Nevertheless, search engines enable us to find many interesting things and valuable information on the web. However, tailoring search engines to individual needs requires those specialists and is thus prohibitively expensive. This results in a search space not addressed by search engines. Probably, this non-addressed search space does not harbor any valuable information. However, there are reasons to believe that the contrary is true. New emerging disciplines like sentiment analysis show that there are still many things left to mine. Broadening the scope of search, however, means more variety in the design of search engines. Even though we can expect that progress in data mining and information retrieval will yield new emerging search engines that are more powerful and address more user needs, the non-addressed search space will remain significantly big.

To raise our search experiences we propose a search interface that supports the active role of the users: By lowering the technical entry level we empower them to equip search engines with their own search features. We want to enable users to define not only keywords but also essential qualities the retrieved results must have. These qualities cannot be expressed by keywords alone.

To reflect essential qualities in a query we propose to define keywords in combination with descriptive patterns rendering the qualities. As we will see in the next section, these patterns can be essential to retrieve the information we require or to discover the data that correspond to our information need. Our approach is applicable to unstructured information, but we can explain it better in the realm of text information. In Big Data, text is the most prominent type of data anyway.

2 Human-Centered Information Discovery

Information discovery (ID) broadly focuses on identifying semantic correlations among data that stand for a superior concept or meaning, not explicitly expressed by these data. Close collocation of data is often used as an indicator for a meaningful correlation. Mass discovery automatically locates frequently collocated data with the assumption that the findings can be useful to users. We call this process shallow discovery.

If we consider the question "Did the share of women in high-level positions of companies increase in the recent past?" we may get a series of articles when searching the web and using the terms of the question as keywords. By expanding and refining our query terms we may clean the query results from irrelevant documents. The articles retrieved may help us to answer the question. For this purpose, we have to read each text and check every section that may relate to our question. It may turn out, that a text addresses the topic, but reflects the corresponding situation in the 60s or 70s of the past century. To further refine our retrieval results, that is, to fine-tune them in accordance with our information need, we have to scrutinize the provided results. The document collection provided in the first place represents a shallow knowledge of the topic. We consider the more detailed and more relevant sections within the documents as deep knowledge.

The search engine can handle the shallow knowledge the web has on the topic, that is, the index list and stored queries related to the topic. Usually, this collection of documents is the first step in our search for documents that address our information need. It just summarizes our need that may have further ramifications not explicitly stated in the query. There are many reasons for this first vague query representation. One reason is that we cannot completely translate our information need into suitable query terms. If we are interested in the actual situation of women filling senior management positions, we may have a variety of aspects in mind that are hard to express in query terms. "Actual", for instance, may mean 2016, 2015, the past five years, or the most recent decade. However, if we expand our query by all terms reflecting the recent past, we are going to raise drastically the quantity of irrelevant retrieval results.

Implicit concepts, we are interested in, may cover "increase" or "number of positions filled", that is, statistical indicators that answer our query. The keyword "increase", for instance, may not help much, albeit it's an essential concept if we want to know whether a positive effect has occurred in the employment situation of women. We need to further specify the increase we have in mind. It may be increase in absolute or relative figures, but the increase should reflect the increase in number of positions (high-level position) filled by women. It may also address the increased number of companies with women in decision-making bodies. The increased number of men in these bodies may even indicate the contrary to what we link at first with the keyword.

Figure 1 shows the variations of the concept "increase" we are interested in. There are a number of instances of the concept "increase": "increase by 14 %", "increase from 10 to 14", "increased by a good three percentage points", or "virtually no increase over 2014". Furthermore, increases vary over industries and economic sectors, too. To correctly handle the concept "increase" we need further qualifying data that may be

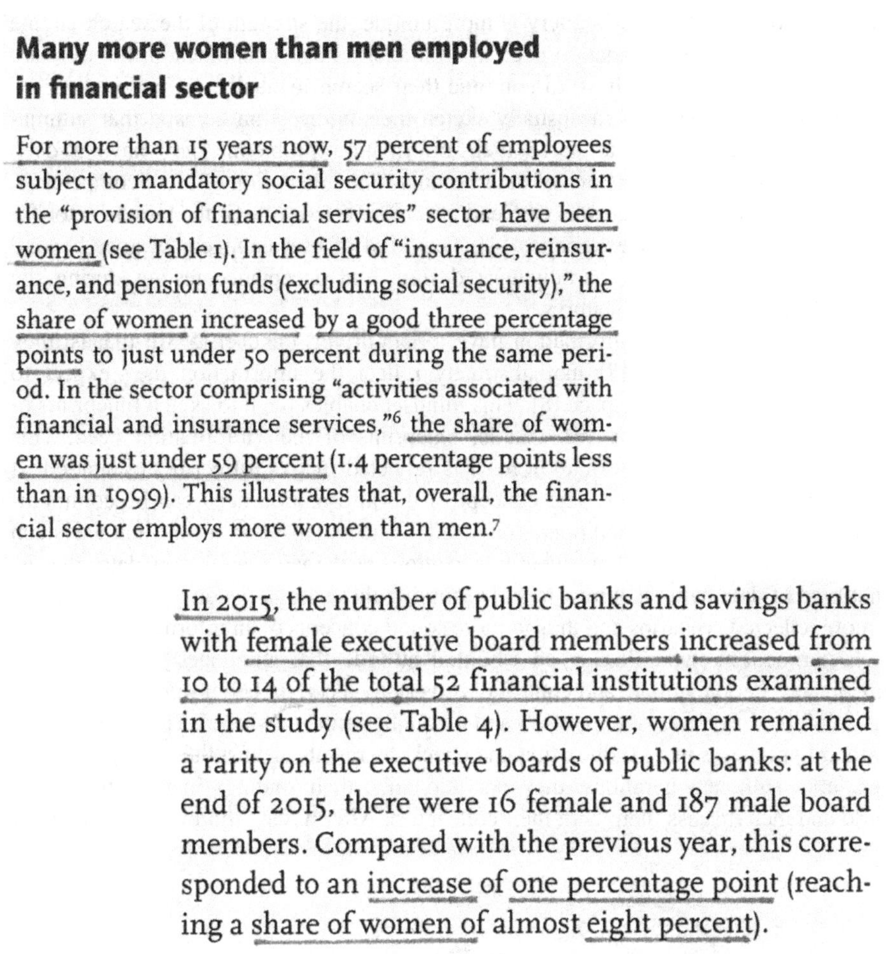

Many more women than men employed in financial sector

For more than 15 years now, 57 percent of employees subject to mandatory social security contributions in the "provision of financial services" sector have been women (see Table 1). In the field of "insurance, reinsurance, and pension funds (excluding social security)," the share of women increased by a good three percentage points to just under 50 percent during the same period. In the sector comprising "activities associated with financial and insurance services,"[6] the share of women was just under 59 percent (1.4 percentage points less than in 1999). This illustrates that, overall, the financial sector employs more women than men.[7]

In 2015, the number of public banks and savings banks with female executive board members increased from 10 to 14 of the total 52 financial institutions examined in the study (see Table 4). However, women remained a rarity on the executive boards of public banks: at the end of 2015, there were 16 female and 187 male board members. Compared with the previous year, this corresponded to an increase of one percentage point (reaching a share of women of almost eight percent).

Fig. 1. Examples of deep knowledge: the variety of presentations of the concept "increase" (of the share of women in high-level positions) [3].

additional keywords, figures, and special characters. These qualifying attributes constitute the deep knowledge about the concept increase.

3   Participatory Design for Self-service Discovery

Even sophisticated search engines can only focus on mass needs for information. To enhance the users' search experience and to avoid confronting the users with too many irrelevant retrieval results, they support users by recommending useful query terms that may detail their need. Recommending keywords, however, only works if the system already identified a critical mass of query term sets that suit the user's keywords expressed so far. If the user's query is more unique, the strength of the search engine diminishes. When an information need is no longer a mass phenomenon the users are on their own, that is, they have to continue their search manually.

Information consumers can usually sketch their information demand that summarizes the data they need to solve their information problem. They have a deep understanding of the foundations of their domain. The integration of more competence, in particular domain competence, can lead to a more active role of the human actor for her or his own discovery experience [4]. This kind of user engagement goes beyond user requirement analysis, participatory design, and acceptance testing during the development of discovery features.

People working with information have a data-driven mindset [5, 6], that is, they resort to mental models [7] that abstractly reflect the information they expect to encounter in their retrieval space [8]. This mindset enables them to sketch blueprints of the things they are looking for, that is, blueprints of their information need. This conceptualization of an information need is reflected in its abstract representation. It has three important qualities: The concept of the information need can be communicated, collectively refined and operationalized. Conceptualization means that users can sketch scenarios showing how their information need may manifest in data, that is, what kind of data patterns it may take. Discussing these scenarios on group level leads to more reflected scenarios and thus to more sound concepts of an information need [9].

Experimenting with data is an essential attitude that stimulates data discovery experiences. People initiate and control discovery by a certain belief - predisposition or bias reinforced by years of expertise - and gradually refine this belief. They gather data, try their hypotheses in a sandbox first and check the results against their blueprints, and then, after sufficient iterations, they operationalize their findings in their individual world and then discuss them with their colleagues. After having thoroughly tested their

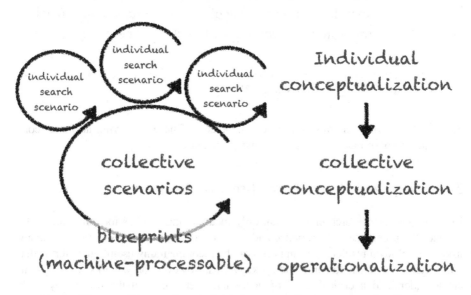

Fig. 2. Discovery lifecycle from individual conceptualization to operationalization.

hypotheses, information consumers institutionalize them to their corporate world, that is, cultivate them in their information ecosystem.

Much like conceptualization, the operationalization of an information need can be an individual or a collective task. Information consumers can express their search scenarios in a way that later on can be processed by machines. These blueprints of search are far from being programming instructions but reflect the users' "natural" engineering knowledge. The machine then takes the blueprints and identifies these information scenarios in data, even though the blueprint abstracts away many details. The language knowledge and their mental models constitute shallow knowledge necessary and sufficient to engineer statements that are processable by the search engine [10, 11]. After reflecting the corporate blueprint they may get hints for further discoveries and the participatory cycle starts anew (see Fig. 2).

4 Pattern Language for Discovery

A good starting point therefore is the language of information consumers. To avoid any irritations or ambiguities, people try to be quite precise in their descriptions. Even though these descriptions are composed of natural language terms and statements, humans are quite good in safeguarding literal meaning in their descriptions. For us, the data-driven mindset becomes evident when users can turn their domain and shallow engineering knowledge into machine instructions suitable for the precise detection and extraction of the facts they expect to discover. The users are in the position to express their domain knowledge on a certain level of abstraction. If the technological entry level for tagging their domain knowledge suits the users' engineering knowledge we can expect them to develop operable representations of their information need [12].

4.1 Design Principles

The blueprint of an information need serves two purposes: they reflect semantic qualities of the discovery scenario the search engine shall detect in data. Simultaneously, they are the building blocks of the meta-language that, when correctly syndicated, support data integration and sharing. While syndicating metadata along their domain competence, users foster implicitly active compliance with organizational data governance policies.

Information discovery starts with information extraction (IE) [13, 14] that distills text or even scattered documents to a germ of the original raw material. IT experts engineer information extraction systems that operate on templates for the facts to be extracted. Labelled slots constitute these templates whereby the labels represent annotated terms.

Self-service information discovery starts with user-driven IE. The users first have to engineer their extraction templates that can also be considered as entity recognizers. This means, a certain amount of engineering is indispensable in IE. The key question is whether information consumers have the necessary engineering knowledge to handle discovery services on their own. This (shallow) engineering knowledge is assumed to be acquired easily and thoroughly specific to the task at hand [15]. The assumption in self-service discovery is that users with their domain competence and shallow engineering knowledge are in the position to manage a certain level of data discovery and information sharing on their own.

The users' blueprints may be simple and concise, but they are comprehensive enough to cover their request. This, in turn, fosters the control of the discovery process. A template with, say eight to twelve slots, can comprehensively cover real-world requests in small-scale domains. This low level of complexity makes it easy for the information consumer to manually control discovery. Whenever they encounter unfilled slots or mistakenly filled slots they may check the corresponding document for obvious errors. On the other hand, they may adapt their blueprint if the representation of a fact appears to be sound in text, but the slots do not consistently correspond to the qualities of the fact.

Our discovery language, developed along the paradigm of simplicity [16], is a meta-language that serves the description of named entities on different levels of complexity. It enables users to define patterns for concepts rendered by simple entities like "date", "birthday", "address", or "increase" that gradually increase in complexity when hierarchically combined into larger constructs. The constituting elements (keywords and/or character patterns) of such entities are not necessarily juxtaposed in a text, in particular if we consider more complex concepts like "vendor" or "buyer" in a contract, that may consist of the named entities "name", "address", probably "birthday" or "social security number", "tax payer number", and "nationality". Furthermore, these elements may be scattered over a large section of the contract and do not always appear in the same sequence. There may be also text (or data) elements in between that are irrelevant for the user. These elements have or may take the character of stop words.

4.2   Language Syntax

The discovery language thus enables the definition of patterns that precisely reflect the information entities the users are looking for. The patterns help to locate relevant information by fading out irrelevant sections. The patterns may become quite complex. The limits of real estate, for instance, can be a combination of geographic directions, addresses, and street names. However, the users know the characteristics of the entities they are looking for. In turn, they can sketch an abstract representation or blueprint of these entities. Sketching means they describe what elements may appear together, in a strict or arbitrary order, over a narrow or broad range. They add significant leading or trailing elements if appropriate. The blueprints themselves can be used as elements and thus become building blocks of a more complex pattern.

On its lowest level, our discovery language completely works with Regular Expressions. They are a very useful instrument when it comes to identify patterns in text and in unstructured data, in general. Unfortunately, Regular Expressions are powerful, but absolutely not user-friendly. They require special skills and are not easy to handle, in particular, when they are addressing complex, i.e. real-world, patterns. Besides, Regular Expressions representing high level facts are extremely complex and barely manageable, even for professionals. Their application also has limitations, when relevant elements (qualities) of facts are too dispersed over the data set, that means when too much "noise" appears between facts or their qualities.

We therefore propose a language that adopts Regular Expressions but shields users from their complexity. It provides users with a stock of labelled Regular Expressions addressing entities like "word", "tax payer number", "percentage", "phrase", "decimal" etc. Instead of defining Regular Expressions, the users compose their patterns by resorting to these basic patterns or to the patterns they have already defined by themselves. The syntax serves to describe how facts, as the constituent parts of the fact requested by the user, appear as sequences of word patterns in data. The corresponding descriptive pattern gradually aggregates into the complex pattern for the requested information. Internally it translates the users' instructions into complex Regular Expressions and applies it to the text or unstructured data.

As already pointed out, the language provides a set of basic variables that cover patterns like "date", "percentage", "zip code", etc.

The users take these basic language elements and define more complex patterns. The following expressions support the identification of companies in texts:

```
name,names = Words."Inc.";"company";"GmbH";"S.A."
street,streets = numeric.Words.ordinal;numeric."st."
city = Words.zipcode.Words:country
company,companies = name,street,suite,city
```

On the left side of the equation the user defines the name of the pattern. The right side of the equation lists the sequence of pattern elements. The pattern can be assigned to a singular term and optionally also to its corresponding plural term. When defining their own patterns, people intuitively apply both forms as you see in the first pattern ("Words").

The operators have the following functions:

- The dot indicates strong sequence ("followed by"). The element indicated before the dot must be located before the one indicated after the dot. In "street", there is a number followed by one or more words, followed by an ordinal or numeric expression that finally is followed by a keyword (put in quotes).
- Comma means weak sequence. The elements are expected to appear sequentially in the data but in any order. One or more elements may even be absent. The pattern "company" consists of the patterns "name", "street", "city" we defined before and the basic pattern "suite" (provided by the discovery language).
- The semicolon is used to indicate an exclusive combination. One of the elements must be present. The company name terminates with one (and only one) keyword as indicated in the example.
- A leading question mark indicates that an element or group of elements can be optional, that is, the corresponding pattern can but need not be located in the data.
- For the text examples of Sect. 2 (see Fig. 1) we can define some of the patterns as follows:

```
share = percentage."employee".industry sector."women";
"share of women"; ("female".Words).?percentage
share increase = share,"increase",percentage;range
```

The output of the extraction process is simply rendered in XML, in order to enable a smooth integration into follow-up processes for data analytics, visualization, reporting and the like. The slots (with annotated terms) capture the facts according to the users' pattern definitions render them by XML elements. Basic patterns are treated like primitive data types; entity elements that correspond to them are not explicitly tagged.

The extracted data for the example may appear in the following XML format:

```
<share increase>
    <share>
        female executive board members
    </share>
    <range>
        from 10 to 14
    </range>
</share increase>
```

In the end, we get a semantic representation of concepts that resembles a thesaurus. However, it is not a general thesaurus, rather an individual one ("share of women in high-level positions"), adapted to the specifics of the respective domain and information need. Furthermore, it isn't either a strict thesaurus where all its concepts are tightly integrated. It's rather a collection of more or less loosely coupled fractions of a thesaurus, with its fractions dynamically changing both, in their compositions and relationships among each other. It is thus more suitable to consider semantic badges as ingredients of a common vocabulary. This vocabulary, in turn, is the asset of the information consumers. They manage it in cooperative authorship.

First experiments with our discovery language addressed about 2500 documents (economic reports, real estate contracts with related certificates, diagnosis reports from radiology and product descriptions, to mention the most prominent ones) distributed over dozens of data sources. In the first place, these samples may seem small to validate a pattern language or to underpin its scalability. However, the inherent character of basically unstructured data distributed over different sources reflects the nature of the challenge we face in data discovery. The language applied in the documents addressed is quite uniform and not narratively complex. The document samples cover this language in its entirety, and thus scale for even larger collections. In many information ecosystems we barely have to deal with highly complex narrative forms. Due to this fact, we can consider this approach as scalable also towards thematic areas outside the domains addressed so far, as long as the narrative nature is relatively uniform.

5 Conclusion

Today's search engines are powerful. They changed the way we deal with information and turned into one of the most valuable information source we have. However, there is a chance and probably even a need to provide users with an appealing retrieval experience that reaches beyond what's possible today. To say, "Just formulate a query and you will get thousands of interesting results! Take what you need!" reflects a strategy doomed to failure.

Information consumers want the information that exactly meets their particular needs. They expect a certain variety of information echoing the diversity of their information need and appreciate more meaningful information for their analytics, reporting, or whatsoever. The more retrieval systems meet the expectations of information consumers the higher are the advantages. These can be manifold, far beyond business success such as growing revenues and market shares.

This affects information governance in general and Big Data governance in particular. It should include semantic search and consider participatory design as design paradigm. There are many discovery tasks that serve individual, ad hoc, and transient purposes. Main stream discovery, in contrast, supports reoccurring discovery requests commonly shared by large user communities and operates on large data collection, including sometimes the entire Web. We can conceive manifold scenarios for non-mainstream discovery. Users may have to analyze from time to time dozens of failure descriptions or complaints, for instance. The corresponding data collections are personal or shared among small groups and consist of bunches of PDF files or emails, for instance, barely documents on the Web. Dynamically changing small-scale requests would mean permanent system adaptation, which is too intricate and too expensive in the majority of cases. With a flexible self-service solution like our discovery language information consumers can reap the benefits of data discovery and sharing and avoid the drawbacks of mainstream discovery.

The actual version of the our discovery language described here is available on sourceforge.net: http://sourceforge.net/projects/mydistiller/.

References

1. Shneiderman, B.: Designing for fun: how can we design user interfaces to be more fun? Interactions **11**(5), 48–50 (2004)
2. Robertson, T., Simonsen, J.: Challenges and opportunities in contemporary participatory design. Des. Issues **28**(3), 3–9 (2012)
3. Holst, E., Kirsch, A.: Financial sector: share of women on corporate boards increases slightly but men still call the shots. DIW Econ. Bull. **6**, 27–38 (2016)
4. Clement, A.: Computing at work: empowering action by "low-level users". Commun. ACM **37**(1), 52–64 (1994)
5. Pentland, A.: The data-driven society. Sci. Am. **309**(4), 64–69 (2013)
6. Viaene, S.: Data scientists aren't domain experts. IT Prof. **15**(6), 12–17 (2013)
7. Norman, D.: Some observations on mental models. In: Gentner, D., Stevens, A. (eds.) Mental Models. Lawrence Erlbaum, Hillsdale (1987)
8. Brandt, D.S., Uden, L.: Insight into mental models of novice internet searchers. Commun. ACM **46**(7), 133–136 (2003)
9. Elbeshausen, S., Womser-Hacker, C., Mandl, T.: Searcher heterogeneity in collaborative information seeking within the context of work tasks. In: Proceedings of the 5th Information Interaction in Context Symposium, pp. 327–329 (2014)

10. Sawyer, P., Rayson, P., Cosh, K.: Shallow knowledge as an aid to deep understanding in early phase requirements engineering. IEEE Trans. Softw. Eng. **31**(11), 969–981 (2005)
11. Chin, G., Rosson, M.B., Carroll, J.M.: Participatory analysis: shared development of requirements from scenarios. In: Proceedings of the ACM SIGCHI Conference on Human factors in Computing Systems, pp. 162–169 (1997)
12. Heymann, P., Paepcke, A., Garcia-Molina, H.: Tagging human knowledge. In: Proceedings of the Third ACM International Conference on Web Search and Data Mining, pp. 51–60 (2010)
13. Cowie, J., Lehnert, W.: Information extraction. Commun. ACM **39**(1), 80–91 (1996)
14. McCallum, A.: Information extraction: distilling structured data from unstructured text. ACM Queue – Soc. Comput. **3**(9), 48–57 (2005)
15. Fan, J., Kalyanpur, A., Gondek, D.C., Ferrucci, D.A.: Automatic knowledge extraction from documents. IBM J. Res. Dev. **56**(3.4), 5:1–5:10 (2012)
16. Magaria, T., Hinchey, M.: Simplicity in IT: the power of less. IEEE Comput. **46**(11), 23–25 (2013)

Federated Query Evaluation Supported by SPARQL Recommendation

Gergő Gombos[1(⊠)] and Attila Kiss[1,2]

[1] Eötvös Loránd University, Budapest, Hungary
{ggombos,kiss}@inf.elte.hu
[2] J. Selye University, Komárno, Slovakia
kissa@ujs.sk

Abstract. The usage of the semantic data is complicated for non-expert users, because the data are on many different SPARQL endpoints and the users need to know the URL of the endpoints. The federated systems are good solution for this problem. These systems interpret the SPARQL query and find the endpoints that can answer the query. Another advantage of the federated systems is it can connect the datasets with one simple query. This means some part of the data is found on different endpoints and the system can connect them. In order to do this the system needs information about the datasets that are stored by endpoints. We know two types for this. The first uses a catalog and stores the information in it. The system makes this information up-to-date at times. The second solution uses ASK query to decide which endpoint can answer the query. The queries run on every endpoint on every time. In this paper, we improve these federated systems. The basic idea is to reduce the number of the available endpoints. Our solution uses the SPARQL recommendation technique. This technique offers triple patterns to the user when the user writes the query. When the system asks new recommendation from the endpoints, it gets some information about the endpoints. This information is useful for the federated systems. It is enough to use only these endpoints given by the recommendations.

In this paper, we extend the recommendation technique with new recommendation type that is based on the rdfs:range predicate. We present a query cost model that represents the number of the queries that need to the federated query evaluation. We present the recommendation information is enough for the evaluation and we make experiments on two federated systems (FedX, DarQ).

Keywords: SPARQL · Federated · Recommendation · LOD Cloud

1 Introduction

A lot of semantic data are available in the LOD Cloud. We can reach these datasets with SPARQL queries via the SPARQL endpoints, but the non-expert user has trouble to find these endpoints. The user needs to know the URL of

© Springer International Publishing Switzerland 2016
S. Yamamoto (Ed.): HIMI 2016, Part I, LNCS 9734, pp. 263–274, 2016.
DOI: 10.1007/978-3-319-40349-6_25

the endpoints and needs to know which endpoint stores the data that the user wants to use. When the user found an endpoint another problem is that the user does not know the structure of the dataset. The structure is needed for the SPARQL query. When the non-expert user found endpoint and know the structure of the dataset, how can he write SPARQL query easier. The federated systems give a solution for the first two problems. A federated system knows the URLs of the endpoints, and it knows which endpoint can answer the SPARQL query. A federated system contains more components. It has a query parser that splits the query of the user to subqueries. After that, it searches the endpoint for all subqueries. This phase is the source selection phase. Finally, it makes the answer from the subresults that come from the endpoints. All components have challenges. For example, a good question in the source selection is how we can decide which endpoint can answer the subquery? We know two techniques for this question: the catalog technique and the ASK technique. The catalog technique stores information about the endpoints. For example, it stores all predicates that are available on the endpoints. It can reach with simple SPARQL query. This information needs to be up-to-date, so the system needs to call the endpoints to refresh the information. The question is how and when we can do this? Our solution uses the recommendation. It has predicates information about the endpoints and we use this information to update the catalog.

The ASK technique does not use any stored information about the datasets of the endpoints. It asks every time the endpoints with simple SPARQL queries. The ASK query returns simple true/false value based on the endpoint can answer the subquery or not. The data are up-to-date on every time to choose endpoints for evaluations, because the query runs on the live endpoints. The disadvantage of the ASK technique is it runs on every endpoint every time. Our solution is similar to the catalog technique. We reduce the number of the possible endpoints with the information that comes from the recommendations. When we get recommendation, we know that endpoint can answer the subquery. In this paper we concentrate only the source selection problem.

The data are stored in the LOD Cloud and it has an important property. Data can connect to other data stored in another datasets. This property is true on the semantic data. We can write query that uses more endpoints and connect the data together. These queries are called federated queries. Since the SPARQL 1.1 we can do this with the SERVICE keyword. This keyword needs an endpoint URL and the triple patterns that run on that endpoint. The variables connect the triple patterns in the query. We mentioned earlier, we need to know the URL of the endpoint and we need to know the structure of the datasets. These limitations make the query writing complicated. The earlier presented systems solve these problems too because when we write a SPARQL 1.0 query (without SERVICE), the federated system can decide which endpoints answer the subquery. After that, the system merges the results to the final answer. Another problem is that we do not know the datasets of the endpoints. The recommendation systems give a solution for these problems. Some recommendation systems work like the autocomplete in the SQL environment. This technique offers possible values with the prefix of the values. For example, when we write a property the system offers the properties that have this prefix value. In this case, we need to know some prefix to the system can offer.

Another solution offers triple patterns to the user based on the semi-finished query. In this case, the user only needs to choose from the triple patterns to make a SPARQL query. In our previous work [4] the recommended triple patterns come from a federated system. Therefore, the final query will be a federated query. The system gets the necessary information from the recommendation, so when the query is finished it can reduce the number of the necessary endpoints.

The system that we presented in our previous paper first queries the possible types of the endpoints. The user can choose from this list that want to use. After that, the system asks the endpoints about the types. It asks the possible predicates to these types. It works with simple SPARQL query, so the endpoints are able to answer the query easier. A predicate has *rdfs:range* properties typically. This property gives more information about a dataset. The *rdfs:range* property gives the range of a predicate. The range is a type, so we can make more recommendation with this information because we can query the predicates of this type. This recommendation adds more help to the user to write SPARQL query.

A simple SPARQL query has a following structure: $SELECT + variables + WHERE + conditions$. The variable part contains the variables that we want to ask. The condition part contains triple patterns that filter the results. All result line must fulfill the conditions. The recommendation systems offer these triple patterns to the user. The federated systems use these triple patterns to make the subqueries and answer the final query.

In this paper, we present that we can configure the federated systems with the recommendation system. We get recommended triples and we can use the predicates for the evaluation. The evaluation needs less time when it selects only the necessary endpoints.

The rest of the paper is organized as follows. Section 2 introduces the cost model of the evaluation of the federated systems and our solution. Section 3 shows the related works in the topic of federated systems and SPARQL GUI. Section 4 presents the challenges of the paper. Section 5 presents the extended recommendation algorithm and the cost of this technique. Section 6 evaluates the algorithm and techniques with some statistics. Finally, Sect. 7 summarizes our results.

2 Preliminaries

In this section we introduce some basic concepts. We present the source selection strategies. We present a cost model that represents the number of the necessary request to evaluate a federated query.

2.1 Source Selection

We mentioned earlier the query parser divides the query to subqueries and the source selection searches the possible endpoints that can answer the subqueries.

This is an important part of a federation system. There are two possible methods to choose endpoint: catalog technique and the ASK technique. The *Catalog technique* stores information about the endpoints. It uses this information to choose the endpoints. If some information is not up-to-date, the system cannot answer the SPARQL query. Therefore, the system needs to update the information about the endpoint. The *ASK technique* runs ASK query to know the endpoint can answer the subquery. It queries all the endpoints with every subquerie. This technique uses only the URL of the SPARQL endpoints. The disadvantage is it uses a lot of queries, but the advantage is it does not need to store information about the endpoints.

2.2 Query Cost Model

We present a cost model of the federation systems. The model represents the number of the query that need for the evaluation. First, we present a basic model and later we present the specific model for the source selection techniques. The model contains a configuration part and a source selection part. The configuration part is the number of the queries that need for the configuration of the federated system. The source selection part is the number of queries that needs to the selection of endpoints, and that needs to the evaluation of the subqueries. Let n the number of the endpoints.

$$Cost_{MaxEval}(n) = Cost_{conf}(n) + Cost_{subQuery}(n) \tag{1}$$

$$Cost_{conf}(n) = (\sum_{i=1}^{n} Cost_{subConf}) * count(triple) \tag{2}$$

$$Cost_{subQuery}(n) = (\sum_{i=1}^{n} Cost_{EPQuery}) * count(subQuery) \tag{3}$$

The Eq. 1 shows the maximal number of requests need for the evaluation of a federated query. The cost depends on how many endpoints are configured in the system (n), because all endpoints need to be configured and all endpoints need to query during the evaluation. The first part (Eq. 2) of the cost is the configuration part. The system collects information about the endpoint $(Cost_{subConf})$. This information is used by the source selection. It also depends on the number of the configured endpoints. In the worst case the system uses all the endpoints, and it needs to configure all the endpoints. The second part (Eq. 3) of the cost is a querying part. This part needs for the evaluation of the subqueries $(Cost_{EPQuery})$. The worst case is when every subquery runs on every endpoint, but the system does not use usually all the endpoints because the source selection decreases the number of the endpoints.

3 Related Work

3.1 Federated Systems

Rakhmawati et al. [10] presented the federated systems in a survey. They showed the federated system components and the available evaluation strategies.

They presented the source selection techniques, too. They called that ASK Query and the Data catalogue.

Verborgh et al. [15] mentioned the availability of the SPARQL endpoints is low. They offer a client-side solution for this problem. Their idea is the client does not send complex query to the endpoint. It uses a pipeline of the simpler queries. It is similar to the recommendation technique where the system runs simple query for the triple patterns.

Buil-Aranda et al. [1] analyzed the federated SPARQL evaluation strategies. They found some federated system do not answer correctly all queries because all endpoints have result size limitation. They compared the evaluation strategies.

We use in this paper two federated systems that use the two mentioned source selection strategies. One is the Darq [9] (distributed ARQ). It is an extension of the Jena [6] ARQ to support federated SPARQL queries. The data source selection is based on the preconfigured properties.

Another system that we use is the FedX [14]. The FedX is an optimization technique for the SPARQL federated queries. It cannot use any information about the endpoints it uses only ASK query for source selection.

3.2 Autocomplete, Recommendation

Hoefler mentioned in his paper [5] that the SPARQL is difficult for non-expert users. The users do not know URL of the endpoints or do not know which data store on it. He observed the user know the spreadsheet applications like Excel. The idea is to make the semantic data into tabular form.

Campinas mentioned too in his paper [2] that the Semantic Web usage is difficult because writing a SPARQL query is complicated. He implemented a data-based auto-completion that recommends items that can be predicates, classes or named graph. Their aim is to make an easy-to-use library.

Kramer et al. [7] presented a SPARQL index technique for autocomplete. It works on the temporary query. When the user writes a '?' or a '<' symbol the system recommends variables or IRIs based on the earlier queries. In our case the recommendation uses the federated system and LOD Cloud for recommendation.

Lehmann and Bühmann [8] presented a technique for making SPARQL query. Their solution is based on the question-answer and the positive learning techniques. The system makes recommendation based on the user selection. The selection is the base of the next iteration. The recommendation runs until the query is found or it is a not learnable query.

Rietveld et al. implemented the Yasgui [11], the user-friendly SPARQL client. It is a web based SPARQL client. It uses a proxy to reach the endpoints. It has an autocomplete function for the prefixes, namespaces and properties from multiple endpoints, but it uses only one endpoint to evaluate the query.

We presented our previous work [4] a recommendation technique with federated system. It recommends only the prefixes and the properties of an *rdf:type*. In this paper, we extend this technique with a more usable recommendation.

Saleem et al. presented the HiBISCus [12], a hypergraph based approach for source selection for federation system. They tested their system with Darq and Fedx, too.

4   Challenge

Our goal is to reduce the number of the endpoints that necessary for the evaluation. The reduction is based on the recommendations that come from the recommendation system. The main idea is the recommendation has information about the endpoints that enough to answer the query. Every time when the system gets new recommended triples it gets predicate information. This information is up-to-date every time. Another advantage is when the endpoint does not response on a recommendation request the system knows this endpoint does not need for evaluation. The recommendation technique reduces the number of endpoints that will use for evaluation. In this paper, we do not want to make a new evaluation strategy or join order technique. We use the available federated systems and we make a better configuration with the recommendation system. The challenge is how we can use this information for better configuration. The configuration of a federated system is static. With the recommendation we can change the configuration for a faster evaluation.

Another aim is to extend the recommendation technique. In our previous work we presented the recommendation technique. It uses only the *rdf:type* and the predicates of a type. We can use another predicates to get new recommendation. The usable predicate is a *rdfs:range*.

5   Technique

First, we extend the earlier presented technique. In previous paper, we use only the prefix, the *rdf:type* and its predicates. We extend this recommendation with the *rdfs:range*.

5.1   Recommendation Technique

The earlier presented algorithm first collects the available types from the endpoints. It can do it with simple SPARQL query.

It makes recommendations from the types. The recommendation is a triple where the subject is a variable that is not used in the query. The predicate is the *rdf:type* and the object is the new type. We get another information with this recommendation because the new type has *rdf:type* predicate information. We store this information about the endpoints.

Another function of the system is the *predicate recommendation* that makes new triple pattern based on the temporary query. The input of the function is a variable and the type of the variable. The federated system asks all the endpoints with this type. We request some entities that have this type and we query the predicates of the entity. We store these predicates in a map to reduce the duplicated predicates. Finally, we prepare recommendations with the new predicates. The subject of the recommended triple is the variable that is in the input of the function. The predicate is the new predicate and the object is a new generated variable that is generated from the input variable and the predicate name. The new predicate has information about the endpoint, too. We store the new information from the new predicate. We get the predicates with simple queries. If we know a predicate we can ask the range of this predicate (*IdentityRangeQuery*) and if the object is a variable we can make a new recommendation to this variable. We ask the range and we use the technique mentioned earlier.

IdentityRangeQuery : `SELECT DISTINCT ?id WHERE {`
`<sometype> rdfs:range ?range .`
`?id rdf:type ?range . }`

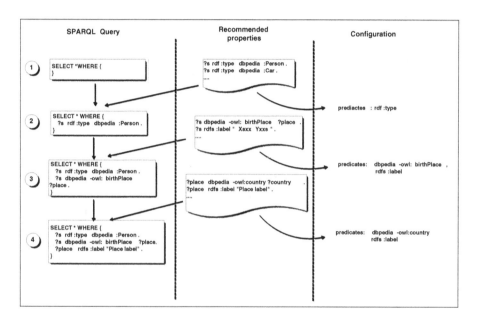

Fig. 1. SPARQL writing with recommendation and information recovery.

We present the algorithm in an example on Fig. 1. On the left side we see the SPARQL. In the first step it is empty. The system recommends some types (in example: *Person, Car*). With this the system gets some predicates (*rdf:type*) information. We accept the *Person* type and we get new recommendations (*dbpedia-owl:birthPlace and rdfs:label*) and the system stores the new predicates (*dbpedia-owl:birthPlace, rdfs:label*). We select the *rdfs:birthPlace* and the system knows with the help of the range predicate the type of the *?place* variable. It is *dbpedia:Place* and recommends new predicates for the *?place*. The system updates the predicate information of the endpoint.

5.2   Recommended Information Is Enough

The Algorithm 1 selects the necessary endpoints. The *EPQ* variable represents the set of the necessary endpoints (see line 2). Let the *UserSelect* a list that

---
Algorithm 1. Select necessary endpoints

1: **function** COLLECTENDPOINTS( )
2:      $EPQ = \{\}$
3:      $UserSelect = List < TP_1, TP_2, TP_3, ... >$
4:      **for all** $tp \in UserSelect$ **do**
5:          **for all** $e \in Endpoints$ **do**
6:              **if** answer(e,tp) **then**
7:                  EPQ $\cup$ e
8:              **end if**
9:          **end for**
10:     **end for**
11: **end function**
---

represents the selected triple patterns that chose the user (see line 3). We check the selected triple pattern which endpoint can answer (see line 6). If the endpoint can answer the triple pattern, it is necessary for the evaluation.

Remark 1 (Recommended Information Is Enough.) Let EPQ the set of the endpoints that are necessary for the evaluation. Let Endpoints the set of all endpoints that the system knows. Let the UserSelect a list of triple patterns that the user choses. Then $\exists$ tp $\in$ UserSelect, e $\in$ Endpoints, answer(e,tp) $\Rightarrow$ e $\in$ EPQ

Proof. The federated system needs for the evaluation that all the triple patterns (TP) belong to an endpoint. If the TP belongs to the endpoint, the endpoint can answer the TP. We prove this statement indirectly. Let e an endpoint that can answer the TP, but the e endpoint does not exist in the EPQ. That means the TP does not come from that endpoint, but the user selected it. Every recommendation comes from the endpoints, so the TP comes from e, and the e endpoint can answer the TP and it pushed to the EPQ.

5.3   Query Cost of Federated Techniques

In the previous section we presented the information recovery from the recommendation. In Sect. 2.2 we showed the number of request of the query evaluation. Now we describe the cost of the two source selection techniques.

Query Cost of ASK Technique. The ASK technique makes queries every time to every endpoint. This is equal to the basic $Cost_{conf}$. The $Cost_{subquery}$ is less because the system does not run the subquery on every endpoint. It uses only endpoints that are selected by configuration phase. Let m the number of the selected endpoint and $(m < n)$.

$$Cost_{askSubquery}(m) = (\sum_{i=1}^{m} Cost_{EPQuery}) * count(subQuery) \qquad (4)$$

Cost of Catalog Technique. The catalog technique uses preconfigured information about the endpoints. This section runs independently from evaluation. The cost of the configuration is 0 in the evaluation phase. In this case, the system uses only the endpoint that is selected by the configuration. It is similar to the ASK technique. The disadvantage of this technique is the configuration is not up-to-date. It is necessary to collect information about the endpoints.

Cost of Recommend Configuration. The recommendation technique uses the ASK technique during the query creating. It serves the configuration to be up-to-date. The advantage of this technique is it reduces the number of the endpoints because it selects endpoints that are used during the query creating.

Cost Comparison. Let $recommend(n) \leq n$. The $recommend(n)$ reduce the number of the endpoints based on the recommendation.

$$Cost_{catalog}(recommend(n)) \leq Cost_{catalog}(n) \tag{5}$$

$$Cost_{ASK}(recommend(n)) \leq Cost_{ASK}(n) \tag{6}$$

When we use the catalog technique the system reads the configuration and it asks only that endpoints that can answer the subquery. When we use the recommendation technique we do not change the federated systems. We change only the configuration with the recommendation. It means the catalog technique reads less endpoint configurations when it uses the recommendation. Without the recommendation the technique checks all endpoint configurations, but in point of request view the two cases are the same. The Eq. 5 represents that the cost when we use the recommendation is less than without the recommendation.

When we use the ASK technique the system asks all the endpoints with ASK query. On query phase it queries the necessary endpoints where the predicates are. The cost of the ASK technique is more expensive than the catalog technique because it asks the endpoints on configuration phase too. When we use the recommendation technique with the ASK technique the number of the requests are smaller because the configuration phase uses less endpoints. It uses only the endpoints that come from the recommendation. The Eq. 4 represents that the cost when we use the recommendation is less than without the recommendation.

6   Experiments

We evaluated our techniques with two related systems. We used the Darq [9], because it uses statistics about the endpoints and we used the FedX [14] because it uses the ASK technique. We have run both from java code on a Virtual Machine. This VM has Intel Xeon X5650 CPU (4 core, 2,67 GHz) with 4 GB memory. We installed two Virtuoso endpoints [3] (ver. 06.01) on two computers. The computers have Intel Core i5 650 CPU (4 core, 3,2 GHz) with 4 GB memory. Both Virtuoso store the FedBench datasets. First Virtuoso stores the NyTimes and the Jamendo datasets and the second stores the DBpedia, LinkedMDB and the Geonames datasets. We configured the Virtuosos to reach the datasets separately. We used the FedBench [13] Cross-Domain queries to evaluate our model. We have run all queries one time for warm-up and five times for the statistics.

When we used the FedX we set all the endpoint for comparison. When we used the DarQ we configured all endpoints with the RDFstat generator.

Figure 2 shows the runtime with and without recommendation. The left figure shows the query 1 and 2, the right figure shows the query 4 and 6 and the middle figure shows the query 3 and 5. The query 7 runs out of memory in both cases. The Darq does not support the UNION and the unbounded queries. In the federated benchmark the query 1 has UNION operator. In this case, the result is the same with and without recommendation and it does not have answer. The query 6 has unbound variable, but we get answer and better result with recommendation.

Figure 3 presents the runtime of the FedX system. We experienced the runtime of all queries was better with recommendation except query 6. It has the same runtime in both cases because the recommendation sets all the endpoint for the evaluation.

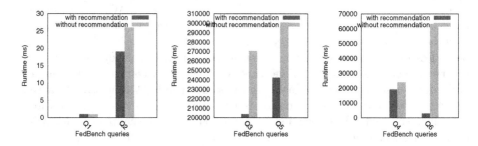

Fig. 2. Runtime with the DarQ (Color figure online)

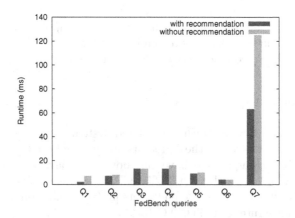

Fig. 3. Runtime with the FedX (Color figure online)

7   Conclusions

The source selection is an important part of a federated system. There are two source selection strategies. One stores information about the endpoint and it uses that information to select the endpoints. This technique has a problem. The catalog needs to be up-to-date. The system has to update this with queries. Another technique is the ASK technique where the system runs ASK queries to know which endpoint can answer the triple pattern. This technique asks all the endpoints with every triple pattern. We reduced the number of the endpoints with a recommendation technique.

The recommendation technique is a user-friendly interface to write SPARQL easier. It is similar to the autocomplete function of the SQL. When the user writes the SPARQL query the system runs simple queries on the endpoints to make recommendation. The recommendations are triple patterns. These triple patterns used by the user in his query. In this paper, we extended our recommendation technique with new extension that uses the *rdfs:range* predicates. We used the recommendation system to get information about the endpoints. We used this information to set the federated system configuration. We presented the algorithm for getting the information. We compared our result with two federated systems: the Darq and the FedX. We have seen that the recommendation can help the federated system to evaluate the query.

In the future we would like to make a library for further applications and we would like to make a web page where this technique can work in order to the non-expert users can use it.

Acknowledgments. Authors thank Ericsson Ltd. for support via the ELTE CNL collaboration.

References

1. Buil-Aranda, C., Polleres, A., Umbrich, J.: Strategies for executing federated queries in SPARQL1.1. In: Mika, P., et al. (eds.) ISWC 2014, Part II. LNCS, vol. 8797, pp. 390–405. Springer, Heidelberg (2014)
2. Campinas, S.: Live SPARQL auto-completion. In: ISWC 2014 Posters and Demonstrations Track, pp. 477–480 (2014). CEUR-WS.org
3. Erling, O., Mikhailov, I.: RDF support in the virtuoso DBMS. In: Pellegrini, T., Auer, S., Tochtermann, K., Schaffert, S. (eds.) Networked Knowledge-Networked Media. SCI, vol. 221, pp. 7–24. Springer, Heidelberg (2009)
4. Gombos, G., Kiss, A.: SPARQL query writing with recommendations based on datasets. In: Yamamoto, S. (ed.) HCI 2014, Part I. LNCS, vol. 8521, pp. 310–319. Springer, Heidelberg (2014)
5. Hoefler, P.: Linked data interfaces for non-expert users. In: Cimiano, P., Corcho, O., Presutti, V., Hollink, L., Rudolph, S. (eds.) ESWC 2013. LNCS, vol. 7882, pp. 702–706. Springer, Heidelberg (2013)
6. Jena, A.: Semantic web framework for Java (2007)

7. Kramer, K., Dividino, R.Q., Gröner, G.: Space: SPARQL index for efficient auto-completion. In: International Semantic Web Conference (Posters and Demos), pp. 157–160 (2013)

8. Lehmann, J., Bühmann, L.: AutoSPARQL: let users query your knowledge base. In: Antoniou, G., Grobelnik, M., Simperl, E., Parsia, B., Plexousakis, D., De Leen-heer, P., Pan, J. (eds.) ESWC 2011, Part I. LNCS, vol. 6643, pp. 63–79. Springer, Heidelberg (2011)

9. Quilitz, B.: DARQ-federated queries with SPARQL (2006)

10. Rakhmawati, N.A., Umbrich, J., Karnstedt, M., Hasnain, A., Hausenblas, M.: Querying over federated SPARQL endpoints–a state of the art survey (2013). arXiv preprint arXiv:1306.1723

11. Rietveld, L., Hoekstra, R.: YASGUI: not just another SPARQL client. In: Cimiano, P., Fernández, M., Lopez, V., Schlobach, S., Völker, J. (eds.) ESWC 2013. LNCS, vol. 7955, pp. 78–86. Springer, Heidelberg (2013)

12. Saleem, M., Ngonga Ngomo, A.-C.: HiBISCuS: hypergraph-based source selection for SPARQL endpoint federation. In: Presutti, V., d'Amato, C., Gandon, F., d'Aquin, M., Staab, S., Tordai, A. (eds.) ESWC 2014. LNCS, vol. 8465, pp. 176–191. Springer, Heidelberg (2014)

13. Schmidt, M., Görlitz, O., Haase, P., Ladwig, G., Schwarte, A., Tran, T.: FedBench: a benchmark suite for federated semantic data query processing. In: Aroyo, L., Welty, C., Alani, H., Taylor, J., Bernstein, A., Kagal, L., Noy, N., Blomqvist, E. (eds.) ISWC 2011, Part I. LNCS, vol. 7031, pp. 585–600. Springer, Heidelberg (2011)

14. Schwarte, A., Haase, P., Hose, K., Schenkel, R., Schmidt, M.: FedX: optimization techniques for federated query processing on linked data. In: Aroyo, L., Welty, C., Alani, H., Taylor, J., Bernstein, A., Kagal, L., Noy, N., Blomqvist, E. (eds.) ISWC 2011, Part I. LNCS, vol. 7031, pp. 601–616. Springer, Heidelberg (2011)

15. Verborgh, R., et al.: Querying datasets on the web with high availability. In: Mika, P., et al. (eds.) ISWC 2014, Part I. LNCS, vol. 8796, pp. 180–196. Springer, Heidelberg (2014)

Evaluation of a System to Analyze Long-Term Images from a Stationary Camera

Akira Ishii[✉], Tetsuya Abe, Hiroyuki Hakoda, Buntarou Shizuki, and Jiro Tanaka

University of Tsukuba, Tsukuba, Japan
{ishii,abe,hakoda,shizuki,jiro}@iplab.cs.tsukuba.ac.jp

Abstract. Recording and analyzing images taken over a long time period (e.g., several months) from a stationary camera could reveal various information regarding the recorded target. However, it is difficult to view such images in their entirety, because the speed at which the images are replayed must be sufficiently slow for the user to comprehend them, and thus it is difficult to obtain valuable information from the images quickly. To address this problem, we have developed a heatmap-based analyzing system. In this paper, we present an experiment conducted using our analyzing system to evaluate the system and identify user processes for analyzing images provided by a stationary camera. Our findings should provide guidance in designing interfaces for the visual analytics of long-term images from stationary cameras.

Keywords: Data visualization · Big data management · Evaluating information · Information presentation · Heatmap · Surveillance system · Visual analytics · Lifelog

1 Introduction

Recording and analyzing images over a long time period (e.g., several months) from a stationary camera could reveal various information regarding the recorded target. For example, if department store staff members install a stationary camera to produce aerial images of a floor, then the recorded images can provide useful data for evaluating the layout of the floor. However, it is difficult to view such images in their entirety, because the speed at which the images are replayed must be sufficiently slow for the user to comprehend them, and thus it is difficult to obtain valuable information from the images quickly.

To address this problem, a considerable amount of research has explored the analysis of images from stationary cameras based on image recognition techniques, with the aim of revealing specific information [5,7,14]. On the other hand, we can focus on visual analytics [12,13] to make discoveries by observing unknown objects or phenomena that have not been established beforehand.

With this motivation, we have developed an analyzing system [8,9] with a heatmap-based interface, designed for performing visual analytics on long-term

© Springer International Publishing Switzerland 2016
S. Yamamoto (Ed.): HIMI 2016, Part I, LNCS 9734, pp. 275–286, 2016.
DOI: 10.1007/978-3-319-40349-6_26

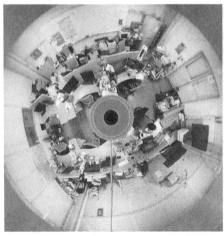

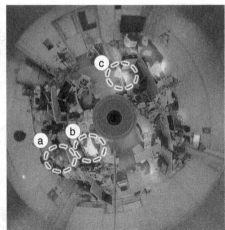

Fig. 1. Omni-directional camera image.

Fig. 2. Image consisting of two heatmaps: (a) a red colored heatmap representing changes of the images in a specific timeframe and (b) a green colored heatmap representing another timeframe. The image contains areas (c) overlaid with red and green colored heatmaps. (Color figure online)

images from a stationary camera (e.g., Fig. 1). This allows the user to analyze long-term images by displaying periods in which the images are changing. It also provides a heatmap that represents the changes to images within a specific timeframe. This heatmap serves as a summary of changes taking place within the timeframe. In addition, this system allows the user to compare two different timeframes by displaying two heatmaps (Fig. 2).

In this paper, we improve our heatmap-based analyzing system [9], and conduct an experiment with our system to evaluate it and identify user processes for analyzing images provided by a stationary camera. The result of our experiment shows that the participants can discover many facts regarding the recorded target quickly (an average of 24 discoveries in 30 min). We also observe that the discoveries can be classified according to five properties. Our findings in this paper are summarized as follows:

– Five properties that can classify the discoveries that the participants obtain using each function of our analyzing system.
– The revelation of the participants' analyzing processes that lead to these five properties.

Those findings should provide guidance in designing interfaces for the visual analytics of long-term images from stationary cameras.

2   Related Work

Interfaces for analyzing images from stationary cameras have recently been explored. Romero et al. proposed Viz-A-Vis, which displays 3D heatmaps [10], and evaluated their system [11]. Their visualization system is different from ours, but we use their evaluating method as a reference. Viz-A-Vis provides 3D heatmaps that summarize the movement of people and objects within a certain timeframe. In contrast, our system provides 2D heatmaps. These 2D heatmaps let the user know where and when changes have frequently occurred during certain timeframes, and provide an easy comparison of two different timeframes. This allows the user to locate events of interest from the images. TotalRecall [3] focuses on transcribing and adding annotations on audio and video recorded at the same time for a hundred thousand hours. While the visualization of their system is similar to ours, ours focuses on comparing two different timeframes using different colored heatmaps. HouseFly [2] presents audio-visual data recorded in several rooms simultaneously using multiple cameras. Their system generates heatmaps and projects the heatmaps onto a 3D model of the recorded space. MotionFinder [1] generates a heatmap as a summary of the images recorded by a surveillance camera, which shows traces of movements across the scene. While that system is similar to ours in generating heatmaps, our research focuses on user discoveries that are obtained by observing heatmaps, and on the processes leading to such discoveries.

Image analyzing methods using crowdsourcing have also been recently explored. Zensors [4] detects objects in images from a stationary camera using crowdsourcing, and notifies users of changes in an image. While Zensors employs crowdsourcing to analyze the images for a specific purpose, our system allows users to analyze images by observing heatmaps by themselves for visual analytics.

Furthermore, automated image analyzing methods have been explored. VERT [6] is a technique to evaluate a summary of an automatically generated video by comparing it with one made by users. By contrast, we provide an analyzing system to users and evaluate the discoveries users obtain with our system.

3   Implementation

This section describes a specification of our system. Our system consists of a recording system and an analyzing system. The recording system obtains images from two stationary cameras that were mounted on the ceiling of the authors' laboratory rooms, preprocesses the images for the generation of a heatmap, and stores the images to NAS (network attached storage). The analyzing system generates heatmaps using the stored images, and presents the heatmaps to users.

3.1   Recording System

We run the recording systems that store the images from omni-directional cameras (Sharp Semiconductor LZ0P3551) mounted on the ceiling of our laboratory (two rooms with sizes of approximately $7.50\,\mathrm{m} \times 7.75\,\mathrm{m}$ ($58\,\mathrm{m}^2$) and

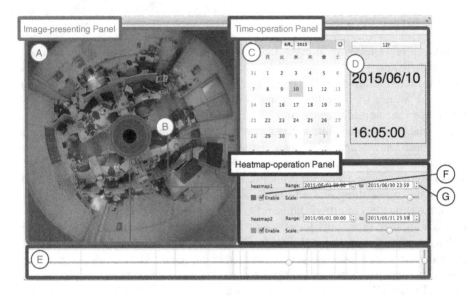

Fig. 3. Our analyzing system using heatmaps.

7.5 m × 15.0 m (113 m^2), and heights of approximately 2.5 m and 2.7 m, respectively) with a 608 × 608 pixels spatial resolution at 1 fps (frames per second). This frame rate is a frequently employed in the video archives of surveillance systems, and results in the recording system producing 86,400 frames per day. The recorded images are stored to NAS (QNAP TS-859 and TS-859 Pro+). The recording systems run on two computers (MacBook Pro 13-inch Late 2011 and MacBook Pro Retina 15-inch Early 2013).

3.2   Analyzing System

Our analyzing system generates heatmaps using the images stored on NAS, and presents the heatmaps to users. Figure 3 illustrates our analyzing system, which consists of Image-presenting Panel, Time-operation Panel, and Heatmap-operation Panel.

Image-Presenting Panel. A camera image view (A) displays a camera image at the date and time (D). Users can select a part (B) of the image (A) for further analysis.

Time-Operation Panel. The system applies blue color to the calendar (C) and the time slider (E), with the density depending on the amount of the movement in the area (B). This function allows users to find a range that they wish to analyze, and reduces the time used to analyze unnecessary images.

Heatmap-Operation Panel. Our system displays two different heatmaps with two different colors (red and green), each of which can be turned on/off using the two checkboxes (F). Users can specify date and time ranges for the heatmaps using the date/time range pickers (G). Activated heatmaps are overlaid with the camera image view (A), as shown in Fig. 2.

Our analyzing system summarizes the movement of people and objects in a specified timeframe based on the number of changes of pixels in the camera images. The more movement there is in the image (A), the more densely the pixel is colored. The more movement there is in the area (B), the more densely the calendar (C) and the time slider (E) are colored. Therefore, our system allows users to recognize areas with little or much movement within a specified timeframe at a glance. Moreover, users can compare movement in two different timeframes by using two heatmaps.

4   Experiment

We conducted an experiment to examine which discoveries users obtained and how, using each function provided by our analyzing system.

4.1   Participants

Four participants (three males, one female) aged between 22 and 23 were recruited for the experiment. Note that the rooms recorded by the stationary cameras consisted of the laboratory of the participants. None of the participants had previously used our system, nor did they have prior knowledge regarding our system.

4.2   Apparatus and Experimental Environment

We employed a MacBook Pro 13-inch Mid 2010 (CPU: 2.4 GHz Core 2 Duo, RAM: 4 GB, OS: Mac OS X 10.9.5) as the computer for running our analyzing system. We recorded the whole experiment with a video camera, a voice recorder, and screen capture software (QuickTime Player 10.3).

4.3   Procedure

First, we informed the participants of the purpose and the procedure of the experiment. We then informed the participants that the reward for participation in the experiment included not only a basic reward, but also a bonus depending on the number of discoveries. After the basic explanation, we explained the use of our analyzing system to the participants. We then asked them to engage with the system until they felt that they completely understood how to use it, as a practice. We employed the images in which the participants were not recorded for the practice.

In the analyzing task, we asked the participants to use our analyzing system for 30 min, during which time they should attempt to make as many discoveries as possible and inform the experimenters about each of these using think aloud protocol. In addition, we asked the participants to inform the experimenters of the facts that led them to each discovery (e.g., the color of the heatmap is dense in certain areas, as described in Sect. 5.3). In this analyzing task, we used images that were recorded over six months (July 1, 2014 to December 31, 2014; 4,416 hours; approximately 32 million images) using the stationary camera. Note that the participants were recorded in the images for this analyzing task.

After the analyzing task was completed, we asked the participants to answer a questionnaire related to our system. The experiment took approximately 60 min in total.

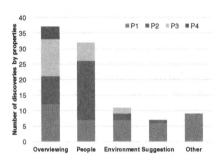

Fig. 4. Number of discoveries by properties. (Color figure online)

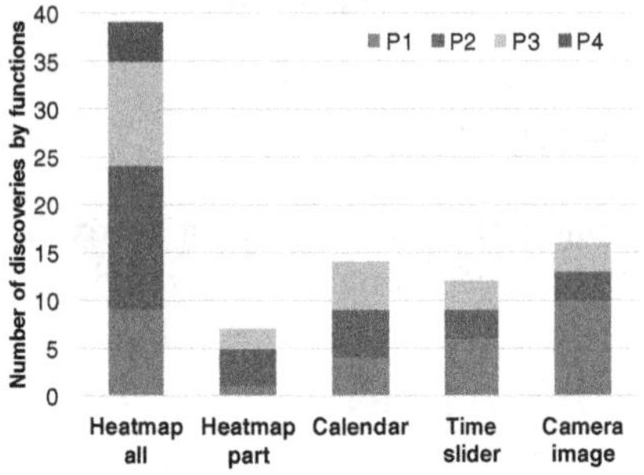

Fig. 5. Number of discoveries by functions. (Color figure online)

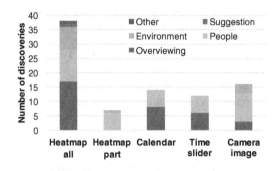

Fig. 6. Number of discoveries by functions. (Color figure online)

5   Result

5.1   Discoveries and Classification

In the experiment, the participants (P1–P4) had an average of 24 discoveries (Total = 96, SD = 13.7). P1 had 41 discoveries, P2 had 31 discoveries, P3 had

20 discoveries, and P4 had four discoveries. Each participant obtained discoveries that were related to her/his colleagues or situations regarding the room. Furthermore, three participants obtained discoveries that related to themselves. We classified the discoveries by the following five properties, with reference to [11]. The result is presented in Fig. 4.

Discovery

> **Overviewing.** Discoveries obtained by paying attention to the entire image.
>
> **People.** Discoveries obtained by paying attention to the people in recorded images.
>
> **Environment.** Discoveries obtained by paying attention to the environment (e.g., objects in recorded images and changes in the appearance of the room).

Discovery Related to the System

> **Suggestion.** Opinions/discoveries that are related to the analyzing system (e.g., requests to extend functionality, proposals of a new function, and ideas to improve the system).
>
> **Other.** Other opinions/discoveries (e.g., suggestions for applications of our system).

We also classified the discoveries by the five functions of our analyzing system by considering which function the participants used when they obtained discoveries (Fig. 5). In this classification, one discovery is classified into multiple functions if participants used more than one functions for the discovery.

Heatmap/All. Discoveries obtained by paying attention to the whole heatmap, (A) in Fig. 3.

Heatmap/Part. Discoveries obtained by paying attention to a part of the heatmap, (B) in Fig. 3.

Calendar. Discoveries obtained by paying attention to the color of the calendar, (C) in Fig. 3.

Time Slider. Discoveries obtained by paying attention to the color of the time slider or comparing different images by operating the time slider, (E) in Fig. 3.

Camera Image. Discoveries obtained by paying attention to the camera image, (A) in Fig. 3.

As shown in Figs. 4 and 5, we found that the discoveries depended on the participant or the function used, based on the color pattern of each chart. P1 made more discoveries using Time slider and Camera image than other participants. P1 realized that movement occurred in a specific area from a heatmap, and then observed images in that area. P1 made many discoveries that were classified under Suggestion or Other, thus providing ideas for potential applications of our system. Figure 4 suggests that only P2 made more People discoveries than Overviewing ones. This is because P2 made more discoveries using Heatmap/part function than other participants, as shown in Fig. 5. The main reason that P2 made more discoveries using Heatmap/part function was that P2 used two heatmaps to compare different timeframes several times. The distribution of the functions used by P3 was similar to that for P2. However, the distribution of the properties was different. This is because P3 tended to make discoveries by seeing things roughly (e.g., there were many people at a certain timeframe) using Heatmap/all function. As shown in Figs. 4 and 5, the number of discoveries by P4 was extremely low. Because all of the discoveries by P4 were classified into Overviewing and obtained using Heatmap/all function, we might fail to explain P4 sufficiently how to use our system or the intent of the experiment. In addition, from the videos that we recorded of the whole experiment using a video camera, we note that P4 hardly used any of the functions except for Heatmap/all.

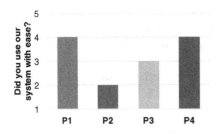

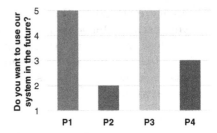

Fig. 7. Did you use our system with ease?

Fig. 8. Do you want to use our system in the future?

Figure 6 shows the number of discoveries classified by functions. Heatmap/all was commonly used. Heatmap/part and Camera image were used mainly to make People discoveries. Calendar and Time slider were only used for Overviewing or People discoveries.

5.2 Qualitative Results

We asked participants to complete a questionnaire that consisted of two questions: *"did you use our system with ease?"* and *"do you want to use our system in the future?"* Each question included a five-point Likert scale styled form (1 = strongly disagree, 5 = strongly agree) and a comment form. The results are presented in Figs. 7 and 8. As shown in Figs. 7 and 8, the scores provided by P2 were lower than for the others. While P2 skillfully use all functions, he stated that *"the analyzing was fun for me, but I do not conceive application examples"* in the questionnaire. Furthermore, P2 provided many requests for extending the functionality, proposals for new functions, and ideas to improve our system. On the other hand, P1 and P3 awarded relatively high scores. From the videos that we recorded of the whole experiment and the comment form of the questionnaire, we conclude that the participants enjoyed looking back on and analyzing their research days.

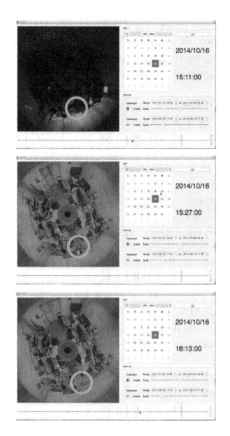

Fig. 9. P1 was aware of the time when a student placed something on the shelf in the laboratory.

Fig. 10. P2 was aware that he often stood up from his seat when he was in the laboratory.

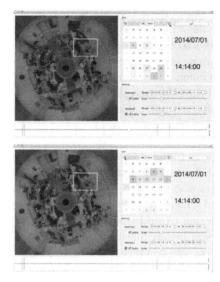

Fig. 11. P3 was aware that he was frequently in the laboratory from late August to early September.

Fig. 12. P3 was aware that the screens of these two monitors were frequently changing.

Fig. 13. P4 was aware that some students were in the laboratory at the end of the year.

5.3   Analyzing Processes

In this section, we describe some of the analyzing processes of the participants. To examine each participant's analyzing processes, we analyzed the screen captures. We found that all of the participants first browsed the images recorded in July, and then browsed the images recorded in August and later in the sequence. After that, each participant acted differently.

P1 discovered that at around 16:00 on October 16th a person placed an object on the shelf in the laboratory, as shown in Fig. 9. We classified this discovery as *People–Camera image*. P1 browsed the images recorded from July to December, and discovered that an object was placed on the shelf in the laboratory at a particular time (the green circles in Fig. 9). In order to reveal the time, P1 first used Calendar function, and then revealed the date. Next, P1 used Time slider function to find that there was no object present at 15:11, and found that the person began placing the object at 15:27 and that the process of placing the object was completed at 16:13. Thus, P1 arrived at the conclusion stated above.

P2 discovered that he often left his seat while he was in his laboratory, as shown in Fig. 10. We classified this discovery as *People–Time slider*. P2 first selected the area of his seat within the image, as shown in Fig. 10. Then, P2 used Calendar function, and explored each timeframe in which he was in his laboratory. As a result, P2 noticed that the blue part of Time slider was not continuous, but rather discrete, and concluded as above. Note that this discovery reveals that our tool is useful for self-behavioral analysis, because this discovery by P2 was related to himself.

P3 discovered that he was in his laboratory more frequently between late August and early September than other timeframes, as shown in Fig. 11. We classified this discovery as *People–Calendar and Heatmap/part*. P3 first selected the area of his seat within the image, as well as P2. Then, P3 used Calendar function, browsed the images recorded from July to December, and noticed that the color of the calendar was dense between late August and early September. Therefore, P3 concluded as above. In addition, P3 noticed that the color of the heatmap was dense in certain areas (the green circles in Fig. 12), and discovered that there were computer monitors in those areas. We classified this discovery as *Environment–Heatmap/all*. After P3 inspected the calendar, he noticed that the color of the heatmap was dense in the areas where the generating timeframe of the heatmap was one day, and concluded as above. Moreover, P3 discoveried that one of the computer monitors displayed a screen saver, while the other displayed a clock.

P4 discovered that there were many students present at the end of the year, as shown in Fig. 13. We classified this discovery as *Overviewing–Heatmap/all*. P4 browsed the images recorded in December, and examined the calendar. P4 set the generating timeframe of the red heatmap to July, and that of the green heatmap to December. At this time, P4 compared the two heatmaps, and she noticed that the density of the green colored heatmap was higher. Therefore, P4 concluded as above.

6   Discussions

In our experiment, we employed images that recorded the participants, in order to ensure consistency in the experimental condition of the participants. As a result, there were many discoveries made that related to the participants themselves. To be precise, 11 of the 96 discoveries (approximately 11.4 %) consisted of such discoveries. Two participants (P3 and P4) stated in the questionnaire that "*I looked back on my life pattern, and my motivation to go to the laboratory increased.*" Therefore, we surmise that our system is useful for analyzing the users themselves.

There was a bias present in the functions of our system that the participants in the experiment chose to use (there was one participant who did not use all of the functions). Therefore, we propose that we should limit the available functions depending on the purpose of the analysis. For example, if a user wants to perform an analysis regarding Environment, then only Heatmap/all and Camera image functions should be provided, considering Fig. 6. In addition, we plan to explore to possibility of reusing the analyzing processes that we found in our research, to provide a wizard that is specialized for each analyzing purpose. As a result, the wizard would enable users to perform an analysis without having a deep knowledge of our system.

7   Future Work

In our experiment, we used images in which the participants were recorded. Because this is a particular situation, we will conduct a further experiment using images in which the participants have not been recorded, and reveal which participants obtain discoveries in such a situation.

All of the participants that were recruited for the experiment had a computer science background. Therefore, we will recruit participants that have different backgrounds to conduct a further experiment examining which discoveries they will make using our system and how.

In the experiment, we used images recorded over only a six-month period. However, because we also have images recorded over a period of more than 20 months and continue to record images, we plan to conduct a further experiment using the longer-term images. In addition, we plan to apply our system with images recorded in different locations (e.g., a hallway or a large shared room).

8   Conclusion

In this paper, we have improved our system for recording and analyzing images using a stationary camera. In addition, we have conducted an experiment to evaluate our analyzing system, and examined what participants discover using each function of the system. The result of the experiment was that the participants made an average of 24 discoveries, which we classified by five properties and by five functions of the system. Furthermore, we revealed the analyzing processes of the participants. We believe that those findings provide guidance in designing interfaces for the visual analytics of long-term images from stationary cameras.

References

1. Buono, P.: Analyzing video produced by a stationary surveillance camera. In: Proceedings of the International Conference on Distributed Multimedia Systems, DMS 2011, pp. 140–145 (2011)
2. DeCamp, P., Shaw, G., Kubat, R., Roy, D.: An immersive system for browsing and visualizing surveillance video. In: Proceedings of the International Conference on Multimedia, MM 2010, pp. 371–380. ACM, New York, NY, USA (2010)
3. Kubat, R., DeCamp, P., Roy, B.: TotalRecall: visualization and semi-automatic annotation of very large audio-visual corpora. In: Proceedings of the 9th International Conference on Multimodal Interfaces, ICMI 2007, pp. 208–215. ACM, New York, NY, USA (2007)
4. Laput, G., Lasecki, W.S., Wiese, J., Xiao, R., Bigham, J.P., Harrison, C.: Zensors: Adaptive, rapidly deployable, human-intelligent sensor feeds. In: Proceedings of the 33rd Annual ACM Conference on Human Factors in Computing Systems, CHI 2015, pp. 1935–1944. ACM, New York, NY, USA (2015)
5. Leykin, A.: Visual human tracking and group activity analysis: a video mining system for retail marketing. Ph.D. thesis, Department of Computer Science and Cognitive Science, Indiana University (2007)
6. Li, Y., Merialdo, B.: VERT: automatic evaluation of video summaries. In: Proceedings of the International Conference on Multimedia, MM 2010, pp. 851–854. ACM, New York, NY, USA (2010)
7. Corporation, N.E.C.: Fieldanalyst. http://www.nec-solutioninnovators.co.jp/sl/fieldanalyst/. Accessed 1 Feb 2016. (in Japanese)
8. Nogami, R., Shizuki, B., Hosobe, H., Tanaka, J.: An analysis support interface using frame difference for a video from a stationary camera. In: Proceedings of the Interaction 2011. Information Processing Society of Japan (2011). (in Japanese)
9. Nogami, R., Shizuki, B., Hosobe, H., Tanaka, J.: An exploratory analysis tool for a long-term video from a stationary camera. In: Proceedings of the 5th IEEE International Symposium on Monitoring and Surveillance Research, ISMSR 2012, vol. 2, pp. 32–37 (2012)
10. Romero, M., Summet, J., Stasko, J., Abowd, G.: Viz-A-Vis: toward visualizing video through computer vision. IEEE Vis. Comput. Graph. 14(6), 1261–1268 (2008)
11. Romero, M., Vialard, A., Peponis, J., Stasko, J., Abowd, G.: Evaluating video visualizations of human behavior. In: Proceedings of the SIGCHI Conference on Human Factors in Computing Systems, CHI 2011, pp. 1441–1450. ACM, New York, NY, USA (2011)
12. Thomas, J.J., Cook, K., et al.: A visual analytics agenda. IEEE Comput. Graph. Appl. 26(1), 10–13 (2006)
13. Wong, P.C., Thomas, J.: Visual analytics. IEEE Comput. Graph. Appl. 24(5), 20–21 (2004)
14. Xing, Y., Wang, Z., Qiang, W.: Face tracking based advertisement effect evaluation. In: The 2nd International Congress on Image and Signal Processing, pp. 1–4 (2009)

The Effect of the Arrangement of Fuzzy If-Then Rules on the Performance of On-Line Fuzzy Classification

Tomoharu Nakashima[(⊠)]

Osaka Prefecture University, Gakuen-cho 1-1,
Naka-ku, Sakai, Osaka 599-8531, Japan
tomoharu.nakashima@kis.osakafu-u.ac.jp

Abstract. This paper presents an experimental study on the performance of online fuzzy classifiers. First, a formulation is given for the fuzzy classifier that is used in this paper. Then, online learning techniques that were proposed in the machine learning community are applied for the fuzzy classifier. As there are several parameters that should be specified by humans in the fuzzy classifiers, a series of computational experiments are conducted in order to investigate the effect of those parameters on the classification performance of the online fuzzy classifiers. It is shown that the arrangement of fuzzy if-then rules dramatically improve the on-line classification performance.

Keywords: On-line learning · Fuzzy if-then rule · Classification

1 Introduction

Information explosion in recent years has brought the need for those information systems that can deal with a massive volume of data within a reasonable computational time. Not only the data are growing, but also the property of the data changes over time. Even the source of the data might change itself over time, making the previous data rather obsolete.

On-line learning is one of the promising methods for the circumstances described above. On-line learning methods modify the models such as classifiers and regression functions based on a few training patterns. They can be applied for learning problems with an intractably large number of training patterns. If the number of training patterns is too large to handle at once, only a small subset of the training patterns is used to train a learning model and incrementally update it using another small subset of the training patterns. On-line learning techniques are also useful in dynamic problem where the true input-output relation or the true classification boundaries changes over time. In this case, available training patterns at each time can be used to update the learning model.

There are several machine learning approaches for on-line learning including confidence-weighted learning [1] and passive-aggressive learning [2]. These approaches are proposed for linear classifiers. The weights of a linear classifier are adaptively updated once a training pattern are newly available. The weight update for both passive-aggressive and confidence-weighted learning is conducted so that the amount

© Springer International Publishing Switzerland 2016
S. Yamamoto (Ed.): HIMI 2016, Part I, LNCS 9734, pp. 287–295, 2016.
DOI: 10.1007/978-3-319-40349-6_27

of weight change is minimized while the loss function of the new training patterns is zero or probabilistically small.

Fuzzy rule-based systems have been shown their good performance in classification tasks [3]. In the case of classification, a fuzzy classifier is constructed from a given set of training patterns. The fuzzy classifier consists of a set of fuzzy if-then rules. In this paper, fuzzy if-then rules with antecedent fuzzy sets and a consequent real value are considered for the fuzzy classifier. The antecedent fuzzy sets are assumed to be given a priori by using human knowledge. The consequent real values are obtained by using some learning technique from given training patterns.

Although the fuzzy systems have been shown to be effective for classification, the classification problems have been assumed to be static. That is, true classification boundaries did not change but only remained still. In this paper, two on-line learning algorithms are introduced to fuzzy rule-based classification systems in order to handle dynamic classification where the true classification boundaries changes over time. As on-line learning algorithms, the paper focuses passive-aggressive learning and confidence-weighted learning.

First, it is shown that a fuzzy classification system can be viewed as a linear classification system in a high-dimensionally mapped space. Next, the formulation of the on-line learning algorithms is provided for fuzzy classification systems. Then, a series of computational experiments are conducted in order to investigate the classification performance of on-line fuzzy classification systems. In the computational experiments, two on-line classification problems are used where a two-dimensional training pattern is randomly generated with a rotating classification boundary at each time step.

2 Fuzzy Classifier

A fuzzy classifier consists of fuzzy if-then rules. Let us assume that the classification problem has the dimensionality of n. It is also assumed that there are only two-classes in the classification problem in a unit space $[0, 1]^n$ without losing generality. The following type of fuzzy if-then rules is used for the fuzzy classifier in this paper:

$$\text{Rule } R_j : \text{If } x_1 \text{ is } A_{j1} \text{ and } x_2 \text{ is } A_{j2} \text{ and} \ldots \text{and } x_n \text{ is } A_{jn}$$
$$\text{then } b_j, \quad j = 1, 2, \ldots, N, \tag{1}$$

where R_j is the label of the j-th fuzzy if-then rule, $A_j = (A_{j1}, A_{j2}, \ldots, A_{jn})$ is a set of antecedent fuzzy sets for R_j, b_j is the consequent real value, and N is the number of fuzzy if-then rules in the fuzzy classifier. The number of fuzzy if-then rules is determined once the fuzzy partition for each attribute is determined by a human user. For example, if three fuzzy sets are used for each attribute in a four-dimensional classification problem, then the total number of generated fuzzy if-then rules is $3^4 = 81$. For the antecedent fuzzy sets, any type of membership functions can be used while this paper considers only triangular-type fuzzy membership functions. Figure 1 shows the triangular-type membership functions with various fuzzy partitions (from two to five

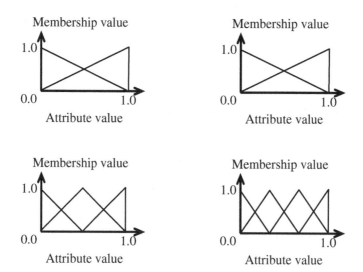

Fig. 1. Triangular-type membership functions

fuzzy sets for an attribute). The membership functions are homogeneously distributed. That is, the width of the fuzzy sets are equal except the rightmost and leftmost ones. Those membership functions are half of the others.

Let $\vec{x} = (x_1, x_2, \ldots, x_n)$ be an unknown pattern for a fuzzy classifier to classify. The classification rule of the unknown pattern is given as follows:

$$\vec{x} = \begin{cases} \text{Class 1}, & \text{if } \sum_{j=1}^{N} b_j \cdot \mu_j(\vec{x}) > 0, \\ \text{Class 2}, & \text{otherwise}, \end{cases} \tag{2}$$

where $\mu_j(\vec{x})$ is the compatibility of the j-th fuzzy if-then rule with the unknown pattern, which is calculated using multiplication of membership values as follows:

$$\mu_j(\vec{x}) = \mu_{j1}(x_1) \cdot \mu_{j2}(x_2) \cdot \ldots \cdot \mu_{jn}(x_{jn}), \tag{3}$$

where $\mu_{ji}(x_i)$, $i = 1, 2, \ldots, n$, is the membership value for the i-th attribute x_i.

3 On-Line Learning Techniques

On-line learning techniques in this paper incrementally update the parameters of classifier models. The parameter update occurs every time a new training pattern becomes available. It is assumed that only a single pattern becomes available at a time. Let us define $\vec{x}_t$ as the training pattern that is available at Time t. The class of the training pattern $\vec{x}_t$ is defined as c_t ($c_t \in \{1, 2\}$). It is assumed that only one training pattern becomes available at each time step. This section introduce a linear classifier as the conventional method as well as two on-line learning methods that are applicable to the linear classifier.

3.1   Linear Classifier

The class of an n-dimensional pattern $\vec{x} = (x_1, x_2, \ldots, x_n)$ is determined by the following rule:

$$\vec{x} = \begin{cases} \text{Class 1,} & \text{if } \sum_{i=1}^{n} w_i x_i + w_0 > 0, \\ \text{Class 2,} & \text{otherwise,} \end{cases} \tag{4}$$

where $\vec{w} = (w_0, w_1, w_2, \ldots, w_n)$ is a weight vector. The weight vector is determined so that the classification error of the linear classifier is minimized in terms of a given set of training patterns. Typically, a least mean squared method is used. However, this is not exactly applicable in this paper as there is no training pattern available for training the linear classifier model. It is also possible that the classification boundary changes over time. There are implicit requirements in the least mean square method that all training patterns are available for training and the classification boundary stays still and never changes.

The assumption in this paper is that not all training patterns are available before training classifier models but gradually made available over time. Thus the classifier model requires to perform on-line learning where the model adapts itself every time a new training pattern becomes available.

3.2   Passive-Aggressive Learning

The training of the linear classifier described in Subsect. 3.1 is generally formulated as an optimization problem where the weight vector $\vec{w} = (w_0, w_1, \ldots, w_n)$ is determined in a way the error between the target class of training patterns and the classification results by the linear classifier is minimized. This formulation is possible if all the training patterns are available at a time. However, this paper considers a different situation where not all training patterns are available but only a limited number of training patterns is available at each time step. Crammer [10] proposed an on-line learning called passive-aggressive learning in order to tackle this special situation of training linear classifiers. The passive-aggressive learning uses the following hinge function for calculating the error between the target class and the classification result:

$$l_{\text{hinge}}(\vec{x}, c, \vec{w}) = \max(0, 1 - c \times \vec{w} \cdot \vec{x}), \tag{5}$$

where $\vec{x}$ and c are a training pattern and its target class. This hinge loss function gives the degree of errors in terms of the current weight vector $\vec{w}$. In most of the cases, there exist multiple weight vectors that makes the value of the loss function. The weight vector is modified so that the amount of the update is minimized. Thus the optimization problem at time t is formulated as follows:

$$\vec{w}^{t+1} = \arg\min_{\vec{w}} \frac{1}{2} ||\vec{w} - \vec{w}^t||^2 \tag{6}$$

$$\text{subject to } l_{\text{hinge}}(\vec{x}^t, c^t, \vec{w}) = 0 \tag{7}$$

where $\vec{w}^{t+1}$ is the updated weighted vector which will be used at the next time step, and $\vec{w}^t$, $\vec{x}^t$, and c^t are the current weight vector, the available training pattern and the target class at time t.

3.3   Confidence-Weighted Learning

The passive-aggressive learning in Subsect. 3.2 has shown its powerful on-line performance in classification and is already used in real-world systems. There is, however, a disadvantage in this method that the learning technique is too sensitive to noisy data. In order to overcome this problem, confidence-weighted learning technique was proposed by Dredze and Crammer [1]. This learning technique assumes that the weights in the linear function are not real values, but follows Gaussian probability distributions. In this way, each weight has two parameters: the mean value and the width of a Gaussian function. The mean value shows the probable value of the corresponding weight, and the width shows the confidence in the mean value. When the confidence in the mean is low, the width of the Gaussian function is large while the width is small when the confidence is high. In the update of the Gaussian functions, the mean value will not largely modified when the width is small as the confidence in the mean value is high. On the other hand, when the width of the Gaussian function is large, the mean value will be moved largely because it is not sure if the current mean value is appropriate or not.

Now that the weight vector $\vec{w}$ follows the Gaussian function, it is written as

$$\vec{w} \sim N(\vec{\mu}, \Sigma), \tag{8}$$

where $\vec{\mu}$ and Σ are the mean vectors and the co-variance matrix, respectively. When a training pattern $\vec{x}^t$ becomes available with its target class c^t for training the linear function at time t, the update of the weight values are performed so that the amount of the modification should be minimized subject to the restriction that the probability of correct classification for the new training is higher than η. This is written as an optimization problem that is formulated as follows:

$$(\vec{\mu}^{t+1}, \Sigma^{t+1}) = \arg\min_{\vec{\mu}, \Sigma} D_{KL}(N(\vec{\mu}, \Sigma)||N(\vec{\mu}^t, \Sigma^t)), \tag{9}$$

$$\text{subject to } \Pr_{\vec{w} \sim N(\vec{\mu}^t, \Sigma^t)} \{c^t \cdot (\vec{w} \cdot \vec{x}^t) \geq 0\} \geq \eta, \tag{10}$$

where D_{KL} is the Kalback-Leibler divergence between the two Gaussian distributions.

3.4   Applying the On-Line Learning Techniques to Fuzzy Classifiers

The on-line learning techniques in Subsects. 3.2 and 3.3 can be applied to fuzzy classifiers. Equations (2) and (4) are the classification rule for an input pattern by a fuzzy classifier and a linear classifier, respectively. They can be seen as the same if the membership values of fuzzy if-then rules is treated as an input vector in a mapped space. That is, the fuzzy classifier performing a linear classification in the mapped space by the fuzzy if-then rules. In the mapped space, $\vec{\mu}(\cdot)$ is the input vector and $\vec{b} = (b_1, b_2, \ldots, b_N)$ can be viewed as the weight vector in the linear classification. In this perspective, the fuzzy classifier can be updated in an on-line manner using either the passive-aggressive learning or the confidence-weighted learning.

If the passive-aggressive learning is applied to the fuzzy classifier, the vector of the consequent real values $\vec{b}$ is updated by solving the following optimization problem:

$$\vec{b}^{t+1} = \arg\min_{\vec{b}} \frac{1}{2} ||\vec{b} - \vec{b}^t||^2 \tag{11}$$

$$\text{subject to } l_{\text{hinge}}(\vec{\mu}(\vec{x}^t), c^t, \vec{b}) = 0 \tag{12}$$

where

$$l_{\text{hinge}}(\vec{\mu}(\vec{x}^t), c^t, \vec{b}) = \max(0, 1 - c^t \times \vec{b} \cdot \vec{\mu}(\vec{x}^t)) \tag{13}$$

In the case of the confidence-weighted learning, the consequent real values of fuzzy if-then rules are assumed to follow Gaussian functions with the mean vector $\vec{\mu}_b$ and the co-variance matrix Σ_b. Then the parameters are modified by solving the following optimization problem:

$$(\vec{\mu}_b^{t+1}, \Sigma_b^{t+1}) = \arg\min_{\vec{\mu}_b, \Sigma_b} D_{KL}(N(\vec{\mu}_b, \Sigma_b) || N(\vec{\mu}_b^t, \Sigma_b^t)), \tag{14}$$

$$\text{subject to } \Pr_{\vec{b} \sim N(\vec{\mu}_b^t, \Sigma_b^t)} \{c^t \cdot (\vec{b} \cdot \vec{\mu}(\vec{x}^t)) \geq 0\} \geq \eta, \tag{15}$$

4   Arrangement of Fuzzy If-Then Rules

The classification performance of the on-line fuzzy classifier can be determined by the arrangement of fuzzy if-then rules. The arrangement of fuzzy if-then rules is determined by the configuration of the antecedent fuzzy sets. Figure 1 shows four configurations of the antecedent fuzzy sets. Two fuzzy sets through five fuzzy sets are used to divide the attribute value. If two fuzzy sets are used for each attribute in an n-dimensional classification problem, the number of fuzzy if-then rules generated for this problem is 2^n. In general, let K the number of fuzzy sets used for each attribute. Then the total number of generated fuzzy if-then rules is K^n. This means that the number of the generated fuzzy if-then rules exponentially increases with the number of fuzzy sets per axis in high-dimensional problem. Since an intractably large number of fuzzy if-then rules hinders from training fuzzy classifiers, it should be always noticed that the number of fuzzy sets should be minimized as much as possible. For static classification problem, there are various way of reducing the number of generate fuzzy if-then rules using evolutionary algorithm (for example, see [3]). However, to the best knowledge of the author, there is not an effective method for dynamic problems that are the focus of this study. This will be the future work.

5 Experiments

5.1 Experimental Setting

A synthetic problem is prepared for investigating the classification performance of the on-line fuzzy classifier. In the synthetic problem, the input space in a two-dimensional unit space $[0, 1]^2$ is divided into two subspaces by a line, which is the true classification boundary. Then, the classification boundary rotates by one degree centering at the point $(0.5, 0.5)$ every time step. A two-dimensional real vector is also generated using uniformly random values from the input space with the class label that is determined from the current classification boundary. The procedure of the computational experiment in this section is written below:

1. Randomly initialize the weights of a linear classifier or the consequent values of a fuzzy classifier. If the weight follows a Gaussian probability distribution, the parameters of the distribution is randomly determined.
2. Evaluate the classification performance of the classifiers.
3. Set $t = 0$.
4. Randomly generate an input vector from the input space. The class label of the input pattern is determined from the true classification boundary at time t. If the generated input vector lies exactly on the classification boundary, abandon the vector and re-generate the input vector.
5. Update classifiers using the generated input vector along with the class label.
6. Evaluate the classification performance of the current classifiers.
7. Terminate the procedure if $t = 720$. Otherwise increment t and go to 4.

Evaluation of the classifiers in Procedures 2 and 6 is done by first partitioning the input space into 10,000 (i.e., 100 × 100) grids and compare the classification results at each crossing-point of the grid and its true class label. The true class label is obtained from the classification boundary at each time step. During the computational experiments, three versions of the passive-aggressive learning (see [3]) and the confidence-weighted learning techniques are used.

5.2 Experimental Results

The computational experiments in Subsect. 5.1 was repeated 10 times with different random initializations of classifiers and the averaged performance evaluation (i.e., the average correct classification rate over 10,000 crossing-points of the grid) is obtained.

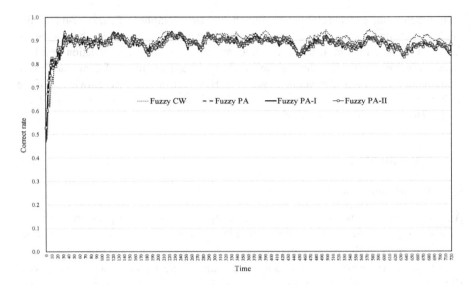

Fig. 2. Experimental results by fuzzy classifiers

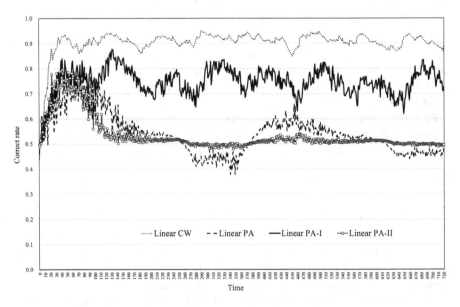

Fig. 3. Classification results by linear classifiers

The experimental results are shown in Figs. 2 and 3. The classification results by the fuzzy classifiers are shown in Figs. 2, and 3 shows the classification results by the linear classifiers. From these figures, we see that the fuzzy classifiers successfully follow the movement of the true classification boundary while it is not the case for some of the linear classifiers.

6 Conclusions

This paper investigated the classification performance of on-line fuzzy classifiers. Passive-aggressive learning and confidence-weighted learning are considered as on-line learning techniques in this paper. It is shown that the fuzzy classifier can be seen as a linear classifier in the mapped space from the original input space into the high-dimensional space that are spanned by the fuzzy if-the rules. A series of computational experiments are conducted to show the effective ness.

References

1. Dredze, M., Crammer, K.: Confidence-weighted linear classification. In: Proceedings of the 25th International Conference on Machine Learning, pp. 264–271 (2008)
2. Crammer, K., Dekel, O., Keshet, J., Shalev-Shwartz, S., Singer, Y.: Online passive-aggressive algorithms. J. Mach. Learn. Res. **7**, 551–585 (2006)
3. Ishibuchi, H., Nakashima, T., Nii, M.: Classification and Modeling with Linguistic Information Granules: Advanced Approaches to Linguistic Data Mining. Springer, Berlin (2004)

An Efficient Scheme for Candidate Solutions of Search-Based Multi-objective Software Remodularization

Amarjeet Prajapati[✉] and Jitender Kumar Chhabra

Computer Engineering Department, NIT Kurukshetra, Kurukshetra, India
amarjeetnitkkr@gmail.com, jitenderchhabra@gmail.com

Abstract. Multi-objective search-based software remodularization approaches are used to rearrange the software elements into modules by optimizing several quality criteria. These search-based approaches can find out better quality regrouping solutions compared to the traditional (analytical based) remodularization, if the suitable encoding for the candidate solutions is used. In this paper, we propose an efficient encoding scheme for candidate solutions and use this scheme to remodularize the object-oriented software using genetic based multi-objective evolutionary algorithm. This proposed representation helps in improving human-computer interaction, and semantic based, efficiently-designed and error-free information gets transferred to the computing system through it. To assess the effectiveness of the proposed approach, we evaluate it over six real-world software systems of different characteristics. Further, the approach is compared with the existing encoding scheme (i.e., GNE representation scheme). Experiments show that the proposed approach produces better results in terms of quality, convergence speed and execution time compared to GNE representation scheme.

Keywords: Software remodularization · Search based software engineering · Multi-objective optimization · Object-oriented systems

1 Introduction

Software Remodularization: Software systems, in particular, object-oriented systems are initially designed and created in a modular way. However, over time, modularity of a system often degrades due to improper placement of software elements into the modules [1]. The ill-modular structure of software system makes it difficult to understand, maintain and evolve [2]. To improve the modularity of software system the maintainers reorganize the software components into the modules and such process is generally known as software remodularization [3]. Software remodularization problem generally involves large set of conflicting criterion, competing constraints, ambiguous and vague information [4]. Hence, solving remodularization problem is very complex and time consuming task. Consider the problem of finding a remodularization of software system that satisfies a given modularity criterion. In such a problem, there can be very large/infinite remodularization alternatives and different sets of modularization can be good solutions. Furthermore, modularization needs to satisfy various competing

© Springer International Publishing Switzerland 2016
S. Yamamoto (Ed.): HIMI 2016, Part I, LNCS 9734, pp. 296–307, 2016.
DOI: 10.1007/978-3-319-40349-6_28

constraints related to the modularity. In such case, identification of an overall good modularization solution is highly desirable for the maintainer, but not easy to obtain through an automated process.

Software remodularization techniques can be broadly categorized into analytical-based and search-based remodularization. Several analytical analysis based techniques have been presented in the research literature for software remodularization [3, 5–7]. These approaches guarantee to find an optimal solution, but require exponential computational time. Hence, such approaches can be more suitable for small size problems. On the other hand the search-based remodularization approaches do not guarantee the best optimal solution, but are able to find near optimal solution in a reasonable time.

This paper uses the search-based remodularization approach and primarily concerns with the problem of rearranging the source code classes into a set of modules of a system whose modularization has degraded due to the maintenance. For such a system some classes may no longer be in suitable modules and thus remodularization of the system become highly useful for improving the software quality. Our aim is therefore to search the whole space of possible modularizations to see if there exists a better grouping of classes in various modules.

Search-Based Multi-objective Software Remodularization: The term "Search-Based Software Engineering" was first given by Harman and Jones [8]. Since then lot of research has been carried out in this direction. As addressed by Harman and Jones [8], the problems to be solved by the SBSE usually require more efforts, the solution is highly intricate, and the software developer is ready to wait for the output. The search-based approach provides a lower human cost solution, freeing the software developer to work on other issues that require creativity and imagination.

To solve any problem using search-based technique, problem needs to be refor-mulated as a search-based optimization problem. For that, it will be necessary to define the following there key ingredients (1) representation of candidate solution; (2) fitness function; and (3) manipulator operators. Proper design of these ingredients has major influence on the performance of search-based software remodularization. The main contribution of this paper is a new and efficient representation of candidate solutions, which helps in improving the human computer interaction (HCI) as software devel-opers (humans) interact with the computer based optimization process through this representation. An efficient representation eases the process of inputting the suitable data to the computing systems ensures the transfer of correct data from humans to computers and has a major impact on performance of computing of this data at the machine end [9].

Good representation of the candidate solutions is critical to the convergence speed of the search-based technique and the quality of obtained results [10]. Most of the existing search-based remodularization approaches use the integer based representation namely GNE (Group Number Encoding) for candidate solution [4, 10–14]. It is most widely used solution representation approach in both single and multi-objective search-based software remodularization. It is represented as an n-sized integer vector, where the value $0 < c_i \leq n$ of the ith class indicates the cluster which the ith class is assigned. A remodularization solution with the same value for all the classes means that all classes are placed in the same cluster, while a solution with all different values (from

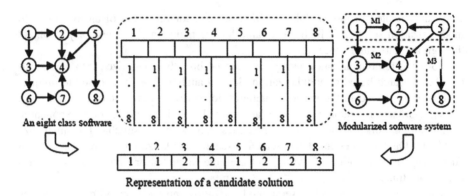

Fig. 1. Illustration of candidate solution using GNE representation

1 to n) means that each classes is in a separate module. The disadvantage of this representation is that it is highly redundant. Figure 1 illustrates an example of the GNE representation.

Above-mentioned integer-based representation approach has been successfully used in many research papers for solving the search-based software remodularization problems. However, major drawback of this representation is that it generates many redundant solutions, which increases the search space and hence execution time. For example, consider software consisting of 7 classes being grouped into 3 modules, the vector (1,1,2,1,2,3,3), (3,3,1,3,1,2,2) and (2,2,3,2,3,2,2) all represent same modularization solution, which places classes 1,2 and 4 in one module, classes 3 and 5 in another module and which places classes 6 and 7 in a third module. Hence, such similar modularization solutions increase the search space.

To minimize the redundancy, we propose a new representation technique in search-based multi-objective software remodularization framework. The new representation is an important task which facilitates an efficient human and computer interaction. Transformation of the software structure into new transformation is a manual or semi automated process usually and optimization is a computer based processing task. The proposed representation requires a clear comprehension of semantics of the structure so that a suitable human computer interaction (HCI) can be planned. The proposed approach for software remodularization is able to produce better solution with faster convergence compared to the previous approach.

The rest of the paper is organized as follows. Section 2 presents relevant research literature. Section 3 describes a framework of the proposed search-based multi-objective software remodularization. Section 4 presents the experiments, results and analysis. Section 5 concludes with future work.

2   Related Works

A large number of research works have been proposed in the literature to support the automatic software remodularization [3, 4, 7, 14–19]. Most of the existing software remodularization approaches are based on analytical techniques [3, 7, 15, 17] or search-based optimization techniques [4, 14, 16, 19]. In search-based approaches, once a software system is framed as a search problem, there are many search algorithms can be applied to solve the problem.

The encoding of the candidate solution is an important activity for the performance of the search problem. In the research literature of search-based software remodularization, many representations have been used such as binary code, floating point number, grey code and integer numbers. However, for search-based software remodularization problem, integer number representation has been found to be more suitable than other representations [4]. Here, we discuss those prevailing approaches which are close to our proposed work.

Mancoridis et al. [11] were the first who formulated the software remodularization problem as search based optimization problem and applied Hill-Climbing and Genetic Algorithms to optimize it. They used an integer based representation techniques to represent the candidate solution. Thereafter, Mitchell and Mancoridis [16] used the same representation technique in Hill-Climbing and Genetic Algorithm for development of Bunch, a tool supporting automatic software remodularization. Praditwong et al. [4] also used the same representation in a new evolutionary algorithm named as two-archive multi-objective evolutionary algorithms to address the software remodularization problems. Abdeen et al. [20] also applied evolutionary algorithms with same representation to modularize the source code classes into packages by automatically minimizing the package dependencies of object-oriented software system. Later, Abdeen et al. [13] extended the same work by formulating the problem as a multi-objective optimization and performed optimization using a multi-objective evolutionary algorithm.

Apart from the above search-based software remodularization, there are some more representations in evolutionary clustering literature. In 1998 Falkenauer [21, 22] proposed a encoding for a variable-length genetic algorithm. The encoding is carried out by separating each individual in the algorithm into two parts: c = [l | g], the first part is the element section, whereas the second part is called the group section of the individual. In [23], research each vector is a sequence of real numbers representing the K cluster centers. For an N-dimensional search space, the length of a clustering solution is N*K words, where the first N positions, represent N dimensions of the first cluster centre and next N positions represent those of the second cluster centre, and so on.

3 Proposed Approach

To improve the performance of search-based software remodularization especially multi-objective search-based software remodularization, this paper proposes a new efficient representation technique for the candidate solution. The considered multi-objective search technique is based on the Non-dominated Sorting concepts [24]. The general structure of the proposed search-based multi-objective software remodularization is given in Fig. 2.

The approach is divided into two main parts. In first part, the software system which is to be re-modularized, is parsed and classes, packages and dependencies between all pairs of classes is extracted. Using the extracted information, initial

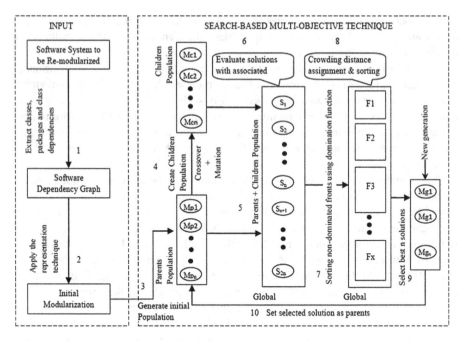

Fig. 2. Overview of search-based multi-objective remodularization process

modularization solution is encoded with the proposed representation technique (in Sect. 3.1). In the second part, the multi-objective evolutionary algorithm (i.e., non-dominated sorting based genetic algorithm) is applied to the initial remodular-ization solution. The algorithm starts by generating initial population from the initial modularization solution. The child population is generated from the initial population by applying the crossover and mutation operators. Next, parent and children popula-tions are combined and a global population is generated. The global population is evaluated with the associated quality measurement. Now the candidate solutions in the global population are categorized according to their dominance. Non-dominated solutions are given a rank of 1; the candidate solutions dominated only by non-dominated candidate solutions are given a rank of 2; candidate solutions domi-nated only by the previous are given a rank of 3, and so on. After ranking, the new parent population for further generation is generated from the non-dominated solution. The algorithm evolves a population from generation to generations by applying crossover, mutation, and selection on the candidate solutions.

3.1 Representation of Candidate Solution

For software engineering domain's search-based optimization algorithms, first and critical issue is the representation of candidate solutions [9]. In case of software remodularization problem there is a need to identify each possible correct combination of re-modularizing a software system. Representation must be chosen carefully so that there is one and exactly one candidate representation per modularization.

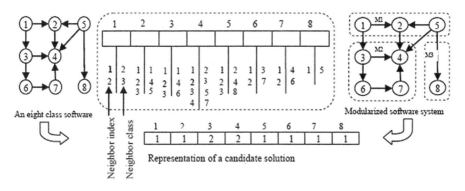

Fig. 3. Illustration of candidate solution representation to an 8 class software remodularization problem.

The approach we adopted in this paper is inspired by the work presented in [25]. In our search-based software remodularization, each modularization solution is represented as a vector of integers ($c = [c1, c2, ..., cn]$), where n is the number of classes in the software dependency graph. In this representation, each c_i is an index between 1 and number of topological neighbors for classes i. When $c_i = 1$, class i is located in the same module as its first neighbor; when $c_i = 2$, it is located in the same module as its second topological neighbor; etc. Figure 3 illustrates the proposed neighbor based encoding scheme.

Conceptually speaking, representing the candidate solutions by means of topological neighbors as discussed above, is usually more computationally efficient than using GNE representation scheme described in Sect. 1. The main reason of improved efficiency is that the search space formed by the proposed approach contains reduced number of redundant solutions compared to the GNE representation. This new representation provides a very good interface for human computer interaction. Software developers (humans) prepare this representation by comprehending the semantics of the structure and at the same time this representation helps in feeding error-free, efficiently-designed and less-redundant data to computing framework. Based on this efficient HCI, relevant, correct & desired information gets transferred to the optimization algorithm which then produces the near optimal solutions in lesser time with better quality.

3.2 Population Initialization

The creation of initial population has a major impact on the efficiency of the search-based evolutionary algorithms. The good initialization of population solution can improve the efficiency of the algorithms. If initial population is generated in such a way that their solutions have a better ability to reach an effective optimal solution, evolutionary algorithm converges quickly [25]. The initial population for the proposed approach is generated using a combination of random initialization and modules generated from K-means algorithm [26].

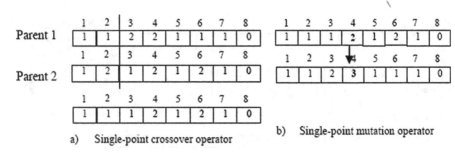

Fig. 4. Illustration of single-point crossover and single-point mutation operators

3.3 Crossover and Mutation

In our search-based software remodularization, for crossover operation, parents are selected using the standard tournament selection method. The crossover process has the following four steps: (1) two parents are selected using the tournament algorithm, (2) a single random point pair is selected at which both parents split, (3) a new individual candidate solution is generated with vector head of first parent and vector tail of second parent, (4) an individual solution in the population is replaced with new individual solution. In mutation operation, a byte is randomly reset to an integer in the feasible set. Figure 4 illustrates the single point crossover and mutation operator.

3.4 Objective Functions

We use five objective functions to optimize our search-based multi-objective: (1) coupling (to minimize), which corresponds to the number of inter-edges (edges between classes in different modules); (2) cohesion (to maximize), which corresponds to the number of intra-edges (edges between classes in the same module); (3) Intra-modular Coupling Density (ICD) [18] (to maximize); (4) number of classes per package (to minimize); (5) number of packages in the system (to minimize).

4 Experiments, Results and Analysis

This section illustrates the results obtained through the experimentation of proposed representation techniques and existing representation techniques by incorporating it into NSGA-II, a multi-objective evolutionary algorithm [24].

4.1 Collecting Results from the Experiments

Since the NSGA-II algorithm is a stochastic optimizer, it can generate different results for the same problem instance from one cycle to another. For this reason, we collect the results for analysis by performing 30 independent simulation runs for each problem instance. As the algorithm is a multi-objective evolutionary optimizer, each running cycle produces a set of trade-off solutions instead of single solution. However, the purpose of this paper is to demonstrate the usefulness of proposed representation techniques over the software remodularization problem. So we select that single solution which has the highest ICD value in the set of trade-off solutions of each run.

4.2 Studied Software Systems

We performed an empirical study for the proposed coupling schemes over six different object-oriented software systems with different size and characteristics. The main characteristics of the systems examined are given in Table 1. For each system, the version number, number of classes, and number of are mentioned in respective rows. All these software systems are based on the java programming language and are open-source or free-software projects.

Table 1. Characteristics of software systems

Systems	Version	#Classes	#Connections
Jstl	1.0.6	18	20
JavaCC	1.5	154	722
JUnit	3.81	100	276
Java Servlet API	2.3	63	131
XML API DOM	1.0.2	119	209
DOM 4J	1.5.2	195	930

For all software systems, we first analyzed and examined different types of modules and libraries and then removed Omni-present classes such as common libraries, utilities and other domain primitive modules because they do not contribute to any main service.

4.3 Results and Analysis

In this section, we present the software remodularization results obtained by NSGA-II algorithm by incorporating the proposed representation technique. The results are evaluated and compared with existing representation in terms of Intra-modular Coupling Density (ICD), Number of Classes per Packages (NCP) and Execution time. The results are statistically analyzed by two-tailed t-test with 95 % confidence level ($\alpha = 5$ %).

ICD as an assessment criterion: First we present the results of the experiments that compare the ICD values obtained from the proposed approach and the existing approach. Table 2 presents the results comparing proposed and GNE representation scheme. The results clearly indicate that the proposed representation technique performs significantly better to the GNE representation approaches for all software systems. For example, if we consider the Jstl system, ICD value of the proposed representation (i.e., 0.8621) is significantly larger than ICD value of the GNE representation. Hence, results clearly indicate that the remodularization solutions obtained through the proposed technique have better coupling and cohesion compared to the existing GNE representation.

NCP as an assessment criterion: The results of NCP metric are demonstrated in Table 2. Similar to the ICD metric, results of the proposed approach also perform better in terms of NCP metric. For example, NCP value of the proposed approach on average for all software systems is 4.5 (i.e. 4.5 classes per package), while it is 1.5 for GNE, which is very small. Hence, the proposed approach produces remodularization solutions with better class distribution among the packages compared to GNE representation.

Table 2. Results obtained through proposed and GNE representation

Systems	Intra-modular coupling dependency			Number of classes per package			Execution time (in ms)	
	Proposed	GNE	t-test	Proposed	GNE	t-test	Proposed	GNE
Jstl	0.8621	0.5273	<0.0001	2.5714	1.3254	<0.0001	672	734
Javacc	0.5673	0.3342	<0.0001	4.3561	1.4327	<0.0001	115859	163645
JUnit	0.6341	0.4014	<0.0001	5.8824	1.7857	<0.0001	51956	64338
Java Servlet API	0.5267	0.2756	<0.0001	4.1562	1.5366	<0.0001	8436	9514
XML API DOM	0.5593	0.3668	<0.0001	4.7179	1.8524	<0.0001	149617	183569
DOM 4J	0.5867	0.3237	<0.0001	5.5758	1.4325	<0.0001	171205	231542

Execution time as an assessment criterion: Execution time has a significant influence on the usability of a software remodularization algorithm, especially if the software developers follow an iterative and incremental approach for remodularization the software systems. For example, if the developer uses the slow algorithm to obtain a baseline remodularization solution, modifying the system accordingly may be a time consuming process due to frequent remodularization. Therefore, we evaluated the execution time of the proposed representation technique for software remodularization and compared it with existing GNE. We run algorithm in the environment of Microsoft Windows 7 with 32 bits on Intel Pentium 4 process at 2.4 GHz and 2 GB of RAM and the algorithms are implemented in jMetal 4.5 frameworks. Table 2 shows the running time performance of the remodularization techniques for all eight software systems. The experimental results clearly show that the proposed representation technique for search-based software remodularization is the most time efficient compared GNE representation.

ICD values vs. number of generation: The next experiment is performed to see the growth trend in ICD values with respect to the number of generations for each variant of search-based multi-objective software remodularization (i.e., proposed and GNE representation). Figure 5 demonstrates the ICD growth speed with respect to the number of generations for six problem instances. The vertical axis in these figures shows the ICD value for modularized system. The horizontal axis shows the number of generations. The minimum number of generation is considered 10*N and the maximum

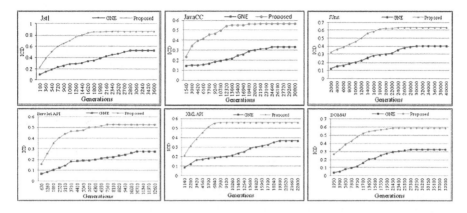

Fig. 5. ICD value vs. number of generation

number of generation is considered 200*N, where N is the total number of classes in the system.

The results demonstrated in Fig. 5 clearly indicate that the growth trend of ICD value of proposed representation scheme for all software system is better compared to the GNE representation scheme. The proposed representation scheme is able to reach the steady state in very small number of generations. However, the GNE representation scheme can only reach at steady state after very large number of generations. For example, after generation 100*N the proposed representation keeps a steady ICD value in all problem instances. However, GNE representation scheme can only reach a steady state until to generation 160*N or later.

5   Conclusion and Future Work

This paper presents a search-based multi-objective optimization approach for software remodularization problem. The approach uses a new and efficient encoding scheme for candidate solutions which ensures a good semantic-based, efficiently-designed, less-redundant and error-free human computer interaction. The approach regroups the classes of the software system by optimizing five objective functions (i.e., coupling, cohesion, Intra-modular Coupling Density (ICD), number of classes per package, and number of packages in the system). The new neighbor based candidate solution representation reduces redundant remodularization solutions from the search space. The approach is evaluated over six real-world software systems and results are compared with the existing integer based representation approach. Experiments show that the proposed approach performs better than the existing integer based representation (i.e., GNE representation) approach in terms of Intra-modular Coupling Density (ICD), number of classes per package, convergence speed as well as execution time.

References

1. Zanetti, M.S., Tessone, C.J., Scholtes, I., Schweitzer, F.: Automated software remodularization based on move refactoring: a complex systems approach. In: Proceedings of 13th International Conference on Modularity (MODULARITY 2014), pp. 73–84. ACM, New York, NY, USA (2014)
2. Bavota, G., Gethers, M., Oliveto, R., Poshyvanyk, D., Lucia, A.D.: Improving software modularization via automated analysis of latent topics and dependencies. ACM Trans. Softw. Eng. Methodol. **23**(1), 1–33 (2014)
3. Anquetil, N., Lethbridge, T.C.: Experiments with clustering as a software remodularization method. In: Proceedings of Sixth Working Conference on Reverse Engineering, pp. 235–255 (1999)
4. Praditwong, K., Harman, M., Yao, X.: Software module clustering as a multi-objective search problem. IEEE Trans. Softw. Eng. **37**(2), 264–282 (2011)
5. Beyer, D., Noack, A.: Clustering software artifacts based on frequent common changes. In: Proceedings of the 13th IEEE International Workshop on Program Comprehension (IWPC 2005), pp. 1092–8138 (2005)
6. Serban, G., Czibula, I.-G.: Restructuring software systems using clustering. In: 22nd International Symposium on Computer and Information Sciences, pp. 1–6 (2007)
7. Maqbool, O., Babri, H.A.: Hierarchical clustering for software architecture recovery. IEEE Trans. Softw. Eng. **33**(11), 759–780 (2007)
8. Harman, M., Jones, B.: Search based software engineering. J. Inf. Softw. Technol. **43**(14), 833–839 (2001)
9. Harman, M. Hierons, R, Proctor, M.: A new representation and crossover operator for search-based optimization of software modularization. In: Proceedings of the Genetic and Evolutionary Computation Conference, pp. 1351–1358. Morgan Kaufmann Publishers, New York (2002)
10. Doval, D., Mancoridis, S., Mitchell, B.S.: Automatic clustering of software systems using a genetic algorithm. In: Proceedings Software Technology and Engineering Practice, STEP 2099, pp. 73–81 (1999)
11. Mancoridis, S., Mitchell, B.S., Rorres, C., Chen, Y., Gansner, E.R.: Using automatic clustering to produce high-level system organizations of source code. In: Proceedings of 6th International Workshop on Program Comprehension, pp. 45–52 (1998)
12. Bavota, G., Carnevale, F., De Lucia, A., Di Penta, M., Oliveto, R.: Putting the developer in-the-loop: an interactive GA for software re-modularization. In: Fraser, G., Teixeira de Souza, J. (eds.) SSBSE 2012. LNCS, vol. 7515, pp. 75–89. Springer, Heidelberg (2012)
13. Abdeen, H., Ducasse, S., Sahraoui, H.A.: Modularization metrics: assessing package organization in legacy large object-oriented software. In: Proceedings of WCRE 2011, pp. 394–398. IEEE Computer Society Press (2011)
14. Barros, M.: An analysis of the effects of composite objectives in multi-objective software module clustering. In: Proceedings of the Fourteenth International Conference on Genetic and Evolutionary GECCC-12, pp 1205–1212 (2012)
15. Wiggerts, T.A.: Using clustering algorithms in legacy systems remodularization. In: IEEE Working Conference on Reverse Engineering, pp. 33–43 (1997)
16. Mitchell, B.S., Mancoridis, S.: On the automatic modularization of software systems using the bunch tool. IEEE Trans. Softw. Eng. **32**(3), 193–208 (2006)
17. Anquetil, N., Denier, S., Ducasse, S., Laval, J., Pollet, D.: Software (re)modularization: fight against the structure erosion and migration preparation (2010)

18. Abreu, F.B., Goulao, M.: Coupling and cohesion as modularization drivers: are we being over-persuaded. In: Fifth European Conference on Software Maintenance and Reengineering, pp. 47–57 (2001)
19. Mkaouer, W., Kessentini, M., Shaout, A., Koligheu, P., Bechikh, S., Deb, K., Ouni, A.: Many-objective software remodularization using NSGA-III. ACM Trans. Softw. Eng. Methodol. **24**(3), 1–45 (2015)
20. Abdeen, H., Ducasse, S., Sahraoui, H., Alloui, I.: Automatic package coupling and cycle minimization. In: Proceedings of the 16th Working Conference on Reverse Engineering, pp. 103–112. IEEE CS Press, Lille, France (2009)
21. Falkenauer, E.: The grouping genetic algorithm–widening the scope of the GAs. Proc. Belg. J. Oper. Res. Stat. Comput. Sci. **33**, 79–102 (1992)
22. Falkenauer, E.: Genetic Algorithms for Grouping Problems. Wiley, New York (1998)
23. Maulik, U., Bandyopadhyay, S.: Genetic algorithm-based clustering technique. Pattern Recogn. **33**(9), 1455–1465 (2000)
24. Deb, K., Agrawal, S., Pratap, A., Meyarivan, T.: A fast and elitist multi-objective genetic algorithm: NSGA-II. IEEE Trans. Evol. Comput. **6**(2), 182–197 (2002)
25. Cotilla-Sanchez, E., Hines, P.D.H., Barrows, C., Blumsack, S., Patel, M.: Multi-attribute partitioning of power networks based on electrical distance. IEEE Trans. Power Syst. **28**(4), 4979–4987 (2013)
26. Hartigan, J., Wong, M.: Algorithm AS 136: a K-means clustering algorithm. J. Roy. Stat. Soc. Ser. C **28**(1), 100–108 (1979)

Dynamic Sampling for Visual Exploration of Large Dense-Dense Matrices

Philipp Roskosch[1], James Twellmeyer[2], and Arjan Kuijper[1,2(✉)]

[1] Technische Universität Darmstadt, Darmstadt, Germany
[2] Fraunhofer IGD, Darmstadt, Germany
kuijper@igd.fraunhofer.de

Abstract. We present a technique which allows visual exploration of large dense-occupied similarity matrices. It allows the comparison of several dimensions of a multivariate data set. For the visualization, the data are reduced by sampling. The access time to individual elements is an ever increasing problem with increasing matrix size. We examine various database management systems and compare the access times for different problem sizes. The visualization responds to user interaction and allows the focus to specific areas within the data. For this, the data is filtered according to user interests and the visualization is refined with subsamples of the filtered data. The context is preserved in this process. The focus allows the discovery of relationships that would otherwise remain hidden.

1 Introduction and Motivation

VIS-SENSE is an international research project. Fraunhofer IGD is one of six partners involved in this project [4,6,18]. Visual Analytics techniques [12,13] are developed that the handling of large and complex data sets of IT-Security to improve international network security [20,21]. The data are compared with each other. Thus large similarity matrices occur with up to $100,000 \times 100,000$ entries. With a visualization of these matrices, homogeneous groups within the data set are examined on similarities or differences [15]. We develop a sampling algorithm that enables displaying all matrices in parallel on a standard computer and monitor. Our algorithm satisfies a real-time requirement, so load times for the user are not noticeable. In addition, we take the idea from [7] and adjust the sample visualized to the user interest. By interacting with the visualization, data with certain properties are increasingly displayed and thus replace less interesting data. For a better overview, we discuss an interaction process and emphasizing added elements. By increasingly choosing additive data with certain characteristics, the distribution of the sample deviates more and more from that of the data set. If the distribution is uniformly distributed at the beginning, it will be more and more adapted to the user's interest through interaction.

© Springer International Publishing Switzerland 2016
S. Yamamoto (Ed.): HIMI 2016, Part I, LNCS 9734, pp. 308–318, 2016.
DOI: 10.1007/978-3-319-40349-6_29

We have implemented the concept of Degree of Interests in a whole new way. In contrast to previous approaches, no DOI function is needed that calculates a value for each date. We work with multivariate data, which have no specific context. Unlike e.g. in geographic data there is no natural distance between objects, but only a calculated similarity. In [7] the DOI is calculated from a specified center. Our data have only an abstract distance or similarity between them. After the initial sample, the user receives context information from the data set. He does not choose a center initially, but rather determines by interaction with the visualization the data that are relevant to him and thereby gradually gets a larger focus on certain parts. We use the characteristics of the data for the determination of *interesting* subsets. Thus, computing power and memory is saved because an explicit calculation of the DOI does not take place of irrelevant data. In [3] it is made clear that each record is just a sample of real-world data. If a sub-sample is used for a visualization the accuracy is only slightly affected. The same is observed for algorithms with higher complexity. A waiver of the last thousandth accuracy enables the calculation of complex algorithms in reasonable time [9]. This behavior is confirmed in this work. It is not possible to visualize the entire data set with all its dimensions in parallel. Sampling allows the examination of a smaller subset of the complete data set with the same statistical properties. The findings and analysis, which are made possible in this way, are of exactly the same quality as when the complete data set is considered. This results from the fact that essential characteristics of the data set are also pronounced available in a sufficiently large sample [10,11].

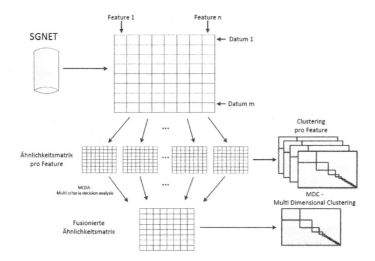

Fig. 1. VIS-SENSE pipeline.

2   Pipeline

The data for the research extracts VIS-SENSE[1] from WOMBAT[2]. In this project, safety raw data were collected and analyzed. See Fig. 1 for the full pipeline. The analytical results provide detailed information about individual records and are therefore provided along with the raw data. The data are collected with SGNET [14], a distributed honeypot system. It automatically learns the behavior of network protocols with techniques from bioinformatics and can handle attacks of any kind. Each attack is classified with the *epsilon-gamma-pi* model of Crandall et al. [2]. The information stored has as a result a high level of granularity and provides a good basis for further processing with the Triage Framework [19].

In this framework, each data item is assigned a category and depending on this only certain – not all – attributes used for further analysis. The term feature is used in the remainder instead of attribute. For each datum, a so-called feature vector is created, which summarizes the features of the datum. This process is called attack feature selection. A similarity matrix is then created from the collected data for each feature. A similarity matrix or dissimilarity matrix is a set of distances between all pairs of data of a data set [8]. The similarity is derived directly from the dissimilarity and vice versa.

The similarity metric depends on the characteristics of the feature [19]. It creates many large similarity matrices, the number is determined by the number of features, the size of the individual matrices by the size of the data set. In the phase graph-based clustering, these matrices are clustered and thus combined homogeneous groups. The clustering algorithm used is not specified by Triage. In VIS-SENSE, an algorithm is used, that recognizes the dominant sets [16] within an adjacency matrix. Reasons for this are, inter alia, a variable number of clusters and parallelization issues [19].

In the third and final step, an MCDA - Multi-Criteria Decision Analysis - is performed. The values of the similarity matrices of all features are combined with aggregation functions and there a similarity matrix is created, which is determined by all features. It is also clustered. This clustering is called MDC - Multi Dimensional Clustering. Because of the many dimensions (features) an aggregation of all values is not trivial. Dependencies of individual features with each other must be recognized and taken into account in the aggregation function. OWA - Order Weighted Averaging functions and Fuzzy Integrals like the Choquet integral, solve these problems (see. [Thod]). Due to the high complexity of this method, the results are not transparent. For the viewer of the MCDA matrix it is not clear how the values were calculated or composed. This is exactly of interest. The goal of MCDA is to assign different malware derivatives to a superclass. The superclasses are investigated and similarities and features with large deviations found. The key factors as sought that are responsible for the outcome in MCDA. With this knowledge, distinct malware groups can be graded better.

---

[1] http://www.vis-sense.eu/.
[2] http://www.wombat-project.eu/Projekt.

For example, suppose there is a cluster in the MCDA whose elements all have identical values of the individual features, apart from the MD5 hash, then it is assumed that the binary was only slightly changed. With this knowledge a heuristic can be created, with which other derivatives of this malware class can be found.

For this analysis, all matrices are visualized in parallel and the calculated clusters are highlighted. Marks in a matrix are transmitted to all other matrices. When a cluster of feature X is marked, it can be seen how the elements are distributed in the other matrices. The data set is very large, it covers up to 10,000 data. The matrices thus contain up to $10,000 \times 10,000$ entries. For the visualization of such large amounts of data the limits of traditional PCs are quickly reached. If the memory should still be sufficient, the resolution of the monitor is not nearly high enough. For this reason, the data must be reduced. For this we use sampling, since dealing with very large amounts of data is possible while not adversely affecting the validity of the visualization [3]. An increase in the amount of data to up to 100,000 elements is planned. Assuming that an element of a similarity matrix is one byte in size, and 20 of these matrices exist, the amount of data is about 186 GB. From this set submatrices are created using a sample of the node set. The elements required are distributed randomly in principle, with the result that each element is read one by one. Important here is a scaling data management. If the access time to the individual elements increases with the number of stored items, then the use of the program with a real-time request is not feasible. We examine in this context the performance of two different database concepts [1] (Fig. 2).

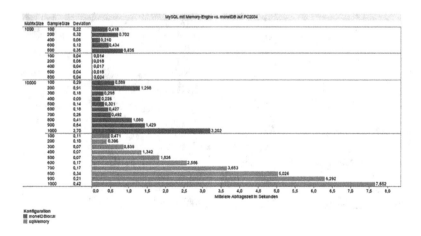

Fig. 2. Comparison of two configurations: (1) MonetDB standard configuration, Data on standard hard disk, 4 GB RAM, Intel Core i3-2120 CPU at 3,3 GHz mit 2 Kernels/4 Threads vs. (2) MySQL with Memoryengine, data in RAM, 24 GB RAM, Intel Xeon E5645 at 2,4 GHz with 6 Kernels/12 Threads.

3   Results

We develop a concept that allows the visualization of large similarity matrices. A similarity matrix is the representation of a graph as an adjacency matrix. There are various visualization types for the display of graphs. The node-link diagram is often used and provides a good overview [5]. For larger graphs, node-link diagrams quickly reach their limits. Especially in densely populated graphs, it is difficult to create a suitable layout. An alternative to node-link diagrams is the matrix representation. Here the edge weight is mapped usually on color or transparency. This representation has its strengths especially in large, densely populated matrices. An ordering of the rows/columns plays an essential role. Is the arrangement unfortunately selected, no information can be obtained from the visualization [5]. We investigated a variety of techniques to visualize large graphs. Of interest is on the one hand filtering by interestingness, on the other hand, a reduction by sampling. Due to the large amount of data and number of dimensions, the data for visualization must be greatly reduced. The goal is the two techniques combine together. For the selection of displayed nodes in the matrices, a sample of the complete set of nodes is needed. After starting the VIS-SENSE environment the sample should be evenly distributed. By interacting with the user the distribution changes and adapts to the User Interests.

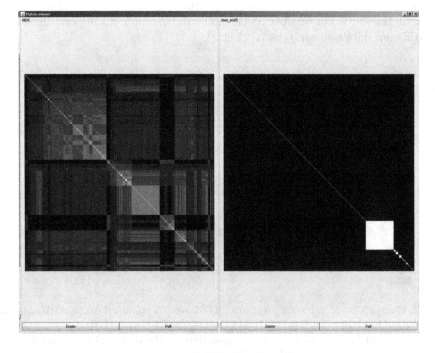

Fig. 3. Initial sampling 1

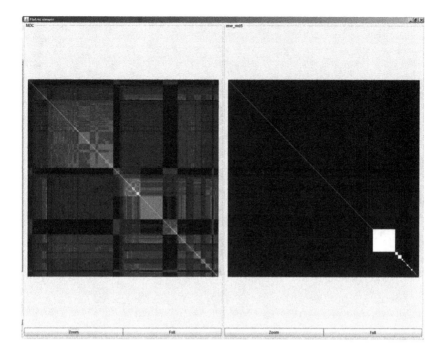

Fig. 4. Initial sampling 2

For visualization properties we use a SGNET record including approximately 14,000 nodes, each with 22 features. For each feature, there is a similarity matrix and cluster information. The information is in text files that have a total size of about 12 GB. We implemented our system in MySQL. For our evaluation, we examined technical and visual aspects. The technical parts deal with the access times to large similarity matrices in different database configurations. The visual aspect describes the effects of our dynamic subsampling on the visualization in relation to the conservation of the context at the simultaneous focus on specific areas.

4 Visual Impressions

With a small matrix $(1,000 \times 1,000)$ configuration 2 is a clear advantage. The processing time increases only very slightly with the sample size, and is even with a relatively large sample less than 0.1 s. MonetDB is in absolute terms with configuration 1 is also very fast, but in a direct comparison can not keep up with the memory engine of MySQL. Much more interesting are matrices with sizes of $10,000 \times 10,000$ entries. Here MonetDB shows its strengths. The access times are only slightly different for small sample sizes compared to the 1000×1000 matrix. Creating a 1000×1000 entries large sample is with 3 s in a noticeable

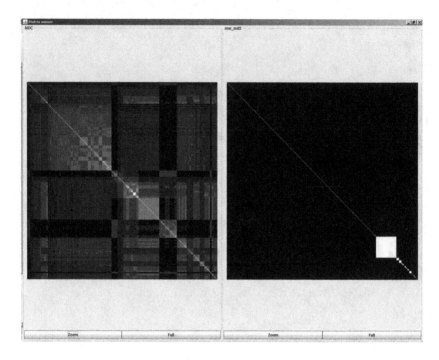

Fig. 5. Program start

area, but is compared to configuration 2 very good. Full results can be found in [17].

We have built our implementation on an existing project. This system has defined the way of visualizing matrices. To deal with the size of the data, it has used a static sample of the data. Thus, always the same subset of the data was visualized and the visualization also remained the same. After successful implementation of our dynamic sampling was necessary to clarify the extent to which the visual impression or the user's knowledge are affected.

4.1   Initial Sampling

In a static sample as a data source, a segment of the data is displayed and this does not change. The most striking characteristics can be seen in it. In our case, these are the largest clusters of a matrix. If only these are of interest, such a sample fulfilled his request. The visualization serves mainly the analysis of the MCDA matrix whose clusters represent relationships of all features. Here the size of a cluster represents the frequency of occurrence in the data set and is thus an indicator of the importance of this relationship. It is not said that smaller clusters represent an unimportant or useless connection, though. A statement about the importance is to be taken by an analyst. For a sample, it is possible that smaller clusters are not represented by any node in the sample and are therefore not

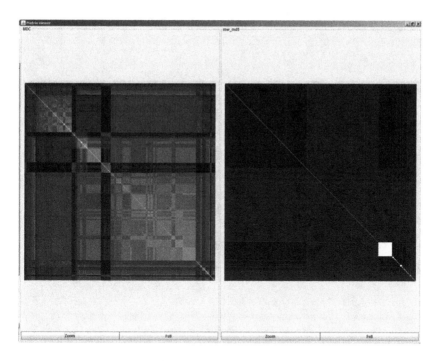

Fig. 6. First subsampling

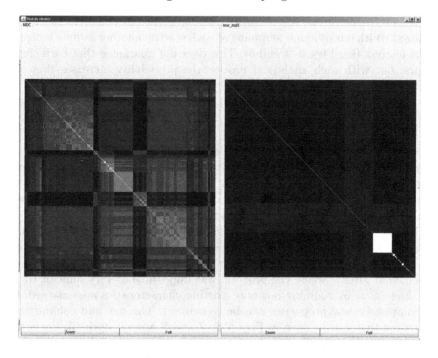

Fig. 7. Second subsampling

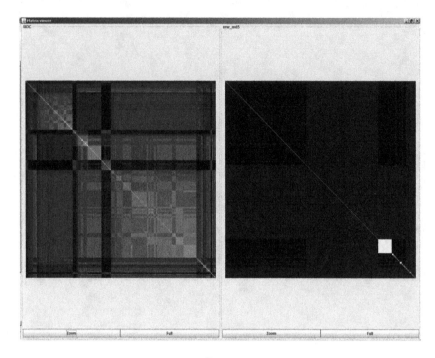

Fig. 8. n^{th} subsampling

visualized. With our dynamic sampling at each startup another sample is created for the analyst (see Figs. 3, 4 and 5). This does not guarantee that each cluster appears, but with each analytical process the probability increases that each cluster was examined at least once.

4.2 Subsampling

As with the initial sampling our implementation shows its strengths in the study of small clusters. If a cluster represented by relatively few nodes the statement about the distribution of these nodes in the clusters of the other feature is not meaningful. With our program nodes are subsampled from the selected cluster and there is a greater focus on this area realized (see Figs. 5, 6, 7 and 8).

Thus, a representative quantity is provided to detect the distribution, or to understand the emergence of this cluster in the MCDA. In the figures it is clear that for the feature mw_md5 after multiple zooming a cluster, noise can be seen, that after starting the program was impossible or very difficult to see. This shows that by zooming not only existing characteristics are enlarged, but also completely new properties can be recognized. The row and column array of matrices that can be seen in Figs. 5, 6, 7 and 8 are not optimal. For a final assessment of the new findings by subsampling, the rows and columns would have to be arranged accordingly. There is no upper limit on the number of nodes that must be present for each cluster in the sample. During the analysis, it can happen that only nodes of one cluster are displayed. The context is in this case completely lost and the program must be restarted. That would be an exemplary approach for improvements and enhancements. Regardless of this, the benefits of dynamic subsampling are clear.

5 Conclusions

Three issues appear to be important: storage, loading, and visualization: (1) The data must be stored for further processing as appropriate. The volume presents in today's resources are not a problem. The time required to insert in a database can be realized with appropriate methods of data base systems in a reasonable time. (2) Access to the data is the biggest problem. By sampling data to non-contiguous positions are read from memory. This is a process that challenges the weaknesses of a hard disk. We were able to show that these weaknesses can be compensated with MonetDB. (3) We have extended the visualization with our technique and allow focusing parts of the data. We discussed many functions that bring visibility and usability.

References

1. Abadi, D.J., Madden, S.R., Hachem, N.: Column-stores vs. row-stores: how different are they really? In: ACM SIGMOD International Conference on Management of Data, pp. 967–980 (2008)
2. Crandall, J.R., Wu, S.F., Chong, F.T.: Experiences using minos as a tool for capturing and analyzing novel worms for unknown vulnerabilities. In: Julisch, K., Kruegel, C. (eds.) DIMVA 2005. LNCS, vol. 3548, pp. 32–50. Springer, Heidelberg (2005)
3. Dix, A., Ellis, G.: By chance enhancing interaction with large data sets through statistical sampling. In: Advanced Visual Interfaces, pp. 167–176 (2002)
4. Eicke, T.N., Jung, Y., Kuijper, A.: Stable dynamic webshadows in the X3DOM framework. Expert Syst. Appl. 42(7), 3585–3609 (2015)
5. Elmqvist, N., Do, T.N., Goodell, H., Henry, N., Fekete, J.: ZAME: interactive large-scale graph visualization. IEEE PacificVIS 2008, pp. 215–222, March 2008
6. Engelke, T., Becker, M., Wuest, H., Keil, J., Kuijper, A.: MobileAR browser - a generic architecture for rapid AR-multi-level development. Expert Syst. Appl. 40(7), 2704–2714 (2013)
7. van Ham, F., Perer, A.: Search, show context, expand on demand: supporting large graph exploration with degree-of-interest. IEEE TVCG 15(6), 953–960 (2009)
8. Han, J.: Data Mining: Concepts and Techniques. Morgan Kaufmann Publishers Inc., San Francisco (2005)
9. Helsgaun, K.: An effective implementation of the Lin-Kernighan traveling salesman heuristic. Eur. J. Oper. Res. 126(1), 106–130 (2000)
10. Kuijper, A., Florack, L.: The relevance of non-generic events in scale space models. Int. J. Comput. Vis. 57(1), 67–84 (2004)
11. Kuijper, A., Olsen, O.F.: Transitions of the pre-symmetry set. In: 17th International Conference on Pattern Recognition, ICPR 2004, pp. 190–193 (2004)

318 P. Roskosch et al.

12. von Landesberger, T., Bremm, S., Kirschner, M., Wesarg, S., Kuijper, A.: Visual analytics for model-based medical image segmentation: opportunities and challenges. Expert Syst. Appl. **40**(12), 4934–4943 (2013)
13. von Landesberger, T., Kuijper, A., Schreck, T., Kohlhammer, J., van Wijk, J.J., Fekete, J., Fellner, D.W.: Visual analysis of large graphs: state-of-the-art and future research challenges. Comput. Graph. Forum **30**(6), 1719–1749 (2011)
14. Leita, C., Dacier, M., Wicherski, G.: SGNET: a distributed infrastructure to handle zero-day exploits. Technical report, EURECOM+2164, Eurecom, February 2007
15. Nazemi, K., Stab, C., Kuijper, A.: A reference model for adaptive visualization systems. In: Jacko, J.A. (ed.) Human-Computer Interaction, Part I, HCII 2011. LNCS, vol. 6761, pp. 480–489. Springer, Heidelberg (2011)
16. Pavan, M., Pelillo, M.: Dominant sets and pairwise clustering. IEEE Trans. Pattern Anal. Mach. Intell. **29**(1), 167–172 (2007)
17. Roskosch, P.: Dynamisches sampling zur visuellen exploration von groen dichtbesetzten matrizen. Technical report, TU Darmstadt (2013)
18. Stein, C., Limper, M., Kuijper, A.: Spatial data structures to accelerate the visibility determination for large model visualization on the web. In: Web3D 2014, pp. 53–61 (2014)
19. Thonnard, O.: D22/d5.2 root causes analysis: experimental report. Technical report, FP7-ICT-216026-WOMBAT, WP5 - Threats Intelligence, FP7-ICT (2011)
20. Zhou, X., Kuijper, A., Veldhuis, R.N.J., Busch, C.: Quantifying privacy and security of biometric fuzzy commitment. In: IEEE International Joint Conference on Biometrics, pp. 1–8 (2011)
21. Zhou, X., Wolthusen, S.D., Busch, C., Kuijper, A.: A security analysis of biometric template protection schemes. In: Kamel, M., Campilho, A. (eds.) ICIAR 2009. LNCS, vol. 5627, pp. 429–438. Springer, Heidelberg (2009)

Interaction Design

Analysis of Hand Raising Actions for Group Interaction Enhancement

Saizo Aoyagi[(⊠)], Michiya Yamamoto, and Satoshi Fukumori

School of Science and Technology, Kwansei Gakuin University,
Nishinomiya, Japan
{aoyagi,michiya.yamamoto,fukumori.s}@kwansei.ac.jp

Abstract. Hand-raising is a way of expressing the intention or communication. The authors are going to create a communication field where people can express their intention freely. This study evaluates impressions of hand-raising motions for communication participants.

Keywords: Hand raising · Embodied communication · Embodied interaction · Group interaction enhancement

1 Introduction

Hand-raising is a motion that represents an active participation in classroom learning, and it is very important for learners to raise their hand in the classroom [1, 2]. Nevertheless, not all learners can actively raise a hand but it is thought to be important to promote learners' to raise their hands in classroom [3].

The authors proposed the concept of a communication enhancement system which is shown in Fig. 1. This system measures learners' actions using cameras and other sensors and promotes learners to raise hand by giving appropriate feedback based on measured data, using embodied media technology, such as Computer Graphic (CG) characters or robots.

However, there is a huge problem in building this system. The hand-raising motions suitable for feedback are not known. This is because hand-raising motions have not been focused on in academic studies; perhaps, psychological factors of hand raising were studied in an educational area [1, 2].

The purpose of this study is to reveal relations between typical motions of hand-raising and their impressions. In this study, impressions of hand raising motions are evaluated in two situations—single character situation and classroom situation, as described in the next section.

2 Method

In the analysis of this study, hand-raising motions of CG characters are used as targets of impression evaluation as they can reproduce motions exactly. The authors extracted five typical motions of hand-raising using motion capture technology and cluster

© Springer International Publishing Switzerland 2016
S. Yamamoto (Ed.): HIMI 2016, Part I, LNCS 9734, pp. 321–328, 2016.
DOI: 10.1007/978-3-319-40349-6_30

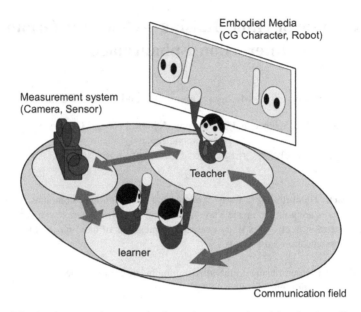

Fig. 1. Concept of communication enhancement by raising-hand media.

analysis [4]. These motions are converted into these for CG characters from motion captured data, as shown in Fig. 2 and Table 1 and used for this study.

Motions A and B are fast and high motions, motion B being the highest and fastest one. Motions D and E are slow and low motions, motion E being the lowest and slowest one. Motion C is in the middle position.

In this study, impressions of hand raising motions are evaluated through two experiments. In the first experiment, each hand-raising motion of CG characters is evaluated when a character raises a motion (single character situation). The first

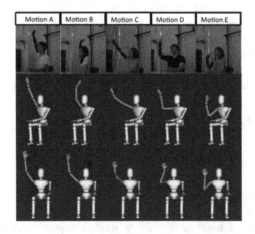

Fig. 2. Typical hand-raising motions of Japanese students.

Table 1. Average height, speed and angle of hand-raising motions.

Motion	Height (%)	Speed (mm/s)	Angle(°)
A	85.3	2806.7	145.4
B	92.9	4710.9	162.5
C	81.7	2089.5	162.8
D	65.1	2069.8	94.9
E	46.8	1558.0	58.4

experiment is conducted to reveal motions' impressions mainly for someone who watches and picks hand-raising learners.

In the second experiment, these motions are evaluated in a situation in which some CG characters raise their hands at the same time (classroom situation). The second experiment is conducted to reveal motions' impressions mainly for learners who raise hand by themselves.

3 Impression Evaluation of Hand-Raising Motions of a Single Character

3.1 Purpose and Method

The purpose of the experiment is to measure impressions of hand-raising motions in a situation wherein each motion is raised by only one character. Impressions of hand-raising motions are then evaluated.

CG characters are projected on a screen by using a projector (EPSON EB-1735W) and five motions are reproduced, as shown in Fig. 2. Participants of the experiment show and evaluate them.

The experiment has two sub situations. The first is normalized-rank approach, shown in Fig. 3. Participants watch five CG characters at the same time, and each of them reproduces a different motion, as shown in Fig. 2. Participants compare these motions in three aspects. Participants are twenty people aged between 19 and 24 years (ten males and ten females).

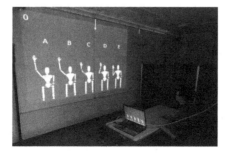

Fig. 3. Experimental scene of normalized-rank approach comparison of hand-raising.

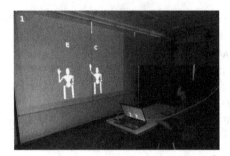

Fig. 4. Experimental scene of paired comparison of hand-raising.

The second is paired-comparison, as shown in Fig. 4. Participants watch two characters in each trial and reproduce two different motions, as shown in Fig. 2. All pairs of motions are compared through this situation. Participants are twenty people aged between 21 and 24 years (ten males and ten females).

3.2 Results and Discussion

Results of the normalized rank approach analysis are shown in Fig. 5. Participants evaluate and compare motions in the three aspects shown at the bottom of Fig. 5. The three aspects are "Arrange motions in the order of good impression", "Arrange motions in the order you feel like picking" and "Arrange motions in the order he/she seems to be picked".

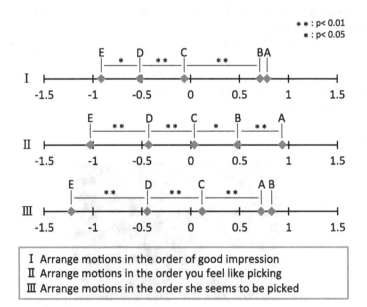

Fig. 5. Results of normalized-rank approach analysis of hand-raising motions.

In Fig. 5, the right side denotes that a participant has agreed to an item. For example, motion A in item I has the best impression. From results, motions A and B are highly evaluated in all three aspects while motion C is moderately evaluated. Whereas, motions D and E have relatively bad impression. To summarize, high hand-raising motions are highly valued in giving a good impression or activeness in representation of intention.

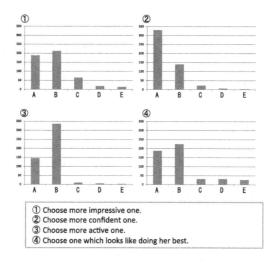

Fig. 6. Bradley-Terry model of impressions for hand-raising motions.

Next, participants answer four questions in paired-comparison; "Choose more impressive one", "Choose more confident one", "Choose more active one" and "Choose one which looks like doing her best". Thurstone's paired comparison is conducted and results are summarized using Bradeley-Terrymodel [5], as shown in Fig. 6. The height of blue bars depicts the "strength" of motions. The higher the blue bar, higher is a more rated in paired-comparison.

In all four questions, motions A and B are highly evaluated. In addition, motion A wins to motion B in question 2, however, motion B wins to motion A in question 3.

Results of normalized-rank approach and paired-comparison conclude that high and fast motions have relatively good impressions. The results of paired-comparison show that effects of speed and height is not linear. Motion B being the fastest and the highest still loses to Motion A in question 3 in Fig. 6. This fact shows that impressive hand-raising is not the same as active hand-raising. When the authors make embodied media, as shown in Fig. 1, suitable speed and height of hand-raising media depends on its objective.

4 Impression Evaluation of Hand-Raising Motions in Classroom Situation

4.1 Purpose and Method

The purpose of the second experiment is to reveal motions' impressions mainly for learners who raise their hand by themselves, in a classroom-like situation where many other learners exist around.

In the experiment, the scene of a classroom and fifty-five CG characters are projected on a screen, as shown in Fig. 7. Participants are explained that they are in a classroom with a teacher asking for a comment. They are requested to evaluate impressions for each scene in the five aspects described later.

Each CG character raises the hand in motion B or E, which are the same as motions used in the first experiment described in Chap. 3. This is because motion B is represents good-impression motions while motion E represents bad-impression motions. In addition, the number of characters that reproduce each motion is thought to be a factor of impressions in this situation and then two situations are set; when all the characters raise their hands in the same motion and when only five characters raise their hands in the same motion.

To summarize, there are four situations; (a) all characters raise their hands in motion A (High-All), (b) all characters raise their hands in motion E (Low-All), (c) Only five characters raise their hands in motion A (High-Five), and (d) only five characters raise their hands in motion E (Low-Five), as shown in Fig. 7.

Participants are twenty people aged between 21 and 24 years old (ten females and ten males).

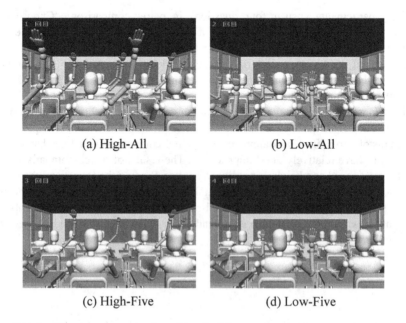

(a) High-All   (b) Low-All

(c) High-Five   (d) Low-Five

Fig. 7. Situations for evaluation of hand-raising motions in classroom situation.

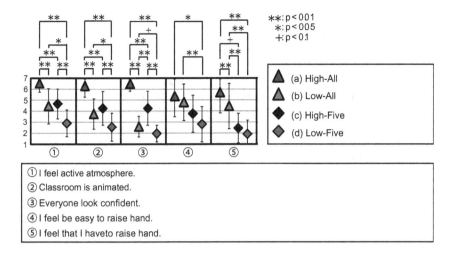

Fig. 8. Results of Wilcoxon signed-rank test of impression evaluation of hand-raising motions.

4.2   Results and Discussion

In the experiment, five aspects are considered on a 7-point scale. Results are analyzed using Wilcoxon signed-rank test and Bonferroni method. These five aspects are (1) "I feel active atmosphere", (2) "classroom is animated," (3) "everyone look confident", (4) "I feel be easy to raise hand" and (5) "I feel that I have to raise hand". Results of the analysis and the considered aspects are shown in Fig. 8.

In results of questions 1 and 2, there are significant differences except for comparison between (b) Low-All and (c) High-Five. In results of question 3, all pairs have significant differences. In results of question 4, comparisons between (a) High-All and (d) Low-Five, and between (a) Low-All and (d) Low-Five show significant differences. In results of question 5, almost all pairs show significant differences.

Results of the experiment imply that high hand-raising and homogeneity (all learners act as the same) of the classroom are important to build good impressions generally. Nevertheless, there are some minor differences between questions.

In questions 1 and 2, which are about impression of a whole classroom, effects of hand-raising and homogeneity are similar. In question 3, which is about confidence, it is important to raise hand in high and fast motion or slow and low motion, but homogeneity is relatively, not important. However, in questions 4 and 5, which are about promoting effect for hand-raising, homogeneity is very important while height and speed are not so important comparatively.

5   Summary

In this study, some impressions of typical hand-raising motions are evaluated through two experiments; each motion is reproduced by a single CG character or groups of CG characters raise hand being surrounded by a participant. According to the results of experiments, high and fast hand-raising generally gives a good impression. In addition, there are some implications from results.

For impressions for the watcher of hand-raising, if hand-raising which looks active is needed, very fast (about 4710 mm/s) motion is suitable. If hand-raising which looks confident is needed, moderately fast (about 2806 mm/s) motion is suitable.

In the classroom situation, if promotion of hand-raising is required, homogeneity of classroom members' action is very important. However, if the atmosphere of classroom is focused on, speed and height of hand-raising are suitable for intervention.

This study revealed relations between motions and impressions of hand-raising. Implications are limited to classroom situation; however, it is thought to be useful to implement the concept of communication enhancement by raising-hand media shown in Fig. 1.

References

1. Fuju, H.: A study on the relationships between kyosyu (hand raising), self-efficacy, outcome-expectancy and outcome-value (in Japanese). Jpn. J. Educ. Psychol. **29**(1), 92–101 (1991)
2. Fuse, M., Kodaira, H., Ando, F.: Positive class participation by elementary school pupils: motivation and differences in grade and gender (in Japanese). Jpn. J. Educ. Psychol. **5**(4), 534–545 (2006)
3. Hirata, M., Chibana, Y.: A study on pupils' self expression in through their active participation in an element classroom -developing a recognition scale of self expression- (in Japanese). Bull. Fac. Educ. Univ. Ryukyus **83**, 67–99 (2013)
4. Aoyagi, S., Kawabe, R., Yamamoto, M., Watanabe, T.: Hand-raising robot for promoting active participation in classrooms. In: Yamamoto, S., de Oliveira, N.P. (eds.) HIMI 2015. LNCS, vol. 9173, pp. 275–284. Springer, Heidelberg (2015). doi:10.1007/978-3-319-20618-9_27
5. Hirotsu, C.: A goodness of fit test for the Bradley-Terry model by a multiple comparisons approach (in Japanese). Qual. Jpn. Soc. Qual. Control **13**(2), 141–149 (1983)

Content Authoring Tool to Assign Signage Items to Regions on a Paper Poster

Akira Hattori[1(✉)], Hiroshi Suzuki[2], and Haruo Hayami[2]

[1] Faculty of Global Media Studies, Komazawa University, Tokyo, Japan
hattori@komazawa-u.ac.jp
[2] Faculty of Information Technology, Kanagawa Institute of Technology,
Atsugi, Kanagawa, Japan
{hsuzuki,hayami}@ic.kanagawa-it.ac.jp

Abstract. This paper describes a content authoring tool for our Hyper Panel system. This content authoring tool makes it possible to assign signage items, such as pictures and movies, according to the layout of a paper poster. Users can do that by dragging and dropping regions and signage items on the poster image. We developed a prototype of the content authoring tool as a web application and evaluated it. The results indicated that our content authoring enables users to understand how to use it and to almost correctly relate signage items to the corresponding regions on a paper poster in an intuitive method.

Keywords: Digital signage · Paper poster · Content authoring tool · HTML5

1 Introduction

There is an increasing proliferation of digital signage [1]. They are now found in many public spaces such as train station, airports, hotels, shopping malls, etc. Compared with traditional paper-based media such as paper posters, digital signage can deal with a wide range of content types and makes it possible to easily update the content. Some of them supports interactions between the viewers and the displays using touchscreens, gesture technologies and mobile devices [2]. However, few studies have so far been made at combining digital signage and paper-based media. The latter has been used for years and is readily available. Thus, we have been developing "Hyper Panel system" to make extensive use of both advantages of digital signage and paper-based media by integrating them [3]. The Hyper Panel system enables an intuitive operation to show signage items such as pictures and movies related to the regions on a given paper poster. When a viewer of the Hyper Panel system attaches a small device with supersonic sensors which we developed in our previous study to the paper poster, the coordinate values of the device are acquired and the signage items corresponding to the position are shown on his/her tablet terminal.

A digital signage system typically consists of one or more displays, one or more media players and a content management system [1, 2]. The latter is responsible for providing capabilities for content authoring and delivery. So far, we developed a fundamental mechanism of the Hyper Panel system to support interactive display of signage items. We believe that developing a content management system for the Hyper

S. Yamamoto (Ed.): HIMI 2016, Part I, LNCS 9734, pp. 329–338, 2016.
DOI: 10.1007/978-3-319-40349-6_31

Panel system produces the intended effect. Therefore, in this paper, we propose the content authoring tool of our Hyper Panel system. We discussed it in [4]. However, we have not compared it with other method yet. Most content authoring tools of the existing digital signage provide a function to define the screen layout. With this function, users can segment the screen into a variety of areas for various purposes. However, such a segmentation function is inadequate for use in our Hyper Panel system because it requires that signage items are assigned according to the layout of a paper poster.

2 Related Work

There has been an increasing interest in interactive digital signage [5, 6]. Our Hyper Panel system also has interactivity. A digital signage system typically consists of one or more displays, one or more media players and a content management system [1, 2]. A large number of studies have been made on the development of digital signage systems. These studies focused on reflections on and lessons from long-term use of a digital signage [7], user-generated signage contents [8, 9], an interactive digital signage [10, 11], etc. Some of them combined paper-based media such as maps and posters with digital information [12, 13]. They make use of near-field communication technology. However, little attention has been given to the content management system. To solve inefficiency and scalability issues introduced by use of proprietary signage content formats, Dayarathna, M., etc. proposed a method of using XML to describe signage contents and evaluated the flexibility in signage content authoring [14]. Their system has a function to manage signage contents, but it does not provide a function to make the screen layout. Takata, S., etc. developed a digital signage system that is low-cost and easy to introduce in small stores [15]. Their system has a function to manage signage contents on the web. However, it handles only a movie file and does not manage the screen layout. Commercial and open-source digital signage systems have a function to manage signage contents. The function allows users to design a screen layout and to make a content with multi areas displaying different items. However, such a function is inadequate for use in our Hyper Panel system because users cannot assign signage items according to the layout of a paper poster in an intuitive environment.

3 Hyper Panel System

Hyper Panel system provides signage items according to the layout of a given paper poster [3]. This system treats any regions on the paper poster as hyperlink anchors that allow viewers to obtain detail information about the content of the region on their mobile devices such as smartphones and tablet terminals. To realize this feature, we developed a small device with supersonic sensors, which is called "viewpoint tag". When a viewer of our Hyper Panel system attaches the viewpoint tag to a given paper poster, the coordinate values of the tag are acquired and the signage items corresponding to the position are shown on his/her mobile device. With this mechanism, the Hyper Panel system makes extensive use of both advantages of digital signage and paper-based media. Figure 1 shows a prototype of the Hyper Panel system which we developed. A content management system is necessary for the Hyper Panel system to produce the intended effects. In the next section, we propose the content authoring tool for our Hyper Panel system.

viewpoint tag

Fig. 1. Prototype of Hyper Panel system

4   Content Authoring Tool

4.1   Outline

Our content authoring tool is based on a client-server model and has five functions. They are (1) to register poster images, (2) to assign signage items to regions for display on a paper poster placed on our Hyper Panel system, (3) to change the size and position of the regions and the assigned signage items, (4) to preview the assignment, and (5) to provide the assignment information to a media player of the Hyper Panel system. The database of our content authoring tool has three tables to manage the assignment information. They store poster images, regions on paper posters, signage items related to the regions, respectively. The relationships are created among these tables.

By the way, those who manage contents of a digital signage are not always technically savvy. Therefore, it is important that such non-technical users of a content management system can easily understand how to properly use it. This is why our content authoring tool provides users with an intuitive environment.

4.2   Functions

(1) **To register poster images**

This function is to add an image file of a paper poster. When registering a new poster, users specify the paper size and orientation and our content authoring tool obtains the size of the poster image. When the content authoring tool provides a content created for a paper poster to a media player of our Hyper Panel system, it converts the coordinates of the regions contained in the content from pixels to millimeters using the paper size and the image size of the poster. This conversion makes it possible to create a content in accordance with the size of a poster.

(2) **To assign signage items to regions**

This function is to assign signage items according to the layout of a paper poster. Users can specify a region to which they want to assign signage items by dragging and dropping on the poster image. If the specified new region does not overlap with any regions registered before, it is added to the database and drawn as a rectangle on the poster image. The database stores two coordinate pairs, which are the upper-left and the lower-right corners, and brief description for each region. Once a region is added, users can relate signage items by dragging and dropping the files into the region.

(3) **To change regions and signage items assigned**

This function is to change the size and position of regions added to the database and signage items related to them. When changing a region, users click the region on a poster image and drag it to the desired size and position. This manner is similar to the way that general office software and graphics software employ. They can remove any signage items from a list of the items related to the clicked region.

(4) **To preview assignment.**

This function is to check if signage items are correctly assigned according to the layout of a paper poster. When users click a region, the signage items related to the region is overlaid to the poster image in sequence. With this function, they can determine the appropriateness of the size and position of the regions and the signage items related to them together.

(5) **To provide the assignment information.**

This function is to output assignment information in XML format. This information is about the relation between regions and signage items. It contains the coordinates of regions converted to millimeters and the URLs of the signage items related to the regions to lead a media player of our Hyper Panel system to the items. This function is available as WebAPI. When the media player sends the information about a paper poster displayed on the Hyper Panel system to the function, it can obtain the assignment information corresponding to the poster. Using this information, it shows signage items on a viewer's mobile device in accordance with the position where the viewer attaches a viewpoint tag on the paper poster.

4.3   Implementation

We developed the content authoring tool as a web application with each function accessed as an individual web page. We implemented the server-side functionality using PHP and MySQL. Assignment information is stored in the database (MySQL). This information is available through the WebAPI provided by our content authoring

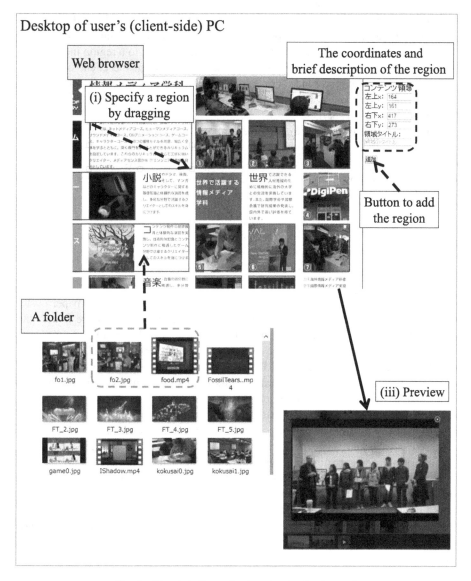

Fig. 2. User interface of out content authoring tool

tool in XML format. At the client-side, we implemented the functionality using HTML5 and Javascript with Fabric.js, which is a Javascript library that works with HTML5 canvas and provides interactive object model on the top of canvas element [16]. We made good use of the library to specify and draw regions on a poster image by dragging a mouse (see (i) in Fig. 2).

When a new region is added to the database, a rectangle is drawn in blue to indicate the region on the poster image. It can be moved and resized by dragging and dropping and the results are immediately reflected in the database. We also implemented the function to relate signage items to regions using HTML5 File API and Drag and Drop API. These two APIs make it possible for users to do this assignment by dragging and dropping signage items, which are files saved on their PC, to a region indicated by a blue rectangle on a poster image (see (ii) in Fig. 2). When the client-side scripts communicate with the server-side scripts to add a new region and relate signage items, they send the coordinate pairs of the region and the files to the server-side scripts through Ajax using jQuery.

The function to preview the assignment allows users to see if signage items are correctly assigned according to the layout of a paper poster. When a region is clicked on the poster image to preview the assignment, the signage items related to the region are overlaid on the poster image and users can view them one after another (see (iii) in Fig. 2). To implement this feature, we used Zoombox plugin of jQuery.

5 Evaluation

5.1 Experiment

In order to see if users can easily and correctly assign signage items to a paper poster with our content authoring tool, we conducted an experiment to compare it with the method to make assignment information in XML format using a text editor. Three university students participated in the experiment. In this paper, we call them participant A, B and C. Participant A and B major in a computer-related discipline, while participant C does not. Participant B and C assigned signage items using our content authoring tool before using a text editor. Participant A did that in reverse order. For the purpose of this experiment, we measured the time it takes the participants to assign signage items by a stop-watch. The participants gave us the start and end signs of the trials. We also asked the experimental participants to answer questions about the usability of our content authoring tool after assigning with both methods.

In this experiment, we used a poster to introduce a department at a university. The participants related 50 signage items to 10 regions on the poster. To do that, we gave them a printed A4-size poster to show the regions, a printed poster and a list to show what items are related to which regions, and a printed assignment information in XML format as a sample. The following is the sample:

```
<paper src="poster.jpg">
<contents pos="100,100,200,200" title="region1">
<picture src="pic1.jpg"/>
<picture src="pic2.jpg"/>
<movie src="mov.mp4"/>
</contents>
<contents pos="250,300,500,400" title="region2">
<picture src="pic3.jpg"/>
<picture src="pic4.jpg"/>
</contents>
</paper>
```

The participants assigned the signage items in accordance with these instructions. Using a text editor, they looked up coordinates of the regions with a general graphics software. About a network environment in the experiment, participant A and B used WiMAX connection, while participant C used optical fiber.

5.2 Results

Table 1 summarizes the time taken for the participants to complete the assignment of the signage items. The asterisk (*) and plus (+) marks in the table indicate that the participants used our content authoring tool before a text editor before and that the participant does not major in computer-related discipline and used optical fiber, respectively. As you can see, participant B and C completed the assignment using our content authoring tool for 4 min and 19 min faster than when making the assignment information in XML format, respectively. On the other hand, participant A did the assignment in almost the same time with either method. Participant B and C alternated between adding a region and relating signage items to the region, while Participant A related all signage items after registering all of regions. All participants used the function to preview after finishing relating all signage items. Participant B used a text editor with the function to support making a file in XML format. After creating the XML file, the participant checked it using a web browser. Participant A and C used a text editor bundled with operating system. All participants made the assignment information in XML format after looking up all coordinates of the regions with a graphics software.

Table 1. Results of the assignment

Participant	Our content authoring tool	Text editor
A	27' 30"	27' 43"
B*	23' 48"	27' 49"
C*,+	17' 17"	36' 14"

In the questionnaires, all participants chose our system to a question which method was easy to understand. The reasons were the follows:

- I specified coordinates of regions in an intuitive method.
- Assignment on a poster image made it possible to easily understand what I was doing.
- It is how to imagine because I could add signage items on a poster image.

We also asked the participants about ease of use of our content authoring tool with 5 categories: very easy, easy, neither easy nor difficult, difficult, and very difficult. They answered "easy" to questions on how to specify a region on a poster image and relate signage items to it. The reason was "Dragging and dropping is easy". They also answered "easy" to a question on how to preview the assignment. Only participant C used the function to change regions and signage items. The participant answered "I was a little confused because I had to move to the page to use the function".

5.3   Discussion

The results of the questionnaires suggest that our content authoring tool provides an environment in which users can assign signage items according to the layout of a paper poster with having an intuitive understanding of what they are doing. This is because all of the functions are available by drag and drop on a poster image. Users can easily understand how to use our content authoring tool even though they are not technical-savvy.

We discuss the results of the assignment of signage items with our content authoring tool. Participant B and C correctly related all signage items to the indicated regions, while Participant A related the same signage item to the indicated region multiple times. The number of such assignment was 7 items. However, there was no item that the participant forgot to relate. Six of them were intended to be related to the first region of the list given as instructions and the rest was the largest file size in the signage items. Actually, the participant had related signage items one after another before the last upload was completed. After all signage items were related, the participant noticed that the upload of signage items had not been complete and related the items again, but the participant did not noticed the multiple assignment and did not used the function to change the assignment. We think that a lack of the upload progress information of signage items caused such multiple assignment of the same item. Such progress information would help users know how long have to wait for the upload. In fact, when the participant understood the feature that our content authoring tool do not show the upload progress information, there was almost no multiple assignment. It is also useful to make it impossible to relate the same signage item to the same region more than one time.

As for the assignment information in XML format, participant A and B did not make any grammatical mistakes, but they made some typing mistakes. For example, they described more than one element for the same signage items in an element for a region to relate some different items to. On the other hand, participant C made both mistakes. The participant did not input a space between attributes, a diagonal (/) to denote an end tag, quotation marks for attribute values, and some end tags. These mistakes can be solved using a text editor with the function to support making a file in XML format. However, such a tool is not used widely, especially for non-technical people. A simple user interface like our content authoring tool is suitable for such users.

Participant C was able to assign signage items faster than the others did using our content authoring tool. The one reason is probably the usage of optical fiber network. In addition, unlike the others, the participant used the function to change the assignment. When using it, the participant also checked if signage items was correctly related, so he hardly used the function to preview the assignment.

These suggest that with progress information, our content authoring tool make it possible more effectively and efficiently, that is, more correctly and quickly assign signage items according to the layout of a paper poster.

6 Conclusion

In this paper, we proposed a content authoring tool for our Hyper Panel system. This content authoring tool makes it possible to assign signage items according to the layout of a paper poster. Users can specify regions and related signage items there on a poster image. As the results of the experiment described in this paper, we found that our content authoring tool provide an easy to understand environment in which users can almost correctly assign signage items in an intuitive method. However, there is room for improvement on its usability. We need to introduce measures to prevent users from relating the same signage items to the same region multiple times. It is also necessary to unify the functions to assign signage items and to change the assignment. These would lead to the improvement in the effectiveness and efficiency of our content authoring tool, which are our future work. In addition, we would like to make use of our Hyper Panel system in various fields, for example, a town guide and education. We have to evaluate it based on the field trials.

References

1. ITU Telecommunication Standardization Sector: Digital signage: the right information in all the right places. ITU-T Technology Watch report (2011)
2. Davies, N., Clinch, S., Alt, F.: Pervasive Displays: Understanding the Future of Digital Signage. Morgan & Claypool, San Rafael (2014)
3. Suzuki, H., Hattori, A., Sato, H., Hayami, H.: Hyper panel system: display system for poster layouts with detailed contents. In: Stephanidis, C. (ed.) HCII 2015 Posters. CCIS, vol. 529, pp. 45–50. Springer, Heidelberg (2015)
4. Hattori, A., Suzuki, H., Hayami, H.: Contents authoring tool for relating pictures and movies to positions on a paper poster. IPSJ J. Inf. Process. Soc. Jpn. 57(1), 270–279 (2016)
5. Want, R., Schilit, B.N.: Interactive digital signage. Computer 45(5), 21–24 (2012). IEEE
6. Veenstra, M., Wouters, N., Kanis, M., Brandenburg, S., Raa, K., Wigger, B., Moere, A.V.: Should public displays be interactive? Evaluating the impact of interactivity on audience engagement. In: Proceedings of the 4th International Symposium on Pervasive Displays, pp. 15–21. ACM, New York (2015)

7. Clinch, S., Davies, N., Friday, A., Efstratiou, C.: Reflections on the long-term use of an experimental digital signage system. In: Proceedings of the 13th International Conference on Ubiquitous Computing, pp. 133–142. ACM, New York (2011)

8. Jose, R., Pinto, H., Silva, B., Melro, A., Rodrigues, H.: Beyond interaction: tools and practices for situated publication in display networks. In: Proceedings of the 2012 International Symposium on Pervasive Displays, 6 p. ACM, New York (2012)

9. Kanis, M., Groen, M., Meys, M., Veenstra, M.: Studying screen interactions long-term: the library as a case. In: Proceedings of the International Symposium on Pervasive Displays 2012. ACM, New York (2012)

10. Chen, Q., Malric, F., Zhang, Y., Abid, M., Cordeiro, A., Petriu, E.M., Georganas, N.D.: Interacting with digital signage using hand gestures. In: Kamel, M., Campilho, A. (eds.) ICIAR 2009. LNCS, vol. 5627, pp. 347–358. Springer, Heidelberg (2009)

11. Kim, E., Lee, H.J., Lee, D.H., Jang, U., Kim, H.S., Cho, K.S., Ryu, W.: Efficient contents sharing between digital signage system and mobile terminals. In: 15th International Conference on Advanced Communication Technology, 2013, pp. 1002–1005 (2013)

12. Borrego-Jaraba, F., Ruiz, I.L., Gomez-Nieto, M.A.: A NFC-based pervasive solution for city touristic surfing. Pers. Ubiquit. Comput. 15(7), 731–742 (2011). Springer-Verlag, London

13. Reilly, D., Rodgers, M., Argue, R., Nunes, M., Inkpen, K.: Marked-up maps: combining paper maps and electronic information resources. Pers. Ubiquit. Comput. 10(4), 215–226 (2006). Springer-Verlag, London

14. Dayarathna, M., Withana, A., Sugiura, K.: Infoshare: design and implementation of scalable multimedia signage architecture for wireless ubiquitous environments. Wireless Pers. Commun. 60(1), 3–27 (2011). Springer US

15. Takata, S., Hayashi, K., Tamatsu, K., Yamagishi, Y., Nagase, H.: Development and use of a digital signage system for revitalizing regional shopping districts. Knowl. Manag. E-Learn. 6 (4), 426–439 (2014). Laboratory for Knowledge Management & E-Learning, Faculty of Education, University of Hong Kong

16. Fabric.js. http://fabricjs.com/

Motion Control Algorithm of ARM-COMS for Entrainment Enhancement

Teruaki Ito[1(✉)] and Tomio Watanabe[2]

[1] Tokushima University, 2-1 Minami-Josanjima,
Tokushima 770-8506, Japan
tito@tokushima-u.ac.jp
[2] Okayama Prefectural University, 111 Tsuboki,
Souja, Okayama 719-1197, Japan
watanabe@cse.oka-pu.ac.jp

Abstract. It is very common nowadays to communicate with a remote person over the network, using a free communication software. However, several drawbacks are pointed out as open issues, such as lack of tele-presence or lack of entrainment in communication. This study proposes an idea of remote individuals' connection through augmented tele-presence systems called ARM-COMS: ARm-supported eMbodied COmmunication Monitor System and tackles these issues. ARM-COMS is composed of a tablet as an ICT (Information and Communication Technology) device and a desktop-type robotic arm, which manipulates the tablet. ARM-COMS is based on the two types of modes, or intelligent tablet mode (IT-mode) and intelligent avatar mode (IA-mode). Under these modes, ARM-COMS has three types of functions; namely, autonomous positioning (AP), autonomous entrainment movement (AEM), and autonomous entrainment positioning (AEP). This paper presents the basic concept of ARM-COMS and its critical challenges, followed by the experimental analysis of motion control to check the feasibility of AEM function of ARM-COMS.

Keywords: Embodied communication · Augmented tele-presence robotic arm manipulation · Human interface · Remote communication

1 Introduction

Nowadays, ICT (Information and Communication Technology) devices enable real-time remote communication over the network. Ranging from the high-qualified commercial systems at the top of the range to freely downloadable application software at the bottom, various choices are available for remote communication [1]. The network-based remote communication is a convenient tool. However, it addresses several critical issues, such as lack of tele-presence feeling and lack of relationship feeling in communication [2].

As for the lack of tele-presence feeling in remote communication, the idea of mobile robot-based remote communication proposes one solution to this issue. The effectiveness of these approaches in remote communication has been shown by

© Springer International Publishing Switzerland 2016
S. Yamamoto (Ed.): HIMI 2016, Part I, LNCS 9734, pp. 339–346, 2016.
DOI: 10.1007/978-3-319-40349-6_32

experimental studies using a mobile robot [4, 12]. Embodiment of an agent using anthropomorphization of an object [8] also shows an interesting idea towards the higher presence of a remote participant [11].

Tele-presence robots provide the tele-presence of the operator in the remote site and even enable to do some kinds of tele-operating tasks remotely. Some robots provide a basic function to support distance communication using several critical technologies such as face image display of the operator [9], remote-drivability to move around, tele-manipulation as well as the basic communication functions such as "talk", "listen", and "see" [5]. However, it is recognized that there is still a gap between robot-based video conference and face-to-face one.

A robotic arm-typed system with mobile function has undertaken a new challenge. For example, Kubi [7], a non-mobile arm type robot, allows the remote user to "look around" during their video call by commanding Kubi where to aim the tablet using intuitive remote controls over the web. Moreover, an idea of enhanced motion display using a moving object has also been reported [10]. However, the movement of human body as non-verbal movement of the remote person is still an open issue.

Considering the critical aspect of entrainment in human communication [13], this research challenges the two issues, which are the lack of tele-presence feeling and the lack of relationship in communication [3]. This paper presents an overview of ARM-COMS (ARm-supported eMbodied COmmunication Monitor System) for connecting remote individuals through augmented tele-presence systems.

2 ARM-COMS (ARm-supported eMbodied COmmunication Monitor System)

2.1 Basic System Overview of ARM-COMS

ARM-COMS is composed of a desktop type mechanical robotic arm, which holds a tablet PC, such as a smart phone, and dynamically manipulates its position and movement autonomously. This autonomous manipulation is controlled by the head movement of a master person whom the tablet represents in remote communication. The head movement of the master person can be recognized by a portable motion sensor, such as a Kinect [6] sensor, and its detected signals are transferred to the PC under which ARM-COMS is connected over the network.

First, a user establishes a connection to the remote ARM-COMS, which is located at a remote site when a remote communication starts. ARM-COMS mimics the movement of its master person as an avatar in communication as if the master person on a remote site is virtually present at the local site. On one hand, ARM-COMS works just like a general mobile robot which supports the remote communication, by way of remote control manipulation over the network. However, ARM-COMS provides more than what is offered by general tele-presence robots, on the other hand. Figure 1 shows the general overview of ARM-COMS and the three critical and unique challenges to which this research is pursuing. These challenges differentiate the ARM-COMS from general tele-presence robot.

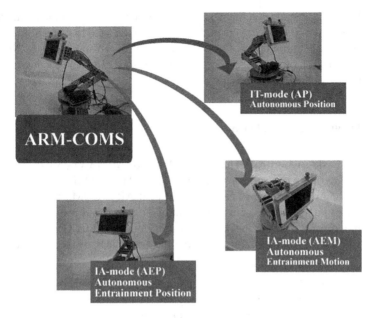

Fig. 1. Challenges of ARM-COMS

2.2   Two Critical Modes of ARM-COMS

ARM-COMS works as an intelligent ICT device on a local site as well as an intelligent remote avatar system who represents its master person on a remote site (Fig. 1). The former performs as an intelligent tablet which is called *IT-mode* herein after, whereas the latter performs as an intelligent avatar module which is called *IA-mode* herein after.

Tablet PC or smartphone is one of the very popular mobile ICT devices today. As a typical situation in using a tablet PC, a user holds the devise in left hand and manipulates it on the touch screen with right fingers. In addition to that, the device is often set to a holder on an office table, a driving seat of a vehicle, or a bed at home. AP (Autonomous Position) function of IT-mode of ARM-COMS enables the tablet PC autonomously and automatically approaches to the user when needed, for example at the time of incoming phone call, or at the time of lost-and-found of tablet.

ICT devices allow us not only to retrieve information, but also to communicate with others over the network. However, when we compare video communication with face-to-face communication, there is a significant difference. When we talk with somebody in a face-to-face meeting, what we share is not merely the same physical space, but also an invisible communication space or atmosphere. As a result, entrainment between the participants occurs during the conversation. However, when we talk with somebody over the network, we can only see the face on the screen and cannot share the same physical space. As a result, this kind of entrainment is different from that of a face-to-face meeting.

Since the entrainment is associated with physical movement of a person, AEM (Autonomous Entrainment Motion) function of IA-mode enables a dynamic movement of a tablet PC during remote communication for entrainment acceleration by mimicking the head movement of its master person. In addition to the head movement of a person, AEP (Autonomous Entrainment Position) function of IA-mode in ARM-COMS enables the expression of relationship between the persons. The next section covers the critical challenges of ARM-COMS.

2.3   Challenges in ARM-COMS

Autonomous Position Control. The first challenge of ARM-COMS tackles the issue of autonomous position control, where a tablet PC on ARM-COMS autonomously and automatically approaches to us when we need it as if ARM-COMS understands when we want. For example, suppose a user is working at a desk and receives an incoming video conference call. Considering what the use is doing, ARM-COMS autonomously takes the table PC in front of the user to urge the acceptance of the connection.

Autonomous Entrainment Movement Control. The first Challenge mentioned above does not directly relate to video communication. However, the second and the third challenges below are directly related to video communications. It has been reported that entrainment among participants emerges during conversation if the participating subjects share the same physical space and engage in the conversation [14]. However, this kind of entrainment in a face-to-face meeting is different from that of remote communication. Tracking the head movement of a speaking person in a remote site, ARM-COMS manipulates the tablet PC as an avatar to mimic the head movement of the remote person so that entrainment emerges as if the local person interacts with the remote person locally. ARM-COMS mimics the head movement on a remote site to represent the speaking person on a remote site.

Autonomous Entrainment Position Control. The third challenge of ARM-COMS deals with an autonomous entrainment position control. In a face-to-face meeting, each person takes a meaningful physical position to represent the relationship with the others, or to send non-verbal messages to others. A closer position would be taken for friends, showing close relationship, whereas a non-closer position would be taken for strangers, showing unfriendly relationship [5]. ARM-COMS controls a tablet PC to dynamically locate an appropriate position in space and to explicitly represent the relationship with other participants, by sending non-verbal messages. For example, the tablet PC would be approaching to the speaking person to show that the remote person is interested in the talk.

3   Motion Control Using a Prototype System of ARM-COMS

A prototype of ARM-COMS system has been developed to study the feasibility of the proposed ideas. The prototype system is a five axis robotic arm controlled by a microcontroller using gesture signals detected by a motion sensor. The prototype is designed to mimic the basic human head motion as the AEM function, which is one of

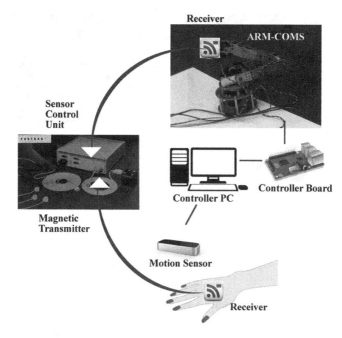

Fig. 2. Experimental setup

the challenges of ARM-COMS. Focusing on the typical human head gestures including; nodding motion for affirmative meaning; head shaking motion for negative meaning; and head tilting motion for unsure meaning, the previous paper reported the basic control results [11]. Redesigning of the prototype system, the motion control algorithms of the prototype are also updated. This section presents the experimental results of motion control by these updates.

Figure 2 shows the setup of this experiments. Since the motion range of head movement is not so wide, this experiment used a hand gesture to analyze the motion of the ARM-COMS. In this experiment, ARM-COMS is controlled by gesture signals detected by a non-contact hand motion sensor. Therefore, a subject could freely manipulate hand gestures without any attachment. However, for data collection, a small receiver was attached to the back of the hand and terminal portion of ARM-COMS.

As the results of program updates, ARM-COMS could mimic the hand gesture motion based on the motion sensor control. From the experimental date, three types of hand gestures were selected to show the feasibility of head gesture motions, nodding, shaking and tilting, as shown in Figs. 3, 4 and 5. In each case, the hand gestures were repeated three times in a consecutive manner.

Figure 3 shows the snapping gesture of hand motion, which is identical to nodding gesture of head movement. The blue line shows the snapping gesture conducted three times in a consecutive manner, whereas the red line shows the corresponding ARM-COMS motion.

Figure 4 shows the twisting gesture of hand motion, which is identical to head shaking gesture of head movement. The blue line shows the snapping gesture

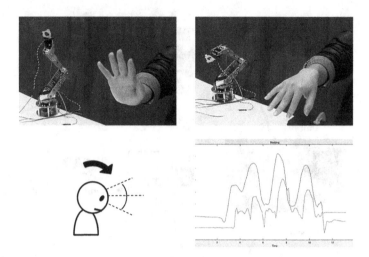

Fig. 3. Analysis of nodding motion (Color figure online)

conducted three times in a consecutive manner, whereas the red line shows the corresponding ARM-COMS motion.

Figure 5 shows the turning back gesture of hand motion, which is identical to head tilting gesture of head movement. The blue line shows the snapping gesture conducted three times in a consecutive manner, whereas the red line shows the corresponding ARM-COMS motion.

From the experimental results of the selected three types of movements, timing of ARM-COMS movement was almost corresponded to the master motion of the hand gestures. However, the trajectories of ARM-COMS were not identical to the original trajectories of master motion of hand. Jerky movement observed in ARM-COMS needs

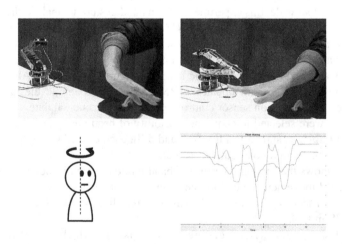

Fig. 4. Analysis of head shaking motion (Color figure online)

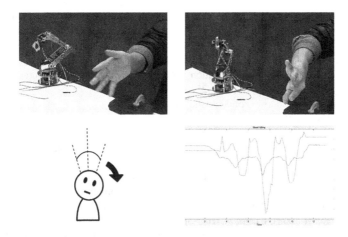

Fig. 5. Analysis of head tilting motion (Color figure online)

to be resolved before applying to the head motion gesture expression in remote communication.

4 Concluding Remarks

The paper presented an idea of active display monitor named ARM-COMS with the two types of modes in ARM-COM system, or IT-mode and IA-mode, followed by the three challenges based on these modes. The three basic functions of AP, AEM and AEP were also presented. The future goal which ARM-COMS is pursuing is not only the tele-presence feeling of a remote person, but also implicitly shows the relationship between the remote person and the local participants by way of the entrainmental behavior of a table PC manipulation.

Acknowledgement.   The author would like to acknowledge Yuki Kawakami, Madihah Maharof, all members of Collaborative Engineering Labs at Tokushima University, and Center for Technical Support of Tokushima University, for their cooperation to conduct the experiments.

References

1. Abowdm, D.G., Mynatt, D.E.: Charting past, present, and future research in ubiquitous computing. ACM Trans. Comput.-Hum. Interact. (TOCHI) **7**(1), 29–58 (2000)
2. Greenberg, S.: Peepholes: low cost awareness of one's community. In: Conference Companion on Human Factors in Computing Systems: Common Ground, Vancouver, British Columbia, Canada, pp. 206–207 (1996)
3. Ito, T., Watanabe, T.: Three key challenges in ARM-COMS for entrainment effect acceleration in remote communication. In: Yamamoto, S. (ed.) HCI 2014, Part I. LNCS, vol. 8521, pp. 177–186. Springer, Heidelberg (2014)

4. Kashiwabara, T., Osawa, H., Shinozawa, K., Imai, M.: TEROOS: a wearable avatar to enhance joint activities. In: Annual Conference on Human Factors in Computing Systems, pp. 2001–2004 (2012)
5. Kim, K., Bolton, J., Girouard, A., Cooperstock, J., Vertegaal, R.: TeleHuman: effects of 3D perspective on gaze and pose estimation with a life-size cylindrical tele-presence pod. In: Proceedings of CHI 2012, pp. 2531–2540 (2012)
6. Kinect. https://dev.windows.com/en-us/kinect
7. Kubi. https://www.revolverobotics.com
8. Osawa, T., Matsuda, Y., Ohmura, R., Imai, M.: Embodiment of an agent by anthropomorphization of a common object. Web Intell. Agent Syst. Int. J. **10**, 345–358 (2012)
9. Otsuka, T., Araki, S., Ishizuka, K., Fujimoto, M., Heinrich, M., Yamato, J.: A realtime multimodal system for analyzing group meetings by combining face pose tracking and speaker diarization. In: Proceedings of the 10th International Conference on Multimodal Interfaces (ICMI 2008), Chania, Crete, Greece, pp. 257–264 (2008)
10. Ohtsuka, S., Oka, S., Kihara, K., Tsuruda, T., Seki, M.: Human-body swing affects visibility of scrolled characters with direction dependency. In: Society for Information Display (SID) 2011 Symposium Digest of Technical Papers, pp. 309–312 (2011)
11. Sirkin, D., Ju, W.: Consistency in physical and on-screen action improves perceptions of tele-presence robots. In: HRI 2012, Proceedings of the Seventh Annual ACM/IEEE International Conference on Human-Robot Interaction, pp. 57–64 (2012)
12. Tariq, A.M., Ito, T.: Master-slave robotic arm manipulation for communication robot. In: Proceedings of 2011 Annual Meeting on Japan Society of Mechanical Engineer, vol. 11, issue 1, p. S12013, September 2011
13. Watanabe, T.: Human-entrained embodied interaction and communication technology. In: Fukuda, S. (ed.) Emotional Engineering, pp. 161–177. Springer, Heidelberg (2011)
14. Wongphati, M., Matsuda, Y., Osawa, H., Imai, M.: Where do you want to use a robotic arm ? And what do you want from the robot? In: International Symposium on Robot and Human Interactive Communication, pp. 322–327 (2012)

IVOrpheus 2.0 - A Proposal for Interaction by Voice Command-Control in Three Dimensional Environments of Information Visualization

Lennon Furtado[✉], Anderson Marques, Nelson Neto,
Marcelle Mota, and Bianchi Meiguins

Graduate Program in Computer Science,
Federal University of Pará, Belém, Brazil
lennonsfurtado@gmail.com,
anderson.gmarques@gmail.com, dnelsonneto@gmail.com,
bianchi.serique@gmail.com, mpmota@ufpa.br

Abstract. Several studies point out the importance of interaction in Information Visualization (InfoVis) field to the success of good data visualization. The interaction researches in InfoVis have encouraged the use of non-conventional interfaces, besides the traditional keyboard and mouse, such as voice commands, gesture controls, among others. This work aims to present aspects of design, development and evaluation of an interface for voice commands to interact in InfoVis 3D applications. The InfoVis technique used as usage scenario is the 3D Scatterplot. In addition, for speech recognition is used Coruja Software, to support Brazilian Portuguese. Finally, usability tests will be presented for a first evaluation of the interface and interaction proposal. The tests used the approach of user tasks to evaluate InfoVis sub-tasks. And as qualitative measurement is used NASA Task Load-Index methodology, which identifies the user's total workload in the different tasks performed.

Keywords: Information visualization · Ivorpheus · Voice interaction · Scatterplot 3D · Brazilian portuguese

1 Introduction

Several studies point out the importance of interaction to information visualization (InfoVis) area, particularly the interplay between interaction and cognition [1–4]. This interplay, combined with the demands from increasingly large and complex datasets, has directed the InfoVis area to seek different ways to interact as alternative to the traditional mouse and keyboard.

The interaction focusing on Natural User interfaces (NUI) paradigm [6] appears as a promising alternative to interactions by conventional means. These NUIs are based on how people interact in the physical world, for instance, through gestures, touch, sketch and speech. This paper will address the NUI by Voice Users Interface (VUI) in InfoVis 3D environment.

© Springer International Publishing Switzerland 2016
S. Yamamoto (Ed.): HIMI 2016, Part I, LNCS 9734, pp. 347–360, 2016.
DOI: 10.1007/978-3-319-40349-6_33

Thus, this work aims to present aspects of design, development and evaluation of an interface for voice commands to interact in InfoVis 3D applications. To test the interaction proposal, was developed an InfoVis tool (IVOrpheus) that uses the 3D scatterplot technique, and to represent data, it uses three spatial dimensions: x, y, and z-axes. And three visual channels: color, shape, and size. The tool allows interaction by mouse and keyboard or voice commands in Brazilian Portuguese, which is performed by Coruja Software [14]. Good practices in VUI were adopted for the application design, as the voice commands automatic adaptability to the used dataset and the dynamic generation of the grammars used in the speech recognition system.

To test the proposal efficacy, usability tests with 10 users were performed to evaluate the application interface with and without interaction by voice. This usability test measured the time spent to complete the tasks by each user, and user's workload using NASA Task Load Index [12]. The test tasks approach 4 of the 12 interaction tasks proposed by Heer and Shneiderman [3], which are: Visualize - specify a visualization of data by setting the axes, Filters - reduce the analysis data set, Select - Pointing to an item or region of interest, Navigate – apply zoom and rotate in the visualization.

Thus, this paper presents the results obtained in the usability test as good practices to assist researchers in development of InfoVis tools to approach the Command-and-Control Voice User Interface. In addition, the role and difficulties present in VUIs were addressed, since the uses of VUIs are underexplored in infoVis area.

2   Application

IVOrpheus [18] is an information visualization tool that uses scatterplot 3D technique, using three spatial dimensions (X, Y and Z) and three visual channels (color, shape and size) to represent data. Moreover, the tool accepts input by voice commands in Brazilian Portuguese.

2.1   Conceptual Aspects

IVOrpheus follows the basic guidelines of a good InfoVis tool, defined by [4] and commonly referred to as the InfoVis mantra, which are: overview of data - user should have a general idea of the data for analysis; semantic zoom - focus on a subset of the data; filters - reduce the analysis data set; and details on demand - present data that are not visually represented (hidden data).

Interface. The first guideline for building IVOrpheus environment is that both interactions by keyboard and mouse and by voice commands will share the same interface. In the development of the interface were considered six main guidelines [5, 11]:

- Home equivalent: a command/button that returns users to a known starting point;
- Back equivalent: a command/button that allows the user to backup one-step at a time;

- Meaningful communication: user should easily identify the commands available for interaction and their meaning, and get help about them on the available commands on the screen;
- Minimal user action: the commands should be simple on each screen. And the input data should be on the screen;
- Consistency and standardization in interaction and screens: forms of interaction and standardization of screens are maintained, as well as the commands in different contexts for similar operations;
- Speaker independent.

The IVOrpheus interface is divided into four main areas, as shown in Fig. 1: the Options bar (1), the Preview area (2), the Legend area (3), and the Menu bar (4). In all areas, each option presented on the screen can be performed by voice command, or mouse click.

The labels of buttons and menus are the commands available for interaction by voice. For example, speaking the voice command "Filter" can access the filter option. The following voice commands are available and visually displayed on the Option bar: "open", "save", "screenshot", "help", "legend" and "details". The Menu bar is enabled only after a database is loaded into the tool, and has the following initial commands: "configure", "filter" and "interact". All this commands are available in Brazilian Portuguese.

Features. The IVOrpheus features follow the main characteristics of a good visualization tool. Below, such features are presented:

Configure/Filter: you can configure or filter the axes x, y, z, and the visual channels color, shape and size. Figure 2 presents an overview of the features set. The setting or filtering of the axes can be either applied to categorical data (discrete values), as continuous data (floating values) and the visual channels color, shape, and size can be applied only for categorical data.

Interaction: In order to manipulate the visualization, the interaction can be applied to rotate, translate, increase or decrease the size of the chart. In addition, the interaction has the "initial state" and "stop" functionalities, as presented in Fig. 2, because IVOrpheus system continuously increment or decrement zoom, rotation, and translation. The stop functionality is used to pause the increment or decrement of these values. While the "initial state" button returns the visualization to their initial values of zoom, rotation and translation.

Options Bar: features contained in this bar are present throughout the execution of the tool, and the user can say these global rules at any time. For instance, the command "Open" can be used at any time to open and load a new base. The "screenshot", "legend", and "details" commands will only be enabled after an already configured loaded base. The option "screenshot" allows the user to capture the current screen, and share the user`s discovers via email or other means of communication. While the "details" option calls the details panel, where the user can configure which attributes are wanted to receive extra information and make such extra details visible when selecting a point.

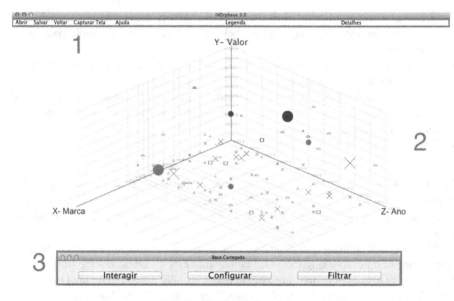

Fig. 1. IVOrpheus Interface.

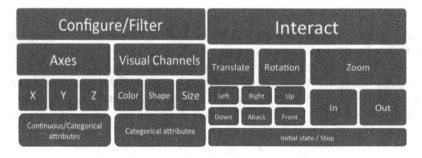

Fig. 2. Interaction by voice/mouse in IVOrpheus software

IVOrpheus as well as all information visualization tools must meet the basic functionality to meet the definition established by Shneiderman [13]: "Overview first, zoom and filter, then details on demand", since all of these features have been accomplished by IVOrpheus application in its features.

3 Usability Test

In this section is presented the test with users, participants and their profiles; procedure for the test; and the analysis of the results.

3.1 Procedure

Participants were presented to IVOrpheus tool through a training video and after that, it was applied a questionnaire to identify the user profile. Therefore, the tests start by giving the users the tasks and at the same time the users performance time was recorded. Upon completion of the tasks, it was administered the questionnaire to identify the level of difficulty in each scenario. And finally, the post-task questionnaire, NASA-TLX, was presented to the user, so that the users workload was measured.

3.2 User's Profile

To identify the different users profiles, a pre-task questionnaire was applied. With the following questions:

1. Do you know the Cartesian plan/space for 2 and 3 dimensions?
2. Have you ever used any software in order to analyze a data table, example: Excel® (Microsoft) Numbers® (Apple) or other?
3. Do you make use or have made use of any application on your phone or computer using the voice as a input, for example, personal voice assistant, such as: the SIRI® Apple or Samsung S Voice® of? If so, how often (rarely or occasionally or frequently)?
4. Are you familiar with applications that use the three spatial dimensions in mobility from the user viewpoint, i.e. the camera, as Blender®, Zbrush®, Autodesk 3D Max®, among others?

Below, are shown in Table 1 the results of the questionnaire where the first five columns represents mouse users and the other five columns, the speech interface users.

It is observed that due to the popularization of personal assistants in various embedded systems, users have had previous contact with the voice interaction technology, even by the fact that the frequency of use of voice software is a secondary mean of interaction. As can be seen, most of the users in Table 1 rarely make use of this technology. The use of three-dimensional environments is underutilization, due to the fact that most software and applications make use of two dimensions.

3.3 Training Video

It was presented, to all the volunteers who performed the tests, a training video lasting 7 min, which had the following points: introduction to visualization tool IVOrpheus, presentation of the interface and its functionalities. Thereupon, it was shown an example of how to open and load a base, and how to configure the spatial dimensions (x, y, and z) and visual channels (color, shape and size). Then, the users were introduced to the use of categorical and continuous filters. Finally, it was shown to the users how to use the details on demand function.

Table 1. Questionnaire to identify user's profiles. Legend, R- rarely, OC-occasionally and OF-often.

	User 1(Mouse)	User 2(Mouse)	User 3(Mouse)	User 4(Mouse)	User 5(Mouse)	User 1(Voice)	User 2(Voice)	User 3(Voice)	User 4(Voice)	User 5(Voice)
1	Yes	Yes	Yes	Yes	Yes	Yes	No	Yes	Yes	Yes
2	Yes	No	Yes	Yes	Yes	Yes	Yes	Yes	Yes	Yes
3	Yes (R)	Yes (OC)	Yes (R)	Yes (OC)	No	Yes (R)	Yes (R)	Yes (OC)	Yes (R)	Yes (OF)
4	Yes	No	No	Yes	No	No	No	No	Yes	Yes

3.4 Tasks

Each user had 18 min to complete the tasks. If the users do not finish in time, the remaining tasks would be unanswered and the volunteer would be asked to complete the NASA-TLX post-task surveys and questionnaire to identify the level of difficulty of the scenarios. In the tests, it was used a database of cars from the 80 s, which contained 789 records and 16 attributes (7 continuous and discrete 9). Using this base, it was presented the following tasks to the users:

- Configure the X-axis to brand, Y-axis to value and Z-axis to year. And find the most valuable car in 1986 between BMW, Isuzu and Dodge brands. After finding it, apply the zoom in it, and centering the point that represent the most valuable car on the center of the screen.
- The IVOrpeus tool start with a loaded base set with the following attributes on the X-axis (brand), Y-axis (value), and Z-axis (year). Configure the visual channels color to cylinders, shape to type and size to traction. After that, find out what is the most valuable car in the value range of \$ 22,965 and \$ 34,875 and using the legend, write the quantity of cylinders, type and traction of the most valuable car in that range.
- Select the car with the following dimensions X-axis (brand: Toyota), Y-axis (value: \$11248), Z – (year: 1981), Color – (cylinders: 4), Shape – (type: Hatch), and size - (traction: 4 × 4). Use the details on demands functionality to select the desired point, and find the number of doors and fuel of the desired car.

3.5 Time

The user had at his disposal 18 min to fulfill all the tasks presented in the list. To measure user performance, tasks were timed as showed in Table 2, which illustrates the time spent by the group of mouse users. Table 3 shows the time of the group of users who used the speech interface to complete the tasks.

Table 2. Time of tasks and its subtasks (Mouse)

	Task 1	Configuring Spatial Dimensions	Categorical Filtering	Zoom/ Rotate	Task 2	Configuring Visual Channels	Continuos Filtering	Understand visualization / Rotate	Read Legend	Task 3	Filters	Details on Demand	Total Time
User 1	01:37	00:34	00:30	00:33	04:51	01:52	01:39	00:17	01:12	02:20	02:17	00:03	08:47
User 2	03:18	00:55	02:08	00:15	04:12	01:33	00:46	00:33	01:20	01:30	01:18	00:12	08:27
User 3	04:27	01:32	02:37	00:18	03:31	01:55	00:48	00:11	00:37	01:15	00:59	00:16	09:13
User 4	03:55	00:59	02:26	00:30	04:28	00:48	01:34	00:20	01:46	02:06	01:58	00:08	10:29
User 5	01:31	00:33	00:46	00:11	03:49	00:40	00:56	00:46	01:27	00:58	00:53	00:05	06:17
Avarage	02:57	00:54	01:41	00:21	04:10	01:21	01:08	00:25	01:16	01:37	01:29	00:08	08:38

Table 3. Time of tasks and its subtasks (Speech Interface)

	Task 1	Configuring Spatial Dimensions	Categorical Filtering	Zoom/ Rotate	Task 2	Configuring Visual Channels	Continuos Filtering	Understand visualization / Rotate	Read Legend	Task 3	Filters	Details on Demand	Total Time
User 1	03:36	01:37	01:36	00:23	05:02	01:52	01:39	00:07	01:24	03:00	00:00	03:00	11:38
User 2	03:50	01:35	01:34	00:41	04:26	01:07	01:43	00:13	01:23	00:00	00:00	00:00	08:16
User 3	04:55	01:17	03:18	00:20	04:21	00:47	01:41	00:08	01:45	01:37	01:28	00:09	10:53
User 4	05:33	01:47	02:58	00:48	07:48	03:16	01:32	01:29	01:31	02:57	02:49	00:06	16:18
User 5	02:30	01:40	01:26	00:24	05:53	01:02	01:11	00:53	02:47	01:29	01:18	00:11	09:52
Avarage	04:04	01:35	02:10	00:31	05:30	01:36	01:33	00:34	01:46	01:48	01:07	00:41	11:23

3.6 Questionnaire to Identify the Level of Subjective Difficulty During the Execution of Tasks and Subtasks (Scenarios)

After the completion of the tasks, users receive the post-task questionnaire to identify the level of subjective difficulty during the execution of tasks and subtasks (scenarios). This questionnaire consisted of a Likert scale [15] with five levels: very easy, easy, medium, hard and very hard. In Tables 4 and 5 is presented the results of the questionnaire for mouse group and the voice group respectively.

3.7 Nasa-Tlx

The user's workload was evaluated with the NASA Task Load-Index [12], which is used to identify the overall workload in the different tasks and the main sources workload. Workload is defined by Hart [12] as a "hypothetical construction cost incurred by a human operator to achieve a given performance level". The NASA TLX is estimated in six subscales (physical demands, mental, time, effort, frustration, and performance). Each of these dimensions has twenty discrete levels to print the user's workload. The smaller the value of each scale, less is the weight of that scale in the final workload and vice versa. Shortly after the user identifies the value of each scale, it was used a sequence of 15 questions, in order to balance and better approach the

Table 4. Post task questionnaire results for mouse users.

Difficulty Level	User 1	User 2	User 3	User 4	User 5	Average
Task 1	Easy	Easy	Medium	Easy	Hard	Medium
Configuring Spatial Dimensions	Easy	Easy	Medium	Very Easy	Medium	Easy
Categorical Filtering	Medium	Easy	Medium	Very Easy	Medium	Easy
Zoom/Rotate	Easy	Very Easy	Medium	Medium	Very Easy	Easy
Task 2	Hard	Medium	Medium	Hard	Very Easy	Medium
Configuring Visual Channels	Medium	Medium	Medium	Very Easy	Very Easy	Easy
Continuos Filtering	Hard	Easy	Medium	Very Easy	Very Easy	Easy
Read Legend	Very Easy	Medium	Medium	Very Hard	Very Easy	Easy
Task 3	Medium	Easy	Medium	Very Easy	Very Easy	Easy
Details on Demand	Medium	Easy	Medium	Very Easy	Very Easy	Easy

overall workload felt by the volunteer. It is shown in Table 6 the results of NASA TLX to the users who used the mouse and Table 7 shows the results to the users who used the natural interaction interface. Finally it is shown in Table 8 averages of two groups.

3.8   Results Analysis

The analysis verifies the requisites, functionality, effectiveness, efficiency, utility, and usability pointed by Mazza [15], which serve as indicators to attest good usability features in an information visualization software.

To measure the functionality, it is needed to verify the possibility, through the use of interaction by natural user interface, of doing all the actions that are achived by conventional means (mouse and keyboard). This is the proposal of this work, and to achieve that, it was created the IVOrpheus information visualization tool. This tool includes all the functionalities provided for Visualization Mantra. Which are:

- Overview: view of a configured base in its entirety;
- Zoom: allows the user to zoom in/out a chart. Thus, the user observes clusters and trends in the data;
- Filters: allows the user to remove information from visualization, thus leaving to be analyzed only relevant information;

Table 5. Post task questionnaire results for speech interface users

Difficulty Level	User 1	User 2	User 3	User 4	User 5	Average
Task 1	Easy	Medium	Easy	Easy	Easy	Easy
Configuring Spatial Dimensions	Easy	Very Easy	Easy	Easy	Easy	Easy
Categorical Filtering	Easy	Medium	Easy	Easy	Easy	Easy
Zoom/Rotate	Easy	Very Easy	Medium	Easy	Easy	Easy
Task 2	Medium	Hard	Medium	Medium	Medium	Medium
Configuring Visual Channels	Medium	Hard	Easy	Easy	Easy	Medium
Continuos Filtering	Easy	Medium	Medium	Easy	Easy	Easy
Read Legend	Medium	Hard	Easy	Medium	Medium	Medium
Task 3	Hard	Hard	Medium	Easy	Easy	Medium
Details on Demand	Hard	Hard	Medium	Easy	Easy	Medium

Table 6. NASA-TLX results (Mouse)

NASA-TLX	TLX-Score	Mental Demand	Physical Demand	Temporal Demand	Effort	Frustration	Performance
User 1	24.16	71	3	3	23	2	43
User 2	29.16	71	3	2	45	3	51
User 3	19.84	49	0	0	3	0	67
User 4	17.66	20	0	75	0	0	11
User 5	22.49	39	5	20	30	15	26

- Details on demand: facilitates the user to obtain additional details about a point beyond the axis values and visual channels.

All these features were included for both mouse and speech interfaces, making possible, through the use of a natural interaction interface, to do all actions performed by conventional means of interaction.

To measure the fficacy, it is needed to verify if the proposed interaction allows the users to complete all tasks.

During the test with users, all participants who used the mouse completed all the tasks. While those who used the voice, four out of five (4/5) of users, were able to complete all the tasks, unless a volunteer who had difficulties in the third task, specifically the sub-task of applying details on demand. Because, that user has

Table 7. NASA-TLX results (Speech Interface)

NASA-TLX	TLX-Score	Mental Demand	Physical Demand	Temporal Demand	Effort	Frustration	Performance
User 1	34.82	60	5	36	50	35	23
User 2	73.47	80	16	92	70	80	42
User 3	19.66	25	0	6	11	50	26
User 4	14.17	64	11	19	11	16	16
User 5	9.82	54	2	2	5	17	24

Table 8. Results average to mouse and speech interface groups.

NASA-TLX Averages	TLX-Score	Mental Demand	Physical Demand	Temporal Demand	Effort	Frustration	Performance
Mouse Group Average	22.49	50	2.2	20	20.2	4	39,6
Speech Interface Average	30.38	56.6	6.8	31	29.4	39.6	26.2

extrapolated the time the task was given as incomplete. Therefore, it can be concluded the efficacy of the voice interaction in 80 % of the studied cases.

To measure the efficiency, it is needed to verify if the use of voice input allows a shorter time and a smaller workload in performing the tasks.

As can be seen in Tables 2 and 3, the first task had an average time for mouse of 02:57 s and for speech interface of 04:04 s. This means that the mouse was 28 % faster than the voice, and the other subtasks from task 1 follow the same trend. To configure the axes x, y and z. The mouse had an average 44 % lower than the voice. While the sub-task to apply a categorical filter was only 23 % and zoom and rotate was 33 % faster.

The pattern is repeated in the second task with an average time by mouse 25 % faster, also configure color, shape and size mouse had a 16 % less time.

The same goes for filtering continuous values, which had a 27 % lower time by mouse. To read the visualization and interact with the mouse persisted faster with a difference of 27 % compared to voice. And read legend, again, the mouse excelled with 29 % faster than voice.

In the third task, the mouse had the advantage of being with an average 11 % faster. The most significant case where the mouse had a much shorter time, then the voice was in the details on demand, the average was 81 % faster than speech interface. This happens because selecting a point by voice requires a much greater complexity than just clicking a point with the mouse.

Underlining this, the total time to perform all the tasks had a difference of 12 % between mouse and voice.

To measure the usability, it is needed to verify if the speech interface use was simple and intuitive enough for the completion of tasks.

To certify the software's usability, it was been proposed to users to answer two post tasks questionnaires. The first one was the questionnaire to identify the level of subjective difficulty during the execution of tasks and sub-tasks, which the result can be seen in Tables 4 and 5, as shown in these tables the frequency of difficulty for mouse was very easy (15), easy (10), medium (20), hard (4) and very hard (1). And for speech interface the frequency of difficulty was very easy (2), easy (26) medium (15), hard (7) and very hard (0).

In general, a larger number of values are between the very easy, easy and medium levels. Therefore, the average values show that the interaction by mouse was easy to interact and the voice interaction due to have a higher frequency between easy, medium and hard levels was an average medium difficulty to interact.

After the questionnaire aimed at measuring the level of difficulty of tasks, the users were asked to fill in the NASA-TLX questionnaire, which measures the workload for the tasks, as can be seen in Tables 6, 7 and 8.

It can be observed that physical demand was 68 % lower when using the mouse. It is likely that due to the user actually be more accustomed of using the mouse to interact with the computer than voice. Also this has led to a temporal demand 36 % lower in mouse group than speech interface, and consequently a 32 % less effort in using the mouse.

One of the greatest weighting factors to natural user interface was frustration, which achieved a 90 % greater when compared to the mouse. This factor influence on all scales measured, mainly in the subjective performance of the user, which was 51 % better in mouse than in the voice.

Frustration has its relevance in the test, because it identifies the user's discomfort during the taks execution. This means that higher the frustration higher is the workload experienced by the user, as shown in TLX score that was 26 % better in mouse than in the speech interface.

In relation to time, workload and difficulty level, the mouse proves to be efficient, while the voice shows to be effective.

To measure the utility, it is needed to verify if in which context speech interface better benefit the user.

The voice input has the role to meet a wider range of users. For instance, users with motor problems or users without sensation in the hands, both can make use of IVOrpheus system to interact with a dataset. Thus, reaching the objective presented by Alan Kay [17], which is as more "friendly" is the interaction between man and machine, greater is the range of people reached.

4 Final Considerations and Future Works

In this work, an information visualization tool in three-dimensional environment was developed using the visualization technique scatterplot 3D, with voice input-based interface. During the tool's implementation process, good practices were adopted related to grammars management used in the Coruja Software. These practices were:

- Sort the voice commands into two types: voice commands independent of the selected base (Global Command) and commands related to the attributes belonging to each database (Local Commands);
- Take into account the ASR (Automatic Speech Recognition) tool limitations: to determine the voice commands, take into account possible restrictions in used ASR, for example, recognition difficulties of some phonemes;
- Choose commands near user's natural language (UNL): For example, the tool should allow the user to enter the number (34427) the way the user says this number in everyday life. That is, as (thirty-four thousand, four hundred twenty-seven). In opposed to make the user dictate the number one by one. I.e. (three, four, four, two, seven);
- Local commands: perform preprocessing on database in order to adjust the attributes present in the database in a readable form for the ASR system.

Based on the results of usability testing, it was observed that most users, who used the voice as input, had a high frustration and workload for the tasks completion. This may have been enlarged, because the voice recognition process sometimes generates erroneous outputs, mainly because of ambient noises or the user's speech pace, among other issues.

Thus, these events directed the research to the following question: "Which approach the use of voice in information visualization technique of scatterplot 3D has greater efficiency in reducing the cognitive load and time of the user? ". As pointed out by usability test, the approach of using voice with the aim of mimic a mouse, have lower efficiency as well as time and workload using standard interaction interface (keyboard and mouse). However, the use of a natural user interface was shown effective, because it allowed most of the users to finish all the tasks displayed.

This observation guides the future of IVOrpheus application, to meet a proposed voice interaction more efficient and that requires less cognitive effort from the user.

Knowing that, for future work, the IVOrpheus system will address the use of the interaction by voice through dialogue, using the principle presented in the works [8–10], leaving the invisible interaction interface to the user, where it should not stick to interface commands, such as buttons and panels. However, it was only introduced the desired question and the system presented a visualization as response.

Moreover, it was proposed certain improvements and additions in the current tool features. Among them are:

- The implementation of configure visual channels for continuous values, such as color assume a range of colors based on continuous values;
- Add functionality to sort the data on the axes of ascending or descending order according to the user's choice;
- Enabling the derivation of data from the selected base, for example, table generating continuous averaging values, thereby generating new tables within the selected base;
- Implement functionality to save the user state, so the users can continue their progress from where it left off, or can share their findings with others;
- Create section for user notes, or allow that the user can comment by voice discoveries in the database;

- And, finally, to extend user tests for viewing by dispersing points in two dimensions and compare with the current tests, ascertaining the increment/decrement of a dimension increases or decreases the time, difficulty, and exerting workload by the user.

References

1. Card, S., Mackinlay, J., Shneiderman, B.: Readings in Information Visualization - Using Vision to Think. Morgan Kaufmann, San Francisco (1999)
2. Chi, E.H., Riedl, J.: An operator interaction framework for visualization systems. In: Proceedings o the InfoVis, pp. 63–70 (1998)
3. Heer, J., Shneiderman, B.: Interactive dynamics for visual analysis. ACM Q. 10(2), 30–55 (2012)
4. Pike, W.A., Stasko, J.T., Chang, R., O'Connell, T.A.: The science of interaction. Inf. Vis. 8(4), 263–274 (2009)
5. Lee, B., Isenberg, P., Riche, N.H., Carpendale, S.: Beyond mouse and keyboard: Expanding design considerations for information visualization interactions. IEEE Trans. Vis. Comput. Graph. 18(12), 2689–2698 (2012)
6. Wigdor, D., Wixon, D.: Brave NUI World: Designing Natural User Interfaces for Touch and Gesture. Morgan Kaufmann, San Francisco (2011)
7. Munteanu, C., Jones, M., Whittaker, S., Oviatt, S., Aylett, M., Penn, G., Brewster, S., Alessandro, N.: Designing speech and language interactions. In: Proceeding, Systems, pp. 75–78. ACM, New York (2014)
8. Sharma, R., Yeasin, M., Krahnstoever, N., Rauschert, I., Cai, G., Brewer, I., Maceachren, A., Sengupta, K.: Speech–gesture driven multimodal interfaces for crisis management. Proc. IEEE 91(9), 1327–1354 (2003)
9. Sun, Y., Leigh, J., Johnson, A., Lee, S.: Articulate: a semi–automated model for translating natural language queries into meaningful visualizations. In: Proceedings of the 10th international conference on Smart graphics, EUA, pp. 184–195 (2010)
10. Cox, K., Grinter, R., Hibino, S., Jagadeesan, L., Mantilla, D.: A multi–modal natural language interface to an information visualization environment. J. Speech Technol. 4, 297–314 (2001)
11. Beasley, R., Farley, K.M., O'Reilly, J., Squire, L., Farley, K.: Voice Application Development with VoiceXML. Sams, Indianapolis (2001)
12. Hart, S., Staveland, L.: Development of NASA–TLX (Task Load Index): Results of empirical and theoretical research. In: Hancock, P.A., Meshkati, N. (eds.) Human Mental Workload. North Holland Press, Amsterdam (1988)
13. Shineiderman, B.: The eyes have it: a task by data type taxonomy for information visualizations. In: IEEE Symposium on Visual Languages, 1996, Proceedings, pp. 336–343 (1996)
14. Silva, P., Batista, P., Neto, N., Klautau, A.: An open--source speech recognizer for Brazilian Portuguese with a windows programming interface. In: The International Conference on Computational Processing of Portuguese (PROPOR) (2010)
15. Likert, R.: A technique for the measurement of attitudes. Arch. Psychol. 140, 1–55 (1932)
16. Mazza R.: Introduction to Information Visualization, p. 125. Springer Publishing Company, Inc., New York (2009)

17. Kay, A.: A personal computer for children of all ages. In: Proceedings of the ACM Annual Conference— Vol. 1 (1972)

18. Furtado L., Miranda B., Neto N., Meiguins B.: IVOrpheus - a proposal for interaction by voice commands in three-dimensional environments of information visualization. In: Computer and Information Technology; Ubiquitous Computing and Communications; Dependable, Autonomic and Secure Computing; Pervasive Intelligence and Computing (CIT/IUCC/ DASC/PICOM), Liverpool, pp. 878–883 (2015)

A Sketch-Based User Interface for Image Search Using Sample Photos

Hitoshi Sugimura, Hayato Tsukiji, Mizuki Kumada, Toshiya Iiba,
and Kosuke Takano$^{(\boxtimes)}$

Department of Information and Computer Sciences,
Kanagawa Institute of Technology, Atsugi, Japan
{s1121157, s1321033, s1321155,
s1221125}@ccy.kanagawa-it.ac.jp,
takano@ic.kanagawa-it.ac.jp

Abstract. In this paper, we present a sketch-based user interface for a content-based image search using sample photos. Our sketch-based user interface diverts a part of the images and their color extracted from sample photos, which are obtained from image resources, such as an image search result, to a sketch, and supports a user to draw a more practical sketch as a query. This feature of the proposed sketch-based user interface allows a user to make a sketch-based query according to the thought and image of the user by painting and decorating the sketch using fragments of images snipped from sample photos and their colors. Thus, the proposed sketch-based user interface can help a user to make a sketch for the image retrieval by leveraging objects and colors that actually appear in images and photos. In the experiment using our proto-type, we evaluated the feasibility of our approach.

Keywords: Content-based image retrieval · Interaction design · Query by sketch · User interface · Sample photos

1 Introduction

In the field of the content-based image retrieval (CBIR) [1], a sketch-based query is a query for an image search that is performed by drawing a sketch that represents the user's thought and image. A sketch-based query allows us to obtain the desired images by intuitively sketching what we want to query, even if we cannot have any query keywords.

However, we often redraw our sketch by improving the colors and shapes until a search system returns appropriate images. A user's repeated redrawing would decrease the convenience of the sketch-based query. Furthermore, even if we sketch well what we want to query, we might not find the objective images when there is no image that has the similar features of color and shape as the user's sketch in an image database. For example, we usually draw a sketch using a few colors, not like a photo where various colors appear. Therefore, there is a possibility that appropriate images will not be obtained in the search result when using a sketch-based query because the sketch does not include the colors that appear in target images in the image database (Fig. 5).

© Springer International Publishing Switzerland 2016
S. Yamamoto (Ed.): HIMI 2016, Part I, LNCS 9734, pp. 361–370, 2016.
DOI: 10.1007/978-3-319-40349-6_34

In this study, we present a sketch-based user interface (sketch UI) for an image search using sample photos. Our sketch UI provides the function of diverting a part of the images and their colors extracted from sample photos, which are obtained from image resources, such as an image search result, to a sketch and helps a user to draw a more practical sketch as a query. This feature of the proposed sketch UI allows a user to make a sketch-based query according to the thought and imagination of the user by painting and decorating the sketch using fragments of images snipped from sample photos and their colors. Thus, the proposed sketch UI can help a user to make a sketch for the image retrieval by leveraging objects and colors that actually appear in images and photos.

In this study, we implemented a prototype of an image search system with a sketch-based user interface that is available through a Web browser. To achieve basic functionality for CBIR, we used a histogram intersection method [1] and a perceptual hash method [3] for the color and outline comparison between images, respectively. In the experiment using our prototype, we evaluated the feasibility of our approach. In the experiment, we prepared 97 images and 8 patterns of sketch-based queries to compare our proposed sketch UI with a baseline approach with a simple sketch functionality. The experimental results showed that our proposed sketch-based user interface could reduce the cost of making a sketch-based query and increase the opportunity for a searcher to obtain the desired images from an image database, especially when a color feature is a significant factor for the image search.

2   Motivating Example

The query-by-sketch image retrieval system [2, 6] allows a user to draw a sketch and retrieve the desired images based on the sketch by applying the content-based image retrieval (CBIR) method [4, 5]. One of the merits of query-by-sketch image retrieval is the flexibility to make an image-based query; however, there is a possibility that the features of a sketched image input as a query do not match those of the target images in the database in the retrieval process because a user freely chooses colors and draws various types of shapes in the sketch. As a result, the image retrieval system cannot return the desired images to the user according to the sketch-based query.

A relevance feedback method for the query-by-sketch image retrieval is proposed, where a searcher obtains objective images by selecting relevant images in the search result and adding their features to the original query [2, 7, 8]. In [2, 8], the semantics extraction from query images using the relevance feedback was studied. In [2], a query-by-sketch image retrieval method was proposed to reduce the semantic gap between low-level features and high-level semantics by adopting relevance feedback. In addition, He et al. presented a leaning method for capturing the semantics of images through the relevance feedback [8]. Furthermore, in [7], Shen et al. proposed a method for optimizing the relevance feedback search by query prediction based on the previously executed iterations' queries. However, these methods cannot always allow us to represent our thoughts and images as a query because the composed image query consists of the features of whole images that the searcher selects as relevant. For example, suppose that a searcher inputs a sketch of an apple as a query and selects an image where one apple appears as a relevant image from the search result through the relevance feedback process. In this case, the image retrieval system will return images that are similar to the selected apple image in the second search result. In this example, when the searcher wants to obtain an image of a tree with many apples, the desired images will not appear in the higher ranking of the search result, unless an image with a feature of a tree is also associated with the composed image query in the relevance feedback.

We incorporate two functions into our sketch UI using sample photos in a target image database: (1) a function of the color palette creation based on colors appearing in the sample photos, and (2) a function of the sketch patch using image fragments snipped from the sample photos. Figures 1 and 2 show examples of these two functions. In the upper illustration of Fig. 1, a user chooses colors in his/her head to sketch an apple; however, as a result, a system might return irrelevant images in the search result. On the other hand, in the lower illustration of Fig. 1, we can see that the user can obtain the proper images of apples in the search result by painting the sketch in a red color, and a shine color appeared in a sample photo of an apple. To support this function, the proposed sketch UI dynamically creates a color palette by extracting colors appearing in sample photos so that a user can choose the colors in the photo for the sketch.

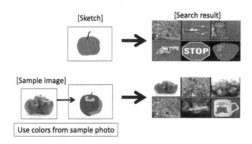

Fig. 1. Example of color extraction from the sample image (Color figure online)

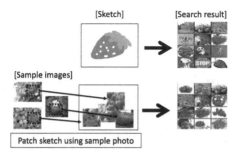

Fig. 2. Example of the sketch patch using a sample image (Color figure online)

When a user does not have a talent for painting, the user may not draw a good sketch and cannot obtain the desired images in the retrieval process, as shown in the upper illustration of Fig. 2. To help a user to draw an expressive sketch, our sketch UI provides the sketch patch function to extract what the user wants to draw by snipping parts of images from sample photos and adding them to the user's sketch. The lower illustration of Fig. 2 shows an example of the sketch patch function. In this example, the desired images of strawberries are retrieved in the search result by extracting partial image fragments of strawberries from three sample photos and adding them to the sketch.

3   Proposed System

Figure 3 shows an overview of our image search system with the proposed sketched-based user interface (sketch UI). Our image search system allows a user to input a sketch-based image as a query and return the search result from an image database by applying the conventional CBIR method. Figure 4 shows the design of our sketch UI. The sketch UI mainly consists of (A) color palette, (B) sketch canvas, (C) search result, (D) image pool for sample photos, and (E) query history.

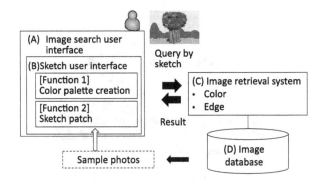

Fig. 3.   System overview

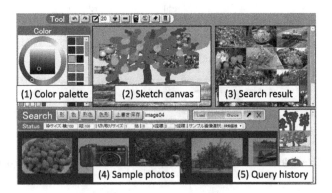

Fig. 4.   Image search interface

Using the sketch UI, a user first draws a sketch on the sketch canvas by choosing colors from the color palette. Then, an image search result is shown in the search result area according to the user's sketch. If there are images that the user wants to divert in the search result, those images can be copied to the image pools for use as sample photos. Here, the color list on the color palette is updated based on the colors in the sample photos. Furthermore, the user extracts image fragments that he/she wants to use by snipping them from the sample photos and adding them to the sketch. By repeating these sketch steps, the user can obtain the desired images from the image database.

3.1   A Function of Color Palette Creation

When a user draws a sketch for the image search, the user does not know what colors should be used to efficiently obtaining the objective images. The function of the color palette creation helps a user to choose proper colors for drawing a sketch by extracting colors actually appearing in a set of sample photos in advance and showing them in the color palette.

The color palette consists of a basic color list and a sample photo's color list. The sample photo's color list on the color palette is updated based on the colors appearing in the sample photos. Each sample photo in the image pool is extracted to n colors c_1, c_2, c_3,..., c_n. Then, the number of pixels for each n colors is calculated for all sample photos, and the colors on the sample photo's color list are sorted according to the pixel number. Colors that are not used in the sample photos do not appear in the sample photo's color list. In addition, the initial colors on the sample photo's color list are extracted from all target images in the image database.

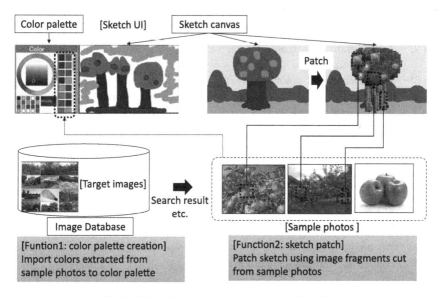

Fig. 5. Main functions of the sketch user interface

3.2   Function of the Sketch Patch

The sketch patch helps a user draw a practical sketch by extracting regions that the user wants to copy by snipping them from a sample photo and adding them to the user's own sketch. First, the user selects a point (x_c, y_c) where the user wants to patch the sketch on the canvas; then, the user selects a region from a sample photo. Figure 6 shows an example where a user selects a rectangular region, where top-left coordinate is a point (x_s, y_s) and the width and height are w and h, from a sample photo. In this example, the user patches the snipped regions of apples with a scale s to the specified point (x_c, y_c) on the canvas.

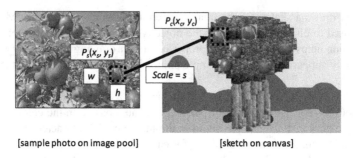

[sample photo on image pool]   [sketch on canvas]

Fig. 6. Example of the sketch patch using a sample photo

3.3   Image Retrieval Method

We apply a conventional image retrieval method for the CBIR. First, we calculate the edge similarity using a histogram intersection method [1] as follows:

Step 1:   Images are reduced to n-colors $c_1, c_2, c_3, ..., c_n$

Step 2:   A histogram h is created for each image based on the number of pixels for the n-colors

Step 3:   The similarity of colors between a sketch image I_s and a target image I_t is calculated using the histogram intersection method. Suppose that the score of the similarity of colors is S_c, and the histograms for I_s and I_t are h_s and h_t, respectively:

$$S_c(I_s, I_t) = \frac{\sum_{i=0}^{n} \min(h_s[i], h_t[i])}{\sum_{i=0}^{n} h_s[i]} \tag{1}$$

Next, to calculate the edge similarity between two images, we apply an average hash method [3] and a hamming distance, as follows:

Step 1:   An image is resized to a $n \times n$ pixel image, and the color of the image is converted to a grayscale color image

Step 2:   The average value of the grayscale color values is calculated for all pixels in the image

Step 3:   When the grayscale value of a pixel in the image is greater than the average value, the pixel is set to 1; otherwise, the pixel is set to 0. Thus, an $n \times n$ bit array is created for the $n \times n$ pixel image

Step 4:   The hamming distance between two bit arrays B_s and B_t for a sketch image I_s and a target image I_t is applied to calculate the score S_e for the edge similarity between I_s and I_t:

$$S_e(I_s, I_t) = hamming\_distance(B_s, B_t) \tag{2}$$

Finally, we calculate the similarity score $S_{c,e}$ between a sketch image I_s and a target image I_t in terms of color and edge using the color score S_c and edge score S_e:

$$S_{c,e}(I_s, I_t) = \alpha S_c + (1 - \alpha)S_e \tag{3}$$

where $\alpha(0 \leq \alpha \leq 1)$ is a parameter for weighting each score.

4   Experiments

4.1   Experimental Environment and Method

In the experiment using our prototype, we evaluated the feasibility of our proposed method. We prepared 97 images, including 10 correct images of a tree with apples, for the evaluation. In addition, using three sample photos, as shown in Fig. 6, we sketched 8 patterns for image queries (Fig. 7). To make each sketch, we did not change the shapes of a tree with apples and the other background objects.

Fig. 7. Sample images

In Fig. 7, the pattern (1) is an initial sketch image that is used as a baseline for the comparison, and the patterns (2) to (8) are drawn based on the combination of the proposed method. We compare each pattern of the sketch-based queries in terms of the recall-precision and the drawing cost of the sketch. In addition, we set the weighting parameter α to 0.2, 0.4, 0.6, and 0.8 in the Eq. (1).

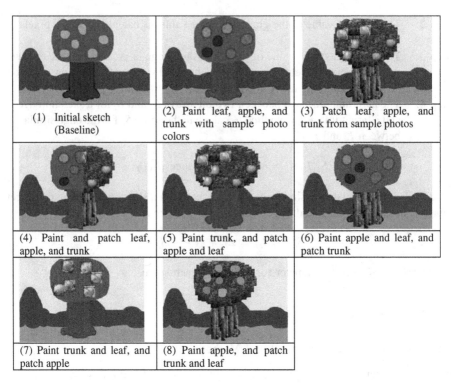

Fig. 8. Query sketch images

4.2 Experimental Results

Figure 9 shows the search results of a recall-precision graph for $\alpha = 0.2, 0.4, 0.6, 0.8$ using the 8 query sketch images shown in Fig. 8. Figure 9 shows that the precision of the search results using the query images (2) to (8) is better than the baseline query image (1) for all four cases.

In addition, when α is a larger value, the tendency of each recall-precision graph varies and the precision of the sketch images using the proposed method is much better than the baseline query image. This result indicates that the proposed sketch patch function is useful when we consider color a more important factor for the image search. At $\alpha = 0.2$ and 0.4, the precision of sketches (3), (5), and (7) is better; therefore, the color red of the apple images from the sample photos positively effects the search results. Meanwhile, when α is a smaller value, the tendency of each recall-precision graph becomes similar, and the shape in all sketched is almost the same.

Furthermore, in terms of the drawing cost, we found that it took a long time to complete a sketch when we used the sketch patch function. On the other hand, it took less time when we drew a sketch by choosing colors from sample photos. Therefore, to find sample photos that have effective colors, a user should draw a shape and paint it using some basic colors and then gradually increase the amount of image patches from

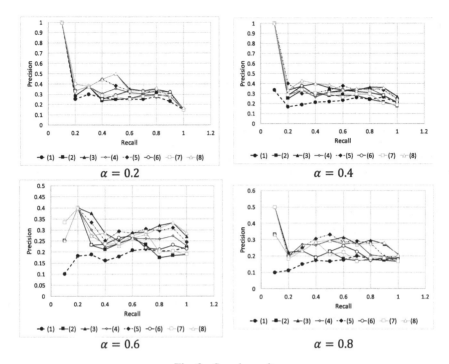

Fig. 9. Search results

the sample photos by leveraging our sketch patch function for retrieving the desired images in a shorter time.

5   Conclusion

In this study, we proposed a sketch-based query user interface (sketch UI) using sample photos to support a user's drawing for an image search. Our sketch UI provides two functions: color palette creation and sketch patching using sample photos. These two functions allow a user to efficiently draw a sketch using colors and parts of images extracted from sample photos. The experimental results using our prototype show that our sketch UI can improve the precision of the initial image search result. In terms of the cost of drawing a sketch, we confirmed that we can draw a sketch in a short time and can find the desired images using both colors and parts of the image from sample photos. In addition, a user can obtain the desired images in a shorter time by initially using some basic colors and then gradually increasing the amount of image patches from sample photos.

In our future work, we will improve the usability of the proposed sketch UI. In addition, we will evaluate the effectiveness of our sketch UI based on comparison with other image retrieval systems.

References

1. Swain, M.J., Ballard, D.H.: Color indexing. Int. J. Comput. Vis. **7**(1), 11–32 (1991)
2. Ohashi, G., Hisamori, T., Mochizuki, K.: Query-by-sketch image retrieval system using relevance feedback. J. Jpn. Soc. Fuzzy Theory Intell. Inform. **19**(5), 537–545 (2007)
3. Klinger, E., Starkweather, D.: The open source perceptual hash library. http://www.phash.org. (Accessed Dec 2015)
4. Ashley, J., Flickner, M., Hafner, J., Lee, D., Niblack, W., Petkovic, D.: The query by image content (QBIC) system. In: Proceedings of the 1995 ACM SIGMOD International Conference on Management of Data (SIGMOD 1995), p. 475 (1995)
5. Lew, M.S., Sebe, N., Djeraba, C., Jain, R.: Content-based multimedia information retrieval: state of the art and challenges. ACM Trans. Multimedia Comput. Commun. Appl. **2**(1), 1–19 (2006)
6. Springmann, M., Kopp, D., Schuldt, H.: QbS: searching for known images using user-drawn sketches. In: Proceedings of the International Conference on Multimedia Information Retrieval (MIR 2010), pp. 417–420 (2010)
7. Shen, H.T., Jiang, S., Tan, K.-L., Huang, Z., Zhou, X.: Speed up interactive image retrieval. Int. J. Very Large Data Bases Arch. (The VLDB J.) **18**(1), 329–343 (2009)
8. He, X., Ma, W.-Y., King, O., Li, M., Zhang, H.: Learning and inferring a semantic space from user's relevance feedback for image retrieval. In: Proceedings of the Tenth ACM International Conference on Multimedia (MULTIMEDIA 2002), pp. 343–346 (2002)

Proposal and Evaluation of a Document Reader that Supports Pointing and Finger Bookmarking

Kentaro Takano[1(✉)], Shingo Uchihashi[1], Hirohito Shibata[1],
Kengo Omura[1], Junko Ichino[2], Tomonori Hashiyama[3],
and Shunichi Tano[3]

[1] Research and Technology Group, Fuji Xerox Co. Ltd., 6-1 Minatomirai,
Nishi-ku, Yokohama, Kanagawa 220-8668, Japan
{kentaro.takano,shingo.uchihashi,hirohito.shibata,
kengo.omura}@fujixerox.co.jp
[2] Faculty of Engineering, Kagawa University, 2217-20 Hayashi-Cho,
Takamatsu-city, Kagawa 761-0396, Japan
ichino@eng.kagawa-u.ac.jp
[3] Graduate School of Information Systems,
The University of Electro-Communications, 1-5-1 Chofugaoka,
Chofu, Tokyo 182-8585, Japan
{hashiyama,tano}@is.uec.ac.jp

Abstract. Pointing and finger bookmarking effectively support reading from paper. However, current electronic media do not support these operations. Readers are discouraged to trace or point text with fingers on popular touchscreen tablet devices because the gestures may cause undesired view changes. Also, bookmarking with the current interface does not provide the ease of finger bookmarking. For solving the problems mentioned above, we proposed a document reader that provides seamless switching between pointing/tracing and touch operations, and integrate features that simulate finger bookmarking by using simple gestures. The results of two experiments (proof reading and cross reference reading between pages) show that participants performed the tasks faster with the proposed system than with the conventional touchscreen systems.

Keywords: Active reading · Pointing · Tracing · Finger bookmarking

1 Introduction

Pointing and finger bookmarking effectively support reading from paper [1]. Tracing text while reading can help skipping over the text, and pointing at documents act as a temporary placeholder that help going back and forth between various locations within the document [2]. Finger bookmarking helps to flip over to other pages faster [3].

These behaviors effectively support reading from paper, but current electronic media do not support them. For example, unlike pointing using both hands, mouse cursors are not able to point multiple points at once [4]. Ironically, readers tend to hesitate to point or trace the text in the documents on a "touch" screen device, fearing

© Springer International Publishing Switzerland 2016
S. Yamamoto (Ed.): HIMI 2016, Part I, LNCS 9734, pp. 371–380, 2016.
DOI: 10.1007/978-3-319-40349-6_35

that unexpected behavior may occur [2]. Early works indicate that bookmarking with the current interface does not provide the ease of finger bookmarking [3, 5].

In this paper, we will propose a document reader that encourages readers to point and trace documents while reading from a touch panel device by preventing unintended operations to be triggered, as well as functions equivalent to finger-bookmarking. Our proposed system enables to tangibly handle documents in an intuitive manner, such as tracing the text across the screen using fingers and pointing at the text. Also, our proposed system aims to mimic the ease of finger bookmarking on paper documents.

2   Proposed System

2.1   Preventing Unintended Touch Operations

In general, unintended operations due to touching the touch panel can be prevented by temporarily disabling touchscreen operations. However, disabling or enabling touch-screen operations by switching back and forth between modes can hinder time efficiency [6].

To shorten the operation time, main operations are assigned to the dominant hand and mode change operations are assigned to the non-dominant hand. This enables for some operations to overlap [7]. As illustrated in Fig. 1 (top), with our proposed system, users slide their thumb diagonally upward to switch from the "reading mode" that does not accept touchscreen to the "operation mode" that accepts touchscreen operation. To encourage the use of the non-dominant hand, the area that detects this gesture is limited to the left side of the screen for a reader whose dominant hand is the right. The screen is switched from the operation mode to the reading mode by taking the hand off the screen as in Fig. 1 (bottom).

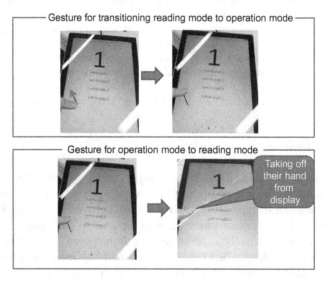

Fig. 1. Gesture for reading mode to operation mode (top), Gesture for operation mode to reading mode (bottom)

2.2   Imitating Finger Bookmarking

Some studies have attempted to imitate finger bookmarking electronically [8, 9]. Wightman proposed a page navigation interface in which bookmarks are placed by turning physical tabs that are attached to the hardware they have designed [8]. Yoon proposed a touch-bookmark interface where the user touches and holds the page to be bookmarked. As long as the page is held, the user can flip to other pages and the bookmarked page can be referred to at any time [9]. These systems make bookmarking easy and simple.

However, even with these systems, the reader has to consciously decide whether or not the page is note-worthy enough that they may want to refer back to, and act upon this decision to leave a bookmark of some sort. On the other hand, when using paper, the reader does finger bookmarking subconsciously, not giving much thought of whether they will actually go back to the bookmarked page. To encourage using finger bookmarking functions, it is desirable to improve usability of the finger bookmarking interface to the subconscious level as on paper documents. Also, it is observed that the reader is most likely to return to the first page they started looking through the pages [1], so we thought a system simulating finger bookmarking should automatically bookmark the starting page.

Therefore, we propose a system that automatically records the first page of where the series of page operations start. As described in the previous subsection, we have designated the default mode of the touchscreen device to the reading mode. The mode needs to be switched in order to turn the page, and the page where the reader is on when the mode switch operation is triggered, is automatically bookmarked. When the thumb is slid down diagonally, the screen will show the bookmarked page (Fig. 2). In the operation mode, page thumbnails are displayed in the bottom of the screen so that the mode can be identified visually.

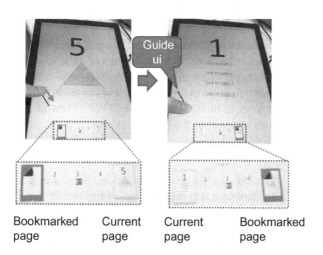

| Bookmarked page | Current page | Current page | Bookmarked page |

Fig. 2. Gesture for move back to bookmarked page

3   Evaluation

We conducted two experiments to evaluate the effectiveness of our proposed system by comparing it with conventional reading systems. The aim of Experiment 1 was to confirm whether our proposed system encouraged pointing to text and improved reading performance. The aim of Experiment 2 was to evaluate the effects of the finger bookmarking interface.

3.1   Experiment 1: Proof Reading

Hypothesis. This experiment contains the following two hypotheses.

Hypothesis 1. There will be more pointing to the text in the document with our proposed system than with a conventional system.

We think that users are less hesitant in pointing at the screen if they know any unintended actions are not triggered when they accidently touch the screen. Thus, we hypothesize that our proposed system will encourage pointing.

Hypothesis 2. Reading from our proposed system will be faster than reading from a conventional system for proof reading.

We think that our proposed system, in comparison to a conventional system, can help find errors more efficiently due to the fact that there will be more pointing at the text.

Method.

Design and Participants. The experimental design was a one-way within-participants design. The factor was a media condition (conventional system and proposed system). Each participant performed all conditions and performed two trials in each condition. The order of the media used in their trials was counterbalanced to cancel the overall effects of the trial order.

Participants were 24 Japanese native speakers (all right-handed). They were in their 20's or 30's. Each participant had more than three years of experience using a PC, more than ten months of experience using touchscreen devices, and corrective eyesight of more than 14/20. Another condition that we included in the recruitment process was for the participant to have a score of 600-700 on the TOEIC (Test of English for International Communication) test within the last two years.

Materials. We created documents for the experiment based on articles from Japanese newspapers.

One document was used in a single task. Each document was one page long. In each text document, the Japanese text and its English translation were printed and we intentionally included errors: mismatches between the Japanese text and the corresponding English translation. We included five errors in each document, such as "father," written in Japanese, and "mother," written in the corresponding portion in English.

Task. The task was to find inconsistences between the text described in Japanese and its English translation. The time limit was six min. The task trials were terminated when participants detected all five errors or when the time limit was reached.

Media Condition. The following two systems were used:

- Proposed system: Each document was displayed with our proposed interface.
- Conventional system: Documents were displayed using a normal tablet reader that triggered page turns, etc. by swiping and tapping motions. The appearance was made to look exactly the same as our proposed system.

Apparatus. The tablet used in the experiment was Surface Pro 3 (Microsoft Corp). The operating system was Windows 8.1.

Results and Discussions. Figure 3 presents the number of observed pointing to text behaviors per minutes. We counted pointing by watching the video of the experiment. We counted the number of times that a finger was pointing at the screen, regardless of whether it was touching the screen or not. The error bar shows the standard error of the mean. It is the same throughout this paper.

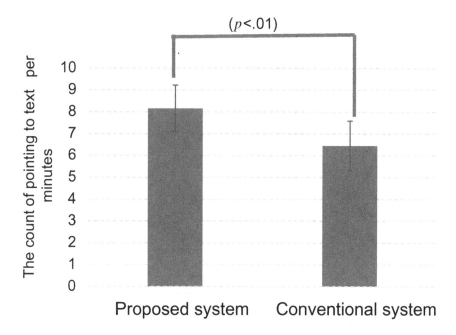

Fig. 3. The number of pointing to text per minutes

A paired t-test revealed a significant difference between the media [$t(23) = 3.1$, $p < .01$]. Participants pointed to the text 26.5 % more when using our proposed system than when using the conventional system. This supports our first hypothesis that there would be more pointing to the text in the document with our proposed system than with the conventional system.

We argued that there were less pointing for the conventional system because users were afraid that it may cause unintended actions. 12 out of 24 participants triggered unintended actions using the conventional system. In the interview afterwards, the participants reported that, "we accidently touched the screen because we were focused with the task." We consider that the unintended actions triggered by pointing made users aware of the gesture and refrain from repeating.

Figure 4 presents the number of error detection per minutes.

A paired t-test revealed a significant difference between the media [$t(23) = 2.9$, $p < .01$]. Participants detected 31.7 % more errors using our proposed system than using the conventional system. This supports our second hypothesis that reading from our proposed system would be faster than reading from the conventional system for proof reading.

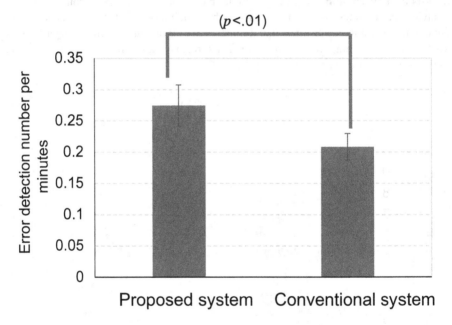

Fig. 4. The number of error detection per minutes

These results indicated that our proposed system effectively support proof reading by encouraging pointing to text. Furthermore, in the interview afterwards, a participant reported that, "(Even in the conventional system) I would point the text without touching the screen, but my fingers would start to shake so I could not point at the exact location." "I could point at the exact location (using our proposed system) and it was less tiring." Our proposed system not only encouraged pointing, but it helped in pointing at the exact location because the finger could be placed there.

3.2 Experiment 2: Cross-Reference Reading Between Pages

Hypothesis. This experiment contains the following hypothesis.

Hypothesis. Reading from our proposed system will be faster than reading from a conventional system for cross-reference reading between pages.

We hypothesize that reading efficiency will improve with our proposed system with a feature that simulates finger-bookmarking, compared to a conventional system without this feature, because going back and forth between pages will be easier.

Method.

Design and Participants. The experimental design was a one-way within-participants design. The factor was a media condition (conventional system and proposed system). Each participant per-formed all conditions and performed two trials in each condition. The order of the media used in their trials was counterbalanced to cancel the overall effects of the trial order.

Participants were 24 Japanese native speakers (all right-handed). They were in their 20's or 30's. Each participant had more than three years of experience using a PC, more than ten months of experience using touch-panel devices, and corrective eyesight of more than 14/20.

Materials. We created documents for the experiment based on the statistical data provided by the Japan Paper Association. The document was 17 pages long: 2 of the pages were the front and back cover, 14 pages contained only graphs, and one page contained only text.

We intentionally included errors: mismatches between the content of the text and the information presented by the graphs. We included 21 errors in each document. For example, the text says that the collection rate of paper recycling in Belgium is 52 %, but the graph indicates 53 %.

Task. The task was to find inconsistences between the information obtained from the text and the graphs. The time limit was six minutes. The task trials were terminated when participants detected all 21 errors or when the time limit was reached.

Media Condition. The following two systems were used:

- Proposed system: We used our proposed system as a document viewer.
- Conventional system: We used Adobe Reader DC as a document viewer. We explained various page navigation features provided by the application and did not restrict their use to complete the task.

Apparatus. The apparatus was same as experiment 1.

Results and Discussions.
Figure 5 presents the number of error detection per minutes.

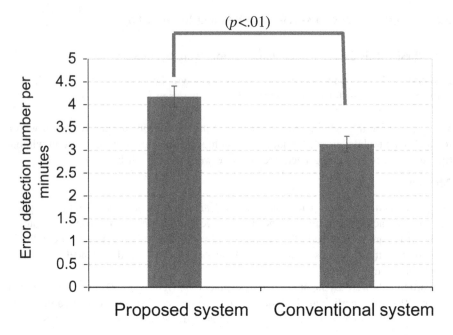

Fig. 5. The number of error detection per minutes

A paired t-test revealed a significant difference between the media [$t(23) = 7.6$, $p < .01$]. Participants detected 33.2 % more errors when using our proposed system than when using the conventional system. This supports our hypothesis that reading from our proposed system would be faster than reading from the conventional system for cross-reference reading between pages.

In the interview afterwards, participants commented on the proposed system saying, "There was minimal stress because I could flip right back to the intended page," "I could use it like paper (finger-bookmarking)." On the other hand, on the conventional system, a participant said, "Thumbnails were okay, but I didn't memorize which pages the graphs were on, so it was a struggle to have to check the thumbnails for the pictures each time I wanted to go back." Thumbnails are effective, but these comments suggest that finger bookmarking is more efficient for going back and forth between pages.

4   Conclusion

In this paper, we proposed a document reader that prevents unintended reactions to occur from misinterpreted pointing and tracing, and integrates a feature that enable bookmarking at ease, much like finger bookmarking.

We verified the effectiveness of our system by the two experiments. The first experiment revealed that our proposed system enabled detecting errors more quickly than when using a conventional system in proof reading. Also, pointing to text was performed more frequently using our proposed system than using the conventional system. These results indicate that our proposed system effectively support proof reading by encouraging pointing to text.

The second experiment revealed that our proposed system enabled detecting errors more quickly than using a conventional system in cross-reference reading between pages. This suggests that finger bookmarking supported going back and forth between pages.

In this study, we verified the effectiveness of our proposed system when the readers were reading individually. We will continue to verify the effectiveness of our proposed system when several people refer to documents for collaborative discussion. Pointing is frequently done during discussion when a reader wants to efficiently communicate a certain point [10]. Therefore, there is a possibility that our proposed system that encourages pointing would support smooth communication. We need to compare the communication process between our proposed system and conventional system in the future to further verify this.

Trademarks.

- Microsoft® and Windows® are trademarks or registered trademarks of Microsoft Corp.
- Adobe® Reader is a trademark or registered trademark of Adobe Systems Inc.
- All brand names and product names are trademarks or registered trademarks of their respective companies.

References

1. Takano, K., Shibata, H., Ichino, J., Hashiyama, T., Tano, S.: Microscopic analysis of document handling while reading paper documents to improve digital reading device. In: Proceedings of the OZCHI 2014, pp. 559–567. ACM Press (2014)
2. Shibata, H., Takano, K., Tano, S.: Text touching effects in active reading: the impact of the use of a touch-based tablet device. In: Abascal, J., Barbosa, S., Fetter, M., Gross, T., Palanque, P., Winckler, M. (eds.) INTERACT 2015. LNCS, vol. 9296, pp. 559–576. Springer, Heidelberg (2015)
3. Shibata, H., Takano, K., Omura, K., Tano, S.: Page vavigation on paper books and electronic media in reading to answer questions. In: Proceedings of the OZCHI 2015, pp. 526–534. ACM Press (2015)
4. Takano, K., Shibata, H., Omura, K.: Effects of paper on cross-reference reading for multiple documents: Comparison of reading performances and processes between paper and computer displays. In: Proceedings of the OZCHI 2015, pp. 497–505. ACM Press (2015)
5. Alexander, J., Cockburn, A., Fitchett, S., Gutwin, C., Greenberg, S.: Revisiting read wear: analysis, design, and evaluation of a footprints scrollbar. In: Proceedings of the CHI 2009, pp. 1665–1674. ACM Press (2009)
6. Shibuya, Yu., Kawakatsu, H., Murata, K.: A web browsing method on handheld touch screen devices for preventing from tapping unintended links. In: Kurosu, M. (ed.) HCII/HCI 2013, Part IV. LNCS, vol. 8007, pp. 491–496. Springer, Heidelberg (2013)

7. Lank, E., Ruiz, J., Cowan, W.: Concurrent bimanual stylus interaction: a study of non-preferred hand mode manipulation. In: Proceedings of the GI 2006, pp. 17–24. ACM Press (2006)
8. Wightman, D., Ginn, T., Vertegaal, R.: TouchMark: Flexible document navigation and bookmarking techniques for e-book readers. In: Proceedings of the GI 2010, pp. 241–244. ACM Press (2010)
9. Yoon, D., Cho, Y., Yeom, K., Park, J.: Touch-Bookmark: a lightweight navigation and bookmarking technique for e-books. In: Proceedings of the CHI EA 2011, pp. 1189–1194. ACM Press (2011)
10. Takano, K., Shibata, H., Omura, K., Ichino, J., Hashiyama, T., Tano, S.: Do tablets really support discussion?: Comparison between paper, tablet, and laptop pc used as discussion tools. In: Proceedings of the OZCHI 2012, pp. 562–571. ACM Press (2012)

An Advanced Web-Based Hindi Language Interface to Database Using Machine Learning Approach

Zorawar Singh Virk[✉] and Mohit Dua

Department of Computer Engineering,
National Institute of Technology, Kurukshetra, India
zorawarvirk@yahoo.ca, er.mohitdua@gmail.com

Abstract. NLIDB (Natural Language Interface to Database) system is a key step to many areas like Database Mining, Search Engines, Medical Science, Artificial Intelligence etc. Existing literature reveals that Natural Language Interfaces were extensively studied from the 1970's to 1990's. The paper proposes a NLIDB system namely Advanced WB-HLIDB (Web based Hindi Language Interface to Database using Machine Learning Approach) that uses the natural language as Hindi language and is based on the Machine Learning technique. The main features that have been introduced are Web Based Graphical User Interface to the system along with the use of Clustering and Similarity functions. This paper discusses the use of Similarity approach instead of the 'Like' approach which had been in practice till recently. Various other components such as multiword selection, recognizing misspelled words, storing of successful queries, auto complete function, built in keywords etc. have also been implemented.

Keywords: NLIDB · WB-HLIDB · HLIDB · Machine learning · Data mining · Similarity functions · KNN algorithm · Hindi shallow parser

1 Introduction

As there is a volatile growth in the field of Internet, the need of the hour for organizations that provide services like information storage, access as well as the information analysis is also increasing at an amazingly high rate. These days, there is too much of the data that needs to be maintained in organizations, companies and university's databases. Only the individuals who are familiar with formal query languages such as SQL, can directly use or access this data. Thus the primary motivation behind studying and implementing a Natural Language Interface to Database System is to allow the user to access as well as maintain the database in the form of natural language query and extend this to any given database in general. Information in a NLIDB system is mainly stored in a structured manner in the form of tables. Thus giving the user an option to query the database by asking questions in natural language instead of a query language like SQL (Structured Query Language) can be of great convenience since the user need not remember the syntax for various queries. Here, Natural Language refers to the typical or the common language that is widely spoken and understood like English or Hindi.

© Springer International Publishing Switzerland 2016
S. Yamamoto (Ed.): HIMI 2016, Part I, LNCS 9734, pp. 381–390, 2016.
DOI: 10.1007/978-3-319-40349-6_36

Similarity measures have become an extremely popular tool in machine learning. One of the biggest problem that haunts the NLIDB system is that of Data Mining. Data Mining refers to the manner in which the useful entities are extracted or retrieved accurately and efficiently from a database containing large volumes of raw data. This is done using a process known as approximate data matching process which further relies on the concept of different similarity functions. The concept of similarity can be different depending on particular domain, task or dataset available. It is desirable to learn similarity functions from training data to seize the correct notion of distance for a particular task available in a given domain.

1.1   NLIDB Areas

Various methods as well as software have been designed so as to solve this problem, but these methods or software do not have the ability to handle complex queries. In the field of Medical Science, NLIDB systems can enable the patient or any general concerned user to access information related to any medical disease or illness, medicines, preventions and precautions etc. This is extremely useful in areas where those who provide information are far less than those who need information.

Another area where NLIDB systems can prove to be immensely convenient is Railway enquiry. In a country like India, which has one of the world's largest railway networks, there is tons of information regarding time tables of thousands of trains running on different routes across the country. Thus having a NLIDB System which can handle all user queries related to the railways can be really beneficial. This type of system simplifies the process of data retrieval as well as data management from databases without making it mandatory for the users to have any prior knowledge regarding the formal query language syntax.

Hence, NLIDB is very appropriate solution for users to express their queries. But as the internet availability as well as the need for these kind of systems increases another aspect of the hour that needs to be addressed is to increase the scope as well as the portability of these type of systems.

2   Related Work

Research in the area of Natural Language Interfaces (NLIs) has been started from the early fifties. From the end-user point of view natural language is easy to use as it is used every day in human to human communication, and is therefore considered as a useful and efficient way for people to interact with computers. Versions of NLIDB had come in the late 60's and early 70's. A number of NLIDB systems have been developed since. Lunar [1] system was built to answer the queries regarding the samples brought back from the moon.

SQ-HAL [2] system was designed to have multiuser support as well as being database and platform independent. Khalid, M.A [3] described QA system which used the information extraction module to make the training data of classifier and this system was designed for English language. HLIDB [4] discussed the various issues, challenges and techniques involved in building an NLIDB. The article also proposes an approach to reduce costs involved in system's development and its adoption by the user.

One of the latest addition to this area is the DHIRD [5] system. This system is designed for accepting queries in English as well as the Hindi language. This system makes use of the Stanford Parser [6] and the Hindi Shallow Parser [7] for English and Hindi language, respectively. The developed system uses its own Tokenizer so as to run Hindi Shallow parser on Windows platform whereas earlier the parser was only compatible to work upon the Linux environment.

3   Architecture

The architecture of this Web Based Hindi Language Interface to Database using Machine Learning Approach mainly consists of three basic components namely Linguistic, Query Translator & the Query Executor Module. These components are illustrated in the Fig. 1.

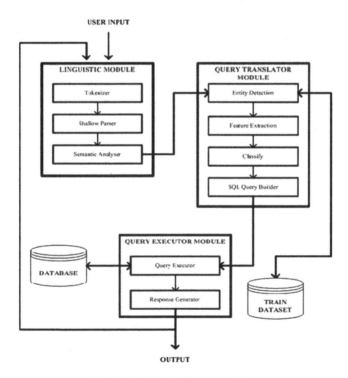

Fig. 1. Architectural representation

3.1   Linguistic Module

All the tasks related to the language of the query such as query entering, preprocessing of the query, semantic analyzing are dealt in the linguistic module. This linguistic module further has three components namely Tokenizer, Shallow Parser and Semantic Analyzer. The work of Tokenizer is to break the query in to different useful tokens. Shallow Parser is used for parsing the input query and for generating the syntax tree. The output of the shallow parser acts as input to the Semantic Analyzer. All the useless tokens are discarded. Matching of the useful tokens with their corresponding English word is done by the Semantic Analyzer. Therefore, important information such as table name, field name (columns name), conditions, function etc. are distinguished by the Semantic Analyzer.

3.2   Query Translator Module

The Query Translator Module has a wide role to play in this system. Query translator module has four components namely Entity Detection, Feature Extraction, Classify, SQL Query Builder. Entity Detection is responsible for the implementation of the similarity check, so as to closely match the misspelled or incomplete words with the correct words.

Feature Extraction is responsible for the generation of feature matrix based on the number of known tokens in each query. On the basis of the output from the Feature Extraction component, classification is done using the Matrix along with the concept of K-Nearest Neighbors (KNN) Algorithm [8].

SQL Query Builder is responsible for creating the queries which are complete in SQL aspect with the help from the previous components. For example:

Input Query: उन सभी विधारथीयो के अनुकरमानुक और अंक बताओ जनिका नाम दीपक है

SQL Query: select rollno, marks from students where name = 'deepak'

3.3   Query Executor Module

The Query Executor Module comprises mainly of two subcomponents Query Executor and Response Generator. The aim of the Query Executor is to take the SQL query from the Query Builder, the part of Query Translator Module and establishes a connection so as to execute the query on the given database which is provided to the Query Executor. Depending on how the system is being used, Response Generator has various functionalities such as displaying the result in the correct format, finding the accuracy rate or assisting in the training of the system. The Result will be shown as output to the user. In case the system is being used for training purpose then the result from the Response Generator will be again fed to the system itself as described in Fig. 1.

4   Implementation

4.1   Web-Based Interface of the System

Using web techniques such as JSP, Eclipse IDE, Apache Tomcat Server a special Graphical User Interface has been developed that is Web Based so as to increase the scope as well as making it more user friendly. Using the Web Based Graphical User Interface end user enters the input sentence in Hindi language and gets the results in the Hindi language as well. The Hindi language interface shows a number of fields like the Successful Queries Dropdown, Query Textbox, Keyboard Button, Search Button and a Result area. This developed interface is shown in the Fig. 2.

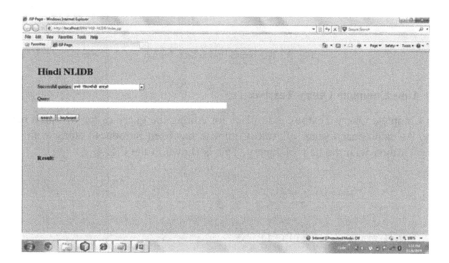

Fig. 2. Graphical user interface

4.2   Keyboard and Search Button

Keyboard has also been included in the developed system so as to make typing of the query much easier and simple. On clicking of the Keyboard Button a keyboard of the helping words or tokens open up. Using this user can simply click on the predefined given words instead of typing the words, the clicked words will directly appear in the Query Textbox. Search Button has been provided to start the query execution process. The query gets executed on clicking the Search Button and the result get displayed as the output. The functionality of the Keyboard as well as the Search button has been illustrated below in Fig. 3.

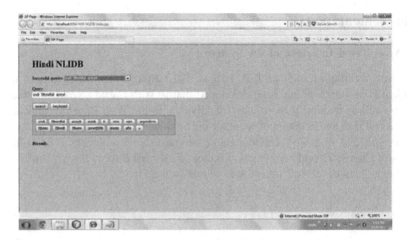

Fig. 3. Keyboard and search button

4.3   Auto Complete Query Textbox

Auto Complete Query Textbox is in place for editing the query or for writing a new query. An additional feature of Auto Complete has been introduced along with the Query Textbox with the help of Jquery. This is shown in the Fig. 4.

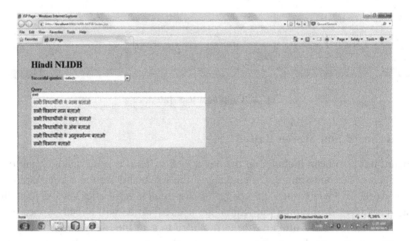

Fig. 4. Query textbox with AutoComplete feature

4.4   Successful Queries Drop Down

Successful Queries Drop Down is based on the query execution history and contains list of all the queries that have been executed effectively. Figure 5 shows the Successful Queries Drop Down list.

Fig. 5. Successful queries drop down list

5 Testing and Results

For two strings, it describes the similarity of two strings to the length of the longest prefix common to both strings. When the user types the query in the question field sometimes only half the word gets typed or the word is misspelled. Then, from the String Similarity measure working at the back-end, the String Matching function gets the actual word and retrieves the answer according to the question.

The Similarity Functions used to check the accuracy of the system are Euclidean Similarity [9], Jaccard Similarity [10], Dice Similarity [11], Cosine Similarity [12], Smith Waterman Similarity [13], Levenshtein Similarity [14] functions. Results according to these Similarity Functions for multi phrase word and misspelled words matching are based on experiment.

The word used to evaluate these different Similarity functions along with the accuracy rates on different Similarity functions shown in Table 1 is विधार्थी नाम..

Table 1. Accuracy values of different similarity functions

	विधार्थी नाम	विधार्थी- नाम	विधर्थी नम	विधार्थी	नाम
	T1	T2	T3	T4	T5
Cos. Sim.	1	0	0	0.70710677	0.70710677
Dice Sim.	1	0	0	0.6666667	0.6666667
Euc. Dist.	1	0.22540335	0.2928932	0.5527864	0.5527864
Jacc. Sim.	1	0	0	0.5	0.5
S.W Sim.	1	0.8333333	0.9	1	1
Lev. Sim	1	0.9166667	0.8333333	0.6666666	0.25

Graph associated with these implemented accuracy values is shown in Fig. 6 below.

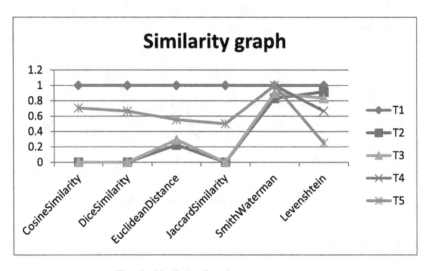

Fig. 6. Similarity function accuracy graph

Depending on the above shown results as well as the graph, Smith Waterman Similarity function is selected as the most suitable Similarity function as it has the most accurate results for most of the test cases. The system described in the paper has been implemented using the Smith Waterman Similarity function.

The result of the query execution is illustrated below in Fig. 7.

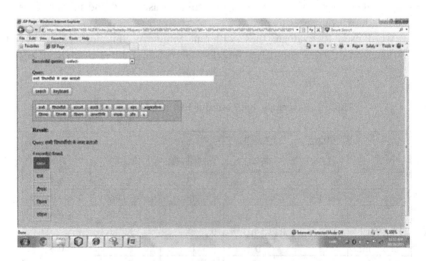

Fig. 7. Snapshot of executed query result

6 Conclusion and Future Work

The paper discusses the implementation of Advanced Web-Based Hindi Language Interface to Database using Machine Learning approach. The Similarity functions have been tested on the developed system to make the system more accurate. The system has been made Web Based and has been provided with the functionality of Auto Complete feature to increase the scope and make it more user friendly respectively. The future scope of the implemented system can have use of multiple languages in a single system along with inclusion of data base independent characteristics.

References

1. Woods, W.A., Kaplan, R.M., Webber, B.N.: The lunar sciences natural language information system: Final Report. In: BBN Report 2378, Bolt Beranek and Newman Inc., Cambridge, Massachusetts (1972)
2. Shingala, P.V.: Enhancing the relevance of information retrieval by querying the database in natural form. In: International Conference on Intelligent Systems and Signal Processing (ISSP), pp. 408–412. IEEE (2013)
3. Khalid, M.A., Jijkoun, V., de Rijke, M.: Machine learning for question answering from tabular data. In: 18th International Workshop on Database and Expert Systems Applications, pp. 392–396, DEXA (2007)
4. Dua, M., Kumar, S., Virk, Z.S.: Hindi language graphical user interface to database management system. In: 12th International Conference on Machine Learning and Applications, pp. 549–554. IEEE, Florida (2013)
5. Kumar, R., Dua, M., Jindal, S.: Domain-independent Hindi language interface to relational database. In: International Conference on Computation of Power, Energy, Information and Communication, pp. 81–86. IEEE (2014)
6. Stanford Parser. http://nlp.stanford.edu/software/index.shtml
7. Hindi Shallow Parser. http://ltrc.iiit.ac.in/analyzer/hindi/
8. Guo, G., Wang, H., Bell, D.J., Bi, Y., Greer, K.: KNN model-based approach in classification. In: Meersman, R., Schmidt, D.C. (eds.) CoopIS/DOA/ODBASE 2003. LNCS, vol. 2888, pp. 986–996. Springer, Heidelberg (2003)
9. Marukatat, S., Methasate, I.: Fast nearest neighbor retrieval using randomized binary codes and approximate euclidean distance. J. Pattern Recognit. Lett. **34**, 1101–1107 (2013). Elsevier
10. Sarawagi, S., Kirpal, A.: Efficient set joins on Similarity Predicates. In: International Conference on Management of Data (SIGMOD 2004), pp. 743–754. ACM (2004)
11. Ye, J.: Multicriteria Decision-Making method using the Dice Similarity Measure based on the Reduct Intuitionistic Fuzzy sets of Interval-Valued Intuitionistic Fuzzy Sets. J. Appl. Math. Modell. **36**, 4466–4472 (2012). Elsevier
12. Sahami, M., Heilman, T.: A web-based kernel function for measuring the similarity of short text snippets. In: 15th International Conference on World Wide Web, pp. 377–386. ACM (2006)

13. Mott, R.: Maximum likelihood estimation of the statistical distribution of smith waterman local sequence similarity scores. Bull. Math. Biol. **54**, 59–75 (1992). Springer

14. Cohen, W., Ravikumar, P., Fienberg, S.: A comparison of string metrics for matching names and records. In: American Association for Artificial Intelligence (2003)

MapCube: A Mobile Focus and Context Information Visualization Technique for Geographic Maps

Björn Werkmann$^{(\boxtimes)}$ and Matthias Hemmje

Department of Multimedia and Internet Applications, Fernuniversität Hagen,
Universitätsstr. 1, 58097 Hagen, Germany
{Bjoern.Werkmann,Matthias.Hemmje}@fernuni-hagen.de
http://www.lgmmia.fernuni-hagen.de

Abstract. A problem inherent in many mobile applications are the form factor restrictions imposed by mobile devices that directly translate into limited screen real estate available to the application. In particular geographic spatial tasks can be more difficult to perform. This paper addresses this information visualization problem in light of the use case real-time ridesharing. Here, the consequence of limited screen real estate is that ride-matching information might be situated at off-screen locations while the driver is following navigation instructions. The MapCube implementation relies on 3D perspective projection and transparency as the basis for screen reuse, to implement *bending*, which makes this information visible again, by reusing screen already occupied by the navigation view. It demonstrates the use of depth-cues which invoke preattentive visual processing to avoid composite-fusing of the transparent foreground layer with the 3D background, to improve perceptibility. The MapCube solution is quantitatively evaluated in a user study.

Keywords: Focus+Context · Peripheral awareness · Off-screen locations · Mobile devices · Spatial cognition · Geographic maps

1 Introduction

This paper presents a novel *Information Visualization* (IVIS) technique called *MapCube* technique which supports visualizing geographic information spaces within the confines of limited screen real estate as found on mobile devices. Using this technique, any kind of event associated with locations on- or off-screen, can seamlessly be visualized with minimal disruption to a main task, that currently requires a geographic map on screen.

This paper addresses this IVIS problem in the light of a *Location Based Service* (LBS) use case supporting real-time ridesharing or dynamic ridesharing, defined by [1] as a "Paratransit-like service [that] allows travelers to be joined in real-time to provide taxi-like responsiveness", which will subsequently simply be called ridesharing.

© Springer International Publishing Switzerland 2016
S. Yamamoto (Ed.): HIMI 2016, Part I, LNCS 9734, pp. 391–402, 2016.
DOI: 10.1007/978-3-319-40349-6_37

To capture this use cases more precisely, the term *Focus Task* (FT) is helpful. The term encapsulates the two meanings of focus as related to a user task. Firstly, a FT is a task that the user is currently and continuously performing, on which the user is *focused*. Secondly, to perform the task, the *focus view*, a display the user requires for performing the task, is *focused* on certain information that is pertinent to the task. The goal of this paper is to address situations, where the focus view more specifically implies that a limited geographic area is visible and displayed on screen as focus view, whereas surrounding areas remain off-screen. For the ridesharing use case, the FT is following navigation instructions on a car navigation display.

Ridesharing entails re-routing the driver to pick up a passenger en-route. The intended use case aims at allowing drivers to be involved in a decision making process to increase the number of matched rides [2] by allowing the driver to perceive possible benefits while identifying passengers that are possible ridesharing-matches, going beyond established ride-matching algorithms without user feedback, such as [3]. This includes support to allow previously neglected *Ride Match Criteria* (RMC) to be considered during such decision making. Deciding whether or not to pick up a passenger is a second task that becomes relevant in addition to the FT. These additional RMC could now become relevant in the context of the decision making, e.g., the location of a *Point Of Interest* (POI) relative to the detour-route, towards the pick-up-point of the potential passenger, which are all off-screen but at the same time highly decision relevant.

The RMC relevant to the use case are similar to those objects identified by [4] in relation to *elementary actions* in context of a LBS, i.e. inherently spatial *Geographic Information Objects* (GIOs), with geometries including points, polylines, polygons, as well as topological relationships among such objects. These kind of GIOs and relationships among them will be called *Complex Geographic Context* (CGC), to distinguish them from simple points, as detailed in Sect. 3. Displaying this CGC is a requirement for the IVIS technique to be employed. In this way, it becomes e.g. possible to present the driver with certain POIs such as a gas station, parks and similar, relative to the current position, the passenger's position and the connecting route of the detour. The information pertinent to this second task is to be displayed on-screen without interrupting the FT which defines a requirement for the IVIS technique to be employed.

The following section will review existing IVIS techniques that are candidates for a solution.

2   Related Work

This section introduces IVIS techniques that directly address the challenges of the ridesharing use case

For overview+detail visualization techniques, e.g. as introduce by [5], the two views for focus and context are spatially separated. This technique is useful in many situations, for mobile devices though, the restricted space disallows *Context Areas* (CAs) of larger extent. An issue of a more general nature that stems from the spatial separation of focus and context, is that it is more difficult for the user to develop an integrated mental model [6]. As pointed out by [7], humans remember layout in space with respect to our vantage point using *egocentric coordinates*. The fact that focus and context are actually two different views, is problematic in this respect as the frame of reference established while performing a task within the *Focus Area* (FA), is based on *egocentric coordinates*. Also, visually linking an object inside to objects outside the FA that are only visible in the overview, is not directly possible, but required to show the route towards the passenger.

Using pan+zoom to control the map content, is an example for temporal separation of focus and its context within the information space. Focus and context are not integrated for pan+zoom techniques, and the temporal separation requires the user to memorize information when changing views. Ultimately, the inherent need to leave the focus view is not acceptable while the user is performing a FT such as the navigation of the ridesharing use case.

The techniques that are part of the focus+context category integrate both views more seamlessly by presenting the focus embedded into the context. Building on earlier work in [8], Furnas introduces *generalized fisheye views* with [9], a general framework for dealing with the space limitations that computer displays impose, by treating context differently from the focus, e.g. using distortions to reduce the context size.

[10] presented an application where a planar graph with cities as nodes is adapted based on the selected focus node. Non linear magnification fields [11] have been introduced as a more abstract representation form for these distortions, and were further developed by [12] and applied to an existing geographical map redering.

[13] introduces *glue* in addition to focus and context, extending upon the fisheye concept to achieve geographical map renderings that provide focus+context map renderings on mobile devices.

The Perspective Wall [14] is an early example of a focus+context view that can easily be applied to geographic map data applying a visual transfer function [15] to context, similar to a perspective projection. Later work, the Document Lens [16] extended this principle and used a truncated square pyramid as projection surface in 3D to provide focus and context within a text document. What remains problematic for focus+context views in general when regarded with respect to the small screen real estate available on mobile devices, is that like in the case of the pyramid sides significant screen real estate is occupied at all times, hence also affecting the FT.

The final category of cue-based techniques is related to visual cues such as color hue and saturation used to highlight or de-emphasize some of the visualized objects, as well as cues that act as proxy for the actual object, e.g. arrows within the FA that provide context by pointing at locations off-screen. A similar technique was introduced by [17]. It is able to describe more attributes of off-screen objects. The idea is developed further by a solution called Halo [18] where POIs at off-screen locations are surrounded by circles that are just large enough to reach into the visible FA. In this way the user can judge the distance and location of the POIs based on the arc position along the screen edge, as well as curvature and size of the visible arc segments. It could be difficult though, to look at the arc segments and determine the relationship of a POI to an off-screen street or highway or indicate the street itself.

In summmary, overview+detail and pan+zoom are not suitable due to the separation of focus and context, cue-based techniques lack expressiveness, and existing focus+context techniques deprive the FT of space. The following section will describe the MapCube visualization technique that addresses these challenges.

3   MapCube

The *MapCube Focus and Context Model* (MFM) as depicted in Fig. 1 summarizes the kinds of GIO-geometry the MapCube needs to be able to display, relates them to visualization as well as *Location Context* (LC) aspects of the ridesharing use case and LBS in general, giving examples for CGC. The term LC encapsulates a combination of the spatial distributions from focus+context in IVIS with a specialization of context as defined by [20], emphasizing spatial aspects.

Region 1 at the center corresponds to the area immediately surrounding the current position of the user. It is the FA that is displayed on-screen, surrounded by the light gray area representing the CA that is off-screen. The *Level Of Detail* (LOD) for this region is appropriate for giving navigation instructions to the user. Showing instructions for both *near* and *far* destinations, have both to be supported by the MapCube conceptual model as indicated by the arrows

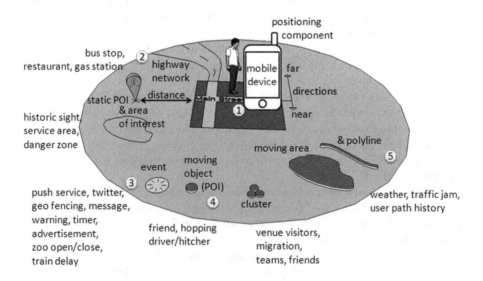

Fig. 1. MapCube focus and context model [19].

to the right of region 1. This means, in particular with respect to CAs, that very far destinations need to be supported, and consequently a CA with large extent within the geographic information space needs to be considered.

All of the following regions region 2 to region 5 pertain to GIOs that are further away from the current location, that are context objects inside the LC.

Region 2 groups GIOs that are independent of time. Besides the highway network as example of polyline data, region 2 contains all the geometry types that must be visualized and gives some examples of the kind of context these can represent, including only static context, i.e., location, path, area or thematic attributes that do not change over time.

Region 3 introduces time, in the sense of an *event*, meaning that the state of a certain location changes, e.g., a possible ride-match candidate that is communicated to the driver.

Region 4 introduces the case that the location of a point changes, it is a *moving object* [21], e.g., also allowing for cluster formation.

Finally, region 5 extends this notion of geometry change over time to polylines and areas. In light of the ridesharing use case a relevant example are traffic jams.

3.1 Visualization Constraints

The following paragraphs will bring requirements stemming from the problem statement derived from ridesharing use case, into the domain of constructing a visual form, as described in [22], as part of the reference model of IVIS, or IVIS pipeline. Derived from the requirements of the ridesharing use case, the following lists *visualization constraints* that the MapCube model has to comply to:

- Not changing the on-screen size or position of the focus view associated with the FT map and *User Interface* (UI)
- Not changing size or position of the already displayed objects
- Not removing already displayed objects

With respect to the first point, this means in particular the FA required for the FT must still occupy the complete screen. The information necessary for the FT remains visible and unchanged inside the FA. The mental model established within the FA, in terms of egocentric coordinates, is also maintained as a frame of reference for new information the LC. The maintained FA includes for example the road network and the highlighted road to follow. Requiring these constraints to be fulfilled, seamless transition from the focus view to a view including LC is possible without disturbing the FT.

3.2 Real World Analogy

This section is related to the *visual form* of the IVIS pipeline. Building on the *visual constraints* described in the previous section, it provides an overview of how visual form is create that satisfies these constraints, introducing a *real world analogy* that is the basis for subsequent *visual mappings*, *visual structures*, and

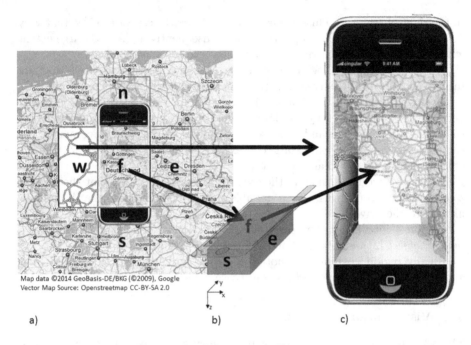

Map data ©2014 GeoBasis-DE/BKG (©2009), Google
Vector Map Source: Openstreetmap CC-BY-SA 2.0

a)   b)   c)

Fig. 2. MapCube concept illustration.

views [22]. The MapCube conceptual model starts from the premise of a simple solution idea. The solution idea is to start from the *physical* or *real world analogy* of a geographic paper map, and a card board box. Simply gluing a cross shaped section of the map onto the box as shown in Fig. 2a and b, is the first step. The map portion on the display of the phone is the lid of the box, the area marked f for focus, at the center of the marked CAs to the west, north, east and south. Taking the lid off and looking into the box allows for looking at the inner walls. Of course with the physical analogy, only the card board is visible as the map was glued to the outside. Imagining the map paper and card board to be translucent plastic instead, makes the map visible on the inside of the box as well, the map is visible from behind. This is the geographic map context that is to be shown in addition to the already visible map portion that is on the lid. Looking into the box in such a way that all four walls are equally visible as depicted in Fig. 2c, presents a view similar to what is intended for the MapCube conceptual model. In case of the MapCube the lid is not taken off, but the visible map portion is rendered partially transparent to keep the FA visible and display the CA at the same time, visible behind the FA, as depicted in the illustration in Fig. 2c. This visualization strategy represents an extension of the substrate folding [22]. In an extension of substrate folding [22], the particular use of the 3D cube metaphor, perspective projection, and transparency is termed *bending*, as previously off-screen content is bent back into view.

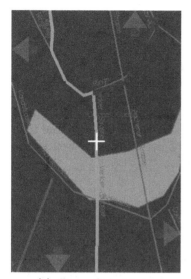

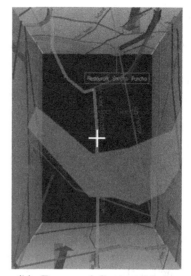

(a) Focus Only Mode

(b) Focus and Context Mode

Fig. 3. MapCube display rendering.

A number of *Perceptibility Problems* (PPs) have been identified, of which the most pressing are that coherent perception of 3D space is lost, and composite fusing [23], i.e., ambiguity in associating a shape with foreground or background. In a prototypical implementation, the *Evaluation Prototype* (EP), these have been addressed, most importantly by modelling the GIOs inside the CA as actual 3D objects that are part of the 3D background. These objects are placed inside the cube, attached to the cube faces. Figure 3 shows the prototypical implementation of this conceptual model of the MapCube. Figure 3a shows the *Focus Only Mode* (FOM), with a red route in the upper right corner, leaving the screen towards the destination that remains invisible off-screen. Figure 3b shows the *Focus and Context Mode* (FCM) where the FA is transparent to reveal how the the route continues as 3D tube towards the destination inside the CA. Here, the GIOs are modelled as actual 3D objects to be able to take advantage of 3D depth cues such as *shape-from-shading* [23] to invoke preattentive visual processing [24,25] that aids distinguishing between focus objects in the foreground and context objects that are part of the three dimensional background.

4   Evaluation

Several aspects of the MapCube technique are relevant with respect to evaluation. Before using the technique in a real life setting for example, the most important aspect are safety considerations, including the risk of distraction introduced by the MapCube technique. This aspect is left as future work because the aspect of showing feasibility of the prototypical implementation (and satisfaction of basic usability requirements in light of PPs) needs to be addressed first. Hence, the goal of the evaluation presented in this section is to investigate the feasibility and usability of the MapCube IVIS technique that satisfies the IVIS requirements identified for the use case of real-time ridesharing.

A summative evaluation that employs an empirical, quantitative method, by means of a user study was performed to compare the MapCube EP with a best of class technique that satisfies some of the constraints of the use case, the Halo technique. This evaluation shows the feasibility of the solution as well as the effectiveness of the solutions implemented to address the PPs.

4.1   User Study

Following the approach of [26] to perform the evaluation, a *usability metric* is defined that allows for comparing the two techniques. These metrics formalize the measurement of quality of the techniques. The summative evaluation is concerned with two *usability dimensions* [27]. First, the *effectiveness* (i.e. "is the user able to complete the task" [28]) which is measured by means of the usability metric *error rate*. Second, the *efficiency* (i.e. "the amount of effort required to complete the task" [28]) which is measured by means of the usability metric *time-on-task*. These two *dependent variables* are determined for two groups, created by variation of the *independent variable* "visualization technique".

To acquire these measurements, a user task is defined that allows for comparison of the two techniques. At the same time it reveals whether perceptibility issues of the MapCube technique have been addressed successfully. Six hotels are positioned at off-screen locations and the user task is to count POIs that are located in the vicinity of a hotel. An incorrect number POIs is counted as an error for the respective hotel, yielding the *error rate* as average across all hotels and participants. The evaluation frame work measures the *time-on-task* of each participant for all six hotels and computes the average for all participants. For Halo, both the hotel and POIs are represented using arc segments. For the MapCube they are represented as 3D objects embedded into the geographical map rendering as described before (i.e., attached to the cube faces).

Every participant performs the user task with both visualization techniques. To avoid carryover effects the first technique uses a different test data set. The measurements are averaged regardless of the data set. The test data is comprised of real locations. The POIs are tourist attractions in the vicinity of hotels selected in then Cologne area in Germany.

4.2   Results

The evaluation was performed with 10 participants. Each of them performed the user task with both visualization techniques, i.e., overall 20 overall 20 experiments were performed revealing measurements for each of the two IVIS techniques' usability metrics in the dimensions of *error rate* and *time-on-task*.

The MapCube *error rate* is 2.1 (standard deviation 1.5) which is half the Halo *error rate* of 4.2 (standard deviation 1.4). This means the MapCube performs better in terms of effectiveness. The MapCube *average time-on-task* is 52.3 (standard deviation 7.78). It is roughly half that of the Halo *average time-on-task* which is 93.8 (standard deviation 22.26), i.e. the MapCube is better in terms of efficiency.

For both measures the difference in population means is due to the varied independent variable "visualization technique". This has been shown by a one-way *Analysis of Variance* (ANOVA). For the underlying measurements a statistically significant effect of the visualization technique can be reported with 95 % confidence (F-quantile $F_{1,18} = 4.41$, degrees of freedom for 2 groups and 2 measurements for each of the 10 participants). For the *error rate* with an F-statistic of $F(1, 18) = 7.85 > F_{1,18}$, and for the *time-on-task* with an F-statistic of $F(1, 18) = 16.5 > F_{1,18}$.

5   Summary and Outlook

This paper set out to investigate the feasibility of an IVIS technique that could satisfy the requirements identified for the use case of real-time ridesharing. The presented MapCube model and IVIS technique, is the proposed solution. The MapCube prototype was built to evaluate this solution.

The MapCube proved to be usable and outperformed a competing technique that is considered efficient. The prototype allows *screen reuse* as intended and can be used effectively to display geographic map portions that would otherwise remain invisible off-screen or merely hinted at. In particular the type of geometry that cannot be easily hinted at (such as, e.g., lines and shapes, as well as relationships between objects) are supported by the MapCube. The additional map portions are presented within an unchanged frame of reference in egocentric coordinates, that are in line with the mental model the user developed while pursuing the FT of following navigation instructions. Because of this, for a GIO that would otherwise remain invisible off-screen, visually linking becomes possible (e.g., by drawing a line along the route to that object within the geographic map rendering). Using transparency to transition from the FOM (which is used while pursuing the FT) to the FCM makes the technique unobtrusive and suitable to display event-related off-screen CGC that is only temporarily visible without interrupting the FT. As described before, the particular fashion of substrate folding termed *bending* allows perceiving of spatial relationships, shapes, map symbols, and text for CGC that would otherwise be off-screen. *Bending* a large off-screen information space back into view directly addresses the use case problem to be able to deal with *far-scattered* CGC.

Successfully ameliorating the PPs brought about by screen reuse, and doing so by employing 3D depth cues, makes a good case for choosing a 3D metaphor that enables use of these cues. An approach that is in principle applicable to any kind of focus+context with context of large 2D extent, that needs to be displayed within minimal screen real estate such as found with mobile devices. With the MapCube the additional constraint of having a FT can be satisfied.

As pointed out with respect to the evaluation, the investigation of in-situ safety considerations of the car-related usage scenario are mandatory before it is possible to apply the MapCube in a real-life ridesharing systems. With respect to future work, it is intended to encapsulate the MapCube prototype's software by means of a software wrapper and application user interface that will allow for a seamless plug and play integration into visual user interface frameworks as well as graphical and web-based user-interface implementation technologies. This will require an operationalization of the IVIS reference model into a middleware software technology that can support the MapCupe Focus and Context Model from a software engineering point of view and allow for seamless and cost-effective plug and play integration with current state-of-the-art 2D and 3D display technologies.

Furthermore, the goal of our future work is the quality assessment and improvement of usability aspects of the existing prototypical MapCube implementation (based on Java, JOGL) and improved versions of the prototypical software implementation. Improvements are to be identified and evaluated with appropriate academic rigor, employing, e.g., further user studies. Especially an apriori study is to be devised (and described) to reveal existing usability problems with respect to learnability, effectiveness, efficiency, satisfaction as well as the overall utility of the technique in mobile application contexts. It will answer questions like: Is the technique indeed helpful? Can pertinent information be gathered, even at a glance?

To this end, several test data sets will be devised and considered for all usability evaluations. The identified problems are to be addressed by means of source code changes to the Java program of the prototypical implementation or a functionally equivalent implementation using WebGL or X3Dom. A related aspect that will be investigated independently is the impact of the technique regarding the FT (e.g. following car navigation instructions) and usage scenario (e.g., driving a car). This will for example answer the questions whether the technique can cause confusion during time sensitive critical situations, e.g. while driving.

References

1. Hwang, M., Kemp, J., Lerner-Lam, E., Neuerburg, N., Okunieff, P.: Advanced Public Transportation Systems: State of the Art Update 2006 (2006)
2. Agatz, N., Erera, A., Savelsbergh, M., Wang, X.: Optimization for dynamic ridesharing: a review. Eur. J. Oper. Res. **223**(2), 295–303 (2012). ISSN: 0377-2217
3. Smirnov, A., Shilov, N., Kashevnik, A., Teslya, N.: Openstreetmap-based dynamic ridesharing service. In: Popovich, V., Claramunt, C., Schrenk, M., Korolenko, K. (eds.) (IF AND GIS 2013). LNGC, pp. 119–134. Springer, Heidelberg (2014)
4. Reichenbacher, T.: Mobile Cartography: Adaptive Visualisation of Geographic Information on Mobile Devices. Verlag Dr. Hut, Munich (2004)

5. Hornbæk, K., Bederson, B.B., Plaisant, C.: Navigation Patterns and Usability of Overview+Detail and Zoomable User Interfaces for Maps (2001)
6. Grudin, J.: Partitioning digital worlds: focal and peripheral awareness in multiple monitor use. In: Proceedings of the SIGCHI Conference on Human Factors in Computing Systems, pp. 458–465. ACM (2001)
7. Dykes, J., MacEachren, A.M., Kraak, M.-J., Association, I.C.: Exploring Geovisualization. Elsevier, Amsterdam (2005). ISBN: 0-08-044531-4 978-0-08-044531-1
8. Furnas, G.W.: The FISHEYE View: A New Look at Structured Files. Morgan Kaufmann, San Francisco (1981)
9. Furnas, G.W.: Generalized fisheye views. SIGCHI Bull. **17**(4), 16–23 (1986)
10. Sarkar, M., Brown, M.H.: Graphical fisheye views of graphs. In: Proceedings of the SIGCHI Conference on Human Factors in Computing Systems, pp. 83–91. ACM, Monterey, California, United States (1992). ISBN: 0-89791-513-5
11. Keahey, T.A., Robertson, E.L.: Nonlinear magnification fields. In: IEEE Symposium on Information Visualization, pp. 51–58 (1997)
12. Rase, W.D.: Fischauge-Projektionen als kartographische Lupen. Salzburger Geographische Materialien **26**(2), 115–122 (1997)
13. Yamamoto, D., Hukuhara, K., Takahashi, N.: A focus control method based on city blocks for the focus+ glue+ context map. In: 2010 IEEE 24th International Conference on Advanced Information Networking and Applications Workshops (WAINA), pp. 956–961. IEEE (2010)
14. Mackinlay, J.D., Robertson, G.G., Card, S.K.: The Perspective wall: detail and context smoothly integrated. In: Proceedings of the SIGCHI Conference on Human Factors in Computing Systems. CHI 1991, pp. 173–176. ACM, New York, NY, USA (1991). ISBN: 0-89791-383-3
15. Farrand, W.: Information Display in Interactive Design. Doctoral thesis (1973)
16. Robertson, G.G., Mackinlay, J.D.: The document lens. In: Proceedings of the 6th Annual ACM Symposium on User Interface Software and Technology, pp. 101–108. ACM, Atlanta, Georgia, United States (1993). ISBN: 0-89791-628-X
17. Zellweger, P.T., Mackinlay, J.D., Good, L., Stefik, M., Baudisch, P.: City lights: contextual views in minimal space. In: CHI 2003 Extended Abstracts on Human Factors in Computing Systems, pp. 838–839. ACM, Ft. Lauderdale, Florida, USA (2003). ISBN: 1-58113-637-4
18. Baudisch, P., Rosenholtz, R.: Halo: a technique for visualizing off-screen locations. In: Proceedings of the SIGCHI Conference on Human Factors in Computing Systems, pp. 481–488. ACM, Ft. Lauderdale, Florida, USA (2003). ISBN: 1-58113-630-7
19. Werkmann, B., Heutelbeck, D., Hemmje, M.: Map-Based Focus and context visualization for location based services. In: Proceedings of 6th GI/ITG KuVS Fachgespräch Ortsbezogene Anwendungen und Dienste, Bonn (2009)
20. Nivala, A.M., Sarjakoski, L.T.: An approach to intelligent maps: context awareness. In: The 2nd Workshop on'HCI in Mobile Guides (2003)
21. Güting, H., Almeida, T.D., Ding, Z.: Modeling and querying moving objects in networks. VLDB J. **15**(2), 165–190 (2006)
22. Card, S.K., Mackinlay, J., Shneiderman, B.: Readings in Information Visualization: Using Vision to Think, 1st edn. Morgan Kaufmann, San Francisco (1999). ISBN: 1-55860-533-9
23. Ware, C.: Information Visualization: Perception for Design, 514 pp. Morgan Kaufmann, San Francisco (2004). ISBN: 978-1-55860-819-1
24. Sun, J.Y., Perona, P.: Preattentive perception of elementary three dimensional shapes. Vis. Res. **36**(16), 2515–2529 (1996). ISSN: 0042–6989

25. Ramachandran, V.S.: Perceiving shape from shading. Sci. Am. **259**(2), 76–83 (1988)
26. Lewis, J.R.: Usability testing. Handb. Hum. Fact. Ergon. **12**, e30 (2006)
27. Bevan, N.: Measuring usability as quality of use. Softw. Qual. J. **4**(2), 115–130 (1995)
28. Tullis, T., Albert, W.: Measuring the User Experience: Collecting, Analyzing, and Presenting Usability Metrics (Interactive Technologies), 336 pp. Morgan Kaufmann, San Francisco (2008). ISBN: 0-12-373558-0

Human-Centered Design

Design Education at the Cross-Roads of Change

Denis A. Coelho[⊠]

Human Technology Group, Department of Electromechanical Engineering,
Centre for Mechanical and Aerospace Science and Technology,
Universidade da Beira Interior, 6201-001 Covilhã, Portugal
denis@ubi.pt, denis.a.coelho@gmail.com

Abstract. The paper advocates for designer immersion while deploying design research methods and design leadership within teamwork. Design educators need to prepare students to take on these roles with confidence, while working at the crossroads between business, culture, design and ergonomics, as well as other specialties according to the nature of the problem at hand. Are there ways design education can support individuals in valuing their uniqueness and transforming their passion and drive into competitive advantage? By helping them develop the curiosity that is needed to discover and select meaningful problems, preparing them to understand context, human activities and the aspirations of the person and of society, educators can get them posed for transformative and actionable creativity that students will then be more likely to engage in, and therefore enthusiastically generate, create and develop relevant and inspiring solutions.

Keywords: Attitudes · Design stages · Design education · Metaphors

1 Introduction

This paper is based on an invited talk delivered by Denis A. Coelho, Professor at the University of Beira Interior, delivered February 1, 2016, at the School of Design of the Hong Kong Polytechnic University.

This (Fig. 1) is a metaphor to the changing world we live in, and to the cycles it inevitably goes through. With this call-up, we intend to juxtapose the movement that is taking place in our world to phase-out fossil fuels, replacing them with renewable energies and capping over-consumption of resources with an even more radical movement of going back to basics, that advocates for rural renaissance, and for a return to a mostly agrarian subsistence model, closer to self-sufficiency, even though this may be seen as a throwback in terms of human and economic development. We think that it is possible to combine these two perspectives and that somewhere in between there is a middle ground that we should collectively seek and work together to jointly achieve. There is definitely a lot of transformation heading our way, we have a choice to either react to it as it happens or we can honestly try to take the lead on change and position ourselves in the frontline or ahead of the fundamental changes that are bound to occur in our economic and social systems. Many people believe that designers are potentially

S. Yamamoto (Ed.): HIMI 2016, Part I, LNCS 9734, pp. 405–412, 2016.
DOI: 10.1007/978-3-319-40349-6_38

Fig. 1. Undated black and white stock picture taken in Kent, Oregon

well versed in the knowledge and in the skills necessary to become leaders in this transformational process, requiring forward looking, focusing on problems, working across disciplines, participating in teams and leading them by example and inspiration, while also adopting a systems perspective and focusing on people.

In its latest redefinition of industrial design the professional practice committee of the International Council of Societies of Industrial Design stresses that designers must be well versed in acquiring "a deep understanding of user needs through empathy and apply a pragmatic, user centric problem solving process to design products, systems, services and experiences". This is where we have contributed to the discipline of Product Design, leading and offering guidance and support to design students in placing the person at the centre of the design process. However, this focus does not entail a detachment from the context, the activity, or the systems perspectives. On the contrary, we strive to get past the often misleading assurance conferred by design requirement specifications, and get our feet on the ground and carry out fieldwork, such as that which is involved in systemic analysis, making use of ethnographic methods to enrich our systems perspective and to foster the creation of real and shared value. Hence we advocate for designer immersion while deploying design research methods and design leadership within teamwork, hence as educators we need to prepare our students to take on these roles with confidence, while working at the crossroads between business, culture, design and ergonomics, as well as other specialties according to the nature of the problem that is at hand and is being tackled.

This is not an easy task and there are many challenges that we encounter in a design educator role. A few of the questions that we are bound to ask ourselves are: How do we not only show them how to design but also get them on their own path and possibly guide them and especially nurture their own trailing of the meta processes through which as individual design students, they flourish as designers and become independent, resourceful and self confident in their abilities and power to change the world, one design at a time? So are there ways design education can support individuals in valuing their uniqueness and transforming their passion and drive into competitive advantage? By helping them develop the curiosity that is needed to discover and select meaningful problems, preparing them to understand context, human activities and the aspirations of the person and of society, we can get them posed for transformative and actionable creativity that they will then be more likely to engage in, and therefore enthusiastically generate, create and develop relevant and inspiring solutions.

2 An Internal Design Compass Metaphor

When a design process is driven by love and passion you can see it in the results, and when it's not, or something gets in between, hijacking it from that truthfulness and wholeness, the results tend to give it away. So, a combination of technical skills and abilities and passionate drive to design which we expect in a product and industrial designer must be balanced and placed in an internal and external dialogue throughout the design process. The paper suggests thinking metaphorically of an internal compass that will help to strike the balance in this skilful, artful and technical process of designing. This metaphor is presented in detail in this section.

Each project and each individual designer benefits from developing a tailored approach and a bespoke design method. I see my role as a facilitator helping individuals unleash their creative power, helping them find their uniqueness and establish confidence in their creative abilities and be willing to take risks in an unorthodox creative stance, tapping in to their inner creative fountain and assisting them in structuring the design process. Recognizing the need to adopt different attitudes and engage suitable abilities throughout the process directs their sage power to the actions conducive to success in the stages of the process. So, let me start with tuning in, empathizing.

2.1 Tuning in

To be able to appreciate the uniqueness in our surroundings and the authenticity of those we interact with and appreciate their differences, respect them, understand them, we need to know ourselves fairly well. In a design context this could be fostered by product personality profiling and even individual personality, team building exercises and games such as "visualize the inner child" in the interactions with others, to foster empathy and tuning in to their reality, aspirations and problems. As an example, consider Fig. 2, depicting a project which was actually built on her personal choice to empathize with young children and articulate sustainability in toy design methods.

2.2 Discovering

The next attitude I would like to bring up is the "exploring" and discovery mode. Observing and engaging in fascination for the new findings whether brought up from literature or from explorative field work or even more structured approaches from ethnography in a more external dialoguing and contemplative attitude. This might involve getting immersed and following what is interesting in context. Don't hold back, dive in as much as possible, let the world fascinate you and then map it and pin point problems.

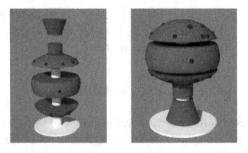

Fig. 2. Toy design concept developed from empathizing (Fernandes & Coelho 2013)

In this project (Fig. 3), the student wanted to work with his original territory. This map is the result of the systemic analysis of a semi-artisanal cheese production process, with inputs, outputs, flows, wastage and those red areas which are critical points. And then a few of those critical points were tackled by different design students – the design of the pens where sheep –big horned ones are milked, a new direction for the logo design (there are many small producers, there is a problem with identifying the certified original authentic product at the point of sale), and a hand tool prototype to improve the quality and the ergonomics of the manual process of excess cheese chip removal at the cheese dairies necessary for homogeneous ripening of the cheese.

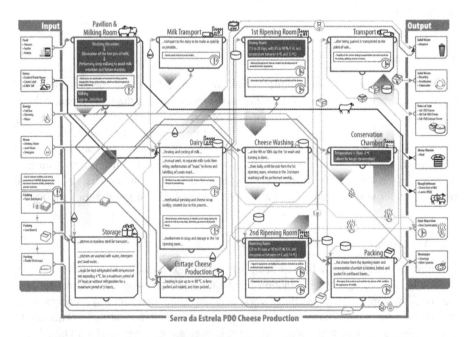

Fig. 3. Systemic design map example (Carrola, Couvinhas & Coelho 2014)

2.3   Flowing

And now we have flowing, sparking innovation, generating alternatives and focusing on positivity to get meaningful results. All the interdisciplinary building blocks at the basis of product design education and the empathic understanding and discoveries previously accomplished really support generating a stream of conceptual solutions embedding positivity and hope, springing from this attitude of flow, tapping into your inner creative fountain and letting the innovative stream boil over, while looking out for the constructive aspects of each idea and adding on and building upon those in succession.

In this project (Fig. 4), the student, a car design aficionado, explored in several iconic roadster models how the drive technology and solution had constrained the design of the car body, and then went on to conceptualize a solution aiming at dealing with the range anxiety problem for electric vehicles (EVs), but keeping a systems perspective, so this concept combines car design, with modular ergonomic batteries and quick exchange stations with some automation (varying degrees conceivable) and a digital network system for booking and capacity management.

Fig. 4. System design: EV, batteries and infrastructure design (Camboa & Coelho 2010)

2.4   Choosing

And now we have "choosing", since multiple paths or concepts are available, navigating them from an inner perspective keeping an eye out for those choices that inspire and arouse emotion, of course refining towards satisfying any other applicable requirements which might involve validation efforts, e.g. usability evaluation of functional prototypes, or focus groups on scenarios, or other feasibility studies, but those aren't really the only important ones, not if something truly novel is to emerge from this process.

These are two streams of the same culturally inspired design project (Fig. 5), the top half was created by one student who worked from literature, making a survey of Portuguese culture and Portuguese speaking countries culture, and then she used the product personality assignment technique to transfer the more flattering cultural attributes into product features. Another student made a collection of existing iconic designs in the same cultural areas and compared these with established design icons from other cultures (Italy, Scandinavia, Germany), and she went on to isolate the differentiating unique aspects of Portuguese and Lusophone design and these are some of the design concepts springing from this other stream in the project.

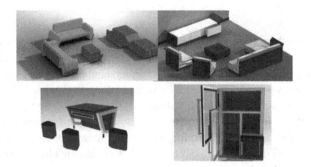

Fig. 5. Culturally inspired design (top images: Cunha Silva & Coelho 2011; bottom images: Simão & Coelho 2011)

2.5 Developing

And now we get to the stage of "developing", which is something typically associated with the work of a product designer, bringing in additional human factors and ergonomics knowledge, drawing, detailing, prototyping, building mock ups, conducting user trials, modelling, presenting, more design research, protecting and communicating the results of the design process, working like busy bees going on from task to task, giving it all and bringing others on board to share a vision and tap into their specific skills complementing your own skill set (Fig. 6). So this is I dare to say the most active and energetic attitude in the whole array of design stages. You summon your abilities,

Fig. 6. A representation of the plethora of development activities in product design (patchwork illustration by Denis A. Coelho & Tiago E. P. Carrola, based on stock images)

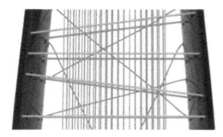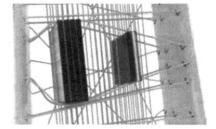

Fig. 7. A bionic design project example (based on the method presented by Versos & Coelho 2011)

Fig. 8. Representation of the internal design compass metaphor: from top centre and clockwise: Tune In, Discover, Flow, Choose and Develop (patchwork illustration and artwork by Denis A. Coelho & Tiago E. P. Carrola)

setup support, activate your execution and leadership skills, get to work developing your design, coordinating everybody else, but checking back regularly on your context and potential users to assure your detailed solution remains faithful to its inspiring essence and then work harder to bring it to the world, whether as entrepreneur or with the support of crowd-funding or other solutions.

This is a biomimmicry design project (Fig. 7). We tackled bionics from the methods at first and then developed a two pronged approach and took it to the application level. One stream flowed as a process going from a problem (stacking of books and discs) to a solution sought with inspiration from nature (spider web). In the lower stream (depicted in Fig. 7), we worked in the opposite direction, starting from the natural structures in bones and trees and looking for an application where the combination of strength with elasticity and resilience would be relevant, and this design, is only achievable through additive manufacturing, like 3D printing of suitable polymers (it is designed for a corn based natural polymer that is biodegradable).

3 Conclusion

Naturally, reiterations, moving back and forth, shifting attitude according to the advances and setbacks in the design project are contingent to this compass metaphor (Fig. 8), hence the central checker board that represents the possibility of any kind of moves.

To wrap-up, everything I said so far about the design process is easier said than done. That is why design students and young designers need advisers to help them sort the complexity out, focus on what they are good at and help them to bootstrap their passion placing it at their service so that it may self-sustainingly pull themselves farther.

References

Fernandes, S.A., Coelho, D.A.: Toy design: a methodological perspective. Int. J. Des. Objects **7** (1), 51–64 (2013)

Carrola, T.E.P., Couvinhas, A.F., Coelho, D.A.: Manufacturing Analysis of the serra da estrela PDO cheese under the perspective of systemic design. In: Proceedings of Human Factors in Organizational Design And Management–XI & Nordic Ergonomics Society Annual Conference –46 (2014). URL: http://proceedings.dtu.dk/fedora/repository/dtu:2221/OBJ/x023.97-102.pdf

Camboa, A.S., Coelho, D.A.: SharE- an engineering system concept proposal for sustainable personal mobility. Int. Rev. Mech. Eng. **4**(1), 106–111 (2010)

da Cunha e Silva, A.S., Coelho, D.A.: Transfering portuguese and lusophone cultural traits to product design: a process informed with product personality attributes. Des. Principles Pract. **5**(1), 145–163 (2011)

Simão, C.S., Coelho, D.A.: A search for the portuguese cultural identity reflected in the design of products. Des. Principles Pract. Int. J. **5**(3), 171–194 (2011)

Versos, C.A., Coelho, D.A.: An approach to validation of industrial design concepts inspired by nature. Des. Principles Pract. Int. J. **5**(3), 535–552 (2011)

Clarification of Customers' "Demand" in Development Process

Shin'ichi Fukuzumi[✉] and Yukiko Tanikawa

Knowledge Discovery Research Laboratories, NEC Corporation,
Kawasaki, Japan
s-fukuzumi@aj.jp.nec.com

Abstract. HCD is a method to give better UX to stakeholders and to provide system and product with high usability for users and stakeholders. When system and product with high usability could be developed, it is easy to verify their usability by usability test. However, it is difficult to check whether these products or system achieve that a user wants to really do it which required in UX white paper. To verify what is thing that users want to do, we discuss what is necessary for development process by analyzing how to take in customer needs to specification from the view point of software engineering and HCD. We propose a phase "acquisition of user demand" before "clarification of user needs" and "specification of user requirements" which are activities of HCD process.

It is important to clarify "demand" and to separate solving by requirements to system and besides that, and both customers' and developers' shall be recognize that to satisfy the customer' needs to the system is not same as to realize customers' "demand".

Keywords: HCD · SWE · Quality · Requirements · Development process

1 Introduction

In 2010, ISO9241-210 "Human-centred design for interactive system" which is an ergonomic related standard about human centered design was published [1], discussion related human centered design (HCD) and user experience (UX) which is newly defined in this standard becomes active in IT business field. This standard is put to practical use as an example which shape HCD concept. Figure 1 shows the relationship among each HCD activity. As shown in this figure, HCD has four activities. These are applied to each development process shown in Fig. 2. HCD is a method to give better UX to stakeholders and to provide system and product with high usability for users and stakeholders [2]. When system and product with high usability could be developed, it is easy to verify their usability by usability test [3]. However, it is difficult to check whether these products or system achieve that a user wants to really do it which required in UX white paper [4].

To verify what is thing that users want to do, we discuss what is necessary for development process by analyzing how to take in customer needs to specification from the view point of software engineering and HCD.

© Springer International Publishing Switzerland 2016
S. Yamamoto (Ed.): HIMI 2016, Part I, LNCS 9734, pp. 413–420, 2016.
DOI: 10.1007/978-3-319-40349-6_39

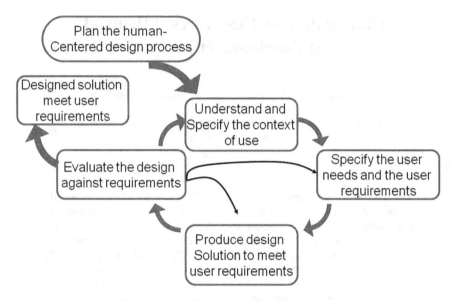

Fig. 1. The relationship among each HCD activity

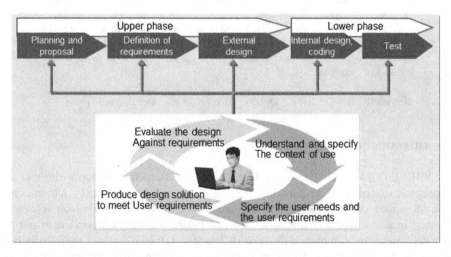

Fig. 2. The relationship among HCD activities and development process

2   Functional Requirements and Non-functional Requirements

Important factors for developing software are to consider what kinds of peculiar features of software for fulfill both explicit and implicit customer needs [5]. The peculiar features of software can be separate feature of functions and feature of quality (Fig. 3). The former is that software operation which transforms input to output, the latter is that

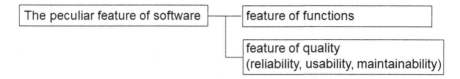

Fig. 3. The peculiar feature of software

extent which provides feature of functions to users suitably. The latter examples are reliability, usability, maintainability, and so on. In ISO/IEC25030, requirements of software products define functional requirements and non-functional requirements (quality requirements, administration requirements (e.g. price, delivery date)) [6]. The feature of quality in the peculiar feature of software describes above includes non-functional requirements. This means not only software development but also system development.

2.1 Requirements Items in Software Engineering

Generally, software, system and service are mainly development based on software engineering. After definition of requirements specification phase were prescribed as development process. It is easy to evaluate whether developed system satisfy their requirements or not because the relationship between development phase includes requirements specification, external design, internal design and function development and each test phases is clear shown in Fig. 4 [8].

Requirement definition in this defines needs related to function development as requirements describes below. Function requirements are that software operation which

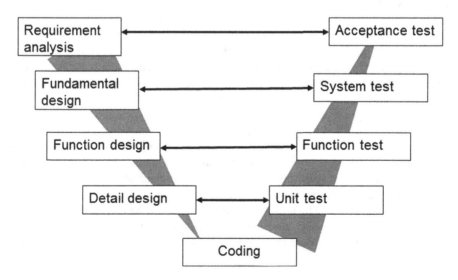

Fig. 4. V-model for development

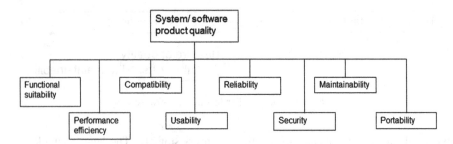

Fig. 5. Product quality model [9]

transforms input to output, it is easy to evaluate or judge whether functions can be realized or not. However, it is difficult to define non-functional requirements and quality requirements and determine requirement level. So, it is also difficult to evaluate or judge whether these requirements can be realized or not.

In software engineering, there is no process to define non-functional requirements which is "extent which provides feature of functions to users suitably" because development process defines after requirement definition phase.

For this issue, ISO/IECJTC1SC7 standardized schematization of quality. About products, quality divides into eight quality properties as shown in Fig. 5 (product quality), it is easy to take quality into requirements [9].

2.2   Requirements Items in HCD

However, development process in software engineering does not prescribe the way to build in policy or use of user and stakeholders as requirements. Currently, user needs analysis include quality is carried out in requirements specification phase, and product quality and quality in use are dealt with in this phase. To realize this analysis in upper phase, concept of HCD (human centered design) is applied. The concept of HCD prescribes to get context of use of system (if the system exists, the use of this system and if system is newly developed, imaginable usage) and to clarify users and stakeholders' needs in more upper phase of development process. By these, it is easy for developers to define requirements specification in development process [1]. HCD defines activities from plan and proposal phase to evaluation phase in development process. In plan and proposal phase, a method how to clarify customer needs is studied [10].

In this, "Needs" is aims of system. This includes not only functional needs but also non-functional needs (e.g. how to use). Of course, it is necessary to develop system (software/service). However, especially the latter, it is difficult to define above needs as requirements and to evaluate and judge whether these requirements can be realized or not.

Recently, ISO/IEC 25010 in SQuaRE (System and software quality requirements and evaluation) defines quality model shown in Fig. 6 (Quality in use) and try to take quality into requirements. Moreover, ISO/IECJTCSC7 try to be able to measure these quality [11].

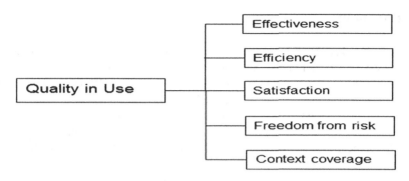

Fig. 6. Quality in use model [9]

3 International Standards Related Functional/Non-functional Requirements

There are some international standards about requirement definition, functional/non-functional requirement clarification, development process and quality property described in Sects. 1 and 2. Figure 7 shows the relationship among these standards (SQuaRE and HCD).

This figure shows that SWE quality standards are closely related to ergonomic related HCD standards. Especially, to standardize HCD four activities format in quality standard means that constitution of SQuaRE is conscious of not only development process but also lifecycle of product and system. ISO/IEC25063 "context of use description" in SQuaRE series [12] targets to be able to describe users' usage of product and system, not mention "users want to do". This describes in the next section.

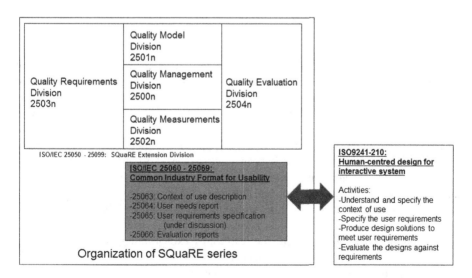

Fig. 7. Relationship among functional/non-functional requirements and HCD

4 "Demand"

For users and stakeholders, is the aim to use the system? In fact, it is important for them to realize what they want to do ("demand"). It is different whether system is necessary.

As described in Sect. 1, HCD is a method to provide better UX. UX white paper [4] shows that experience includes "before use", "during use", "after use" and "through total usage". "Users want to do" can be verify through experience in each step (Fig. 8).

However, currently, to get what they want to do ("demand") is not defined in not only development process but also HCD. Due to this, objectives (value) which users and stakeholders would like to realize cannot be understand by development fields though developers can get the view point of "use system".

We propose a phase "acquisition of user demand" before "clarification of user needs" and "specification of user requirements" which are activities of HCD process.

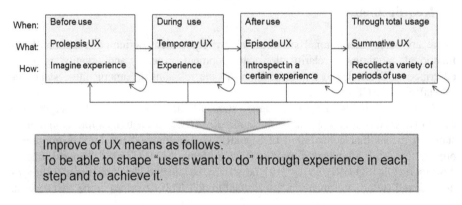

Fig. 8. UX step [4]

4.1 Example

For example, we consider problems and solutions of immigration in international airport. Main problems are considered to be "congestion reducing" and "judgment of safety, reassurance and accuracy". In case of transforming these problems to items which would like to realize in system, target is "efficiency", or "automation" about recognition function. Of course, if these functions are installed in the system, the time for recognition will be shortened. However, it is difficult for users themselves smoothly who do not use the immigration system daily to carry out a flow of a series of authentication a management government service was doing personally. Because of this, congestion is not reduced. Safe and accurate review and judgement will be carried out by automation, but it is difficult for users to feel "reassurance". From this, to solve main problems shown firstly, it is necessary to realize not only efficiency and automation as functions of system but also items except system requirements, e.g. instruction of users to system terminals, navigation of operation, fundamental UI design, sense of security a staff can be called anytime.

4.2   Proposal

Thus, it is important to clarify "demand" and to separate solving by requirements to system and besides that, and both customers' and developers' shall be recognize that to satisfy the customer' needs to the system is not same as to realize customers' "demand" (Fig. 9).

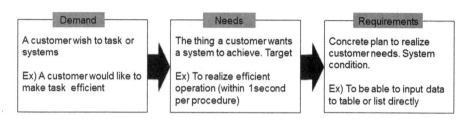

Fig. 9. Relationship among "demand", "needs" and "requirements"

5   Conclusion and Current Situation

This paper points out an important issue about getting users' demand in development process. Though SWE and HCD define the process about clarification of customer needs and user requirements definition, the process about users' demand does not define in development process. This paper proposes that this task shall be included in the process.

Currently, ISOTC159SC4WG28 jointly with ISO/IECJTC1SC7 discuss a HCD and quality related standard focused to user requirements (ISO CD25065). In this standard, "demand" is clearly positioned in development process.

References

1. ISO9241-210: Human-centred design for interactive systems (2010)
2. Tanikawa, Y., Suzuki, H., Kato, H., Fukuzumi, S.: Problems in usability improvement activity by software engineers - consideration through verification experiments for human-centered design process support environment. In: Yamamoto, S. (ed.) HCI 2014, Part I. LNCS, vol. 8521, pp. 641–651. Springer, Heidelberg (2014)
3. ISO/IEC 25062: Software engineering.— Software product Quality Requirements and Evaluation (SQuaRE) .— Common Industry Format (CIF) for usability Test Reports (2005)
4. Roto, V., Law, E., Vermeeren, A., Hoonhout, J. (ed.): Use Experience White Paper - Bringing clarity to the concept of user experience, Result from Dagstuhl Seminar on Demarcating User Experience, September 15–18, 2010, pp. 1–12 (2010)
5. Nonaka, M., Azuma, M.: Systems and Software Quality: 5. Non-Functional Software Requirements Definitions: For Creating Quality Software, Information processing society of Japan, vol. 55, No.1, pp. 31–37, January 2014 (in Japanese)
6. ISO/IEC25030: Software engineering -Software product Quality Requirements and Evaluation (SQuaRE) –Quality Requirements (2007)

7. IEEE CS, ACM: Software Engineering 2004: Curriculum Guidelines for Undergraduate Degree Programs in Software Engineering (2004). http://sites.computer.org/ccse/
8. V-Modell XT (2005). http://www.v-modell-xt.de
9. ISO/IEC 25010: Software engineering. -Software product Quality Requirements and Evaluation (SQuaRE) - System and software quality models (2011)
10. Okubo, R., Tanikawa, Y., Fukuzumi, S.: Proposal for a method to clarify customer needs using HI (Human Interface) patterns. In: Proceedings of the 5th International Conference on Applied Human Factors and Ergonomics AHFE 2014, pp. 4097–4108 (2014)
11. ISO/IEC25022: Systems and software engineering – Systems and software Quality Requirements and Evaluation (SQuaRE) – Measurement of quality in use (2016)
12. ISO/IEC25063: Systems and software engineering – Systems and software Quality Requirements and Evaluation (SQuaRE) – Context of use description (2014)

Product Awareness Between Consumers and Designers – A Family Dining Table Design as Example

Ming-Hsuan Hsieh[1(✉)] and Chia-Ling Chang[2]

[1] Department of Computer-Aided Industrial Design,
Overseas Chinese University, Taichung, Taiwan, ROC
mhhsieh@ocu.edu.tw
[2] Department of Education Industry and Digital Media,
National Taitung University, Taitung, Taiwan, ROC
idit007@gmail.com

Abstract. Recently, consumer-oriented design has become the key for product development. However, due to a lack of effective consumer opinions by designers, leading designers and consumers have differences on product awareness. This study is based on the Cognitive Structure Model, to understand the differences between designers and consumers based on the family dining table. The purpose is to aid designers in obtaining an understanding and consensus with the consumer for their products. This research used Mind Mapping to work with Means-End Chain to perform designers' cognitive approach followed by an implication matrix of consumer awareness survey. The results can be used to divide the designers and consumers awareness into four parts: "positive consensus", "negative consensus", "designer subjective perception" and "subjective perception of consumers". Finally, there is a streamlined Hierarchical Value Map to show the product design guidelines. The family dining table design focused on the steps of product design ideas. The focus is to assist the industry to accurately grasp the designer and consumer awareness of consensus and to work out effective product development direction.

Keywords: Consumer-oriented design · Cognitive similarities and differences · Family dining table · Design guidelines

1 Introduction

Nowadays, in order to meet the varieties needs of consumers, many manufacturers use consumer-oriented design approach to product development. However, because of different lifestyles and values differences between designers and consumers, resulting in product implied meaning is not exactly the same. The significance of the product come from cognition, it is precisely consumers to buy or not (Zanoli and Naspetti 2002; Kapoor and Kulshrestha 2009). Consumer-oriented design is not only facing designers and consumers cognitive difference (Chuang et al. 2001), but also the majority of consumers are unable to clearly and fully describe their needs, leads designers encounter difficulty truly understand their preferences (Chang et al. 2006). Because of

© Springer International Publishing Switzerland 2016
S. Yamamoto (Ed.): HIMI 2016, Part I, LNCS 9734, pp. 421–432, 2016.
DOI: 10.1007/978-3-319-40349-6_40

expression of the views of consumers out there are limits, during consumer research, it is necessary to focus on how to form the understanding of consumer demand, as well as more depth cognitive similarities and differences between designers and consumers.

Kleef et al. (2005) pointed out that the new product development process is divided into opportunity identification, development, optimization and launch. Opportunity identification is the involvement of consumers in unmet needs. It will strongly influence the quality of new product development. Alam and Perry (2002) analysis of consumer the order of importance in various stages of development of new products. Idea generation ranked first, it showed the impact of consumer opinion in this stage. If manufactures can lead consumers' opinions and views in early stages of idea generation, to eliminate the idea is not feasible, it will reduce unnecessary losses.

Although awareness and consumer demand in the product development process is important, but for designers, there are still big differences between consumer awareness, on the major factors causing differences are as follows: (i) Through designers' traditional brain storm, it can only reflect the designer's personal knowledge. It would be too subjective. (ii) When the consumers involved in the design, subject to the limited experience and knowledge of the conditions, it is difficult to have a breakthrough innovation. Therefore, designers should not be limited in the comments made by the consumer directly, but must further guide consumers into unfamiliar or unknown field. (iii) The interpretation of designers sometimes does not meet the same as consumers. It will help filter product ideas by clearly understanding of differences between the two sides on the type of the product awareness. This study will present "Family dinning table" as the theme, the use of Cognitive Structure Model (Hsieh et al. 2013) allows designers product ideas generation obtain the agreement between consumers, to help work out the correct design guidelines.

2   Literature Review

In Sects. 2.1 and 2.2, we will review Mind Mapping and Means-End Chain, through these combinations to perform designers' cognition. Section 2.3 is introduction of Implication Matrix, through this matrix to quantify the association between two elements among respondents, in order to obtain consumer awareness.

2.1   Mind Mapping

When the design theme is determined, designers can be carried out to develop new product ideas using mind mapping. When drawing a Mind Map, there are several tips (Gelb 1998; Buzan 2002; Reed 2005): (i) Text or image rendering central of the paper, then extending the trunks. (ii) On an extension of the branch, just write a keyword, any ideas are free to play, uncritical. (iii) All of the branches of each node to form a structure, trunks and branches are in different thickness. (iv) There are two ways of brain storming, Brain Flow is a keyword to associate another keyword, then think of the next keyword; and Brain Bloom is a keyword to associate many keywords. (v) Meet thoughts blank, a few lines may be added after the keyword, it will induce brain tries to fill it. (vi) BOIs (Basic Ordering Ideas) is principle classification through thinking system. Mind Mapping is a release of brain potential graphical tool that can be administered in accordance with the hierarchical classification and association between them conceived to help designers with creative ideas lead to unlimited and reorganized in ideas of creating new thinking structure.

2.2 Means-End Chain

Means-End Chain proposes product is stored hierarchically in memory of consumers, as product attributes, consumption consequences and personal values in linkage, if an attribute links to more abstract values, then this property is important (Chiu 2005; Ferran and Grunert 2007; Klenosky 2002). "Attribute" is the characteristic of the product or service physical or observable; "consequence" is the benefits or consequences by using the product obtained; value means a highly abstract motivation to guide usage behavior. Means-End Chain is a good way to find what makes product or service more important, to help investigators appreciate the experience and knowledge of consumers. This method presents the extracts of cognitive structures, an one-to-one linear type links cognitive concepts (Voss et al. 2007). Details from a low level attribute to high level value of the process, explain the motivations of consumers' view, the product information is interpreted and what elements are important to know.

2.3 Implication Matrix

Rekom and Wierenga (2002) considers the Implication Matrix as a link between the concepts, the matrix of rows and columns, are classified as the elements, row-items present means and column-items present ends. Implication Matrix is found as a gap of qualitative and quantitative findings, as to quantify the relationship between the elements, the higher values between the two elements, the stronger connection. (Leão and Mello 2007; Veludo-de-Oliveira et al. 2006). With statistics all respondents mentioned a number of times between two elements of links, it can aggregate implication Matrix (Phillips and Reynolds 2009).

3 Cognitive Structure Model Process

Section 3.1 use Mind Mapping to present a product awareness of a designer. These data will be used to guide the consumer as well. Section 3.2 Applying Implication Matrix, so that consumers will pairwise elements rated hierarchically in attributes-consequences and consequences-values. It makes consumers fully express their opinions. Section 3.3 the distinction between the designer and the consumer awareness of the similarities and differences, to obtain the cognitive consensus as to develop products based on the design guidelines.

3.1 Development of Designers' Cognition

Establish an effective BIOs (Basic Ordering Ideas) is an important key to draw drawn a mind map. It will allow ideas to go along with others to organize the structure. This method is a keyword association process, broken down into several categories or hierarchically stages, so that the brain's Reflections in a natural structure, which is the main idea after the presentation, followed by secondary ideas which quickly and easily promote the formation. This study applied BOIs Means-End Chain architecture, from inside out for the values-consequences-attributes, the idea for the hierarchical classification, as shown in Fig. 1. Mind Mapping in depicting the relationship between keywords and description, will thin continually, screening and understand information and to support the decision of affection.

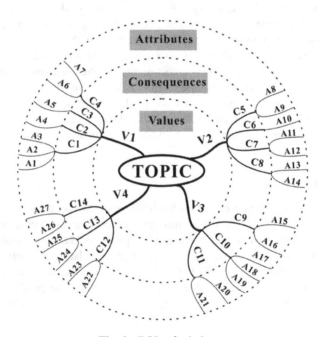

Fig. 1. BOIs of mind map

3.2 Understand Consumer Perceptions

Attributes, consequences, values generated from mind maps for the development of attributes-consequences (AC) consequences-values (CV) basic on questionnaires of Implication Matrix. In other words, to investigate the use of a these elements of consumer awareness by Implication Matrix, whereby to guide consumers connect important elements. This study collected Scale questionnaire, directly from respondents rating elements pairwise. Figure 2 depicts the form of AC Implication Matrix, as well as CV Implication Matrix. Application of Implication Matrix contains understanding of consumer awareness, to realize the knowledge of product cognitive structure from Consumers.

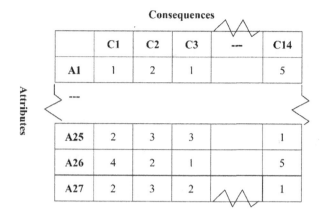

Fig. 2. Form of AC Implication Matrix

3.3   Consumer and Designers Cognition

Designers and consumers will have the same perception and differences in two types, each of which may be divided into two zones, a total of four blocks as Fig. 3. In Fig. 3, $A_i - C_j$ presents a attributes–consequences link, $A_i \nleftrightarrow C_j$ presents no any attributes–consequences link; $C_j - V_k$ presents a consequences–values link, $C_j \nleftrightarrow V_k$ presents no any consequences–values link. The description of these four blocks as follow:

(i)   Designer and Consumer have same cognition (D = C): same cognition two types, one is the designers and consumers are considered this linked $(A_i - C_j; C_j - V_k)$ as a "positive consensus"; the other One is that the designers and consumers are no such link $(A_i \nleftrightarrow C_j; C_j \nleftrightarrow V_k)$ as a "negative consensus".

(ii) Designer and Consumer have different cognition (D ≠ C): there are two different types of cognition, one is that the designers have this link $(A_i - C_j; C_j - V_k)$, and consumers thinks that no such link $(A_i \nleftrightarrow C_j; C_j \nleftrightarrow V_k)$, as "designers subjective"; another One is that the designer has no such link $(A_i - C_j; C_j - V_k)$; but the consumers think there is this link $(A_i - C_j; C_j - V_k)$, as "consumers subjective".

Designers and consumers are both considered this link $(A_i - C_j; C_j - V_k)$. This block represents designers and consumers to reach a consensus on cognition, which can be used as preliminary product design guidelines. In order to present this Means-End Chain of this block clearer, we will adopt Hierarchical Value Map (HVM). HVM Construction is to contain the resulting of Implication Matrix data analysis. It represents the majority of people in most of the ideas most of the time to help researchers to understand the current market environment.

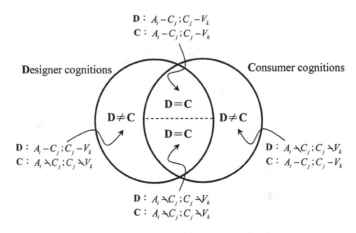

Fig. 3. Consumer and designers cognition

4 Practice

In this chapter will use "parent-child table design" as an example. At first, the designer followed mind mapping tips, conduct creative thinking, to produce 20 "attributes", 10 "consequences" and 4 "values". Then through Implication Matrix integrate 82 respondents are among the elements associated with the score to clarify designers and consumers in the "parent-child table Design" the similarities and differences cognition link. Win the final with streamlined HVM performance "positive consensus" from designers and consumer awareness. In this block obtain the important link as a product design guidelines.

4.1 Designers to Mind Mapping New Product

Used by three designers with mind mapping brainstorming session, which lasted for 1 h. Mind Mapping values for trunk generate levels of "fun", "inspiration", "safety" and "Memories", a branch of extending obtained consequences, then the next layer of branches extending attributes. Designers take their experience and knowledge, combined with keyword stratification and classification principles, creative thinking process to clarify the designer of "parent-child table" cognitive structure, the results as shown in Fig. 4.

4.2 Implication Matrix Consumer Awareness Survey

In Fig. 4, the elements can be used to construct AC and CV Implication Matrix. Attributes are listed in the rows, and consequences are listed in columns, it produces an AC matrix. In matrix respondents answer preview all attributes and the connection of consequences. 5-point rating scale, a very strong association 5 points, strongly associated with 4 points, 3 points ordinary, little relevance 2 points, 1 point associates.

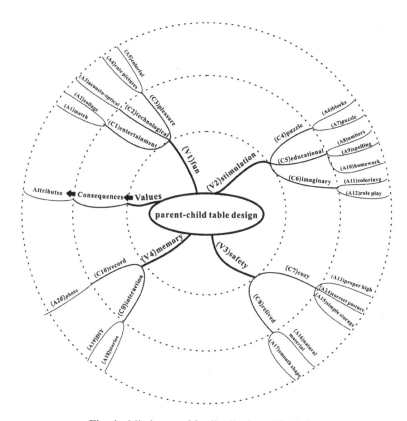

Fig. 4. Mind map of family dinning table design

The same, CV matrix lists the consequences and values. Questionnaire (contains AC and CV scales) distributed a total of 101 respondents, the final sample is 82, respond to 81 %.

An aggregate Implication Matrix was then produced based on the data provided by the 82 respondents, as shown in Table 1. The formula for calculating the association weight of each cell in the aggregate AC Implication Matrix is as follows:

$$\overline{A_i C_j} = \frac{\sum_{(i,j)=(1,1)}^{(37,18)} A_i C_j}{N} \tag{1}$$

where i is the number of attributes, ranging from 1 to 37; j the number of consequences, ranging from 1 to 18; N the number of respondents, which value is 92; $\overline{A_i C_j}$ the average association rating between the attribute i and the consequence j, ranging from 1 to 5.

In addition, Table 1 sums up all the elements' "mean ratings" $(\overline{X}A_i)$ to further calculate the intensity of each linkage, which is discussed in more detail in the next section.

Table 1. AC Implication Matrix summary of family dinning table design

Attributes	Consequences										$\overline{X}A_i$ (To)
	C1	C2	C3	C4	C5	C6	C7	C8	C9	C10	
A1	4.11	2.53	3.03	3.75	3.77	3.25	2.65	1.63	2.94	2.11	2.98
A2	3.54	2.34	3.34	3.37	3.40	3.62	2.43	1.60	3.19	2.49	2.93
A3	3.90	3.39	3.66	2.25	2.97	2.54	2.88	1.76	3.75	2.37	2.95
A4	3.52	1.88	4.00	2.35	3.15	2.93	2.34	2.11	3.37	1.87	2.75
A5	3.30	2.37	3.85	2.77	3.27	3.34	3.02	2.39	3.09	1.98	2.94
A6	3.88	2.78	3.44	4.21	3.82	3.67	2.93	2.52	3.63	2.46	3.33
A7	3.69	1.90	3.16	3.83	3.50	3.06	2.75	2.40	3.29	2.04	2.96
A8	1.74	2.23	2.29	3.71	4.10	2.35	1.94	2.19	2.22	2.28	2.51
A9	3.16	2.56	2.94	3.49	3.95	2.62	2.21	2.73	2.71	2.51	2.89
A10	1.58	1.74	1.53	3.08	4.26	1.78	1.67	3.71	2.66	2.79	2.48
A11	3.79	1.68	3.78	3.29	3.11	4.18	3.36	2.31	3.89	3.73	3.31
A12	3.86	3.01	3.97	2.94	3.64	4.06	2.94	2.44	3.84	3.03	3.37
A13	1.55	1.52	3.26	1.55	2.03	1.56	3.89	3.47	2.78	1.54	2.32
A14	1.62	1.61	2.99	1.52	2.87	1.52	3.47	3.82	2.48	1.65	2.36
A15	1.67	1.56	3.48	1.66	3.31	2.13	4.08	3.33	2.80	1.59	2.56
A16	1.80	1.69	3.39	1.61	2.73	1.60	3.63	4.23	1.71	1.72	2.41
A17	2.45	1.82	3.33	1.63	2.12	1.50	3.24	3.92	1.98	1.61	2.36
A18	3.42	2.05	3.47	3.09	3.79	3.11	2.91	2.75	4.02	2.39	3.10
A19	3.95	2.73	3.93	3.48	3.96	3.84	3.49	3.00	3.51	3.26	3.52
A20	3.57	2.98	3.86	2.83	2.90	3.13	3.10	3.14	4.01	4.14	3.37
$\overline{X}C_j$ (From)	3.01	2.22	3.34	2.82	3.33	2.79	2.95	2.77	3.09	2.38	

To conserve space, we use code number to represent each attribute and consequence.

$$\overline{X}A_i = \frac{\sum_{j=1}^{18} \overline{A_i C_j}}{n} \tag{2}$$

where i is the number of attributes, ranging from 1 to 37; j the number of consequences, ranging from 1 to 18; n the total number of consequences, with the value of 18; $\overline{X}A_i$ is the mean association rating of attribute i, ranging from 1 to 5.

4.3 Using Streamlined Hierarchical Value Map Develop Product Design Guidelines

Figure 4 Mind Mapping has a link, in Tables 1 and 2 indicates shaded by representatives designer's own awareness. On the other hand, referring to Nielsen (1993) mentioned five-point scale of the average (mean) if greater than 3.60 (in Tables 1 and 2 are shown in bold), in this question is "positive" of the score, which means consumers believe that two elements of the association is significant. Both shaded and bolded link made both designers and consumers "positive consensus"; just having shade without bold means "designer subjective"; only bold and no shaded stands for "consumer subjective"; neither shaded nor bold represents designers and consumers to achieve "negative consensus", the result is divided four blocks as shown in Fig. 5. Figure 5 to i.

Table 2. CV Implication Matrix summary of family dinning table design

Consequences	Values				
	V1	V2	V3	V4	$\overline{X}C_j$ (To)
C1	4.25	2.68	1.83	3.20	2.99
C2	3.40	2.73	2.05	2.31	2.62
C3	4.02	2.51	3.01	3.44	3.25
C4	3.84	4.18	1.99	2.99	3.25
C5	3.13	4.04	2.39	2.61	3.04
C6	3.75	3.93	2.00	2.74	3.11
C7	2.63	1.94	3.48	3.04	2.77
C8	2.01	1.82	4.08	2.07	2.50
C9	3.91	3.77	3.66	3.79	3.78
C10	3.34	2.85	2.94	4.11	3.31
$\overline{X}V_k$ (From)	3.43	3.05	2.74	3.03	

To conserve space, we use code number to represent each consequence and value.

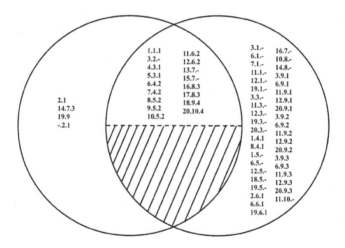

Fig. 5. Designers and consumer awareness of similarities and differences (Fig. symbol "-" represents the missing)

j.k Representative $A_i - C_j - V_k$ link, for example 8.5.2 representative the link of A8-C5-V2. In the block of Negative consensus contains too many links without valuable discussions, we tried to neglect with a slash.

Figure 5 in the "positive consensus" block, there are a total of 14 full Means-End Chain, and three incomplete. The strength of each link can be found in Tables 1 and 2, to link aggregation in each From and To values. For example: A7 → C4 → V2, A7 From a value of 0, To is 2.96; C4 elements From a value of 2.82, To value of 3.25; V2 elements From a value of 3.05, To a value of 0, therefore, total link strength:

$$(0 + 2.96) + (2.82 + 3.25) + (3.05 + 0) = 12.08$$

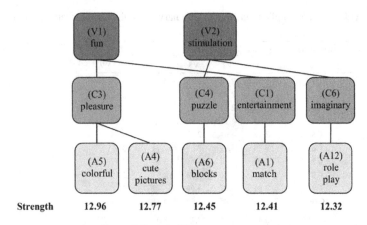

Fig. 6. Streamlined hierarchical value map

It will be to complex and can't really identify the importance of the links if we put all elements in "positive consensus" block. Therefore, designers need to follow their own demand to find out the strength of several former links to define design guidelines. Figure 6 is drawn out the top five of the links, the chain A5 → C3 → V1 is the most critical 1, link strength is 12.96, it can be called critical path, describes the respondents emphasis on "rich colors" attribute, hope to create "pleasure" through this property, and make "fun" between parents and children.

5 Conclusion

There were many methods to elicit consumer demand, but these methods are mostly for processing and interface features of the decision. Designers and consumers understand the differences in cognitive structure and factors, and then guide the design approach is a relatively less explored area of research. Therefore, this study focuses on the application of mind mapping to develop the concept of family dinning table. The Implication Matrix reads the respondents on a clear definition of designer and consumer awareness of similarities and differences, in order to solve the problems of the designer in the conceptual stage which is easy encounter the ideas are too idealistic and uncertainly consumer demand.

From this study "Family dinning table Design" during the practical exercises in the application of cognitive structure can be found the following advantages. (i) The consumer can effectively participate in the design. Consumers in the product development process plays an important role, their views can be understood sooner the better, because the designers can eliminate their own subjective concept. (ii) To divide the similarities and differences between designers and consumer awareness. It's not only understand the cognitive difference, but also to help designers more objective understanding of their own ideas positioning in the consumer market. (iii) Design guidelines have drawn statistical basis. Through investigation and analysis contains in a Implication Matrix by the consumer directly score the elements of connected level, divided by four blocks, then from the "positive consensus" block calculates the most important links. It can assist the designer more clear and easily to define design guidelines. In this case only take "positive consensus" account. To use this block as a product design guidelines, you can try to discuss "designer subjective" and "subjective consumers" in the future, in order to prevent ignore potential product concept. In summary, this study cognitive structure mode program that allows designers to brainstorm mind mapping to present a perception of a product. Contains Implication Matrix for consumer surveys to clarify the difference between the designer and the consumer's cognitive structure. Streamlined HVM can see important links, to help designers to have an effective product design guideline.

Acknowledgement. This study was supported by the Ministry of Science and Technology of the Republic of China (MOST 104-2221-E-240-001).

References

Alam, I., Perry, C.: A customer-oriented new service development process. J. Serv. Mark. **16**(6), 515–534 (2002)

Buzan, T.: How to Mind Map: The Ultimate Thinking Tool That Will Change Your Life. Thorsons, London (2002)

Chang, H.C., Lai, H.H., Chang, Y.M.: Expression modes used by consumers in conveying desire for product form: a case study of a car. Int. J. Ind. Ergon. **36**(1), 3–10 (2006)

Chiu, C.-M.: Applying means-end chain theory to eliciting system requirements and understanding users perceptual orientations. Inf. Manag. **42**(3), 455–468 (2005)

Chuang, M.C., Chang, C.C., Hsu, S.H.: Perceptual factors underlying user preferences toward product form of mobile phones. Int. J. Ind. Ergon. **27**(4), 247–258 (2001)

Ferran, Fd, Grunert, K.G.: French fair trade coffee buyers' purchasing motives: an exploratory study using means-end chains analysis. Food Qual. Prefer. **18**(2), 218–229 (2007)

Gelb, M.J.: How to Think Like Leonardo da Vinci: Seven Steps to Genius Every Day. Delacorte, New York (1998)

Hsieh, M.-H., Huang, C.-Y., Luh, D.-B., Liu, S.-F., Ma, C.-H.: An application of implementing a cognitive structure model to obtain consensus from consumers. Int. J. Des. **7**(2), 53–65 (2013)

Kapoor, A., Kulshrestha, C.: Consumers' perceptions: an analytical study of influence of consumer emotions and response. Direct Mark. Int. J. **3**(3), 186–202 (2009)

van Kleef, E., van Trijp, H.C.M., Luning, P.: Consumer research in the early stages of new product development: a critical review of methods and techniques. Food Qual. Prefer. **16**(3), 181–201 (2005)

Klenosky, D.B.: The "pull" of tourism destinations: a means-end investigation. J. Travel Res. **40**(4), 385–395 (2002)

de Souza Leão, A.L.M., Benício de Mello, S.C.: The means-end approach to understanding customer values of a on-line newspaper. Braz. Adm. Rev. **4**(1), 1–20 (2007)

Nielsen, J.: Usability Engineering. Academic, Boston (1993)

Phillips, J.M., Reynolds, T.J.: A hard look at hard laddering: a comparison of studies examining the hierarchical structure of means-end theory. Qual. Mark. Res. Int. J. **12**(1), 83–99 (2009)

Reed, W.: Mind Mapping for Memory and Creativity. Forest, Tokyo (2005). (in Japanese)

Van Rekom, J., Wierenga, B.: Means-end Relations: Hierarchies or Networks? An inquiry into the (a) Symmetry of Means-end Relations. ERIM Report Series Research in Management, Erasmus University, Rotterdam (2002)

Veludo-de-Oliveira, T.M., Ikeda, A.A., Campomar, M.C.: Discussing laddering application by the means-end chain theory. Qual. Rep. **11**(4), 626–642 (2006)

Voss, R., Gruber, T., Szmigin, I.: Service quality in higher education: the role of student expectations. J. Bus. Res. **60**(9), 949–959 (2007)

Zanoli, R., Naspetti, S.: Consumer motivations in the purchase of organic food: a means-end approach. Br. Food J. **104**(8), 643–653 (2002)

User Interface Developing Framework for Engineers

Hiroyuki Miki[1(✉)], Kunikazu Suzuki[2], and Tsuyoshi Suzuki[2]

[1] Oki Consulting Solutions Co., Ltd., Tokyo, Japan
hmiki@cf.netyou.jp
[2] Oki Electric Ind. Co., Ltd., Saitama, Japan

Abstract. These days, web applications are widely used on not only desktop PCs but also tablet PCs and smartphones. For developers of web applications, productivity and effectiveness (usability and accessibility) are big issues to respond to customers' high expectations for web applications. This paper focuses on the development of business use web by system engineers and programmers, and proposes a design framework featuring usability/accessibility guidelines, UI (design) patterns, which connect usability/accessibility guidelines, sample programs, and some other components. The framework aims at high flexibility, productivity, and effectiveness (usability and accessibility) for various developments of business use webs.

Keywords: User interface · Development framework · User experience · Usability · Accessibility · Human-centered design

1 Introduction

These days, web applications are widely used on not only desktop PCs but also tablet PCs and smartphones. This trend has been encouraging advances of their User Interfaces (UIs) dramatically such as multi touch interfaces.

For developers of web applications, productivity and effectiveness (usability and accessibility) (Fig. 1) are big issues to respond to customers' high expectations for web applications [10]. Since a lot of development efforts are spent to the development of UIs, they are big concerns for the developers.

There are largely three ways to develop UIs of web sites which take usability and accessibility into account. First is Human-Centered Design [5, 9, 10] in which multi-disciplinary team members consisting of usability professionals, system engineers, web designers, and programmers, work together to achieve high usability and accessibility. In this case, since many people join the development, achieving high productivity is not easy. Second is a developer centered approach. Skilled system engineers and programmers refer to usability and accessibility guidelines/style guides [8] and/or use some tool such as Content Management System (CMS) [11] to create web sites. Because of low availability of usability professionals and/or severe budget, this second approach is also popular these days. Third is between the first and the second. Skilled system engineers and programmers consult usability professionals and/or web designers and use some tool to develop web sites.

© Springer International Publishing Switzerland 2016
S. Yamamoto (Ed.): HIMI 2016, Part I, LNCS 9734, pp. 433–441, 2016.
DOI: 10.1007/978-3-319-40349-6_41

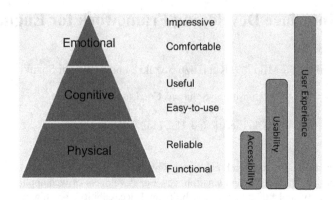

Fig. 1. Effectiveness: usability and accessibility [10]

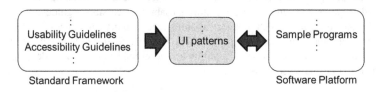

Fig. 2. Productivity: UI (design) patterns and sample programs

As far as business use webs (business webs in short) such as for application, reporting, procurement, and so on, are concerned, since they tend to have relatively fixed task sequences and allow modest GUI parts and screen designs, the second and the third approach have been taken in many cases. However, productivity and effectiveness (usability and accessibility) of the development are not easy to handle. For example, Japanese committee of e-government web systems reported many problems of UIs [2] and published the standard guidelines for national information systems [6] to reduce the problems.

This paper focuses on the second way for the development of business use web, and proposes a design framework featuring usability/accessibility guidelines, UI (design) patterns, which connect usability/accessibility guidelines, sample programs (Fig. 2), and some other components (Fig. 3). UI patterns are a collection of typical templates of screens which are accompanied by usability/accessibility notes [13]. The framework aims at high flexibility, productivity, and effectiveness (usability and accessibility) for various developments of business use webs.

In the following, after briefly explaining common methods and this approach in the section two, the proposed framework is explained in the section three followed by future plan and conclusion.

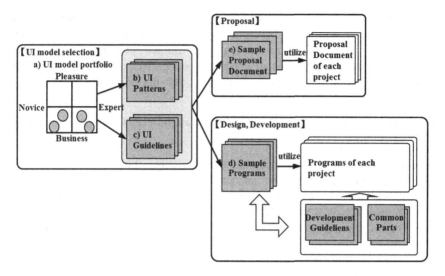

Fig. 3. Overview of the proposed framework

2   Approach to Productivity and Effectiveness (Usability and Accessibility)

2.1   Common Methods

Among others, four common methods are explained below.

- Guidelines on usability and accessibility
- Style guide
- UI (design) patterns
- Content Management System

Firstly, guidelines on usability and accessibility have been used for a long time [1, 3, 4, 7]. Such guidelines are sometimes provided with coding guidelines to help software engineers implement the guidelines correctly. Since the guidelines are general enough to support a wide variety of applications, they tend to require basic knowledge of usability and accessibility, and trainings to be useful for software engineers. As a result, they are not used well by software engineers in general.

Secondly, style guide is a material which explains details of specific screen designs. Usability/accessibility guidelines are often referred to explain details of design decisions. It is usually used at a renewal of web sites. Although it is also useful to promote third party's' development of related web sites [8], it tends to be too specific to the original web site.

Thirdly, UI patterns are a collection of typical templates of screens which are accompanied by usability/accessibility notes [13]. Since UI patters are more general than style guides and can be basis of CMS, they are flexible for various uses. Because of its flexibility, this paper uses UI patterns.

Fourthly, CMS is a system used to create and manage the content of a web site. Since there are different kinds of web platforms such as PCs, tablet PCs, and smartphones, CMS is more used to easily create and manage different platforms by one system. However, as far as business webs are concerned, since specifications are decided by a orderer, flexibility of CMS sometimes falls short of the development.

2.2   This Approach: UI Patterns to Bridge a Gap Between Guidelines and Sample Programs

Before starting this project, there were standard guidelines of basic usability and accessibility to support system engineers, and a web application framework to support software programmers in the company (Oki Electric). Since accessibility standards (JIS X 8341-3 [7] based on W3C WCAG2.0 [12], and so on) are not easy to understand for system engineers and programmers, a document which explains them was created by usability professionals to support developments of government-related web sites. Although the document has been used well, usability issues and the productivity issue have not been handled systematically.

This project started to handle usability issues and the productivity issue well in addition to accessibility issues. To start this project, basic policy was created by core members.

1. Since actual needs of system engineers and programmers are not well articulated, initial new materials such as UI patterns and sample programs should be small enough to get more feedbacks from them. This process should be repeated until the materials obtain good appraisals from them. More advanced and expensive framework such as CMS is considered as a future issue.

Based on this policy, multidisciplinary team consisting of usability professionals, web designers, software platform engineers, and system engineers started Human-Centered process. Initial interviews of related engineers revealed the following opinions.

- Agree that productivity and effectiveness (usability and accessibility) have priority to cope with.
- Need several sets of UI patterns if possible.
- Concerned with too modest aesthetics of UI patterns
- Need an up-to-date framework.
- Need support to use the framework.

Related engineers recognized the issues and they seemed to come up with reasonable requests that well reflect their past experiences. Of special note was their concern on flexibility.

Getting the feedbacks, the following policies were added to the basic policy.

2. In order for both system engineers and programmers to easily understand both UI patterns and sample programs, same examples of the same web site should be used in UI patterns and sample programs.

3. All of UI patterns, sample programs and examples should be more aesthetically pleasing than modest business web sites for a wide applicability. For this reason, travel reservation webs are adopted to explain UI patterns and sample programs.

3 Proposed Framework

Figure 3 shows the overview of the proposed framework. It consists of (a) UI portfolio, (b) UI patterns, (c) UI guidelines, (d) sample programs, and (e) sample proposal document. Components (a), (b), and (d) are main parts of the framework, which are supposed to be used alphabetically. Components (b) and (d) use the same examples of the travel webs. On the other hand, other components, (c) and (e), are supposed to be used only when necessary. Component (c) should be referred when the orderer requires high quality of usability/accessibility since it is a detailed material of usability/accessibility. Component (e) should be referred when to create and submit a proposal document at a competitive bidding. This framework will continuously support the activities from a proposal till an implementation in order to reduce usability and reduce development costs.

Throughout the framework, usability points are categorized into five aspects based on the Japanese electrical government guidance: (1) page layout and visual design, (2) ease and understandability of use, (3) easiness to understand instructions and the state, (4) error prevention and the handling, (5) help and support.

Whilst, accessibility points are categorized into nine aspects: (1) compliance to the standards such as JIS X 8341 series, (2) easiness to understand instructions and the state, (3) localization, (4) alternate image information, (5) indexing, (6) keyboard operation and the focus, (7) multimedia, (8) prevention of time change expression and bouts attack, (9) navigation.

Five components of the framework are explained hereafter.

3.1 UI Portfolio

UI model portfolio is provided as an initial document for the system engineer to talk with the orderer about what kinds and tastes of web site the orderer wants to be constructed. It consists of two axes with four quadrants; vertical axe is for pleasure or business use, horizontal one is for novice or expert use. With screen images of four quadrants, the system engineer can articulate orderer's potential requirements.

3.2 UI Guidelines

UI guidelines consist of updated usability guidelines and accessibility guidelines. The usability guidelines, which consist of over two hundreds of well-known guidelines, are sorted by added degree of importance to easily find important ones (Table 1). The accessibility guidelines consists of JIS X 8341-3 [7] and its descriptions. UI guidelines should be referred when the orderer requires higher quality of usability/accessibility than those written in UI patterns since they are detailed materials of usability/accessibility.

Table 1. UI guidelines

Japanese e-government	title	guidelines	Score
3)understandability of instruction and status	form and data input	Forms pre-warn the user if external information is needed for completion (e.g. a passport number)	6
		The site makes it easy to correct errors (e.g. when a form is incomplete, positioning the cursor at the location where correction is required)	6
		Fields in data entry screens contain default values when appropriate and show the structure of the data and the field length	5
		Forms allow users to stay with a single interaction method for as long as possible (i.e. users do not need to make numerous shifts from keyboard to mouse to keyboard).	5
		Forms are validated before the form is submitted	4

3.3 UI Patterns

In general, business use webs include tasks to be completed which consist of step by step procedures. Compared with general use webs, they consist of stereotypical screens such as login screen and form-filling screen.

UI patterns provide six basic screen patterns: portal, log-in, menu, search condition, search result, and form-filling input (Table 2, Fig. 4). For system engineers, actual screen designs based on UI patterns will contribute to efficient and effective clarification of orderer's requirements through discussions.

Table 2. Six UI patterns of business use webs

#	UI pattern	Description
1	Portal	Providing various entrances to the user to respond to users' various needs.
2	Log-in	Accepting information for log-in from the user.
3	Menu	Showing menu items and accepting menu selection by the user.
4	Search condition	Accepting search conditions from the user.
5	Search result	Showing search results and accepting modifications of search conditions.
6	Form-filling input	Accepting various inputs from the user

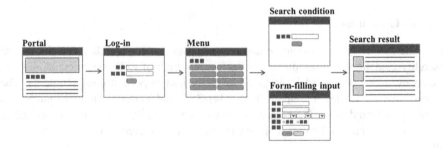

Fig. 4. Relations of six UI patterns of business use webs

In order to create actual screen design based on UI patterns, examples will serve as useful references. Considering the tendency that recent business use webs are more like general use webs such as Electric Commerce web sites, examples of travel reservation webs are added to UI patters (Fig. 5). Since they includes all of six patterns and are more aesthetic than conventional business use webs which use modest GUI parts of operating systems, they will serve as useful references.

Figure 5 shows an example of log-in screen where the following four points are explained as special notes.

- Only the minimum necessary elements should be used in order for the user to go through it effortlessly.
- Appropriate guidance should be provided to non-registered users as well as registered users.
- First input field should be focused to allow instant input by the user.
- Guidance for the user who forgets password should be provided.

Since it was pointed out in the initial interviews that system engineers tend to focus on details of each screen too early before the overall design, the overall design is explained before the explanations of six UI patterns.

3.4 Sample Program

Sample programs are html and Java programs of the examples of six UI patters. Programmers can more understand usability/accessibility points written in UI patters through reading codes of sample programs.

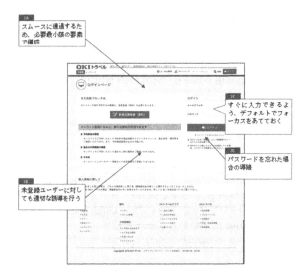

Fig. 5. Example of log-in screen

3.5 Sample Proposal Document

This document provides a typical example of the proposal document of business use webs which describes usability/accessibility well. It includes (1) requirements definitions (methods to ensure good usability/accessibility, methods to minimize variance, and so on), (2) skill requirements, and (3) development process. It is provided to reduce the work of creating a proposal document.

4 Future Plan

Until now, except for (a) UI portfolio, the first versions of five components have been created: (b) UI patterns, (c) UI guidelines, (d) sample programs, and (e) sample proposal document. Second interview of these components will be conducted within a month. After the second interview, the five components will be modified for a trial use.

After the trial, productivity and effectiveness (usability and accessibility) will be examined again by the interview. Considering its results, the entire framework will be reconsidered for better use.

5 Concluding Remarks

This paper focused on the development of business use web by system engineers and programmers, and proposed a design framework featuring usability/accessibility guidelines, UI (design) patterns, which connect usability/accessibility guidelines, sample programs, and some other components. The framework aimed at high flexibility, productivity, and effectiveness (usability and accessibility) for various developments of business use webs.

Although this framework was created based on initial interviews of related engineers, the choices of the framework await engineers' evaluation. Engineers will simulate their usage of this framework and will come up with both advantages and disadvantages of it.

References

1. Apple: iOS human interface guidelines. https://developer.apple.com/library/ios/documentation/UserExperience/Conceptual/MobileHIG/
2. Committee of e-government guideline: usability survey of e-government, 20 April 2009. https://www.kantei.go.jp/jp/singi/it2/guide/kaisai_h20/dai2/sankousiryou2.pdf
3. Hartson, R., Pyla, P.S.: The UX Book: Process and Guidelines for Ensuring a Quality User Experience. Morgan Kaufmann, San Francisco (2012)
4. ISO 9241-110: Ergonomics of human-system interaction – Part 110: Dialogue principles. ISO (2006)
5. ISO 9241-210: Ergonomics of human-system interaction – Part 210: Human-centred design for interactive systems. ISO (2010)
6. IT promotion office of Japan: Standard guidelines on national information systems. Japanese Government (2014)

7. JIS X 8341-3: Guidelines for older persons and persons with disabilities-Information and communications equipment, software and services-Part 3: Web content. JIS (2010)
8. Knight, A.: Apple, Google & Starbucks: Inside the Web Design Style Guides of 10 Famous Companies. http://blog.hubspot.com/marketing/web-design-style-guide-examples
9. Kohno, I., Fujii, H.: User-centered approach for NEC product development. In: Stephanidis, C. (ed.) Posters, Part I, HCII 2011. CCIS, vol. 173, pp. 48–52. Springer, Heidelberg (2011)
10. Miki, H.: User experience evaluation framework for human-centered design. In: Yamamoto, S. (ed.) HCI 2014, Part I. LNCS, vol. 8521, pp. 602–612. Springer, Heidelberg (2014)
11. Wordpress. https://ja.wordpress.com/
12. W3C WCAG2.0: Web Content Accessibility Guidelines (WCAG) 2.0. https://www.w3.org/TR/WCAG20/
13. Zenbou, H., Ogawa, T.: Approach of applying design technology to system development process: from HCD to UX design. Fujitsu **64**(2), 119–126 (2013)

Agile Human-Centred Design: A Conformance Checklist

Karsten Nebe[✉] and Snigdha Baloni

Rhein-Waal University of Applied Science,
Friedrich-Heinrich-Allee 25, 47475 Kamp-Lintfort, Germany
Karsten.Nebe@hsrw.eu, snigdha.baloni@gmail.com

Abstract. Agile development is gaining popularity in industries in recent years. For more than a decade there have been researches about the integration of agile development and Human-Centred Design (HCD) so that organizations can benefit from the best of both. However, such approaches are being performed in-house and often not published broadly. What are best practices for the integration? Do these integration approaches affect the methodology of agile development? Or, are the principles of HCD being influenced by the aggregation of both methodologies? Agile human-centeredness needs to be assessed in relation to a reference model. Such a reference model did not exist. This paper provides a checklist that can be used to assess the user-centeredness of the agile processes. The checklist is based on DIN ISO 9241-210 in combination with best practices from agile human-centred design approaches and is evaluated by experts feedback.

Keywords: Agile development · User-centred design · Integration · Process assessment · Capability maturity model

1 Introduction

Software development frameworks have been evolving since there was a need to make software development more manageable and efficient [8]. Agile development processes were developed to overcome the recognized drawbacks of traditional sequential approaches [28]. Agile processes are iterative and incremental and lightweight. Another prevalent methodology is the User-Centred Design (UCD). UCD is a multi-disciplinary design approach, which emphasizes user involvement for clear understanding of requirements and tasks [14, 19]. UCD is based on iterations of design and evaluation. It is considered the solution to better user experience and usability. Various researches show that adoption of agile development is increasing day by day [2, 35]. In addition, some researches show that cost-benefit tradeoffs have become a key consideration for adopting UCD methods in product development [19]. Agile development processes allow delivering high quality products in a short period of time. On the other hand, UCD gives us the end user empathy to build more usable products with higher user satisfaction [26]. In order to achieve benefits from the advantages of both of these methodologies, a variety of researches have been done in the past few decades to integrate these two process models. Some of the significant integration strategies and frameworks are discussed in Sect. 2.2.

© Springer International Publishing Switzerland 2016
S. Yamamoto (Ed.): HIMI 2016, Part I, LNCS 9734, pp. 442–453, 2016.
DOI: 10.1007/978-3-319-40349-6_42

It is also observed that there is research data available for the assessment of agile processes and UCD processes, some of which are discussed in Sect. 3. Though there are various methods available to assess the agility of an agile process, there seems to be a lack of data available for assessing the user-centeredness of an agile process or vice versa, the agility of a UCD process. This paper explores possibilities to assess the ability of such organizations to perform human-centred design in agile development process environments.

2 Agile Development and HCD

Today, many industries have adopted agile development methodologies and the level of agile adoption is high and rising [2, 35]. The most popular agile approaches are Scrum and Extreme Programming [9, 20]. Compared to the traditional process models, agile methodologies are used for a dynamic environment where requirements, technologies and deadlines are changeable. Agile methods are structured keeping in mind that real world requirements are likely to change. Their basic values are interaction, collaboration and adaptability [17]. Agile models are considered as lightweight as they do not consider extensive documentation, and prefer informal and frequent communication over procedures [5, 17, 20, 27]. The iterative nature of agile development helps to concurrently work on smaller set of features to over the course of time form the bigger system. Large projects are therefore often implemented in series of small projects, delivering the customer a finished, tested and working implementation on a regular basis which can be more valuable to the customer than a document or a changeable overall design [1]. Agile development is not just about the agile values and practices but is also about managerial or organizational policies. Since all the values and principles are theoretical and there is no unique way to implement them, these can be perceived and implemented differently in different organizations [5, 27]. It's the core characteristics that are shared and the focus is on the basic principles of agile software development as explained in the Agile Manifesto.

According to Nielsen [23], the biggest risk of agile methods is that it is created by programmers or developers and focuses mainly on the implementation. Less importance or effort is given to usability. With the increase in the importance of user experience in system development for the past few decades, the need of more usable products has grown. User-centred design (UCD) is an approach that intends to make usable and useful products by keeping end-users in the center of the development process. The idea behind UCD is to gain a strong understanding of the user and the user's tasks and requirements [19]. This is done in an iterative manner with creating alternative solutions and testing them with users continuously. ISO 9241-210 [14] defines requirements and recommendations on human-centred approaches to design and shows how HCD can be effectively used and organized in a company's environment. As it is a management standard and it does not provide the methods and techniques needed for the implementation.

2.1 Comparison of Agile Development and UCD

Agile and UCD have the same goal of creating high quality products, but there are always differences in practices involved in each process. This is one of the reason integrating these two processes is a challenge for decades. The following aspects sum up the similarities along with the differences between the two perspectives:

I. While agile and UCD are both iterative, there is difference in what is being iterated [3, 9, 27]. Agile methods iterate over application code or a smaller set of features that can be implemented. Iterations in agile are done during development. UCD iterates over user requirements and interaction design. Rannikko [27] states that a factor to keep in mind while integrating agile and UCD would be to make UCD incremental as well. In UCD practices, the user requirements are gathered and design solutions are being tested iteratively before the actual development begins. Making UCD incremental would mean to do user requirements elicitation and development of design alternatives for a short set of features iteratively. This makes it easier to be integrated with an agile process.

II. Both the processes are user-centred or human centric. Agile and UCD principles all involve the user throughout design and development process. The difference here is that in UCD users are the end users of the product, i.e., users that would actually use the product, but agile processes rarely differentiate between customer and end-users [3, 27]. In order to integrate these two perspectives, there needs to be real end-user involvement in all the stages. In agile process there is no end-user involvement for evaluation of the design by definition. For agile to be more human-centred participation of end-users during designing and evaluation is needed to get feedback and achieve improvements continuously.

III. Both the approaches emphasize effective teamwork and communication [3, 27]. Agile development process gives importance to face-to-face communications and keeping the team together, motivated and self-organized, which relates to the UCD principles as well. Another characteristic of UCD approach is that the whole team is supposed to design and develop keeping in mind the end-user [27].

IV. Rannikko [27] points out that agile methodology works effectively in projects where requirements are not clear in the beginning. But agile methodologies do not mention how these requirements are being gathered. Agile teams depend on the customer for their requirements. In the case where the requirements are not clear to the customer, the team has to figure out by themselves and build something to ask the customer if the solution is what they expected. To save costs on changes of prior implementations, it is better to have done UCD practices before implementation. UCD methodology traditionally does up-front analysis, requirement gathering and design. Some high-level UCD practices, if integrated with agile, can help overcome such risks.

V. In agile development developer based testing is done on a daily basis and apart from this testing there is customer/user acceptance testing that can be done after every iteration or Sprint (in Scrum), but it lacks any usability evaluation testing. Even though the developer and expert would be taking care of the usability, the real evaluation is complete only when it is tested with the end-users as well [27].

Evaluation in agile means acceptance from the customer who actually verifies if all the requirements are met and all functionalities implemented. There is less focus on usability of the system or product by default. UCD puts emphasis on the users and evaluates the system by testing with real users, which highlights usability defects and technical problems as well.

2.2 Agile and UCD Integration Approaches

Growths in research about agile and UCD integration have started to address the previously mentioned differences through different approaches. Past research showed how usability requirements were treated insufficiently in agile methods and which gaps need to be filled with UCD activities to make products more usable [5]. Silva et al. [32] did a systematic literature review of agile and UCD integration processes and propose an integration framework. This framework is almost similar to the approach that Fox et al. [10] came up with after interviewing 10 participants adapting or working in integration projects across America, Canada and Europe. Fox et al. came up with a Generalised, a Specialist and a Generalist-Specialist approach that was being used by most of the participants. Findings from their research show how the two methodologies are getting integrated in software industry. None of the processes followed by each participant was identical, but they had some commonalities. The authors constructed a high level representation of the similarities in the approaches and called it Agile-UCD General Process Model (AUGPM) [10]. Nebe and Paelke [21] also did a comparison of various kind of agile and UCD integration processes. They pointed out that every integration process has a distinct focus and does integration on one of the three levels, namely, on the level of Standards, Process Model or Operational process. The AUGPM developed by Fox et al. [10] is not only a very general approach, it also details the procedures to be followed. They not only confirmed the Sy model [33] but also showed that Sy's model is not limited to one organization. They have detailed the approaches by describing who performs which activities in the team. They also mention the output expected from every stage and every iteration and what should be the next steps, which was not provided in the details by Sy. Though AUGPM is a general approach that was designed with the similarities of processes followed by the participants of the study. Fox et al. also found distinct differences that they described as three different approaches for integration of UCD and agile. The approaches that emerge are different in the aspect that who executes which role in the process. These approaches are described with significant details. When looking into related work of integration of agile and UCD, it can be seen that most of approaches developed fit into one of the three approaches below proposed by Fox et al. [10]:

- The Specialist approach: In this approach, the team members are distinctly divided into UCDS (UCD Specialist) and development teams. There are three main groups, the users/customers, the UCDS, and the development team.
- The Generalist Approach: This approach uses two main groups, the user/customer and the developers that also act as UCDS. Developers that act as UCDS may or may not be formally trained UCDS. But they must have some informal or self-taught UCD skills. The roles that developers play are the main difference between the Specialist and Generalist approach.

- The Generalist Specialist Approach: In this approach there exists a team member that not only has formal UCD training but also has extensive software development experience. This member is a Generalist as well as a Specialist. Generalist because he can contribute in development task as well as perform UCD tasks and Specialist because he can also act as a UCD specialist.

3   Assessment of Agile- and UCD-Processes

A current state analysis is the first and typical step in a process to start any improvement endeavors in an organization. In software engineering and usability engineering process assessments are a widely used practice to this [16]. Datta [4] proposed a metric, the Agile Maturity Index (AMI) based on five software project dimensions, namely, Duration, Risk, Novelty, Effort and Interaction. The score obtained helps organization to decide the best fit methodology for a given project. Sidky [31] introduced the Sidky Agile Measurement Index (SAMI) which is based on the number of agile practices adopted by an organization. The "agile potential" of the organization depends on the number of agile practices being followed. SAMI has five agile levels and each level correlates with a set of principles and practices stated in the Agile Manifesto. Patel and Ramachandran [25] introduced in their paper the Agile Maturity Model (AMM) for agile software development environments. AMM is based on the agile software development values, practices and principles and is designed to improve and enhance the agile methodology being followed.

Apart from various research data and maturity models, there are many checklists and questionnaire available online that can be used for assessing the agility. For example, the Karlskrona test [30] provides an eleven-point questionnaire to analyze the agility of the existing process. The Agile Maturity Self Assessment consists of six questions based on the agile principles answered using the seven scale of Expertise [24]. Additionally there are the Nokia test [18] available online which is more specific to Scrum process, and the 42 point test: How Agile are You? [34] and the Scrum Master checklist [15]. These checklists mentioned are just a few from the many available online.

Various approaches have also been proposed and used to analyze and assess the current state of a UCD process. Earthy [6] introduced the Usability Maturity Model (UMM) to assess the level of maturity of an organization with regard to its capabilities to perform human-centred design. It is also known as the INUSE process assessment model [16]. This process assessment model is based on the software process assessment model defined in ISO 15504-2 in 1998 (This has been revised by ISO/IEC 33002 in 2015) [13]. The INUSE processes model consists of six levels of capability (Incomplete; Performed; Managed; Established; Predictable, Optimising). There are certain process attributes associated which each level of capability. These attributes determine whether a particular capability level is achieved. This process assessment model developed by INUSE project is well documented with all the details on how the assessment is to be performed. The process descriptions of the INUSE processes model was later published as a technical report ISO 18529 [12, 16]. Jokela [16] summarizes and contrasts various usability capability assessment approaches. He also came up with a new assessment approach KESSU UPA. KESSU UPA consists of a new UCD process model, a three dimensional process-performance model and the implementation of the assessment as a workshop.

As shown, various researches and approaches to assess the agility of an agile process and also to assess the user-centeredness of a UCD process exist. Many frameworks and approaches have been already developed to get the benefits of both, some of which have been discussed already in this paper. But still, there is a lack of research data that would help in assessing the agile processes or the integrated agile-UCD processes for their user–centeredness [29]. Many organizations are willing and trying to integrate UCD in their agile development process these days. But therefore it is necessary to first assess the principle user-centeredness of the agile processes.

In the following section we explore the possibilities to measure the user-centeredness of an agile process applied in an organization, which would also help in knowing the capability of the organization using agile processes to perform HCD.

4   Checklist for User-Centredness of Agile Processes

The aim of this paper is to find a solution to measure the user-centeredness of a given agile process. It is relevant to mention here that this work is not aiming to assess an organization's process implementation maturity level. It attempts to assess the user-centeredness (as per the UCD values, principles and activities) of a given agile process model being followed (as per the agile principles, values and activities). For the purpose of this paper, it is important to have a basic definition for the process methodology in question that defines their principles, values and activities. The rest of the research is then performed depending on the basic definition of these process methodologies that are taken into consideration.

All developed processes are based on agile development methodologies principles, values and activities that are defined in the Agile Manifesto. The research work done for this paper also considers the Agile Manifesto for the basic agile definition while assessing a given agile process. To measure the user-centeredness of a UCD process there are various approaches available as discussed in previous section. The standard ISO/TR 18529 is one of them. As explained already, ISO/TR 18529 introduces the Usability Maturity Model, but it is yet to be investigated whether this model can be used for assessing user-centeredness of agile or integrated agile-UCD processes.

Here, ISO 9241-210 is chosen as reference model for assessing the user-centeredness of a process. With no assumption of any design process, it provides a HCD perspective that can be integrated into different design and development processes in a way that is applicable to the particular context. It describes how HCD can be planned and integrated into all phases of the product life cycle. The Annex B in the standards describes a sample procedure for assessing applicability and conformance. It provides a checklist that can be used to analyze whether HCD is being followed in a given process. Therefore, requirements and recommendations are listed in a checklist sequentially. The standard clearly states that the checklist is provided as guidance and must not be used as a substitute of the standard. Each requirement and recommendation is stated as a single point in a separate row. Most of these requirements and recommendations have components. Every such component is stated as an entry in a separate row. Achievement of a requirement or recommendation depends on satisfying each of its components as well. Figure 1 displays a snapshot of this checklist showing the header attributes.

Clause/ subclause	Requirement or recommendation	Applicability		Conformance		
		Yes/No	Reason not applicable	Yes	No	Comments
4	Principles of human-centred design					
4.1	Whatever the design process and allocation of responsibilities and roles adopted, a human-centred approach should follow the principles listed [in 4.1].					

Fig. 1. Table B.1 (of ISO 9241-210) checklist header snapshot

To check the fulfillment of the requirements and recommendations, first the checklist is reviewed by experts to know which of these clauses are actually applicable for the project or process. This is documented by Yes/No in the third column with a justification in the fourth column, in case that particular clause is not applicable. Next, the clauses, which are marked as applicable, are then reviewed to determine whether the project or process conforms to those requirements and recommendations. How this is determined is not stated in the standard. It may vary from project to project and organization to organization.

For the intention of this paper the authors used this checklist as it defines HCD by principle and analyzed whether agile principles match or interfere.

4.1 Development of the Agile-HCD-Conformance Checklist

The checklist of ISO 9241-210 was analyzed for the purpose of this paper, exploring whether it would be possible to use this checklist to assess the user-centeredness of agile processes. To do so, each of the 103 entries in the checklist was examined whether it is applicable to agile development process (by definition as per the agile manifesto). This brought to light the gaps in agile development process, by definition, considering which the process can be made more human-centred. The analysis of the checklist was done in three steps: First, all 103 entries of the checklist were analyzed to find which entries or clauses of the checklist are actually valid enough when considering an agile development process. This was done to first eliminate the entries, which are completely unrelated to agile development. Second, the clauses in which a agile development process needed to be adapted in order to become human-centred were determined. Third, the gaps found in agile development processes were analyzed and recommendations as to how these gaps can be filled were provided. These recommendations are based on the state of the art research approaches (integration of agile and UCD as discussed in this paper).

During analysis of the checklist, it was found that all clauses of the checklist were valid enough to be used for assessing an agile process for its human-centeredness. All 103 entries of the checklist passed the first step of the analysis. In the second step of the analysis, 90 clauses could be found where agile processes need to be adapted in order to fulfill the requirement listed. By doing this, gaps in agile development processes (by definition) were determined. Lastly, the identified gaps were analyzed and a solution was given for every such clause. For example, consider the following clause from the checklist: "Clause 4.3 (under point 4. Principles of Human-Centred Design): User involvement should be active." This particular checklist clause is valid to be used for the assessment of an agile process. But when the HCD principles are considered, a gap is observed in agile processes even though agile methodology does involve users/customers (see 2.1.II). In HCD, user involvement should be active throughout the project life cycle and especially during the early stages. As defined in ISO 9241-210, the real end-users must be involved during requirements gathering where, if needed, low fidelity prototypes must be included to get more definite user requirements and understanding of the users tasks. Moreover, in HCD end-users must also be involved during designing. The designs must then be tested with real users to get their feedback for improvements before the actual implementation starts. In the end, a user-centred evaluation must be performed as the final step after implementation is done. As per the agile definition, the first point to note is that agile does not differentiate between users and customers [3, 27]. Second point to note is that agile processes does not emphasize on user involvement during the early stages and user evaluation during the design phase. Following this procedure the analysis highlighted gaps in agile development processes. Then, recommendations for improvement could be given. For the above example, it is recommended to involve real users in the early stages (e.g. Sprint Zero) as well as during the agile development process, especially by the involvement of real end users during requirements analysis and elicitation. In addition, the user needs to also be involved to evaluate the designs apart from just testing the implementation at the end [7, 10].

Every entry in the checklist was analyzed as per the process explained above. This resulted in the development of a new extended version of this checklist having the same clauses as in ISO 9241-210 checklist but with agile gap findings and additional recommendations for implementation of HCD. This extended list can help filling the gaps and makes agile processes human-centred. This Agile-HCD-Conformance Checklist can be found at the URL [22]. The extended checklist is quite similar to the ISO 9241-210 checklist with a slight difference. Columns one and two remain the same, i.e., first being the clause or sub clause number and the second the requirement or recommendation. The third and fourth column contains information related to the applicability of that clause to agile process (by definition). The third column is filled with Yes/No depending whether that recommendation or requirement is applicable to the agile process according to the agile definition. In case a recommendation or requirement is not applicable, the reason is mentioned in the fourth column. These basically determine the gaps. The fifth and the last column contains the recommendations to make the agile process more human-centred based on the related work already done in integration of agile and UCD.

4.2 Evaluation of the Agile-HCD-Conformance Checklist

To evaluate if the checklist could be used to assess an organization's ability to perform human-centred design in an agile development processes and whether it provides means for the implementation, expert feedback was needed. Experts must have a strong knowledge of agile development processes, based on their educational background or work experience of years in agile development projects along with having certifications related to agile processes (like the Scrum Master certification).

The statements, which are present in the "Applicable to agile process (by definition)? (Y/N)" and "Reason not applicable" columns of the checklist, are the entries of the checklist, which were needed for the evaluation through experts. These describe the gaps of human-centeredness in agile processes, which need to be filled. Therefore an online evaluation questionnaire was created (*For future studies input is still needed. Please help and support by providing expert input at* [22]). Each question of the questionnaire consists of the specific requirement or recommendation as in the original checklist, followed by the agile applicability statement from the developed new checklist. Every question was comprised of two parts. One was the requirement or recommendation clause and the second was the "Applicable to agile process (by definition)? (Yes/No)" and the "Reason not applicable" statement. The participants were asked to give their feedback for each agile applicability statement, i.e., whether they agree or disagree with the given statement (multiple choice). They were also provided with separate text boxes to write their comments after every question.

The online questionnaire was sent to 12 experts. Five responses were received. By looking at the results, similar trends could be identified. The evaluation report with the responses of the participants along with their comments can be found at the URL (Nebe [22]). In summary it shows that the experts mostly agree with our findings.

Keep in mind, while analyzing and proposing the Agile-HCD-Conformance Checklist, the purpose of this research was not to analyze for operational process implementation, but was a focus on fundamental agile development principles. Some of the experts' responses unconsciously compared the checklist entries with the given agile process they were following in their organization. Such responses were excluded. Also, not all negative responses from experts meant that they disagree with our checklist statement. In few situations, experts state a negative response but after reading their comments it was understood that they actually disagreed with the actual checklist statement for agile, which was what expected and explained in our "reasons not applicable" section. In some few cases it was seen that our "Reason not applicable" statement is not clear enough and the responses from the experts helped us to refine "Reason not applicable" statement in the new version of our checklist.

Altogether it can be said, that the Agile-HCD-Conformance Checklist can be used as a good source for the assessment of the user-centeredness of agile processes and can be a used as a guideline for setting up new agile HCD processes.

5   Summary, Conclusion, Discussion and Outlook

This research explored approaches of assessment for agile processes and human-centred design (HCD) processes. It was important for this work to understand the underlying basic principles and values of both the methodologies. In addition, state of the art research about strategies for the integration of agile and UCD are reported. Even though, many integration approaches exist, there is still a gap of principal recommendations and practices for the integration of agile and HCD processes. The authors present an approach that give guidance for such integration based on principles and best practices of agile processes and user-centeredness. The standard ISO 9241-210 was chosen to explore the possibilities of assessing the user-centeredness of agile processes. Based on this, the Agile-HCD-Conformance Checklist [22] was developed so that it can be used as a source for the assessment of the user-centeredness of agile processes. The Agile-HCD-Conformance Checklist was evaluated with experts. Minor refinements were done after the evaluation results analysis. It is concluded that the research was successful in finding the gaps that would help the agile process to adapt and perform HCD. The Agile-HCD-Conformance Checklist, also provides recommendations on how the gaps found in agile process can be filled. Recommendations are given based on state of the art researches in the field of integration of agile and UCD.

Due to the limitation of time, the evaluation is based on feedback of five experts. Given the time, more feedback could have been gathered that might have helped to refine the findings more and make it more concrete. *If you are interested in supporting this approach and future work, please provide your expertise in filling the questionnaire* [22]. *Thanks a lot.*

This research leads to a vast area for research questions in the area of measuring the user-centeredness of an agile process or an integrated user-centred agile process. Moreover, it also leads to questions in the area of measuring the agility of a user-centred design process or an integrated agile user-centred process. Further research can also be done to develop a maturity index to analyze whether an agile process can be put in a level of maturity in terms of user-centeredness or vice-versa.

Acknowledgements. We are very grateful to all the participants in this study without whom this analysis would not have been possible, and to Jonathan Yen for his support in finalizing this paper.

References

1. Armitage, J.: Are agile methods good for design? Interactions **11**(1), 14–23 (2004)
2. Bustard, D., Wilkie, G., Greer, D.: The maturation of agile software development principles and practice: observations on successive industrial studies in 2010 and 2012. In: 20th IEEE International Conference and Workshops, pp. 139–146. IEEE, Scottsdale (2013)
3. Chamberlain, S., Sharp, H., Maiden, N.: Towards a Framework for Integrating Agile Development and User-Centred Design. http://www.ime.usp.br/~marivb/ihc3.pdf
4. Datta, S.: Agility measurement index – a metric for the crossroads of software development methodologies. In: Proceedings of the 44th Annual Southeast Regional Conference, pp. 271–273, New York (2006)
5. Düchting, M., Zimmermann, D., Nebe, K.: Incorporating user centered requirement engineering into agile software development. In: Jacko, J.A. (ed.) HCI 2007. LNCS, vol. 4550, pp. 58–67. Springer, Heidelberg (2007)
6. Earthy, J.: Usability Maturity Model: Human Centredness Scale. http://www.idemployee.id.tue.nl/g.w.m.rauterberg/lecturenotes/usability-maturity-model%5B1%5D.pdf
7. Ferreira, J., Nobel, J., Biddle, R.: Agile development iterations and UI design. In: Proceedings of Agile 2007, pp. 50–58. IEEE, Washington (2007)

8. Fowler, M.: The New Methodology. http://www.martinfowler.com/articles/newMethodology.html

9. Fox, D.: Agile Methods and User-Centred Design: How These Two Methodologies are Being Integrated in Industry (M.Sc. thesis), University of Calgary (2010). http://pages.cpsc.ucalgary.ca/~maurer/uploads/Publications/Agile_UCD.pdf

10. Fox, D., Sillito, J., Maurer, F.: Agile methods and user-centred design: how these two methodologies are being successfully integrated in industry. In: AGILE 2008, Conference, pp. 63–72. IEEE, Toronto (2008)

11. Iver, R.M., Campbell, B.: Accelerating your organization's agile adoption. In: Agile 2010 Conference, Orlando (2010). http://www.robbiemaciver.com/documents/presentations/A2010-Agile%20Maturity%20-%20Presentation.pdf

12. ISO/IEC, ISO/TR 18529 Ergonomics – Ergonomics of Human-System Interaction – Human-Centred Lifecycle Process Descriptions (2000)

13. ISO/IEC, ISO/IEC 15504-2 Information Technology – Process Assessment – Part 2: Performing an Assessment (2003)

14. ISO/IEC, ISO 9241-210 Ergonomics of Human System Interaction-Part 210: Human-Centred Design for Interactive Systems (2010)

15. James, M.: A ScrumMaster's Checklist. http://www.scrummasterchecklist.org/

16. Jokela, T.: Assessment of User-Centred Design Process As a Basis of Improvement Action. http://herkules.oulu.fi/isbn9514265513/isbn9514265513.pdf

17. Lan, C., Ramesh, B.: Agile software development: ad hoc practices or sound principles? IT Prof. **9**, 41–47 (2007). IEEE

18. Little, J.: The Nokia Test. http://agileconsortium.blogspot.com/2007/12/nokia-test.html

19. Mao, J., Vredenburg, K., Smith, P.W., Carey, T.: User-centred design methods in practice: a survey of the state of the art. In: Proceedings of the 2001 Conference of the Centre for Advanced Studies on Collaborative Research, p. 12. IBM Press (2001)

20. McInerney, P., Maurer, F.: UCD in agile projects: dream team or odd couple? Interactions **12**, 19–23 (2005)

21. Nebe, K., Paelke, V.: Usability-engineering-requirements as a basis for the integration with software engineering. In: Jacko, J.A. (ed.) HCI International 2009, Part I. LNCS, vol. 5610, pp. 652–659. Springer, Heidelberg (2009)

22. Nebe, K. (2016). https://www.hochschule-rhein-waal.de/de/fakultaeten/kommunikation-und-umwelt/organisation/professoren/prof-dr-karsten-nebe/publikationen-0

23. Nielsen, J.: Agile Development Projects and Usability, Nielsen Norman Group, on 17 November 2008. http://www.nngroup.com/articles/agile-development-and-usability/

24. Page-Jones, M.: The Seven Stages of Expertise in Software Engineering. http://www.wayland-informatics.com/The%20Seven%20Stages%20of%20Expertise%20in%20Software.htm

25. Patel, C., Ramachandran, M.: Agile maturity model (AMM): a software process improvement framework for agile software development practices. OALib (2014). http://www.oalib.com/paper/2761472#.VAmwFcKSySo

26. Patton, J.: Hitting the target: adding interaction design to agile software development. In: Proceedings of OOPSLA 2002 OOPSLA 2002 Practitioners Reports, pp. 1-ff. ACM, New York (2002)

27. Rannikko, P.: User-centred design in agile development. M.Sc. thesis, University of Tampere. http://tampub.uta.fi/bitstream/handle/10024/82310/gradu04854.pdf?sequence=1

28. Salah, D.: A framework for the integration of user centred design and agile software development processes. In: 2011 33rd International Conference on Software Engineering (ICSE), pp. 1132–1133. IEEE, Honolulu (2011)

29. Salah, D., Paige, R., Cairns, P.: Integrating agile development processes and user centred design- a place for usability maturity models? In: Sauer, S., Bogdan, C., Forbrig, P., Bernhaupt, R., Winckler, M. (eds.) HCSE 2014. LNCS, vol. 8742, pp. 108–125. Springer, Heidelberg (2014)
30. Seuffert, M.: Karlskrona test. http://mayberg.se/learning/karlskrona-test-online
31. Sidky, A.: A structured approach to adopting agile practices: the agile adoption framework. Ph.D. dissertation, Computer Science, Virginia Tech, Blacksburg (2007). http://scholar.lib.vt.edu/theses/available/etd-05252007-110748/
32. Silva, D.T., Martin, A., Maurer, F., Silveira, M.: User-centred design and agile methods: a systematic review. In: Agile Conference (AGILE) pp. 77–86. IEEE, Salt Lake City (2011)
33. Sy, D.: Adapting usability investigations for agile user-centred design. J. Usability Stud. **2**, 112–130 (2007). http://uxpajournal.org/wp-content/uploads/pdf/agile-ucd.pdf
34. Waters, K.: How Agile Are You? (Take This 42 Point Test). http://www.allaboutagile.com/how-agile-are-you-take-this-42-point-test/
35. Williams, L.: What agile teams think of agile principles? Commun. ACM **55**(2), 71–76 (2012)

Understanding the Dynamics and Temporal Aspects of Work for Human Centered Design

Kate Sellen[(✉)]

Ontario College of Art and Design University, Toronto, Canada
ksellen@faculty.ocadu.ca

Abstract. This paper explores an information theoretic approach to identifying strategies in work practices in dynamic contexts using blood issuing for the operating suite as a case study. Going back to conceptual models of strategies indicated in early human computer interaction work, together with contemporary representation of work practices in dynamic healthcare contexts, the concepts of temporality and pace are explored. This exploration highlights a number of strategies that may be generalizable and could be used to guide inquiry in the early stages of design. Attending to potential general work practice strategies that can arise in response to dynamics and temporal aspects of a particular setting and its conditions, by focusing observations and contextual inquiry for instance, has the potential to avoid idealized conceptions of work practices and inform system design.

Keywords: Human-centred design · Task analysis · Cognitive systems · Workarounds · Task representation · Temporality

1 Introduction

Human centred design techniques began to be applied to human computer interaction in medical settings nearly two decades ago, as these techniques were developed for use in other domains but also in response to the call for better understanding of issues related to Information technology specific to healthcare (HIT).

The adoption of HIT has not been universally successful. Often the proximal cause of HIT failure is identified as a lack of HIT adoption or resistance from clinicians and staff [1–3]. However, the prevalence of issues that have been identified with HIT relating to workflow, communication, ease of use, system design, and usefulness, suggest a gap between the HIT systems as designed and their fit with the work practices they are intended to support. Calls for different strategies for system design and implementation have been growing in response to these reports [4–6] – a challenge well suited to a human centric approach.

There are now many examples of a human centric approach combining cognitive science, human computer interaction, and human factors engineering techniques at multiple levels of analysis of HIT, including the individual, team, group, and institution [7–9]. However, how might we develop design strategies from these investigations that support human centric design in the early stages of system design – taking into account highly dynamic and temporal aspects of work practices in the healthcare context?

© Springer International Publishing Switzerland 2016
S. Yamamoto (Ed.): HIMI 2016, Part I, LNCS 9734, pp. 454–461, 2016.
DOI: 10.1007/978-3-319-40349-6_43

1.1 Representing Dimensions and Temporal Dynamics

There are approaches to system design that include dynamic and temporal aspects, for example, Cognitive Work Analysis (CWA) and its use for assessing work domains in settings that include surgical procedures, critical care, and emergency room diagnosis, among others [10, 11] and resiliency engineering is also relevant here.

CWA is one of a suite of tools that support Ecological Interface Design [12]. A growing theme among researchers experimenting with CWA for strategy analysis is the challenge of conceptualizing the mapping between a work practice strategy and the dynamics of the work practice and the representations that can be used in practice for system design [13, 14]. Resiliency is an approach which includes concepts that allow for recognition and representation of dynamics and temporality, including a stated aim to design in order to support flexibility to respond to changing demands in a work system [15, 16]. An human centric approach to design could be supported by some of the concepts central to resiliency [18–20], however understanding strategies to support resiliency and representations is also a challenge.

The common issue of how to conceptualise work practice strategies, task dimensions, and temporal dynamics for system design motivates the theoretical exploration of this paper through the lens of a case study on blood ordering. The starting point of which is not CWA or resiliency engineering but how researchers have explored temporality and pace in healthcare and human computer interaction and in particular concepts that may be useful to understanding work practices.

2 Case Study

This paper discusses some of the theoretical implications of the findings from a multi-site sociotechnical study of the introduction a new system of blood ordering into a variety of surgical suites covering different scales and types of surgery. This study provided an opportunity to investigate the context and characteristics of the work practices of the surgical suite. Analyses of critical incidents and interviews highlighted the issue of the dynamics of certain aspects of the work of blood ordering. This included volumetric dynamics and temporal dynamics – a change in pace or urgency of the blood need and pace of the task of blood ordering that was not accounted for in the design of the system under study [20].

3 Temporal Dynamics

3.1 Temporality

In more recent work, human computer interaction research has turned to questions of supporting complex and unfolding work practices over time [21]. In particular, the concept of temporality has been explored in studies of information and information transfer between members of healthcare teams, and work organization and mobility have informed new thinking [22, 23]. The conceptual diagram (Fig. 1) illustrates the potential interplay of pace and the concept of temporal dynamics.

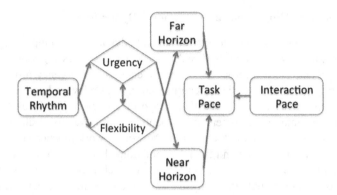

Fig. 1. Conceptual diagram of temporal aspects of medical work with the addition pace concept (adapted from Reddy et al. [23, 24].)

Where temporal trajectories describe the change over time of a situation or its unfolding over time, temporal rhythms describe recurring patterns, for instance the recurring pattern of checking a patient's pulse or ordering blood, and temporal horizons describe a foreseeable segment of activity and its timespan.

Flexibility and urgency determine the temporal horizon chosen (see Fig. 1). If there is greater flexibility and little urgency for a task a distant time horizon could be chosen by an individual. For instance filing a patient report could be postponed to the end of a shift. Equally, a near time horizon could be chosen if filing the report could make way for other tasks that are less flexible. Seen through this lens, the task of the HCI researcher/designer is to enable the work practices of managing and constructing time horizons, temporal rhythms, and temporal trajectories.

3.2   Information Theoretic Approach

Pace usually refers to the rate of speed at which an activity proceeds, whether it be walking through a museum or completing a surgery. The pace of an activity might be determined by a number of factors including the goal or motivation for the activity, spatial characteristics of the activity, and the circumstances of the individuals or team involved (are they busy or not). Many researchers in HCI have explored and exploited the notion of pace to move the design of interactive systems forward but mainly in the context of its more obvious meaning e.g. the pace of walking through a tourist experience, the pace of a game, or the pace of a museum experience [25–27].

Alan Dix introduced the concept of pace to interaction research in 1998 [28]. Using an experimental conferencing system to conduct much of the research, the analysis focused on the pace of communication between individuals working on a team and the pace of the tasks they were trying to achieve. Analysis of the conversations between individuals highlighted the issues that can arise when pace of communication and pace of task do not match. Drawing on concepts from information theory, the analysis described pace using the concepts of communication channels, bandwidth, reception,

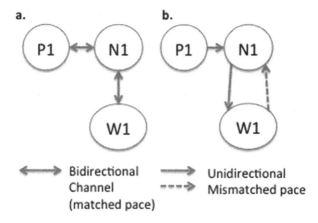

Fig. 2. Information theoretic conceptual diagram of open loop interaction (a) and closed loop interaction (b), to illustrate pace (adapted from Dix [28]).

control loops, and process control. Drawing on primarily on the work of Dix [28] the following example explores the concept of pace using the case of blood ordering (Fig. 2).

If a physician in an OR requests a blood order during surgery, a nurse usually receives the order verbally (P1 to N1), the verbal communication channel allows bidirectional communication between the nurse and the physician and so clarifications can be made. The nurse must complete the blood order by interacting with the work artifacts available to him/her (W1), feedback on the task to the physician can happen most efficiently if the pace of interaction with the work artifact matches the pace of the physician's task of getting the blood transfused in time (Fig. 2a closed loop control system). Often the interaction channel with the work artifact (W1) will not have the same pace as the communication between the physician (P1) and the nurse (N1). In this case an open loop control system is experienced (Fig. 2b open loop control system). The successful execution of the task under open loop control system conditions can only be accomplished if the task is predictable i.e. the physician must have confidence that ordering blood takes approximately 8 min and that this can be relied upon. Some characteristics will be revealed as inflexible to the influence of the work artefacts i.e. the circumstances of the patient that lead to a need for transfusion, the temperature at which red blood cells must be stored, and quantity of red blood cells needed. If there is a lack of predictability or the work artifacts do not have the same pace as the task, then a mismatch may be inevitable at some point in the interaction and a break down may occur. When there is a mismatch, some form of adaptation is likely.

3.3 Emergence of Workarounds

For the purpose of this paper it is the predictions about coping strategies, which emerge as a result of a mismatch in pace between task and interaction represented in Fig. 1, which will be applied to an exploration of blood ordering. In an ideal situation the task pace matches the interaction pace. Dix [28] identifies several different possible strategies noting that if a channel of interaction is too slow to meet the needs of the task then people will adapt by reducing the total interaction with the inadequate channel. This could be by *delegation, laziness/eagerness, or multiplexing.*

As Dix predicted "cooperation can only succeed if the pace of interaction is sufficient for the task" [cf. 28]. Indeed, the work practices that emerge out of a period of adaptation are a series of workarounds to accommodate the challenging issue of task pace not matching interaction pace. Faced with this mismatch OR teams adapted using the strategies predicted by Dix, namely by:

- Delegating
- Eagerness
- Multiplexing

Dix even notes in conclusion on the subject of time-critical tasks that "such tasks are often of a safety critical nature and it is obviously important to know whether peoples coping strategies will be sufficient for emergency situations". Details of these examples can be found in previous work [20]. For the reader two additional examples are described here to support the discussion.

(1) Strategy 1: One adaptation involved skipping safety steps in the labeling and checking of blood units to achieve shorter temporal horizons. This *eagerness* suggests that staff in the OR have developed a strategy of interacting with the new fridge that allows them flexibility. The 'no scan' is used most often in a situation where the dimensions of their task are at an extreme (high number blood units needed, shortest time available, extreme trauma case).

Note that Dix's concept of Laziness [cf. 28] did not apply in the case of blood ordering since the pace of the task of retrieving blood was never slower than pace of interaction available.

(2) Strategy 2: Gradual realization that a better match could be made between the pace of task and the pace of the interaction channel through *delegation* to support staff, who work primarily outside of the OR rooms, was reflected in the software logs. These revealed that support roles encountered fewer interaction errors with the ERBI system than other roles (X^2 (9, N = 3210) = 51.2, p = <.001). So their interactions had a more predictable time horizon.

4 Discussion

4.1 Dynamics and Temporality

This exploration focused on the work practices of operating room staff as they develop strategies for incorporating interaction with a new technology into their work practice. From this we will discuss the implications of an understanding of pace in particular, for designing interactive systems.

An analysis that gives prominence to *pace* shifts the conversation from one about information and knowledge provision to one about the dynamics of work practices and tasks. This is particularly useful for HCI endeavors that seek not to support a task with information and knowledge to enhance knowledge based decision making but to replace a task with an interactive system to support primarily actions. As Dix [cf. 9] points out "…work has some associated pace and we should expect that this pace and the pace of interaction are well matched."

Using the notion of pace to articulate dimensions of work practice adaptation that have implications for design, an information theoretic approach [28] can be extended to include contemporary concepts of temporality and temporal horizons [22, 23].

The temporal horizon for the OR nurse retrieving a unit of red blood cells for a patient, would be different from a porter's temporal horizon for the same activity. Using the concept of the temporal horizon may help in understanding the dynamic nature of the task itself, and the circumstances of the individual healthcare worker. The idea of pace is key here. The pace of activity necessarily quickens when a close temporal horizon is called for, whereas, a distant temporal horizon may accommodate a slower pace or result in postponement of activity.

Dimensions and strategies of work practice that emerge from this exploration to consider that could be used to inform design based on this exploration of dynamics and temporality include: *delegation, laziness/eagerness, or multiplexing* in response to high to low volumes in tasks, compressed to extended time frames, routine to exceptional cases, novice to expert staff mix, or staff mix in general, and the artefacts available. Early phases of understanding the context and requirements gathering for design could be informed by a strategy that includes deliberate attention to these dimensions and strategies.

5 Conclusion

This exploration of the dynamics of pace and temporality in medical work was supported by examining both concepts of temporality and concepts of pace. The case study of blood ordering and the emergence of workarounds, in response to a new artefact that required adaptations in work practices, revealed examples of work practice dynamics that indicate a number of dimensions that are relevant in representing dynamics of healthcare settings in order to guide design. These dimensions offer a possible framework to guide contextual inquiry at the beginning of system design to better serve a human centric approach.

References

1. Wager, K.A., Lee, F.W., White, A.W.: Life after a disastrous electronic medical record implementation: one clinic's experience. Ann. Cases Inf. Technol. Appl. Manag. Organ. **3**, 153–168 (2001)
2. Freudenheim, M.: Many hospitals resist computerized patient care. The New York Times, C6 (2004)

3. Connolly, C.: Cedars-Sinai doctors cling to pen and paper. The Washington Post, 21 (2005)
4. Karsh, B.T.: Beyond usability: designing effective technology implementation systems to promote patient safety. Qual. Saf. Health Care **13**(5), 388–394 (2004)
5. Karsh, B.T., Brown, R.: Macroergonomics and patient safety: the impact of levels on theory, measurement, analysis and intervention in patient safety research. Appl. Ergon. **41**(5), 674–681 (2010)
6. Pagliari, C.: Design and evaluation in eHealth: challenges and implications for an interdisciplinary field. J. Med. Internet Res. **9**(2), e15 (2007)
7. Laxmisan, A., Hakimzada, F., Sayan, O.R., Green, R.A., Zhang, J., Patel, V.L.: The multitasking clinician: decision-making and cognitive demand during and after team handoffs in emergency care. Int. J. Med. Inform. **76**(11), 801–811 (2007)
8. Patel, V.L., Zhang, J., Yoskowitz, N.A., Green, R., Sayan, O.R.: Translational cognition for decision support in critical care environments: a review. J. Biomed. Inform. **41**(3), 413–431 (2008)
9. Horsky, J., Kaufman, D.R., Oppenheim, M.I., Patel, V.L.: A framework for analyzing the cognitive complexity of computer-assisted clinical ordering. J. Biomed. Inform. **36**(1), 4–22 (2003)
10. Nemeth, C.P., Kowalsky, J., Brandwijk, M., Kahana, M., Klock, P.A., Cook, R.I.: Before I forget: how clinicians cope with uncertainty through ICU sign-outs. In: Proceedings of the Human Factors and Ergonomics Society Annual Meeting, vol. 50, no. 10, pp. 939–943. SAGE Publications, Chicago, October 2006
11. Nemeth, C., Wears, R.L., Patel, S., Rosen, G., Cook, R.: Resilience is not control: healthcare, crisis management, and ICT. Cogn. Technol. Work **13**(3), 189–202 (2011)
12. Vicente, K.J., Rasmussen, J.: Ecological interface design: theoretical foundations. IEEE Trans. Syst. Man Cybern. **22**(4), 589–606 (1992)
13. Cornelissen, M., McClure, R., Salmon, P.M., Stanton, N.A.: Validating the strategies analysis diagram: assessing the reliability and validity of a formative method. Appl. Ergon. **45**(6), 1484–1494 (2014)
14. Ashoori, M., Burns, C.M., d'Entremont, B., Momtahan, K.: Using team cognitive work analysis to reveal healthcare team interactions in a birthing unit. Ergonomics **57**(7), 973–986 (2014)
15. Dekker, S.W.: Doctors are more dangerous than gun owners: a rejoinder to error counting. Hum. Fact. J. Hum. Fact. Ergon. Soc. **49**(2), 177–184 (2007)
16. Woods, D.D.: Behind Human Error. Ashgate Publishing Ltd., Farnham (2010)
17. Lin, L., Vicente, K.J., Doyle, D.J.: Patient safety, potential adverse drug events, and medical device design: a human factors engineering approach. J. Biomed. Inform. **34**(4), 274–284 (2001)
18. Carthey, J., De Leval, M.R., Reason, J.T.: Institutional resilience in healthcare systems. Qual. Health Care **10**(1), 29–32 (2001)
19. Beuscart-Zéphir, M.C., Pelayo, S., Bernonville, S.: Example of a human factors engineering approach to a medication administration work system: potential impact on patient safety. Int. J. Med. Inform. **79**(4), e43–e57 (2010)
20. Sellen, K., Chignel, M.: Pace and temporality in safety critical medical work: concepts for understanding adaptation behaviors. In: Workshop Proceedings, HCI Research in Healthcare: Using Theory from Evidence to Practice. Workshop. International Conference on Human Factors in Computing Systems (2014)
21. O'hara, K., Kjeldskov, J., Paay, J.: Blended interaction spaces for distributed team collaboration. ACM Trans. Comput.-Hum. Interact. **18**(1), 1–28 (2011). doi:10.1145/1959022.1959025

22. Reddy, M., Dourish, P.: A finger on the pulse: temporal rhythms and information seeking in medical work. In: Proceedings of the 2002 ACM Conference on Computer Supported Cooperative Work, New Orleans, Louisiana, USA (2002)
23. Reddy, M.C., Dourish, P., Pratt, W.: Temporality in medical work: time also matters. Comput. Supported Coop. Work **15**(1), 29–53 (2006). doi:10.1007/s10606-005-9010-z
24. Reddy, M.C., Shabot, M.M., Bradner, E.: Evaluating collaborative features of critical care systems: a methodological study of information technology in surgical intensive care units. J. Biomed. Inform. **41**(3), 479–487 (2008). doi:10.1016/j.jbi.2008.01.004
25. Cheverst, K., Davies, N., Mitchell, K., Friday, A., Efstratiou, C.: Developing a context-aware electronic tourist guide: some issues and experiences. In: Proceedings of the SIGCHI Conference on Human Factors in Computing Systems, The Hague, The Netherlands (2000)
26. Galani, A., Chalmers, M.: Production of pace as collaborative activity. In: CHI 2004 Extended Abstracts on Human Factors in Computing Systems, Vienna, Austria (2004)
27. Mark, G., Voida, S., Cardello, A.: "A pace not dictated by electrons": an empirical study of work without email. In: Proceedings of the 2012 ACM Annual Conference on Human Factors in Computing Systems, Austin, Texas, USA (2012)
28. Dix, A.: Pace and interaction. In: Proceedings of the Conference on People and Computers VII, York, United Kingdom (1993)

User Centered Design Methods and Their Application in Older Adult Community

Joash Sujan Samuel Roy[1](✉), W. Patrick Neumann[1], and Deborah I. Fels[2]

[1] Department of Industrial Engineering, Ryerson University, Toronto, Canada
{joash.sujan,pneumann}@ryerson.ca
[2] Ted Rogers School of Information Technology Management, Ryerson University,
Toronto, Canada
dfels@ryerson.ca

Abstract. Older adults have unique perspectives on technology use that may involve having acquired disabilities, be more likely to be novice users and have more life experiences/biases that can influence user testing results. This literature review is aimed at assessing the application of basic User Centered Design (UCD) Instruments with Older Adults. 41 research articles published between 1988 and 2015 were gathered from different databases. Papers were included if the target audience was older adults and were analyzed only if the primary data collection instrument was any of the following: Questionnaire, Focus Groups, Cultural Probe, Diary Study, Think Aloud protocol, Interviews, Paper prototyping. The major findings from the resources reviewed showed that the application of UCD methods in older adults were commonly used to measure illness and understand their daily lives, experiences and living conditions. Only a few instruments such as Cultural Probe, Think Aloud Protocol and Paper Prototyping were used in the development of technology or devices. Many UCD methods may exist, but none appears to be a superior way to gather requirements. All methods have limitations when applied in an older adult context. A new design method approach should be developed to accommodate older adults in technology development process.

Keywords: User Centered Design methods · Older adults

1 Introduction

Measuring and fulfilling requirements of older adults in the development of assistive devices can result in successful products, reduce product recalls and avoid frequent design modifications [1]. Despite an increasing older adult population, organizations and researchers tend to concentrate on producing technologies aimed at younger audiences. This is because companies want products that suit the masses so that profits are maximized or it is too difficult to engage older adults [2]. As a result older adults have been left out of the development process, particularly of assistive technologies, or are being consulted at the end of the design process (Peterson 2013). Additionally, although some scientists and engineers adopt the practice of involving end users in the early stage of the product development process, different factors impact the quality of data collected

© Springer International Publishing Switzerland 2016
S. Yamamoto (Ed.): HIMI 2016, Part I, LNCS 9734, pp. 462–472, 2016.
DOI: 10.1007/978-3-319-40349-6_44

such as the use of proxies instead of real end users [1]. As a result there is an increasing recognition that poor usability increases risk for the user [1].

Capturing needs and desires as well as system requirements from older adults is part of a human-centered approach to design and development. According to ISO standard 13407 "The human centered design (HCD) process is intended to help those responsible for managing hardware and software design, and processes to identify and plan effective and timely human centered activities" (1999, p. 21). Along the continuum of HCD is inclusive design, which refers to designing for everyone by considering diverse abilities [3]. Applying the principles of inclusive design can aid designers in serving those needs and can enhance safety and agency for the individual [4]. Devices developed by designers without understanding specific needs dissatisfy the users therefore resulting in product failure.

Existing needs analysis techniques used UCD provide some methods that may be used in the design process to capture the needs and priorities of older adults. In this paper, UCD methods will be presented and discussed with respect to their applicability, use and usefulness in the context of designing assistive technologies for older adults. Although there are many tools available, very little information has been generated on the extent to which they have been used in designing for older adults. The goal of this study was to search literature involving older adults as target group and assess the use of basic UCD instruments among them.

2 Methods

Literature searches were conducted in the following electronic databases: Proquest, Science Direct, Google Scholar, SAGE research methods and Springer. The time range was from 1988 to 2015.

The following search terms related to UCD methods were used Questionnaires, Diary Study, Cultural Probe, Focus Groups, Interview Study, Paper Prototyping, Think Aloud Protocol and Questionnaire which were identified from Interaction Design by Preece et al. [5]. The terms were combined with terms related to the target population: Older adults and Assistive Technology.

Articles were selected through a scanning process: abstracts and conclusions were scanned. About 35 potential references were identified which included reports, internet sources and books. The inclusion criterion is that the target group of the research study must be older adults. The documents were analyzed only if the above mentioned UCD instruments were used as a primary method for data collection or design evaluation with older adults. This helped narrow down articles to proceed with the assessment of UCD instruments in an older adult context.

3 User Centered Design Methods

3.1 Questionnaire

Questionnaires are often used in psychological and social science studies, although the instrument specific to HCI or user need analysis context is comparatively lower [6]. Here we summarize the feasibility and ways in which questionnaires have been used with older adult populations.

According to a study conducted by Troyer and Rich [7] questionnaires have been used as a meta-memory self-reporting tool, which allows the researcher to measure the everyday memory issues happening among the targeted older adult population. Twenty-one items that addressed various emotions and perceptions of concern to the participants' current memory ability were used in the questionnaire. A mood and feeling questionnaire was included as a measure of the subjective memory ability of the participants and was found to be in larger correlation with Meta memory tool ability.

Another study conducted with older adults having subjective memory complaints aimed to develop a questionnaire to measure the perceptions of older adults' help seeking behavior [8]. The illness perception scale consisted of two different scales: the identity scale and causal scale. Additional measures were taken using the Geriatric Depression Scale (GDS) and Memory Functioning Scale (MFQ) to capture depression level due to memory impairment and to assess their memory complaints. Although these questionnaires were being used to understand the older adult's perception, designers can use the Illness Perception Questionnaire (IPQ) as an additional construct to the needs analysis questionnaire to analyze the user experiences rather than asking what they need.

Results from a study conducted by Muntinga et al. [9] shows the designed questionnaire to measure the client centeredness of a home care service resulted in a cognitive burden imposed on the older participants due to various characteristics such as length and comprehensibility. The authors suggest that this may be the result of questions composed with the unavailability of standards or hypotheses derived from the small population.

Based on the findings from the articles, most of the scenarios where questionnaires were used with older adults tended to gather information on their social life, illness, psychological ability and opinion. No papers were found where questionnaires were used as a primary tool to gather user needs.

3.2 Focus Groups

The focus group method is a very important qualitative tool for exploring a particular topic which is exploratory [10]. Six papers were identified where focus groups have been used as a primary method of data collection. Researchers from the World Health Organization Quality of Life (WHOQOL) field centres conducted a focus group that aimed at eliciting key concepts of life among older adults in a multi-cultural scenario [10]. Since the sessions were conducted at multiple locations a new set of guidelines for conducting the sessions was established which included a timeframe for conducting the group, number of groups, preparation for conducting the groups, procedure and structure of the focus groups discussion [11]. The guidelines were designed for adults over 80 years of age and four to six members in each group. The focus group discussions were well structured but most of the centres were only able to partially complete their discussion due to the many strict guidelines set by WHO.

The benefit of the focus group method is that it creates an interaction between the moderator and the participants: it allows the moderator to get a full explorative view of the participants without decontextualization [12]. Claes insists if a discussion is being conducted among a diverse population with age as the only criterion, it would narrow the focus, which involves the risk of fixating on a solution and leaving other relevant solutions unexplored. Hence, the diversity of the sample population needs to be taken into account. Moderators conduct the focus group session by jumping into the discussion topic which might leave the participants unaware that the topic is in a biased situation.

To address this issue, researchers from the University of Salford implemented a round table concept where participants are brought together and thoroughly briefed about the topic for which the discussion is being held [13]. An increase in the confidence level of the participants about the topic to be discussed was observed.

Findings from the papers reviewed shows that although there are multiple ways of conducting a focus group, there are many key issues that need to be mentioned. As indicated by Mehta when selecting a user sample for the focus group session, steps must be taken to ensure cultural equivalence, language equivalence, age consideration, and cognitive-ability [14]. The topic of the focus group should also address a specific issue that the sample population has been facing every day, because they will have better insight of problems known and that they regularly experience.

The above studies were concentrated on gathering information to assess the mental ability, behaviour and identifying the problem faced in conducting focus groups with older adults. Although older adults often mention the problems they encounter in their daily activities, the data must be careful reviewed by experts to identify their needs. There were three major criteria that must be followed while conducting a focus to design efficient products for older adults [15]. The first was focus groups should collect data to understand and investigate how older adults managed their activities. The second was understanding how older adults are currently coping with or have coped with the problem. Finally, findings from this data must be applied in the design and development process so that designers can create or modify existing system or tools.

Results from the papers reviewed show that the focus group method can be an effective way to identify user needs even if it is time consuming and resource intensive. However, it has been accepted by older community, because it helps them put forward their opinion in a supportive environment [16].

3.3 Cultural Probe

When the designer does not know the group of participants for whom the products are being developed, it is difficult to understand the culture, attitude, behaviour and preferences. According to [17], cultural probes are a way to identify user needs. This method involves using digital cameras, diaries, paper prototyping and other materials. The major criterion in conducting a culture probe activity is that the design kit should contain materials that will support the goal of the researcher. Also, the researcher should not make any addition or modification of the kit halfway through the process to justify the results [18].

For this study there were eight papers were identified where cultural probe was used as a primary method of data collection. Concerns have been raised about cultural probes being rationalized by the user's intent of analyzing the data [18]. Hence, they suggest that the cultural probe technique should be used to encourage subjective engagement. Based on the articles analyzed most studies conducted with the cultural probe as a methodology focused on understanding user needs rather than assessing the individual's ability. From research conducted by [18–20, 44] on using cultural probe as a technique for requirements gathering for developing assistive technology it can be established that cameras and diaries are the most common probe material to capture rich data. However, a diary study is considered as a separate UCD method that has been widely used to understand the illness behaviour of the older adults which will be discussed later in this article. Also findings from the above sources show that the relation between cultural probe and design was not the primary way to apply design to the new technologies but it can point the designer in a direction where there was a need for assistive technology.

The cultural probe method is an efficient way to capture user experiences and data but another qualitative UCD method is required to elicit further information relevant to the design [19]. The cultural probe alone cannot provide the data we need unless another method is adopted to discuss about the findings because analyzing the used probe will provide data on how the probe has been used, whereas a questionnaire or interview session is required to gather their views and experiences on using the probe. There are limitations with certain items used in the cultural probe, such as photo – map documentation, journey map and postcards. These probes require more effort in their preparing and evaluation than other probes, but they provide a higher degree of insight. However, because they require higher effort from participants, they are valuable as tools to capture data from older adults [21].

3.4 Diary Study

Diary study has been used widely among medical researchers where patients are requested to keep a track of their treatment or diagnosis in the form of a diary. Five papers were identified where diary study have been used as a primary data collection method. A diary provides rich data of an individual's daily experience [23] and provides researchers with progressive and rich information. However, analyzing enormous amount of qualitative data is the most tedious part of the diary study where the process lasts between few days to several months based on the volume of data collected [25].

The methodology is commonly used common among medical and psychological researchers. The way older adults tackle their problems is not straightforward and diary study helps researchers understand the depth of the individual needs, as it varies across symptoms and each individual might be dealing with different problems ranging from acute to chronic conditions [24]. A study conducted by [25] where the researchers used diary study and quantitative method to identify the effects of meditations on chronic pain, and sleep. Results from twenty seven participant's diaries provided depth in the experience of older adults, which a quantitative method could not provide. This is because the participants were able explain their feedback and record them every day, rather than answer survey questions at the end of the treatment. Also, studies conducted by [23, 45, 46] used diary study as a primary method to collect data from older adults concerning their illness behaviour and their interpretations of symptoms of illness.

Results from the articles reviewed shows that diary studies have been used widely in medical research to understand an older adult's illness and the effect of treatment on them, but has not been used as an instrument to identify design requirements for assistive technology or devices. Although the diary study can be an effective way of collecting rich data and are found to be less expensive than focus groups or interview methods, the cumbersome process of analyzing the data collected makes it less desirable [23].

3.5 Think Aloud Protocol

The think aloud protocol requires people to say out loud everything that they are thinking and trying to do [16]. The think aloud protocol has been commonly used in usability studies. It is useful in studies highlighting problems faced by a participant while carrying out a task or process [15]. The HCI protocol involves participants being asked to verbalize what they are doing as they navigate through screen, pages and menus in a test interface [27]. Five published articles were reviewed where think aloud protocol is used as a primary User Design method.

In the case of older adults it must be confirmed that the individual knows about product or activity [15]. To tackle this issue, [15] implemented a task-based approach where users are asked to complete certain tasks in a multimedia interface rather than exploring the system. This helps the users to understand the flow of the system, rather than being frustrated and withdrawing while the study is in progress. Think aloud protocol is an effective method of understanding the user's view on a product [15]. The same approach is adopted by [28] where the author used scenario based think aloud protocol to evaluate an online diagnosis tool with the help of older adults [28]. The most common issues faced are deviation from task protocols [27], familiarity with the product or tool [15, 28], and balancing user frustration with another task. For older adults, cognitive ability may also add complications to verbal protocol analysis.

Moderators need to understand that for certain older adults the process of thinking aloud and navigating will be a dual task and sometimes users perform these simultaneous tasks poorly due to their possibly limited cognitive and motor ability. To address this problem, users can be asked to complete the task first without verbalizing and later perform the task again by thinking aloud [15]. Although this method seems to be promising, there are chances to include bias or performance variations as the users becomes familiar with the system while performing the task second time. This methodology can be very challenging while conducting study with people who are Deaf. To address this issue, a gestural think aloud protocol can be used where the Deaf participants use American Sign Language that is interpreted in real-time (for hearing researchers) to describe as they perform the task [29]. Based on the findings from the articles collected, it is evident that the think aloud protocol is often used as a user evaluation tool in the HCI studies with older adult participants.

3.6 Interviews

There are three major types of interviews; open ended, structured and semi structured [30]. Unlike the focus group and think aloud protocol the interviewer imposes control on the conversation. Structured interviews have been used in scenarios where the designers need feedback on a product or design [16]. For this study seven papers were reviewed where interview technique was used as a primary data collection instrument from older people.

Research conducted by [31, 32, 48] used an unstructured method and semi structured method to examine the challenges faced by older adults having schizophrenia, analyze the ways in which older adults with psychiatric disability experience pain and social relations, and to developed a patient diagnoses system [31]. Findings from above scenarios showed the author's aim was focused on understanding the older adult's perception and experiences [32]. Hence, the concept of unstructured general interview technique was adopted as it provided the richest source of data compared to the other interview techniques [30]. The absence of the structured framework can allow the participant's view on the issue to be the focus [33]. The use of semi structured interviews has enabled the collection of rich data on individual experiences and also the interviewer acquires the intended information [34].

The interview technique helps the researcher capture the intended information in a qualitative form, but it has not been used in studies involving more than 15 to 20 older adults since each session takes place between 60 to 90 min, and the health and mental condition of each individual makes the process more complicated. Results from the studies reveal that structured interview technique is often used to gather feedback and ratings from older participants on the assistive products or treatment received, and the unstructured interview technique is used to gather information on older adult's perceptions of illness or the experiences in the daily life. Based on the findings from the articles referred, interview technique was never used to gather user requirements from older adults.

3.7 Paper Prototyping

"A paper prototype is a visual representation of what the System will look like. It can be hand drawn or created by using a graphics program. Usually paper prototype is used as part of the usability testing, where the user gets a feel of the User Interface" [35, p. 11]. The low fidelity paper prototyping requires more cognitive load as the participant has to put together the designer's explanation of the concept and can become frustrating when performing the process for multiple scenarios. Hence, it is not efficient among older participants. Another reason that the paper prototyping will be harder for the older adults is that most individuals lack design vocabulary [36]. But, studies suggest that older people worked well when designers were instructed by participants on features and design needed in the device interface or product, which results in high fidelity prototyping which were more accurate than the prototypes created by the older participants. To address this issue narrative scenario based prototyping has been designed which includes storyboards and videos. This may be an apt solution, because it is valuable for portraying context dependent nature [37]. This methodology of prototyping slows down the designer as it requires much coding to write. It also involves more modifications than the low fidelity designs. Although this method requires users to expend a significant amount of cognitive effort, results based on the studies conducted in articles [35–37, 49–52]; show that the paper prototyping has been widely and successfully used in HCI studies among older adults to design computer application interfaces and interactive products.

4   Conclusions

Based on the articles reviewed, more importance has been given to collecting qualitative data from the end-user likely because this type of data provides rich details about user experiences. In general, paper prototyping and cultural probes have been used to identify typical user needs, and the diary study method has been used to understand the behaviour of individuals.

Although the above reviewed methods can be efficient tools for collecting data from older adult users, they require participation and user involvement throughout the design and development process either in home or in a laboratory environment. Since these processes require the user's participation over a period of time, they can impose a burden among the participants to varying degrees. This is particularly true for people with dementia or partial memory deficiency, which may make many of these tools unsuitable for these user groups.

Older adults with cognitive disabilities were identified as a key group for whom specially adapted tools were needed. Even though researchers have been adopting the interview and observational methods for individuals with dementia, several issues persist. Use of the interview technique tends to result in less valuable data and fewer responses in terms of user needs. Use of the observational method can help designers understand problems and concerns, but generate less information about the user experience. Culture probes and diary studies can be used by designers to more efficiently design assistive technologies or products for older adults with intermittent memory loss or dementia,

In conclusion, a new design approach is needed that builds upon, but still uses, the core conventional methods. This would address the need to design a new user needs method by enhancing the existing methods and giving a voice to people with cognitive issues. For older adults in this category, involvement should not just be as participants in the study or test, but also they should be given the opportunity convey their issues, how it affects their daily life and express the need to address the problem by means of inclusive design and assistive technology development. As part of the future work, new tools or method should be created to help designers to identify user requirements of the older adults.

Acknowledgements. Funding for this work was generously provided by the Age-Well National Centre of Excellence.

References

1. Martin, J., Murphy, E., Crowe, J., Norris, B.: Capturing user requirements in medical device development: the role of ergonomics. Physiol. Meas. Physiol. Meas. **27**(8), R49–R62 (2006)
2. Eisma, R., Dickinson, A., Goodman, J., Syme, A., Tiwari, L., Newell, A.: Early user involvement in the development of information technology-related products for older people. Univ. Access Inf. Soc. **3**, 131–140 (2004)
3. Etchell, L., Yelding, D.: Inclusive design: products for all consumers. Consum. Policy Rev. **14**(6), 1–1 (2004). Accessed 29 Feb 2016
4. Shah, S., Robinson, I.: User involvement in healthcare technology development and assessment. Int. J. Health Care Qual. Assur. **19**(6), 500–515 (2006)
5. Preece, J., Rogers, Y., Sharp, H.: Data gathering. In: Interaction Design: Beyond Human-Computer Interaction, 3rd edn., p. 232. Wiley, New York
6. Årsand, E., Demiris, G.: User-centered methods for designing patient-centric self-help tools. Inform. Health Soc. Care **33**(3), 158–169 (2008)
7. Troyer, A., Rich, J.: Psychometric properties of a new metamemory questionnaire for older adults. J. Gerontol. Ser. B Psychol. Sci. Soc. Sci. **57B**(1), P19–P27 (2002)
8. Hurt, C., Burns, A., Brown, R., Barrowclough, C.: Perceptions of subjective memory complaint in older adults: the illness perception questionnaire – memory (IPQ-M). Int. Psychogeriatr. **22**(5), 750–760 (2010)
9. Muntinga, M., Mokkink, L., Knol, D., Nijpels, G., Jansen, A.: Measurement properties of the client-centered care questionnaire (CCCQ): factor structure, reliability and validity of a questionnaire to assess self-reported client-centeredness of home care services in a population of frail, older people. Qual. Life Res. **23**, 2063–2072 (2014)
10. Hawthorne, G., Davidson, N., Quinn, K., Mccrate, F., Winkler, I., Lucas, R., Molzahn, A.: Issues in conducting cross-cultural research: implementation of an agreed international protocol designed by the WHOQOL group for the conduct of focus groups eliciting the quality of life of older adults. Qual. Life Res. **15**, 905–905 (2007)
11. Oudsten, B.L., Lucas-Carrasco, R., Green, A.M., Group, T.W.: Perceptions of persons with Parkinson's disease, family and professionals on quality of life: an international focus group study. Disabil. Rehabil. **33**(25–26), 2492–2492 (2011). Accessed 29 Feb 2016
12. Claes, R., Heymans, M.: HR professionals' views on work motivation and retention of older workers: a focus group study. Career Dev. Int. **13**(2), 95–111 (2008)
13. Raynes, N., Coulthard, L., Glenister, C., Temple, B.: Age does not come alone: Identifying and implementing older people's views of quality in home care services. Qual. Ageing Older Adults **5**(1), 24–31 (2004)
14. Mehta, K.: The challenges of conducting focus-group research among Asian older adults. Ageing Soc. **31**, 408–421 (2011)
15. Fausset, C., Mayer, A., Rogers, W., Fisk, A.: Understanding aging in place for older adults: a needs analysis. PsycEXTRA Dataset **53**, 521–525 (2009)
16. Pattison, M., Stedmon, A.: Inclusive design and human factors: designing mobile phones for older users. PsychNology **4**(3), 267–284 (2006)
17. Boehner, K., Vertesi, J., Sengers, P., Dourish, P.: How HCI interprets the probes. In: Proceedings of the SIGCHI Conference on Human Factors in Computing Systems - CHI 2007, pp. 1–1. Accessed 25 Feb 2016 (2007)
18. Caleb-Solly, P., Flind, A., Vargheese, J.: Cameras as cultural probes in requirements gathering — Exploring their potential in supporting the design of assistive technology. In: 2011 24th International Symposium on Computer-Based Medical Systems (CBMS), pp. 1–6 (2011)

19. Wherton, J., Sugarhood, P., Procter, R., Rouncefield, M., Dewsbury, G., Hinder, S., Greenhalgh, T.: Designing assisted living technologies 'in the wild': preliminary experiences with cultural probe methodology. BMC Med. Res. Methodol. **12**, 188–188 (2012)
20. Brown, M., et al.: Using cultural probes to inform the design of assistive technologies. In: Kurosu, M. (ed.) HCI 2014, Part I. LNCS, vol. 8510, pp. 35–46. Springer, Heidelberg (2014). Dickinson, A., Newell, A., Smith, M., Hill, R.: Introducing the Internet to the over-60s: developing an email system for older novice computer users. Interact. Comput. **17**, 621–642 (2005)
21. Thoring, K., Luippold, C., Mueller, R.M.: Opening the cultural probes box: a critical reflection and analysis of the cultural probes method (n.d.). Accessed 17 Feb 2016
22. Lallemand, C.: Dear diary: using diaries to study user experience. User Experience Magazine, 1 August 2012
23. Musil, C., Ahn, S., Haug, M., Warner, C., Morris, D., Duffy, E.: Health problems and health actions among community-dwelling older adults: results of a health diary study. Appl. Nurs. Res. **11**(3), 138–147 (1998)
24. Verbrugge, L.M., Ascione, F.J.: Exploring the iceberg. Med. Care **25**(6), 539–569 (1987)
25. Morone, N., Lynch, C., Greco, C., Tindle, H., Weiner, D.: "I felt like a new person." The effects of mindfulness meditation on older adults with chronic pain: qualitative narrative analysis of diary entries. J. Pain **9**(9), 841–848 (2008)
26. Terry, W.: Everyday forgetting: data from a diary study. Psychol. Rep. **62**, 299–303 (1988)
27. Chung, J., Chaudhuri, S., Le, T., Chi, N., Thompson, H., Demiris, G.: The use of think-aloud to evaluate a navigation structure for a multimedia health and wellness application for older adults and their caregivers. Educ. Gerontol. **41**, 916–929 (2015)
28. Luger, T., Houston, T., Suls, J.: Older adult experience of online diagnosis: results from a scenario-based think-aloud protocol. J. Med. Internet Res. **16**(1), e16 (2014)
29. Roberts, V., Fels, D.: Methods for inclusion: employing think aloud protocols in software usability studies with individuals who are deaf. Int. J. Hum.-Comput. Stud. **64**, 489–501 (2005)
30. Fontana, A., Frey, J.H.: Interviewing: the art of science. In: D. (ed.). The Handbook of Qualitative Research, pp. 361–376 (1994). Accessed 29 February 2016
31. Jones, K.: The unstructured clinical interview. J. Couns. Dev. **88**, 220–226 (2010)
32. Mccann, T., Clark, E.: Using unstructured interviews with participants who have schizophrenia. Nurse Res. **13**(1), 7–18 (2005)
33. Moyle, W.: Unstructured interviews: challenges when participants have a major depressive illness. J. Adv. Nurs. **39**(3), 266–273 (2002)
34. Wang, R., Korotchenko, A., Hurd, L., Mortenson, B., Mihaildis, A.: Power mobility with collision avoidance for older adults: user, caregiver, and prescriber perspectives. Prim. Health Care **50**(9), 1289 (2014)
35. Vijayan, J., Raju, G.: A new approach to requirements elicitation using paper prototype. Int. J. Adv. Sci. Technol. **28**, 11–11 (2011)
36. Hawthorn, D.: Interface design and engagement with older people. Behav. Inf. Technol. **26**(4), 333–341 (2007)
37. Sellen, K., Massimi, M., Lottridge, D., Truong, K., Bittle, S.: The people-prototype problem. In: Proceedings of the 27th International Conference on Human Factors in Computing Systems - CHI 2009, pp. 635–638 (2009)
38. Tsolidis, G.: Migration, Diaspora and Identity Cross-National Experiences, p. 161. Springer, Dordrecht (2014)
39. Fisk, A.: Guiding the design process. In: Designing for Older Adults Principles and Creative Human Factors Approaches (2nd edn.), p. 37. Taylor & Francis, London (2004)

40. Cunliffe, A., Gladman, J., Husbands, S., Miller, P., Dewey, M., Hardwood, R.: Sooner and healthier: a randomised controlled trial and interview study of an early discharge rehabilitation service for older people. Age Ageing **33**, 246–252 (2004)
41. Mojtabai, R.: Clinician-identified depression in community settings: concordance with structured-interview diagnoses. Psychother. Psychosom. **82**, 161–169 (2013)
42. Massimi, M., Baecker, R., Wu, M.: Using participatory activities with seniors to critique, build, and evaluate mobile phones. In: Proceedings of the 9th International ACM SIGACCESS Conference on Computers and Accessibility - Assets 2007, pp. 155–162 (2007)
43. Mehta, K.K.: The challenges of conducting focus-group research among Asian older adults. Ageing Soc. **31**(03), 408–421 (2011). Accessed 16 Feb 2016
44. Leonardi, C., Mennecozzi, C., Not, E., Pianesi, F., Zancanaro, M., Gennai, F., Cristoforetti, A.: "Knocking on elders' door." In: Proceedings of the 27th International Conference on Human Factors in Computing Systems - CHI 2009 (2009). Web
45. Stoller, E.P.: Interpretations of symptoms by older people: a health diary study of illness behavior. J. Aging Health **5**(1), 58–81 (1993). Web
46. Stoller, E.P., Forster, L.E., Portugal, S.: Self-care responses to symptoms by older people. Med. Care **31**(1), 24–42 (1993). Web
47. Gill, A.: Current think aloud practices. Thesis,d University of Guelph. Print
48. Nordström, M., Dunér, A., Olin, E., Wijk, H.: Places, social relations and activities in the everyday lives of older adults with psychiatric disabilities: an interview study. IPG Int. Psychogeriatr. **21**(02), 401 (2009). Web
49. Dickinson, A., Newell, A.F., Smith, M.J., Hill, R.L.: Introducing the internet to the over-60s: developing an email system for older novice computer users. Interact. Comput. **17**(6), 621–642 (2005). Web
50. Rice, M., Alm, N.: Designing new interfaces for digital interactive television usable by older adults. Comput. Entertain. (CIE) **6**(1), 1 (2008). Web
51. Siek, K.A., Khan, D.U., Ross, S.E., Haverhals, L.M., Meyers, J., Cali, S.R.: Designing a personal health application for older adults to manage medications: a comprehensive case study. J. Med. Syst. **35**(5), 1099–1121 (2011). Web
52. Cesar, P., Chorianopoulos, K., Jensen, J.F.: Social television and user interaction. Comput. Entertain. (CIE) **6**(1), 1 (2008). Web
53. Massimi, M., Baecker, R.M., Wu, M.: Using participatory activities with seniors to critique, build, and evaluate mobile phones. In: Proceedings of the 9th International ACM SIGACCESS Conference on Computers and Accessibility - Assets 2007 (2007). Web

Haptic, Tactile and Multimodal interaction

Effect of Physiological and Psychological Conditions by Aroma and Color on VDT Task

Takeo Ainoya and Keiko Kasamatsu[✉]

Faculty of System Design, Tokyo Metropolitan University, Hachioji, Japan
kasamatu@tmu.ac.jp

Abstract. There is research that color and smell improve arousal during VDT task. As the psychological effect of the harmony of colors and aroma, there is research that is being considered from the side of the sympathetic-parasympathetic activity. In this research, we focused on the harmony relationship of aroma and color, these harmonious relationship was examined the physiological and psychological effects of VDT work. From the psychological aspect, aroma has given a good effect, there was a tendency to feel calm by the aroma and color of the investigation. From the physiological aspect, it tends to be stabilized when there is a aroma during task, the effect of the color has been suggested to be susceptible than aroma. If applied to the design to suit its influence on purpose, it is possible to some effective design for the purpose.

Keywords: Aroma · Color · Physiological · Psychological · Design

1 Introduction

It has been made various studies about the relation between the colors and aroma. Koike et al. [1] investigated whether aroma reduce psychological stress and enhance concentration of attention during mental arithmetic. The results indicate that temporal aroma presentation mainly changes brain activity and thus improves concentration of attention. There were researches which had extract dimensions in impressions of colors and fragrances, and had examined their harmonious relationship [2–4].

It is known that the aroma has the effect of changing the concentrate state and stress state. For example, the aroma of mint series is effective to concentrate and lavender is effective to relieve tension. It is a well-known fact that there is such an effect only in the aroma, in addition to this, further effects are expected by stimulating the other senses. Therefore, in this study, we focused on the vision and olfaction. We examined the effect of adding a color to aroma. Specifically, we were focusing on the aroma and color harmony of effect, it was to investigate the physiological and psychological effects in VDT work.

In this research, we focused on the harmony relationship of aroma and color, these harmonious relationship was examined the physiological and psychological effects of VDT work.

© Springer International Publishing Switzerland 2016
S. Yamamoto (Ed.): HIMI 2016, Part I, LNCS 9734, pp. 475–482, 2016.
DOI: 10.1007/978-3-319-40349-6_45

2   Methods

2.1   Participants

Participants were sixteen (eight males and eight females). They were normal in the vision and olfaction in everyday life, and were in good health.

2.2   Aromas

The aromas were Eucalyptus globulus and Citrus sinensis. These are Chemotypes essential oil (Pranarom International). Eucalyptus globulus is effective to concentration and Citrus sinensis is effective to relax condition.

2.3   Colors

The participant selected the colors (on the screen of the PC) each fitting into two types of aroma on experiment description date. Cotton wool that has dropped a few drops of essential oil was in the case. Participants sniffed the aroma by opening the lid, chose the color that fits with its aroma from the Windows color palette. The screen colors which were selected by participants was showed on Fig. 1.

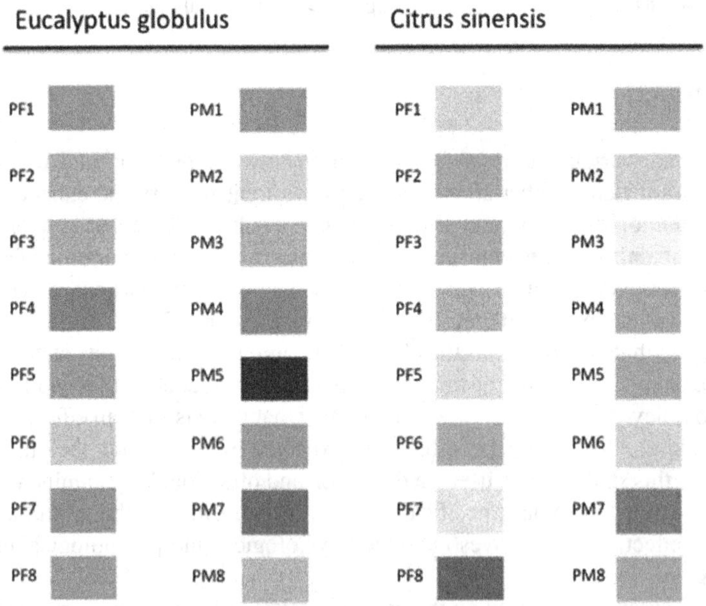

Fig. 1.   The screen color (Color figure online)

2.4 Conditions

The conditions were the following six.

(1) eucalyptus globulus and color which participant felt to be harmonized with euca-
     lyptus globulus
(2) citrus sinensis and color which participant felt to be harmonized with citrus sinensis
(3) eucalyptus globulus and color of (2)
(4) citrus sinensis and color of (1)
(5) no aroma and color of (1)
(6) no aroma and color of (2)

2.5 Task

The task was two-digit addition mental arithmetic task. The mental arithmetic formula
was displayed on screen. The experimental time was 20 min. The color of display screen
was selected by each participant. For the screen of display, the area around number
formula was white, the number formula was black and the color of the other peripheral
area was selected by the participant.

2.6 Questionnaire

The information of participants was age, sex, and likes and dislikes of aroma. The mood
assessment before and after the task, the impression evaluation was carried out after the
task. The mood assessment items were nineteen. The impression evaluation items were
fifteen.

2.7 Physiological Indices

The measured physiological indicators were electroencephalograph, electrocardiograph, and electrodermograph (Fig. 2). The content of alpha wave (8–12 Hz) and beta
wave (12–20 Hz) were calculated. The electrocardiograph was analyzed by the
frequency analysis and calculated LF/HF. The electrodermograph was calculated the
integral value.

Electroencephalograph   Electrocardiograph   Electrodermograph
(MindWave)   (RF-ECG)   (Nexus-32)

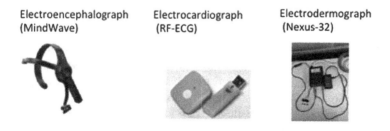

Fig. 2. The measurement devices

2.8 Procedure

The experiments were carried out in the following procedure each a condition.

- Facesheet (only on first experiment) + mood assessment
- Physiological indices attached
- Rest of 1 min
- The task start (for twenty minutes)
- Rest of 1 min
- After the task, impression evaluation and mood assessment

The participant was conducted an experiment once for 6 conditions. For a different aroma of the conditions, it was carried out after a period of time more than one week as a general rule.

3 Results and Discussion

The result likes and dislikes of aroma used in the experiment was as Fig. 3. Other than one person was answered that like citrus sinensis. Half of the experimental participants answered that like eucalyptus globulus, was a aroma that favorite divided. Then, the results of mood assessment, impression evaluation, and the physiological indices is stated.

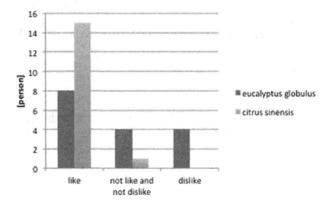

Fig. 3. Preference for aromas (Color figure online)

Mood Assessment. Here, we describe items effect of color and aroma was observed. For the "refreshing" item, the score is low if there is no aroma. It was shown to feel refreshing when there is aroma (Fig. 4). For information about "dark", because it was lower in the citrus sinensis, aroma citrus sinensis soften the dark feelings (Fig. 5). For the "restless", if the color and aroma is correct, restless score is low. In other words, there is a tendency to feel the harmony of color and aroma calm down. In other words, the aroma has a positive impact on mood. In particular, aroma of citrus was to brighten the feeling. In addition, there is a tendency to feel calm by the harmony of aroma and color.

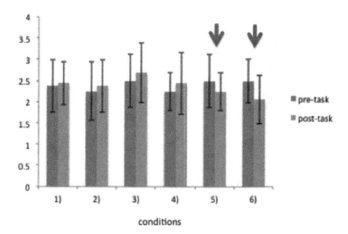

1) eucalyptus globulus and color which participant felt to be harmonized
with eucalyptus globulus
2) citrus sinensis and color which participant felt to be harmonized
with citrus sinensis
3) eucalyptus globulus and color of 2)
4) citrus sinensis and color of 1)
5) no aroma and color of 1)
6) no aroma and color of 2)

Fig. 4. The score of refreshing on mood assessment (Color figure online)

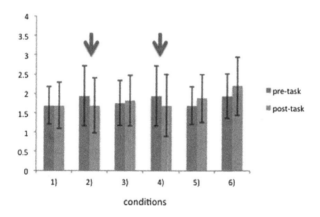

Fig. 5. The score of dark on mood assessment (Color figure online)

Impression Evaluation for Harmony of Color and Aroma. For information about "favorite" and "bright", citrus sinensis also on the screen of the same color was high evaluation (Fig. 6).

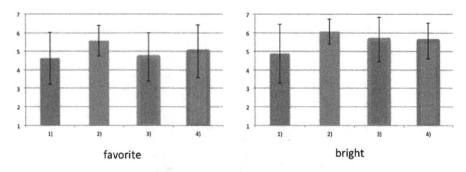

favorite   bright

1) eucalyptus globulus and color which participant felt to be harmonized
with eucalyptus globulus
2) citrus sinensis and color which participant felt to be harmonized
with citrus sinensis
3) eucalyptus globulus and color of 2)
4) citrus sinensis and color of 1)

Fig. 6. The score of "favorite" and "bright" on impression evaluation

Physiological Indices. On the integral value on electrodermal activity, in conditions that are watching the screen of the color matches the citrus sinensis, integral value was low trend. It was showed this has been a state of being relaxed (Fig. 7).

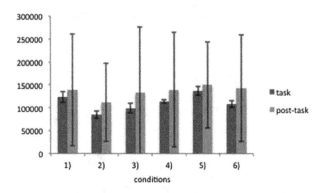

Fig. 7. The integral value of electrodermal activity on task and post-task (Color figure online)

LF/HF of ECG was slightly lower value of eucalyptus globulus than citrus sinensis during task. Relaxing effect by the aroma of eucalyptus globulus appeared. Moreover, the value after work at the time of the E screen there was a high tendency. After the task was over, it was shown to stress state is getting stronger (Fig. 8).

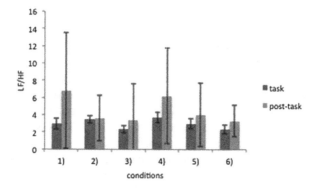

Fig. 8. LF/HF on task and post-task (Color figure online)

For alpha wave content of brain waves, the value after task under the conditions of citrus sinensis of aroma were elevated. That is enough to feel relieved after the task is stronger than the other conditions (Fig. 9).

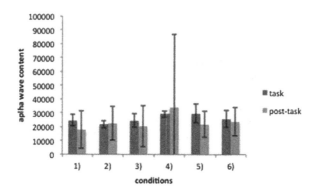

Fig. 9. Alpha wave content on task and post-task (Color figure online)

It was recognized that if there was a harmony of color and aroma in the VDT work, there was a physiological and psychological effects. This can be said to be evidence to support the implicit knowledge that is felt experientially. Some designers have been empirically acquire such a capability and knowledge and have applied to conventionally products and space. Not only designers, by design in cooperation with researchers, such as ergonomics expert, taking advantage of the evidence in the upstream process of the design process has an important role. Based on this evidence, to develop a design methodology that applies such design thinking is effective to propose products and spaces with a new value. In the future, we will be working on a new development of evidence-based design methodology as one of the design approach.

4 Conclusion

The harmonious relationships between colors and aromas were examined the physiological and psychological effects of VDT work.

There is a possibility that the aroma has a positive impact on mood after task. In particular aroma of citrus sinensis soften the dark feelings after task. In addition, there was a tendency to calm down when the color and aroma are matched. Electrodermal activity tended to stable if there was a aroma in the task. LF/HF was observed relaxing effect by eucalyptus globulus than citrus sinensis during the task.

From the psychological aspect, aroma has given a good effect, there was a tendency to feel calm by the aroma and color of the investigation. From the physiological aspect, it tends to be stabilized when there is a aroma during task, the effect of the color has been suggested to be susceptible than aroma. In other words, aroma and color affects even if they are not noticed by yourself. If applied to the design to suit its influence on purpose, it is possible to some effective design for the purpose. In this study, we will aim to develop the design process to take advantage of evidence data for corporate with designer and researcher in the future.

References

1. Koike, T., Yamada, H., Kaneki, N., Kamimura, H.: Psycho-physiological responses to mental arithmetic with temporal aroma presentation. Trans. Jpn. Soc. Kansei Eng. **12**(special issue 1), 229–237 (2013)
2. Miura, K., Saito, M.: Harmony between colors and fragrances: effect on dimensions of impressions. Kansei Eng. Int. J. **11**(1), 1–11 (2012)
3. Jingu, H.: Representation of smell and common sense. In: Proceedings of 36th Congress on Japan Ergonomics Society, pp. 68–69 (1995)
4. Miura, K., Saito, M.: Harmonious color model with fragrances. Color Res. Appl. **37**(3), 219–232 (2012)

Topographic Surface Perception Modulated by Pitch Rotation of Motion Chair

Tomohiro Amemiya[1]($\boxtimes$), Koichi Hirota[2], and Yasushi Ikei[3]

[1] NTT Communication Science Laboratories,
3-1 Morinosato Wakamiya, Atsugi, Kanagawa 243-0198, Japan
amemiya.tomohiro@lab.ntt.co.jp
[2] Graduate School of Information Systems,
The University of Electro-Communications,
1-5-1, Chofugaoka, Chofu, Tokyo 182-8585, Japan
[3] Graduate School of System Design, Tokyo Metropolitan University,
6-6 Asahigaoka, Hino-shi, Tokyo 191-0065, Japan
http://www.brl.ntt.co.jp/people/t-amemiya/

Abstract. The paper investigates multimodal perception of a topographic surface induced by visual and vestibular stimuli. Using an experimental system consisting of a motion chair and optic flow on a wide screen, we conducted a user study to assess how congruence or incongruence of visual and vestibular shape cues influence the perception of a topographic surface. Experimental results show that the vestibular shape cue contributed to making the shape perception larger than the visual one. Finally, the results of a linear regression analysis showed that performance with visual unimodal and vestibular unimodal cues could account for that with visuo-vestibular multimodal cues.

Keywords: Vestibular sensation · Self-motion · Multisensory · Motion platform

1 Introduction

The emergence of consumer-friendly head mounted displays with high frame rates and wide angle, such as Oculus Rift, easily provides the general public with an immersive virtual reality experience. Thanks to the progress in video technology and the recent spread of video presentation equipment, we can watch stereoscopic movies and large-screen high-definition videos in our private living rooms much more easily than before. Other sensory information, such as tactile, olfactory, or vestibular information, could be added to further enhance the presence of these audiovisual contents [1,2]. If sensory stimuli can be fully optimized, it is expected that a highly effective system can be developed with inexpensive, simple, and small equipment.

For contents such as driving games, it is very hard to create a highly realistic experience just with audio-visual high-definition technologies because the

© Springer International Publishing Switzerland 2016
S. Yamamoto (Ed.): HIMI 2016, Part I, LNCS 9734, pp. 483–490, 2016.
DOI: 10.1007/978-3-319-40349-6_46

sense of body motion is strongly involved in the experience. Thus, we must consider building a new framework to present a body motion stimulus when we design contents related to body motion. In driving simulators, humans generally detect velocity information using visual cues, and acceleration and angular acceleration information using mechanical ones (vestibular and tactile sensations). The organs that sense acceleration can be stimulated by mechanical (e.g., motion chairs [3]), electrical (e.g., galvanic vestibular stimulation [4]), and thermal means (e.g., caloric tests). Electrical stimulation can be achieved with a more inexpensive configuration than other methods can. However, although it affects anteroposterior and lateral directions differently, there have been no reports that it affects the vertical direction. In addition, its effect is changed by the electrical impedance of the skin. In thermal stimulation, cold water is poured directly into the ear, which is not a suitable experimental stimulus with computer systems. Therefore, motion chairs have been the *de facto* standard to create a sensation of full body motion in vehicles.

A driving experience is generally created by vehicle velocity and body motion caused by the topography of the road. Much research has been reported that velocity perception can be modulated by visually induced self-motion illusions [5] or tactile motion information [6,7]. On the other hand, the perception of the topography has not been well studied. Most conventional research has used motion chairs with six degrees of freedom to reproduce exact physical information, but such chairs tend to be expensive and large.

In this study, to move the user's body and induce a shape perception, we choose a motion chair (Kawada Industries, Inc.; Joy Chair-R1) with two degrees of freedom in roll and pitch rotations; it does not move in the vertical direction. However, one study has shown that humans more strongly perceive the shape of an object during active touch from the force profile applied to the finger than from the position profile of the finger [8]. This implies that the shape perception could be induced by local changes in topographic information without vertical movement, although the shape perception by the finger and by the body will differ. To verify the hypothesis that shape perception could be induced by body tilt, we constructed an experimental system using the simple two-DOF motion chair to present body tilt with optical flow and conducted a user study to classify the perceived shape based on visual and vestibular cues.

2   User Study

2.1   Participants

Ten male participants, aged 19–33 years, participated in the experiments. Because it has been reported that women experience motion sickness more often than men [9], only male participants were recruited. They had no recollection of ever experiencing motion sickness. All participants had normal or corrected-to-normal vision. They had no known abnormalities of their vestibular and tactile sensory systems. Informed consent was obtained from the naive participants before the experiment started. Recruitment of the participants and experimental procedures were approved by the NTT Communication Science Laboratories Research Ethics Committee, and the procedures were conducted in accordance with the Declaration of Helsinki.

2.2 Apparatus

Visual stimuli were radial expansions of 700 random dots. The size of each dot was 81.28×10^{-3}m. Resolution was 1024×768 pixels (XGA). A visual stimulus was presented by a projector on the floor (NEC; WT600J). We used a 100-in. screen. The distance between the participant and the screen was 1.72 m. Participants wore an earmuff (Peltor Optime II Ear Defenders; 3M, Minnesota, USA) to mask the sound of the motion chair.

The motion chair and the visual stimulus were controlled by different computers on a network with distributed processing. Stimulus presentation was controlled by Matlab (The Mathworks, Inc., Natick, MA, USA) using Cogent Graphics Toolbox developed by John Romaya at the LON, Wellcome Department of Imaging Neuroscience, and Psychophysics Toolbox [10]. Synchronization of the stimuli was performed over the network. Position control was adopted to drive the motion chair by applying a voltage proportional to the desired angle with a microprocessor (Microchip Inc.; PIC18F252) and a 10-bit D/A converter (MAXIM; MAX5141).

2.3 Procedure

The experimental task was to report whether the shape they ran over was a bump (convex upward), a hole (concave), or a flat surface (plane) by pressing keys of a numeric keyboard labeled 'bump', 'hole' and 'flat'. No feedback was given during the experiment. Ratings of motion sickness on a seven-point scale (1: not at all, 4: neither agree nor disagree, 7: very much) were also collected. Three optical-flow conditions (Bump/Hole/Flat) $\times$ 3 motion-chair conditions (Bump/Hole/Flat) $\times$ 3 velocity conditions (20, 30, or 40 m/s) $\times$ 10 trials (a total of 270 trials) were conducted. Subjects had 15-minute breaks after every 28 trials, but could rest at any time. A typical experiment lasted about three hours and thirty minutes.

In each trial, a stimulus combination of optical-flow and motion-chair conditions was presented in a random order. Participants were seated in the motion chair with their body secured with a belt. They were instructed to keep their heads on the headrest of the chair and not to move the neck. Figure 1 shows the experimental procedure. Participants were instructed to watch the fixation point on the screen during the trial. After five seconds, the stimuli were presented for 20 s.

The shape was expressed by titling the chair forwards and backwards as shown in Fig. 2, i.e., modifying the pitch rotation which corresponded to the

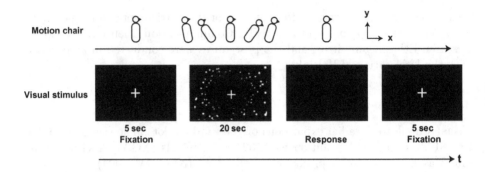

Fig. 1. Experimental procedure.

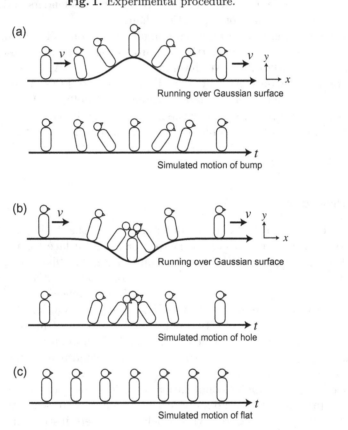

Fig. 2. Tilt of the motion chair when running over a bump (a), hole (b), and flat (c).

tangential angle on the surface. We adopted the shape profile ($y = f(x)$) as a Gaussian surface ($N(\mu, \sigma^2)$). The maximum of the tilt of the motion chair,

$$\theta_{max} = \tan^{-1}(\frac{d}{dx}f(x)|_{x=\mu\pm\sigma}), \qquad (1)$$

was set to 13.5°. After ten seconds from the start, the height was at the maximum (i.e., $x = \mu$). The translational velocity was calculated by $v = dx/dt$. The slope of the shape was set as $\sigma = 1.1$, which was determined by the rotational velocity of the actuators in the motion chair.

3   Results and Discussion

3.1   Shape Classification

The average probabilities of classifying perceived shapes by visuo-vestibular stimulation are shown in Fig. 3. Each row of graphs is the condition of bump, hole, or flat of vestibular stimuli and each column of graphs is the probability of classifying the surface as bump, hole, or flat. Note that we merged the velocity conditions (20, 30, and 40 m/s) because there were not large difference across them.

We applied an arcsine transformation to the probabilities P as $\phi = \arcsin(\sqrt{P})$ to meet the initial assumption of an analysis of variance (ANOVA) test. Then, a two-way repeated measures ANOVA was performed on ϕ. The result showed main effects of the motion-chair condition (F(2, 18) = 13.46, $p<.001$, $\eta_p^2 = .599$ for the bump stimuli; F(2, 18) = 12.05, $p<.001$, $\eta_p^2 = .572$ for the hole; F(2, 18) = 16.10, $p<.001$, $\eta_p^2 = .641$ for the flat) and of the optical-flow condition (F(2, 18) =9.28, $p<.005$, $\eta_p^2 = .508$ for bump; F(2, 18) =7.24, $p<.005$, $\eta_p^2 = .446$ for hole; F(2, 18) =17.48, $p<.001$, $\eta_p^2 = .660$ for flat), but the interaction between motion-chair and optical-flow conditions was not significant ($p>.10$), except for flat (F(4, 216) = 7.72, $p<.001$, $\eta_p^2 = .125$). This would be because participants mostly classified the shape as 'flat' due to a lack of information for judging the shape in the condition where both conditions were flat.

The comparison of the effect sizes between conditions shows that vestibular stimulation (i.e., stimulus by the motion chair) affected shape perception greater than visual stimulation (i.e., stimulus by optical flow). This suggests that the tilt of the chair, 13.5°, was large enough to judge the shape independent of visual stimuli since the threshold of tilt perception was 2.2° [11].

It has been argued that all motion sickness arises from either visual or vestibular rearrangements [12]. It would be possible that a sensory conflict caused by our experimental stimuli produces motion sickness, resulting in misjudgment of shape perception. However, subjective ratings of motion sickness from all subjects were not larger than 2, which means that the experimental stimuli did not generate motion sickness.

3.2   Perceptual Model

Since we did not observe an interaction between motion-chair and optical-flow conditions, we built a linear model of multimodal integration from unimodal shape perception as

$$\phi_{12} = w_1 \phi_1 + w_2 \phi_2 + b \tag{2}$$

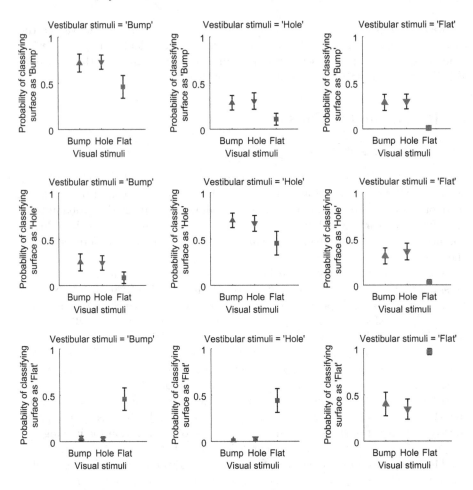

Fig. 3. Probabilities of classifying surfaces as bump, hole, or flat.

where ϕ_i is the angular transformation value of the response ratio, w_i is the weight of each factor of the modality (vision, $i = 1$; vestibular sense, $i = 2$; multimodal of vision and vestibular sense, $i = 12$), and b is the intercept. Independent variables are the responses from visual stimuli of either a bump or hole under the flat motion-chair condition (ϕ_1) and from motion-chair stimuli of either a bump or hole under the flat visual condition (ϕ_2). Dependent variable ϕ_{12} is the response from visual and motion-chair stimuli of either a bump or hole.

The result shows that the coefficients of determination were $R^2 = 0.57$ for the shape perception of a bump and $R^2 = 0.58$ for that of a hole and that the responses from visual and motion-chair stimuli were able to be explained with the linear regression (ps< .001). In both cases, the weight of vestibular sense was larger than that of vision (bump $w_1 = 0.45$, $w_2 = 0.68$; hole $w_1 = 0.43$,

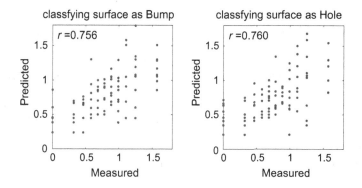

Fig. 4. Scatter plot of values predicted by the obtained regression formula and actual values of the multisensory effect.

$w_2 = 0.64$). This is in line with the effect sizes of the ANOVA we mentioned above. Figure 4 shows a scatter plot of values predicted by the obtained regression formula and actual values of the multisensory effect.

4   Conclusions and Future Work

In this paper, we reported a perceptual integration of visuo-vestibular stimulation to generate convex or concave perception of a topographic surface. We used a motion chair and optic flow on a wide screen and conducted a user study to assess the influence of congruence or incongruence of visual and vestibular shape stimuli on the perception of a topographic surface. Results show that the vestibular shape cue contributed to the shape perception more than the visual one. Finally, we built a perceptual model of sensory integration, and the results of a linear regression analysis showed that performance with visual unimodal and vestibular unimodal cues could account for that with visuo-vestibular multimodal cues. Future work includes conducting a further experiment with different parameters in an attempt to augment the effect of visual stimuli or weaken the effect of the vestibular sensory stimuli.

Acknowledgements. The work was supported by the National Institute of Information and Communications Technology (NICT) of Japan.

References

1. Ikei, Y., Abe, K., Hirota, K., Amemiya, T.: A multisensory VR system exploring the ultra-reality. In: Proceedings of the 18th International Conference on Virtual Systems and Multimedia (VSMM). IEEE (2012)
2. Ikei, Y., Shimabukuro, S., Kato, S., Komase, K., Okuya, Y., Hirota, K., Kitazaki, M., Amemiya, T.: Five senses theatre project: sharing experiences through bodily ultra-reality. In: Proceedings of the IEEE Virtual Reality 2015, pp. 195–196 (2015)

3. Huang, C.-H., Yen, J.-Y., Ouhyoung, M.: The design of a low cost motion chair for video games and MPEG video playback. IEEE Trans. Consum. Electron. **42**(4), 991–997 (1996)
4. Maeda, T., Ando, H., Amemiya, T., Nagaya, N., Sugimoto, M., Inami, M.: Shaking the world: galvanic vestibular stimulation as a novel sensation interface. In: Proceedings of the SIGGRAPH Emerging Technologies, p. 17 (2005)
5. Riecke, B.E., Schulte-Pelkum, J., Caniard, F., Bulthoff, H.H.: Towards lean and elegant self-motion simulation in virtual reality. In: Proceedings of the IEEE Virtual Reality Conference, pp. 131–138 (2005)
6. Riecke, B.E., Väljamäe, A., Schulte-Pelkum, J.: Moving sounds enhance the visually-induced self-motion illusion (circular vection) in virtual reality. ACM Trans. Appl. Percept. **6**(2), 7:1–7:27 (2009)
7. Amemiya, T., Hirota, K., Ikei, Y.: Perceived forward velocity increases with tactile flow on seat pan. In: Proceedings of the IEEE Virtual Reality Conference, pp. 141–142. IEEE Computer Society, Los Alamitos (2013)
8. Robles-De-La-Torre, G., Hayward, V.: Force can overcome object geometry in the perception of shape through active touch. Nature **412**(6845), 445–448 (2001)
9. Lentz, J.M., Collins, W.E.: Motion sickness susceptibility and related behavioral characteristics in men and women. Aviat. Space Environ. Med. **48**(4), 316–322 (1977)
10. Brainard, D.H.: The psychophysics toolbox. Spat. Vis. **10**, 433–436 (1997)
11. Guedry, F.E.: Psychophysics of vestibular sensation. In: Kornhuber, H.H. (ed.) Vestibular System Part 2: Psychophysics, Applied Aspects and General Interpretations. Handbook of Sensory Physiology, vol. VI, pp. 316–322. Springer, Heidelberg (1974)
12. Reason, J.T., Brand, J.J.: Motion Sickness. Academic Press, London (1975)

Mel Frequency Cepstral Coefficients Based Similar Albanian Phonemes Recognition

Bertan Karahoda[1], Krenare Pireva[1(✉)], and Ali Shariq Imran[2]

[1] Faculty of Computer Science and Engineering, UBT, Pristina, Kosovo
{bkarahoda,krenare.pireva}@ubt-uni.net
[2] Faculty of Computer Science and Media Technology,
Norwegian University of Science and Technology (NTNU), Trondheim, Norway
ali.imran@ntnu.no

Abstract. In Albanian language there are several phonemes that are similar in pronunciation like /q/ - /ç/, /rr/ - /r/, /th/ - /dh/ and /gj/ - /xh/. These phonemes are difficult to distinguish by human ear even for native speaking Albanians from different regions. The task becomes more challenging for automated speech systems, recognizing and classifying Albanian words and language due to the similar sounding phonemes. This paper proposes to use Mel Frequency Cepstral Coefficients (MFCC) based features to distinguish these phonemes correctly. The three layers back propagation neural network is used for classification. The experiments are performed on speech signals that are collected from different male and female native speakers. The speaker independent tests are performed for analyzing the performance of the classification. The obtained results show that the serial MFCC features can be used to classify the very similar speech phonemes with higher accuracy.

Keywords: Albanian phonemes · Similar phonemes classification · Serial MFCC features · Neural network classifier · Back propagation network

1 Introduction

Most of the current speech recognition techniques are designed to distinguish words. The word recognition is difficult to maintain since the system should be trained for each new word that is added in the database. A phoneme recognition approach could avoid this continual challenge, as a complete training could be made by using all possible phonemes of that particular language [1].

Although the Albanian language is widely spoken language, there are few works conducted to the Albanian phoneme recognition in some multilingual approaches [2]. Also, there is a lack of Albanian speech corpus which makes it difficult to conduct experiments for Albanian speech recognition systems. In Albanian language however, there is a problem when processing phoneme for recognition, as there are couples of phonemes that sound very similar but in fact are different, like the phonemes strong /rr/ and light /r/. Also the accent

© Springer International Publishing Switzerland 2016
S. Yamamoto (Ed.): HIMI 2016, Part I, LNCS 9734, pp. 491–500, 2016.
DOI: 10.1007/978-3-319-40349-6_47

of Albanian language differs from region to region. This further adds to the difficulty of correctly recognizing these phonemes.

Many speech phoneme recognition techniques are proposed by various researchers for several languages [1,3,4,7]. In speech recognition approaches, extracting the features that describe best the characteristics of the speech signal content is the most important process for further processing the speech signals. For feature extraction, the MFCC [3], the Linear Prediction based Cepstral Coefficients (LPCC) [5], and Wavelet Transform (WT) [6] based methods are widely used. Other techniques are also used for speech recognition. In [7,8], the MFCC is combined with wavelet transform to increase the speech recognition performance. In [9], the fuzzy modeling approach is proposed for speech phoneme recognition, whereas, in [10] the auditory based scale-rate filter selection method is presented. Researchers in [11] suggested a new feature extraction method called Fisher Weight Map for speaker independent phoneme recognition.

Furthermore, the neural networks and hidden Markov models are widely used for speech signal classification [12,13]. Each of the aforementioned methods describes the characteristics of the speech signal under consideration, and justify the need to use a specific method, as to increase the recognition rate in their particular contribution. Since there is no work conducted to the similar Albanian phonemes recognition, in this work the significance of MFCC features are investigated for Albanian language and its ability for classifying the similar phonemes. MFCC features are widely used in automatic speech and speaker recognition. They were introduced by Davis and Murmelstein in the 1980s, and have been used in many systems ever since [3,7,8].

The rest of the paper is organized as follows. Section 2 presents the proposed method describing feature extraction and classification process. Section 3 discusses the experimental results while the conclusion is provided in the last section.

2   Proposed Method

The proposed method consists of four major steps as shown in Fig. 1: (a) speech detection; to detect speech part within a signal, (b) noise removal; to remove any unwanted noise from the speech signal, (c) Mel Cepstrum analysis; to extract discriminative features useful for phenoms classification, (d) and artificial neural network; to classify amongst different Albanian phonemes from speech signals. Each of the steps are discussed further in the following subsection.

2.1   Speech Detection

The speech detection is the first major step. In speech detection part, the start time of the initial consonant is detected while looking for a sudden increase of amplitude and intensity. Also, from this point is the beginning of the processing phase. Once the speech is detected from the signal, the next step is to remove any unwanted noise from it.

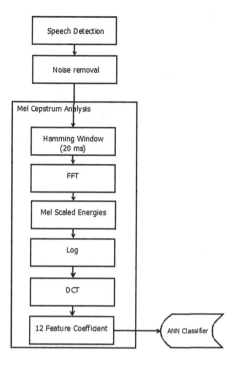

Fig. 1. Block diagram of proposed method

2.2 Noise Removal

The purpose of pre-processing steps is to remove any unwanted noise from the speech signal. As the Albanian phonemes sound very similar, therefore, it is important to obtain a better quality signal by removing unwanted noise. This will help obtain better features from the speech signal, ultimately improving classification results. The pre-emphasis filter is usually used as the first stage in processing the speech signals which improve the Signal to Noise Ratio (SNR). Furthermore, it is used to enhance specific speech information in higher frequencies and to calibrate the energy to analyse the wide spectrum of the speech signal. The pre-emphasis filter is expressed as follows [14]:

$$y(n) = x(n) - a * x(n - 1) \tag{1}$$

The pre-emphasis filter coefficient used in our proposed method is set to 0.95, whereas, x(n) and y(n) are the values of input and output respectively.

2.3 Mel Cepstrum Analysis

The next step in the proposed method is to extract features for classification by performing Mel Cepstrum analysis on the speech signal.

The mel-scale frequencies reflect the human auditory system frequency response which are obtained from linear frequency f by using the Eq. (2):

$$Mel(f) = 2595log(1 + \frac{f}{700})$$

(2)

For the various number of equally spaced mel frequencies the triangular filters are generated for linear frequencies obtained from Mel scaled frequency. Each filter is then multiplied with the Fourier spectrum of the original signal to obtain the log of the energies for Mel spaced filter banks. The discrete cosine transform (DCT) is used as the final step for obtaining the MFCC. The detailed steps are explained further in the following subsection.

2.4 Feature Extraction

The feature extraction process is as follows:

1. The detected speech signals are divided into 20 ms time intervals by using the hamming window. The overlap between the windows is set to 10 ms. The purpose of this overlap is to eliminate the spectral leakages. This is achieved because the time intervals of the hamming window is 20 ms and by keeping an overlap of half of the window size, spectral leakage can be avoided.
2. For each windowed signal the fast Fourier transform (FFT) is performed next to obtain the frequency amplitudes. The 20 Mel scaled filter banks are generated for the frequency range 300–5500 Hz, where most of the speech signals energies are concentrated. Fig. 2 shows the used mel filter banks and the frequency intervals.
3. Each Mel scaled filter bank is multiplied by windowed Fourier spectrum to obtain the energies of each filter bank.
4. Then DCT of the log of the energies obtained for 20 Mel scaled filter bank is computed and the first 12 coefficients of the DCT transform are used as feature vector for one windowed signal.
5. For approximately six-windowed signal the same procedure is repeated to obtain the 70 coefficients serial feature vector which corresponds to the approximately 70 ms time duration. Figure 3 shows the feature vectors obtained for the phoneme /rr/ from two different speakers.

2.5 Artificial Neural Network Classifier

The last step in the proposed method is the classification of Albanian phonemes using the extracted feature vectors. The three-layer backpropagation neural network is used for phonemes classification. The 70 coefficients feature vector obtained as a result of feature extraction process is fed to the 70 neurons in input layer. The 30 neurons are used in hidden layer and 8 neurons in output layer to classify the 8 different phonemes.

The speech phonemes from 4 male and 4 female speakers are used for training the network which created a total of 64 training samples for 8 phonemes. The structure of the used neural network classifier is given in Fig. 4.

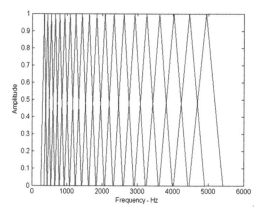

Fig. 2. Mel scaled filter banks

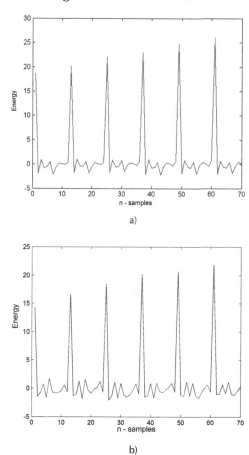

a)

b)

Fig. 3. The n-sample feature vectors; (a) Phoneme /rr/ female speaker, (b) phoneme /rr/ male speaker

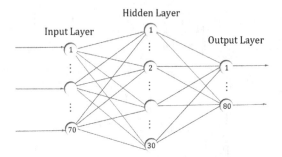

Fig. 4. Neural network structure (70 neurons in input layer, 30 neurons in hidden layer and 8 neurons in output layer)

3   Results

Due to the unavailability of Albanian language database, the speech samples are collected manually from people originally from different regions with diverse ascent. The speech signals are collected from 23 male and female speakers in silent environment with 48000 sample rate, which makes a total of 184 isolated phoneme signals. From those 184 phonemes, 64 of them are used for training the backpropagation neural network, and the rest 120 phonemes are used for testing.

All the speech signals contain the initial consonant followed by the vowel. The signal energies are computed for 20 ms durations, to detect the beginning of the initial consonants, the signal is subjected to the threshold. The threshold level is set to 0.2 in our case which is calculated experimentally. 120 phonemes from 15 male and female participants were used for testing which were not included in training set. The trained backpropagation network is tested with all 120 test phonemes, the results of which are discussed further.

Two types of tests are carried out, the first one is performed for each phoneme individually in separate classes as shown in Table 2, whereas, in the second test we have divided each pair of similar phonemes into four classes as shown in Table 1. The recognition tests is performed for each of these classes, as each class has different characteristics from other phonemes pairs. The tests are performed without using any filter for noise reduction.

Table 1 shows the correct recognition rates for each class which is calculated based on the number of correct recognitions. The highest recognition rate was achieved in the third class /rr-r/, whereas, the lowest recognition rate were in /dh-th/ class. The average recognition rate for all classes combined together is 72 %.

Table 2 shows the correct recognition rates for each phoneme in individual classes.

Table 1. Recognition performance for 4 phonmes classes

Phoneme classes	ç-q	dh-th	rr-r	gj-xh
Correct classification rate (%)	82	50	95	60
Overall performance (%)	72			

Table 2. Recognition performance for each phonmes classes

Phoneme classes	ç	q	dh	th	r	rr	gj	xh
Correct classification rate(%)	60	66.7	46.7	53.3	86.7	93.3	73.3	66.6
Overall performance(%)	68.3							

As it is seen in Table 2, the best recognition rate was obtained for the phoneme /rr/ followed by /r/, and the worst recognition rate was for phoneme /dh/. The overall recognition rate achieved is 68.3 % as depicted in Table 2, which makes the difference between the performances of two tests to 3.7 %, as can be compared from the overall performance from two tables (Tables 1 and 2).

For showing the number of correct and incorrect prediction compared to the actual outcomes, we used the confusion matrix. In order to compute the sensitivity, precision and accuracy rates, the confusion matrix for a two class classifier has been used [15]. Table 3 summarizes different attributes of the confusion matrix.

Table 3. Confusion matrix 2x2, for two classes (positive and negative)

		Prediction	
		P	N
Actual	P ´	TP(true positive)	FN (false negative)
	N´	FP(false positive)	TN (true negative)

- TP (true positive) is the number of correct predictions that an instance is positive,
- FN (false negative) is the number of incorrect of predictions that an instance negative,
- FP (false positive) is the number of incorrect predictions that an instance is positive,
- TN (true negative) is the number of correct predictions that an instance is negative,

The sensitivity or Recall rate (TPR) is the proportion of actual positive cases which are correctly identified. It is expressed as the proportion of number that are TP of all the numbers that are actual positive (TP+FN):

$$TPR = \frac{TP}{TP + FN} \tag{3}$$

Precision or Positive Predictive Value (PPV), is the proportion of positive cases that were correctly identified. It is expressed as the proportion of the number that are TP, of all the numbers that outcome positive (TP+FP):

$$PPV = \frac{TP}{TP + FP} \tag{4}$$

And, the accuracy (ACC) is the total number of predictions that were correct, calculated with Eq. (5), as follows:

$$ACC = \frac{TP + TN}{P + N} \tag{5}$$

The sensitivity, precision and accuracy rates for each phoneme class are represented in Table 4.

Table 4. Confusion matrix representing the sensitivity, precision and accuracy

Phonemes	ç	q	dh	th	r	rr	gj	xh
Sensitivity (%)	27	40	40	50	80	33	27	33
Precision (%)	33	40	67	50	43	50	31	33
Accuracy (%)	84	85	90	88	84	88	83	83

The accuracy of the classification for the individual 8 classes test is above 80 % for all the phoneme classes, whereas, the precision is above 60 % in the phoneme /dh/, and above 50 % in /th/ and /r/. The average accuracy rate is 86 %.

4   Conclusions and Future Work

The Albanian phonemes /ç/ - /q/, /rr/ - /r/, /th/ - /dh/ and /gj/ - /xh/ are very similar in pronunciation. They are also difficult to distinguish by human ear in a spoken Albanian language. This paper proposed a method for accurately recognizing Albanian phonemes using the MFCC based features and the three layers back propagation neural network. The combination of MFCC features and neural network classification model was able to classify the similar phonemes with acceptable recognition rate.

The overall performance for four phoneme classes was 72 %, where for each phoneme class the overall performance was 68.3 %. If we compare the recognition rate of other languages that used the same feature extraction method MFCC, for example, in Thai speech [1], the vowel was recognized with 67.71 %, whereas, the initial consonant with 63.82 %. Comparing to that, the results of this paper are satisfactory, even though the classification accuracy is still very low.

In general, the difference between the overall performances of four classes of similar phonemes and the eight classes of individual phonemes are found to be miniscule, which shows that the MFCC based features can be used to classify speech signals which are very similar in pronunciation, with acceptable results. The accuracy of recognition rate was calculated using confusion matrix which resulted with 86 % of accuracy.

As a future work, the paper can be extended further by applying other feature extraction algorithms for speech recognition and evaluating the classification results using Bayes classifier and SVM. Further comparisons can also be made from the results obtained by other classifiers.

References

1. Theera Umpon, N., Chansareewittaya, S., Auephanwiriyakul, S.: Phoneme and tonal accent recognition for THAI speech. Exp. Syst. Appl. **38**(10), 13254–13259 (2011)
2. Caranica, A., Buzo, A., Cucu, H., Burileanu, C.: Speed@ mediaeval 2015: Multi-lingual phone recognition approach to query by example STD (2015)
3. Dabbaghchian, S., Sameti, H., Ghaemmaghami, M., BabaAli, B.: Robust phoneme recognition using MLP neural networks in various domains of MFCC features. In: 2010 5th International Symposium on Telecommunications (IST), pp. 755–759, December 2010
4. Sharifzadeh, S., Serrano, J., Carrabina, J.: Spectro-temporal analysis of speech for spanish phoneme recognition. In: 2012 19th International Conference on Systems, Signals and Image Processing (IWSSIP), pp. 548–551, April 2012
5. Zbancioc, M., Costin, M.: Using neural networks and LPCC to improve speech recognition. In: 2003 International Symposium on Signals, Circuits and Systems SCS 2003, vol. 2, pp. 445–448 (2003)
6. Sahu, P., Biswas, A., Bhowmick, A., Chandra, M.: Auditory ERB like admissible wavelet packet features for timit phoneme recognition. Int. J. Eng. Sci. Technol. **17**(3), 145–151 (2014)
7. Tavanaei, A., Manzuri, M., Sameti, H.: Mel-scaled discrete wavelet transform and dynamic features for the persian phoneme recognition. In: 2011 International Symposium on Artificial Intelligence and Signal Processing (AISP), pp. 138–140, June 2011
8. Xue-ying Zhang, X., Bai, J., zhou Liang, W.: The speech recognition system based on bark wavelet MFCC. In: 2006 8th International Conference on Signal Processing, vol. 1 (2006)
9. Halavati, R., Shouraki, S.B., Zadeh, S.H.: Recognition of human speech phonemes using a novel fuzzy approach. Appl. Soft Comput. **7**(3), 828–839 (2007)
10. Fartash, M., Setayeshi, S., Razzazi, F.: A scale-rate filter selection method in the spectro-temporal domain for phoneme classification. Comput. Electr. Eng. **39**(5), 1537–1548 (2013)
11. Muroi, T., Takiguchi, T., Ariki, Y.: Speaker independent phoneme recognition based on fisher weight map. In: 2008 International Conference on Multimedia and Ubiquitous Engineering MUE 2008, pp. 253–257. IEEE (2008)

12. Rahman, M., Islam, M.: Performance evaluation of MLPC and MFCC for HMM based noisy speech recognition. In: 2010 13th International Conference on Computer and Information Technology (ICCIT), pp. 273–276, December 2010
13. Paulraj, M., Bin Yaacob, S., Nazri, A., Kumar, S.: Classification of vowel sounds using MFCC and feed forward neural network. In: 2009 5th International Colloquium on Signal Processing Its Applications CSPA 2009, pp. 59–62, March 2009
14. Muda, L., Begam, M., Elamvazuthi, I.: Voice recognition algorithms using MEL frequency cepstral coefficient (MFCC) and dynamic time warping (DTW) techniques. arXiv preprint (2010). arXiv:1003.4083
15. Visa, S., Ramsay, B., Ralescu, A.L., Van Der Knaap, E.: Confusion matrix-based feature selection. In: MAICS, pp. 120–127 (2011)

Minimal Virtual Reality System for Virtual Walking in a Real Scene

Michiteru Kitazaki[1](✉), Koichi Hirota[2], and Yasushi Ikei[3]

[1] Department of Computer Science and Engineering,
Toyohashi University of Technology, Toyohashi, Aichi, Japan
mich@cs.tut.ac.jp
[2] Graduate School of Information Systems,
The University of Electro-Communications, Tokyo, Japan
hirota@vogue.is.uec.ac.jp
[3] Graduate School of System Design,
Tokyo Metropolitan University, Tokyo, Japan
ikei@tmu.ac.jp

Abstract. Various sensory stimuli are required to accomplish a fully virtual walking system because walking is related to multimodal sensations. We developed a minimal virtual walking system and evaluated it using psychological factors. The system consisted of a real-scene optic flow and rhythmic foot vibrations. We tested the effects of vibrations synchronized with optic flow and the size of the visual field on the sensations of virtual walking and found that synchronized, two-channel foot vibrations with a 3-D optic flow elicited the virtual walking sensation. A larger visual field enhanced the footstep sensation during walking.

Keywords: Walking · Virtual reality · Optic flow · Vection · Tactile sensation · Vibration

1 Introduction

Walking consists of multisensory sensations and a sensory-motor integrated action. When we walk, we see optic flow, hear sounds, feel airflows, and place feet on the ground while we move our legs and arms in a complex and well-designed manner. We are consciously aware of some of them, but unconsciously aware of others. Therefore, it is difficult to develop a comprehensive virtual reality system to provide virtual walking sensations. Instead, we are focusing on a minimal system for experiencing virtual walking in a real scene.

Optic flow is one of the strongest stimuli that makes us perceive self-motion. A coherent motion presented in a large visual field induces a sensation of self-motion (vection; Fig. 1) [1, 2]. Because walking is a kind of self-motion, vection is effective in producing a virtual walking sensation.

Leg movements are required to walk around in the real world. Omni-directional treadmills and leg support actuator systems enable users to walk in place [3, 4]. These systems utilize the brain's motor commands and user's proprioceptive information

© Springer International Publishing Switzerland 2016
S. Yamamoto (Ed.): HIMI 2016, Part I, LNCS 9734, pp. 501–510, 2016.
DOI: 10.1007/978-3-319-40349-6_48

Fig. 1. Schematic example of real-scene optic flow

from body movements. Thus, users have to actually move their legs in these systems. We would like to provide a virtual experience of leg movement during walking without actually moving the legs. Leg movement during waking is a rhythmic action, and walker's feet strike the ground rhythmically. Thus, rhythmic, tactile stimulation to the soles of the feet may induce a sensation of walking.

We combined visual motion display (vection) and vibration stimuli on both feet. Rhythmic stimulation to the feet may induce spinal central pattern generators to produce an active walking sensation [5, 6]. The system consists of a walking recording system and a walking experience system.

2   Walking Recording System

The recording system captured stereo motion images from two cameras (GoPro HERO 3,1280 × 720 pixels, sampling at 30 Hz) attached to a participant's forehead (Fig. 2) to obtain optic flow. The interocular distance was 6.5 cm, which is similar to an average person's interocular distance [7]. Acceleration sensors (ATR-promotion TSND121, sampling at 1 kHz) were placed on the person's left and right ankles to obtain the timing of foot strikes on the ground synchronized with optic flow (Fig. 3). We recorded walking scenes of two persons (heights: 175 cm and 178 cm) in two different locations (Fig. 4).

Fig. 2. Two cameras mounted on a walker's forehead to capture stereo motion images or 3-D optic flow.

Fig. 3. Two acceleration sensors placed on left and right ankles to extract the timing of footsteps on the ground.

Fig. 4. Two visual scenes captured for experiments

3 Walking Experience System

For the walking experience system, 3-D (stereo) motion images with binocular disparity were presented on a head-mounted display (HMD; SONY HMZ-T1, 1280 × 720 pixels, 45 × 25.3 degrees of visual angle, 60 Hz, and Oculus Rift DK2, 960 × 1080 pixels, 90 × 110 degrees of visual angle, 60 Hz) and rhythmic vibration stimuli were presented to the left and right heels in sync with the walker's sight (Fig. 5). The sound of footsteps were recorded and processed through a low-pass filter at 120 Hz (duration 150 ms; Fig. 6 left). The recording was used to produce tactile vibrations on the observer's feet using vibro-transducers (Acouve Lab Vp408; Fig. 6 right).

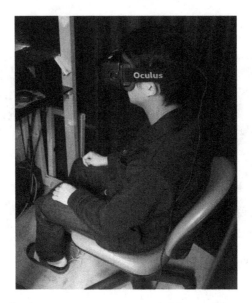

Fig. 5. Two visual scenes captured for experiments

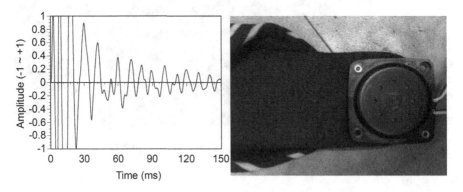

Fig. 6. (Left) Vibration profile. (Right) A vibro-transducer attached to a shoe

4   Experiment 1

Ten naïve participants (undergraduate and graduate students) participated in the experiment after providing a written informed consent. This study was pre-approved by the Committee for Human-subject Studies of Toyohashi University of Technology.

We presented visual motion images to participants using the HMD (SONY HMZ-T1) with and without vibrations on their heels. In half of the trials, participants observed the walker's leg and foot movements at the beginning of walking experiences to enhance syncing foot vibrations with visual walking. Then, they observed a scene of others walking forward. Participants were asked to rate the quality of their experience for vection, walking, footsteps, and telepresence after observing each scene for 25 s. Participants' responses were measured by using a visual analogue scale (VAS; Fig. 7). They moved a mouse cursor to indicate how they perceived each sensation. Moving the mouse left was for the least sensation and right was for the most sensation. We digitized the analogue responses to integral scales of 0–100.

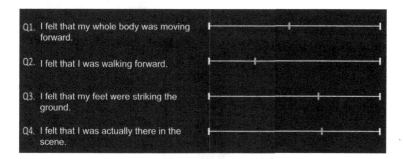

Fig. 7. Visual analogue scale for participants' responses

Participants rated two vibration conditions (with or without vibrations), two visual conditions (with or without visual walking at the beginning), two scene heights, and two locations.

We performed repeated measures ANOVA (two vibration conditions × two visual conditions) for each rating. Vection was perceived more with foot vibrations than without vibrations (main effect of vibration conditions: $F(1,9) = 20.739$, $p = .0014$; Fig. 8), and enhanced with visual walking at the beginning (main effect of visual walking conditions: $F(1,9) = 5.172$, $p = .0490$).

A walking sensation was perceived more with foot vibrations than without vibrations (main effect of vibration conditions: $F(1,9) = 23.876$, $p = .0009$; Fig. 9). There was no significant effect of visual walking or interaction.

Footstep sensations were perceived more with foot vibrations than without vibrations (main effect of vibration conditions: $F(1,9) = 13.345$, $p = .0053$; Fig. 10). There was no significant effect of visual walking or interaction.

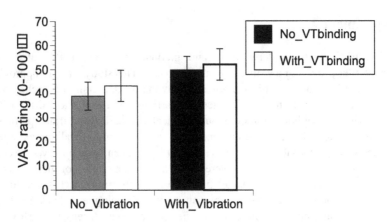

Fig. 8. Results of vection sensation

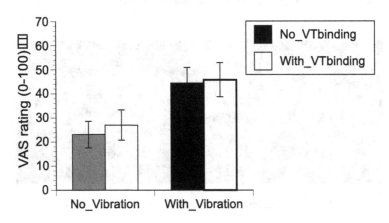

Fig. 9. Results of walking sensation

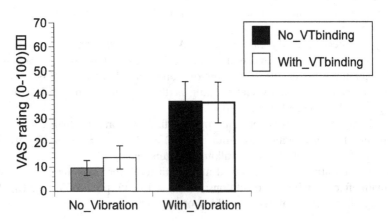

Fig. 10. Results of footstep sensation

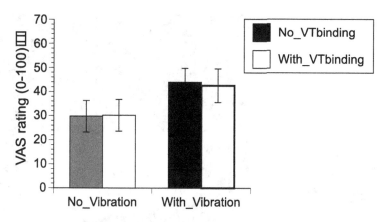

Fig. 11. Results of telepresence sensation

Telepresence was perceived more with foot vibrations than without vibrations (main effect of vibration conditions: $F(1,9) = 21.360$, $p = .0013$; Fig. 11). There was no significant effect of visual walking or interaction.

5 Experiment 2

Fifteen naïve participants (undergraduate and graduate students) performed the experiment after providing a written informed consent. This study was pre-approved by the Committee for Human-subject Studies of Toyohashi University of Technology.

We presented the same stimuli to participants using another HMD (Oculus Rift DK2) with and without vibrations on their heels. The Oculus Rift DK2 has a much larger visual field of view (90(width) × 110(height) degrees of visual angle) than the HMD of Experiment 1 (45 × 25.3 degrees of visual angle). However, we presented the visual stimuli in 66.4 × 37.2 degrees (604 × 254 pixels) at the center of the display because of a limitation of the captured image size (Fig. 12).

Participants observed leg and feet movement of walkers at the beginning of walking experiences in all trials. They rated the quality of their experience for vection, walking, footsteps, and telepresence after observing each scene for 20 s. They performed three repetitions of all combinations of two vibration conditions (with or without vibrations), two scene heights, and two locations in random order.

We conducted two-railed, single sample t-tests for the vibration conditions. All of the vection ($t(14) = 2.527$, $p = .0121$), walking ($t(14) = 3.454$, $p = .0019$), footstep ($t(14) = 3.500$, $p = .0018$), and telepresence ($t(14) = 2.399$, $p = .0155$) sensations were stronger with the foot vibrations than without the vibrations (Fig. 13).

To investigate effects of the visual field size of the HMDs, we compared the data of Experiment 1 and Experiment 2 for the common conditions (with or without foot vibrations, and with the visual walking scene at the beginning; Fig. 14). We conducted two-way ANOVA (two visual sizes × two vibration conditions) for each rating. All of the vection ($F(1,23) = 9.703$, $p = .0049$), walking ($F(1,23) = 22.865$, $p = .0001$),

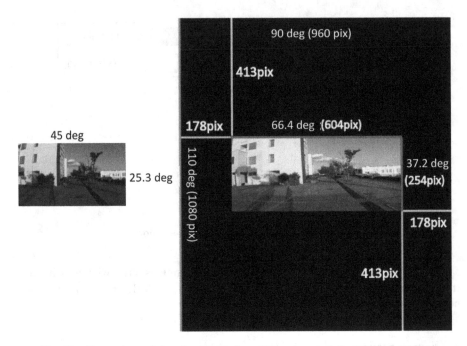

Fig. 12. Comparison of the visual field size of Experiments 1 (Left) and 2 (Right)

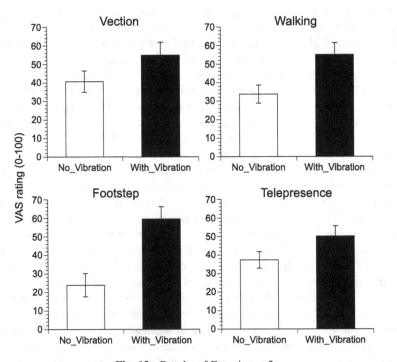

Fig. 13. Results of Experiment 2

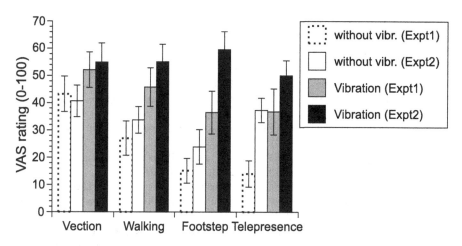

Fig. 14. Comparison of results of Experiment 1 and Experiment 2

footstep (F(1,23) = 18.370 p = .0003), and telepresence (F(1,23) = 11.978, p = .0021) sensations were stronger with the foot vibrations than without the vibrations. Only the footstep sensation was improved by a large visual field (F(1,23) = 4.738, p = .0400), and the others were not significantly improved (vection p = .9903, walking p = 3423, telepresence p = .3596). There was no interaction (ps > .354).

6 Conclusion

Subjective ratings of an active walking experience, including vection, footsteps, and telepresence, were improved with rhythmic vibrations on the heels of participants' feet. These results suggest that our minimum walking experience system, which has only 3-D visual motion images and two channel foot vibrations, gave users an active walking sensation to a certain extent.

The walking experiences, except for the footstep sensation, might not be affected by the size of visual stimuli. However we need further investigation because the number of subjects was not very large (N = 10, 15), and also the difference of visual size was not large (about two times in area size).

In the next step, we are going to present walking sensations on different surfaces such as soft sand or hard concrete roads by modulating foot vibrations.

Acknowledgments. This research was supported in part by the SCOPE program (141203019), and a Grant-in-Aid for Scientific Research (A) (#26240029 and #15H01701). We thank Atsuhiro Fujita, Takaaki Hayashizaki, Katsuya Yoshiho, Keisuke Goto, and Shohei Ueda for data collection and analysis.

References

1. Dichgans, J., Brandt, T.: Visual-vestibular interactions: effects on self-motion perception and postural control. In: Held, R., Leibowitz, H.W., Teuber, H.L. (eds.) Handbook of Sensory Physiology, vol. 8, pp. 755–804. Springer, Heidelberg (1978)
2. Kitazaki, M., Sato, T.: Attentional modulation of self-motion perception. Perception **32**, 475–484 (2003)
3. Iwata, H.: Walking about virtual environments on an infinite floor. In: Proceedings of IEEE VR 1999, pp. 286–293 (1999)
4. Iwata, H., Yano, H., Nakaizumi, F.: Gait Master: a versatile locomotion interface for uneven virtual terrain. In: Proceedings of IEEE VR 2001, pp. 131–137 (2001)
5. Gravano, S., Ivanenko, Y.P., Maccioni, G., Macellari, V., Poppele, R.E., Lacquaniti, F.: A novel approach to mechanical foot stimulation during human locomotion under body weight support. Hum. Mov. Sci. **30**, 352–367 (2011)
6. Cheron, G., Duvinage, M., De Saedeleer, C., Castermans, T., Bengoetxea, A., Petieau, M., Seetharaman, K., Hoellinger, T., Dan, B., Dutoit, T., Sylos Labini, F., Lacquaniti, F., Ivanenko, Y.: From spinal central pattern generators to cortical network: integrated BCI for walking rehabilitation. Neural Plast. **2012**, 375148 (2012)
7. Dodgson, N.A.: Variation and extrema of human interpupillary distance. In: Proceedings of SPIE, 5291, Stereoscopic Displays and Virtual Reality Systems XI (2004). doi:10.1117/12. 529999

Designing Effective Vibration Patterns
for Tactile Interfaces

Daiji Kobayashi$^{(\boxtimes)}$ and Ryogo Nakamura

Chitose Institute of Science and Technology, Hokkaido, Japan
{d-kobaya, b2121580}@photon.chitose.ac.jp

Abstract. Tactile interfaces presenting vibration stimuli are able to communicate confidentially and silently. Recent advances have enabled the users of mobile devices to create their own vibration patterns using software installed on their devices. Our research investigated vibration patterns with the aim of realizing a method that would allow elderly Japanese users to design memorable vibration patterns. Our previous study led to the conclusion that the vibration patterns characterized by the pronunciation of the message could be effectively recognized by the user. Thus, we now present an experimental study based on the proposed message-to-vibration pattern conversion method for designing comprehensible vibration patterns. First, the effectiveness of vibration patterns characterized by Japanese pronunciation factors such as the beat or the alteration in accent was evaluated. Further, we experimented with vibration patterns created by using the volume of the user's voice during pronunciation. The results confirmed the effectiveness of the method of voice volume-to-vibration patterns.

Keywords: Tactile interface · Vibration pattern · Notification message

1 Introduction

Mobile devices such as cellular phones and smartphones notify their users of incoming calls or messages by using a vibrating alert. Tactile stimuli such as vibrations were first considered as a medium of communication in the 1950s. For example, Geldard's fundamental article [4] about the perceptual characteristics of vibration stimuli referred to vibratory intensity discrimination, temporal discrimination, and learning curves for communication using "vibratese language." The letters or some prepositions of the "vibratese language" were made by using five thoracic buzzes representing vibration stimuli composed of two dimensions, i.e., intensity and duration. In this way, the researchers focused on improving the efficiency of the communication through tactile and haptic sensory modalities. More recently, users of the latest mobile devices are able to create their own vibration patterns for different notifications from the device by tapping on the touchscreen. Our previous study involved using a smartphone to test and evaluate the idea of creating and using vibration patterns on such mobile devices [7]. In these studies, the vibration patterns were of constant duration and intensity, similar to Morse code, and the respective vibration patterns presented different notification messages such as "The battery is running out", "You have a call"; therefore, the participants had to learn and memorize the correspondence between the vibration

© Springer International Publishing Switzerland 2016
S. Yamamoto (Ed.): HIMI 2016, Part I, LNCS 9734, pp. 511–522, 2016.
DOI: 10.1007/978-3-319-40349-6_49

pattern and the corresponding notification message in advance. The experimental results suggested that the number of vibration patterns participants were able to recognize could be fewer than five; however, we found that it was a cue to allow memorable vibration patterns to be created such that they are characterized by the pronunciation of the notification message. In this regard, we observed that most of the participants used to create their own vibration patterns based on their respective tempi and rhythms when they spoke the message. These results were experimentally confirmed by another study using a custom-built vibration mouse including a vibrating motor. However, the pronunciation factors that affect the recognition of the vibration pattern as a specific message were not clarified [6].

As to the Japanese language, we not only considered phonograms in which the pronunciation and the letter coincide but also ideographs that have their own meanings. The form of an ideogram suggests the meaning is the key to understanding the message conveyed by the letter. The ideograms and the meanings are cued to remember each other. From this point of view, 'tactons' or 'tactile icons', from the concept of the ideograph, are a sort of vibration stimuli created from audial rhythms. Tactons have been researched from both the physiological and sensory points of view [9, 10]. On the other hand, a message written in Japanese phonograms such as Kana represents the pronunciation of the message. Thus, according to our previous studies, comprehensible vibration patterns that represent the pronunciation of a message could be used to approximate the phonological vibration pattern. Therefore, we have been researching the requirements for creating comprehensible phonological vibration patterns.

Japanese phonetics is based on the concept that the phonetic characteristics include accent, rhythm, intonation, tempo, and so on [4]. Thus, from the perspective of phonetic characteristics, we tried to make and evaluate vibration patterns based on the tempo of pronunciation [6, 7].

This study proposes using vibration patterns with the phonetic characteristics of the accent of pronunciations to determine the requirements of designing comprehensible vibration patterns. Thus, two types of vibration patterns, namely tempo-based vibration patterns and accent-based vibration patterns were compared by experimentally obtaining the participant's tactile comprehension using a vibration mouse. In this regard, the method according to which the tempo-based vibration patterns are designed was proposed in the previous study [6]. Thus, we designed the tempo-based vibration patterns based on the existing method. We produced the accent-based vibration patterns by creating vibration patterns that were similar to the pronunciations using our custom-built controller for the vibration mouse and then evaluated the patterns by assessing participants' tactile comprehension experimentally.

2 Evaluation of Tempo-Based and Accent-Based Vibration Patterns

2.1 Method

Vibration Mouse and the Control System. Although we evaluated the vibration patterns using not only the vibration mouse but also a smartphone in our previous studies, the characteristics of memorable vibration patterns for the participants were about the same for both of these tactile interfaces. However, the vibration mouse is able to generate a vibration wave with larger amplitude, which is controlled by changing the voltage applied to the vibrating motor in the vibration mouse. Therefore, we used the vibration mouse to produce a wider range of vibration patterns in this study.

The vibration mouse was made by attaching a vibrating motor (S.T.L.JAPAN CL-0614-10250-7) to a computer mouse (DELL MO56UOA) and is able to present vibration stimuli with an averaged vibrational wave velocity of 2.3 mm per second. The power voltage for activating the vibrating motor attached to the mouse was controlled using a high-precision analog I/O terminal (CONTEC AIO-160802AY-USB) and a personal computer (DELL XPS 8300) running Windows 8.1 Pro Japanese edition. The voltage applied to the vibration motor was controlled by the I/O terminal with our custom software. In addition, the vibration mouse simultaneously functioned as the computer mouse with two buttons and a scroll wheel.

Designing Two Types of Vibrational Notification Messages. Two types of vibration pattern were evaluated. The tempo-based vibration pattern should be composed of vibrations of constant duration and intensity as shown in the lower portion of Fig. 1; however, the amplitude of the vibrational wave velocity measured at the surface of the vibration mouse was rough with a delay according to the digital oscilloscope (Tektronix DPO2024B) to which a vibrometer (MotherTool VB-8205SD) was attached as vibration sensor as shown in the upper portion of Fig. 1. Although the respective vibration durations and the gap between the durations were decided based on a young individual's reading of the message, the duration of vibrations was chosen from 100, 200, and 400 ms based on a previous study [8].

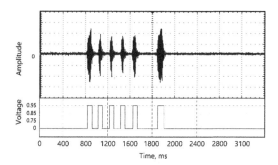

Fig. 1. Example of a vibrational waveform on the surface of the vibration mouse (upper). The vibration is rough and the amplitude is varied in spite of applying power voltage constantly to the vibrating motor (lower).

On the other hand, the accent-based vibration patterns were designed according to an accentual dictionary of the Japanese language [1] and other reference books on Japanese linguistics. Concretely, we estimated the perceptual duration of vibration at 180 ms per mora based on the average duration of mora in Japanese reading. In the same way, we decided that the gap between vibration durations for choked sound was

240 ms and the duration of a long vibration was 380 ms. Further, the voltage applied to the vibrating motor was classified into three levels according to the alteration in accent. Therefore, the vibration waveform on the surface of the vibration mouse in case of presenting an accent-based vibration pattern was as shown in the upper portion of Fig. 2.

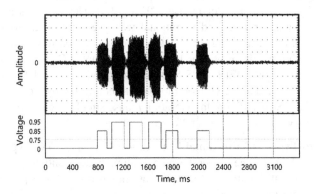

Fig. 2. Example of voltage shifts for presentation of the accent-based vibration pattern (lower) and observed vibrational waveform on the surface of the vibration mouse (upper). This example shows the vibration pattern for presenting the same notification message that is shown in Fig. 1.

Our experiment involved creating two sets of vibration patterns and each set included the same six notification messages in advance. The two sets of vibration patterns were designed based on the method of designing tempo-based and accent-based vibration patterns of each. The six notification messages were Japanese sentences representing the following: "The bath is ready," "The battery has been recharged," "You forgot to turn off the light," "You've got mail," "Clean your kitchen," and "The bus is due to arrive."

Although we researched vibratory patterns from the view of vibratory perception, in practice, the vibrating sound normally perceived in the context of using the vibration mouse is produced on a desk or a table. In other words, the vibration patterns would not only be perceived by the user's vibratory perception but also by their auditory perception. Therefore, in this experiment, the participants tried to evaluate the vibration patterns without covering their ears.

Participants. We selected 33 male students ranging from 21 to 24 years of age and 3 female students ranging from 21 to 23 years of age as participants. The users of the vibratory interfaces had to be able to perceive the vibration patterns; however, one male student could not perceive the vibration pattern correctly through the experiment. Therefore, the experimental data of 35 students were analyzed in this experiment.

Experimental Procedure. The experiment was applied within-subjects design and the participants tried to correlate the notification messages with the tempo-based vibration patterns in the first trial, whereas the second trial was used for evaluating the accent-based vibration patterns. The procedure followed during each trial was divided into two steps. Firstly, participants were expected to learn the correspondence between the notification messages and the vibration patterns using the software we developed. The software featured a learning window and a trial window. The learning window included six buttons indicating the different notification messages and a "Next" button in the lowest part of the window as shown in Fig. 3. Using this window, the participant was able to produce the vibration patterns on the vibration mouse by using the mouse to select a button on the screen. Participants were able to learn the correspondence between the vibration patterns and the notification message repeatedly until they internalized the relations. After the learning procedure, the participants clicked the "Next" button to progress to the next step upon which the learning window on the screen was replaced with the trial window as shown in Fig. 4.

Fig. 3. Learning window for confirming the correspondence between the notification message and vibration pattern.

After relaxing a while, the six vibration patterns were randomly presented to the participants one by one. The participants tried to correlate the messages with the vibration patterns by using the vibration mouse to select the answer from six notification messages or by selecting "I could not recognize it" in the right column of the trial window as shown in Fig. 4. Participants' answers were recorded by the software and their opinions about the ease of learning and ability to recognize the vibration patterns were further assessed in an interview after all the trials.

Fig. 4. Trial window for testing six vibration patterns

2.2 Results

Number of Correct Answers. We measured the comprehensibility of the notification message communicated by the vibration pattern by counting the number of correct answers by the participants for the two different kinds of vibration patterns: tempo-based and accent-based. As a result, the number of correct answers in the case of using tempo-based vibration patterns averaged 3.63 (SD = 1.43), although the number of correct answers in the case of using accent-based vibration patterns averaged 3.86 (SD = 1.56). The result of a two-sided test of statistical significance using a level of significance of 0.05 indicated that the difference between those averages were not statistically significant ($p = .55$). Thus, we concluded that the comprehensibility of both types of vibration patterns was almost the same.

Participants' Opinions. The outcome of the interviews conducted with participants determined that 15 of the 35 participants believed that tempo-based vibration patterns were comprehensible. Meanwhile, 20 of the 35 participants preferred the accent-based vibration patterns because of comprehensibility. As far as the characteristics of the pronunciation of notification messages are concerned, 32 of the 35 participants said that the vibration pattern representing the notification message including choked and/or long sounds was easy to learn regardless of the types of vibration patterns.

As for the reason for their preference for vibration patterns of either one of the two types, most of the participants not only pointed out the easiness to learn the correspondence between the notification messages and the vibration patterns but also mentioned the ease of imagining the pronunciations from the vibration patterns after learning.

2.3 Discussion

Although the number of correct answers for the respective types of vibration patterns was almost the same, participants' opinions suggest that the ease with which the pronunciation of the notification messages is imagined is an important factor in designing vibration patterns. In addition, the result of our previous study suggests that the pronunciation of the notification message depended on the person; therefore, the vibration patterns representing the pronunciation should be designed following the user's pronunciation. However, the vibration patterns for the experiment in this study were not designed according to the pronunciation of respective participants; instead, they were designed based on the pronunciation of a young individual. Further, the easiness of imagining the pronunciations from the vibration patterns varies between individuals. That is, for some people, neither of these types of vibration pattern would provide a sufficient cue to imagine the pronunciations of notification messages. In this regard, the above results confirmed our previous knowledge, even though the previous study only included the vibratory perception of the vibration pattern.

This explains why the number of correct answers for both types of vibration patterns seem to be almost the same. Nevertheless, it is difficult to describe both of the types of vibration pattern as being comprehensible.

In addition, the number of correct answers was almost the same as in our previous studies [6, 7]; therefore, it seemed that the vibrating sound of the vibration mouse has an insignificant effect on the perception of vibration.

2.4   Summary of Evaluation

Although the above results did not enable us to clarify a comprehensible type of vibration pattern, we found that neither the tempo-based nor the accent-based vibration patterns have sufficient cues to represent the pronunciation of the notification message. This suggested the need to develop a method to design a more comprehensible vibration pattern and encouraged us to design a new vibration pattern including more cues. Our aim was therefore to imagine the pronunciation of notification messages using a vibration pattern that includes characteristics of both tempo-based and accent-based vibration patterns.

3   Designing Vibration Patterns Based on the User's Voice

We designed more comprehensible vibration patterns by focusing on the voice of the user of the vibration mouse, because voice or pronunciation could include characteristics of both the tempo and accent of speech. However, it is necessary to develop a new method to reflect the characteristics of the pronunciation on the vibration pattern. In this regard, one approach to creating a vibration pattern would be to convert the voice into vibratory stimuli. Thus, we developed a converter that amplified the speech signal and applied voltage to the vibrating motor in the vibration mouse. The vibration pattern produced by the converter was named "voice-based vibration pattern" and was evaluated together with the other two types of vibration patterns from the viewpoint of comprehensibility.

3.1   Developing a Converter for the Voice-to-Vibration Pattern

The new system for generating vibratory stimuli by the vibration mouse consisted of a capacitor microphone (SONY ECM-PCV80U), a personal computer (DELL XPS8300), the converter we developed, and the vibration mouse. The circuit of the converter was a modification of the circuit of a sound level meter as shown in Fig. 5.

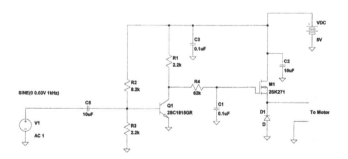

Fig. 5. Circuit diagram of the converter

The converter was driven by both the audio signal from the headphone jack and 5 V supplied via the USB (universal serial bus) port of the personal computer. The audio signal was output by playing a recorded audio file using our custom software and the microphone. Thus, the user had to record his/her pronunciation of notification messages and create the audio files in advance before presenting the vibration patterns as described later. The audio file consisted of data generated by analog-to-digital conversion at a sampling rate of 44.1 kHz with a 16-bit quantization rate.

The voltage applied to the vibrating motor was supplied from the output jack of the converter. Figure 6 shows the change in the waveform inputted as an audio signal including the pronunciation of the notification message to the vibrational waveform on the surface of the vibration mouse. The waveforms in Fig. 6 were measured and recorded by the digital oscilloscope at both points A and B of the circuit; however, the vibratory waveform C was measured by attaching the vibration sensor of the vibrometer. Comparing the waveform of the audio signal and the amplitude of vibration on the vibration mouse indicated that the tempo and accent mostly seem to be the same, though the amplitude of vibration has a lag time compared with the waveform of the audio signal.

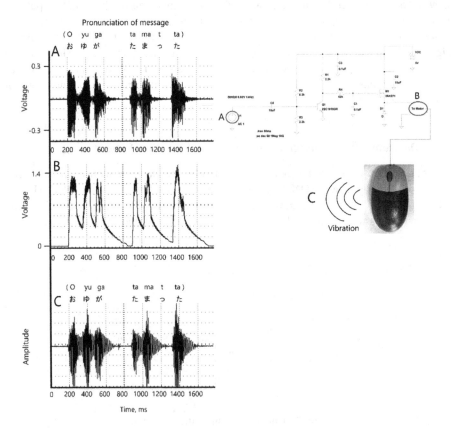

Fig. 6. Example of waveforms recorded at points A and B in the circuit of the converter and the amplitude of vibration on the surface of the vibration mouse (indicated as waveform C).

3.2   Creating Three Types of Vibration Patterns

We evaluated the voice-based vibration patterns by using eight notification messages consisting of the six notification messages used in the former experiment and the additional messages "Clean your toilet" and "The TV program is starting." These eight notification messages were converted into three types of vibration patterns, namely tempo-based, accent-based, and voice-based. However, the voice-based vibration patterns had to be produced by the respective participants in advance of their trials using our custom software.

On the other hand, the tempo-based and accent-based vibration patterns were created based on the pronunciation of the young individual who was used in the former experiment.

3.3   Experiment

The experiment was with-in-participants design and conducted for three conditions using tempo-based, accent-based, and voice-based vibration patterns for the same eight notification messages. The participants were required to evaluate the comprehensibility of the three types of vibration patterns. However, the vibration patterns were not only evaluated in terms of their comprehensibility but also from a learnability perspective in the context of daily use. In other words, we assumed vibration patterns requiring more understanding from the user as being less effective. In this regard, the data would not provide a clear indication as to the learnability if participants were given opportunities to understand the correspondence between the vibration patterns and notification messages as far as they considered it necessary. Thus, participants were intentionally allowed few opportunities to understand the correspondence between the vibration patterns and the notification messages before the trials in this experiment.

The software for learning and evaluating tempo-based and accent-based vibration patterns was used as well as the experiment described before. However, this time the window for software learning included eight buttons indicating the different notification messages. Each button was only available once and the software presented the vibration pattern on the vibration mouse only once. As for learning and evaluating voice-based vibration patterns, we employed additional custom-built software for use in the experiment. The software had three functions: recording the user's speech, understanding the vibration patterns based on the recorded speech, and evaluating the vibration patterns one by one.

Procedure. In the experiment, the participants repeatedly evaluated the eight tempo-based, accent-based, and voice-based vibration patterns; therefore, participants repeatedly attempted understanding and correlating the notification messages with the vibration patterns three times in a similar way as follows. In addition, participants were required to listen to white noise with a headphone because we had little idea of the tactile perception stimulated by the voice-based vibration patterns.

Firstly, participants evaluated the tempo-based vibration patterns following the same procedure used in the former experiment. More specifically, after the participants experienced all eight vibration patterns one by one, they tried to randomly correlate the eight notification messages with the vibration patterns presented and answered the message they recognized by choosing from the list of eight notification messages and clicking the answer on screen using the vibration mouse.

Secondly, the accent-based vibration patterns were learned and evaluated in the same way as the tempo-based vibration patterns.

Lastly, the subjects recorded the eight notification messages for presenting the corresponding voice-based vibration patterns using the microphone and the custom-built software as shown in Fig. 7. Participants were required to check the voice-based vibration patterns after recording their speech of the notification message and were able to try to record again until they were satisfied with the voice-based vibration pattern they produced. Further, they tried to tune the volume level using a keyboard, because the amplitude of the voice-based vibration pattern converted directly by the converter was changed according to the volume level of sound. About this point, the volume of the voice depended on the participant's voice; therefore, quiet talkers were required to increase the volume level in order to present voice-based vibration patterns more clearly.

Fig. 7. Scene showing a participant recording his speech of eight notification messages one by one using the custom-built software.

Before the trials, participants recorded their speech of the eight notification messages after which they had one opportunity to check or learn the respective voice-based vibrational message based on their speech converted by the converter. After relaxing a while, they tried to correlate the notification messages with the randomly presented voice-based vibration patterns and provided their answers on the screen. After completing all the trials, participants were interviewed to obtain their opinions about the effectiveness of the vibration patterns.

Participants. The participants were 19 male students ranging from 21 to 23 years of age and 11 female students ranging from 19 to 22 years of age. Although all participants were physically unimpaired and were able to perceive the vibration stimuli from the vibration mouse, two participants admitted to finding it difficult to understand any of the notification messages of the vibration patterns. Further, an additional participant was unable to create voice-based vibration patterns at maximum speech volume because she was a silent speaker. Therefore, the experimental data of 27 participants were analyzed in this experiment.

Result and Discussion. Based on the experimental data, the correct answers for each type of vibration pattern were averaged and compared as shown in Fig. 8. Further, we analyzed the variance and the difference among the three types of vibrations. The results showed that the difference was statistically significant ($F(2, 78) = 3.17$, $p = .048$) and the results of multiple comparisons of the three types showed that the significance probability between voice-based and tempo-based ($p = .074$) and between voice-based and accent-based ($p = .089$) were significant using a level of significance of 0.1. Thus, it seemed that voice-based vibration patterns were more comprehensible than the other two types especially when the user is allowed little opportunity to understand the correspondence between the vibration pattern and the notification message.

Our analysis of the participant opinions indicated that 24 out of 27 participants preferred the voice-based vibration pattern; however, 2 of the 27 participants preferred the tempo-based, whereas 3 of the 27 participants preferred the accent-based vibration. Those participants who preferred the voice-based pattern said that the vibration more closely reflected his/her speech than the other types.

Although the voice-based vibration pattern seemed to be effective, further analysis indicated that the number of correct answers was reduced when the vibration pattern represented a monotonous notification message. This could lead to a decrease in the comprehensibility of voice-based vibration patterns.

4 Conclusion

This study led to the development of an appropriate method for designing a vibration pattern through experimentation. We found the voice-based vibration pattern, including the characteristics of the user's pronunciation, could be more effective than the other patterns. However, the comprehensibility of a voice-based vibration pattern could be reduced by the specific characteristics of pronunciation such as monotonous notification messages. Therefore, this problem should be addressed to improve the effectiveness of the method.

References

1. Akinaga, K. (ed.): Nihongo Akusento Jiten [Japanese Accent Dictionary]. Sanseido, Tokyo (2015)
2. Brewster, S., King, A.: An investigation into the use of tactons to present progress information. In: Costabile, M.F., Paternó, F. (eds.) INTERACT 2005. LNCS, vol. 3585, pp. 6–17. Springer, Heidelberg (2005)
3. Brown, L.M., Brewster, S.A., Purchase, H.C.: Multidimensional tactons for non-visual information presentation in mobile devices. In: ACM International Conference Proceedings Series, vol. 159, pp. 231–238 (2006)
4. Geldard, F.A.: Adventures in tactile literacy. Am. Psychol. **12**, 115–124 (1957)
5. Kashima, T.: Kiso kara manabu Onseigaku [Studying Phonetics from the Basics]. 3A Corporation Online, Tokyo (2002)

6. Kobayashi, D., Mitani, H.: Designing memorable tactile patterns. In: Yamamoto, S., Abbott, A.A. (eds.) HIMI 2015. LNCS, vol. 9172, pp. 396–404. Springer, Heidelberg (2015). doi:10.1007/978-3-319-20612-7_38

7. Kobayashi, D., Nakano, M.: Designing memorable tactile patterns for older adults. In: Proceedings 19th Triennial Congress of the IEA (2015)

8. Kobayashi, D., Takahashi, K.: Designing understandable vibration patterns for tactile interface. In: Yamamoto, S. (ed.) New Ergonomics Perspective, pp. 259–266. CRC Press, London (2015)

9. Rinker, M.A., Craig, J.C., Bernstein, L.E.: Amplitude and period discrimination of haptic stimuli. J. Acoust. Soc. Am. **104**(1), 453–463 (1998)

10. Tan, H.Z., Reed, C.M., Duriach, N.I.: Optimum information transfer rates for communication through haptic and other sensory modalities. IEEE Trans. Haptics **3**(2), 98–108 (2010)

Relationship Between Operability in Touch Actions and Smartphone Size Based on Muscular Load

Kentaro Kotani[1(✉)], Ryo Ineyama[1], Daisuke Hashimoto[2],
Takafumi Asao[1], and Satoshi Suzuki[1]

[1] Department of Mechanical Engineering, Kansai University, Osaka, Japan
{kotani,k270053,asao,ssuzuki}@kansai-u.ac.jp
[2] Graduate School of Science and Engineering, Kansai University, Osaka, Japan
k311848@kansai-u.ac.jp

Abstract. The objective of this study was to examine the changes in muscular loads of the forearm/hand areas and in the subjective responses associated with operability and discomfort levels when participants performed touch action on different sizes of smartphones. In the experiment, finger motions and electromyograms (EMGs) of three muscles were recorded during reciprocal tapping tasks with the smartphones while participants were in the seated position. Three sizes of smartphones as well as one with a small soft keyboard for minimizing dynamic thumb motions as an intervention were provided. The data showed that muscular loads on the thumb abduction and flexion of the proximal interphalangeal joints of the finger were affected by the size of the smartphone used. A large smartphone with the keyboard intervention successfully reduced the muscular load for abduction of the thumb and, as a second-order effect, the force for holding the smartphone by using finger flexors. The subjective ratings of difficulty in touch action were significantly affected by the size of smartphone, and the subjective ratings of difficulty in gripping the smartphone were also affected by the size of smartphone. The results implied that both input method for reducing the amount of thumb abduction and key layout for reducing reach by the thumb are recommended to reduce the muscular loads for operating large smartphones.

Keywords: Touch action · Smartphone · Operability · Musculoskeletal disorders

1 Introduction

The recent development of mobile phones with touch displays, including smartphones, has led to an increase in incident cases of musculoskeletal disorders (MSDs). Many studies have focused on the relationship between the use of mobile phones and the factors associated with MSDs. Gustafsson, et al. [1] used electromyography to compare thumb postures and physical loads in relation to mobile phone tasks (such as texting messages), gender, and history of musculoskeletal symptoms. They found that participants with musculoskeletal symptoms had different behavior patterns which

S. Yamamoto (Ed.): HIMI 2016, Part I, LNCS 9734, pp. 523–530, 2016.
DOI: 10.1007/978-3-319-40349-6_50

emphasize lower muscle activity levels for thumb abduction and for fast thumb motions with fewer pauses. Berolo, et al. [2] evaluated the use of mobile phones and its association with the subjective pains of the upper extremity, upper back, and neck. They concluded that the association between the use of hand-held devices and musculoskeletal symptoms raised concern over the intensive use of such devices. These results suggested that the use of mobile phones was related to the potential risk of MSDs.

Under the current development of smartphones, the design of smartphones has become diversified, including the popularity of large-size displays. When the size of the display becomes large, the display area being operated by the thumb needs to be increased. This use of the thumb results in unstable grasping of the device. The emergence of these adverse effects may prompt an increase in the risk of MSDs. Kietrys et al. [3] reported the risk of MSDs accompanied by the growing size of touch-screen devices by monitoring muscular activities by using electromyography for thumb motions and static loads for gripping. They compared a variety of devices, including physical keypad devices and touch screen devices with sizes ranging from 3.5 to 9.5 inches, and found a trend toward high finger flexor, wrist extensor, and trapezius muscle activities when participants used both hands on a device with a large display area. Their results are convincing that it would be important to investigate the effect of smartphone size on operability based on the muscular load when participants use only one hand, which is now the typical operation by smartphone users.

Therefore, the objective of this study was to empirically investigate the changes in muscular loads and in subjective responses associated with operability and discomfort levels of participants when they used different sizes of smartphones.

2   Methods

2.1   Participants

We conducted a laboratory study in which five right handed male subjects, whose ages ranged from 20 to 22 years, participated in the study. Based on the interview, all of the participants regularly used smartphones to send/check SMS messages or to play social games. Their corrected visions were better than 20/30. Each participant gave a written informed consent prior to beginning the study. No history of or symptoms associated with musculoskeletal pains in the upper extremity or the neck were reported at the time of the interview.

2.2   Experimental Apparatus

Figure 1 shows the setup for the experiment. Finger motions were recorded by high speed video camera (HAS-L1, DITECT) with a microzoom unit (JF17095 M, SPACECOM). Muscle activity was measured with a bioamplifier (BA1104 m EMG, Nihon Santeku, low-pass frequency of 1000 Hz, TC: 0.03 s). These signals were synchronized with a sampling rate of 100 Hz at the data logger (GL900, GRAPHTEC). Three types of smartphones were used. Table 1 summarizes the properties of the smartphones and includes their dimensions and weights. In addition to the three smartphones, a large smartphone with a modified soft keyboard (Type Large2) was also tested. The dimensions of the Large2 as compared to the Large are shown in Fig. 2. The size of the soft keyboard in Large2 was as the same as that in the Small condition. The new size of the keyboard was designed to see the effect of redesigning the size of the keyboard.

Table 1. Dimension of the smartphones used in the experiment

Condition	Dimension	Weight
Small (iPhone5S, Apple)	H 123.8 mm W 58.6 mm T 7.6 mm	112 g
Medium (iPhone6, Apple)	H 138.1 mm W 67.0 mm T 6.9 mm	129 g
Large (iPhone6plus, Apple)	H 158.1 mm W 77.8 mm T 7.1 mm	179 g
Large2 (iPhone6plus, Apple) with modification of soft keyboard size 74 %)	H 158.1 mm W 77.8 mm T 7.1 mm	179 g

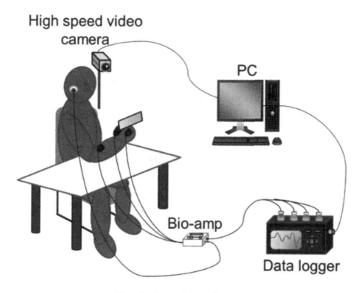

Fig. 1. Experimental setup

2.3 Experimental Protocol

Participants performed reciprocal tapping tasks with smartphones while participants were in the seated position. They used their right hand to hold the smartphone and used their right thumb for the task. They rested their right elbows on a table during the task.

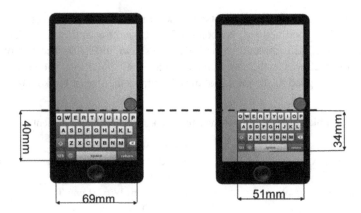

Fig. 2. Smartphones with modification of soft keyboard size. Left: Large condition and Right: large 2 condition, in which the size of large condition was used with modification where the soft keyboard was set to confine the area for the thumb motion.

A total of nine characters ('q', 't', 'p', 'a', 'g', 'l', shift key, 'v', and backspace keys) were selected for the task and were entered with a QWERTY soft keyboard with tap-based touch action. A yellow marker was attached to the surface of the smartphone (see Fig. 3) to define the default position, and participants were asked to enter the characters three times, in reciprocating motions, by starting from the default position each time.

The muscular loads in three muscles in the right forearm/hand areas were registered by electromyography. Table 2 summarizes the muscles and their roles associated with the musculoskeletal motions used in this study. After the task was completed, participants

Fig. 3. Smartphone showing the default position (yellow marker) and the keys used for the task (marked in red circles) (Color figure online)

Table 2. Muscles and their functions used in the study

Muscle	Motion
Abductor pollicis brevis (APB)	Abduction of the thumb
Flexor digitorum superficialis (FDS)	Flexion of the PIP joints of fingers
First dorsal interosseous (FDIM)	Abduction/flexion of MP joint of the index finger

were asked to fill out the subjective evaluation form, where they reported the operability, the ease of holding the smartphone, and the level of fatigue suffered from the task on the Likert scale of one to five.

2.4   Data Analysis

For the analysis of electromyogram (EMG)data, band-pass filtering between 5 Hz and 300 Hz was used, followed by root mean square processing, as described by Gustafsson, et al. [1]. The EMG signals during the task were then normalized by the EMG data for standardized contraction protocol, where participants were asked to perform a 5-s maximum contraction. The normalized EMG signal (%maximum voluntary contraction (%MVC)) was assigned to represent the muscular load for each touch action on the display. The onset of touch action was set to the time the thumb started motion from the yellow marker, and the offset of touch action was set to the time the thumb landed on the designated character. Segmentations of videotaped motions were completed manually. A repeated measures analysis of variance was performed on the %MVC and on the subjective ratings for the size of smartphone. P-values less than 0.05 were considered statistically significant, and a post hoc Tukey's significant difference test was applied to determine if differences existed between the measures collected for each size of smartphone.

3   Results and Discussion

3.1   Relationship Between Size of Smartphone and the Muscular Load

Figure 4 shows changes in the muscular load by the size of the smartphone. The muscular loads on two measured muscles were affected by the size of the smartphone ($F (3, 176) = 7.44$, $p < .01$ for FDS, $F (3, 176) = 3.82$, $p < .05$ for APB). However, the muscular loads on the FDIM were not affected by the size of the smartphone ($F (3, 176) = 1.72$, NS). For FDS, the muscular load during the task using the Large smartphone was higher than when using the other smartphones, including the Large2 smartphone. For APB, the result was slightly different: The muscular load during the task using the Large smartphone was marginally significantly higher than when using the Small smartphone, and it was significantly higher than when using the Large2 smartphone. The result apparently indicated that a large smartphone with an intervention to confine the area to be operated by the thumb motions indeed successfully reduced the muscular load for abduction of the thumb and, as a second order effect, reduced the force for holding the smartphone using finger flexors.

Among the three muscles, the muscular load for APB was high, ranging from 20 to 45 % MVC and also showed large differences in the muscular load between the Large and the Large2 smartphone conditions. On the other hand, the muscular load for FDIM was relatively low, and the differences between conditions were small, from 5 % to 10 % MVC. The muscular loads obtained in this study were relatively higher than in the previous study [3] using touch devices with 3.5 to 9.5 inch displays with both hands, with that study showing 8.9 to 26.2 % MVC for APB and 5.9 to 19.4 % MVC for FDS. The relatively high muscular load in this study may come from the task of performing two functions with one hand, i.e., participants had to move the thumb while securely grasping the smartphone at the same time. Especially high muscular load for APB during touch operation was also observed by Xiong and Muraki [4], who compared two sizes of buttons on a smartphone touch screen and concluded that the muscular load for touching the keys by the thumb was due to the increase of the thenar eminence grip. Their results showed that a significant decrease of APB during touching of small keys required less thenar eminent grip. This is consistent with our study, in which participants performed tasks with the Large2 condition which required touch action with a relatively upright thumb posture.

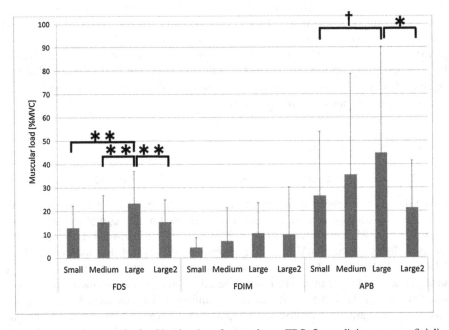

Fig. 4. Changes in muscular load by the size of smartphone. FDS: flexor digitorum superficialis, FDIM: first dorsal interosseous, APB: Abductor pollicis brevis. **: $p < .01$, *: $p < .05$, †: $p < .1$.

3.2   Relationship Between Size of Smartphone and the Subjective Ratings

Figure 5 shows changes in subjective ratings by the size of the smartphone. Subjective ratings of difficulty in touch action were significantly affected by the size of the smartphone (F (3, 16) = 5.68, p < .01), and subjective ratings of difficulty in gripping the smartphone were also affected by the size of the smartphone (F (3, 16) = 10.08, p < .01). For both ratings, touch action with a large smartphone showed the highest difficulty ratings. There were no significant differences between the ratings obtained for small and medium smartphones. Although the EMG difference was apparent between the Large and the Large2 conditions, differences in subjective ratings were not present.

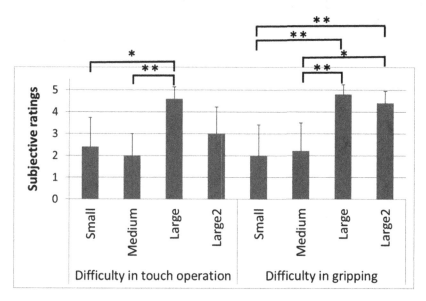

Fig. 5.   Changes in subjective ratings by the size of smartphone. **: p < .01, *: p < .05,

4   Conclusion

In this study, both the muscles associated with gripping the smartphones and the muscles for thumb abduction were affected by the size of the smartphones. High muscular loads measured in participants using a large smartphone were reduced by modifying the size of the soft keyboard on the display to confine the area for thumb motion. Overall, the results implied that input methods to reduce the amount of thumb abduction and key layouts to reduce thumb reach are recommended to reduce the muscular loads for operating large smartphones.

Acknowledgements. Part of the present study was funded by Advanced-biomedical sensing technology research group Kansai University, and Kakenhi of the Japan Society for the Promotion of Science (26560036). The authors would like to thank Yosuke Sano during the data collection.

References

1. Gustafsson, E., Johnson, P.W., Hagberg, M.: Thumb postures and physical loads during mobile phone use – a comparison of young adults with and without musculoskeletal symptoms. J. Electromyogr. Kinesiol. **20**, 127–135 (2010)
2. Berolo, S., Wells, R.P., Amick, B.C.: Musculoskeletal symptoms among mobile hand-held device users and their relationship to device use: a preliminary study in a Canadian university population. Appl. Ergon. **42**, 371–378 (2011)
3. Kietrys, D.M., Gerg, M.J., Dropkin, J., Gold, J.E.: Mobile input device type, texting style and screen size influence upper extremity and trapezius muscle activity, and cervical posture while texting. Appl. Ergon. **50**, 98–104 (2015)
4. Xiong, J., Muraki, S.: An ergonomics study of thumb movements on smartphone touch screen. Ergonomics **57**(6), 943–955 (2014)

Why Is Tactile Information not Accurately Perceived?

Accuracy and Transfer Characteristics of Visualized Schematic Images Induced by Perceived Tactile Stimuli

Keisuke Kumagai(✉), Kazuki Sakai, Kentaro Kotani,
Satoshi Suzuki, and Takafumi Asao

Department of Mechanical Engineering, Kansai University, Osaka, Japan
{k194690,k447583,kotani,ssuzuki,Asao}@kansai-u.ac.jp

Abstract. In this study, we focused on the visualization of tactile information, where people mapped the set of perceived tactile stimuli to the visible images. This empirical study was intended to determine these characteristics of visualization. Participants were asked to draw a set of two straight lines, given as tactile information perceived on their palm. Geographical differences between the original and perceived lines categorized into displacement, rotation angles, and scaling rates were analyzed by applying affine transformation. The participants drew significantly more deviating lines for subsequent lines. Participants also tended to draw the lines shifting downwards. The tendency to deviate the lines downwards was presumably explained by the psychological effects related to cautious behavior towards actions away from their bodies, i.e., participants were, in an involuntary manner, restrained to draw the lines at the upper part of the tablet, which was physically away from the body trunk, yielding a trend that many lines tended to be drawn nearer to the body.

Keywords: Tactile display · Tactile stimuli · Visualization · Short-term memory · Tactile spatial information · Affine transformation

1 Introduction

There have been a numerous reports associated with tactile displays as a potential alternative for the Braille system. Tactile displays can transmit various information to its users, including characters and shapes, by presenting physical stimuli to the skin. The need to develop tactile displays stems from the fact that the proportion of visually disabled persons who can read Braille is quite low (only 12.7 %) [1], and it is difficult for people with acquired blindness to learn Braille [2].

With regard to previous studies on tactile displays, in the study of Mizukami et al. [3], an experiment was conducted where participants were given a set of characters by presenting the vibrotactile information perceived from their palm. They reported that the correct response rates for complex characters such as "A" and "F" were approximately 60 %. Mine et al. [4] conducted an experiment where participants were asked to identify hiragana characters by tracing their palm with a touch pen used for smartphones,

© Springer International Publishing Switzerland 2016
S. Yamamoto (Ed.): HIMI 2016, Part I, LNCS 9734, pp. 531–538, 2016.
DOI: 10.1007/978-3-319-40349-6_51

reporting that there was an apparent trend between certain shapes with a low recognition rate and the wrong answers. They found that the average correct answer rates were 57.79 % among all participants. These studies commonly reported that the correct answer rates for characters presented by tactile display were low; although various approaches have been discussed, no clear solutions regarding the improvement of recognition rates have been found till date.

In this study, we focused on visualization, visually representing internal concepts formulated through the transmission process to tactile information. Wake et al. [5] suggested that visualization was the process from which we generate image-based information obtained through tactile perception in the brain temporarily; people then recognize the information by matching it with a set of long-term memory images. However, it is not clear how accurately tactile images are visualized. Therefore, considering that perceived tactile information is geometrically distorted from its original information, factors adversely affecting the correct recognition of tactile information can be clarified by evaluating the distortion generated through the process of visualization.

Therefore the objective of this study was to empirically examine the accuracy of visualization of tactile information and the existence of a trend in distortion through the process of visualization by directly comparing the participants' visualized images with their original images.

2 Method

Figure 1 shows the schematic diagram of the apparatus. Compressed air was generated by an air compressor (Hitachi Koki EC1430H2), and the air-jet stimuli were presented by means of a 12 × 12 air-jet array controlled by a precision pressure regulator (CKD RP2000-8-08-G49PBE). The pressure level and airflow duration were controlled by an electro-pneumatic regulator (CKD EVD-1900-P08 SN), and the selector used for determining the location to generate stimuli was controlled by electromagnetic valves (KOGANEI025E1-2).

In this experiment, tactile stimuli were presented to the middle of the palm. The level of air pressure was set to 100 kPa, and the duration of each air jet emission was 100 ms. Each trial consisted of presenting two line-shaped stimuli. After two sets of line-shaped stimuli were presented to the participants, they were asked to draw two perceived lines on the tablet. Instructions were given to the participants such that the perceived stimuli should be drawn as per what they just perceived. The inter-stimulus interval between two straight lines was 2000 ms. Prior to the stimulus presentation, an auditory signal was given for preparation. Each set included 240 trials; a total of three sets were conducted in three days. A set is divided into three subsets to confirm the existence of a daily-based difference in geometric transformation of tactile information through visualization.

Six right-handed university students (20 to 24 years of age) participated in the experiment.

Owing to the geometrically precise coupling between the palm and the nozzle matrix, the hand location to the nozzle plate was aligned so that all tactile stimuli were

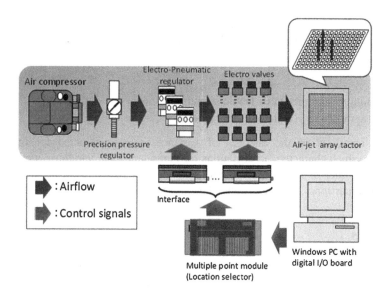

Fig. 1. Overview of the experimental apparatus

properly applied to the surface of the palm. The hand location was then digitized so that the participants could relocate their hands easily at the identical location.

Ear plugs and headphones with white noise had to be worn by the participants to minimize any clues they may obtain from sounds generated by air-jet emission.

Comparisons between the original and the visualized tactile stimuli were calculated by applying affine transformation. Geographical differences between the original and perceived lines were categorized into displacement [px], rotation angles [deg], and scaling rates [-], for further analysis.

The amount of deviation categorized as three characteristics are derived as follows; displacement t [mm]

$$t = \sqrt{\left(M'_x - M_x\right)^2 + \left(M'_y - M_y\right)^2} \tag{1}$$

M_x, M_y Midpoint coordinates of the preceding line stimulus
M'_x, M'_y Midpoint coordinates of the subsequent line stimulus

rotation angles θ [deg]

$$\cos\theta = \frac{C_x C'_x + C_y C'_y}{|\vec{C}||\vec{C'}|} \tag{2}$$

θ Angle between two lines
scaling rates A [-]

$$A = \begin{cases} \frac{C'L}{CL} \text{(if } C'L > CL) \\ \frac{CL}{C'L} \text{(if } CL > C'L) \end{cases} \tag{3}$$

CL Length of the presented tactile stimuli
$C'L$ Length of the visualized tactile stimuli

Repeated measures of the analysis of variances were conducted for the above parameters which characterized deviations for the independent variables, including the sets and the order of line stimuli. Significant relationships were further analyzed by multiple comparisons. The significance level was set to 0.05 for the comparison.

3 Results

Figures 2, 3, and 4 show the average displacement, rotation angles, and scaling rates for two consecutive stimuli in each set. These figures represent how accurately the tactile stimuli were visualized; note that they do not show how the perceived stimuli deviated from the original stimuli.

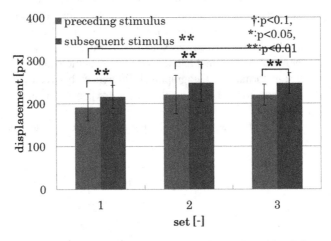

Fig. 2. Changes in displacement of visualized stimuli from the given stimuli for two consecutive stimuli. (Color figure online)

According to Figs. 2, 3, and 4, the participants perceived that preceding stimuli averaging 210.3 px (about 17.5 mm) deviated from the given stimuli and also perceived that the subsequent stimuli averaging 236.6 px (about 19.7 mm) deviated from the given stimuli. Participants perceived the stimuli, which were displaced on an average of 14.5 % in rotation and approximately 28.3 % in average size changes.

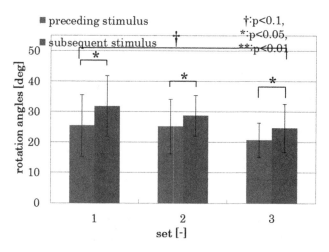

Fig. 3. Changes in rotation angles of visualized stimuli from the given stimuli for two consecutive stimuli. (Color figure online)

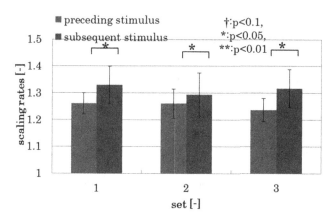

Fig. 4. Changes in scaling rates of visualized stimuli from the given stimuli for two consecutive stimuli. (Color figure online)

Further, the only displacement that was significantly different is for the set (F (2, 2) = 729, p< 0.01).

The deviations for each of the three categories were significantly different between the preceding stimulus and the subsequent stimulus (F (1, 2) = 1240, p< 0.01 for

Table 1. Number of incorrect answers categorized by the direction of deviation

Participant	Up	Upper Right	Right	Lower Right	Down	Lower Left	Left	Upper Left
A	38	18	57	111	200	177	76	43
B	35	33	52	73	138	201	123	65
C	40	38	50	97	228	173	37	57
D	31	39	86	96	195	174	61	34
E	32	47	101	179	154	115	56	34
F	30	43	58	170	158	121	99	41

displacement, $F(1, 2) = 27.1$, $p < 0.05$ for rotation angles, and $F(1, 2) = 19.5$, $p < 0.05$ for scaling rates). The result revealed that deviations from the origin were significantly different between the preceding stimulus and the subsequent stimulus. As shown in Figs. 5, 6 and 7, the deviations of subsequent stimuli were larger than those of the preceding stimuli.

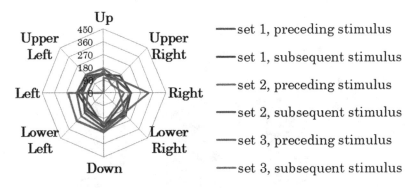

Fig. 5. Deviation by the direction shown in pixels [Participant D]. (Color figure online)

The deviations, including the direction of the deviation, was further analyzed. Table 1 shows the number of incorrect answers categorized by eight directions of deviation.

According to Table 1, the number of incorrect answers tended to shift downward for all participants.

Figure 5 shows the deviation by the above eight directions for the performance by participant D, as an example. As seen in Fig. 5, responses were made that deviated downwards; and the deviation was small when they responded upward, in most cases.

4   Discussion

An empirical study to evaluate visualization of tactile information revealed that errors were present between visualized tactile images and the original tactile images. As reported by the process of modality conversion, where participants who responded by drawing with their hands caused the decay of tactile information [6]. In this study, when participants were asked to visualize and draw a set of two straight lines given as tactile information on their palm, the modality conversion occurred twice, such as Tactile → Vision → Movement of the arm in this experiment; thus the possibility of deviation was smaller at the stage of Tactile → Vision conversion.

In addition, displacement, rotation angles, and scaling rates were significantly different following the order of given stimuli. The deviation of the preceding stimuli was smaller than that of the subsequent stimuli, and the accuracy of the tactile information dropped significantly. This loss of accuracy for the subsequent stimuli was interpreted as the participants not being able to memorize the tactile information of the subsequent stimuli accurately enough to represent them on the tablet, due to a lack of available memory resources for the second stimuli.

The number of incorrect answers shifted downward for all participants. In the previous study [7], an experiment was conducted where participants were asked to answer by providing the locations and the directions of stimuli given as tactile information perceived on their palm. They reported that participants perceived the stimulus position shifting downward, which was consistent with this study. Thus the trend to perceive the stimuli downward would be categorized into as one of the conversion characteristics.

It was also revealed that the deviation upwards decreased, whereas the deviation downward increased. According to Kikuchi et al. [8], the psychological effect related to cautious behavior towards actions away from the body was present; therefore participants were, in an involuntary manner, restrained to draw lines at the upper part of the tablet, which was physically away from the body trunk. This yielded trends where many lines tended to be drawn at near to the body, which was the bottom part of the tablet. Such psychological behaviors may have resulted in suppressed deviation for upward movement.

5   Conclusion

In this study, participants were asked to draw a set of two straight lines given as tactile information perceived on their palm. Geographical differences between the original and perceived lines categorized as displacement, angle of rotation, and the rate of scaling were analyzed by applying affine transformation. As a result, two lines were compared with respect to deviations from the original lines; it was revealed that the participants drew significantly more deviated lines when the subsequent line was given. Participants also tended to draw lines downwards.

Subsequent lines were drawn rather differently from the original line owing to the limitation of short-term memory. It was interpreted that participants could not memorize the geographical information of the subsequent lines accurately enough to represent them on the tablet due to a lack of available memory resources for the second lines. The tendency to deviate the lines downwards was presumably due to the psychological effect related to cautious behavior towards actions away from their bodies, i.e., participants were, in an involuntary manner, restrained to draw lines at the upper part of the tablet, which was physically away from the body trunk, yielding trends where many lines tended to be drawn near the body.

Acknowledgements. Part of the present study was funded by Advanced-biomedical sensing technology research group Kansai University, and Kakenhi of the Japan Society for the Promotion of Science (26560036).

References

1. Ministry of Health, Labour and Welfare, Social Welfare and War Victims' Relief Bureau, Department of Health and Welfare for Persons with Disabilities, Handicapped children and physically handicapped people's survey result: Ministry of Health, Labour and Welfare, p. 49, p. 64 (2008)
2. Haga, Y., Matsunaga, T., Mizushima, M., Totsu, K., Esashi, M.: 2D pin display for blind aid using SMA micro actuator. In: The 3rd JSME Symposium on Welfare Engineering, pp. 197–199, Tokyo (2003)
3. Mizukami, Y., Uchida, K., Sawada, H.: Tactile transmission by higher-level perception using vibration of shape memory alloy thread. Inf. Process. Soc. Jpn. **48**(12), 3739–3749 (2007)
4. Mine, J.: Investigation on recognition rate of Hiragana when using character communication techniques by transmitting point-movement information via sense of touch. Department of Computer Science and Engineering School of Fundamental Science and Engineering, Waseda University (2015)
5. Wake, H., Wake, T.: Perception of tactile letters by fingertip. In: 6th Sensory Substitution Symposium, pp. 63–67 (1980)
6. Posner, M.I.: Characteristics of visual and kinesthetic memory codes. J. Exp. Psychol. **75**(1), 103–107 (1967)
7. Sato, H.: Presentation for tactile letter information using flick motions and its evaluation, Unpublished Master's thesis, Kansai University (2015)
8. Kikuchi, H., Iwaki, S.: Accuracy of reproduction of object locations by Haptic Kinesthesi. Inf. Process. Soc. Jpn. **J96-D**(1), 25–34 (2013)

Multimodal Information Coding System for Wearable Devices of Advanced Uniform

Andrey L. Ronzhin[1(✉)], Oleg O. Basov[2], Anna I. Motienko[1],
Alexey A. Karpov[1], Yuri V. Mikhailov[1], and Milos Zelezny[3]

[1] SPIIRAS, 39, 14th Line, St. Petersburg 199178, Russia
ronzhin@iias.spb.su
[2] Academy of FAP of Russia, 35, Priborostroitelnaya, Orel 302034, Russia
[3] University of West Bohemia, Pilsen, Czech Republic

Abstract. The paper presents a mathematical model of a subsystem for multimodal information coding. Analytical expressions for the quality and speed of information transmission are obtained. The results of experimental studies of the developed multimodal information coding system are presented. The requirements for using the developed model and system for data processing in wearable devices of advanced uniform are discussed.

Keywords: Multimodal information · Coding algorithms · Uniform · Wearable devices · Data transmission · Energy consumption reduction

1 Introduction

Nowadays, there is a need to improve speech compression, to increase the efficiency of using network resources of a mobile communication system, and to consider new features of modern communication systems development. Therefore, it is of great importance to work out new coding methods and algorithms as well as to improve the existing ones. The solution to this problem is connected with the creation of the effective multimodal information coding systems for wearable devices of advanced.

Even now, there are prerequisites to reject the traditional principles for separating transmitted information into communication services and to implement polymodal infocommunication systems (PICS). Such systems imply a coherent set of data processing and information storage, telecommunication networks, which operate under a single management for the purpose of collecting, processing, storage, protection, transmission and distribution, display and use of multimodal information, taking into account the meaning of the transmitted messages, the identity of users, their mood, physiological and psycho-emotional state. To estimate user state, parameters are implemented of non-invasive registration methods functioning during communication and duty work of users [1–9].

It should be noted that a multimodal information coding system is one of the most important elements of PICS, as the quality indicators of the procedure for multimodal information coding determine the upper bound to the quality of communication provided in the chain "soldier-squad-platoon-company" [10]. Unlike traditional telecommunications, transmission of information via PICS is carried out in the form of a set of

© Springer International Publishing Switzerland 2016
S. Yamamoto (Ed.): HIMI 2016, Part I, LNCS 9734, pp. 539–545, 2016.
DOI: 10.1007/978-3-319-40349-6_52

signals of the modalities corresponding to the main channels of interpersonal communication [11]. The signals of the individual modalities (speech, lip movement, eye movement, movement of the facial muscles, gestures, handwritten keyboard input, or input via sensors), processed in the subscriber terminal of the soldier, are transmitted together through hardware and software means of communication and further along the existing communication channels of data network.

It is obvious that the maximum amount of information is transferred from the subscriber to the subscriber via visual and acoustic communication channels. However, depending on the situation, there is always a technical possibility to allocate bandwidth to transmit additional data by means of efficient compression of the signals of modalities.

The analysis shows that the following contradictory objectives are the most relevant to a multimodal information coding system for wearable devices of advanced uniform:

- to increase the quality of encoding messages while maintaining one of the speeds of multimodal information transmission;
- to adaptively reduce the speed under conditions of multimodal information transmission via data networks with varying parameters (e.g., along radio channels) without degradation of the qualitative assessments of encoding messages.

The solution to the formulated tasks will improve the efficiency of interpersonal communication in the chain "soldier-squad-platoon-company" by increasing the amount of information about military personnel state necessary for making adequate managerial decisions during combat operations. However, such an approach is in conflict with the traditional principle of providing communication services and informatization to the users of a data transmission network. It is required to validate scientific and methodical modeling tools, including mathematical ones; to determine potential and ultimate characteristics of PICS for the total number of modalities in each managerial situation; to choose an apparatus for estimating parameters of data network during multimodal information transmission.

2 Model of Multimodal Information Coding System

The synthesis of PICS requires the development of theoretical models to assess the quality of encoding multimodal information with given resources of data transmission network (DTN) and a volume required for transmission of the maximum number of messages of different modalities with the specified quality and rationale for the choice of methods of transmitting such messages based on simulation results.

In view of the existing models of speech and video codecs, a set-theoretic model of a multimodal information coding system with multi-parameter adaptation can be represented as follows (Fig. 1). We consider the parametric coding of redundant messages and propose a universal representation of signals of different modalities in the following form. The input of a multimodal information coding system can be described as the sets of messages from sources of different modalities $\left\{ \vec{A}_w \right\}$, $w = \overline{1, W}$. The internal sub-system parameters are:

(1) source (modalities) number W;

(2) number K_w of the values $w = \overline{1, W}$ of a random variable describing the w-th message source in analysis period T_A;

(3) mapping type of a parametric analysis G_{PA}, determined by a mode of creation, combination and mapping of a parameters set $\vec{X}_w$ of the analyzed messages $\vec{A}_w$;

(4) number $p_w, w = \overline{1, W}$ and a representation of coding parameters $\vec{X}_{w,j}, j = \overline{1, p_w}$ of multimodal information sources;

(5) mapping mode $G_{Kw,j}$, $w = \overline{1, W}$, $j = \overline{1, p_w}$, which determines the quantization procedures of the observed parameters of multimodal information sources;

(6) number o_j of quantization levels for each of the observed parameters of information sources $(j = \overline{1, p_1 + \ldots + p_W})$, which determine the cardinality of subsets of coding parameters $\{C_j\}$ at DTN input;

(7) mapping mode of a statistical analysis G_{SA}, which determines the classification procedure of initial messages from W sources;

(8) number H of states of user terminal $\overline{CMT}$, which determines a set of information capacity distribution modes of a communication channel by sets of coding parameters of W sources, where

$$\overline{CMT} = \left\{ No_{G_{K1,1}} \right\} \times \ldots \times \left\{ No_{G_{K1_p}} \right\} \times \ldots \times \left\{ No_{G_{KW,1}} \right\} \times \ldots \times \left\{ No_{G_{KW,pW}} \right\}$$
$$\times \{o_1\} \times \ldots \times \{o_p\} \times \ldots \times \{o_{p1 + \ldots + pW - 1} + 1\} \times \ldots \times \{o_{p1 + \ldots + pW}\}$$

where $No_{G_{KW,pW}}$ is a number of a mapping $G_{Kw,j}$, $w = \overline{1, W}$, $j = \overline{1, p_1 + \ldots + pW}$. Values $o_j = 1$ provide possibility of exclusion of j subspaces from structure of space of coding parameters. In a particular case of one-to-one correspondence between the values o_j and mappings $G_{Kw,j}$, the set $\overline{CMT}$ will be as:

$$\overline{CMT} = \{o_1\} \times \ldots \times \{o_p\} \times \ldots \times \{o_{p1 + \ldots + pW - 1} + 1\} \times \ldots \times \{o_{p1 + \ldots + pW}\}.$$

For a highly adaptive system, the number of possible states of the user terminal can be infinitely large: $H = |\overline{CMT}| = \infty$.

Given the distortions produced in the encoding and the impact of the communication channel defined by mapping G_{CH}, with known mapping G_{DK}, which uniquely determines a decoding procedure, the mathematical description of the entire coding subsystem relative to the external parameter characterizing the quality of encoding messages of different modalities can be represented as follows:

$$D_{\text{cym}} = \sum_{w=1}^{W} \left(\frac{D_w\left[\{\vec{A}\}, \{\hat{\vec{A}}\}\right]}{P_{C_w}} + \sigma \sum_{q=1}^{W} \left(\frac{D_w\left[\{\vec{A}\}, \{\hat{\vec{A}}\}\right]}{P_{C_w}} - \frac{D_q\left[\{\vec{A}\}, \{\hat{\vec{A}}\}\right]}{P_{C_q}} \right)^2 \right),$$

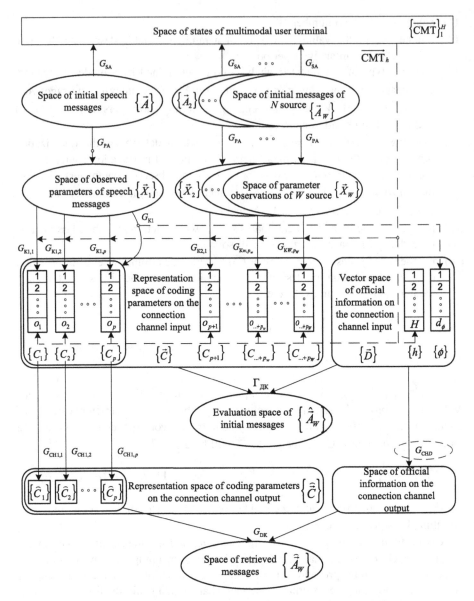

Fig. 1. Model of a multimodal information coding system

where $D_w\left[\left\{\vec{A}\right\}, \left\{\hat{\vec{A}}\right\}\right]$, $w = \overline{1, W}$ is the mean square error between the sets of the initial and recovered messages or noise energy at restoring messages of w source; σ is the empirical coefficient that determines the degree of the influence of penalty; $P_{C_w} = \sum_{i=1}^{U} \vec{A}_{wi}^T \vec{A}_{wi}$ is message energy of the w-th source.

The above-mentioned list of the internal parameters of a multimodal information coding system allows us to formulate the mathematical model of such a system in relation to the external parameter – transmission speed (information output):

$$B_{(W)} = \frac{\log \prod_{w=1}^{W} \prod_{j=p_{w-1}+1}^{p_w} o_j + r + \log d_\phi + \log H}{T_A} \text{ bit/s,}$$

where $r = \left\lceil \log_2 \left(1 + \sum_{i=1}^{t_{INT}} C_n^i \right) \right\rceil$ is a number of check bits, and t_{INT} is the correcting

ability of an error-correcting code; C_n^i is the number of combinations of n by i; $d_\varphi = |\{\varphi\}|$ is the cardinality of a sub-space $\{\varphi\} \in \{\vec{D}\}$, characterizing the set of error-correcting coding modes.

Thus, the obtained formalisms determine the important internal functional features of DTN taking into account the patterns of transmission of data blocks corresponding to the active modalities. The proposed mathematical model of information modality processing is being introduced in the telecommunication system connecting distributed users and a central control station.

3 Coding System for a Multimodal Speech Signal

The coding system for a multimodal speech signal (Fig. 2), developed based on the presented mathematical model is shown in [12]. A set of subjective evaluations (Table 1) shows that introduction of adaption procedure to multimodal speech coding system ensured a high quality reconstruction of the speech signal for transmission speeds $\{V\}$. Furthermore, tests of the subjective listening of the speech signal, encoded (decoded) with the use of algorithms №. 1–3, indicate marked superiority of intelligibility and naturalness of the synthesized speech. They also show superiority of the speaker's voice recognition in comparison with algorithms on FS1015, FS1017 and FS1016 standards correspondingly; at the same time with the use of algorithm №. 4 they point out quality, comparable to standard Full-rate GSM (13 kbps).

Peak computational complexity Q of algorithms is calculated with allowance for the need to fulfill the required number of operations in real time for maximum volumes of VQ codebooks. The transition to the adaptive coding demanded substantial (about twice as much) increase in the amount W of stored information in memory devices due to the need to store the new program segments and additional variants of codebooks. At the heart of improving the quality parameters of the developed algorithms is an in-depth analysis of the speech signal frame and adaption to their parameters, characterized by increased computational complexity of procedures for speech coding. At the hardware level the developed algorithms, in comparison with the similar standard algorithms, require increased efficiency of estimators and additional capacity of memory elements.

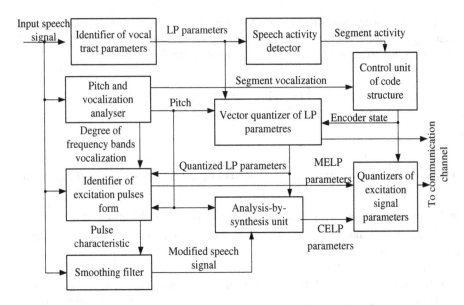

Fig. 2. Generalized structural scheme of the multimodal speech coding system

Table 1. Qualitative characteristics of the multimodal speech coding system

№	V, kbps	Quality of reconstructed speech			Q, MIPS	W, K words
		Syllable intelligibility	Estimation by the method of pairwise comparisons	MOS		
1	1,2	86 %	2,9	3,2	19,2	16,44
2	2,4	92 %	3,5	3,7	28,4	20,5
3	4,8	94 %	4,2	4,2	24,1	29,2
4	9,6	96 %	4,6	4,5	26,7	37,4

4   Conclusion

The wearable and embedded devices of user uniform have limited energy resources that impose constraints on using sensors and methods of data processing and communication. For this reason, the proposed model providing energy optimization during communication via several information modalities is useful for application, and the proposed multimodal speech coding system will be implemented for the organization of military communications in the chain "soldier-squad-platoon-company". Increasing the number of transmitted modalities will allow solving a range of other important practical problems, for example, improving the quality of identification of psycho-physical state of the soldier and other tasks [13–16].

Acknowledgments. This work is partially supported by the Russian Foundation for Basic Research (grants № 16-08-00696-a, 15-07-06774-a).

References

1. Gregory, F.D., Dai, L.: Multisensory information processing for enhanced human-machine symbiosis. In: Yamamoto, S., Abbott, A.A. (eds.) HIMI 2015. LNCS, vol. 9172, pp. 354–365. Springer, Heidelberg (2015). doi:10.1007/978-3-319-20612-7_34

2. Goldberg, D.H., Vogelstein, R., Socolinsky, D.A., Wolff, L.B.: Toward a wearable, neurally-enhanced augmented reality system. In: Schmorrow, D.D., Fidopiastis, C.M. (eds.) FAC 2011. LNCS, vol. 6780, pp. 493–499. Springer, Heidelberg (2011)

3. Tao, X.: Handbook of Smart Textiles. Springer, Singapore (2015)

4. Meng, F., Spence, C.: Tactile warning signals for in-vehicle systems. Accid. Anal. Prev. **75**, 333–346 (2015)

5. White, T.L., Krausman, A.S.: Effects of inter-stimulus interval and intensity on the perceived urgency of tactile patterns. Appl. Ergon. **48**, 121–129 (2015)

6. Ayuso, A.J.R., Lopez-Soler, J.M.: Speech Recognition and Coding: New Advances and Trends. NATO ASI Series, vol. 147. Springer, Berlin (1995). Germany, 464 p.

7. Karpov, A., Ronzhin, A.: A universal assistive technology with multimodal input and multimedia output interfaces. In: Stephanidis, C., Antona, M. (eds.) UAHCI 2014, Part I. LNCS, vol. 8513, pp. 369–378. Springer, Heidelberg (2014)

8. Karpov, A., Akarun, L., Yalçın, H., Ronzhin, Al., Demiröz, B., Çoban, A., Zelezny, M.: Audio-visual signal processing in a multimodal assisted living environment. In: Proceeding of 15th International Conference INTERSPEECH-2014, Singapore, pp. 1023–1027 (2014)

9. Karpov, A., Ronzhin, A., Kipyatkova, I.: An assistive bi-modal user interface integrating multi-channel speech recognition and computer vision. In: Jacko, J.A. (ed.) Human-Computer Interaction, Part II, HCII 2011. LNCS, vol. 6762, pp. 454–463. Springer, Heidelberg (2011)

10. http://yourtactic.com/news/view/12

11. Basov, O.O.: Reasoning of the transition to polymodal infocommunicational systems. In: Distributed Computer and Communication Networks: Control, Computation, Communication. – DCCN-2015, pp. 19–22, October 2015

12. Saveliev, A., Basov, O., Ronzhin, A., Ronzhin, A.: Algorithms for low bit-rate coding with adaptation to statistical characteristics of speech signal. In: Ronzhin, A., Potapova, R., Fakotakis, N. (eds.) SPECOM 2015. LNCS, vol. 9319, pp. 65–72. Springer, Heidelberg (2015)

13. Balatskaya, L.N., Choinzonov, E.L., Chizevskaya, Svetlana Yu., Kostyuchenko, E.U., Meshcheryakov, R.V.: Software for assessing voice quality in rehabilitation of patients after surgical treatment of cancer of oral cavity, oropharynx and upper jaw. In: Železný, M., Habernal, I., Ronzhin, A. (eds.) SPECOM 2013. LNCS, vol. 8113, pp. 294–301. Springer, Heidelberg (2013)

14. Volf, D., Meshcheryakov, R., Kharchenko, S.: The singular estimation pitch tracker. In: Ronzhin, A., Potapova, R., Fakotakis, N. (eds.) SPECOM 2015. LNCS, vol. 9319, pp. 454–462. Springer, Heidelberg (2015)

15. Karpov, A., Ronzhin, A., Kipyatkova, I.: An assistive bi-modal user interface integrating multi-channel speech recognition and computer vision. In: Jacko, J.A. (ed.) Human-Computer Interaction, Part II, HCII 2011. LNCS, vol. 6762, pp. 454–463. Springer, Heidelberg (2011)

16. Potapova, R., Komalova, L., Bobrov, N.: Acoustic markers of emotional state "aggression". In: Ronzhin, A., Potapova, R., Fakotakis, N. (eds.) SPECOM 2015. LNCS, vol. 9319, pp. 55–64. Springer, Heidelberg (2015)

Increasing User Appreciation of Spherical Videos by Finger Touch Interaction

Yuta Sakakibara[✉], Ryohei Tanaka, Takuji Narumi,
Tomohiro Tanikawa, and Michitaka Hirose

Graduate School of Information Science and Technology,
The University of Tokyo, Hongo 7-3-1, Bunkyo-Ku, Tokyo 113-8656, Japan
{sakakibara, r_tanaka, narumi,
tani, hirose}@cyber.t.u-tokyo.ac.jp

Abstract. In this manuscript, we present a system to appreciate spherical videos on mobile devices by using an interface that enables users to play back videos by finger touch interaction. In conventional Virtual Reality (VR) media that use interfaces such as a playback button and a seek bar for videos, users stop watching the videos before viewing the entire content. Previous systems could not effectively attract user interest in content because they are passive media that requires less interaction. In our proposed system, users can touch and manipulate virtual objects interactively, thus increasing user appreciation and achieving a significant VR experience. We evaluated our proposed interface by conducting a demonstrative experiment at a real exhibition. The results showed that with our proposed interface, users scrolled more video frames than with conventional interfaces. In conventional interface systems, many users stopped their experience in the middle of playback before the video ended, and 37 % of the users played the video to the end. However, with our proposed interface, 71 % of the users watched the entire video.

Keywords: Interaction design · Digital museum · Mobile VR · Spherical video · Touch interface

1 Introduction

In a Virtual Reality (VR) environment, the ability to interact with virtual objects improves user experience. Thus, a good design of the interaction in a VR system is important. A VR experience that includes significant interaction enhances user interest and understanding more effectively than a passive VR experience. Therefore, some VR systems incorporate physical interaction by users. Arakawa et al. proposed a reliving video experience system that demonstrates the way in which a camera operator captured the scene by enabling users to move in the same way as the camera operator and by simultaneously showing the corresponding scene on the screen of their handheld devices [1]. Arakawa et al. showed that their proposed interaction techniques are effective in reliving a video experience. If the interaction design in a VR system is not appropriate, users will fail to understand the experience of that system. Therefore, users may lose interest in VR objects and stop their experience before viewing the entire content that the designers prepared and intended to show.

© Springer International Publishing Switzerland 2016
S. Yamamoto (Ed.): HIMI 2016, Part I, LNCS 9734, pp. 546–555, 2016.
DOI: 10.1007/978-3-319-40349-6_53

The popularization of omnidirectional cameras, which can capture spherical images instantaneously, has facilitated the archival of a real space. Additionally, the usage of experiential devices such as tablet devices and head-mounted displays has become widespread. Consequently, a larger number of VR systems with spherical images and videos have been developed. In particular, spherical images are suitable for easy construction of immersive and realistic virtual spaces [2, 3]. A spherical image contains the entire information of the landscape of all angles from a location; therefore, a natural appreciation of spherical images requires manipulation such as a mouse dragging operation, as performed in Google Street View [4]. Several studies have investigated spherical images; the experience of spherical images by using a hand-held device such as a tablet device is known to be immersive and effective in the understanding of geometric space [2, 5–7].

However, the appreciation of spherical videos has two problems. First, conventional video interfaces with a playback button and a seek bar, such as YouTube [8], require few interactions. Thus, the experience of a spherical video with a conventional interface becomes passive. Second, users cannot obtain sufficient information because a part of the region cropped from the spherical image is displayed on a mobile device, and therefore, at a given moment, users can only appreciate a part of the direction of spherical videos that contain plenty of information. Users cannot view all the directions at a given moment; therefore, they may overlook the movement of the main object of the spherical video if the video plays back automatically. These problems make it difficult to continuously retain the interest of the user throughout the playback. Hence, in conventional interfaces without physical interaction, some users gradually lose interest and stop appreciating spherical videos in the middle of the playback.

Therefore, we propose a system with an interface that enables users to play back spherical videos by touching and swiping objects in the spherical movie. In our proposed interface, users are able to directly manipulate the objects in the movie. It is expected that users will frequently interact with virtual objects and will be able to obtain information about the objects because the proposed interface is intuitive; further, the video can be easily played back or stopped according to user preferences. Hence, the proposed interface retains user interest and enables users to completely appreciate the spherical video. In addition, we conducted an experiment in a real exhibition and evaluated the effectiveness of our proposed interface for a spherical VR experience.

2   Related Work

In this section, first, we describe a VR system for the appreciation of spherical images on mobile devices. Second, we describe the use of mouse dragging as an interface for video.

2.1   Mobile Application for Viewing Spherical Images

Virtual spaces constructed by spherical images are more immersive and realistic than the virtual spaces constructed by computer graphics [2, 3]. Okada et al. developed an application named "Manseibashi Reminiscent Window" for mobile devices; with this application, users can appreciate spherical images of the past scene on-site by super-imposing a past-scene image of an actual site onto the present scene. Their proposed system is socially accepted and maintains user interest even in an unattended exhibition. In this system, the virtual camera, which crops a part of the region of the spherical images, is linked with the orientation of the mobile device obtained from the built-in gyro and acceleration sensor. When the user directs a mobile device in a specific direction, the virtual camera turns to the same direction in conjunction with the user movement. Motion-based interaction is known to improve the level of immersion and presence of a VR experience [7]. Therefore, in our proposed system for appreciation of spherical videos, we configure the virtual camera to be connected to the orientation of the mobile device.

2.2 Direct Manipulation Interface for Video

Thorsten et al. proposed an intuitive interface for frame-accurate navigation in video scenes [9]. A dragging operation along the trajectory of the moving object in the scene results in the selection of the appropriate video frame. In the experiment by Thorsten et al., their interface reduced the time required for in-scene navigation tasks by an average of 19–42 % when compared with the time required by a standard seek bar. Additionally, in a survey, users responded that this interface was more natural than conventional interfaces. This interface enables users to navigate an object in video to a specific desired position precisely and quickly; further, the interface is useful in video tasks such as editing video, reviewing sports footage, and verification of video in a trial.

Although the study by Thorsten et al. focused on accurate navigation of objects in video, we apply this technique to play back videos. We aim to develop a mobile system; therefore, in order to play back videos, users must swipe a touchscreen instead of dragging a mouse. We expect that this intuitive swiping interface will be effective in attracting the interest and understanding of the user with regard to the video content. Then, we perform an experiment to evaluate this effectiveness.

3 Design of Proposed System

3.1 Overview

In conventional video interfaces such as playback buttons and seek bars, it is difficult to retain user interest owing to the lack of interaction. Therefore, some users stop their VR experience before the video ends. Further, users cannot view all the angles of spherical images at a given instant of time. Hence, we propose a new interface for playing back spherical videos; in the proposed interface, users can directly manipulate objects by swiping the screen. It is expected that users will intuitively play back spherical video and interact with the virtual object frequently, thus leading to an increase in interest.

3.2 Spherical Video Used in Our System

In our proposed system, we captured spherical video by using an omnidirectional camera, "LadyBug5". The camera is installed at the top of an electric wheelchair and records a video at 10 fps. The camera is approximately 170 cm in height. We captured the departure of a sleeper train, "Hokutosei", from Ueno station, Japan. This train is the main and movable object in our system. The railway has a linear trajectory, and therefore, it is an ideal choice for the proposed interface. We created a movie that captures the train departure from the station for a duration of 90 s. This video consists of 900 frames.

3.3 Playing Back Video by Manipulating Virtual Objects

We propose an interface in which users play back the spherical movie by swiping virtual objects. In this system, we use the spherical video of a departing sleeper train captured from a fixed point. The train moves linearly away from the camera. We can sense the finger touch interaction of the user obtained from the touch screen. When the user swipes the train, the frame of the video is switched depending on the extent of finger movement, considering that the train follows their finger. We implemented this mechanism by creating a virtual train model in the background and calculating its coordinates (Fig. 1). When the trajectory of the train is swiped on the display, this virtual train model moves linearly in the same direction as the finger. Even after the user touch action is complete, the manipulated model maintains its speed owing to inertia. A swipe action in the opposite direction enables the user to navigate the model to the opposite side. In order to allow users to experience the manipulation of a train according to their will, we implemented the interface by linking the coordinates of the virtual model with a suitable video frame. First, we configured three representative combinations of the position of the model with video frames; then, we linearly complemented the other combinations. The touch of a user is valid only when it is on the trajectory of the train, and touching any other region does not influence the playback of the movie. The train can be swiped in the opposite direction to enable reverse play. Based on a user study at a past exhibition at a real museum in Saitama, Japan, we found that many users swipe in the same direction repeatedly in order to accelerate the object. Hence, we reflect this user behavior by introducing a positive rate to increase the speed when the object is continuously swiped in the same direction. This interface is applicable only to the videos containing an object that moves definitely.

Thus, we developed a system for interactive spherical videos based on touching and swiping objects in the video. Users can intuitively play and reverse play a spherical movie at any arbitrary speed, and they can stop at a desired frame easily by manipulating objects in the video. Further, users inevitably focus on a moving object and are expected to be attracted to it. We can reduce the oversight of an important object by designing it as a movable object.

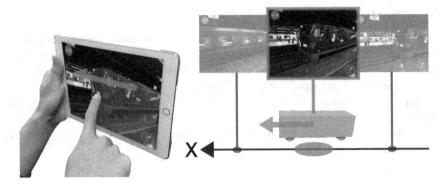

Fig. 1. Proposed system

4   Experiment at a Real Exhibition

We evaluated our proposed interface by conducting a large-scale demonstration experiment at a real exhibition at Gunma, Japan. The subjects were guests who attended this exhibition. The staff in the exhibition room handed out iPad Air 2 devices to the subjects and explained the method to experience our system. The subjects were free to terminate the viewing at their will. We used the spherical video of the departure of a sleeper train, as described in Sect. 3. The exhibition was held for 92 days. We displayed a system with our proposed interface for the initial 43 days and a system with a conventional interface for the remaining 49 days.

4.1   Application

Proposed System. The subjects were able to play and reverse play the spherical movie at any speed voluntarily and stop at the desired frame easily by manipulating the objects in the video. This interface was not familiar to the subjects; therefore, a hand icon was shown on the display, and the icon moved to indicate touch interaction and the direction of swiping (Fig. 2). Further, the train was emphasized by turning on and off a red light before the first touch interaction.

Conventional System. We created a system with a conventional interface for comparison with our proposed interface. The conventional interface consisted of a playback button and a seek bar (Fig. 3). Buttons for playing, reverse playing, and changing the playback speed were provided. The subjects were able to multiply the speed by 2, 4, 8, or 16 during play and reverse play. The seek bar enabled transition between video frames.

Fig. 2. Screenshot of proposed system

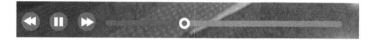

Fig. 3. Conventional video interface

4.2 Detailed Process

The subjects directed their iPad toward a scale railroad model of Hokutosei displayed in the exhibition room (Fig. 4). When the device camera captured the model, the subjects began to appreciate the spherical video. The subjects freely appreciated the spherical video and could quit at any point of time. The values measured by the gyro sensor and the video frames watched were recorded in the background. The total number of subjects who experienced the proposed interface was 1,169, and the number of subjects who experienced the conventional interface was 1,295.

4.3 Results and Discussion

Figure 5 shows the number of times that the subjects interacted; the interaction was in the form of swiping and manipulating the virtual object for the proposed interface and touching buttons and the seek bar for the conventional approach. Although these numbers cannot be directly compared owing to the difference between the interfaces, it can be observed that the proposed interface induced frequent interaction and attracted user interest in the video, as expected. In the case of the conventional interface, 41 % of the subjects did not use the buttons and seek bar, and 77 % of the subjects used them less than twice; therefore, it is likely that the subjects watched the spherical video passively.

The subjects appreciated more video frames in the proposed interface than in the conventional interface. Figure 6 represents the total number of video frames watched in each experience. It is observed that the subjects watched more video frames in the

552   Y. Sakakibara et al.

Fig. 4. Scene at the exhibition

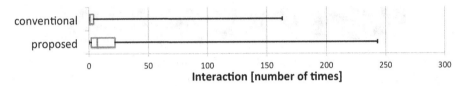

Fig. 5. Total amount of interaction

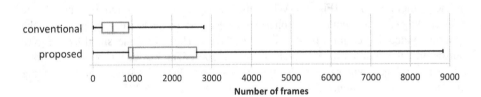

Fig. 6. Total number of watched video frames

proposed interface system than in the conventional interface system. Figure 7 indicates the distribution of the watched video frames for each interface. These graphs indicate the frames that are appreciated greatly. The subjects watched the entire video almost uniformly in the proposed interface system. Based on the slight increase toward the end, it can be inferred that some subjects played back the video in reverse and watched it again even after having watched the entire video. However, in the conventional interface system, the watched frames converge in the first half of the video. It is conjectured that passive video appreciation without appropriate interactions attracts little interest and causes interruption in the experience. Therefore, it is likely that our proposed system has an effect of retaining appreciation after the video ends.

Figure 8 shows the percentage of subjects watching each frame of video. In the system with the conventional interface, the percentage steeply declines as the video

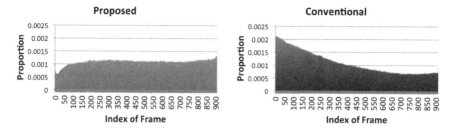

Fig. 7. Distribution of watched video frames

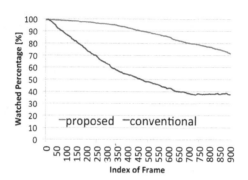

Fig. 8. Percentage of subjects watching each frame (Color figure online)

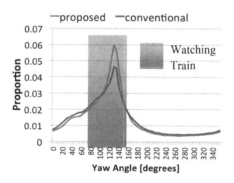

Fig. 9. Distribution of yaw angle of iPad (Color figure online)

progresses to the end; the percentage of subjects who played the video to the end was 37 %. In contrast, 71 % of the subjects watched the entire video in the proposed system. The reason for this result could be that the proposed interface retained user interest.

Figure 9 shows the distribution of the yaw angle of the iPad. The iPad and the virtual camera are linked, and these attitudes are determined by the yaw, pitch, and roll angles. The yaw angle represents the direction that the subjects are looking at in a spherical image because almost all the user rotation in appreciation is along the yaw angle. The difference between the interfaces is small; however, the rate of watching the main objects is slightly higher in the proposed interface. The reason for this result may be that the train was the only large, moving object in the video, and therefore, it stood out. In order to observe the actual effect, we must measure the appreciation activity for a video that has multiple objects or small objects. This experiment can be considered in future work.

5   Conclusion

The design of suitable interaction is essential to achieve an effective VR experience. In this study, we proposed an interface for appreciation of spherical videos. With our interface, users are able to intuitively play back the video by touching and swiping a moving object in the video.

In our experiment at a real museum, it was observed that users interact with virtual objects more frequently. Further, users watched more video frames with the proposed interface, which is intuitive and enables easy manipulation of a spherical video, than with the conventional interface. In addition, the distribution of watched video frames was almost even in the case of the proposed interface. Consequently, in the case of the conventional interface, many users stopped their experience in the middle of a video playback, before the video ended; 37 % of users played the video to the end. However, in the case of the proposed interface, 71 % of the users watched the entire video. The reason for these results is that the experience through a conventional interface is passive and includes few interactions, whereas the experience through the proposed interface provides many interactions and attracts user interest effectively.

A limitation of this study is that the proposed interface cannot be applied to videos that do not have a linearly moving object. Such videos would require the acceptance of user interaction in the form of tapping or pinching in or out.

In future work, we plan to apply this interface to videos that contain multiple moving objects. A VR experience with active selection of interactive objects is subjective and unforgettable [1, 10]. We will determine the appropriate response of virtual objects to user interaction. Further, with the emergence of algorithms for calculating object trajectories by using optical flow fields between neighboring frames in the scene [11], we can apply our proposed interface to spherical VR systems such as virtual tour and live broadcasting to increase the attractiveness of these VR experiences.

References

1. Arakawa, T., Kasada, K., Narumu, T., Tanikawa, T., Hirose, M.: Augmented reality system for overlaying a scene in a video onto real world and reliving the camera operator's experience. In: 2013 IEEE Virtual Reality (VR), pp. 139–140. IEEE (2013)
2. Chen, S.E.: Quicktime VR: an image-based approach to virtual environment navigation. In: 1995 Proceedings of the 22nd Annual Conference on Computer Graphics and Interactive Techniques, pp. 29–38. ACM (1995)

3. Endo, T., Katayama, A., Tamura, H., Hirose, M., Tanikawa, T., Saito, M.: Image-based walk-through system for large-scale scenes. In: VSMM98, vol. 1, pp. 269–274 (1998)
4. Google Street View. https://www.google.co.jp/intl/ja/maps/streetview/
5. Tanaka, R., Narumi, T., Tanikawa, T., Hirose, M.: Attracting user's attention in spherical image by angular shift of virtual camera direction. In: 2015 Proceedings of the 3rd ACM Symposium on Spatial User Interaction, pp. 61–64. ACM (2015)
6. Okada, N., Imura, J., Narumi, T., Tanikawa, T., Hirose, M.: Manseibashi reminiscent window: on-site AR exhibition system using mobile devices. In: Streitz, N., Markopoulos, P. (eds.) DAPI 2015. LNCS, vol. 9189, pp. 349–361. Springer, Heidelberg (2015)
7. Hwang, J., Jung, J., Kim, G.J.: Hand-held virtual reality: a feasibility study. In: 2006 Proceedings of the ACM Symposium on Virtual Reality Software and Technology, pp. 356–363. ACM (2006)
8. YouTube. https://www.youtube.com/?hl=ja&gl=JP
9. Karrer, T., Weiss, M., Lee, E., Borchers, J.: DRAGON: a direct manipulation interface for frame-accurate in-scene video navigation. In: 2008 Proceedings of the SIGCHI Conference on Human Factors in Computing Systems, pp. 247–250. ACM (2008)
10. Narumi, T., Hayashi, O., Kasada, K., Yamazaki, M., Tanikawa, T., Hirose, M.: Digital diorama: AR exhibition system to convey background information for museums. In: Shumaker, R. (ed.) Virtual and Mixed Reality, HCII 2011, Part I. LNCS, vol. 6773, pp. 76–86. Springer, Heidelberg (2011)
11. Brox, T., Bruhn, A., Papenberg, N., Weickert, J.: High accuracy optical flow estimation based on a theory for warping. In: Pajdla, T., Matas, J(. (eds.) ECCV 2004. LNCS, vol. 3024, pp. 25–36. Springer, Heidelberg (2004)

Production of a VR Horror Movie Using
a Head-Mounted Display
with a Head-Tracking System

Kenichi Sera[1,2], Takashi Kitada[1], and Nahomi Maki[2(✉)]

[1] FLAME Ltd., ApolloProcess Building 3F,
1-6-7 Higashi-Azabu, Minato-ku, Tokyo 106-0044, Japan
[2] Kanagawa Institute of Technology,
1030 Shimo-ogino, Atsugi-shi, Kanagawa 243-0292, Japan
maki@ic.kanagawa-it.ac.jp

Abstract. Head-mounted displays (HMDs) that feature a stereoscopic wide-viewing angle and head-tracking function for virtual reality environments have emerged recently. As a result of this development, various contents that use the special qualities of HMDs have begun to be produced suddenly. In this study, we propose a short horror movie for HMDs using a free viewpoint that takes advantage of the features of the head-tracking system.

Keywords: Head-mounted display · 3DCG · Virtual reality

1 Introduction

Head-mounted displays (HMDs) that feature a stereoscopic wide-viewing angle and head-tracking function for virtual reality (VR) environments have emerged recently. A head-tracking system enables the display to follow the movement of a user's head. As a result of this development, various contents that use the special qualities of HMDs have begun to be produced suddenly. HMDs evoke a strong absorbing sense; thus, they are suitable for the production of horror movies. In this study, we propose a short horror movie for HMD that uses a free viewpoint that takes advantage of these features. We create the movie using Oculus Rift VR Development Kit 2.

In directing the horror scenes, we use as reference the "perfect formula" for horror movies as published by King's College London in 2004. This formula indicates that the most important factors of the genre are escalating music, a sense of the unknown, and chase scenes. We direct the horror gimmicks based on this formula.

2 Countermeasure to Problem of HMD

HMD has various advantages that bring a sense of absorption in VR. However, it also has several disadvantages. In this study, we thoroughly consider the way to address such disadvantages.

© Springer International Publishing Switzerland 2016
S. Yamamoto (Ed.): HIMI 2016, Part I, LNCS 9734, pp. 556–562, 2016.
DOI: 10.1007/978-3-319-40349-6_54

Three-Dimensional Drunkenness

The main problem with an HMD is that it easily causes three-dimensional drunkenness that affects the viewer's physical condition. As a result, when users feel the acceleration, they experience vestibular sense and nausea in addition to visual perception. When wearing an HMD, a person may experience 3D drunkenness, which involves a sense of collision, because only two eyes are used while three senses are functioning. The following three situations illustrate how HMD drunkenness occurs:

(i) The user does not know the way from which he/she should move or the screen moves in an unintended direction.

(ii) The screen movement causes sudden acceleration and deceleration or a sharp curve. As long as the screen movement is accelerating, the user experiences a sense of collision that increases in momentum because of sudden acceleration, deceleration, and turn.

(iii) When the Oculus Rift is used, the distance between the actual screen and the eyes is short. Thus, the viewer may experience nausea and eye fatigue after using the device for many hours.

Safety for Viewers

We have to consider safety when wearing an HMD because the user cannot see the surroundings. For example, using the device poses a risk of contact when other people or objects are near the viewer. Furthermore, if the viewer is standing while wearing the HMD, his/her body could become unsteady when the vestibular sense is paralyzed.

Compatibility with Other Devices

A viewer cannot see his/her own hand because Oculus Rift is a non-transparent type of HMD. Therefore, its compatibility with other devices, such as keyboards and controllers, is not good. A viewer who is unaccustomed to keyboards or controllers may have difficulty knowing where certain buttons are located without looking at one's hands. Additionally, once the viewer loses control, he/she has to grab the controllers.

3   Solution to the Problem in HMD

In this study, the following method is conducted to solve the problem stated in Sect. 2.

Solution to 3D Drunkenness

The following three approaches are considered to reduce 3D drunkenness:

(i) The player is placed on a lorry on a stage and a railroad track is placed on the ground, as shown in Fig. 1. The audience can grasp the course as they move forward.

(ii) Rapid turn and acceleration and deceleration are avoided to the utmost. The speed of the lorry decreases as much as possible in this production. Moreover, the lorry is programmed to slow down when it turns perpendicularly and climbs stairs.

(iii) The movie should not be long or should be set up a rest point.

The movie in this project is approximately 4–5 min long.

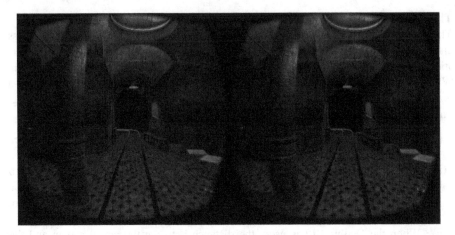

Fig. 1. Railroad placed on the ground

Ensuring Viewer Safety

As mentioned, we have to consider safety because the viewers are unable to see their surroundings while wearing the HMD. For example, when another person or an object is near the viewer, the risk of physical contact occurs. Moreover, the viewer's vestibular sense is paralyzed when using the HMD while standing, so that his/her body is unsteady and in danger of collapsing. To solve this problem, we prepare a stable chair for the viewer to sit on while playing the movie.

Solution to Incompatibility with Other Devices

Parallel use of Oculus Rift and other devices is difficult because of incompatibility. Therefore, we produce a movie that has no room for the player to control. Other devices are unnecessary because the viewer does not have to operate a character to watch the movie.

4   Building a Stage

The entire movie is set in an old and dark hospital. The stage, materials, and gimmicks are built using Unity 3D. The hospital is a two-story building, and the audience rides a coaster and moves from the first to the second floor. A map of the stage is shown in Fig. 2. To the left is the first floor, and to the right is the second floor.

The stage is designed to accommodate the route of the coaster. The coaster passes the doors many times, and the backs of the doors are difficult to see. Thus, the viewer cannot see an upcoming frightening scene. We also made the coaster move straight as much as possible to avoid a measure of 3D drunkenness, and we set the number of corners to a minimum. The route is presented in Fig. 3.

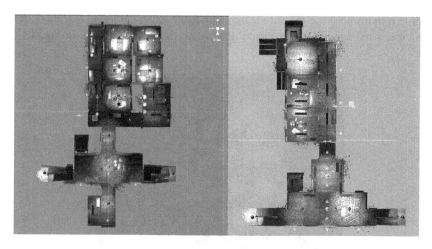

Fig. 2. Map of the stage

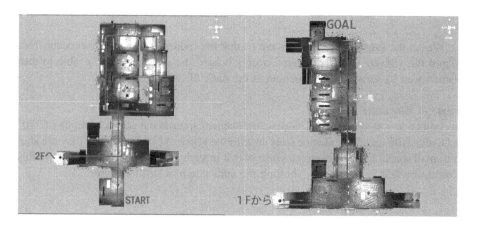

Fig. 3. Map of the route

5 Direction of Horror Movie Using HMD

Using an HMD with a head-tracking system, we produced a short movie through Oculus Rift. We developed several gimmicks that take advantage of the features of the head-tracking system.

Leading the Viewer's Eyes
One of the most important features of this movie is that the players are able to see any direction across a viewing angle of 360°. This condition means that we have to lead the players' eyes such that they can witness and encounter the scary scenes in the movie. In this study, we choose the occurrence of sudden sounds based on the "perfect formula" of the horror genre. For example, we devise a loud banging sound that causes the

player to turn his/her head toward the direction from which the sound is coming. At the same time, a red handprint with blood appears on the wall, as shown in Fig. 4.

Fig. 4. Handprint with blood and the position of sounds

We set the surround speaker system so that the sudden sound may also occur from behind the viewer. When the sound occurs behind the viewer, he/she is able to turn his/her head to see what is happening at the back of the stage.

Sense of Blockade

In contrast to watching a usual display, the scenery spreads out across an angle of 270° in Oculus Rift, and the audience feels an extreme sense of blockade when they are shut in a small space. People develop a sense of fear in such a closed and small space. In this project, the fear is directed by shutting the audience in a small elevator.

Fig. 5. Point of view from a low position

Height of Viewpoint

We also consider the difference in the "scares" produced by varying the height of the viewing angle of the audience. The point of view from a low angle is shown in Fig. 5, and that from a high angle is shown in Fig. 6.

Fig. 6. Point of view from a high position

A comparison between Figs. 5 and 6 shows that a view from a low position gives the viewer a sense of expanse on the stage. Thus, the viewer senses that the viewpoint is weak. The height of the point of view is set to approximately 120–130 cm in this project.

Enclosed Space

In this movie, the coaster enters the elevator and moves underground in the end. The space in the elevator is small and dark, thereby giving the viewer a sense of blockade.

Fig. 7. Inside the elevator

Numerous gimmicks are presented before the viewer arrives to this scene, so when nothing happens in this space, the viewer is being alarmed reversely. The space inside the elevator is shown in Fig. 7.

Approach Close and Hand
One gimmick is that an unidentified ghost attacks the player at the end of the movie. The HMD shows the ghost approaching the player from the front and coming several centimeters close to him/her. The ghost attacks by hanging from the top so that it looks as huge as possible, as shown in Fig. 8.

Fig. 8. The attacking ghost

6 Conclusion

A three-minute horror movie using HMD, which takes advantage of the features of the head-tracking system, was created. We sent questionnaires to the viewers after the viewing and obtained answers such as the following: "I experienced a highly realistic sensation that cannot compete with [the feeling from] any other conventional horror movie" and "I enjoyed the fearfulness of the unfolding actions as I changed viewpoints." This production succeeded in evoking the characteristic fear that is induced by horror movies. However, further applications of the head-tracking function should be explored.

References

1. Reiners, T., Wood, L.C., Bastiaens, T.J.: New landscapes and new eyes: the role of virtual world design for supply chain education. Ubiquitous Learn.: Int. J. **6**, 37–49 (2014)
2. Hager, H., Cakmak, T.: Cyberith virtualiver. In: ACM SIGGRAPH 2014, Emerging Technologies (2014)

Basic Investigation for Improvement of Sign Language Recognition Using Classification Scheme

Hirotoshi Shibata, Hiromitsu Nishimura, and Hiroshi Tanaka[✉]

Kanagawa Institute of Technology, 1030 Shimo-Ogino,
Atsugi, Kanagawa, Japan
s1585009@cce.kanagawa-it.ac.jp,
{nisimura,h_tanaka}@ic.kanagawa-it.ac.jp

Abstract. Sign language is a commonly-used communication method for hearing-impaired or speech-impaired people. However, it is quite difficult to learn sign language. If automatic translation for sign language can be realized, it becomes very meaningful and convenient not only for impaired people but also physically unimpaired people. The cause of the difficulty in automatic translation is that there are so many variations in sign language motions, which degrades recognition performance. This paper presents a recognition method for maintaining the recognition performance for many sign language motions. A scheme is introduced to classification using a decision tree, which can decrease the number of words to be recognized at a time by dividing them into groups. The used hand, the characteristics of hand motion and the relative position between hands and face have been considered in creating the decision tree. It is confirmed by experiments that the recognition success rate increased from 41 % and 59 % to 59 % and 82 %, respectively, for a basic 17 words of sign language with four sign language operators.

Keywords: Sign language · Color gloves · Optical camera · Recognition · Classification · Decision tree

1 Introduction

Sign language is a commonly-used communication method for hearing-impaired or speech-impaired people. Written conversation is another method for communication with physically unimpaired people. However, this method takes some time and cannot transmit the intended message simultaneously to many people. The automated conversion from words to sign language has been investigating recently [1, 2], and it seems to be approaching a practical level. Evolution of animation technology and computer processing ability make this possible.

Although interpretation from sign language to words has also been studied for many years, the technologies have not yet matured to the level of practical use. Specifically, some methods that use a special sensor or device [3, 4] incur a high introduction cost or sensors must be attached to the body. The detection target is mainly limited to hand motions and the hand shape, and finger motion are not observed.

S. Yamamoto (Ed.): HIMI 2016, Part I, LNCS 9734, pp. 563–574, 2016.
DOI: 10.1007/978-3-319-40349-6_55

Therefore, it seems difficult to realize a high recognition performance. The number of recognized words is limited [5, 6]. These technological results are insufficient for practical use. In addition, although the limited scene for usage should be proposed, they have not investigated from aspect of this point in previous studies.

The authors also have been investigating a recognition method for sign language that uses colored gloves [7]. The main feature of our proposed method is to distinguish each finger, and the front and back of the palm. A recognition rate of 83.8 % for 24 words was obtained by the proposed method [8]. The 24 words in this investigation were selected from a Japanese official certification examination for sign language. To make the recognition method practical, the number of words, and the recognition performance must be increased.

This paper presents a recognition method that is appropriate for increasing the number of words with high recognition performance. Classification scheme for words to be recognized has not been included in a conventional investigation, therefore, the recognition performance is thought to degrade according to the increase in the number of words. The authors propose a classification that considers the features of the sign language motion for each word, for example, the size of hand motion and the used hands, that is, one or both for the sign language, etc. A decision tree is introduced for the classification in this study. The recognition process is applied to the words after classification using the decision tree. The number of words to be recognized can be decreased, therefore, a higher recognition performance is expected to be maintained compared with conventional method [8]. The effectiveness of the proposed method was confirmed by the experiment that was carried out by operators wearing colored gloves.

2 Motion Detection and Colored Gloves to Be Used

It is desirable to select commonly used equipment for sign language recognition. This makes it easier to disseminate its usage among many people. At present, smartphones have become consumer devices, and they are equipped with many sensors, including a camera. Their processing capability has also been increasing. The implemented camera sensor and the smartphone's high processing ability will enable the device to recognize sign language and output its translated meaning as text or voice communication.

The following items seem to be necessary to recognize sign language by considering its motion.

(a) Identification of each finger and both hands
(b) Motion detection of wrists/hands and fingers
(c) Hand shape recognition
(d) Discrimination between the two sides of the palm
(e) Relative position of hands and face
(f) Detection of mouth motion and recognition of facial expression

Identifying each finger is one of the important factors for hand shape recognition. Colored gloves are proposed for hand shape recognition [9]. The tip of each finger of the glove has a different color. This makes it easy to identify each finger and can lead to reliable recognition of hand shapes. If we use wrist bands for both hands, the right and

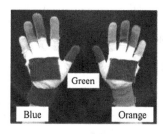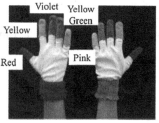

Fig. 1. Proposed colored gloves (Color figure online)

left hand are easily distinguished. In addition, the palms of the hands can be identified by the presence of colored regions. Wrist motions can be monitored by detecting the center of gravity of the regions traversed by the colored wrist bands, and we regard this motion as hand motion. The face position is detected by face recognition using image processing. Therefore, challenges (a)–(e) are considered to be met by using colored gloves.

The colored gloves we designed are shown in Fig. 1. Five colors are used so as to uniquely identify each finger, different additional colors distinguish each wrist, and green patches locate the palms of the hands. Thus a total of 8 colors are proposed to recognize sign language. Background subtraction is used on the camera image to extract 8 colored regions, each being identified by its hue and saturation values [7].

3   Classification by Decision Tree for Sign Language Words

3.1   Application of This Study and Targeted Words

The authors now consider that this investigating method applies to learning tools for sign language. An image of using scenery is shown in Fig. 2. A user watches a sign language sample movie dictionary [10] in order to memorize their motions, and after memorizing he/she tries a motion in front of a camera without the sample movie to review learning. Using this research, the recognition system can output a recognition result from their motion, to be used as a learning tool.

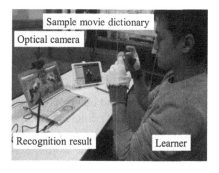

Fig. 2. Application of this research

The 17 basic sign language words are included in this movie dictionary. Therefore, in first stage of this investigation, recognition technologies in this study are investigated for these 17 words. They are shown in Table 1.

Table 1. Sign language words

Word number	1	2	3	4	5	6
Word	You あなた	Thank you ありがとう	No いいえ	Good job お疲れ様	Good morning おはよう	Sorry ごめんなさい
Word number	7	8	9	10	11	12
Word	That's right 1 そうですね1	That's right 2 そうですね2	What? 何？	I see 1 なるほど1	I see 2 なるほど2	Drink 飲む
Word number	13	14	15	16	17	
Word	Nice to meet you 初めまして	Of course もちろん	Good 良い	Be nice よろしくお願いします	I 私	

3.2   Classification of Sign Language Words

There are countless sign language words. It seems to be quite difficult to maintain high recognition performance for a lot of words. Therefore, we propose a classification for sign language words by their characteristics of motion in order to maintain recognition performance. Better recognition performance can be expected by reducing the number of sign language words by classification before the recognition process. The motion characteristics of 17 recognition words are analyzed, and the following features are considered for classification in this investigation.

1. Hands used for sign language: Right hand/Both hands
2. Movement of each hand: Large motion/Small motion
3. Difference of distance between each hand and the face: Large/Small

3.3   Classification by Hand Detection

There are sign language words that are expressed only using the right hand. Therefore, as the first step for classification, the authors proposed classification by the used hands, that is, right hand or both hands. This is decided by the detection of the colored region of blue assigned for the right wrist and orange for the left wrist. Appearance of the wrist in more than one-fifth of the total frames of a sign language motion will indicate that the hand is used.

3.4   Classification by Hand Movement

The authors propose a second classification by the size of hand motion. Some sign language words have large hand motions, and others have little motion. As the same as previous section, the center of gravity of the colored region of each wrist is used for detection of hand movement. Figure 3 indicates an example of the movement of the center of gravity of two sign language motions: the words "Sorry" and "I see". The unit of the y axis indicates a pixel.

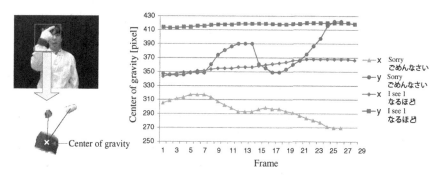

Fig. 3. Movement of center of gravity of the colored region of the wrist

Movement measurement of the hand motion in pixels depends on the number of pixels of used camera and the distance between camera and the colored gloves. Therefore, experimental conditions are set in this investigation as follows. The distance between the camera (Logicool HD ProWebcam 920) and the colored gloves is about 1 m, the image frame size is 800 * 600 pixels, and the frame rate is 30 fps. The hand motion and hand shape are measured based on the results of color detection for the colored regions of gloves. Detection is severely affected by the illumination conditions. Therefore, the experiment was carried out under a constant illumination condition of 230 lx.

Two types of sign language operators were kept in this investigation. One group consisted of operators who learned sign language using a movie dictionary (amateur), and the other group was sign language user in their daily lives (native signer). We consider that the diversity is important in creating a dictionary for sign language recognition. Therefore, the decision tree for classification and the dictionary for recognition were composed of samples generated by an operator pair with an amateur and a native signer. Recognition experiments were carried out by a pair with a different amateur and a different native signer. The operators list is shown in Table 2.

Table 2. Sign language operator list

Name	Role	Sign language skill
Operator A	Making decision tree and dictionary for recognition	Native signer
Operator B	B Same above	Amateur
Operator C	Recognition target	Native signer
Operator D	Same above	Amateur

The movement is evaluated from the average of the movement of the center of gravity of each wrist region, and its average was calculated from the following expression for classification.

Here,

n: the total number of frames of sign language motion data

i: i^{th} frame of motion data

W_x: x coordinate of the of center of gravity of colored region of the wrist
W_y: y coordinate of the of center of gravity of colored region of the wrist

$$\frac{\sum_{i=1}^{n-1} \sqrt{(W_x(i+1) - W_x(i))^2 + (W_y(i+1) - W_y(i))^2}}{n-1} \tag{1}$$

The 17 sign language words were examined by the operators A & B. The data from these two operators are shown in Fig. 4. It is natural that there is some variation between two operators and among each of the sign language words. Here, we introduce the idea of range for each classification criterion. The upper limit for classifying words as small motions, and the lower limit for large motions are defined. The "no decision" range to classify ambiguities in motion size is introduced. This method helps to avoid classification failure; as a result, it contributes to maintaining the recognition performance.

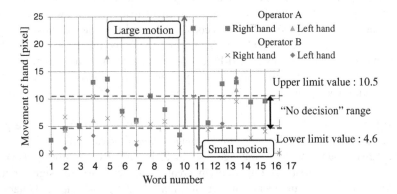

Fig. 4. Movement of the hand motion and classification criterion

3.5   Classification by Distance Between Face and Each Hand

There are differences in the distance between the face and each hand in each sign language word. An example is shown in Fig. 5. The photo on the left shows an example of a large difference in the distance between left and right hand and face (d_R and d_L), and one on the right shows an example of a small difference. d_R is almost equal to d_L in the photo on the right. The authors use this feature as a third classification in our scheme.

The classification criterion is the average value of the difference of the distance between the face and each hand in motion. Its value is calculated by expression (2). Here, the meaning of i and n is the same as expression (1), and the others are as follows.

d_R: distance from the right wrist and the center of the gravity of the face
d_L: distance from the left wrist and the center of the gravity of the face
fs: size of face

Fig. 5. Distance between face and each hand

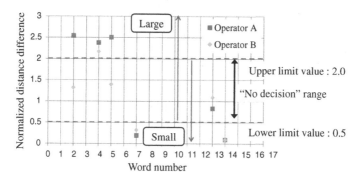

Fig. 6. Distance difference between face and each hand and classification criterion

The distance between the face and hands is normalized using the image size of the face. This prevents any effect from the differences in distance between the sign language operator and the camera. This is a necessary function when this method is applied for practical use. The position and the size of the face are detected using the face recognizer included in OpenCV [11].

$$\sum_{i=1}^{n} \frac{|d_R(i) - d_L(i)|}{fs(i)} \tag{2}$$

Figure 6 shows the distance difference between the face and each hand. This result was obtained by the same two operators obtained the result in Fig. 4. The authors propose the upper limit for classifying as a small distance difference and lower limit for large distance difference the same as Fig. 4. Although some words are included in a common area by the "no decision" range, this avoids discrimination failure at this stage of classification.

3.6   Decision Tree Obtained by Two Operators

The decision tree can be composed by using the results of Sects. 3.3, 3.4 and 3.5. Figure 7 shows a decision tree. The 17 words are each assigned to a group, that is, leaf node. The feature of this classification is that some words belong to multiple groups. This is because the "no decision" range is defined in the classification.

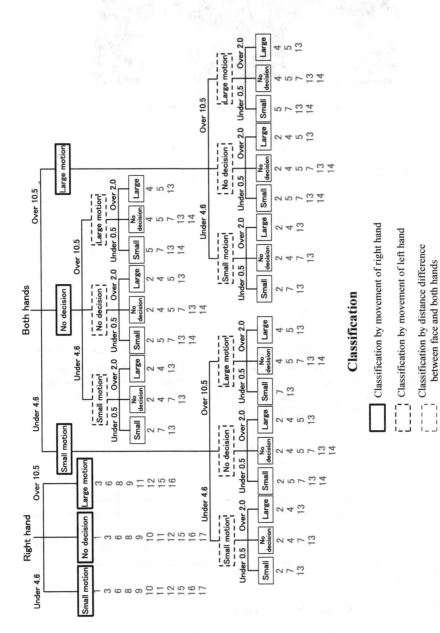

Fig. 7. Decision tree from features of motion and classification result

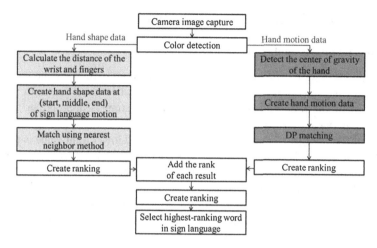

Fig. 8. Flow of recognition method

This helps avoid failure in classification; as a result, this can increase the performance of sign language recognition. The recognition method is applied to each word that is belonged to each group. Since the number of the words in the recognition process can be decreased, higher recognition performance is expected from the proposed method. When a word cannot be classified, recognition using the 17 words dictionary is carried out in this process, for example, in the case of no detection of the right hand.

4   Sign Language Recognition Method

A sign language recognition method after classification that uses hand shape and hand motion recognition is shown in Fig. 8 [8]. At this stage, the hand shape recognition process is applied at the beginning, middle, and the end of a sign language motion. The hand motion recognition process is applied over the span between the beginning and the end of the sign language motion. The identification of the word is based on these results.

Hand shape recognition is based on the hand shape feature vector whose magnitude is the distance between the center of the wrist and the tip of each finger. The magnitude for an invisible finger-tip due to a finger being bent and occlusion is set at zero. The shape recognition result is obtained by selecting the hand shape for which the distance between template feature vectors prepared in advance and the observed target feature vector is smallest [9]. Hand motion can be detected by obtaining the center of gravity of the colored region of the wrist band. The DP matching scheme is applied to motion recognition. Differences in motion sizes are taken into account by normalizing the motion ranges.

5   Recognition Experiments and Evaluation

5.1   Experiment Method

The recognition results after this classification are compared with the recognition results from conventional method, that is, without classification, in order to verify the effectiveness of the proposed method. If the classification is appropriate, it can be expected to the increase recognition success rate.

When the "no decision" range between the upper and lower limit value is smaller, it can be expected that classification errors appear. It is considered to exist appropriate range since the narrow range produces classification errors that directly affect sign language recognition performance. However, narrow range reduces the number of words to be recognized by the classification process, which leads to high recognition performance. Therefore, we carry on recognition experiment by changing this range. There are two ranges shown in Figs. 4 and 6. These ranges were changed simultaneously.

5.2   Experiment Result

First, the recognition results using the conventional method [8] without classification are shown in Table 3. Each number shows each candidate's ranking of words as the recognition result. Namely, number 1 means a successful recognition result for that word. According to Table 3, the recognition success rate was 41 % and 59 % for two operators. The table on the left shows operator C, and the table on the right shows operator D.

Table 3. Recognition results using conventional method

Operator C   Recognition success rate: 41%   Operator D   Recognition success rate: 59%

Next, the recognition results using the proposed method are shown in Table 4. The "no decision" ranges shown in Figs. 4 and 6 were used in this experiment. The black cells indicate that these were eliminated by classification process. In this experiment, classification error wasn't occurred. The classification results are different between operator C and D. However, the number of words to be recognized has been decreased by classification. According to Table 4, the recognition success rate was 59 % and 82 % respectively. In this result, it was confirmed that the proposed method has the effect of improving recognition performance.

Table 4. Recognition results using proposed method

Operator C Recognition success rate: 59% Operator D Recognition success rate: 82%

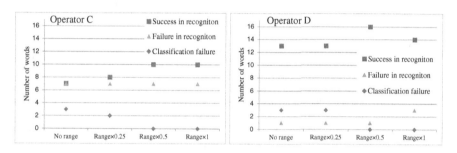

Fig. 9. Change of the recognition performance by "no decision" range

5.3 Change of the Recognition Performance by "no Decision" Range

The "no decision" range affects the recognition performance. The recognition performance was investigated by changing this range and the results are shown in Fig. 9. In this figure, the results on the left were obtained by operator C, and the results on right were operator D. Range ×1 indicates the recognition result from the previous section, that is, the original range. When the original range was changed to range×0.25, classification failures appeared in each recognition result. It was found that a narrow range causes classification failure and a lower success rate. It was confirmed that it is necessary to define an appropriate range in this proposed method to achieve recognition performance.

6 Conclusion

The authors have proposed a classification method for realizing high performance recognition for sign language. The number of recognition targeted motion can be decreased by classification, since multiple motions can be divided into several groups. The recognition method is applied to the motions that belong to each group. The classification process has been defined by considering the features of each sign language motion. In this study, three features are taken into account, that is, the used hand, the range of hand motion and the distance relation between the face and each hand.

The decision tree was created based on these results. The feature of the proposed decision tree is a "no decision" range in order to avoid classification failures. Experiments were carried out to evaluate the recognition success rate using the conventional method and the proposed method for a basic 17 words in sign language. The success rate was confirmed to be increased from 41 % and 59 % to 59 % and 82 %, respectively. The effectiveness of the proposed method has been confirmed by experiments carried out with sign language operators.

References

1. Jen, T., adamo-villani, N.: the effect of rendering style on perception of sign language animations. In: Antona, M., Stephanidis, C. (eds.) UAHCI 2015. LNCS, vol. 9176, pp. 383–392. Springer, Heidelberg (2015)
2. Adamo-Villani, N., Wilbur, R.B.: ASL-Pro: American sign language animation with prosodic elements. In: Antona, M., Stephanidis, C. (eds.) UAHCI 2015. LNCS, vol. 9176, pp. 307–318. Springer, Heidelberg (2015)
3. Baatar, B., Tanaka, J.: Comparing sensor based and vision based techniques for dynamic gesture recognition. In: The 10th Asia Pacific Conference on Computer Human Interaction (APCHI), Poster 2P-21 (2012)
4. Matsuda, Y., Sakuma, I., Jimbo, Y., Kobayashi, E., Arafune, T., Isomura, T.: Development of finger braille recognition system. J. Biom. Sci. Eng. 5(1), 54–65 (2010)
5. Humphries, T., Padden, C., O'Rourke, T.: Basic Course in American Sign Language. T. J. Publishers Inc., Silver Spring (1994)
6. Murakami, K., Taguchi, H.: Gesture recognition using recurrent natural networks. In: CHI 1991 Conference Proceedings, pp. 237–242 (1991)
7. Sugaya, T., Nishimura, H., Tanaka, H.: Enhancement of accuracy of hand shape recognition using color calibration by clustering scheme and majority voting method. In: Yamamoto, S. (ed.) HCI 2014, Part I. LNCS, vol. 8521, pp. 251–260. Springer, Heidelberg (2014)
8. Sugaya, T., Tsuchiya, H., Iwasawa, H., Nishimura, H., Tanaka, H.: Fundamental study on sign language recognition using color detection with an optical camera. In: International Conference on Imaging and Printing Technologies (ICIPT), Mandarin Hotel, Bangkok, Thailand, pp. 8–13 (2014)
9. Sugaya, T., Suzuki, T., Nishimura, H., Tanaka, H.: Basic investigation into hand shape recognition using colored gloves taking account of the peripheral environment. In: Yamamoto, S. (ed.) HCI 2013, Part I. LNCS, vol. 8016, pp. 133–142. Springer, Heidelberg (2013)
10. SmartDeaf: http://www.smartdeaf.com/
11. OpenCV: http://opencv.org/

Empirical Study of Physiological Characteristics Accompanied by Tactile Thermal Perception

Relationship Between Changes in Thermal Gradients and Skin Conductance Responses

Takafumi Shinoda[1($\boxtimes$)], Kouki Shimomura[1], Kentaro Kotani[1], Satoshi Suzuki[1], Takafumi Asao[1], and Shigeyoshi Iizuka[2]

[1] Department of Mechanical Engineering, Kansai University, 3-3-35, Yamate-cho, Osaka, Japan
{k402825,k787947,kotani,ssuzuki,asao}@kansai-u.ac.jp
[2] Faculty of Business Administration, Kanagawa University, Kanagawa, Japan
shigeiizuka@gmail.com

Abstract. This paper presents empirical results regarding emotional changes represented using different thermal gradients by measuring skin conductance responses (SCRs), when providing thermal information with various gradients. Participants attached a probe in their right forearm for thermal stimuli, and SCR measurements were conducted when participants perceived the time to detect a temperature change. The SCR amplitude showed a significant tendency to vary between +0.5 and −0.5 [°C/s] and between +0.5 and −0.3 [°C/s] of thermal gradients. The results of this study showed that differences in clear thermal gradients, such as the comparison between warm and cold stimuli, affected emotion, and differences in detailed thermal gradients, such as the comparison between 0.3 and 0.5 [°C/s] of thermal gradients, did not affect the changes in emotion.

Keywords: Emotion · Skin conductance responses · Thermal gradients · Tactile sensation

1 Introduction

Information presentation technology with tactile stimuli is being widely used for the development of emotion interfaces [1, 2]. A majority of such techniques apply vibratory stimulation [3]. However, the presentation medium using vibratory stimulation has various drawbacks, including potential stress development caused by prolonged stimulation [4]. Thermal perception plays an important role in human activity [5] and affects emotion, sentiment, and pleasantness [3]; thus, a communication device that has an effective interface with humans by using thermal perception is favorable [6].

Akiyama et al. [3] observed changes in emotional states by presenting thermal stimuli along with music as auditory stimuli. They compared subjective feelings of

© Springer International Publishing Switzerland 2016
S. Yamamoto (Ed.): HIMI 2016, Part I, LNCS 9734, pp. 575–584, 2016.
DOI: 10.1007/978-3-319-40349-6_56

emotional states by using two conditions: whether the thermal stimuli are controlled by a designated thermal profile given during music appreciation programs. However, relevant studies show a lack of objective evaluation of emotional changes because most have focused on estimating changes in emotional states subjectively.

In our study, we measured skin conductance responses (SCRs) by using an index for changes, developed by the automatic nerves system that is triggered by thermal stimuli. A change in the SCR amplitude has been regarded as an objective index for emotional changes [7–9]. According to physiological studies [10], SCRs have been considered as an index for resulting in the sweat gland activity, which is controlled by the sympathetic nerves and becomes active when a human perceives a stimulus [11–13]. Thus, the emotion caused by thermal stimulation can be evaluated objectively. Furthermore, estimating the smallest quantity of stimulus required for evoking emotion is possible by clarifying the relationship between the characteristics of thermal stimuli and the SCRs. The results of this study will contribute to the development of a video interface with a more realistic impression by supplemental thermal information.

According to Kenshalo [14], skin temperature, thermal stimulation area, and thermal gradients were the factors influential in the thermal perception of males. This paper focuses on thermal gradients because in the practical use of a tactile device with thermal perception, applying thermal stimulation is necessary, considering its benefit to the users and the difficulty in perceiving the thermal stimulation when the stimulation area is small [15].

The empirical results of this study showed emotional changes represented by different thermal gradients by measuring SCRs when providing thermal information with various thermal gradients.

2   Methods

2.1   Participants

The participants included five college students (with an average age of 22.2 years). All the participants were right handed. Each participant gave written informed consent prior to the beginning of the study.

2.2   Experimental Apparatus

SCRs were measured using a portable bio-amplifier (Polymate, AP1000, NIHON-SANTEKU Co., Japan) with an electrodermal activity (EDA) measurement unit (AP-U30m, NIHONSANTEKU Co., Japan). A thermal stimulator (Intercross-210, Intercross Co., Japan) was used for presenting thermal stimuli. Figure 1 shows the experimental system setup.

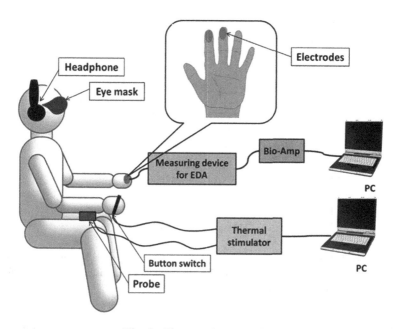

Fig. 1. The experiment system

2.3 Experimental Procedure

As an experimental preparation, participants grasped a button-switch in their right hand, and a probe was attached to their right forearms for providing thermal stimulations. Electrodes (PPS-EDA, TEAC Co.) were attached at the ventral part of the second and third fingers of their left hand for the EDA measurement. All the participants underwent a practice session to learn to press the button-switch as soon as they perceived a temperature change from their thermoneutral state. The thermal gradient was set to 5 levels (−0.5, −0.3, 0, +0.3, +0.5 [°C/s]). Five measurements were performed for each thermal gradient, yielding 25 trials for each participant. The participants used eye masks and headphones to prevent interference with auditory and visual information. The probe and skin temperatures were adjusted to be equal before each trial. Figure 2 shows the diagrammatical view of the temperature adjustment for the coupled areas.

The experimental procedure was as follows.

1. After the practice session, the experiment was started by pre-adjusting the temperature at the probe and skin.
2. The temperature was varied using a designated thermal gradient. Participants pressed the button-switch as soon as they perceived the difference in temperature.
3. Participants filled in a questionnaire regarding the thermal change.
4. Participants took a 1-min break for minimizing the influence of the prior trial.
5. The session ended after 25 repetitions of procedures 2–4.

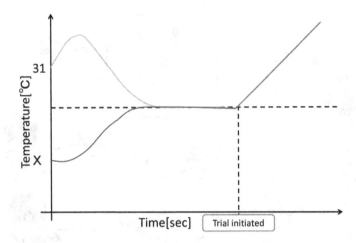

Fig. 2. Temporal changes in the temperature at the probe and the skin. Thermal stimulator was controlled such that the temperature at the probe and the skin was adjusted to be equal before the trial started. (Color figure online)

In addition, the thermal stimulation was stopped when the skin temperature of the participants reached to ± 5 [°C] from their initial temperature if the participants did not respond. In the case of 0 [°C/s], the participants mostly did not respond; thus, the measurement was terminated after 15 s.

2.4   Data Analysis

Regarding the time of motor responses to the thermal stimuli, Harrison et al. [16] reported the time from the onset of the stimulus to that of the reaction. According to them, the reaction time for the neural processing and reaction for the stimulus was estimated at 0.2 [s], and the distance between the area of stimulus presentation and the spinous process of the seventh cervical vertebra was estimated at approximately 1 [m]. These estimations yielded 2.2 [s] for the overall reaction time, assuming the transmission velocity of C-fibers.

Therefore, the perception time of temperature change was set to 0.2 [s], deducting from the time the participants responded using the button-switch. Figure 3 shows the time flow during the trial where participants perceived the thermal stimuli.

The SCR amplitude was analyzed by referencing two preceding studies, that is, a typical peak of SCR amplitude reached a maximum at 6–8 s after stimuli perception [17], and the SCR amplitude was developed within 5 [s] after stimuli perception [18]. Therefore, the peak of SCR amplitude was defined as the reaction that appeared within 5 [s] after the perception time of temperature change, and the highest peak value within 10 [s] was represented as the amplitude value. Figure 4 shows the diagrammatical view of the analysis regarding the choice of the SCR amplitude value.

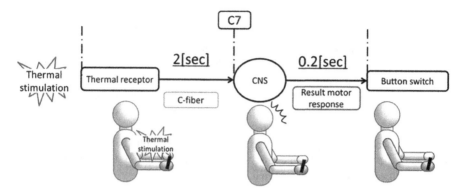

Fig. 3. Time flow of a trial

The perception time of the temperature change and the SCR amplitude were tested for effects due to thermal gradients. The independent variables consisted of the five levels of thermal gradients, whereas the dependent variables comprised the perception time of temperature change and the SCR amplitude. A repeated measures analysis of variance (ANOVA) was performed and a post hoc Bonferroni test was applied if differences existed between thermal gradients.

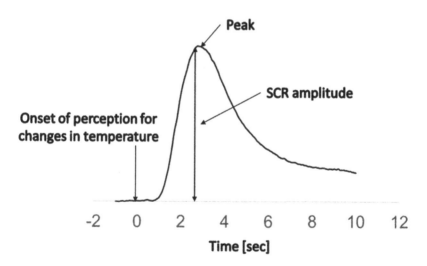

Fig. 4. Determination of peak value for SCR amplitude

3 Results

Figure 5 shows a typical example of SCR obtained in the case of thermal gradient of 0.5 [°C/s]. The solid lines indicate SCR signals, and the dashed lines indicate the time when participants responded.

If the participants failed to respond by the time the trial ended, or no peak values were observed in spite of the response, that trial was not included in the results.

Figure 6 shows the relationship between the thermal gradient and the perception time of temperature change when warm stimuli were applied. Figure 7 shows the relationship between the thermal gradient and the perception time of temperature change when cold stimuli were applied.

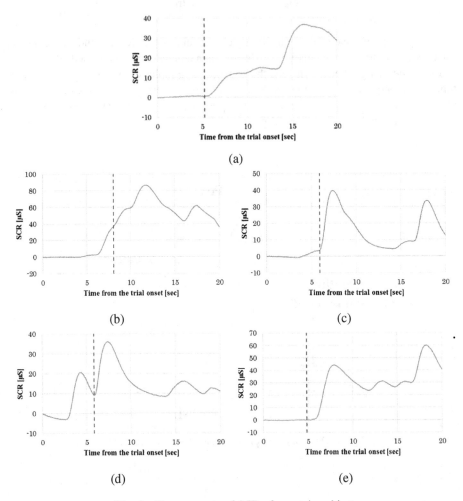

Fig. 5. Measurements of SCR of a certain subject

A significant difference was observed (warm condition: $F(1,48) = 18.35$, $p < .01$; cold condition: $F(1,47) = 31.71$, $p < .01$) as shown in Figs. 6 and 7.

Figure 8 summarizes the standardized SCR amplitudes with the changes in thermal gradients. When the thermal gradient was set to 0 [°C/s], the participants did not respond in all conditions; thus, the SCR value was plotted at 0 [μS] as a reference.

There was a significant tendency ($F(3,87) = 2.95$, $p < .1$) that the SCR amplitude was different between +0.5 and −0.5 [°C/s] and between +0.5 and −0.3 [°C/s] of the thermal gradients.

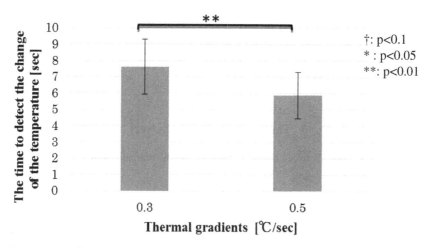

Fig. 6. Relationship between thermal gradients and the time to detect the change of the temperature (warm conditions)

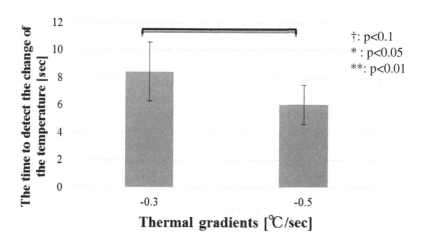

Fig. 7. Relationship between thermal gradients and the time to detect the change of the temperature (cold conditions).

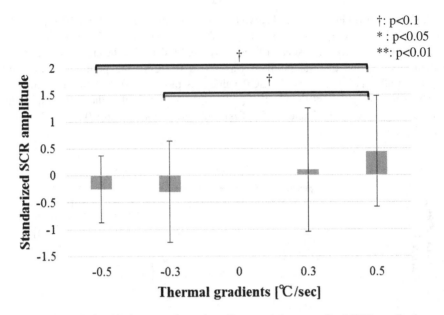

Fig. 8. Relationship between thermal gradients and the normalized SCR amplitudes

4 Discussion

The perception time of temperature change significantly decreased regardless of the stimuli (warm or cold) presented, as the thermal gradients were increased (Figs. 6 and 7). Baba et al. [19] changed the voltage levels applied to a Peltier device to generate different thermal gradients and present various thermal stimuli. They reported that the perception time of temperature change tended to be shorter when thermal gradients were increased. The results of this study are consistent with those of their study. Overall, increasing the thermal gradients was the potential key to the quick perception of temperature change.

ANOVA revealed that a significant difference ($F(3,87) = 2.95$, $p < .05$) in SCR amplitude was present with the difference in the thermal gradients. Therefore, changes in SCR amplitude were due to the difference in the thermal gradients, that is, thermal gradients affected the changes in emotion. Compared to conditions of thermal gradients, the SCR amplitude showed a significant tendency ($p < .1$) to differ when +0.5 or −0.5 [°C/s] and +0.5 or −0.3 [°C/s] of thermal gradients were applied. The results of this study showed that differences in clear thermal gradients, such as the comparison between warm stimuli and cold stimuli, affected emotion, whereas differences in marginal thermal gradients, such as the comparison between 0.3 and 0.5 [°C/s] of thermal gradients, did not show changes in emotion.

Ikeura et al. evaluated psychological changes by using galvanic skin reflex (GSR) when a robot approached participants at different velocity levels [13]. The results of their study suggested that GSR significantly increased when the initial acceleration of the moving robot was high, which differ with the results of our study.

This conflict was due to the modality of perception, that is, the perception mechanism of tactile sensation was different from that of visual information. Humans can perceive changes in a moving object mostly by visual information, whereas they can perceive temperature changes on and off by tactile sensation. Thus, the participants in our study were not sufficiently sensitive to detect the detailed difference in thermal gradients that would cause emotional changes.

Evidence showed that warm stimuli significantly affected emotions compared with cold stimuli. The results reveal that warm stimuli have a potential to offer more clarified information to the users when applying thermal information devices.

5   Conclusions

In this study, thermal stimuli affected emotion, as confirmed by changes in SCR amplitudes. The SCR amplitude had a significant tendency to differ when +0.5 or −.5 [° C/s] and 0.5 or −0.3 [°C/s] of thermal gradients were applied.

This study was limited to interpreting the results regarding the attention level given to the tactile stimuli, that is, the participants were isolated from auditory and visual stimuli and were asked to focus on tactile stimuli. Therefore, the change in SCR amplitudes may arguably be different if the participants were asked to focus on their primary task and the remaining resources were used to detect tactile stimuli. This would be a major consideration for further development of tactile devices.

In the future, we will conduct an experiment evaluating the same procedure with different body parts to determine a body part that may effectively change emotion because of thermal tactile stimuli, instead of the location of the forearm used in this study.

Acknowledgements. Part of the present study was funded by Advanced-biomedical sensing technology research group Kansai University, and Kakenhi of the Japan Society for the Promotion of Science (26560036).

References

1. Fukushima, S.: Emotion interface in the fields of entertainment and communication. J. Robot. Soc. Jpn **32**(8), 692–695 (2014)
2. Fukushima, S., et al.: Emotional vibration: enhancement of emotion using a combination of sound and skin sensation to the Pinna. Virtual Real. Soc. Jpn **19**(4), 467–476 (2014)
3. Akiyama, S., et al.: ThermOn − a novel thermo-musical interface for an enhanced emotional experience. Inf. Process. Soc. Jpn Interact. **2013**, 356–360 (2013)
4. Imae, Y., et al: Characteristics of apparent motion induction by tactile stimuli using air-jet. IEICE Technical report, The Institute Electronics Information and Communication Engineers, pp. 53–56, 2007–2010
5. Doi, K., et al.: Sensory characteristics of temperature and its discrimination in the human palm. Int. J. Affect. Eng. **11**(3), 419–425 (2012)

6. Nishimura, T., et al.: Relationship between press force and sensory characteristics of temperature in Forefinger. Int. J. Affect. Eng. **13**(3), 433–439 (2014)

7. Sato, K.: High-response thermal display unit using spatially distributed warm and cold stimuli. Inf. Process. Soc. Jpn Interact. 923–928 (2012)

8. Mizuno, T., et al: Evaluation of emotional stress in mental workload. IEICE Technical report, The Institute Electronics Information and Communication Engineers, pp. 143–147 (2007)

9. Yamashiro, D., et al.: Sympathetic skin response and emotional changes visual stimuli. No To Hattatsu **36**, 372–377 (2004)

10. Ozawa, S.: Standard Textbook. pp. 218–220, 222–223, 386–387. IGAKU-SHOIN, Tokyo (2014)

11. Numata, K., et al.: Electrodermal conditioning: its significance and research trends. J. Literary Assoc. Kwansei Gakuin Univ. **61**(2), 55–88 (2001)

12. Miyata, Y.: New Physiological Psychology. vol. 1, pp. 27–30, 210–221. Kitaooji Bookstore (1998)

13. Ikeura, R., et al.: Study on emotional evaluation of robot motions based on galvanic skin reflex. Japan. J. Ergon. **31**(5), 355–358 (1995)

14. Kenshalo, D.R.: Warm and cool thresholds as a function of rate of stimulus temperature change. Percept. Psychophys. **3**(2), 81–84 (1968)

15. Abe, M., et al.: Trial of the measurement of the thermal sensitivity in the oral mucosa and lips and lips neighborhood of the young fellow. Japan. J. Sens. Eval. **16**(1), 43–50 (2012)

16. Harrison, J.L., Davis, K.D.: Cold-evoked pain varies with skin type and cooling rate: a psychophysical study in humans. Pain **83**(2), 123–135 (1999)

17. Hata, T.: A trial for quantitative analysis of electrodermal activity by a "lie-detector" electrical kit. Hamamatsu Univ. Sch. Med. Bull. **22**, 35–41 (2008)

18. Hirota, A., et al.: A new index for psychophysiological detection of deception: applicability of normalized pulse volume. Japan. J. Physiol. Psychol. Psychophysiol. **21**(3), 217–230 (2008)

19. Baba, et al.: Development and investigation of a video game interaction that offers termal sensation to users. IPSJ SIG Technical reports, pp. 1–6 (2010)

Using the Office Desk as a Touch Interface

Hirobumi Tomita$^{(\boxtimes)}$, Simona Vasilache, and Jiro Tanaka

University of Tsukuba, Tsukuba, Japan
tomita@iplab.cs.tsukuba.ac.jp,
{simona,jiro}@cs.tsukuba.ac.jp

Abstract. A system that allows a user to easily operate a computer or tablet while working on a desk was devised. In particular, the desk is changed into an input interface that can detect the touch of a hand. A device that acquires the position data of the hand and a software program that operates the computer or tablet using this device were developed. The device, which uses the office desk as a touch interface, was constructed. The device was used in an application for navigating images displayed on a screen, even while doing other work on the desk (e.g., drawing). In future work, the sensors in the device will be improved, and various applications utilizing the device will be developed and experimentally evaluated.

Keywords: Touch interface · Digital desk · Capacitive sensing · Tabletop interfaces

1 Research Objective

Users commonly perform tasks simultaneously while working on a computer or tablet; for example, they might draw a picture on a piece of paper while looking at a given design displayed on the screen of a computer or tablet, or they might answer questions while consulting a reference book displayed on the screen. However, when users want, for instance, to change the reference materials or expand the figure on the screen, they may think it difficult to operate the device. That is, because input interfaces such as keyboard and mouse are outside their working space, they must stop and move their working hand in order to operate them. In light of this example, the goal of the present study is to devise a system by which the user can easily operate a computer or tablet while working on a desk.

2 Our Solution

2.1 Input Interface

Many types of input interfaces, like physical keys (keyboard and mouse), cameras, and microphones, are used to operate a computer or tablet. In this study, the input interface chosen is based on recognition of the working hand. This hand-based interface is intuitive and easy to use. Prior researches have used various devices to detect a hand on

© Springer International Publishing Switzerland 2016
S. Yamamoto (Ed.): HIMI 2016, Part I, LNCS 9734, pp. 585–595, 2016.
DOI: 10.1007/978-3-319-40349-6_57

a desk. For instance, image processing of camera-captured images could detect a hand [1], and Microsoft Kinect v2 and Leap Motion were used for recognizing hand positions and gestures [3]. With Microsoft Kinect v2, it is only necessary to install a camera; however, difficulties due to room lighting, background, and color of the hand arise. Leap Motion placed on a desk recognizes the position gesture of the hand, but it intrudes into the work space and cannot recognize the hand if an obstacle is placed in between the hand and camera.

Given the issues described above, in this study, changing the desk itself into an input interface that can detect touch is proposed. In this way, the user can work without having to change the environment around the desk. When a computer or tablet is operated, the positional data of the hand touching the desk is used. It is therefore necessary to develop a device for acquiring this positional data and a software program for operating the computer or tablet via this device.

2.2 Desk-Touch-Interface

The flow of the proposed desk-touch-interface using a desk is described in Fig. 1.

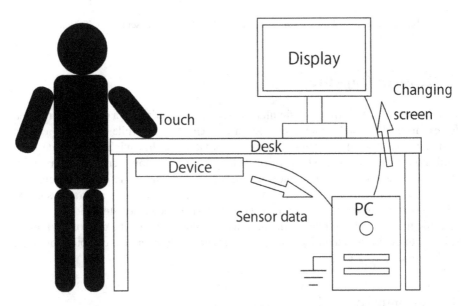

Fig. 1. Desk-touch-interface system

First, the user changes the desk into an input interface, and places a hand on the desk. Then, the developed device (which changes the desk into an input interface) detects the position of the hand and operates the screen of the computer.

3   Implementation Prototype for Detecting a Touch of a Hand

A prototype device for detecting the hand by using the office desk as a touch interface was constructed as shown in Fig. 2. It includes a touch sensor, an acrylic board and RS232C-interface IC. Once the device is installed on the back of the desk and is connected to the computer, it can transmit the positioning data of the hand touching the desk.

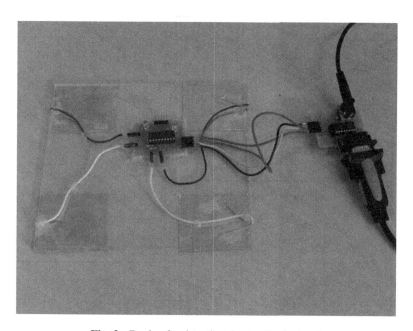

Fig. 2. Device for detecting the touch of a hand

3.1   Structure of the Touch Sensor

The touch sensor is constructed of a resistor, a microcomputer, and aluminium materials. Its function is to detect a hand touching the aluminium material. An outline of the touch-sensor circuit is shown in Fig. 3. When a voltage is applied to the output pin of the microcomputer, the waveform of the voltage at the input pin of the microcomputer changes when a hand touches the aluminium material. An example of the waveform is shown in Fig. 4.

If a hand touches the aluminium material, the speed of rise and fall of the input voltage is reduced by the human body's capacitance, and a delay occurs. The delay is measured by the microcomputer, which can thus detect a touch of a hand. The waveform depends on the value of the resistance, the area of the aluminium material, and the distance between the hand and the aluminium material. Even if a hand does not directly touch the aluminium material, the sensor can detect that a hand is approaching the aluminium material by changing these parameters. To detect a hand on the desk, the device (including the touch sensor) is installed on the back of the desk.

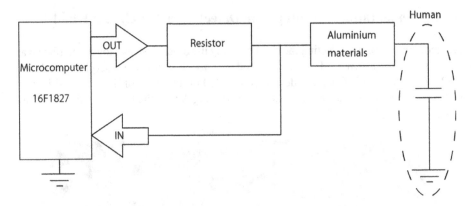

Fig. 3. Outline of touch-sensor circuit

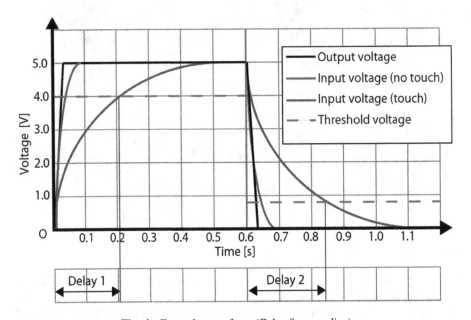

Fig. 4. Example waveform (Color figure online)

3.2   Number of Counts as Delay Time

The delay time is measured by the microcomputer, which uses a variable for measuring delay time, namely, the number of counts between the output-voltage rise (or fall) and the input-voltage rise (or fall). As a sensor value, the number of counts is sent to the host computer. Since number of counts is used instead of measuring real time, the delay time gets longer so that number of counts increases. However, when measured, the number of counts output every time is not stable. The microcomputer therefore calculates the mean of the number of counts and outputs a stable value. A PIC16F1827 microchip was used to output the number of counts. It is connected to both ends of the resistance such as the circuit in Fig. 3. The voltage on input pin is high when input voltage is 2 V, and it is low when input voltage is 0.8 V. The microcomputer's I/O pin is connected to an RS232C-interface IC (model ADM3202AN) to send the number of counts as a sensor value to the host computer.

3.3 Preliminary Experiment of the Touch Sensor

To evaluate the performance of the touch sensor, three experiments were carried out.

(a) Detection of touch on desk

The touch sensor was installed on the back of a desk, and the change in delay when the desk was touched investigated. The experimental conditions are listed as follows:

- Aluminum material area: 50[mm] × 60[mm]
- Resistance value: 1.0 [MΩ]
- Desk material: Wood
- Desk thickness: 30 [mm]

Mean number of counts when a hand touched the desk and when it did not touch the desk are listed in Table 1.

Table 1. Mean number of counts measured in experiment (a)

	Mean number of counts
No touch	7.0
Touch	10.7

The result shows that there is a difference between the values, indicating that a touch can be detected by the sensor.

(b) Changing the position of the hand on the desk

The change in the mean count given by a touch sensor when the hand position on the desk changes was investigated next. A touch sensor like that described in experiment (a) was used. Mean number of counts for the position of the hand are listed in Table 2.

Table 2. Mean number of counts in experiment (b)

	D = 0 [mm]	D = 25 [mm]	D = 50 [mm]	D = 75 [mm]	D = 100 [mm]
No touch	7.0	7.0	7.0	7.0	7.0
Touch	10.7	10.0	9.3	8.4	7.7

"D" is the distance from the center of the sensor to the hand. The results show that as the hand gets further from the sensor, the delay decreases at an almost constant rate. Although only one sensor was used in this experiment, using multiple touch sensors would make it possible to estimate the position of the hand on the desk.

(c) Estimating the position of the hand

Four sensors like those used in experiment (a) were installed 60 mm apart to form the touch positions as shown in Fig. 5. Each sensor is connected to an I/O pin of the microcomputer so that it measures the number of counts when a hand touches five points. That is, four points correspond to four sensors, and one point corresponds to the center of the rectangle created by the four sensors.

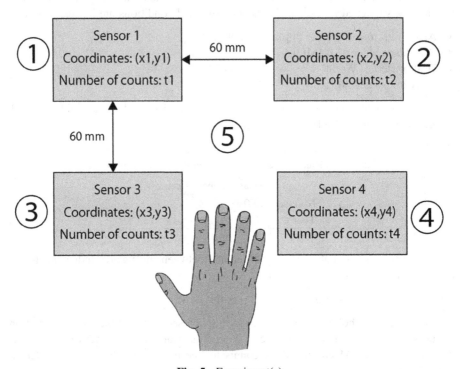

Fig. 5. Experiment(c)

As shown by the results listed in Table 3, the four sensors obtained a different number of counts at each touch point. The values are similar when the same point was touched on different occasions. It is therefore concluded that the position of the hand can be estimated by using the values obtained from the four sensors. However, when the user does not touch the desk, each sensor outputs a different value because the number of counts obtained by each sensor is different (due to individual differences in the internal circuit of each pin).

Table 3. Mean number of counts in experiment (c)

	No touch	①	②	③	④	⑤
Sensor 1	9.2	13.3	12.2	10.0	10.8	12.4
Sensor 2	11.4	14.0	16.4	13.3	13.0	15.6
Sensor 3	10.8	11.5	12.0	14.8	12.5	13.0
Sensor 4	13.1	13.8	13.8	15.4	16.2	15.5

3.4 Normalized Sensor Data

Because the number of counts for each pin differs, the sensor data is normalized. That is, the difference between the number of counts when the desk is not touched and the maximum number of counts when it is touched was determined, and the difference is used to calculate the normalized number of counts, p_n, for every sensor, given as

$$p_n = \frac{t_n - t_{l,n}}{t_{h,n} - t_{l,n}} \times 100 \tag{1}$$

Where $t_{l,n}$ is the number of counts of the nth sensor in case of no touch, $t_{h,n}$ is the maximum number of counts of the nth sensor in case of touch on the nth sensor, and t_n is the number of the counts measured at that time (where n = 1, 2, 3, or 4). By using the normalized value, it is easy to estimate touch position and swipe direction.

3.5 Calibration

The number of counts corresponding to no touch and that corresponding to a touch must be calibrated whenever the device is started and whenever the user changes (because these values are different for each user). The device can be calibrated easily by simply touching the desk. The maximum count is reset whenever the user changes by simply placing a hand on the desk. In case the desk is changed, the user installs the device on the back of the desk and calibration is enabled.

3.6 Detecting a Touch

A threshold of the touch is defined before the touch position is estimated. A touch is taken as detected when the normalized counts exceed the threshold. Three states, namely, "not touch", "tap", "touch" are considered. As described later, these states are used to prevent mistouches. Hand-related information is obtained only in the "touch" state.

3.7 Estimating the Touch Position

The position of the hand is estimated by using the values provided by the four sensors. The coordinates of the position of the hand (hx, hy) are represented as

$$hx = \frac{x_1 \times p_1 + x_2 \times p_2 + x_3 \times p_3 + x_4 \times p_4}{p_1 + p_2 + p_3 + p_4} \tag{2}$$

$$hy = \frac{y_1 \times p_1 + y_2 \times p_2 + y_3 \times p_3 + y_4 \times p_4}{p_1 + p_2 + p_3 + p_4} \tag{3}$$

These coordinates were experimentally estimated by using the device. The experimental conditions are shown in Fig. 6. As described above, the device can acquire the positioning data of the hand, even when a piece of paper or a regular-size notebook are sandwiched between the desk and the hand.

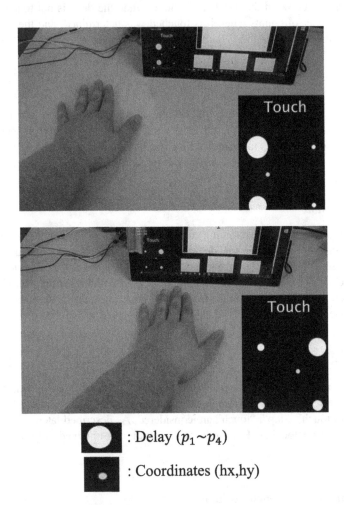

⬤ : Delay ($p_1 \sim p_4$)

▫ : Coordinates (hx,hy)

Fig. 6. Conditions of the experiment

4 Application of the Device

4.1 Outline of the Application

The device was evaluated in an application for operating images displayed on a screen while doing other work on the desk (e.g., drawing). The software used for this application was developed using Processing. A screenshot of the application in action is shown in Fig. 7; (A) indicates the folder containing the image, (B) indicates the main image, and (C) shows a preview of the current image and the previous/next images. Moving the hand on the desk changes the image or the folder. In this example application, when the hand is moved to the left, the main image changes into the previous image. When the hand is moved upwards, the folder is changed. A function to prevent malfunctions is activated by tapping the table twice to lock the screen. It is cancelled by tapping twice again.

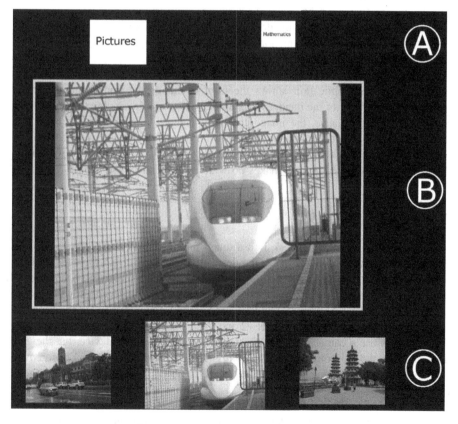

Fig. 7. Screenshot of test application

4.2 Detecting Swipe Direction

The application must be able to detect a swipe movement of the hand. The position data of the hand is used to find the touch point and the release point of the swipe. The swipe movement is then detected by using the difference between the two points.

4.3 Instructions for Operating Application

1. Install the device (by using masking tape) on the back of the desk where the user works. Then connect it to an AC adapter for supplying power
2. Launch the device and the software for changing the screen
3. Calibrate the device started by clicking the mouse on the screen or touching the screen
4. Change an image on the screen. The image in Fig. 7 is displayed when the user starts the software; the image can be changed by the hand moving right and left, whereas the folder can be changed by moving it up and down
5. Lock the screen by tapping the desk twice; cancel the lock by tapping twice again; this function prevents malfunction in case of touching by mistake

   (Steps 4 and 5 are repeated.)

Observations. The application allows the user to change the image and the folder simply by movements of the hand, even if a notebook is sandwiched between the hand and the desk; for instance, the image can be changed while drawing a picture in a notebook with one hand. Sometimes, the software wrongly detects a swipe movement. When no operation is performed, the device reacts to a hand or an arm. However, errors do not occur as long as the user makes no wide movements of the hand.

5 Related Work

Prior research on changing a desk into a touch interface has been reported. Wellner enabled the interaction operation on the desk by recognizing a hand on the desk by using a camera and projecting a picture on the desk with a projector [1]. Xiaojun et al. investigated the touch operation and the position of an appropriate window in order to support work using a desktop computer by installing a touch display in the desk [2]. Efanov et al. used a Microsoft Kinect v2 and Leap Motion for detecting the hand [3]. These studies use a camera, a touch display, and a hand-sensing device, but they are dependent on the environment of the room and the structure of the desk. Moreover, whenever the desk is changed, additional time is needed for reinstalling peripheral elements.

Several studies deal with detecting a hand and using it to interact with a desk. Grosse-Puppendahl et al. conducted research on ubiquitous computing with NFC using capacitance [4]. The receiver of the sensor is placed on the back of the desk, and several transmitters are placed on the desk for measuring capacitance. In this setting, a transmitter device is needed for measuring capacitance. The proposed hand-detection system, user oneself does not need to have a power source. Grosse-Puppendahl et al. also conducted research on recognizing the position of the hand and multi-touch with multi capacitance sensors [5]. This research is similar in part to the present work, although the proposed device makes use of single touch; it is also low cost, uses readily available electronic parts, and its small size allows it to fit in the palm of a hand.

6 Concluding Remarks

A device that enables touch interaction on a desk by using the human body's capacitance was proposed. In addition, the device can detect touch position and swipe movement by using multi sensors. The device was used in an application for operating images displayed on a screen, even while doing other work on the desk. Although a basic application, namely, changing an image, was demonstrated, this application proved to be easy-to-achieve on a computer or tablet by using this device while working on a desk. In future work, the sensors in the device will be improved, various applications utilizing the device will be developed, and the applications will be experimentally evaluated. At this stage, only desks were used for interaction; in future work, using walls or doors for interaction will be considered.

References

1. Wellner, P.: The DigitalDesk calculator: tangible manipulation on a desk top display. In: Proceedings of 4th Annual ACM Symposium on User Interface Software and Technology, pp. 27–33. ACM, New York, NY, USA (1991)
2. Bi, X., Grossman, T., Matejka, J., Fitzmaurice, G.: Magic desk: bringing multi-touch surfaces into desktop work. In: Proceedings of SIGCHI Conference on Human Factors in Computing Systems, pp. 2511–2520. ACM, New York, NY, USA (2011)
3. Efanov, I., Lanir, J.: Augmenting indirect multi-touch interaction with 3D hand contours and skeletons. In: Proceedings of 33rd Annual ACM Conference Extended Abstracts on Human Factors in Computing Systems, pp. 989–994. ACM, New York, NY, USA (2015)
4. Grosse-Puppendahl, T., Herber, S., Wimmer, R., Englert, F., Beck, S., von Wilmsdorff, J., Wichert, R., Kuijper, A.: Capacitive near-field communication for ubiquitous interaction and perception. In: Proceedings of 2014 ACM International Joint Conference on Pervasive and Ubiquitous Computing, pp. 231–242. ACM, New York, NY, USA (2014)
5. Grosse-Puppendahl, T., Braun, A., Kamieth, F., Kuijper, A.: Swiss-cheese extended: an object recognition method for ubiquitous interfaces based on capacitive proximity sensing. In: Proceedings of SIGCHI Conference on Human Factors in Computing Systems, pp. 1401–1410. ACM, New York, NY, USA (2013)

Author Index

Abe, Tetsuya I-275
Abramczuk, Katarzyna I-3
Aihara, Kenro II-40
Ainoya, Takeo I-475
Akakura, Takako II-138
Akasaki, Hina II-103
Alexandrova, Todorka II-103
Amemiya, Tomohiro I-483
Aoki, Ryosuke II-32
Aoyagi, Saizo I-321
Archer, Libby II-445
Asahi, Yumi II-560, II-569
Asao, Takafumi I-523, I-531, I-575
Astell, Arlene J. II-445

Baba, Kensuke I-168
Baloni, Snigdha I-442
Ban, Yuki II-487
Basov, Oleg O. I-539
Beauxis-Aussalet, Emma I-191
Beecks, Christian I-238
Bernardes Jr., João Luiz I-214
Bhatnagar, Raj I-229
Bock, Julie S. I-158
Bordonhos, Pedro I-14
Bröhl, Christina I-191
Byttner, Stefan II-20

Caldwell, Barrett S. II-414
Calero Valdez, André II-402
Cerqueira, Renato I-115
Chan, Jonathan II-454
Chang, Chia-Ling I-421, II-235
Chang, Wen-Chih II-223
Chang, Yu-Shan II-3
Charoenkitkarn, Nipon II-454
Chawla, Priya I-229
Chen, Shanguang I-40
Chhabra, Jitender Kumar I-296
Chien, Yu-Hung II-3
Chignell, Mark II-454
Cho, Hyunkyoung II-244
Chu, Yih-Hsien II-3
Chunpir, Hashim Iqbal II-379, II-391, II-423

Coelho, Denis A. I-405
Curri, Endrit II-391

de Guzman, Chelsea II-454
De Vocht, Laurens I-238
Dias, Paulo I-14
Didandeh, Arman I-103
Dua, Mohit I-381
Duarte, Eduardo I-14

Ellis, Maggie II-445
Englmeier, Kurt I-252

Fahn, Chin-Shyurng I-80
Falkman, Göran II-20
Fels, Deborah I. I-462
Ferreira, Juliana Jansen I-115
Flanagan, Brendan I-127
Floyd, Molly K. I-158
Fujimori, Susumu II-138
Fukumori, Satoshi I-321
Fukuzumi, Shin'ichi I-413
Furtado, Lennon I-347

Giova, Diana II-325
Gombos, Gergő I-263
Goodwin, Leslie I-158
Goubran, Laila II-11
Groh, Rainer I-203

Hakoda, Hiroyuki I-275
Hamann, Tatjana II-402
Han, Chia I-229
Harada, Tomohiro II-501
Hardman, Lynda I-191
Harney-Levine, Sarah II-445
Hasegawa, Shinobu II-168, II-178
Hashido, Rihito II-599
Hashimoto, Daisuke I-523
Hashimoto, Ryo II-32
Hashiyama, Tomonori I-371
Hattori, Akira I-329
Hayami, Haruo I-329
Hayashi, Maho II-256

Hayashi, Ryutaro   II-346
Hayashi, Yuki   II-115
Hayashi, Yusuke   II-126, II-146
Helldin, Tove   II-20
Hemmje, Matthias   I-391
Herrmann, Martin   I-203
Hill, Jordan R.   II-414
Hirano, Takahiro   II-478
Hirashima, Tsukasa   II-126, II-146
Hirokawa, Sachio   I-127, I-168
Hirose, Michitaka   I-546, II-290, II-313,
    II-487, II-599
Hirota, Koichi   I-483, I-501, II-357
Hong, Seungmo   II-278
Horiguchi, Yukio   I-25
Hosono, Naotsune   II-521
Hsiao, Hsien-Sheng   II-3
Hsieh, Ming-Hsuan   I-421, II-235
Hsu, Chia-Chien   II-466
Hsu, Yu-Chin   II-466
Huang, Fei-Hui   II-531
Huang, Weifen   I-40
Hwang, Faustina   II-445

Ichino, Junko   I-371
Ihara, Masayuki   II-32
Iiba, Toshiya   I-361
Iio, Takamasa   II-478
Iizuka, Shigeyoshi   I-34, I-575
Ikeda, Mitsuru   II-115
Ikei, Yasushi   I-483, I-501, II-268, II-357
Imran, Ali Shariq   I-491
Inada, Kaori   II-81
Ineyama, Ryo   I-523
Inoue, Hiromitsu   II-521
Ishida, Tatsuro   II-32
Ishigaki, Ken   II-268
Ishii, Akira   I-275
Itai, Shiroh   II-256
Ito, Noriko   II-336
Ito, Takao   I-136
Ito, Teruaki   I-339

Jackson, G. Cole   I-158
Jiang, Jie   II-454
Jo, Junghoon   II-278

Kaburagi, Hirofumi   II-542
Kąkol, Michał   I-3

Kamiyama, Naoto   II-367
Kammer, Dietrich   I-203
Kang, Yen-Yu   II-589
Karahoda, Bertan   I-491
Karbay, Edibe Betül   II-423
Karpov, Alexey A.   I-539
Kasamatsu, Keiko   I-475
Kashihara, Akihiro   II-168
Kato, Toshikazu   I-179, II-72
Kawamata, Taisuke   II-138
Kawamoto, Kayo   II-146
Kim, Eunseok   II-278
Kim, Jea-In   II-278
Kim, Jungwha   II-278
Kim, Kihong   II-278
Kim, Sunhyuck   II-278
Kimita, Koji   II-197
Kimoto, Mitsuhiko   II-478
Kimura, Koya   II-63, II-550
Kirchner, Bettina   I-203
Kiss, Attila   I-263
Kitada, Takashi   I-556
Kitazaki, Michiteru   I-501
Kobayashi, Daiji   I-511
Kometani, Yusuke   II-159
Kono, Susumu   II-40
Kotani, Kentaro   I-523, I-531, I-575
Kovacs, Tim   II-50
Kuijper, Arjan   I-308, II-300
Kumada, Mizuki   I-361
Kumagai, Keisuke   I-531

Lagebrant, Alice   I-148
Larsson, Håkan   I-148
Lees, David S.   II-414
Liao, Chi-Meng   II-223
Lif, Patrik   I-148
Lin, Ching-Torng   II-466
Lin, Kuen-Yi   II-3
Ling, Chen   I-158
Liu, Wang   I-40
Ludwig, Thomas   II-391

Maeshiro, Midori   I-48
Maeshiro, Tetsuya   I-48, II-90
Maki, Nahomi   I-556
Mannens, Erik   I-238
Marques, Anderson   I-347
Matsui, Tatsunori   II-197, II-209

Matsuka, Hirohito   II-560
Matsumuro, Miki   I-60
Matuszka, Tamás   II-278
Mbilinyi, Ashery   II-168
Meiguins, Bianchi   I-347
Mertens, Alexander   I-191
Meske, Christian   II-434
Mikhailov, Yuri V.   I-539
Miki, Hiroyuki   I-433
Mikkonen, Tommi   II-325
Miller, Michael J.   II-414
Minami, Toshiro   I-168
Misue, Kazuo   I-136
Miwa, Kazuhisa   I-60
Miwa, Yoshiyuki   II-256, II-346
Miyata, Akihiro   II-32
Mizoguchi, Satoshi   II-197
Mori, Hirohiko   II-187, II-579
Morizumi, Ryota   II-569
Mota, Marcelle   I-347
Motienko, Anna I.   I-539
Muramatsu, Keiichi   II-197
Murtagh, Fionn   I-252

Nagaoka, Keizo   II-159
Nagashio, Takuya   II-478
Nakahata, Tomoki   II-478
Nakajima, Kanako   II-103
Nakajima, Tatsuo   II-103
Nakamura, Ryogo   I-511
Nakanishi, Hayato   I-168
Nakanishi, Hiroaki   I-25
Nakanishi, Miwa   II-521
Nakashima, Moriyu   I-25
Nakashima, Tomoharu   I-287
Nakata, Masaya   II-50
Nakata, Toru   II-72
Nakatoh, Tetsuya   I-168
Narumi, Takuji   I-546, II-290, II-313, II-487,
    II-599
Nebe, Karsten   I-442
Neto, Nelson   I-347
Neumann, W. Patrick   I-462
Niese, Christoph   II-300
Nishi, Hiroko   II-256, II-346
Nishimoto, Koshi   II-336
Nishimura, Hiromitsu   I-563
Nojima, Takuya   II-357
Nowaczyk, Slawomir   II-20

Ocharo, Harriet Nyanchama   II-178
Ogawa, Nami   II-487
Oka, Makoto   II-187, II-579
Omura, Kengo   I-371
Osawa, Sohei   II-313
Ota, Hirofumi   II-268

Paik, Jin-kyung   II-244
Park, Hyerim   II-278
Park, Noh-young   II-278
Parush, Avi   II-11
Pashami, Sepideh   II-20
Pireva, Krenare   I-491
Prajapati, Amarjeet   I-296

Rasche, Peter   I-191
Riveiro, Maria   II-20
Ronzhin, Andrey L.   I-539
Roskosch, Philipp   I-308
Rudolph, Dominik   II-434

Saito, Rei   II-50
Sakai, Kazuki   I-531
Sakakibara, Yuta   I-546
Sakamoto, Mizuki   II-103
Sakamoto, Takashi   I-179
Sakata, Mamiko   II-81, II-336, II-511
Sakurai, Sho   II-487
Salo, Kari   II-325
Santos, Beatriz Sousa   I-14
Sato, Hiroyuki   II-50, II-501
Sawaragi, Tetsuo   I-25
Schaar, Anne Kathrin   II-402
Schlick, Christopher M.   I-191
Seaborn, Katie   II-494
Sedig, Kamran   I-103
Segura, Vinícius   I-115
Sei, Natsumi   II-187
Seidl, Thomas   I-238
Seko, Shunichi   II-32
Sellen, Kate   I-454
Sera, Kenichi   I-556
Seta, Kazuhisa   II-115
Shao, Jiang   I-70, I-91
Shen, Zhangfan   I-70, I-91
Shibata, Hirohito   I-371
Shibata, Hirotoshi   I-563
Shimohara, Katsunori   II-63, II-478, II-550

Shimomura, Kouki   I-575
Shimomura, Yoshiki   II-197
Shinoda, Takafumi   I-575
Shiomi, Masahiro   II-478
Shiozu, Yurika   II-63, II-550
Shizuki, Buntarou   I-275
Shoda, Haruka   II-81, II-336, II-511
Stieglitz, Stefan   II-434
Sudo, Yuta   II-72
Sugimura, Hitoshi   I-361
Sugino, Ryota   II-197
Sujan Samuel Roy, Joash   I-462
Suzuki, Hiroshi   I-329
Suzuki, Kunikazu   I-433
Suzuki, Noriko   II-81, II-336, II-511
Suzuki, Satoshi   I-523, I-531, I-575
Suzuki, Shoko   II-103
Suzuki, Tsuyoshi   I-433

Tachibana, Masao   II-589
Tajima, Yusuke   II-501
Takadama, Keiki   II-50, II-501
Takahashi, Naoki   I-179
Takahashi, Takuto   II-346
Takano, Kentaro   I-371
Takano, Kosuke   I-361
Takehana, Kazuma   II-209
Tanaka, Hiroshi   I-563
Tanaka, Jiro   I-275, I-585, II-542
Tanaka, Ryohei   I-546, II-313
Tanaka, Takamitsu   II-589
Tanev, Ivan   II-478, II-550
Tanikawa, Tomohiro   I-546, II-290, II-313,
    II-487, II-599
Tanikawa, Yukiko   I-413
Tano, Shunichi   I-371
Theis, Sabine   I-191
Tian, Yu   I-40
Tolt, Gustav   I-148
Tomita, Hirobumi   I-585
Tomita, Yutaka   II-521
Tsukiji, Hayato   I-361
Tsutsui, Yuhei   II-357
Twellmeyer, James   I-308

Uchihashi, Shingo   I-371
Ueoka, Ryoko   II-367

Van de Walle, Rik   I-238
Vasilache, Simona   I-585, II-542
Verborgh, Ruben   I-238
Virk, Zorawar Singh   I-381
Vogl, Raimund   II-434
von Landesberger, Tatiana   II-300

Wang, Chunhui   I-40
Wang, Haiyan   I-70
Wang, Jun   I-40
Watanabe, Hiroshi   II-32
Watanabe, Masahiro   II-32
Watanabe, Tomio   I-339
Werkmann, Björn   I-391
Whitehead, Anthony   II-11
Wierzbicki, Adam   I-3
Wille, Matthias   I-191
Williams, Elizabeth A.   II-445
Wilms, Konstantin   II-434
Wojdziak, Jan   I-203
Wongwichai, Thongthai   II-589
Woo, Woontack   II-278
Wright, Dave   II-445
Wu, Meng-Luen   I-80

Xi, Hongwei   I-70
Xue, Chengqi   I-91

Yabe, Hiroyuki   II-290
Yamabe, Koko   II-103
Yamaguchi, Hiroki   II-90
Yamaguchi, Rina   II-511
Yamakawa, Yuto   II-256
Yamamoto, Michiya   I-321
Yoshida, Keisuke   II-268
Yoshida, Shunsuke   II-290
Yu, Kuang-Chao   II-3

Zaia, Jaqueline   I-214
Zaina, Luciana   II-391
Zelezny, Milos   I-539
Zhang, Jing   I-70
Zhao, Rui   I-70
Zhou, Lei   I-91
Zhou, Xiaozhou   I-91
Ziefle, Martina   II-402
Zucherman, Leon   II-454

Printed in the United States
By Bookmasters